Rivers of Rock

Rivers of Rock

stories from a stone-dry land

Central Arizona Project Archaeology

by Stephanie Whittlesey

SRI Press, Tucson, Arizona

2003

Published by SRI Press,
a division of Statistical Research, Inc.,
P.O. Box 31865, Tucson, Arizona, 85751

Prepared for the
USDI Bureau of Reclamation,
Phoenix Area Office, P. O. Box 81169, Phoenix, AZ 85069-1169
Contract No. 99-CS-32-0040

ISBN 1-879442-93-0 (cloth)
ISBN 1-879442-94-9 (paperback)

Second printing, April 2004
Printed in the United States of America

Library of Congress Cataloging-in-Publication Data

Whittlesey, Stephanie Michelle.
Rivers of rock : stories from a stone-dry land : Central Arizona Project archaeology / by Stephanie Whittlesey.—1st ed.
p. cm.
Prepared for the USDI Bureau of Reclamation.
Includes bibliographical references and index.
ISBN 1-879442-93-0 (alk. paper)—ISBN 1-879442-94-9 (pbk. : alk. paper)
1. Indians of North America—Arizona—Antiquities. 2. Central Arizona Project (U.S.)—History. 3. Excavations (Archaeology)—Arizona. 4. Colorado Plateau—Antiquities. 5. Arizona—Antiquities. I. Title.

E78.A7 W48 2003
979.1'3—dc21

2003009788

Front cover photo: Little Colorado River. Photograph by Jefferson Reid.

Back cover photo: Stephanie Whittlesey at Monument Valley, Arizona. Photograph by Jefferson Reid.

Section divider photos:
Headwaters: Summit, Rocky Mountain National Park, Colorado. Photograph by Jefferson Reid.

Midstream: Horseshoe Dam and Reservoir. Photograph courtesy U.S. Bureau of Reclamation. Joe Madrigal, Jr., Photographer.

Slackwater: Fannin-McFaland Aqueduct. Photograph courtesy U.S. Bureau of Reclamation. Joe Madrigal, Jr., Photographer.

This book is dedicated to all of Arizona's people, past and present, who loved the land and tried to preserve it for future generations.

Table of Contents

Preface

This book is about landscapes and therefore about three intimately connected things—land, people, and the interaction between land and people. It is first about the land—about Arizona, a stone-dry land of astonishing natural landscape. It is about Arizona's rare and precious sources of water, its dry rivers, its streams of manufactured rock. The stories that fill this book begin with land and water, and so in thanking those who made this book possible, I must first acknowledge the Arizona land that is my home. It has provided inspiration and achingly blue skies, strength, and an appreciation for the play of light through clouds. I am grateful for the blinding crack of hot lightning on desert peaks, the scent of creosote after thunder, and the smell of rain on hot stone.

Second, this book is about people—Arizona's past and present peoples, its history, and its archaeology, to which I have dedicated my professional life. This book tells stories about life in a stone-dry land—the remarkable ways people have invented to live with the land, use its resources, and adapt to its scarce water over the millennia. It goes deeper still to touch on how human lives and cultures have been shaped by land and water. In this sense, it is an ethnography of water. The book is also about one of the most remarkable phenomena in Arizona's history—the Central Arizona Project—and the archaeology that was carried out before the dams and canals were built. I am grateful to the many people who populate this book, from those who lived the stories to those who tell them. Many of the archaeologists who developed the ideas about the past that fill these pages are my friends and colleagues. We have shared campfires and passionate arguments, shoveled dirt, and raised glasses together. It has been a privilege to know them.

Some deserve special acknowledgment for making this book happen. It was funded by the U.S. Bureau of Reclamation, which supported the archaeology reported here. The agency has done a great job of fulfilling its legal and ethical responsibilities to historic preservation, and I am privileged to have been a part of several archaeological projects it has sponsored. Jon Czaplicki of that agency deserves credit for supporting the public-outreach project we called "Modern Rivers, Ancient Times," which includes this book as well as other products. The project is unique in cultural resource management archaeology. We can hope that other agencies will follow Jon's lead in underwriting different kinds of projects—not just the dry, dense, descriptive reports that we archaeologists are accustomed to writing—that will reach out to a public audience and give something back to the people who ultimately make archaeology possible. It has been a pleasure to work with Jon over the years, and as always, I appreciate his patience, vision, and guidance.

Tom Lincoln and Dave Gifford, also of the Bureau of Reclamation, and Gene Rogge, who has a long history with federal archaeology, commented on the draft manuscript. Dale Clauser, former public relations officer at the Bureau of Reclamation, provided unlimited access to the agency's wonderful collection of photographs, videotapes, and other public-outreach materials. I am also grateful to Chris Downum of Northern Arizona University, who as one of the peer reviewers for the project, provided thorough and insightful commentary and suggestions.

Many people at Statistical Research were instrumental. Terry Majewski and María Molina provided managerial and editorial help. María deserves particular thanks for negotiating the sometimes troubled waters of publishing permissions and for putting together the index, which is never an easy job. She is a tremendously good editor, and I hope I can count her as a friend. Graphics manager Cindy Elsner-Hayward and her staff in SRI's graphics department, including Lois Kain and Amelia Natoli, crafted the illustrations and scanned what must have seemed like thousands of slides and photographs. They deserve awards of merit for grace under pressure. Production manager Toni Tallman helped with the nuts and bolts of making a book. SRI's president, Jeff Altschul, ran interference on numerous occasions, and his patience is as unflinching as his belief that public outreach is a critical part of cultural resource management. Carol Ellick offered helpful ideas in the early stages of the project. Kristin Hagenbuckle assisted in locating historical photographs, and Andrea Vermeer helped to research materials.

My deepest thanks go to my husband, archaeologist Jeff Reid at the University of Arizona, who was my traveling companion on many of the excursions described here. He provided most of the wonderful slides of Arizona's spectacular landscapes and captured its consistent ironies on film. As another peer reviewer, he also supplied helpful review comments. His other contributions include typically outrageous humor, cover art, and the book's title, which was conceived on one of our near-monthly excursions to the South Rim of the Grand Canyon. Regardless of what else our life together may have been, it has invariably been interesting.

I must also thank our daughter, Erin Reid, for sharing with us many of the special moments described here. Growing up as she did in an archaeological field camp, archaeology, Arizona's native peoples, and its astonishing natural landscape run as deep in her blood as they do in ours.

I am especially grateful to the many wordsmiths whose poetry and prose illuminate the work. Thank you for allowing me to share your creative words, which express heartfelt emotions about the land and the people, with others. Various publishers and agents helped to secure copyright permissions and I appreciate their hard work and prompt response. The University of Arizona Press, and Ryan Charles in particular, fielded a barrage of requests with grace and efficiency. The Arizona Historical Society deserves thanks for rapidly fulfilling our demand for photographic reproductions.

Bill Benoit is responsible for making the book, taking the manuscript and illustrations from an incoherent set of electronic files to a polished final product. He did a fabulous job of graphic design and layout, and I appreciate the time he spent on making the book visually appealing and artfully designed.

The cats that permit me to share their house actually provided little substantive assistance in the writing and preparation of this book, but their companionship helped the difficult passages to flow more smoothly. I follow Brian Fagan's lead in thanking my feline buddies who, in their own way, are people, too.

Last, this book is about the interaction between people and land—the landscape. The landscape is a seamless rendering of history, a mnemonic for events and times past. It is memory scribed in stone and water, and each person's landscape is unique. Retelling the stories etched in the landscape conjures up unforgettable memories of remarkable people and the ways in which their actions shaped the course of history and extraordinary events. The intertwined stories of the land, the people, and the past presented here are therefore personal ones. I have stood at the Carl Hayden Visitor Center admiring the geometry of Glen Canyon Dam and wondering how it looked before the river was drowned, before McDonald's and golf courses and hotels, when sheep and Navajo herders were the sole inhabitants of the land. Crossing the bridge at Lee's Ferry, I have marveled at its dizzying height above the Colorado River and at how John Doyle Lee was able to ferry wagons and horses across it in a fragile boat so many years ago. I was there when the platform mounds of the Tonto Basin were being excavated, watching as the great adobe pillars and the stone-based granaries emerged from the ground along with many different questions about the past and its meaning. I have viewed the great, blue arch of the highway bridge from the turquoise waters of Theodore Roosevelt Lake. I have survived the destructive power of water, watching in fascinated dread as buildings slid into the Rillito River and bridges collapsed in Tucson during the flood seasons of 1983 and 1993. The stories in my personal landscape are written in water and stone, archaeological sites, and sky.

It should be obvious to readers that I love what I do, and I hope they will enjoy reading the stories in this book as much as I have enjoyed the telling. I extend my thanks to anyone who helped during the project that I may have inadvertently forgotten. I believe that the past is prologue to the present and predictor of our future. I also believe that we are a remarkable species, pitiful in our fears, fearless in our ability to fool ourselves, boundless in our hope. This book is a celebration of our best, and I am profoundly grateful for the opportunity to be its author.

Rivers of Rock

Headwaters

Prologue:

At River's Source

Prologue

"This would be a good country," a tourist says to me, "if only you had some water." He's from Cleveland, Ohio.

—Edward Abbey, *Desert Solitaire*

This book is about water, the literal source of life in America's desert Southwest. In desert lands such as today's state of Arizona, water is more than a substance without which all living things would perish. It is metaphor, symbol, the subject of prayer and ritual. It is toward water's control that much of our technology has been directed. Water has inspired invention, art, belief, expression. Toward water we yearn, leaning as the young corn does toward the sun. This book explores some of water's deeper levels, its hidden meanings and covert significance. It is a book about the unique environment of desert Arizona, the stone-dry land that has presented challenges and offered advantages to its human inhabitants for millennia. It is also about the diverse peoples who have settled in Arizona over the last 10,000 years, each of whom forged a striking adjustment to a land of little rain and uncontrollable rivers. We will learn how the ancient peoples of Arizona and those of modern times conceptualized and symbolized water, how they captured rainfall and controlled rivers to grow their food, how in turn water shaped the form and substance of their lives. Last, the book is about the unique, humanized environments created when people interact with the land on which they live and from which they derive sustenance. All of the stories we will tell begin and end with water.

The ancient nexus among people, the land, and its yield has marked the American Southwest as it does elsewhere and everywhere, from the native peoples of the past, to the fur traders of the historical period, to

The Colorado River near Lee's Ferry, northeastern Arizona.
Photograph by Jefferson Reid.

The Little Colorado River near Cameron, Arizona. PHOTOGRAPH BY JEFFERSON REID.

the Euroamerican settlers of the nineteenth century (Wilkinson 1992:15). This book explores these connections among land, people, and the humanized landscape. Land and water are the foundations of all our stories. Paradoxically, water is the primal force that shaped the desert landscape, polishing and perfecting landforms and topography through eons of geologic time. This surficial aspect of water is easy to see reflected in the smooth curve of stone and the dry washes that weave through the heated stones of desert plains. We will celebrate the remarkable natural beauty of Arizona as molded by water and time. We will assess its diversity and learn of its many natural constraints and abundant resources.

In its water, this land knows no moderation. On the one hand, Arizona is an arid country, a land of little rain. In the 1800s, John Wesley Powell stressed the aridity of the land beyond the hundredth meridian—less than 20 inches of precipitation falls there each year. Farming relying on rainfall alone is difficult and has been considered by some to be impossible, although the history of ancient farming tells otherwise. In some places in the desert Southwest, years pass without water falling from the skies. The rivers are few, and many of them roar through canyons of stone, inaccessible and impossible to harness. Others are rivers of rock, flowing through dry beds for the greater part of the year.

On the other hand, a surfeit of water has often made life difficult for desert dwellers. Although the rain often falls too little or in too few places, sometimes too much of it falls and all at once. The West's great rivers are fed on snowmelt, and when spring thaws combine with warm rains they often overflow their banks, flooding the surrounding land. Such floods swept away the simple irrigation ditches of ancient farmers and the earth-and-rock dams built by pioneer settlers along Arizona's river valleys. Even in the last few decades, raging floodwaters have washed away farms, livestock, and the built environment.

Water over the dam: floodwaters overflowing Horseshoe Dam in the winter of 1993. Photograph by Stephanie Whittlesey.

The most vital water source in the desert Southwest and Arizona is the Colorado River. It has been described as "the most used, the most dramatic, and the most highly litigated and politicized river in this country, if not the world" (Fradkin 1968:15). This book is also about the Colorado River. We will remember what the river was like before it was captured and controlled. It was a river of rock, essentially liquid earth dissolved and transported by erosion and the river's great force—a unique blending of the basic elements composing the desert environment. The Colorado River is also a metaphor for the environmental and cultural diversity of Arizona and the American Southwest. By understanding the Colorado River and its peoples, we will create a context, a cultural geography for telling stories of life in a stone-dry land.

Next, we turn to people and **culture**. Beliefs, values, and technology direct the shape of human cultures in diverse ways. There are numerous means of living with any land, and culture dictates our choices and their forms. Moreover, Arizona contains a remarkable diversity of human societies, ethnic groups, and cultures and has since people first inhabited it. We will explore Arizona's human diversity as well as its natural variability, telling stories of human cultures confronting water's scarcity and excess in diverse, intriguing ways.

In desert lands, water is the invisible shaper of societies, the substance of warfare and political intrigue, the molder of poetry, science, culture, and religion. In these aspects, water represents religion, politics, economics, and aesthetics (Stegner 1981). The need to cope with the Southwest's immoderate water supply and adjust to its capriciousness and vicissitudes has shaped the form and substance of human cultures in Arizona as elsewhere around the world. It is the only weapon we have in the constant battle against aridity. According to historian Michael Meyer (1984:8), water has:

> actuated and dominated an amazing variety of social and economic relationships. It dictated growth patterns, precipitated conflict, influenced the form of governmental institutions, and helped define how different social and ethnic groups related to one another. . . . it came to occupy a unique place in the southwestern psyche. Because of its cardinal role in the daily struggle for survival it was also afforded a telling reverence in southwestern religion, mythology, and lore.

The result of human cultures interacting with their natural environment is a modified environment, a cultural landscape that is a unique blending of the natural and cultural. As each society views the world differently, it also creates a humanized landscape that is distinctive and unique. This book will dip into these deeper, less visible levels of water, exploring how water has influenced culture and how people have altered the land.

We will also dip into contradiction and irony. The desert Southwest is a land of extraordinary paradoxes centering on water and its uses (Wilkinson 1992:16), and we will touch on some of them. Consider these examples—land that was once largely inaccessible and inhabited only

Water and History

In *Rivers of Empire: Water, Aridity, and the Growth of the American West,* historian Donald Worster (1985:19) has pointed to water's tremendous influence:

> Water has been critical to the making of human history. It has shaped institutions, destroyed cities, set limits to expansion, brought feast and famine, carried goods to market, washed away sickness, divided nations, inspired the worship and beseeching of gods, given philosophers a metaphor for existence, and disposed of garbage. To write history without putting any water in it is to leave out a large part of the story. Human experience has not been so dry as that.

sparsely by Native Americans is now open to millions of people who reside here and who come to visit, relax, and enjoy its scenic wonders. So many people are drawn to the wild spaces of the Southwest, lured by vast, empty skies and postcard-perfect vistas, that we are damaging the physical landscape. The Colorado River was once uncontrollable and unusable; it is now so completely controlled and used that its waters no longer reach the sea and have not for several decades. The opening of the West for settlement and the technological mastery that has been achieved over an inhospitable land have sown the seeds of decline by permitting population to far exceed the land's ability to support it. Water and its recreational uses have become a primary lure in a state where natural surface water does not exist. Aqueducts that were planned to carry water to farms now provide water to cities because agriculture has declined.

Perhaps the greatest paradox is the Central Arizona Project—a spectacular, human-made river running uphill more than 300 miles through a desert where little rain falls, and the beds of natural rivers lie dry and barren. It was decades in the making, the source of political and legal debates and much controversy. This book is about the Central Arizona Project, too, because the modern history of water in the Copper State has focused on the construction of this technological wonder. The project built by the U.S. Bureau of Reclamation takes Colorado River water from Lake Havasu and conveys it along underground pipelines and aboveground canals to metropolitan Phoenix and Tucson and various Indian communities. We will discover how the Central Arizona Project was conceived and built.

Cathedral Rock and Oak Creek at Red Rock Crossing near Sedona, Arizona. PHOTOGRAPH BY STEPHANIE WHITTLESEY.

Hayden-Rhodes Aqueduct emerging from Buckskin Mountains tunnel. PHOTOGRAPH COURTESY U.S. BUREAU OF RECLAMATION. JOE MADRIGAL, JR., PHOTOGRAPHER.

On still another level, this book is about **archaeology**. The homes of Arizona's ancient peoples, many of which now lie drowned below reservoirs, were excavated by archaeologists before the Central Arizona Project canals were built and the dams were modified. This work was mandated by federal law, and the scientific information that resulted was used to craft the stories told in the pages of this book. Archaeology uncovers much more than bits of broken pottery and stone tools, the discarded refuse of people now lost to history. Archaeology is the medium by which we learn about ancient life. As historian David Lowenthal (1985:238) has expressed it, "[a]rchaeology inherits the earth; most places contain the debris and cradle the memory of innumerable past events." The earth is a treasury of geological and archaeological history, writes Lowenthal (1985:239), layered in complicated, stratiform fashion.

We will explore these layers to decipher past lives in Arizona. We will tell many stories about water in a stone-dry land—stories of scarcity and excess; the places where water can be found, often hidden and unexpected; the ways ancient peoples diverted water and moved it onto their fields with weirs, dams, and canals; the spiritual means they used to ensure enough water at just the right times. We will discover how Akimel O'odham (Pima) farmers in the eighteenth and nineteenth centuries used Gila River water to cultivate vast fields of winter wheat, corn, squash, beans, and hay. We will hear the heartbreaking stories of Mormon

Falling Stars

. . . for a moment I think I've almost caught a falling star: there is no mystery; there is only paradox, the incontrovertible union of contradictory truths. A falling star which melts into vapor as I grasp it, which flows through my fingers like water, like smoke.

–*Edward Abbey,* Desert Solitaire

The Pillar site in Tonto Basin during excavations sponsored by the U.S. Bureau of Reclamation. Photograph courtesy U.S. Bureau of Reclamation. Joe Madrigal, Jr., photographer.

farmers along the Little Colorado River whose laboriously built and costly dams washed out with depressing regularity every year. We will learn how the great water-control works of our own times were built to master the erratic, magnificent Colorado River.

Finally, this book is about the future as much as it is about the past. Today in Arizona, the greater Southwest, and the United States, we are facing serious issues concerning land, water, population growth, environmental and climatic change, impacts to land and water, and sustainability. To address these issues and shape a landscape for the future, we must understand what did and did not work in the past. Our activities may have unintended consequences that influence people's ability to live with the land in the future. Sometimes the consequences of environmental modifications are highly detrimental, as pointed out by Crumley and Marquardt (1990:73): "we consciously extract coal to provide energy for domestic consumption and industrial production; in the process, we unintentionally produce acid rain, which may have a long-term deleterious effect on agriculture and, eventually, on the health of our own society."

We want the Southwest's land to be everything to us, so historian Charles Wilkinson (1992:16) has written. "[E]veryday citizens expect the western lands to generate wood products, metals, food, and electricity—and, as well, abundant wild animals; stretched-out, pristine vistas; wondrous watercourses; and a deep quiet that stirs in a near-primeval way the contemplation of centuries back and centuries ahead." We cannot have it all, however, and somehow we must reconcile these contradictory expectations. "By understanding the interrelatedness of our natural and cultural landscapes," George Thompson (1995:xiv) has written, "perhaps it is possible, despite our past history, to become better stewards of the land and better caretakers of our fellow human beings and compatriot life forms."

The Central Arizona Project

Water, in the guise of the Central Arizona Project, was the rationale for this book. It is a river of human-made rock, water that flows uphill through cement canals and huge siphons—a vast system of dams, canals, and reservoirs that would dwarf the simple irrigation canals of times past. The Central Arizona Project serves multiple functions for the citizens of Arizona—providing flood control, water conservation and supply, some hydroelectric power, and recreational opportunities. The project was conceived in

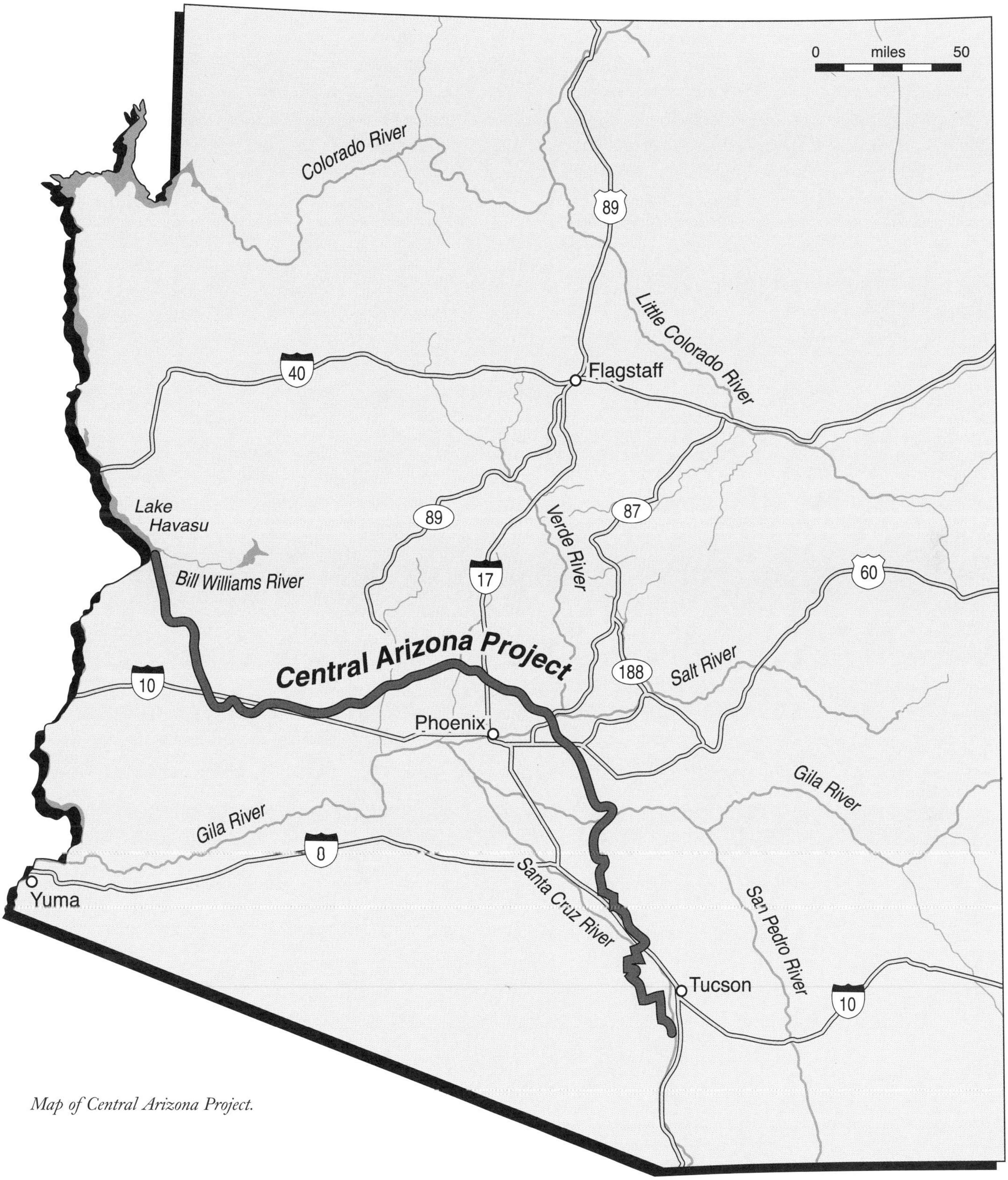

Map of Central Arizona Project.

the late nineteenth century, when irrigation pioneers dreamed of controlling the capricious Colorado River and using its tremendous flow to water Arizona farms. The water first flowed to central Arizona users in 1985, and the project was essentially finished in 1992. We will tell the story of this enormous project in these pages.

During planning and construction of the Central Arizona Project, a series of legally mandated historic and environmental-preservation programs were implemented in the United States. In accord with these laws, the Bureau of Reclamation funded environmental, cultural, and archaeological studies before the Central Arizona Project was built. This work not only preserved **archaeological sites**, habitats, and endangered species but also contributed an enormous body of scientific information. This book tells these stories, too—ways in which the nation grappled with preserving its historic resources and how the Central Arizona Project solved the problem of historic preservation as well as engineering and construction problems.

The scientific contribution of the project was vast, but the information was essentially inaccessible, published in many weighty volumes dense with archaeological jargon. The Bureau of Reclamation wanted something else to serve as a capstone to Central Arizona Project archaeological studies, something that was accessible to all and readable—a product that would summarize results for the public whose tax dollars helped to fund the project. This book is the outcome of that vision. It uses information generated by Central Arizona Project archaeology to craft stories about life in this stone-dry land.

There are many layers to the story of the Central Arizona Project, and poured together, they can be seen as a vast lake of different depths. The uppermost level, the glittering surface of the water, is the story of dam and aqueduct construction. The project has a long, complicated, and often acrimonious history. Politicians fought over the project throughout much of the twentieth century, battling in state and federal legislatures and inside and out of federal courts. The project was expensive, requiring huge quantities of federal dollars to plan, construct, and take care of associated tasks. The Central Arizona Project altered our politics, legislation, and some might say, our way of life itself. We will learn of the battles that were fought, the compromises that were won, and the struggles to build engineering marvels. We will discover how the project and the agency that built it changed over the project's lifetime.

Slide a little deeper into the water, down into the cooler levels where the water grows still, and the Central Arizona Project story becomes one of human culture confronting a land of little rain. It is a story of our struggle with a vast, harsh, arid land and its rare, vital sources of water—a battle to settle, farm, persist, and survive. Through archaeological studies that were legally mandated before the Central Arizona Project could be built, we know a great deal about the people of the past and how they managed to live in a desert land. Although each culture developed its own and often striking ways of living in the desert and using its waters, we will discover some universal truths in the struggle to survive. In this sense, the book can be seen as an **anthropology** of water and of the Colorado River that made the Central Arizona Project possible. It is an **ethnography** of place, a humanized anthology of stories about land and water. Archaeology is the medium through which we tell these stories.

Dive more deeply still, and we are in the cold, dark waters above the lake bottom, where the abstract, ephemeral aspects of human thought influence our concrete actions and behaviors. Each human group interacts with the physical and biological environments in ways that are determined by beliefs, values, perceptions, and culture. The environments are in turn altered by people's interactions. The result is a cultural landscape, a modified or humanized environment—an environment shaped by human thought and action. Anthropologists label this perspective the cultural-landscapes approach, and no better means can be found to understand the history of water control in the Southwest and how we have been able to adapt to, survive, and sometimes thrive in the desert land.

The story of the Central Arizona Project not only reflects Arizona's history, but also mirrors the history of the greater American Southwest and our nation itself. In the struggles to build the project, we can see reflections of larger issues—how to live successfully in a land of capricious resources, the best way to use those resources, and how to preserve and protect the land. We can even glimpse issues of national scope—what sort of nation we envision, the larger role of the federal government, how to form our national land-use and water-use policies. We will tackle some of the larger issues as well.

The perspective taken in this book is an outgrowth of various schools of thought about people and their relationship to the environment. Its most vital and vibrant paradigm is the belief that we, as sentient entities, do not simply "adapt" to whatever challenges the environment presents. Instead, we literally make our environment. How we perceive our environment, label it, derive symbols from it, interact with it, and ultimately how we cherish or destroy it affects the form, culture, and history of human societies. Although historians often stress technology as the root factor shaping people's interactions with the world, the ways in which humans perceive that world is probably more fundamental and profound. Moreover, it is neither the environment nor mankind that is most significant in this equation, but a third intangible element—the *relationship* between people and their land, which writer Mary Austin often emphasized in her musings about the desert West (Trimble 1998:139). In the next section, we turn to a brief overview of this perspective on land and people.

I Have Known Rivers

Poet Langston Hughes writes of rivers:

> I've known rivers:
> I've known rivers ancient as the world and older than the flow of human blood in human veins.
>
> My soul has grown deep like the rivers.
>
> . . . .
>
> I've known rivers:
> Ancient, dusky rivers.
>
> My soul has grown deep like the rivers.
>
> *(Langston Hughes, "The Negro Speaks of Rivers")*

Honanki Cliff Ruin near Sedona, Arizona.
Photograph by Stephanie Whittlesey.

About Cultural Landscapes

Today's anthropologists and archaeologists sometimes use a new way of thinking about how past and present peoples relate to their environment, called the cultural-landscapes approach. Often called cultural-landscapes theory or the cultural-landscapes paradigm, this approach helps us to understand how the physical and biological environments shaped the lives of ancient peoples, and how in turn, people altered the environments to suit their needs. Although it is a relatively new field of inquiry, the roots of the approach lie deep in several disciplines, of which archaeology is only one.

The word "landscape" means much more than a scenic view that can be appreciated for its aesthetic qualities, and the term is used differently among the various disciplines that study landscapes. When geologists speak about landscape, they usually mean features of the land surface and rocks, and "landscape evolution" refers to the processes by which these features came to have their physical properties. Landscape architects are concerned with buildings, parks, and other constructed settings of human habitation. Geographers use the term landscape in many different senses. Other social scientists often employ the word metaphorically, referring, for example, to the "economic landscape." In anthropology and archaeology, landscape has a particular meaning. By speaking of *cultural landscapes*, we emphasize that a cultural landscape is not only created by people, it is one created by *culture*.

A cultural landscape is simultaneously the product of nature and of human interaction with nature. It is the result of people living with the physical and biological environments, interacting with them and modifying them in myriad ways, and modeling worldview, ideology, and cognition upon the land. Cultural landscapes are shaped by the general mental templates that societies use to understand their world, other people's actions, and various physical and natural processes that shape the world. The result is dual—culture is transformed, given substance in the corporeal world, and the environment is transformed by human thought and action. The cultural-landscapes approach is an anthropological, behavioral, and cognitive view of environmental adjustment focusing on geography (Whittlesey 1998a). For these reasons, we can call it *a holistic anthropology of place.*

It is easy to see this interaction with living societies, but what of the past? Archaeological landscapes are the cultural landscapes of the past reconstructed from the archaeological record. When we excavate an archaeological site, archaeologists are most broadly trying to discover how ancient people conceived their world, interacted with it, and changed it over time. Ultimately we want to know how successful ancient peoples were in their adjustment to the environment and how successful the humanized environment was in supporting life. The stories of cultural landscapes in this book have been reconstructed through the medium of Central Arizona Project archaeology.

There are three building blocks of a cultural landscape, whether modern or ancient—land; people and culture; and the interactions between land and people, which create the landscape. The land includes the physical environment, such as landforms and topography, geological formations and rocks, and rivers and streams. It also includes the history of these physical characteristics. Climate is part of the physical environment, too, and is partly a product of geographic location on the globe and partly a product of topography and landform. The plants and animals that populate the land form the biological environment. Variability in the biological environment is a product of climate, geographic location, and other factors, and the biological inhabitants of the earth also have histories. The interrelationship of the physical and biological environments is typically labeled an ecosystem. It is important to remember that the environments are constantly changing. Sometimes the processes of change are easy to see, and at other times take place over such long periods that change is essentially invisible to the human eye. *A landscape, whether contemporary or one that existed in the past, begins with the land and its plant and animal occupants and with climate.*

Sonoran Desert landscape. PHOTOGRAPH BY JEFFERSON REID.

Although founded on the physical and biological environments, the cultural-landscapes approach does not separate the natural world from the human world. John Brinkerhoff Jackson, who was the creator of the modern landscape movement in cultural geography, wrote that "a landscape. . . . is a space or a collection of spaces made by a group of people who modify the natural environment to survive, to create order, and to produce a just and lasting society" (Jackson 1995:43). *Landscapes, then, are created by people.* There is no artificial division between "nature" and "culture" in this view. Charles Darwin laid this misconception to rest long ago—"far from being 'separate' from nature, human beings happen to be biological animals, too" (Flores 1998a:36). As Flores points out, we do not have to choose between humans and nature.

The anthropological approach to landscape is distinguished by its emphasis on cognition, perception, and culture. How people perceive places and conceptualize their environment lies at the core of the cultural landscape. These perceptions are learned and therefore differ from culture to culture. Greider and Garkovich (1994:1) reveal this in their definition of landscape as "the symbolic environments created by human acts of conferring meaning to nature and the environment, of giving the environment definition and form from a particular angle of vision and through a special filter of values and beliefs." Moreover, people often define themselves by their cultural landscapes or humanized environments. These landscapes reflect our self-definitions that are grounded in culture (Greider and Garkovich 1994:1). It is possible to take an extreme view and say that landscapes do not exist outside of people's perception of them. For the individual, a landscape does not exist if the individual is no longer a part of it (Rabbitt 1995:180). Language is a crucial part of culture and cognition. By naming the important features of our world, we give them an established identity (Basso 1996).

A cultural landscape is a humanized environment that has been created by cultural perceptions. These perceptions determine how we interact with the environment, how we exploit and preserve it, the ways in which we shape it and in turn are shaped by it. The importance of cultural values and perception also means that *there is no single cultural landscape of the past or present, but as many different landscapes as there are cultures*, and even potential variations within a single culture.

Canyon de Chelly, northeastern Arizona, and Antelope House cliff ruin. Photograph by Stephanie Whittlesey.

Cultural landscapes have life histories that illustrate the processes by which the land is transformed and becomes an architectural form. The landscape is both medium for and outcome of action and previous histories of action (Tilley 1994:23). Because landscape includes a temporal dimension, a historical explanation on some level is a necessary ingredient of landscape analysis (Roberts 1993:10). A primary goal of archaeological landscape reconstruction is to read the history of human interactions with the environment through time, and the temporal dimension that is typically the domain of archaeology is the best tool for such reconstructions.

The history of human-environment interactions can be read most easily in landscape modifications. People dam rivers and change their courses; they modify the distribution of plants and animals, domesticate them, and sometimes extirpate them. People construct various kinds of settlements and buildings, agricultural features, roads, and much more. In farming the land, people add nutrients to the soil and change its physical properties. The residues of these activities take the form of archaeological sites and activity areas. Landscape history can also be read in the environmental history of any place where people have settled, used environmental resources, or modified the land.

The historical dimension of landscape study is important because what affects the environment also affects people and vice versa. "In interacting with their physical environment," Crumley and Marquardt (1990:73) write, "people . . . make decisions and expend energy according to their own mental models of how the world operates." As Gussow (1995:225) expressed it, "Our landscape is more than a passive backdrop to human events—it is a stage on which we move. The objects and forms on that stage shape our actions, guide our choices, restrict or enhance our freedom, and in mysterious ways even predict our future." Or expressed another way, "Landscapes often are archaeological expressions of . . . cultural transformation" (Hardesty 1999:218).

Why study cultural landscapes? Archaeology has long been a discipline interested in the relationships between people and their environments. The time depth of prehistoric archaeology is a good stage for examining long-term processes of environmental change and how people cope with change. In cultural landscapes, archaeologists can study social as well as environmental change. Contradictions inevitably arise as people interact with the environment, use it as a stage for social and political change, and act out tensions among social groups. The cultural landscape can be seen as the product of conflict resolution (Marquardt and Crumley 1987:7).

For the archaeologist, cultural landscapes are important because they help us to reconstruct intangibles of culture and ideology that are otherwise difficult to study. As Mrozowski and Beaudry (1990:189) expressed it, "It is thus possible to gain insight into the workings of culture in terms of conscious and unconsciously shared notions of order and causality, of reason and sense in human relations, through archaeology by attending to the affective power of the built environment—the total material expressions of landscape and land use."

Using a cultural-landscapes approach, the archaeologist can make sense of vastly different and often competing conceptions of land use through time. As the following chapters will demonstrate, the cultural landscapes of the past and present were extraordinarily different. Each group approached the environment differently, had distinctive sets of beliefs and values, and used the land and water in varied ways. Viewing these differences within a cultural-landscapes approach helps us to understand how these differences came to be and place them in a contextual framework.

Petroglyphs in the lower Verde River valley. PHOTOGRAPH BY STEPHANIE WHITTLESEY.

It is commonplace to say that to understand the present and the future we must understand the past. Connecting the threads of the past to the present, scholars, artists, historians, and archaeologists create a fabric that displays the diversity and richness of Arizona's landscapes. We do this because we recognize that, if perception and beliefs shape the natural environment and how we use it, then we can change these views to make a better, more acceptable context for existence. Joseph Meeker (1997:5–6) phrased it in terms that are readily understood, writing: "however the human mind imagines the world, that is how the world tends to become for humans. If we think of the Earth as a farm, then we behave as if it were one; if we imagine that the Earth is a spaceship, then we manipulate and direct its path toward our chosen goal." We apply to the earth whatever model we have adopted to explain it to ourselves. These models are passed along from generation to generation through cultural traditions and social institutions. Using a cultural-landscapes approach will help us to reconceptualize our environment and its water, to reshape our technology and ideology to deal with the challenges of watering Arizona in the future.

ABOUT THIS BOOK

Our story begins with the Colorado River. Together, the Colorado River and the Central Arizona Project encompass all of Arizona's physical and biological landscapes. We will learn about the land through which the river flows and what the river was like before it was dammed and controlled. We will also learn about the peoples and cultures of the Colorado Basin as background to telling their stories of water use and meaning. We will take an imaginary voyage down the Colorado River from source to delta, looking at its topography and hydrology, its peoples past and present, and some of the important events that affected the river, the land, and the people.

Next, we will turn to the history of water control in the West and construction of the Central Arizona Project—the legal and political battles, the struggle for land and water rights, how the liquid treasure was eventually divided up and allocated among all those who use the river's water. We will discover how the Central Arizona Project and the many ancillary and supporting projects were constructed. These tasks are accomplished in the first part of this book, called *Headwaters*, which provides the background for the stories that we will tell.

The middle section of the book, *Midstream*, examines water use among Arizona's peoples through time. We divide Arizona into three physiographic provinces—Colorado Plateau, mountain Transition Zone, and desert Basin and Range. The Colorado River, the Central Arizona

Magic

Driving late at night through the Onandaga Indian Reservation, Native American writer Joseph Bruchac wound past abandoned fields, broken-down houses, and last the hills set in place by the Holder Up of the Heavens. He writes,

. . . .
& I remember
that this is a land
which has been bright with magic

(Joseph Bruchac, "Three Poems for the Indian Steelworkers in a Bar Where I Used to Drink")

Cliff ruins in the Sierra Ancha, Arizona. Photograph by Stephanie Whittlesey.

Project, or both, crosses each of these provinces, although most of the Central Arizona Project lies within the Basin and Range province and the Sonoran Desert. For each province, we look first at the land. To tell stories about the ways people have used the land and the water through time, we must understand something of the physical and biological environments. We will describe the unique features of each province—landforms, topography, geology and soils, water sources, plants, and animals. We will look at climate, temperature, and rainfall. Because people have singular effects on the land, we must learn about culture as well. We look at some of the people who occupied each province, describing briefly their languages and organization, how they lived with the land, and their subsistence and economy. Last, we look at the ways in which these peoples interacted with the unique environments of each province to create distinctive cultural landscapes, focusing on how they conceptualized water, used it, and controlled it. We will learn how water shaped their lives as we know it through Central Arizona Project archaeology.

The last section, *Slackwater*, is a summary and synthesis. It compares and contrasts what we have learned through Central Arizona Project studies, using a cultural-landscapes approach to examine the ways in which ideology and cultural values have shaped land and water use to create modified, highly humanized environments. The book closes with an appendix describing the legislative background for archaeological and environmental studies and a glossary.

As many different scholars, writers, poets, and ordinary folk have observed, our personal relationship with the land, which is unique to each individual's experience, perceptions, and culture (Trimble 1998:139), determines how we use the land. Scholars, scientists, poets, novelists, and essayists have been writing about the American Southwest and its peoples for centuries. We will look at how some of these people have viewed the land, glimpsing their personal landscapes. I have selected some gems of such writing, along with the oral histories of Native American and Mexican-American peoples, to augment my own impressions.

To achieve the tasks set forth in this book, I have drawn on four ways of describing the modern land and accessing and reconstructing the past: observation, memory, **artifact** and archaeology, and text or history. The gifts of sensory impression and memory provide a framework for describing personal experiences and perceptions of the desert Southwest as it appears today and as we remember it. Barry Lopez (1998:142–143) has perhaps said it best:

> It is through the power of observation, the gifts of eye and ear, of tongue and nose and finger, that a place first rises up in our mind; afterwards it is memory that carries the place, that allows it to grow in depth and complexity. For as long as our records go back, we have held these two things dear, landscape and memory. Each infuses us with a different kind of life.

Artifact, archaeology, and history provide means of going backward in time, delving into the land and landscapes of the past. In his book *The Past Is a Foreign Country,* Lowenthal (1985:xv) has written: "The past is everywhere. All around us lie features which, like ourselves and our thoughts, have more or less recognizable antecedents. . . . Whether it is celebrated or rejected, attended to or ignored, the past is omnipresent." Lowenthal (1985:xv) also lists three ways of knowing the omnipresent past: "Relics, histories, memories suffuse human experience," he has written. "Each particular trace of the past ultimately perishes, but collectively they are immortal." What Lowenthal labeled "relics" is properly the realm of archaeology and the artifacts it uncovers in the houses, sediments, and refuse of ancient times. In addition, as Lowenthal observes, there is history. "History extends and elaborates memory by interpreting relics and synthesizing reports from past eyewitnesses" (Lowenthal 1985:210). Lowenthal broadly defines history to include **prehistory**, natural history, oral narratives, films, fiction, and much more. As used here, "history" typically means textual productions. We combine in this book the descriptive, sensory powers of observation; the sweet nostalgia of memory; human and natural history; and the debris of the past as unearthed by archaeology to help us understand the cultural landscapes of the past.

As the foregoing indicates, there is a general structure to the book. It is not an academic volume, however, and does not have to be read in order from first to last page. Chapter 1 provides an overview of the land, water, and peoples of the Colorado Basin and serves as an introduction to what follows. The reader may wish to begin there. The stories presented in *Midstream* are vignettes—individual tales or viewpoints that dip briefly into what are often complicated issues. Although they are presented in rough chronological order, these stories do not have to be read in that order; each is a stand-alone tale.

This book is a collection of stories, a thesaurus of impressions, descriptions, memories, perceptions, and history about the Colorado River, the land of the American Southwest and Arizona that is at once ethereally beautiful and ambiguously harsh, and the strange dichotomy of water and desert. Writing this book has been an intensely personal enterprise, and the narration reflects the process of one woman coming to grips with the often glorious, sometimes disturbing natural context of life. At the same time, the book is a scholarly enterprise that draws on the facts of history, nature, and archaeology. To ease the transition from one aspect to the other, I have tried to avoid scientific and archaeological jargon as much as possible. Technical terms that appear in boldface print throughout the book are defined in the glossary. Each chapter closes with a section that provides sources to which the interested reader may turn for additional information, including books, journal articles, and World Wide Web sites. Along with impressions, fragments of journals and fiction, and poetry, I have tucked little nuggets of scientific, biographical, and historical information into sidebars to avoid interrupting the flow of the text. All of these asides can be enjoyed individually at the reader's convenience.

This book offers a window into water as the medium that created the textured, nuanced, sometimes baffling, always fascinating cultural landscapes of Arizona's past and present. The landscape is a textual production, a physical metaphor for the discontinuities and shifting meanings that have remade the natural world into a human artifact and have embedded into it images of the past. We find that cultural forms do not necessarily persist across time and space, but are transmuted, constantly changing texture and color. We can create and recreate, reform and reshape our landscapes into a format that will take us into the twenty-first century and farther still. In these stories, descriptions, and recollections, we look at the ordinary as well as the spectacular, the mundane as well as the sacred. "By appreciating the everyday places of our existence,"

Thompson (1995:xiv) has written, "as well as the spectacular places we often can only imagine from afar with the aid of words and pictures, it is possible for us to comprehend what is at risk when we fail to care for those places properly." Our story unfolds with the Colorado River, and we begin our journey with a voyage from its headwaters to its junction with the sea.

For further information, see: Carole L. Crumley (editor), Historical Ecology: Cultural Knowledge and Changing Landscapes *(School of American Research Press, Santa Fe, 1994); Carole L. Crumley and William H. Marquardt (editors),* Regional Dynamics: Burgundian Landscapes in Historical Perspective *(Academic Press, San Diego, 1987); John B. Jackson,* Discovering the Vernacular Landscape *(Yale University Press, New Haven, 1984); George F. Thompson (editor),* Landscape in America *(University of Texas Press, Austin, 1995); Christopher Tilley,* A Phenomenology of Landscape: Places, Paths and Monuments *(Berg, Oxford, 1994); Stephanie M. Whittlesey,* Archaeological Landscapes: A Methodological and Theoretical Discussion. *(In* Vanishing River: Landscapes and Lives of the Lower Verde Valley: The Lower Verde Archaeological Project, *edited by Stephanie M. Whittlesey, Richard Ciolek-Torrello, and Jeffrey H. Altschul, SRI Press, Tucson, 1998).*

A Voyage down the Colorado River:

TRAVELING THE RIVER OF STORIES

1

The way was west, but the way was also down, down, down into the depths of time.

—DONALD WORSTER, *A River Running West: The Life of John Wesley Powell*

TO UNDERSTAND THE CENTRAL ARIZONA PROJECT, we must begin with the Colorado River, for it is the source of the water that flows some 300 miles through cement canals and siphons from Lake Havasu to Tucson. More than just the source of Central Arizona Project water, the river can teach important lessons about larger issues relating to the American West. Encapsulating much of the Southwest's environmental diversity, the river is a metaphor for its geography and landscape. The river also speaks to southwestern history, politics, economy, and ethnic diversity. It runs through a fabled territory of legend, gold, and visions—the American West, where the national movement laid forth in the doctrine of Manifest Destiny culminated and where native peoples confronted the consequences of Euroamerican intrusions. Moreover, the Colorado River and the surrounding land are sacred—they are homeland and emergence places for many of the West's indigenous peoples. The Colorado is also a river of dreams, whose waters bear witness to stories of human hopes, aspirations, successes, and failures through millennia of striving. When we recount the river's stories—whether of geological history, ancient life, or its taming and diversion—we are reading the history of the West.

The Colorado River basin offers a set of peculiar physical paradoxes. Consider this. It contains one of the greatest river systems in America and at the same time one of the greatest deserts in the world (Waters 1984:6). The basin lies entirely beyond John Wesley Powell's hundredth meridian, which defines the limits of land that could be farmed without irrigation. Three of North America's desert ecosystems—Sonoran, Mojave,

Colorado River near Kremmling, Colorado. PHOTOGRAPH BY JEFFERSON REID.

and Great Basin—converge in the basin. Through this stone-dry land flows the dominant river system in the American Southwest. Paradoxically, although the river emerges at the Continental Divide and is fed by snowmelt, it is imprisoned in desert canyons where snow seldom falls. Perhaps most striking, the river has a great watershed and copious flow, yet this water is largely unusable unless tapped by modern technology.

The Colorado River has a number of unique features setting it apart from other American rivers. It is a big river draining a vast area, extending 1,700 miles from the headwaters of the Green River in Wyoming to the Gulf of California. Together with 35 perennial rivers and numerous tributary streams, the Colorado drains more than 256,000 square miles of land in the United States and northern Mexico—equivalent to one-twelfth of the continental United States. Seven western states are included in its drainage basin, which is divided into two segments at Lee's Ferry in northeastern Arizona. The Upper Basin states include Wyoming, Colorado, Utah, and New Mexico, and the Lower Basin states are Arizona, Nevada, and California.

The big river runs wide and deep. Its width varies from 76 to 300 feet; its depth averages 35 feet, but where its erosive force has carved pools it can be more than 100 feet deep. The size of its drainage area and the steepness of its gradient—it drops an incredible two-and-one-half miles in elevation, from a height of 14,000 feet at its headwaters to below sea level (Waters 1984:13)—yield as much as 14 million acre-feet of water each year. Despite its size and magnitude, the Colorado River is not the largest in the West. The Columbia River drains a watershed of equivalent size, yet its *unused* flow is about 12 times greater than that of the Colorado River (Fradkin 1968). Although of comparable grandeur, Waters's (1984:xvii) "great Red River of the West" is hardly as mighty as the Mississippi.

There can be few other rivers in America, perhaps in the world, that traverse such astoundingly variable country. The river and its tributaries drain five physiographic provinces—southern and middle Rocky Mountains, Wyoming Basin, Colorado Plateau, and Basin and Range. The Colorado Plateau—a massive, uplifted series of plateaus whose sedimentary history can be read in colorful layers—forms more than half the Colorado's drainage basin. The country through which the river runs is unparalleled in physiographic, topographic, geologic, and climatic diversity. It contains almost every physical landscape in the West—snow-clad mountains; sagebrush-dotted high plains; slick-rock canyon country; scorched, barren deserts—and even earlier, it sustained a luxuriant, Nile-like delta. Only the chaparral-covered Mediterranean hills and the humid, cool forests of the Pacific Coast are missing. Diverse landscapes create equivalent variety in plant and animal life, some forms of which occur nowhere else in the world. Each landscape yields resources, whether timber, minerals, grasslands, or arable soil.

But the Colorado River Basin is also a country full of danger, fraught with obstacles to human habitation and use—a defiant land daring humans to tame it. It was isolated from the rest of the nation through much of its history, and some of the basin's states were the last to achieve statehood. Remote, inaccessible, distanced from the urban centers of the East by lack of transportation facilities, the Colorado Basin was in essence a foreign country. From the snow-packed, forbidding mountain ranges of the Rockies to the searing heat and scant rain of the deserts, the Colorado River Basin encompasses the West's constraints as well as its advantages.

Unlike spring-fed streams of other regions, the Colorado's precious, highly coveted water derives from snowpack in the mountains of Wyoming and Colorado. Snowmelt in the spring is augmented by isolated areas of high precipitation. Consequently the river is a slave to its source. In years when snowpack is thick and precipitation high, the river is engorged, massive, frightening. In times of drought, it dwindles; the reservoirs expose their bleached bones, and dust boils up from the once-submerged sandy wastes. Those who tapped the river and envisioned the vast development that now depends on its water may have never considered what would happen if snow did not fall on the Rocky Mountains.

Grand Teton National Park, Wyoming. PHOTOGRAPH BY JEFFERSON REID

Because of its source, the river is as variable in its moods as a Victorian maiden. The river fluctuates violently on a seasonal basis and from year to year with the vagaries of winter storms arising in the Pacific Ocean, the accumulation of snow in the headwater ranges and spring runoff, and fluctuations in ocean currents that have been labeled in recent years El Niño (wet cycle) and La Niña (dry cycle). Winter storms

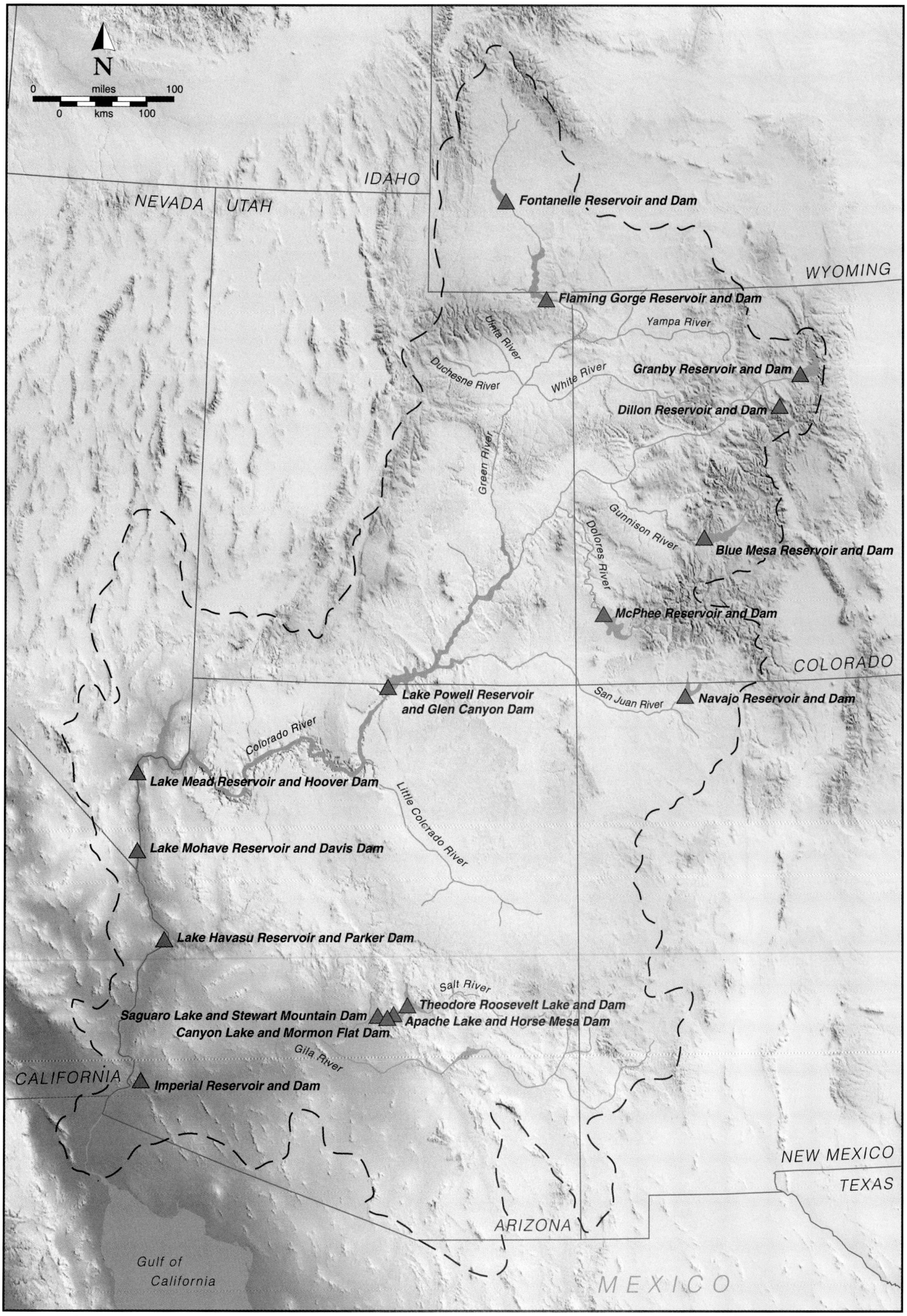

The Colorado Rive Basin, showing the Four Corners of the U.S. Southwest, the Colorado's tributaries, and major water-control projects.

have often generated the most damaging flows. Unlike summer's fierce, localized, and intermittent monsoons coming from the Gulf of Mexico, winter storms originating in the Pacific Ocean are typically widespread and gentle, soaking into the ground. When the volume of water exceeds the soil's capacity to absorb it, runoff begins; it accelerates if rain continues. When warm, late-winter storms add rain to melting snow, the effects can be disastrous. Dams have ameliorated the worst effects of such fluctuations, but the river still varies and will continue to do so.

In millennia of journeying to the Gulf of California, the river has cut canyons of incomparable depth and brilliance, exposing the deeply sedimented history that so fascinated early explorers. These glorious chasms blocked human exploration, use, and settlement and created stultifying impediments for the engineers building dams in the gorges. The river is canyon-bound along most of its length; the longest stretch of unbroken canyon is 283 miles through Marble and Grand Canyons (Waters 1984:13). Much of the Colorado's water is consequently unreachable, held captive by canyons as much as a mile deep. Powell, who was the first Anglo-American to run the river (the Hopi tell of a person who negotiated the river inside a hollow log), was steeped in this irony. When he remembered the canyon country, one of the most arid places in the United States, he remembered the sound of running water. It was "the land of music. . . a land of song" (Worster 2001:333).

Much of the canyon country is formed of soft, easily eroded sedimentary rocks—sandstone, shale, mudstone, and limestone. As the river slices through these naked rocks bare of vegetation that would block runoff and moderate erosion, it becomes a river of rock. The river carries the basin's depositional history in the particles of rock, sand, and silt. Before the dams, the Colorado's sediment volume was extraordinary. In large part, it is this load of liquid rock, along with its delta, that prompted E. C. La Rue to call the Colorado River "America's Nile" in his 1916 report, *Colorado River and Its Utilization*. The Colorado is at times seemingly more solid than liquid (Waters 1984:13). "Too thick to drink, too thin to plow," it was said (Fradkin 1968:182). The suspended, fine sediment colors the water reddish brown, giving the river its name.

During flood events, the quantity of heavy, detrital material sloughed from the stony slopes of the Colorado Plateau is vastly increased. Obeying the laws of gravity, this matter drops out and is redeposited where the river's gradient moderates about 200 miles above the Gulf of California. Over time, the river formed its own delta with this material, cutting off the peninsula and raising its channel higher than the surrounding desert (Waters 1984:14). According to Marc Reisner (1986:122), who penned the classic water-control history *Cadillac Desert: The American West and Its Disappearing Water*, so much sediment was deposited that the raised riverbed forced the river to slip out of its shallow embankments and seek new channels time and again.

Dams have changed these processes by impounding sediment in the river's upper reaches. Before Hoover Dam was built, the Colorado River carried an average annual load of 180 million tons of silt past Yuma. According to writer Russell Martin (1999:32), this figure represents *11 tons* of silt for every acre-foot of water, a load 17 times greater than that of the so-called muddy Mississippi. After the dams, the annual load of 180 million tons of silt was reduced to 13 million tons. The captured silt began to accumulate in Lake Mead, reducing its storage capacity. One reason Glen Canyon Dam was built was to solve this problem (Fradkin 1968:182).

The great river begins with two streams, each heading in the high mountains of the West (see Colorado River Basin map). The Green River is the westerly of the two, rising in the glacial mountains of the Wind River Range in Wyoming. This river is 730 miles long and drains a larger area than the second stream. The Green River falls 9,000 feet in its course, winding its way successively through alpine meadows, sagebrush flats, alkaline wastes, and deep sandstone canyons. The easterly stream is the upper reach of the Colorado River, which until 1921 was known as the Grand River (Fradkin 1968:30). This name change was not unimportant, for it implied that the rights to the water properly belonged to the state of Colorado rather than Utah. The upper Colorado River heads in Rocky Mountain National Park in Colorado. It flows 420 miles to join the Green River in Canyonlands National Park near present-day Moab, Utah. Both the Green and the Grand/Colorado have been argued to be the Colorado's true source. Because of greater length and watershed, Fradkin (1968:35–36) and Worster (2001:155) argued on hydrological grounds that the true beginning of the Colorado is the Green River, and I follow these authors' usage.

There is an indescribable lure of running the river, of abandoning oneself to "the noiseless effortless powerful slide of the Colorado through its burnished chute of stone" (Abbey 1968:173). In the following sections, we trail in the wake of Powell and other explorers, running the rapids without a raft to view the country carved by the river; on our journey, we will seek meaning in the topographic bones of the land. Much of what follows is based on my own travels throughout the Southwest and particularly on two trips my husband and I made to follow the Colorado River from its headwaters at the Green and Grand Rivers to

The Name of the River

Few rivers have carried as many names as the Colorado (Waters 1946). By the mid-1700s, the Colorado had already been named four times by Spanish explorers and missionaries who apparently did not know or remember those who had gone before. Hernando de Alarcón, commander of Coronado's sea force, was the first European to sail up the Colorado River in 1540. He called it El Río de Buena Guía, the River of Good Guidance. Working his way southward in an attempt to rendezvous with Alarcón, another of Coronado's men, Don Rodrigo Maldonado, encountered a broad, red river. On its banks, he saw Native Americans carrying torches, and he named the river El Río de Tizón, meaning Firebrand (or half-burnt wood) in Spanish (Waters 1946:146).

Don Juan de Oñate, first governor of New Mexico, struck westward in 1604. He too encountered the great river, which he named El Río Grande de Buena Esperanza—the River of Good Hope (Waters 1946:152). The indefatigable Padre Eusebio Kino, who began missionary efforts in Sonora and southern Arizona in 1687, named the Colorado El Río de los Mártires (the River of the Martyrs) (Waters 1946:155).

A hundred years or so later, Padre Francisco Garcés made a number of trips to the river country, opening trails that would be followed for centuries. He was the first to make use of the name that would stick (Stevens 1988:5)—Colorado, meaning red or colored earthy shades in Spanish—and astutely observed that it drained a distant, red country (Waters 1946:156). In 1776, Padre Francisco Silvestre Vélez de Escalante named the Colorado El Río del Cosnina, reflecting his party's decision to abandon their route and return home (Waters 1946:161).

Waters (1946:xi) simply calls the Colorado the Great Red River of the West, and this may be the most appropriate name of them all.

Many names were also bestowed on the Green River (Fradkin 1968). The Native American name Seedskeedee meant "prairie chicken river," and it is still applied to landscape features in the area. Franciscan missionary Silvestre Vélez de Escalante gave the first European name, San Buenaventura. Those who followed Escalante called it Río Verde in Spanish and the name was adopted by trappers. Others called it the Colorado, because the easterly stream above the confluence with the Green was at that time called the Grand River. I have been unable to discover the definitive source of this name. Historian Robert Black (1969) contends that the name was of French origin and perhaps bestowed by a trapper. Grand appeared on a map of the region drawn in 1839 (Geary 1999:viii). Other sources, according to Geary, credit John C. Frémont for naming the river and the lake.

In 1921, the Utah legislature introduced and then defeated a bill to change the name from the Green to the Colorado. Colorado lawmakers acted more decisively, and in the same year the Grand River became the Colorado (Fradkin 1968:35).

Yuma, Arizona, in the late spring and summer of 2002—a season of drought, fear, and fire in the American Southwest.

On this journey, we will see the Colorado River region as it is today, a teeming country of well-watered farmlands, ski resorts burdened with the weight of moneyed chic, Indian casinos, blue-water resorts, sprawling urban centers knotted with freeways—the West transformed by water. We will also see the basin as it once was—home to diverse native peoples who wrested a successful living from the often-harsh land, frightening in its immensity to the first European and Anglo-American explorers, a refuge and dreamscape for Mormon pioneers—a stone-hard land with scarce water and limitless spaces. To understand the land, we must go back in time through the landscape of memory, for the river today is not the river that was. Memory and observation together will describe the land and the water, setting a geographic and emotional backdrop for the stories that follow. I will attempt Navajo writer Nasdijj's (2000:49) approach: "I do not have tourist mementos," he states. "What I have are images I attempt to put into words so you get the smell and the feel of the place. Place as it serves the function of telling the story." We will decipher the river of stories and dreams, translating its messages and its history into lessons for now and tomorrow.

Headwaters of the Green River to Canyonlands National Park

The Green River rises in a land of perpetual snow and ice, the Wind River Range in Wyoming. I confess that I have not hiked to its glacial headwaters. The closest I have come is Pinedale, which lies at the foot of the mountains. There can be no doubt that Pinedale is a mountain town. Every inch of wall space in Farley's General Store is covered with the trophy heads of snarling game animals. Pinedale is also home to the Museum of the Mountain Man that celebrates the trappers who explored the upper reaches of the Green River between 1820 and 1840. Above Pinedale rise sharp, glacier-carved peaks—in late May, still shrouded with snow—that shelter the river's mystical source. Writer Philip Fradkin has climbed much closer to the source than I, and he has described it convincingly. Melting glacier water and snow gather at Knapsack Col on the Continental Divide. My map gives the elevation as almost 14,000 feet above sea level. Forming small rivulets, the unnamed stream gathers itself and grows (Fradkin 1968:36):

> into what could almost be called a series of small, thin lakes: paternoster lakes, so called because of their resemblance to the beads of a rosary. A coyote howled and its cries blended with the many different sounds of running water. It was as if the mountains were weeping. There were countless glints of warm light on water and ice as I walked toward the rising sun. . . . The minute, intense reflection of the sun in the tarn almost brought my perception of the source down to a single radiant drop. But on this day there were many sources.

The Green River, Wyoming, looking toward the Wind River Range and the river's headwaters. PHOTOGRAPH BY JEFFERSON REID.

Below, small lakes gleam like Fradkin's rosary beads—Peak Lake, Stonehammer Lake, the Green River Lakes. The topographic map first labels the stream the Green River at the glacial valley of the same name (Fradkin 1968:39). Rushing downhill as if anxious to reach the sea, the stream is fed by a dozen creeks coming off the Grand Teton and Gros Ventre mountain ranges. Elk, moose, bison, and deer once densely populated this country; protected, fat, and relaxed, they survive still in national parks such as Grand Teton and Yellowstone.

An American Symbol

The West is a land of symbols: the cowboy, the warrior of the plains, the horse and the six-shooter. But perhaps no more representative symbol of the West exists than the American bison, commonly known as the buffalo.

—*Exhibit at the entrance to the Buffalo Bill Historical Center, Cody, Wyoming*

Warning distributed at Grand Teton National Park, Wyoming.

As it leaves the mountains, the stream widens and slows, meandering through grassy valleys and sagebrush. This is the classic western landscape—rolling, gray-green country where cowboys still ride against a technicolor backdrop of snow-capped peaks (Fradkin 1968:41). Pronghorn and cattle share the open range, and in late May, the wind still holds a bite. To my eyes, it seems to be desert land—a high, cold desert to be sure, but a desert nonetheless.

At Fontanelle, the traveler encounters Fontanelle Dam, which was built by Reclamation as part of the Colorado River Storage Project. This ambitious project approved in 1956 included Glen Canyon Dam, a story that is told elsewhere in this book. Below the reservoir, the river channel is wide, and cottonwoods line its banks; the boundary cliffs are painted in muted pastel tones of pink, khaki, gray, and olive green. Flocks of white birds float unconcerned on the waters of the Seedskadee Wildlife Refuge. This is an alkaline country, and the water it yields is salty. When Green River leaves Wyoming, its salinity has increased markedly to about one-third of the total at the Mexican border (Fradkin 1968:92).

Fifty miles downstream is Green River, Wyoming. Powell launched his first expedition at this place. In 1869, he took a group of stalwart but inexperienced explorers down the Green and Colorado Rivers in fragile, wooden boats, marveling at the deep geologic history, indescribable scenery, living Native Americans, and evidence of past human occupation. Powell's men floated through Flaming Gorge, into the canyons of today's Dinosaur National Monument, and through the gorges of the Colorado in Utah and Arizona all the way to a Mormon settlement at Callville, Nevada, where the Grand Canyon ended. At that time, the land was terra incognita to Euroamericans. Before Powell, Euroamericans had attempted to follow the Colorado from both directions—from its headwaters to the junction of the Green and Grand Rivers, and up as far as Boulder Canyon from the delta. But no one had successfully negotiated the stupendous, rapid-filled stretch of the great canyons. At that time, the Colorado was an extremely different river than today's dammed and tamed one, with treacherous rapids that were all the more dangerous because they were unexpected. The Powell exploration of 1869 was a voyage of discovery in many ways.

Powell probably chose Green River as his embarkation point because of the railroad, for it enabled him to bring boats and supplies to what was then a sparsely populated and remote setting. The expedition pushed off from an island located just a few blocks from the Union Pacific Railroad station. Today, Expedition Island is a city park where a memorial and plaques recount the historic events that took place there. We noticed that it is also a locale for kayakers to practice their rollover skills. The land

The Green River at Expedition Island. John Wesley Powell launched his boats here in 1869. PHOTOGRAPH BY JEFFERSON REID.

is stark and bleached, white as the trona which is mined there. Bare cliffs rise above the river, little changed from the 1800s as we saw by comparing historical photographs. It took the Powell crew two months and heartbreaking effort to reach the confluence of the Green and Grand Rivers. Today, the trip can be made leisurely by car in just a few days, with plenty of time for sightseeing.

Just south of Green River is Flaming Gorge, named by Powell for the red colors of its sandstone walls. It was the first of the canyons through which the expedition would negotiate a fragile path. Today, the contrast between the deep tones and the pale, chalky country to the north is just as striking as it must have seemed to Powell. According to an exhibit at the Flaming Gorge Dam Visitor Center, Flaming Gorge Dam was built as part of the Colorado River Storage Project, which was designed to "regulate the flow of the Colorado River; provide for flood control and recreation; provide for storage and delivery of water for irrigation, municipal, industrial, and other beneficial purposes; improve water quality; improve conditions for fish and wildlife; and generate electrical power." These lofty goals were achieved by a dam standing 455 feet above the river that required one million cubic yards of concrete and cost more than $65 million. It has created a reservoir with 375 miles of shoreline; no trace remains of the crimson-walled gorge that flamed in Powell's imagination.

Leaving Wyoming, the Green River flows across the northeastern corner of Utah, capturing snowmelt from the Uinta Mountains, the only major east-west range of the Rocky Mountain system and the highest point in the state. The Green loops around Browns Park into the state of Colorado, where it is joined by the Little Snake

Triangulating a Pie

Near the junction of the Green and Grand Rivers, John Wesley Powell's little band of voyagers made camp for the night. Powell recalled the following incident.

> While eating supper we very naturally speak of better fare, as musty bread and spoiled bacon are not palatable. Soon I see Hawkins down by the boat, taking up the sextant—rather a strange proceeding for him—and I question him concerning it. He replies that he is trying to find the latitude and longitude of the nearest pie.
>
> —*John Wesley Powell,* Exploration of the Colorado River and its Canyons

Train station at Green River, Wyoming. PHOTOGRAPH BY JEFFERSON REID.

Flaming Gorge Dam and Reservoir, Wyoming.
Photograph by Jefferson Reid.

River rising in the Medicine Bow Range of Wyoming. The river flows past the Gates of Lodore into the infamous Canyon of Lodore and Dinosaur National Monument. Fradkin (1968:153) has written of this region:

> To watch the Green River disappear at the southern end of Brown's Park into the Gates of Lodore in Dinosaur National Monument, Colorado, and to see it reappear near Jensen, Utah, is to experience the plunge from lush tranquillity into desolate wastes. For me, the Gates of Lodore mark the point where the change begins. . . . The gate's precipitous canyon walls, viewed from the entrance, rise in smooth, massive blocks from the flat terrain of the park. They glow blood-red in the morning. The blocks on either side of the river, it seems, would interlock in a decisive closing should they ever be joined together like the fingers of both hands. The tranquil river, sweeping around a bend, disappears into this fastness, a disappearance made more ominous by its placid surface.

In 1869, Powell also wrote of the Gates of Lodore, penning his observations at sunset when the rosy hues were changing to somber browns and black shadows. To him, it seemed "a dark portal to a region of gloom—the gateway through which we are to enter on our voyage of exploration tomorrow. What shall we find?" (Powell 1895:148). Powell's black musings proved prophetic. Negotiating the Canyon of Lodore, one of the boats, the *No Name*, was wrecked in a furious rapid.

On June 18, 1869, exhausted and weak, they pulled up the boats on a beach that lay directly below the vertical face of an 800-foot-high sandstone cliff. The massive face of Steamboat Rock at the confluence of the Green and Yampa Rivers threw the echoes of the men's voices back across the river, giving Echo Park its name. What a feeling of relief Powell and his men must have felt, having survived the wreck and managing to save barometers, thermometers, and happily, a three-gallon keg of whiskey (Powell 1895:157). Today, looking down toward Echo Park from the overlook in Dinosaur National Monument, the Gates of Lodore are hidden, and the river is just barely visible. A series of mesas resembling river terraces on a huge scale jut out like the steps of a giant staircase. The sense of distance and the massive and overbearing weight of impassive, sculpted stone are overwhelming. The river appears tiny, incapable of carving deep and treacherous canyons and

Dinosaur National Monument. Photograph by Jefferson Reid.

The Green River near Jensen, Utah. PHOTOGRAPH BY JEFFERSON REID.

splintering Powell's little wooden boat. Unlike many of our crowded national recreation areas, Dinosaur is not filled to overflowing with tourists and campers. The air here is still and silent, scented with juniper and sagebrush. Echo Park and Dinosaur National Monument were the scene of the first major battle between conservationists and the U.S. Bureau of Reclamation over the damming of the Colorado River, a story told in Chapter 4.

Leaving Dinosaur National Monument, the Green River loops back into Utah. At Jensen and nearby Vernal, the countryside is bucolic, verdant where irrigation has provided water. It was the middle of August when we passed through, and farmers were cutting alfalfa. Its sweet, grassy scent perfumed the damp, cool air. The contrast between the lush farmland along the river and the bare rock of the canyons was almost painful in its intensity. Resuming its southward course, the Green traverses the Uinta Basin and the dry plateaus of the Uintah and Ouray Reservation. The tourist lacking off-road capabilities must bypass the river here and stick to the blacktop highways that skirt the plateau land. The route to the west goes through the heart of Carbon County, mining country where coal and oil are wrenched from the earth. Just outside Rangely, two golden eagles lifted into the air inches from the hood of our car, almost touching the metal with their wings. In this land, the snow-capped mountains of the Rockies are simply a pleasant memory. But the river remembers, and the memories of glaciers and snow sing in its water.

In historical times, this was the home territory of the Ute Indians. These Native Americans ranged through much of eastern Utah and western Colorado and into parts of Wyoming and New Mexico. They traveled even farther in search of game. In more distant times, this land was home to the ancient people of the archaeological Fremont culture, a poorly understood group that is best known for the striking rock art on the sheer, sandstone walls of the canyons.

Below Green River, Utah, the river snakes its way toward the confluence with the Colorado/Grand River, looping through Labyrinth Canyon into Canyonlands National Park and the upper portions of Glen Canyon National Recreation Area. Here we leave the Green and follow the course of the Colorado from its headwaters in Rocky Mountain National Park. This is a voyage that Powell did not take; one can only wonder how different his trip might have been had he put his boats into the Grand River, rather than the Green.

Water Grandmother

Water Grandmother weaves the world
In the beginning there was only water.
Water Grandmother floated in her basket
In the midst of the waters.
She thought and created the land from her own body
As Spider creates her web, or
As a woman creates her basket.

Interview with Antonio Buck, Jr.
As interpreted by Dr. James A Goss, 1960s
From the exhibit Mountain Family Spirit: Arts and Culture of the Ute Indians
Organized by the Taylor Museum of Colorado Springs Fine Arts Center

HEADWATERS OF THE COLORADO RIVER TO CANYONLANDS NATIONAL PARK

The Colorado, formerly Grand, River is born in Rocky Mountain National Park in today's state of Colorado. A park interpreter told me that the river's source is at La Poudre Pass, and I will have to take his word for it. As Fradkin (1968:45) has observed wryly, to hike to the headwaters is not a simple task. The Colorado River trail leads seven and one-half miles from a picnic area along the river toward the pass. My map gives the elevation as just under 11,000 feet above sea level, and even with a metabolism conditioned by living at 7,000 feet in Flagstaff, Arizona, I was unprepared to tackle the climb. This is an ethereal, otherworldly land, a time out of mind. At the park summit where the road crosses the divide and leads toward the Front Range cities, we were high above the tree line and the clouds, and we shivered in our inadequate clothing. The visible landscape was bare rock, tundra, and snow not yet melted in August. The heart beats faster here, and the lungs strain to reap oxygen from the thin, searing air.

Trailhead to headwaters of the Colorado River in Rocky Mountain National Park, Colorado. PHOTOGRAPH BY JEFFERSON REID.

Rocky Mountain National Park, Colorado, looking toward La Poudre Pass and headwaters of the Colorado River. PHOTOGRAPH BY JEFFERSON REID.

Downstream from the pass, the stream gathers itself into paternoster lakes and boggy meadows. It winds through the narrow Kawuneeche Valley over tumbled stone, gaining strength from other creeks that rise from the Continental Divide. To the west, the peaks of the Never Summer Mountains stand like a movie set. Everything here is green—emerald grass, deeper blue-green and gray-green of conifers, reflections in the water, luxuriant meadows. Even the great antlers of bull elk appear mossy. The river is still a glacial stream, not yet colored by the rosy hues of liquified sandstone. Steely gray and clear, it emerges into Grand Lake, which, according to writer Michael Geary (1999:vii), is the largest natural body of water in Colorado. One of many upscale Colorado River recreation areas, Grand Lake is billed as the Snowmobile Capital of Colorado (Geary 1999:104). Its older names include the Ute Ungarpakareter (Red Lake), Arapaho Batannaach (Spirit Lake), and English Stillwater Lake (Geary 1999).

seepage, not the melting snow of La Poudre Pass, "constitutes the source of the upper Colorado River."

The Colorado–Big Thompson project was one of the earliest efforts to tap the unending flow of the Colorado River, and it is the uppermost of the river's diversion systems. The plan was to collect water from the West Slope, store it, and then transport it to the Front Range cities (Geary 1999:96). This ambitious project by the Bureau of Reclamation was completed in 1959. Water is first funneled into Lake Granby, which is formed where Granby Dam stops the Colorado. On the August day I visited Lake Granby, drought years had brought the water level down. A bleached water line rimmed the edge, and the wind blew dust up from the exposed lake bed. Upstream, Shadow Mountain Dam creates a reservoir that regulates water levels in Grand Lake. Finally, an intake structure at the east end of Grand Lake diverts water into the Alva B. Adams Tunnel for its nearly three-hour journey to Estes Park.

Grand Lake, Colorado, looking toward Mt. Craig, also called "Baldy." PHOTOGRAPH BY JEFFERSON REID.

Lake Granby, Colorado. PHOTOGRAPH BY JEFFERSON REID.

Another search for treasure, this time liquid, followed the Gold Rush years in Colorado (Geary 1999:72). In the 1880s, a simple but bold plan was developed to capture snowmelt and divert it to Fort Collins and Greeley. Built by Chinese, Swedish, and perhaps Japanese laborers, by 1932 the Grand Ditch stretched 14 miles to La Poudre Pass. The ditch can still be seen as an incongruous, brown scar across the green flanks of the Never Summer Mountains. Fradkin (1968:42) credits the Grand Ditch as the first conveyor built to transport water outside the Colorado River Basin. For Fradkin (1968:45), the water lost from the ditch due to

Water that nature destined for the Pacific Ocean now flows to the industries, farms, and ranches of northeastern Colorado (Geary 1999:98).

This part of Colorado bears no resemblance to the rough-and-tumble mining towns that sprang up in the nineteenth century. In places such as Breckenridge, once-ramshackle Victorian buildings have been immaculately restored and now house the accoutrements and service industries of ski chic. These gleaming "painted ladies," their yards brimming with colorful perennials and annuals, line the downtown streets. The cost of watering the landscaping alone must be astronomical. Huge hotels nestle on the flanks of the ski slopes. In such places, it is easy to imagine that soon every square inch of private land will be jammed with homes, ski lodges, and other playgrounds. All of this development depends on water—the farms that spread in the valleys, the boating and fishing on the lakes and reservoirs, skiing and snowmobiling, the many primary residences, ski chalets, and second homes. I wondered how Breckenridge fared in the drought winter of 2001, when ski areas throughout the Southwest closed or relied on artificial snow. No sign of hardship could be seen in its lush, pastel extravagance, however.

At present-day Kremmling, Colorado, the country has eased down from the precipitous mountain slopes to wider, more open land. The river skirts the higher elevations for the remainder of its journey through the state. The Blue River joins the Colorado near Kremmling. The Blue has been dammed far upstream; Dillon Reservoir near the town of the same name collects the Blue's waters. At Dotsero, the river meets Interstate 70 and they run parallel through Glenwood Canyon, Glenwood Springs, Rifle, and on to Grand Junction. Place names reflect the river's original name—Grand Mesa, Grand Hogback, Grand Tunnel Ditch, Grand Valley. At Grand Junction, the Gunnison River joins the Colorado. This major tributary has been dammed, too—near the town of Gunnison, Blue Mesa Reservoir traps the river before it can reach the Colorado.

Southwest of Fruita and Grand Junction—billed as "Colorado's Wine Country"—is Colorado National Monument, where the red-rock country begins. The monument lies on the edge of the Uncompahgre Plateau, an uplifted fault block in which wind and water have sculpted cliffs, deep canyons, and monoliths. Geologist Halka Chronic (1988:83) has cataloged some strange details of the ancient Colorado River's history in this area. More striking than the rock formations is the unforgettable view across the Grand Valley to the northeast toward Utah's Uinta Mountains.

The river rushes through the newly designated Colorado Canyons National Conservation Area and emerges in Utah. There it winds toward the confluence with the Green River through a wilderness of arched and carved rock. Utah State Highway 128 follows the Colorado for some distance northeast of present-day Moab, Utah, through valleys where red sandstone mesas are juxtaposed against the snow-covered La Sal Mountains. The Dolores River joins the Colorado along this stretch. Like so many of the Colorado's major tributaries, the Dolores has been dammed upstream to form McPhee Reservoir.

Moab is an adventure capital, a place where bicyclists, river rafters, and jeep tourists can experience the thrill of well-worn "wilderness." We passed carloads of bicyclists

Colorado National Monument, Colorado, looking toward the Colorado River. Book Cliffs bordering East Tavaputs Plateau in the distance. Photograph by Jefferson Reid.

Along the Colorado River near Moab, Utah, looking toward La Sal Mountains. PHOTOGRAPH BY JEFFERSON REID.

with dozens of mountain bikes strapped to carriers on top of the vehicles. In Moab, it is not water but rock that has been commodified. Rock is not the backbone of the land but an adventure canvas, little more than a backdrop for hiking, climbing, sight-seeing, rock crawling in off-road vehicles, and bicycling; a material that creates rapids for the river runners. Real and artificial rock chipped, painted, and chiseled to emulate the towering, horned figures of Fremont rock art adorns everything from motel signs to gallery art.

At Arches National Park near Moab, weirdly shaped rock formations—delicate arches; thin, vertical fins; spires, turrets, and pinnacles—are silhouetted against the La Sal Mountains. It is a good place to experience firsthand the great physical landscape contrasts of the Colorado Plateau. The park's *Official Map and Visitor Guide* reports that more than 2,000 arches have been cataloged in the park, ranging from 3 feet to more than 300 feet in length. Arches form when thin, curving sheets of sandstone fall away from both sides of a rock fin (Chronic 1988:31–32). Deepening, they ultimately join to form windows and arches. The stone in Arches is a vast canvas for the artistry of the elements—sculpture shaped by the action of wind and water, paintings daubed by mineralization. After a while of stone-gazing, one begins to see rock art on a gigantic scale—portraits of an elderly Navajo woman and her husband; a perfect, young pharaoh with chiseled features;

Stone arch at Arches National Park. PHOTOGRAPH BY JEFFERSON REID.

Arches National Park, Utah, looking toward La Sal Mountains. PHOTOGRAPH BY JEFFERSON REID.

a turtle. I discovered sphinxes and camels, Napoleonic busts, and the heads of Egyptian queens. In late May, it was hot, and visitors vied avidly for the few picnic tables located in the shade of overhanging junipers.

Not far below is Canyonlands National Park, where the Green and the Colorado/Grand Rivers join. Above the confluence, the rivers swoop in lazy meanders created from early Miocene times when they cut across a nearly level plane. Where the rivers shortcut these entrenched meanders, leaving abandoned loops high above the present river level, park lands such as Jackson Hole and Anderson Bottom have formed. The rivers are "docile and easygoing, essentially free from rapids" (Chronic 1988:63). Not so the Colorado River below the confluence. The change to a savage, unpredictable, wild river is forcefully illustrated in Canyonlands National Park. The rivers have shaped "a lonesome, dramatic land of barren canyons, cliffs, buttes, and mesas, a strangely beautiful, awesome valley where erosion rules" (Chronic 1988:58). Several overlooks high above the rivers access the incredible vistas. We chose the Needles Overlook. In this area, the Permian Cedar Mesa Sandstone has eroded along two intersecting sets of joints and faults into a forest of fantastic pinnacles that give the overlook its name (Chronic 1988:61, 65). Neither words nor photographs are adequate to convey the spectacle of vastness and wildness. Only the distant whine of small aircraft and the calls of cattle grazing on the terraces below hinted at a populated world.

The confluence of the Green and Colorado Rivers is often striped with distinct colors, created by each river's sediment load and turbulence (Chronic 1988:64). Sometimes one or the other is more green or clear. The merged streams flow side by side, unmixed, for some distance. We were unable to see this phenomenon, for the river was too far below us, hidden by the panorama of stone. Salt cedar, or tamarisk, has stabilized the sand bars and beaches along this stretch of the river (Chronic 1988). A nonnative plant introduced from the Near East by way of Mexico, salt cedar is a phreatophytic plant—one that has no control mechanism for water. The plant takes as much water as possible and sends it out into the leaves. What the plants do not take up shrinks back into the ground and returns to the water table (Childs 2000:146). This prodigious water user is capable of drying up natural springs (Chronic 1988:64).

Below Canyonlands National Park, the combined Colorado and Green Rivers, from this point on named the Colorado by all, rampage through Cataract Canyon, first named by Powell. Chronic (1988:60) has labeled this canyon "one of the wildest stretches of water in any national park." The Dirty Devil River—another name legacy from Powell's first voyage—meets the Colorado at present-day Hite, and there Lake Powell begins. It is about 200 miles from Cataract Canyon to Glen Canyon Dam at Page—the city that rose from uninhabited ground expressly to house the dam builders. The river enters the present-day state of Arizona near its boundary with Utah, and the portion that traverses Arizona is labeled the lower Colorado River. This 800-mile-long stretch begins just below Glen Canyon and ends at the Gulf of California.

Glen Canyon to Grand Canyon

Like so many other features of the canyon country, Glen Canyon was named by Powell. Of entering the canyon, he wrote: "we have a curious ensemble of wonderful features—carved walls, royal arches, glens, alcove gulches, mounds, and monuments. From which of these features shall we select a name? We decided to call it Glen Canyon" (Powell 1895:232–233). Powell gave its length as 149 miles. Before Glen Canyon Dam, the river from this point southward carried the heavy load of silt, sand, and rock particles that inspired its name. Today, at certain times and in certain lights, the river still flows red. Lake Powell, named for the explorer in a piece of inspired irony, now covers what was once Glen Canyon.

Lake Powell lies in the center of some of the Southwest's most spectacular scenery. To the northwest is the red, slickrock country of the Grand Staircase–Escalante National Monument and the Kaiparowits

Needles Overlook, Canyonlands National Park. Photograph by Jefferson Reid.

Wahweap Marina, Lake Powell, Arizona. PHOTOGRAPH BY JEFFERSON REID.

Plateau. To the north is Capitol Reef National Monument, another extravagantly colored and wildly shaped wilderness of rocks. Just north of Rainbow Bridge National Monument, the Escalante River draining the Kaiparowits Plateau joins the Colorado. Powell's cartographer dubbed the Escalante as "The Unknown River." According to naturalist and poet Ann Weiler Walka (2002:5), it was the last river in the lower 48 states to be mapped. In the winter of 1871–1872, Powell and his brother-in-law Almon Thompson named the river for Padre Silvestre Vélez de Escalante. This is the land of standing rock, as the Ute called it—a land of frozen rainbows, mythology turned to stone. The contrast here between naked red stone and blue water is remarkable and unearthly, a combination both awesome and unnatural. Not sky, not river, Walka (2002:45) has written, Lake Powell is "sleight of hand, illusion, no place."

The region is also the historic and modern home of the Southwest's most populous Native American tribe, the Navajo, or Diné. East of the lake is Navajo Nation land, and over it looms the rounded bulk of one of the Navajo's holy places, Navajo Mountain. The Navajo call it Naatsis'áán, and they know this **laccolithic** dome as the head of Earth Woman, a powerful being who reclines across the Four Corners Region. Powell named it "Mount Seneca Howland" after one of the men who left the expedition, hiked out of the Grand Canyon, and ultimately was killed. The name never stuck, and in 1912, Ellsworth Kolb, one of two brothers who helped to open the Grand Canyon to tourism, first wrote of it as Navajo Mountain.

Capitol Reef National Monument. PHOTOGRAPH BY STEPHANIE WHITTLESEY.

Below Navajo Mountain, the San Juan River joins what is now Lake Powell from the east. Although greater than the Rio Grande in its annual discharge, it was virtually unknown when historian Frank Waters wrote of it in 1946.

The river was named by Spanish explorers after St. John the Baptist. The Navajo view the San Juan as a sacred river, and they say that the rain that nourishes all life sprang from the union of the Colorado and the San Juan. The San Juan has also been dammed, diverted, and tamed to bring water to western cities such as Albuquerque. Wilkinson (1992) has told the story of the San Juan–Chama Project, a technical-engineering marvel with many ramifications for Native Americans.

Upstream of the San Juan–Colorado confluence near the hamlet of Mexican Hat, the San Juan River cuts through naked rock to form great, looping meanders named the Goosenecks. A sign at Goosenecks State Park, which overlooks the spectacle, reads: "GEOLOGISTS CONSIDER THIS PART OF THE RIVER TO BE ONE OF THE FINEST EXAMPLES OF 'ENTRENCHED MEANDERS' ANYWHERE IN THE WORLD." The meanders originated when the river flowed across a relatively flat plain and became entrenched as the Colorado Plateau was uplifted. Four meanders or goosenecks are visible from this point.

The Goosenecks are best viewed from the plateau south of Natural Bridges National Monument. Standing at that overlook and looking southward, the spires and buttes of Monument Valley are visible in the far distance. So many John Ford westerns were filmed in this awesome land of weirdly shaped stone sentinels that Monument Valley has become for many people the quintessential image of the West. It has also become the stereotypical Navajo landscape, where herds of snowy sheep and their velveteen-and-turquoise-clad herders are silhouetted against rippling, red sand dunes. The red sand of Monument Valley is persistent, a stinging rain that stains clothing and shoes.

The land of the Southern Paiute abuts the north side of Glen Canyon and the Grand Canyon to the west. Anthropologists classify them in the Southern Numic branch of the Uto-Aztecan linguistic family. These people once ranged north and west of the Colorado throughout southwestern Utah, the Kaibab Plateau, northwestern Arizona, the Arizona Strip north of the Grand Canyon, and parts of southeastern Nevada and eastern California. As told in their origin story, the Colorado River is the heart of Southern Paiute territory, and the people consider the entire Grand Canyon to be sacred land. In past times, these mobile people lived in small groups based in home territories. They subsisted largely on the products of the hunt and on gathered wild plant foods. Many of the carved buttes, canyons, plateaus, and mesas of the Colorado canyon country bear Southern Paiute names.

At Lake Powell, a historical marker commemorates the place known as the Crossing of the Fathers, El Vado de los

Monument Valley. Photograph by Jefferson Reid.

Padres, which is now covered by water. In 1776, Franciscan friar Silvestre Vélez de Escalante undertook a journey of discovery accompanied by his superior, Francisco Atanasio Domínguez. Leaving Santa Fe, they traveled northward and eventually reached Utah Lake. Their return journey took them across the northern side of the Grand Canyon. They had been warned that the great canyon would block any attempt to cross the river. Not far from the place that would later be known as Lee's Ferry, they found a difficult ford across the Colorado River, which Escalante called El Río Grande de los Misterios, "the great river of mysteries."

A more recent bit of Arizona history also lies under Lake Powell. In the 1870s, the discovery of precious metals in the Grand Canyon brought a flurry of mining efforts (Crampton 1972:153). Perhaps the most daring of the hopeful entrepreneurs was Robert Brewster Stanton. He connected with Frank Brown, a Denver real-estate investor who was seeking to construct a railroad along the Colorado River across the Continental Divide. In 1899, Brown and Stanton surveyed the river. Brown drowned when their boat overturned in Marble Canyon and Stanton, who was a railroad engineer, took up his vision alone. Stanton found a route over which he thought rails could be laid. The Denver, Colorado Canyon & Pacific Railroad was to link the Rocky Mountains with the sea via the Grand Canyon. Prophetically, Stanton proposed to run the railroad on electricity produced by the river's water (Crampton 1972:187). Stanton sought to win financial backing for his proposed canyon railroad and even visited Powell in Washington, D.C., armed with photographs, maps, and facts, but he had no takers.

When his railroad scheme failed, Stanton turned to gold mining in Glen Canyon. He laid claim to virtually the entire length of the canyon and tried to use the river as a giant sluice box. Forty miles downstream from Hite, Stanton installed a massive dredge that in 1899 cost at least a hundred thousand dollars, possibly twice that amount. In April 1901, Stanton reported a net profit of $30. The gold dust was so fine it floated right through the dredge machinery. Dreams of vast fortunes slipped inexorably downstream (Farmer 1999:220). Stanton's dredge remained beached until it was submerged by Lake Powell.

At Lee's Ferry, the Colorado breaks through the cliffs that mark the end of Glen Canyon. Once it was the only place for a 279-mile stretch where a wheeled vehicle could be brought to the water's edge (Crampton 1972:142), and later the site of the only bridge across the Colorado River south of Moab and north of the Grand Canyon. A Mormon refugee from the Mountain Meadows massacre named John D. Lee settled along the river at a place called Lonely Dell at the mouth of the Paria River. By 1873, he was carrying people over the big river on the ferry *Colorado*. After Lee was executed for his role in the massacre, Mormons operated the ferry until 1928, when it was replaced by Navajo Bridge across Marble Canyon (Crampton 1972:146). The river crossing at Lee's Ferry was the point of entry for Mormons coming from Utah to settle Arizona territory. For almost four centuries, Waters (1984:11) has written, Lee's Ferry was "the rendezvous of Spanish, Mormon, outlaw, trapper and traveler alike." One mile below the mouth of the Paria River, all the waters of the upper basin unite to form a single stream where the flow can be measured. Below this point lies the lower Colorado River Basin.

From Lee's Ferry, the Colorado runs south through Marble Canyon. In 1869, Powell (1895:238) named the canyon because it resembled "one great bed of marble a thousand feet in thickness," but the stone is actually hard, polished limestone. The river has hollowed the stone into facsimiles of architectural forms. From the air, Marble Canyon appears to be a virtual crack in the earth, belittling the canyon's actual scale and grandeur. Powell (1895:244) gave its distance as about 65 miles long. The rapids of Marble Canyon are treacherous and can be deadly, as Stanton's experience demonstrates vividly.

On the northwestern side of Marble Canyon rise the Vermilion Cliffs—an immense, uplifted rim marking the edge of the Paria Plateau. Western writer Wallace Stegner (1953:91) labeled it "the most striking and beautiful and persistent cliff-wall in the whole plateau country." The Vermilion Cliffs represent the southernmost step in the colorful, grand staircase leading north to Bryce Canyon National Park—the White, Gray, and Pink Cliffs, which were named in the 1800s by Clarence E. Dutton.

Clarence E. Dutton

Clarence Edward Dutton graduated from Yale in 1860. During the Civil War he was transferred to the U.S. Army Ordnance Corps and remained as a captain after the war. In 1871, he was reassigned to Washington, D.C., where he became part of that city's intellectual corps and acquainted with John Wesley Powell. He was detailed to join Powell's survey in 1875, and for 15 years split his time between the field and the Ordnance Corps. Described by Stephen Pyne (1998:xv) as "geologist, raconteur, explorer, landscape critic," Dutton was the author of the first comprehensive geology of the Grand Canyon, *Tertiary History of the Grand Cañon District* (1882). More than scientist and intellectual, Dutton was a landscape poet, a writer whose glowing words painted the bare stratiform bones of the land in vivid colors. Dutton's epic work established the Grand Canyon as a symbol and rich record of earth history.

Bryce Canyon is perhaps the most famous of the rock wildernesses in this area. The 9,000-foot-high ridge forming the eastern rim of the Paunsaugunt Plateau has been eroded on the eastern edge, to create rock amphitheaters. Its pinnacles, needles, and hoodoos are bathed in pastel tones—

Vermilion Cliffs. PHOTOGRAPH BY JEFFERSON REID.

There are many versions of this tale, and probably all of them hold some kernel of truth. It is a story of fear and betrayal, loyalty and murder, martyrdom and faith. It illustrates the lengths to which some people were driven by the cruelty of life in the American West.

In 1857, a time of fear and rumors, the United States was waging war against what it perceived to be a rebellion in Utah. Mormons and their Indian allies were gathering in response. A party of about 140 immigrants had the misfortune to be passing through Utah on the way to California. Mormons accused them of disrespect and poisoning spring water. The immigrants turned against the Mormons with hostility and threats, setting the two groups squarely against one another. Early in September, the wagon train stopped in the long mountain valley called Mountain Meadows, located in the far southwestern corner of Utah's Dixie. There they planned to rest and prepare for the long journey across barren country that lay ahead.

The Story of John D. Lee and the Mountain Meadows Massacre

Here the story grows murky. Some accounts give that Mormons dressed as Indians fired upon the wagon train, others that Indians were responsible. Whoever the perpetrators, they instigated a pitched battle against the immigrant party that lasted for four days. Then, so the story goes, John D. Lee was ordered to betray the immigrants—offer them safe conduct to Cedar City if they would surrender their arms, then kill them. In her biography of Lee, Juanita Brooks (1985:211–212) has cited the chilling orders.

The unsuspecting immigrants marched between two files of Mormon guards who opened fire on the men and wounded. Indians leaped from an ambush and killed the women and children. In all, fewer than 20 young children survived the massacre. The clothes of the dead were stripped off and the bodies of the murdered immigrants were piled up for burial. Some accounts say that the bodies were left unburied for the creatures of the wild.

Lee reported verbally to Brigham Young. According to Brooks (1985:223), he said that Indians were entirely responsible for the massacre; "no white man was named, not even those who came only to bury the dead."

Life went on, and the aftermath of the massacre built to its inevitable conclusion. The surviving immigrant children were adopted into local families. Lee married Emma Batchelor, a 22-year-old English girl who took her place beside his other wives. The bones of the slain immigrants were gathered and reburied. Someone erected a stone cairn, later destroyed, over the site that read, "VENGEANCE IS MINE SAITH THE LORD, I WILL REPAY." Lee settled into a period of prosperity and, so he assumed, forgiveness.

By 1870, discontent with the policies of its leaders was growing within the church. There was talk of Young's culpability in the Mountain Meadows massacre, particularly his public recognition of those who had taken part. To get him out of the way, Lee was ordered to sell his holdings and move to Kanab. Action was starting against polygamists at the time, and Lee transferred his property to his wives. Then the church ordered him to take one or two wives and move down to the Colorado River crossing. Lee subsequently would be excommunicated.

At the mouth of the Paria River, Lee and Emma built a home in the place she called Lonely Dell. They were living there when John Wesley Powell's second expedition came down the Colorado River, and Emma cooked for the men. In 1872, Lee established a ferry at the crossing under Young's orders. It provided a route for Mormon immigrants crossing into Arizona and eased the tremendous isolation of the place.

The respite in this refuge did not last long. In 1874, Lee was arrested for murder and confined while waiting for his trial. The jury could not reach a verdict, and a second trial was ordered. Lee waited out the time in the state penitentiary in Salt Lake City. The jury for the second trial consisted of men in good standing with the Mormon Church. As Brooks (1985:358) has pointed out, a "conviction by a jury of his peers would be more effective in that it would declare to the world the fact that the church did not uphold Lee nor approve of his actions." The jury brought in a guilty verdict, and 19 years after the horrifying incident, Lee was sentenced to death. Lee did not make the public confession that would have spared his life, but he did write the story of the massacre.

On March 23, 1877, Lee was taken to the scene of the massacre. Before he was executed, he posed for a photograph sitting on the edge of his coffin. Lee was buried near Panguitch, Utah, with his temple robes on top of his body. A simple monument now stands there. In 1961, John D. Lee was reinstated into church membership and blessings. Was it murder, justice, or betrayal? The reader may decide.

For more information, see: Juanita Brooks, John Doyle Lee: Zealot, Pioneer Builder, Scapegoat *(Utah University Press, Logan, Utah, 1985).*

coral, salmon, buttercup yellow, chalky white, gray, and lavender. The pink colors of the Claron Formation rocks come from iron oxides and tiny grains of hematite (Chronic 1988:48). Faults have thrust the ancient lake deposits upward and split them apart. Erosion has carved the uppermost white-rock formation into rectangular shapes that mimic grottoes, Greek temples with columns, and the gothic arches of European cathedrals. To my eye, Bryce's formations resemble elaborate, pastel sand castles on a grand scale.

Marble Canyon ends where the Little Colorado River joins the big river at the edge of present-day Grand Canyon National Park. To reach the confluence, the Little Colorado River flows through land belonging to the Navajo Nation. Coronado's chroniclers called the Little Colorado the Spanish version of "Flax River," a name later adopted by Army surveyor Lieutenant Joseph Christmas Ives. In the 1820s, the father-and-son trapping team of Sylvester and James Ohio Pattie ventured into the canyon country. Although they may have been among the first Anglo-Americans to view the Grand Canyon, historian Richard Batman (1984) has pointed out that Pattie's reminiscences indicate a topographically confused and temporally impossible route. When Pattie (1984:88–89) recorded the following passage, he was probably describing the Little Colorado River canyon, for Batman indicates he often meant that river when he referred to the "Red river":

> On the 28th, we reached a point of the river where the mountains shut in so close upon its shores, that we were compelled to climb a mountain, and travel along the acclivity, the river still in sight, and at an immense depth beneath us. . . . It is perhaps, this very long and formidable range of mountains, which has caused, that this country of Red river, has not been more explored, at least by the American people. . . . April 10th, we arrived where the river emerges from these horrid mountains, which so cage it up, as to deprive all human beings of the ability to descend to its banks, and make use of its waters.

The confluence of the Colorado and the Little Colorado rivers is a sacred place, marking the point where the Hopi emerged into the present world—the Sipapuni, a spring mound in the Little Colorado River gorge a few miles

Hoodoos

The *Hoodoo* is Bryce Canyon National Park's newsletter. Its front page gives the definition of hoodoo as: 1. A pinnacle, or odd-shaped rock left standing by the forces of erosion. 2. (Of African origin) To cast a spell or cause bad luck.

The first, matter-of-fact definition does little justice to the fantastic forms created by erosion. For "erosion is king here," Halka Chronic (1988:48) has written. "And what erosion! Towers and turrets, narrow scalloped walls, and thousands of ornate and fanciful figures." The active agent causing these fairylands of stone is water—rain, frost, snowmelt, and runoff. As for the second definition, the official map and visitor's guide tell us that hoodoos cast their spell on all who visit.

The handiwork of erosion—Bryce Canyon National Park, Utah.
PHOTOGRAPH BY JEFFERSON REID.

upstream from the confluence. The spring produces 100,000 gallons of water each minute. It literally bursts, throwing itself from the point of emergence (Childs 2000:101–102). To the Hopi, springs are entities: not spirits, but simply alive. "They were points where creation came to the surface and spilled out, where a hand could actually reach forward to feel the emergence" (Childs 2000:86). Not far from Sipapuni is another spring that the Zuni claim as their emergence point. Interestingly, "Hydrologists have found that the reservoirs beneath these two ceremonial springs originate in entirely separate parts of Arizona. Their waters differ in age, in fact, by thousands of years" (Childs 2000:101 102).

To the west, on the Arizona Strip, today's Kaibab-Paiute Reservation is set against the western arc of the Vermilion Cliffs in one of the more remote portions of the state. Powell explored this country in the first year of his surveys on the high plateaus. The reservation encompasses Pipe Spring, an important Southern Paiute encampment and holy place that was appropriated by Mormon settlers and today is a national monument.

Powell called the "big Cañon," as it was later labeled by the rather unimaginative Lieutenant Ives, the Great Unknown. The canyon seemed to him ominous; the expedition's stores were low, and although the men appeared as cheerful as they had ever been, their jests rang hollow to the major's ears.

The Covenant with Maasaw

When the Hopi people first emerged into this world, so the story goes, they saw footprints on the earth's surface. The footprints were larger than those of any living person, and they knew they were not alone. Soon they encountered Maasaw—guardian of the earth, fire, and the underworlds. He was wearing a terrible mask. The Hopi petitioned the great being to allow them to live on earth. Maasaw agreed, provided that they make a covenant with him. The people must promise to take care of the earth. The covenant was sealed when the people accepted Maasaw's gifts of corn and a digging stick. Among the many colors of corn offered to the Hopi, they chose blue, knowing it would last forever. Although their life would be one of hardship, it came with the promise of survival. The Hopi have chosen Hopivötskwani, a way of life based on patience, humbleness, and the willingness to endure hardship—the same virtues that enable them to successfully grow crops on the windswept mesas.

The covenant requires that the Hopi people continue to perform ceremonies to ensure the perpetuation of life on earth. Ritual life is focused on making sure that rain in all of its forms—clouds, snow, springs, and rivers—will continue to fall and bring up the sweet, green corn and squash. Because of this covenant and its requirements, Hopi ceremonies symbolically incorporate and pay homage to water, which is the source of all life.

—Traditional

Versions are also told in: Harold Courlander, The Fourth World of the Hopis *(Crown Publishers, New York, 1971); Trudy Griffin-Pierce,* Native Peoples of the Southwest *(University of New Mexico Press, Albuquerque, 2000); Edmund Nequatewa,* Truth of a Hopi: Stories Relating to the Origin, Myths and Clan Histories of the Hopi *(Northland Press and Northern Arizona Society of Science and Art, Flagstaff, 1967).*

How Pipe Spring Got its Name

An interpreter at Pipe Spring National Monument told what is probably an apocryphal story of marksmanship. In 1858, so the story goes, pioneer Jacob Hamblin and party camped at the spring while on an expedition headed to Hopi from St. George, Utah. Someone bet Jacob's brother William that he could not hit a handkerchief tied to the limb of a tree at 50 yards. Because he was known as "Gunlock Bill," this bet may have been a bad idea. When William took the shot, the air pushed ahead of the bullet moved the handkerchief out of the line of fire and he missed. Undeterred, William took up another test—he shot the bottom out of the bowl of a pipe without breaking the sides. The spring was named after that pipe.

The interpreter thought it unlikely that a pioneer in this wild country would have owned a silk handkerchief. Gunlock Bill's feat of marksmanship seems equally improbable. The reader may decide the truth of this story.

Down the Great Unknown

Four years after the first voyage down the Green and Colorado Rivers, John Wesley Powell wrote of the anxiety and even fear that beset the expedition on beginning the journey into the Grand Canyon.

> The flour has been resifted through the mosquito-net sieve; the spoiled bacon has been dried and the worst of it boiled; the few pounds of dried apples have been spread in the sun and reshrunken to their normal bulk. The sugar has all melted and gone on its way down the river. But we have a large sack of coffee. The lightening of the boats has this advantage: they will ride the waves better and we shall have but little to carry when we make a portage . . . .
> We have an unknown distance yet to run, an unknown river to explore. What falls there are, we know not; what rocks beset the channel, we know not; what walls rise over the river we know not.
>
> –*John Wesley Powell,* The Exploration of the Colorado River and its Canyons

GRAND CANYON TO GRAND WASH CLIFFS

A plaque at the South Rim near El Tovar Hotel gives the length of the Grand Canyon from Lee's Ferry to Grand Wash Cliffs as 277 miles. The canyon's average width is 10 miles, but it is more than 200 miles to travel from rim to rim by road. With an average elevation of 8,000 feet above sea level, the North Rim is higher than the South Rim, which averages 7,000 feet. In its course through the canyon, the river drops 2,200 feet.

These bare geographic facts give no conception of the Grand Canyon's incomprehensible size, saturated colors, or immense architectural forms. Artists, poets, writers, scientists, and everyday tourists have all attempted to describe the Grand Canyon and the emotions it generates, but it is a difficult task. "The newcomer does not arrive fully prepared to appreciate the canyon," so historian Donald Worster (2001:325) has written, and it is still harder to capture its spirit. Standing on its rim for the first time, the Grand Canyon appears unreal—a computer-generated image from a high-tech movie, perhaps, or the painted backdrop to an old, technicolor western. The canyon is "by far the most sublime of all earthly spectacles. . . . The sublimest thing on earth" (Dutton 1882:141–143). Mark Neumann, who wrote a fascinating ethnography of the Grand Canyon, and writer Stephen Pyne (1998) have argued that the canyon, like so many other features of the physical landscape, became what people made of it. The canyon was "created" by a series of intellectuals, who by recording the canyon in words and pictures shaped human perceptions that persist today. Neumann (1999:67) has written:

The El Tovar Hotel

The El Tovar Hotel on the South Rim of the Grand Canyon opened in 1905 to house the many tourists who were already flocking to the scenic wonder. The hotel was named for Don Pedro de Tovar, a soldier in Coronado's army. It was designed for the Harvey Company and the Santa Fe railway by Chicago architect Charles Whittlesey, who designed other famous structures in the Southwest. He combined the stylistic elements of a Swiss chalet and a Norwegian villa into a unique architectural blend. The hotel cost a quarter of a million dollars to build and boasted a solarium; a music room; a fifteenth-century, Norwegian-style dining room; a roof garden; a greenhouse to raise vegetables in the snowy season; and telephones (Neumann 1999:27).

El Tovar Hotel, South Rim, Grand Canyon. PHOTOGRAPH BY JEFFERSON REID.

Grand Canyon, South Rim. Photograph by Jefferson Reid.

The "abyss" has been an enduring symbol that marks a cosmogonic site of intellectual challenge, spiritual profundity, and existential gravity and weightlessness. The Grand Canyon has been all of these to people since John Wesley Powell followed the Colorado River into what he called the "Great Unknown." Since that time, the canyon has been a symbolic space cleaved between distanced, scientific interpretations of nature that claim objectivity and control, and spiritual longings for answers to questions over one's place in nature and the cosmos.

The canyon has meant something different to all who have encountered it. Native Americans view it as a sacred place imbued with holy meaning, an Eden where creation stories can be read in stone and water. European explorers, Anglo-American miners and trappers, and road and railroad surveyors found it little more than an egregious obstacle to achieving wealth or connecting place to place—a worthless country, profitless and remote. The French, British, German, and Japanese tourists come to the canyon to seek the spirit of the American West. The canyon has become a spiritual nexus for the western conservation, environmentalist, and wilderness movements. Artists find it a perennial source of inspiration, a muse set in stone.

The same physical attributes that render the Grand Canyon a sublime and inspiring spectacle also present torturous obstacles, although most who view the canyon never see its darker side. The river flows through the canyon in a series of long pools some 40 feet deep interspersed with short, steep rapids created where harder rock stopped the river's ceaseless downcutting. The rapids were a source of immense hardship to the Powell expedition. The men were forced to portage their boats many times over especially difficult places. Glen Canyon Dam has changed the rapids like so much else about the river, but even today, they can be challenging. The river runners who have successfully negotiated the Colorado's rapids have become legendary figures in the annals of canyon history.

The naked rock reflects the sun and little grows on the steeper slopes. Rock slides and falls are ever-present dangers. In their macabre catalog of death in the canyon, ecologist Michael Ghiglieri and physician Thomas Myers (2001:21) list 50 victims of accidental falls. The "easiest" way to reach the canyon floor has always been by foot. The hike down to the bottom of the canyon and back up the other side is 24 miles by steep, strenuous hiking trail. The trails are treacherous, slippery with loose rock, icy in winter, and hazardous with the leavings of the mules that carry less inspired visitors to the canyon bottom and back. Joints ache and swell, muscles strain, the lungs labor. It cannot be done in a single day, although some have tried. During summer storms, side canyons funnel water off the bare slopes into sudden flash floods of nearly inconceivable force and ferocity. People drown, and their bodies are never found. So many people have drowned in flash floods, swimming and rafting accidents, and crossing mishaps that Ghiglieri and Myers (2001) dub the river "The Killer Colorado."

The climate is one of the canyon's worst hazards. The cool air and forests of the rims provide no portent that the canyon floor will be hot, thorny, and perilous. Despite signs warning visitors that hiking in summer's heat can be dangerous, each year tourists overcome with heat prostration and dehydration are hauled out of the canyon. It is difficult to carry enough water to sustain the body on a summer hike—more than two gallons per person per day—and unprepared hikers succumb to the physiological effects of heat and cold (Ghiglieri and Myers 2001:43).

Sign warning hikers to Indian Gardens at Grand Canyon National Park. PHOTOGRAPH BY JEFFERSON REID.

Despite these formidable obstacles, the Grand Canyon was long inhabited by indigenous peoples. From Lipan Point on the South Rim, you can look down to Unkar Delta, one of the largest, river-level stretches of arable land in the canyon, where archaeologists from the School of American Research excavated prehistoric dwellings and farm sites. Exploring a smaller gulch of Bright Angel Canyon, Powell found such ruins and marveled at their location. "It is ever a source of wonder to us," he wrote, "why these ancient people sought such inaccessible places for their homes. They were, doubtless, an agricultural race, but there are no lands here of any considerable extent that they could have cultivated" (Powell 1895:259).

The Spanish were the first Europeans to gaze into the depths of the great canyon. In 1540, Francisco Vásquez de Coronado marched north from Compostela, Mexico, through the new lands in search of treasure. Hearing tales of a large river that ran west into a land where giants lived, Coronado dispatched an exploring party from Zuñi (the fabled Cíbola) under his officer García López de Cárdenas. Their route evidently took them along the Little Colorado River and the present Arizona State Route 64, reaching the South Rim perhaps near Desert View Point. The explorers' estimates of the Grand Canyon's width and depth were the first words written about the Colorado River and its canyons.

They originally estimated that the river was only about six feet wide. An abortive attempt to reach the canyon bottom proved this to be wrong.

The Franciscan priest Francisco Tomás Hermengildo Garcés was another Spaniard who viewed the canyon. More than two centuries after López de Cárdenas, he traveled across the Coconino Plateau to the South Rim. Garcés named the gorge Puerto de Bucarelia after one of the viceroys of New Spain. Although Garcés may have found a road paralleling the Colorado River of potential interest to Spain, it was a rocky one. "I am astonished at the roughness of this country," he wrote, "and at the barrier which nature has fixed therein" (quoted in Fradkin 1968:216).

The first Anglo-American tourists in the late nineteenth century came on horseback, taking three days to ride from Flagstaff. Beginning in 1892, stagecoaches made the trip to the South Rim in one day (Mangum and Mangum 1999) on two alternate routes around the San Francisco Peaks. The round-trip fare from Flagstaff was $20. In 1901, the Atchison, Topeka & Santa Fe railroad extended mining-built tracks to the rim. By 1905, when El Tovar Hotel was built, the railroad and Fred Harvey's hotels allowed visitors to see the canyon in comfort and style. In 1919, Grand Canyon was named a national park (Crampton 1972:206). Shortly thereafter, the automobile democratized the park from a playground for the rich to something within the reach of almost everyone—so much so that traffic congestion and pollution prompted the beginning of shuttle bus service in the 1970s.

Today, the Grand Canyon is one of the world's paramount tourist attractions and the region's greatest commercial industry. In 1998, almost five million people from many nations visited it (Neumann 1999:9). Pyne (1998:116) argued that the Grand Canyon has become a kind of sacred site to Europeans and Americans alike—easily the most spectacular and most distinctive place to seek the spirit and character of the American West. The canyon's topographic features still bear the names of ancient gods and goddesses bestowed by Powell—Venus Temple, Apollo Temple, Wotan's Throne—which reflect the mystic aura of the sublimest place on earth. "There are enough cathedrals and temples and altars here for a Hindu pantheon of deities," Abbey (1968:176) wrote. It is inconceivable to think that Bureau of Reclamation engineers once sought to build dams in Marble Canyon and Grand Canyon.

Below Bright Angel Canyon, the river plunges into Granite Gorge, which Powell labeled the river's "granite prison." It winds past Osiris Temple, Sagittarius Ridge, Powell Plateau, Steamboat Mountain, and Fossil Bay toward the territory of today's Pai peoples. As with Hopi, Zuni, Navajo, and Southern Paiute, the canyon is the spiritual home and sacred place of the Pai. This group of Yuman-speaking people, called the Upland Yumans by anthropologists, includes the Hualapai and Havasupai. Although the Yavapai are linguistically and culturally similar to the other two peoples, in earlier times they were not friendly with the others. Oral history tells a tale of escalating tensions among the people until blood was spilled and the Yavapai split from the other two groups.

According to oral traditions, the Pai people came into existence in southern Nevada at Avi kw'ami or Spirit Mountain, known by the Anglo name of Mount Newberry. The ancestors of today's people moved to Meriwhitica Canyon, a tributary of the Grand Canyon (Crampton 1972:28), where they were taught everything necessary to live in the canyon country—the names of the springs, the uses of plants, how to hunt, and the appropriate ways to live with the land. Although not their place of emergence, the Grand Canyon is the place where the Pai became distinct from neighboring tribes and learned how to live successfully. The rocks are home to the spirits and the souls of the ancestors linger there; each spring and stone has a meaning and a story.

The Havasupai Reservation begins where the canyon loops around Great Thumb Mesa. The Havasupai have inhabited the green and paradisaical canyon bottoms since time immemorial. Their reservation encompasses the well-watered farmlands of Havasu Canyon, also called Cataract Creek Canyon. Havasu Falls, pouring its white veil into the turquoise water, is an inspiring sight to those intrepid enough to hike to the canyon bottom. Garcés was the first European to see Havasu Canyon and the village of the Havasupais. "All the earth here is red," he wrote in 1776 (Crampton 1972:71).

At Lava Falls, basalt boulders create a 30-foot drop where waves crest as high as three-story houses when the river is in flood. There was a cycling wave at the bottom that would burst apart with the crack of a gunshot. Powell ran this rapid in wooden boats—a 15-foot pilot boat and two 20-foot dories. Even today on a far tamer river, the falls inspire fear in river runners. North of Lava Falls, the volcanic bulk of Mount Trumbull stands above the canyon rim.

The Hualapai Reservation is adjacent to the Havasupai country, and the river's traditional significance is symbolized by its central place in the official tribal seal of the Hualapai Nation. On Hualapai lands, the total width of the canyon, excluding the inner gorge called lower Granite Gorge, begins to narrow. There are fewer carved buttresses, buttes, and side canyons, and the descent to the river becomes less tortuous and steep. From Peach Springs, a

Havasupai Medicine Song

This traditional Havasupai song, titled "Havasupai Medicine Song," was transcribed by Leanne Hinton and Lucille Watahomigie.

The land we were given
is right here,
right here.
Red rock
streaked with brown
shooting up high
all round our home.
Red rock
shooting up high
right here.
A spring will always be there
down at its foot
From way back
it is ours
Right down
the center of our land
a line moves,
bright blue-green,
. . . .
all round the water.
This is what I'm thinking.
At the edge of the water
foam is forming,
swirling, swirling.
At the edge of the water
silt is being laid down
in ripples.
This is what I'm thinking.
Water skaters walk,
gliding, gliding.
This is what I'm thinking.
Water grasses growing,
bright blue-green
under the water.

vehicle can be driven down a rocky, rough road to the water's edge, the only place along the Grand Canyon where it is possible to do so. Across the gorge from Meriwhitica is Separation Canyon, where three of Powell's men left the expedition, tired of the hardships and fearing what was ahead. They were thankfully unaware of the worse fate that would befall them. The men were killed when they climbed out of the canyon, some say by Indians. This tale, like so many others, is disputed (see the discussion in Ghiglieri and Myers [2001]).

It was a vast relief for Powell's expedition to come out of the Grand Canyon into the valley with low mountains in the distance—"The relief from danger and the joy of success are great" (Powell 1895:284). It had taken three months and six days to travel from Green River to Grand Wash Cliffs. The startled Mormons at Callville who saw Powell's boats pull ashore thought they were seeing ghosts, for the expedition had been reported lost and everyone drowned.

Since the dams were built, the sense of a vital river ends at Separation Canyon for many. "From here to where the Colorado River ends just short of the Gulf of California, the river is either a wide reservoir, a narrow lined channel, a trickle after being diverted, or a sluggish flow where the used water is returned" (Fradkin 1968:227).

GRAND WASH CLIFFS TO YUMA

The Grand Wash Cliffs represent a fault scarp that demarcates the western end of the Grand Canyon. The Colorado Plateau ends there, and the more open, flatter Basin and Range province begins. From the Grand Wash Cliffs to the end of its journey, the river will mark boundaries between the modern political entities of Arizona, Nevada, and California. At Hoover Dam, the river turns abruptly to the south and begins its descent to the Gulf of California. Hoover was the first of the great dams built on the Colorado River. The edifice straddling Black Canyon, dedicated by President Franklin D. Roosevelt in 1935, is everything a dam should be—"a monument to man's apparent infallibility and triumph over a mighty river" (Fradkin 1968:238).

Hoover Dam is a remarkable edifice—a giant structure resembling some sort of space station or biosphere constructed to shelter earthlings on an alien, watery planet. There is nothing here but rock and water; even the parking lots—engineering marvels in and of themselves—and visitor conveniences are carved out of living stone. Over it all loom the high towers and buzzing lines bringing electricity from the turbines deep within the dam to the homes,

Hoover Dam. Photograph by Jefferson Reid.

The river is a long, thin lake for about 66 miles below Hoover Dam, because Davis Dam north of Bullhead City backs Lake Mojave upstream almost to Hoover. Desert of unimaginable heat and aridity borders the river of rock; each summer, Bullhead City and neighboring Laughlin, Nevada, routinely reach the highest temperatures in the nation. The land here appears as if it had been seared by fire. Rocks are the colors of charcoal and ash, burnt by millennia of sun, blown from the bowels of the earth by volcanic fires. Desert vegetation—the eccentric, multiarmed Joshua trees, creosote, yucca—is sparse, and in the drought year of 2002, it is also dying. What remains of the river's water carries only the faintest memories of ice mountains and wooded slopes. It seems to be hurrying, almost human in its determination to leave behind the acres of burnt rock and find the sea.

casinos, and businesses of California and Nevada. When we visited Hoover Dam in the summer after September 11, 2001, security remained high. Law enforcement was highly visible, and it took a long time to cross the dam.

Behind Hoover Dam, Lake Mead stretches 108 miles upstream to Separation Canyon. Named for Reclamation commissioner Elwood Mead, it is the nation's largest artificial lake. So much lies below the lake: the place where Powell ended his historic trip, Mormon towns, routes of ferries that brought miners to the Nevada gold mines, the drowned ruins of cotton farms, the confluences of rivers. The lake's Overton Arm extends some 50 miles into Nevada, and the Lake Mead Recreation Area continues 70 miles past Hoover Dam southward to Davis Dam. Near Saddle Island, the Colorado is tapped for the casinos and hotels of Las Vegas. In ancient times, this region and the neighboring drainages of the Virgin and Muddy Rivers were home to the people archaeologists label the Virgin Anasazi. The Mojave Desert creeps down to the eastern end of the lake, where the spiky limbs of Joshua trees rise below the Grand Wash Cliffs.

It is possible that Powell may not have been the first Anglo-American on the river. In 1867, a tenderfoot prospector named James White emerged from the river near Callville. He was nearly naked, emaciated, and sunburned, and he told a wild tale. He floated down the river on a makeshift raft, he claimed, to escape an attack by Ute Indians in which his partner was killed. No one really knows how far White floated or if he actually came by the river at all (Ghiglieri and Myers 2001; Worster 2001:133–134).

Southward the river flows, now dividing Arizona and California, through the Mohave Valley and the Fort Mojave Indian Reservation—home to the Mohave, or Ahamakav, "the people who live along the river." Anthropologists group the Mohave with the River Yuman peoples, and their language is similar to that spoken by the Pai, indicating historical continuity between the Yuman peoples living in the upland and lowland regions of the Colorado River. Unlike their Pai neighbors, the Mohave still live in the shadow of the sacred peak of Spirit Mountain (Avi kw'ami).

Past Needles, California, the river creates marshy areas that shelter wildlife. Narrowing, it flows past the northern part of the Chemehuevi Indian Reservation on the California side of the river. The Chemehuevi are a Numic-speaking people who penetrated River Yuman territory in the 1850s and adopted much of their culture, although the Chemehuevi retained their own language. Below the reservation is the remarkable irony of Lake Havasu, a Pai word meaning "blue-green water."

Lake Havasu was formed by yet another of the Colorado's dams, Parker Dam, located at the confluence of the Bill Williams and Colorado Rivers. Colorful brochures tout the lake's paradox—with a year-round temperature averaging 88 degrees Fahrenheit and an average annual rainfall of less than four inches, Lake Havasu is a water-lover's paradise. It also hosts the state's second-largest tourist attraction—London Bridge, transplanted from its green English home to the searing desert by a developer with a sense of humor. Lake Havasu attracts millions of party-bound college students who frolic in the shadow of the bridge's Tudor

Lake Havasu. PHOTOGRAPH BY JEFFERSON REID.

architecture during spring break. In May, we spent a while in a city park downstream from the bridge. Jet skis can be rented for an hour or so of fun on the water. The more permanent residents anchor their boats along the beach, relaxing with coolers at their sides. A homeless woman hunted for loose change in the shallows. Not even the dogs had been forgotten; part of the park complete with fire hydrant had been set apart for canine frolics. We did not linger long; the heat was oppressive, a physical weight. It was impossible to imagine life away from the river.

The river-lake then flows past the Aubrey Hills and the rest of the Chemehuevi Indian Reservation toward Parker Dam. Anthropologist Trudy Griffin-Pierce (2000:247) describes the reservation as "30,000 acres of dry mountains and forbidding desert dotted with creosote and ocotillo." Parker Dam was completed in 1938. It was built to protect land from floods on the Bill Williams and Colorado Rivers, provide hydroelectric power, and supply water to California through the Colorado River Aqueduct. The underground aqueduct is more than 240 miles long. As with the Central Arizona Project, the water must be lifted from the lake level up and over mountain ranges to reach its final destination in California (Waters 1984:348–350). Parker Dam figured prominently in the story of the Arizona-California water wars told in Chapters 2 and 3. When Parker Dam was built, it flooded most of the Chemehuevi Valley (Griffin-Pierce 2000:248). A modern Chemeheuvi woman said, "I have to throw flowers on the water here if I want to honor my people, because that's where they are—underneath" (Trimble 1993:407).

At Parker Dam, the Bill Williams River flows into Lake Havasu from the east, forming the Bill Williams arm of Lake Havasu. The Central Arizona Project begins near the confluence. The diversion facilities include an intake channel, the Havasu Pumping Plant to lift the water nearly a thousand feet up and over the Buckskin Mountains—a feat that can only be appreciated by standing at the plant and looking directly up the vertical face of the mountain—and the Buckskin Mountains Tunnel. Some 1.5 million acre-feet of water are pumped from the lake each year. The $150 million alpha facility is surprisingly small, marked only by

London Bridge at Lake Havasu, Arizona. PHOTOGRAPH BY JEFFERSON REID.

Lake Havasu Pumping Plant, the beginning of the Central Arizona Project. Photograph by Jefferson Reid.

a simple sign that bears the label "U.S. Bureau of Reclamation" and giving no hint of what lies underground. The great engineering marvels that lift water over the vertical rise of the mountain and into the first stretch of the aqueduct are invisible. There was no one to answer my questions. The facility is fenced and locked, the engineers concerned with operations rather than tourists. The single question that filled my mind was "why?" Why begin here, where the water must be pumped skyward? Was there no other place along the river where its flow could be captured and sent on its way across the desert heart of the state? Was it topography that determined its location, or something else?

Below Parker Dam, a highway snakes along the river toward the town of Parker. In May, before summer's fierce and erosive storms, the water was not red but a tropical blue-green. We saw manufactured homes and trailers, a two-story "Bikini Bar and Biker Club" overhanging the water, and a score of boats apparently worth far more than their owners' homes. The silence was broken often by the sound of motors; voices drifted across the water. The Colorado here is truly a river of rock; the canyon walls and the hills above are bare, bereft of any leaf or stem of green. Stunning against this backdrop are the golf courses, the watered, green turf forming mute testament to the power of water to transform naked rock for human purposes.

A golf course along the lower Colorado River near Parker, Arizona. Photograph by Jefferson Reid.

Indian gaming has created improbable, lush resorts that celebrate captured and diverted water. Water flows several stories down artificial waterfalls and into interior lakes at the Blue Water Casino and Resort in Parker, where red-faced tourists can gamble after a day on the river. The water in the hotel where we stayed felt soapy, so soft it seemed impossible to rinse it off. I wondered about its source and what energy must have driven it through pipes into my room, and pondered more unanswered questions: Where did they rid the river of its cocoa-colored silt? Does it lie impounded behind Glen Canyon Dam or in some other concrete prison? What chemicals did they add to make the water potable?

Below Parker, the river opens out through the Colorado River Indian Tribes Reservation. The reservation is home to several groups, including the Chemehuevi and a few transplanted Hopi and Navajo, although the Mohave dominate. Anthropologists divide the lowland Yumans into two groups. Among others, the Delta Yumans include the Cocopah (also spelled Cucupá), and the Quechan and Mohave represent the River Yumans. After extended conflict, a group of Yuman-speaking Maricopa were driven in historical times to live among the Akimel O'odham along the middle Gila River. As Griffin-Pierce (2000:233) has reminded us, the Yuman peoples occupied a territory that for most of its history has been contested ground. The river was "a conduit for vast, sweeping change and the almost constant movement of peoples. From its vantage point Spirit Mountain has seen fierce battles won and lost, the dispersion of many peoples, their decimation by disease, the expansion of an empire, the dismemberment of homelands, and the transformation of the river itself."

The Yuman peoples living along the lower Colorado were once highly dependent on the river for sustenance and livelihood. Although the river tribes were mobile, shifting residence throughout the year to take advantage of inland, desert resources, they also farmed along the river. Each year the river flooded, depositing rich, black soil on its wide floodplain. When it receded, the people sowed

Panic Grass

The Colorado River was life to Yuman-speaking peoples. The delicious grain panic grass (*Panicum sonorum*), known as *shimcha* in the Yuman language, was a dietary staple. The Cocopah and other tribes planted the seeds in the rich, moist soil left after the river overflowed its banks and then receded—a technique called flood-recession agriculture. Each plant yield as many as 2,500 grains (Nabhan 1985:155). The tiny seeds are nutritious, containing about one-fourth protein. The seeds were parched, made into gruel, and patted into cakes. Yields of panic grass and other crops fluctuated with the amount of runoff, but remained rich. Today, no panic grass grows in the river's dry floodplain.

corn, wheat, squash, beans, and panic grass in the mud flats. The river also teemed with native fish, waterfowl, and game in the forests along its edges. "It was the river that made life possible for the River Yuman peoples," Griffin-Pierce (2000:238–239) wrote, "for otherwise the terrain. . . . Would never have supported their dense population."

The desert floor away from the river was an enormous canvas decorated with ritual art. People of the **Patayan culture**, the probable prehistoric ancestors of the Yuman peoples, etched giant figures into the stones of the desert pavement—human, animal, and geometric figures, along with seemingly random lines, spirals, and loops. The stone art, called **geoglyphs** or **intaglios**, retold stories—of creation, the deeds of mythic heroes, and gods. An intricate system of trails marked by cairns and other stone features link the figures. Some trails may represent pilgrimage routes of the

Living with a River

The river was everything to the Yuman tribes of the Colorado River—sustenance, a means of travel, life itself. They learned through the centuries to be comfortable with the river, to use its waters, and to avoid its dangers. The Indians caught squaw fish, suckers, mullet, bony tail, and chub with dip nets, seines, traps, and weirs. Fish were so abundant that they could be scooped up with large, canoe-shaped baskets (Stewart 1983:59). The Yumans also hunted geese, ducks, other waterfowl, beaver, and larger game in the thickets and lagoons. The Mojave swam in the river and ferried its waters on rafts. The Cocopah constructed dugouts of cottonwood and rafts of tule and logs. They floated small children who could not yet swim on large, shallow pottery saucers or baskets. Parents pushed the children ahead as they swam alongside (Drucker 1941:124).

keruk ritual, which symbolizes the journey to the sacred mountain Avi kw' ami. Others may be vital connections between water sources. This is a country, naturalist Craig Childs (2000:14) has written, that is "littered with arcane rock symbols, and death, and rumors of water."

Below the Colorado River Indian Tribes reservation is Ehrenberg, once a port and destination for the steamboats that plied the Colorado River in the nineteenth century. Downstream, the Yuma Proving Ground borders the eastern bank of the river. More improbable than golf courses in the desert are the decommissioned tanks and artillery that adorn the entrance to the facility. Farther to the east is the Kofa National Wildlife Refuge. Then the river sidles past the Chocolate Mountains, molten heaps of "marbled chocolate, off which the heat shimmers" (Fradkin 1968:240). This is desolate land, the most arid of deserts. It is frightening in its immensity, its searing heat, its lack of water.

At Imperial Dam, the All-American Canal diverts water to the Imperial Valley in California. The canal flows through another piece of contested ground and was a site of the Arizona-California water wars. Most of the 1.5 million acre-feet of water destined for Mexico is diverted at Imperial Dam. It is run through the All-American Canal, directed through a power plant, and returned to the river just above the border before being shunted aside for the last time at Morelos Dam. In the 27-mile stretch between Imperial Dam and Morelos Dam in Mexico, the Colorado is little more than a drainage ditch. Below Imperial Dam is the Fort Yuma Indian Reservation where Quechan peoples live, the Laguna Mountains rising to the east, and the modern city of Yuma.

At Yuma, the Gila River flows into the Colorado from the east through a narrow defile between the Laguna and Gila Mountains. The river was one of the important east-west routes linking California with lands to the east and south, carrying explorers, miners, and pioneers westward. The Gila heads in the mountains of New Mexico. Near Phoenix, the Salt River and then the Hassayampa join the Gila. After the confluences, the Gila River loops between the Gila Bend Mountains to the west and the Buckeye Hills and Maricopa Mountains to the east. West of modern Gila Bend, the Gila is dammed by Painted Rock Dam. No longer one of Arizona's major rivers, the Gila's bed is usually dry.

A network of canals here drain the Colorado of much of its last water. Yuma has been transformed by the magic of water. Acres of corn, barley, wheat, and cotton wave below the blast-furnace sun, and the unwary driver may stall behind tractors and wagons full of newly baled alfalfa. There are acres of trailer parks, too, and the air is dense with the smell of agricultural chemicals. At Yuma Crossing, we walked down to the river on a day in mid-May when the temperature topped 100 degrees Fahrenheit, and the air was thick with humidity, seemingly too dense to breathe. In the nineteenth century, the U.S. Army used the Yuma Quartermaster Depot to store and distribute supplies for military posts in Arizona, Nevada, Utah, New Mexico, and Texas. Ocean-going vessels brought supplies from California to Port Isabel at the mouth of the Colorado River, where they were transferred to river steamers.

The Colorado River at Yuma Crossing State Historic Park, Arizona. Photograph by Jefferson Reid.

Leaving Yuma Crossing and the depot, we drove to the west where a vast realm of sand dunes shimmers and sparkles. Early explorers called this 60-mile-long belt of sand dunes the Walking Hills (Stevens 1988:8). Vestiges of the old, wooden corduroy road crossing the dunes can still be seen.

Long before that road was built, Yuma was the end point of El Camino del Diablo, the infamous Devil's Highway that linked Spanish settlements in Sonora with those in California. It continued to be used throughout the nineteenth century, and the graves that line its waysides offer proof of the often deadly journey. The trip along the Devil's Highway was only possible because the seemingly waterless mountains hold tanks or *tinajas*—secret waterholes that conserve precious water even in the dry season. *Tinajas* are pools that develop in rocky watercourses, like bowls beneath a dry waterfall. They are found high in the ***bajadas,*** "where containers have been carved from the rock like secret vases and ollas" (Childs 2000:24). The desert is webbed with trails that converge at *tinajas.* Childs (2000:31) has called these faint lines made by the passage of countless human feet "waterlines"—the opposite of canals, they bring people to water rather than water to people. To discover these sources of water requires the knowledge gained by those who have lived in desert country—knowledge that we, with our dams, canals, and reservoirs, have lost.

Stories of Desert Water

Craig Childs (2000:6) writes of the mystery of desert water and its secret knowledge:

> There are great, natural cisterns out in the desert, marvelous contraptions of rock, but each is buried within miles of difficult land. They are revealed gradually, through patient inquiry, through stories told over hundreds of years.

But the knowledge required to access desert water is fading, lost in the hazy distance of desert mirages (Childs 2000:10):

> The desert cities have their cement aqueducts to siphon distant rivers, and holes are drilled into ten-thousand-year-old banks of groundwater. Familiarity with scattered water holes has become obsolete, left only for the bighorn sheep. Words are now missing from the story of ephemeral waters, severing critical pieces of information. Many people have died while crossing this desert, regardless of their reasons for being there. They died because the story was forgotten.

The Tidal Bore

The coastal tide is called the tidal bore. "A bore," according to Frank Waters (1984:116), "is simply a tidal wave which rushes up between the narrow converging shores of a river in a high and advancing wall of water opposing in turbulent conflict the current of the river itself. Such bores are encountered in but few river mouths in the world." The Colorado River was one. The tidal variation of the Gulf of California ranges from 22 feet to a high of 32 feet. Before the dams were built, the tides rhythmically generated tremendous waves that swept almost 40 miles up the Colorado River. Incoming seawater and outgoing river water collided, creating a wall of water as much as 15 feet high.

In the early 1820s, the Pattie trapping party experienced firsthand the fluctuations of the Colorado River with the tides. Their riverside camp established at low tide was inundated when the tide came in. Pattie wrote (1984:138), "we gathered up our floating blankets, got into our canoes, and held fast to the brushes, until the water fell again, leaving us and our canoes high and dry."

Waters (1984:104–105) tells a grimmer tale of the phenomenal power of the tidal bore. In November 1922, the little 36-ton steamer *Topolobampo* set out from Guaymas with 125 field hands and their families, bound for the cotton fields of the Mexicali Valley. They anchored for the night in midchannel. At midnight, everyone on board was awakened by a terrifying roar—what sounded like a tremendous waterfall downriver. The frightened passengers saw an immense wall of water nearly 15 feet high traveling upriver with "the speed of an express train." There was hardly time for anyone to cry out. "The wave caught the *Topolobampo* squarely abeam," Waters (1984:105) wrote, "snapped the hawsers like threads, and rolled the ship over like a log." Only 39 passengers survived, and of the 86 who drowned, only 21 bodies were ever recovered.

Yuma to the Delta

Not far past Yuma, the river crosses the international boundary. I have heard that it is possible to stand on Morelos Dam and look upstream, where there is a pool of water, and then downstream to a dry riverbed, but I have never seen this myself. Below Morelos Dam, the Colorado River is dry. The only visible water is that dammed in the reservoirs and shunted in the canals and the mirages that shimmer on the blacktop like broken promises.

This was not always the case. The lower Colorado was once a vital, living stream on which many different people depended—Native Americans, Anglo fur trappers, steamboat captains. In the 1820s, James Ohio Pattie (1984:129–130) wrote one of the earliest descriptions of the river that once was. Below the Gila River, the Colorado was a wide, braided stream following a "remarkably circuitous" route. The bottomlands were some 6 to 10 miles wide, and the banks were lined with lofty, thickly set cottonwood trees. In just one morning, the men caught 60 beaver, trapping them on the numerous midstream islands.

Moreover, the river was once navigable as far upstream as Boulder Canyon, where Hoover Dam now stands. The first European to discover the Colorado's possibilities for navigation was the Spaniard Francisco de Ulloa. 1539, he found himself embayed at the head of what he called the Vermilion Sea, surrounded by shoals and muddy waters of an estuary (Sykes 1937:7). He was impressed by the height of the tides, the violence of the tidal currents, and the great expanses of muddy flats. To the Spaniard, the place seemed to be a region of mirages, vast distances, and muddy desolation (Sykes 1937:7).

The river was demonstrated to be navigable a year later. At about the same time that López de Cárdenas was facing the immensity of the Grand Canyon, Hernando de Alarcón sailed some distance up the river from its mouth. Alarcón never made contact with Coronado's land expedition, which was at that time hundreds of miles away.

In 1857, the U.S. Army's Topographical Engineers commissioned Lieutenant Joseph Ives to determine the navigability of the Colorado River above Fort Yuma. Ives was tasked to chart the river's channels and approaches, measure its depth, and calculate its discharge. The lieutenant ordered an iron-hulled, shallow-draft, stern-wheeled boat from a team of shipbuilders in Philadelphia. It was shipped disassembled to San Francisco by way of the Panama Railroad and then to the mouth of the Colorado on the schooner *Monterery* (Sykes 1937:20). To the vast amusement of Indian spectators, the newly christened *Explorer* grounded constantly working up the uncharted river. Near the place where Hoover Dam now stands, the little vessel hit a submerged rock and was damaged badly. Ives gamely pressed on in a wooden skiff, reaching Las Vegas Wash before he turned back (Stevens 1988:7).

The next to profit from the river's bounty were steamboat companies. The discovery of precious minerals in Arizona Territory triggered what has been called "the great Colorado River Rush of 1862" (Lingenfelter 1978:31). Steamboats began to ply the river by the end of the Civil War to provide goods and services to miners, merchants, and speculators. It was a time of "unequalled profits for the river steamers and one of bitter rivalry for the river trade" (Lingenfelter 1978:31). The "Arizona Fleet" carried passengers and freight on sternwheelers as far upstream as the mouth of the Virgin River nearly 600 miles above the Gulf of California. By meeting oceangoing vessels in the Gulf of California, the paddlewheelers provided a transportation link to California and beyond. "Even with the risk of shipwreck the sea route to Arizona was still quicker, cheaper and far more attractive than the overland trek across the Mojave or Colorado deserts" (Lingenfelter 1978:57).

Steamboats such as the *Cocopah, Esmeralda, Colorado,* and *Mohave* and a series of barges made the river a commercial and navigation success throughout the 1860s. New steamers were built and launched from the shipyard at Colorado City, which was later named Yuma. The tidal basin became an effective dry dock and the ultimate place for disposing of worn-out or wrecked craft (Sykes 1937:27). One of these was the *Explorer.* After foundering at Black Canyon, the boat was sold to a local steamboat company, repaired, and used to carry freight. In 1929, a surveying party discovered the remains of an iron, shallow-draft steamer buried in the mud away from the active river channel. It was subsequently identified as the *Explorer* (Sykes 1937:90–92). It had run out of control, drifting out of sight into Mexican territory and eventually running aground.

By the middle of the 1870s, the Colorado Steam Navigation Company was doing about a quarter of a million dollars a year in business, handling some 7,000 tons of freight and about a thousand passengers each year (Lingenfelter 1978:71). Martha Summerhayes, wife of U.S. Army officer John W. "Jack" Summerhayes, recorded the dubious comforts of travel by river steamer. Arriving from San Francisco at Port Isabel in August 1874, they took the steamer *Gila* upriver to Fort (at that time Camp) Mojave.

A Trip by River Steamer

Martha Summerhayes's account of traveling with her husband, first published in 1908, is remarkable for the unusual view it provides of a New England woman confronting the harsh realities of desert life. The Colorado River voyage from Port Isabel upriver to Camp Mojave on the steamer *Gila* took 18 days. Passengers slept on the deck because of the tremendous heat, bathed with the thick, brown river water, and ate what was to Mrs. Summerhayes's refined sensibilities meager fare. Later, she wrote of this journey (Summerhayes 1979:43) as a woman's trip into the unknown.

> I must confess that the history of this great river was quite unknown to me then. I had never read of the early attempts made to explore it, both from above and from its mouth, and the wonders of the "Grand Cañon" were as yet unknown to the world. I did not realize that, as we steamed along between those high perpendicular walls of rock, we were really seeing the lower end of that great chasm which now, thirty years later, has become one of the most famous resorts of this country and, in fact, of the world.

With the coming of the railroad in 1877, the oceangoing steamers and the ports where they had docked were abandoned. The railroad provided easier access to California than the roundabout sea route, and the river towns suffered. Only the upriver trade to the mines and the army at Fort Mojave sustained the river boats, and soon this was lost as

Historic train engine at Yuma Crossing State Historic Park, Arizona, site of the Yuma Quartermaster Depot. PHOTOGRAPH BY JEFFERSON REID.

well. The era of steam navigation ended in 1909 when Laguna Dam was completed, closing the river 14 miles above Yuma.

It is difficult to imagine river boats steaming up and down the Colorado River, and still more difficult to envision the great contrast between that flowing stream and the sere, inland desert. Away from the river, the land is spectacular for its barrenness and vastness—broad wastelands and desert pavements or *pedregales* punctuated by eerie volcanic spires and tanks sculpted in stone. The Sierra Pinacate volcanic fields rise darkly from the Gran Desierto dunes, the rims of its ancient craters gaping like open mouths. Julian Hayden, who spent a lifetime investigating the human history of this desert, said of it that "in complete silence and isolation, it was like what walking on the moon must be" (cited in Reid and Whittlesey 1997:112). Rainless, hosting secret water holes, littered with the bones of the dead—this country of sand and stone is distant indeed from the lush floodplain of the river.

THE COLORADO RIVER DELTA

The delta country remained lush for several decades after the river-boat trade ceased and the first dams were built. In 1922, famed naturalist Aldo Leopold (1949) found that it was impossible to locate the river's actual channel because a hundred green lagoons formed a twisting, turning maze. He described the delta as a veritable jungle. "A verdant wall of mesquite and willow separated the channel from the thorny desert beyond," he wrote (Leopold 1949:142). The verdant habitat supported abundant bird and animal life grown fat eating mesquite and screwbean pods. Small animals were "too abundant to hunt," and jaguar and bear roamed in the thickets.

Still later, Sykes (1937:3) described the Colorado River delta as encompassing more than 3,300 square miles amidst the gravels, sands, and stony pavements of the surrounding desert wasteland. The delta was characterized by a maze of channels, a tremendous tidal bore in the main channel, muddy flats where the river had receded, sloughs, and marshes.

Today, the delta described by Leopold and Sykes has disappeared. No Colorado River water reaches the Gulf of California; it has all been diverted by upstream dams and

Laguna Dam

A U.S. Bureau of Reclamation fact sheet tells the story of Laguna Dam and the Yuma Area Project. As early as 1902, farmers and speculators had envisioned an irrigation project along the lower river centered at Laguna, north of Yuma. The project would include a dam, canals, and levees to control what at that time was a serious flood danger. The dam was a diversion facility that shunted water into two canal systems, the Yuma Main Canal and the Arizona Main Canal. A siphon under the Colorado River enabled the water in the Yuma Main Canal to reach the areas below Yuma. When the dam was completed in 1909, so the fact sheet tells us, "the people of Yuma and surrounding areas were ecstatic. Certainly laborers and engineers were pleased that this challenging task was at last over and that a monument to engineering now stood ready to guide the water of the Colorado River to the hot Southwest." The event was celebrated with a parade down Main Street in Yuma, a barbeque, and train rides over the dam, luring the Chicago White Sox baseball team from its spring training in San Francisco. "Yuma blossomed during the next decade," the fact sheet proclaims.

—*Fact Sheet, U.S. Department of the Interior, Bureau of Reclamation*
Brief History of the Yuma Area Office *(No date)*

Desert Wasteland

The intrepid Padre Eusebio Kino and his military companion Capitán Juan Mateo Manje were among the first to cross the desert wastes lying east of the Colorado River and south of the Gila River—the area now known as the Gran Desierto and the Sierra Pinacate, a volcanic island in a sea of sand dunes. Kino and Manje were seeking to further the interests of the Spanish crown by identifying a land route connecting California and Pimería Alta.

In their travels between 1698 and 1702—across the desert, down the Gila River, down the Colorado River—Kino and Manje proved that "*California no es isla, sino península*"—it was not an island, but a continuous stretch of land above the Gulf of California. They also found that the Colorado River was many times the size of the Gila River, a mighty stream beside which the Gila paled. Kino and Manje were also among the first to travel the notorious and deadly Camino del Diablo—the Devil's highway—that ran from Sonora to Yuma Crossing across the Sierra Pinacate, Tinajas Altas, Cabeza Prieta, and the Gila Mountains (Hartmann 1989:87).

aqueducts. The dams have changed the quality of the water as well as its quantity. Salinity increases downstream as a result of evaporation, water diversion, and irrigation. Salts leached out when water is applied to a field increase the river's salinity when the water is returned (Fradkin 1968:297). No specifications were ever made about the quality of the water promised Mexico by treaty. To give water destined for Mexico a tolerable level of salinity, Congress authorized a desalinization plant. By one estimate, the plant's desalinization procedures would have cost about $300 per acre-foot of water (Reisner 1986:7). The plant operated for only a few months before it was mothballed. A Reclamation fact sheet states that "Because of favorable river conditions in recent years, the Yuma Desalting Plant has been in a state of ready-reserve, capable of operating at full capacity when necessary."

Today, only a few marshy places remain in the delta, and they are artificial. The Cienega de Santa Clara, located 60 miles south of Yuma, is home to almost 300 bird species. The marsh is fed by a canal transporting agricultural runoff water from the Wellton-Mohawk Irrigation District. The district was formed in 1951 to reduce the river water to a tolerable level of salinity for agricultural crops. The canal feeding the *cienega* was initially intended to carry refurbished water coming from the Yuma desalinization plant. The Cocopah still retain more or less worthless fishing rights to the Laguna Salada south of Mexicali. Once said to be boiling with fish brought in by the river, it is now a brackish lake. Marine life and the Mexican shrimp-fishing industry have been threatened by diversion of Colorado River water. It has been estimated that unemployment is as high as 30 percent in the delta area. In the year 2000, a combined Mexican and American group sued the Bureau of Reclamation for violating the Endangered Species Act by depriving the delta of water. Federal officials concluded that the law's reach ends at the border.

AT RIVER'S END

Our voyage down the Colorado River has taken us through a geography of stone and sky, water running red, and cliffs that are the colors of blood, flesh, and bone. It has taken us through the homeland of native peoples and the history of Euroamerican intrusions. We have skirted the contested issues of water and land, although we have journeyed through a dramatic transformation—from a wild river flowing through a sparsely populated, austere land to a highly controlled river whose water supports a dense population, agriculture in places not possible by nature unaided, and recreational pursuits undreamed of by earlier generations.

The river upon which the Lower Yuman tribes depended is gone. The river that the Patties described as a great braided stream, the marshy land rich in birds and fish at which Aldo Leopold marveled, the river that was navigable by steamboat in the nineteenth century—is no more. The impacts on humans and the surrounding land are marked and likely to be enduring. This transformation is well illustrated by the dismal predictions of early explorers whose visions proved less than prophetic. After the *Explorer* ran aground, Ives's exploring party followed the wagon road that Edward F. Beale surveyed and built for the War Department. They descended Peach Springs Canyon to the floor of the Grand Canyon, explored the Havasupai country, and went eastward toward the San Francisco Peaks. He continued on to the Little Colorado River, to the Hopi Mesas, and on to Fort Defiance. Ives's bald statement on the value of the country that hosts one of the world's most prominent tourist attractions has been quoted often—"ours has been the first and will doubtless be the last party of whites to visit this profitless locality. It seems intended by nature that the Colorado River, along the greater portions of its lonely and majestic way, shall be forever unvisited and undisturbed" (exhibit at the Carl Hayden Visitor Center, Glen Canyon Dam; also cited in Worster 2001:130).

In 1859, J. N. Macomb, who explored the river country as far as the junction of the Green and Colorado/Grand Rivers, repeated Ives's dismal assessment: "I cannot conceive of a more worthless and impracticable region that the one we now found ourselves in" (cited in Worster 2001:131).

These early explorers could find nothing of commercial interest in the 630-mile-long stretch of the Colorado River between Moab, Utah, to the place where Hoover Dam would be built—no resources that could be exploited, no viable transportation routes, no westward passage to the sea through the terrible and beautiful canyons. The river that would transform the West was locked in its canyons, unable to water farmland, flowing through a country as arid and impossible to reach as the moon. This was destined to change in dramatic and irrevocable fashion. We turn next to the history of this transformation.

Greeting the Day

Each day in the Akimel O'odham villages of long ago, one of the elder men would stand on top of a *vato* (ramada) just before sunrise to make a speech, awakening the villagers and greeting the day. The speech would go something like this:

Now another day is coming,
Awake from slumber,
Look toward the east,
See the rising of the sun,
Which means another day to toil.
Another day to hunt for meat,
To put the seed in the ground
That the yield might be good,
So our people may not go hungry.
The great Father provided us the sun
To give life to our earth so
That it might give us a good yield.
And that we might see
To hunt our game for meat.
So arise and make use of the day
And do not get in the way
Of the women as they go about
Fixing up the camp and the
Needed task of preparing meals for you.
Many moons, many suns have come and gone
Since our forefathers here on this same ground
Toiled and struggled so that we might
Enjoy life today.
So let us not waste this day.
But get your tools, go out to the field, or
Take down your bow and arrows
And go after the game, so that
Your family will not be in need of meat.
So now I hope you will strive
To make this day the best in your life.

George Webb, *A Pima Remembers*

For further information, see: Craig Childs, The Secret Knowledge of Water: Discovering the Essence of the American Desert *(Little, Brown, and Co., 2000; originally published in hardcover by Sasquatch Books, Seattle, 2000); Halka Chronic,* Pages of Stone: Grand Canyon and the Plateau Country: Geology of Western National Parks & Monuments *(The Mountaineers, Seattle, 1988); Philip L. Fradkin,* A River No More: The Colorado River and the West *(University of Arizona Press, Tucson, 1968); Michael M. Geary,* A Quick History of Grand Lake: Including Rocky Mountain National Park and the Grand Lake Lodge *(Western Reflections, Ouray, Colorado, 1999); Stephen J. Pyne,* How the Canyon Became Grand: A Short History *(Viking Press, New York, 1998); Frank Waters,* The Colorado *(Ohio University Press/Swallow Press, Athens, Ohio, 1984 [an early history, before most of the dams were built]).*

Controlling the Wildest River in the West

2

Water or the lack of it, rivers or their absence, are among the defining characteristics of the West. People as knowledgeable and experienced as John Wesley Powell and Wallace Stegner have urged us to think of the West as arid land, and they were right to do so. What we know from our western past and our own present is that water is one of the critical resources, that in our region it tends to be scarce, and that it has been and is the focus of intense argument and debate, and sometimes the cause of violent confrontation and death.

—Gary Holthaus, *Wide Skies: Finding a Home in the West*

Making the desert bloom, engineering the West's rivers so that farmland would stretch green and fertile where once there had been only sagebrush, sand dunes, and cactus—this was the dream of water control in the arid West. As Worster (1985:68) has reminded us, the word desert has two meanings. On the one hand, it means an unpopulated land, a land without human inhabitants. On the other hand, it means an arid country, a land of little rainfall. Although scholars quibble over how dry a land must be to qualify as a desert, the Desert Botanical Laboratory defined "desert" to mean a place that receives 10 inches of rain or less each year (Worster 1985:69). The consequences of water control in the West have irrevocably altered both meanings, for population has soared with the coming of water to the land. Through technology, we have been able to change the face of the earth itself—for better or worse.

Water control in the desert West centered on the mighty Colorado River, the great stream that Waters (1984:328) called "the wildest river in America." It was an outlaw river, which could flood regularly and drown settlements and farms, yet drop to a mere trickle in dry seasons. The rationale for attempting to control the Colorado was breathtaking in its simplicity—an unused river was worthless. Only when its water was

New Theodore Roosevelt Dam. Photograph courtesy U.S. Bureau of Reclamation. Joe Madrigal, Jr., photographer.

diverted and used to maximum benefit could the Colorado's full potential be realized. For the hydraulic engineers of the late nineteenth and early twentieth centuries, "conservation" had little to do with protecting the rivers, preserving their integrity, or saving them for posterity. Conservation meant putting rivers to work in the most efficient way to maximize production and wealth (Worster 1985:155). The Reclamation Service's earliest dam-building efforts sprang from this philosophy. Even though the Bureau of Reclamation's great dam-building era is over, the philosophy still drives the modern institution that has given over water control in large part to those who use it.

Outlaw River

Many writers, poets, and historians have penned stories about the Colorado River that was. Their tales evoke a river vastly different from the managed stream, the salty trickle, the river of rock that today's river represents. Their stories are epitaphs written on the tombstone of the Colorado's waters.

In telling the history of the Colorado, Frank Waters conjures up a memory. "The Colorado is an outlaw," he wrote.

> It belongs only to the ancient, eternal earth. As no other, it is savage and unpredictable of mood, peculiarly American in character. It has for its background the haunting sweep of illimitable horizons, the immensities of unbroken wilderness. From perpetually snow-capped peaks to stifling deserts below sea level, it cuts the deepest and truest cross section through the continent (Waters 1984:xvii).

And because of this unpredictable, often violent nature, Waters (1946:xviii) believes, those who love it best are also those who fear it most.

Today, those who love the Colorado River fear different things.

Not only the Colorado, but its tributary streams as well, would eventually be harnessed to stop floods and ensure a predictable water supply. Phoenix would be shaped into an agricultural paradise as the waters of the Salt, Verde, and Agua Fria Rivers were dammed and diverted. And after a half-century of debate, legal wrangling, and at least one literal battle, Central Arizona Project water would begin to flow.

The history of water control in the West is a monumental tale, one that enfolds many fascinating stories and subplots. It is, in the words of law professor Charles Wilkinson (1992:223), "an unsettling story that speaks directly to the limits of technical expertise, the treacherous allure of the grandiose solution, and the consequences that can unfold when the government opens its checkbook and closes its regulation manual." It is a story that resounds in the deepest core of our emotions, for it has pitted natural and social elements against each other in struggle, compromise, despair, and triumph. A national ideology of technological mastery, raw independence, and manifest destiny fueled the dreams of individual farmers and settlers that all too often evaporated like water on desert stones when confronted by the practical reality of the arid West. Naked ambition, greed, and questionable ethics battled against the noble ideals of our nation's greatest leaders. Subduing the wildest river in the West is an epic story that illuminates our national and regional history—a window on our past and lessons for the future.

The following pages trace attempts to control the Colorado River in general chronological order, but the stories are self-contained. Each encapsulates a place and a point in time where human dreams and material technology met to change the shape of the land and its water forever.

John Wesley Powell

Although the story of water control in the West actually begins with the prehistoric farmers of plateau, desert, and mountains, most accounts start with John Wesley Powell. Powell's pioneering expeditions down the Colorado River and his subsequent surveys of the plateau province were more than simple adventures or investigations of unknown territory. These experiences would have a profound effect on attempts to control water in the West. In fact, one of Powell's original missions was to study the hydrology of the region toward developing an irrigation system for the rainfall-deficient West (Worster 2001:127). Certainly what he learned in his explorations would influence notions of irrigation technology and its social aspects.

Powell came away from his experiences with a clear and practical understanding of the dramatic ways in which the eastern and western United States differed—perhaps the first intellectual of his time to recognize this. The West was arid country that could not be farmed by rainfall alone. Beyond the hundredth meridian, less than 20 inches of rain

John Wesley Powell

John Wesley Powell was born in 1834 of immigrant English parents, Joseph and Mary Dean Powell. Staunch abolitionists and ardent followers of John Wesley, founder of the evangelic Protestant movement called Methodism, his parents hoped that their son would be a spiritual leader. The family moved a great deal, investing in small farms and carrying the word of God as they went from New York to Ohio and Wisconsin. Powell's early life experiences directed him toward natural history, particularly geography and geology. He attended several colleges but never completed a degree; in his formidable intellectual pursuits he was self-taught. Through the years, while he sought an education and battled with his parents over his future, he discovered rivers. "They flowed through the landscape of his mind like songs of freedom and escape" (Worster 2001:76).

Powell tried teaching, but he was not satisfied with that as a profession. When he was 27 years old, the Civil War broke out, and Powell was among those who answered the call for volunteers. He enlisted in the Union army, rose quickly through the ranks, and was promoted to artillery captain. After he enlisted, he requested leave to marry his half-cousin Emma Dean, whom he had met in Detroit. Soon Powell was thrust into one of the bloodiest battles of the conflict. At Shiloh, he was hit in the right arm as he signaled to his artillery battery to fire. He was taken to Savannah, where his bride of five months waited. He suffered the fate of so many others wounded by bone-shattering musket balls, and the arm was amputated. Powell remained in the army, saw several more battles, and was promoted to major in 1864.

John Wesley Powell's 1869 expedition departing from Green River City, Wyoming. Photograph courtesy Arizona Historical Society, Tucson (AHS Accession No. 43201).

The following year he mustered out of service with a disability pension and returned to civilian life. Powell took up teaching again, but he already had his eyes on the West. A collecting expedition to the Rocky Mountains in 1867 laid the groundwork for the exploration of the Colorado River that would follow in 1869. Powell was indefatigable despite his injury, a man of great intellectual and physical energy.

In 1869, the party of 10 that included the Major's brother, Walter, left Green River City, Wyoming, to tackle the Colorado River. They sailed in four wooden boats—*Emma Dean, Kitty Clyde's Sister, No Name,* and *Maid of the Canyon,* one a 16-foot pilot boat and the remainder 21 feet long. They each carried a 10-month supply of rations, clothing, ammunition, traps, and an assortment of tools, chronometers, sextants, barometers, thermometers, and compasses. Few of the men were trained, and not one was experienced, for they were the first to attempt to follow the Colorado River to the mouth of the Grand Canyon. The mishaps and obstacles—portaging the

(continued on following page)

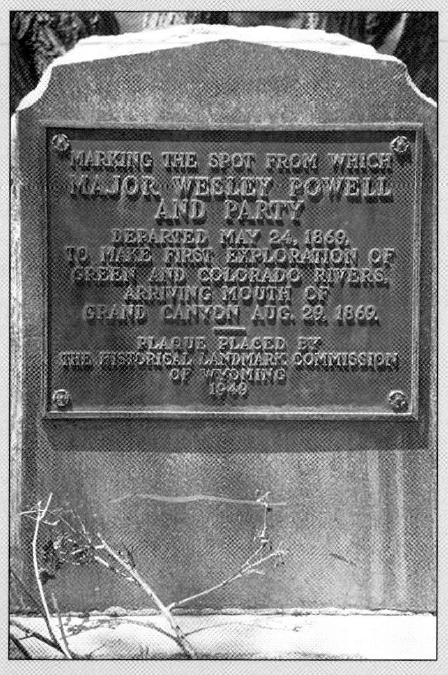

Monument on Expedition Island commemorating the Powell expedition of 1869. Photograph by Jefferson Reid.

boats, "lining" them on ropes, overturning boats that drenched their food and instruments, losing the *No Name,* stranding on sand bars, and enduring illness, injuries, death, and the many raging rapids—were equaled by the wonders they saw, some of them for the first time by Euroamerican explorers. It is astounding to consider what the one-armed Powell accomplished on this voyage. The exploration, according to Worster (2001:260), represented "a triumph of ordinary people confronting an extraordinary landscape."

Following the expedition, Powell directed one of four surveys funded by the U.S. government. Beginning in 1871, he made a second trip down the Colorado River. The Powells' only daughter Mary was born during that exploration. Advised that Congress might not renew the appropriations for his survey unless he published his report, Powell cobbled together information from four years of work between 1869 and 1872 and both canyon trips as *The Exploration of the Colorado River of the West.* Reprinted in 1895 as *Canyons of the Colorado,* this report became the most popular literary product of the western surveys and remains in print today.

In 1873, Powell was appointed special commissioner to look into Indian affairs in the West. These experiences would foreshadow his work in the Bureau of Ethnology. In 1879, Congress consolidated the surveys into the U.S. Geological Survey headed by Clarence King. Powell established the Bureau of Ethnology in the Smithsonian Institution in 1879. Continuing to survey the West, in 1879 he presented his plans for reforming public land laws and promoting irrigation in the comprehensive *Report on the Lands of the Arid Region of the United States.* When King resigned in 1881, Powell was appointed the second director of the U.S. Geological Survey.

Powell resigned from the U.S. Geological Survey in 1894. He remained as titular head of the Bureau of Ethnology, although the practical running (and mismanagement) of the agency was carried out by William McGee. Powell's health declined as he grew older, and the once-vigorous man endured surgery on his amputated arm and suffered a hernia, a stroke, and other illnesses. He died of a cerebral hemorrhage at the family bungalow in Maine in 1902. It was the year that President Roosevelt signed the Reclamation Act into law. Powell was buried in Arlington National Cemetery, and his monument reads simply "Soldier. Explorer. Scientist"—a fitting epitaph for the man who thought to redeem the nation and the West through science.

Although Powell is better known as an explorer and is associated with the U.S. Geological Survey, his studies in anthropology and his directorship of the Bureau of Ethnology, later named the Bureau of American Ethnology, were vital during a time when indigenous peoples were experiencing enormous changes in population, territory, and culture. Powell's dream from the beginning was to found a "science of Man" (Worster 2001). By 1880, the bureau was on its way to fulfilling that vision. Powell organized the Anthropological Society, out of which grew the American Anthropological Association and its journal, *American Anthropologist,* and was also instrumental in founding the National Geographic Society.

John Wesley Powell's life encapsulated many of the trends that swept the nation during that turbulent time in its history—the triumph of science over religion; the immigrant tide that moved west from the old country to the farthest shore of the new world, following "an extravagant dream of geography" in Worster's (2001:38) words; the struggles of a nation grappling with its polyglot citizens of many ethnic groups, its Native Americans, and its multiple cultures; and America's confrontation with the land.

John Wesley Powell with Paiute headman. Photograph courtesy Arizona Historical Society, Tucson (AHS Accession No. 49893).

Two excellent biographies of John Wesley Powell: Wallace Stegner, Beyond the Hundredth Meridian: John Wesley Powell and the Second Opening of the West *(Penguin Books, New York, 1953), and Donald Worster,* A River Running West: The Life of John Wesley Powell *(Oxford University Press, New York, 2001)* fell each year except in isolated pockets, and 20 inches was the minimum amount for farming without irrigation. Western lands were also outstanding for diversity created by variation in elevation, latitude, topography, climate, and soil. The West was, in essence, the opposite of the East, which was wet, capable of being farmed without irrigation, and more geographically uniform in character.

Moreover, the rivers were strikingly different. The few permanent rivers were inconstant, fickle streams. Whereas rivers east of the hundredth meridian are fed by reliable springs and rainfall, most rivers in the arid West derive from mountain snow (Wilkinson 1992:219–222). As a consequence, most of their flow comes in a rush during April, May, and June, when warm spring rains melt winter snows. In addition, annual snowfalls fluctuate, often dramatically. Western rivers "are wildly inconstant, both month to month and year to year" (Wilkinson 1992:222).

Beginning in 1874, the Powell survey built these features of western land and water into its land-classification system. The surveyors routinely distinguished areas that were suitable for cultivation by irrigation from areas that were not. Moreover, Powell was not sanguine about the West's ability to support farming. As early as 1874, in a letter to the House Committee on Public Lands, Powell warned that two-fifths of the nation had a climate so dry that agriculture could not be pursued without supplemental water. Perhaps as little as 1 to 3 percent of the land could be redeemed through irrigation (Worster 2001:348–349).

Powell's river explorations had captured the public imagination at a time when the West was perceived as the promised land—where people of all nations could find a better place and a better chance to fulfill the American dream. Although the recommendations made in Powell's 1879 *Report on the Lands of the Arid Region of the United States, with a More Detailed Account of the Lands of Utah* were designed to permit orderly westward expansion based on realistic expectations, many of his ideas challenged prevailing notions. The report was, in Worster's (1985:133) words, "a model of ecological realism in an unsympathetic age of unbounded expectations." Stegner, who was one of Powell's biographers, was more blunt. The report was more than a revolution in the system of land surveys, policy, tenure, and farming methods in the West. It was also a denial of "almost every cherished fantasy and myth associated with the Westward migration and the American dream of the Garden of the World" (Stegner 1953:212). Powell was striking at the heart of the myths, challenging secular beliefs that were as deeply rooted as religious ones.

The central core of the plan Powell outlined in his report on arid lands was simple. It was necessary to subdue the wild rivers of the West to achieve the greatest possible development of mining, industry, manufacturing, and agriculture (Worster 1985:134). Powell was the first to suggest that the West should become a new kind of hydraulic society based on technological mastery of its rivers. Prophetically, he suggested (Powell 1983:11) that the future development of irrigation would depend on use of the larger streams—one of which was presumably the tricky Colorado that had given Powell so many heart-stopping moments on its rapids. Powell proposed that the "waste waters" pouring down the slopes after storms or when the snows melt in the spring should be captured and stored to achieve the maximum benefit. "The greater storage of water must come from the construction of great reservoirs in the highlands where lateral valleys may be dammed and the main streams conducted into them by canals," he wrote (Powell 1983:13). With these words Powell sketched the outlines of the philosophy on which the Reclamation Service would be built.

To achieve Powell's laudable objectives required a major overhaul of existing land and water laws in the West, however. In his report, Powell included several eminently practical proposals that were based on the facts he had accumulated in his scientific explorations and on his intimate knowledge of the region. Behind Powell's reasoning was a desire to see a flourishing agrarian society, a dream that had been evoked nationally by Thomas Jefferson (Wilkinson 1992:236). Powell sought to halt the insidious spread of water monopolization that had already begun in the 1800s. Investors were able to gain control of large tracts of land and most of its water through manipulating water-rights laws. At that time, there were two basic doctrines of water rights in the United States. The first was developed from English common law. This "riparian principle" or doctrine of "riparianism" held that only people living on the banks of a river could lay claim to its flow; it was ownership of land that established water rights (Worster 1985:88). According to this principle, originally developed in the humid and well-watered British Isles, the rivers belonged to no one. People living along the banks of a stream had rights to use the water as they wished, as long as the flow was not diminished. All landowners bordering a watercourse shared it, regardless of whether they had ever put its water to work previously (Wilkinson 1992:232). This doctrine implied fundamental equality; moreover, people living far from a river were not disadvantaged. In a well-watered land, there was enough for all.

But the West was not a well-watered land. The second principle was the doctrine of prior appropriation that grew out of and was symbiotic with hardrock-mining laws. It stated that the first person to come to a stream and claim its water had acquired it and had priority to exploit it. It did not matter how far from the river that person lived or how the water was used (Worster 1985:88). Miners employed what Wilkinson (1992:232) has called a "simple, primitive rule of capture," which was "first in time, first in right." The California Gold Rush contributed to the adoption of this doctrine. Because few California mines were located adjacent to streams, necessary water was transported to them through flumes and ditches (Fradkin 1968:115). The "due diligence" rule required that a miner use the water actively, just as a claim was worked, in order to keep the water rights. If not used, the water right was abandoned. After the initial appropriation, a water right could be leased or sold. Water was property from the moment it was first put to use (Wilkinson 1992:232–233). In the water-deficient West, the most important factor was putting water to beneficial use, even if this took place a great distance from the source.

Riparianism was essentially biased against economic development. As Stegner (1953:226) has pointed out, "Water is the true wealth in a dry land; without it, land is worthless. . . if you control the water, you control the land that depends on it. In that fact alone was the ominous threat of land and water monopolies." The people who settled the West generally rejected the riparian doctrine and employed the principle of prior appropriation "because it offered them a greater freedom to exploit nature" (Worster 1985:89)—a fact that has been inexplicably ignored by western historians, according to Worster.

Flaming Gorge Reservoir. PHOTOGRAPH BY JEFFERSON REID.

Wilkinson (1992) included the doctrine of prior appropriation in the list of anachronistic and poorly functioning principles that govern use of western resources and which are largely responsible for today's natural-resource problems. These "lords of yesterday," as he has called them, can be traced to the extraordinary era of American westward movement in the nineteenth century. Although they arose under wholly different economic, political, and economic conditions, this battery of antique laws and policies has had a sweeping and pervasive influence on contemporary society. Wilkinson (1992:17–21) believes that inertia, powerful lobbying forces, and lack of public awareness perpetuate the lords of yesterday.

Powell argued that the prior-appropriation doctrine was unworkable for the arid West. It inevitably tended toward monopolization of land, because whoever claimed an upstream right to water could control the land downstream (Watkins 1983:xvi). To rectify this situation, Powell (1983:41) proposed that rights to water required for irrigating any tract of land should inhere in the land itself, and water rights would be part and parcel of land titles. This conviction sprang from Powell's deep understanding of the character of western land and water. The 1862 Homestead Act establishing the 160-acre homestead unit, which was created in the humid East, was absolutely wrong in the arid West. It was too restrictive in a region where there was little or no surface water. Unless the holding fortuitously contained water—and few did—such acreage would be hopelessly unsuited for farming and incapable of supporting the homesteads. Irrigated farms in the West should be only 80 acres in size, Powell believed—half the size of the homestead watered by rainfall but completely sufficient for an irrigated farm. By contrast, 160 acres was woefully inadequate for nonirrigated land, and much more acreage was required for success. Powell believed that such pasture farms, which would be far more common than irrigated farms in the West, should be 2,560 acres in size—16 times the normal homestead. Each 2,560 pasturage farm should have 20 acres of irrigable land with a water right that was inseparable from the land.

Powell's proposals went against the existing provisions of the Desert Land Act of 1877. The act provided settlers with one section (640 acres) of desert land if they could irrigate it within three years. Desert land was defined as all nontimbered land that would not produce an agricultural crop without irrigation. Although remaining true to the Jeffersonian ideal of small, independent landholdings, the act fostered abuses and land-grabbing speculation. Its chief beneficiaries, according to Worster (2001:339–340), were livestock grazers in Montana, Wyoming, and Colorado, many of them syndicates. Because the act did not specify what constituted irrigation, from where the water was to be obtained, or how much water was to be used, anyone could claim as irrigation ditches what were essentially plow furrows. Bureau of Reclamation historian Michael Robinson (1979:8) relates the apocryphal tale of one enterprising claimant who splashed a can of water into a ditch on his land and avowed that he had "reclaimed" it.

To achieve his goals, Powell argued, the existing land-survey system—the General Land Office's standard, rectangular grid—should be scrapped and replaced with one that would give each homestead access to water. Surveys should be based on topography rather than an arbitrary grid, and farms would be as irregular as necessary to give each one water frontage and irrigable soil.

Perhaps most iconoclastic of Powell's proposals and antithetical to the doctrine of prior appropriation was his notion that people organize in cooperative efforts to develop water for irrigation (Stegner 1953:226–228). Maximum development of irrigation would require use of the larger streams, as he had argued, and this could not be achieved by small farmers acting independently (Powell 1983:11). The large rivers—the mightiest of which was the Colorado—required cooperative labor and aggregated capital on an enormous scale to build and maintain diversion and distribution features (Fradkin 1968:65).

Lake Havasu. Photograph by Jefferson Reid.

To achieve the necessary overhaul of land and water laws, in his report Powell offered two sample bills for Congress to consider. The Mormon success in cooperative irrigation ventures had influenced Powell a great deal, as his first proposed bill indicated. He suggested that nine or more people should be able to organize their own cooperative irrigation districts. The lands within a district should be in one continuous tract, and no single individual could own more than 80 acres. Powell's second proposed bill was also highly democratic. It would have authorized pasturage homesteads organized into districts on the public lands. Groups of nine or more people could organize and act cooperatively to set up a grazing district.

Powell envisioned democratic rather than monopolistic, highly efficient use of the diverse lands of the West. The wholesale grabbing of water and land already underway could be avoided by dividing the land into small parcels and putting it under cooperative control, establishing water rights that would inhere with the land, and enabling cooperative irrigation and grazing ventures by individuals rather than corporations. Control could be placed in the hands of a more benevolent authority than the private speculator who was fattening on promoting the myths of the West.

Had Powell's proposals been adopted, they might have changed western history a great deal, but they were not. Powell failed to push his program through Congress (Fradkin 1968:23). In 1879, Congress passed a "gutted" measure that consolidated the surveys and appointed a public-lands commission but did not touch either the existing public land laws or the surveying system (Stegner 1953:239). Powell's proposals effectively constituted a revolution (Watkins 1983:xvii) that alienated too many commercial, corporate, and political interests, particularly those of the railroad monopolies. What Powell proposed "was too sweeping a reform, too methodical a process and too drastic a change for his time, and even possibly for the present" (Fradkin 1968:23). As Robinson (1979:6) has pointed out, a Congress based in humid Washington, D.C., was slow to reform laws that seemed to work successfully there. Powell's ideas also challenged well-entrenched ideologies. There has always been something inherently emotional about the notion of bringing water to the land, of "reclaiming" the West, as Fradkin (1968:24) has pointed out. It was as if water projects were the West's payoff for being a colony to the rest of the nation, or "a 'plundered province,' in the words of historian Bernard DeVoto" (Fradkin 1968:24). Congressmen failed to be wooed by Powell's proposals because they, too, were lost in their own dreams of the West (Worster 2001:359).

The dream that produced the great westward migration of the 1870s was fueled by boosterism (Horace Greeley's directive, "Go west, young man" had galvanized the nineteenth century), optimism, and the extension of the railroad. It was also promoted by some fortuitous climatic events. After 1865, a humid cycle set in that brought above-average rainfall to the Midwest. Coinciding as it did with settlement crossing the hundredth meridian, the climatic transformation was attributed to divine intervention. Its motto was the unique meteorological principle that "rain follows the plow." As the western country was settled and farmed, it was thought, rainfall increased. The exact mechanism by which this took place was never satisfactorily explained, but it acted to bring still more people westward.

The views of naysayers such as Powell, who kept on insisting that the West was indeed an arid land, rang hollow in light of the evidence to the contrary. Rain follows the plow, the boosters argued, and if there was not enough rainfall beyond the hundredth meridian then all farmers needed to do was cultivate the land. Rainfall would increase automatically. Powell the scientist and explorer was characterized as a charlatan and meddler in affairs of which he was ignorant (Watkins 1983:xvii).

Despite the failure of his proposals in Congress, Powell continued his efforts to establish a sane approach to irrigation in the West. In 1888, he was asked to conduct an irrigation survey to investigate the practicability of constructing storage reservoirs for irrigation water, identify the lands that could be irrigated, and designate places where hydraulic works could be located (Worster 2001:473). The Geological Survey administered the survey, which had two divisions—hydrography to conduct the irrigation survey and topography to map the western river basins.

Powell simply could not please the influential power brokers in Congress, however. Senator William Stewart of Nevada spearheaded opposition to the Irrigation Survey that culminated with congressional hearings in 1890. Before the Select Committee on Irrigation and Reclamation of Arid Lands, Powell revealed the shape of the new society that he would like to see in the river valleys of the West. It was in a sense "a strategy of ecological adaptation" (Worster 1985:138). Powell's scheme was to divide the region beyond the hundredth meridian—an area of more than 1.3 million square miles—into natural hydrographic basins or watersheds. These units, not the arbitrary squares of the township and range system developed in the humid East, would organize settlement. The plan would place the jurisdiction, community planning, and use of water resources within the boundaries of the region that generated them. Powell's scheme also placed limits on ownership of irrigated lands and left the use and protection of nonirrigable lands to the districts.

In a few parts of the West other than among the Mormons of Utah, similar schemes had begun in a limited fashion. California's Wright Act of 1887 enabled irrigation districts to form, own water in common, and sell bonds to finance canals and headgates. In New Mexico, the Hispanic community had been irrigating for a century (Meyer 1984), but the full potential of watersheds had never been realized.

Regardless of such limited support, Powell's reform notions were soundly defeated. He was pilloried in the press, and pitched battles continued in Congress. Opposition pivoted upon the provision that lands in the public domain be withdrawn from settlement until the Irrigation Survey was completed. Eventually the Senate killed the Irrigation Survey, and although the Geological Survey appropriations increased, "all the western lands were restored to the old system so riddled with fraud and conflict and so ill-fitted to the conditions of nature" (Worster 2001:506).

Powell would never investigate the irrigation issue officially again, although public officials and private individuals in the United States and foreign countries continued to badger him with questions. He cultivated an intellectual life in Washington, D.C., where he negotiated the political waters of bureaucracy as head of the Bureau of American Ethnology and the Geological Survey. A branch of the latter agency was the forerunner of the Bureau of Reclamation.

Powell's blueprint for a new western society never came to pass, and the federal government would eventually undertake the reclamation of arid lands. The misapplied homesteading laws with their susceptibility to fraud and failure remained in place (Worster 2001:379). Walka (2002:97) speculated about what Powell may have felt at the end of his fruitless battles. "Surely John Wesley, harassed and finally deeply hurt by political adversaries in Washington, turned his mind back toward the Great Unknown. Drifted again on the muddy river slipping through his veins."

The Beginning of Federal Reclamation in the West

John Wesley Powell's vision of a new hydraulic society in the American West would eventually be realized, and the rivers he saw as its salvation would be dammed, diverted, and controlled. But it would not be at the hands of groups of farmers in cooperative irrigation districts as Powell envisioned. Instead, the federal government would step in and take Powell's dreams to reality. Historian Patricia Nelson Limerick (1987) and her colleague William Travis (Limerick and Travis 2002) have stressed the irony of this situation. Westerners have traditionally viewed themselves as rugged individuals who insist on making their own choices and refuse petty regulation. Westerners settled where they wanted, even if the land was not compatible with their dreams, and lived according to individual, rugged, self-reliant terms—until they needed help. When they got themselves into a mess, it was the federal government who stepped in to bail them out. The key role of the federal government in western economy is well written in water (Limerick 1987:138). When the theory that rain follows the plow evaporated like virga on the summer air, the westerner looked to the federal government to rectify the shortfall that had become all too apparent. The government would build the dams and reservoirs, aqueducts and canals that filled in for the rain.

By the end of the nineteenth century, irrigation in the West had become a veritable crusade, a program that seemed to make sense on patriotic as well as economic grounds. The great drought of 1890, which had devastated the Great Plains, galvanized an irrigation movement led by boosters such as the Nebraska journalist William E. Smythe. Resigning from his newspaper post, Smythe moved to Salt Lake City, founded a new journal, *The Irrigation Age,* and began his irrigation crusade. Smythe maintained that the aridity of the West was not a deficit as Powell had proposed but a blessing in disguise. Irrigation was the miracle means by which arid America could be conquered, Smythe maintained (Fradkin 1968:25)—conveniently ignoring the fact that Powell had said it first. Smythe organized the first Irrigation Congress in Salt Lake City and the second in Los Angeles to provide a platform for promoting his theories and schemes.

There was one dissenting voice at the 1893 Irrigation Congress, however, and it was Powell himself. On the final day, the delegates had approved a platform proposing that the federal government build reservoirs and guarantee water (Worster 2001:528). Powell spoke and deflated this pipe dream. There was not enough water in the arid region to carry out all the ambitious projects and dreams that had been envisioned, he proclaimed. Even if expanded, irrigation would prove a limited remedy. He thundered prophetically, "I tell you gentlemen you are piling up a heritage of conflict and litigation over water rights for there is not sufficient water to supply the land" (cited in Worster 1985:132). Powell's protests were ignored, and Smythe's *Conquest of Arid America,* published in 1900, became the bible of the reclamation movement.

State water laws that began to be implemented in the late 1800s sowed the seeds of federal water control. Public ownership and the distribution of water under the doctrine of prior appropriation were becoming established in the Rocky Mountain states. In 1881, Colorado developed a state engineer's office to supervise water claims. Such acts were the first steps to counteract chaotic individualism and toward declaring "that the rivers of the West are in some sense public property and that any private appropriation can only be made under public rules and at public sufferance" (Worster 1985:95). In 1891, the Desert Land Act was revised to prevent rampant abuses, and it was extended to Colorado. California, by contrast, threw together a ramshackle compromise in the 1886 decision of *Lux v. Haggin.* The state adopted the riparian principle but accepted appropriation rights derived from the federal government, which in its Mining Act of 1866 had conceded such rights on the public domain (Worster 1985:107).

Wyoming's governor appointed Elwood Mead, who would later become commissioner of the Bureau of Reclamation, to be the first territorial engineer. Mead developed a water-control system demanding that water users obtain rights through a permit issued by the state engineer. This system limited control by private water users and in theory protected the public interest and the small farmer. By 1919, the Wyoming system would be adopted by several Western states, including Arizona. Water agencies sprang up whose mission, according to Wilkinson (1992:240), was to serve the bidding of the rights holders: to record their rights, make them official, enforce them, and lobby for new projects.

At about the same time, Wyoming Senator Joseph M. Carey introduced the Carey Act of 1894, which provided for the federal government to give up one million acres of land to a state if those lands could be reclaimed and settled. Although the act spurred a spate of canal-building and irrigation projects, Robinson (1979:9) claimed that before 1900 this act failed dismally because private investors were reluctant to invest in irrigation projects. Eight years after it was enacted, only 4 of the 10 eligible states had applied for federal lands, and little acreage had been set aside (Worster 1985:157). According to Robinson (1979:9), only 11,321 acres had been patented under provisions of the Carey Act by 1902.

Irrigation districts further fostered the private interests that were favored by western water policy. These districts were corporate, administrative bodies that held and distributed water and received subsidies for water-development projects. They also maintained revenue-raising authority by means of tax-exempt bonds. As the 1800s drew to a close, then, western water users had developed a system that gave them extraordinary power over the rivers: an unfettered right to extract free water through the doctrine of prior appropriation, a state office to protect rights, and special, publicly funded districts to administer and boost water projects (Wilkinson 1992:242).

Elwood Mead

Elwood Mead grew up in Indiana, obtained degrees in engineering and agriculture, and in 1883 moved west to teach at Colorado Agricultural College in Fort Collins. Mead became involved in water policy in Colorado, but was frustrated by the rejection of his proposals to make water-rights administration a state task. He was given the opportunity to make this happen as state engineer in Wyoming. The legal structure to protect water rights that he developed and implemented was borrowed in a number of other western states. Worster (1985:183) tells us that Mead's dream was to make irrigation a social success and stamp its mold on rural life everywhere in America. His vision of the West was essentially a society formed of small farmers. Lake Mead, the reservoir created by Hoover Dam, is named after him.

PHOTOGRAPH BY JEFFERSON REID.

Despite the initial success of this system, scholars and public figures began to suggest an increasing role for the federal government. As early as 1890, following upon Powell's insistence that the great rivers of the West could only be controlled cooperatively, Brigadier General Nelson Miles had proposed that the necessary capital to control and command the rivers should come from the U.S. government. He also suggested that a single water law should extend over the entire arid region and its irrigation system to replace the existing hodgepodge of conflicting state laws (Worster 1985:139). Seven years later, Hiram Chittenden, in reporting on a survey of potential reservoir sites in Wyoming and Colorado, included an argument that the government should build dams and reservoirs (Worster 1985:159).

Wilkinson (1992:242) has suggested that the great spur to federal involvement was the need for dams. As Powell had observed in his arid-lands report, dams would solve several problems at once. By permitting spring flows to be stored until the irrigation season, the rights of senior and junior water users could be preserved. The erratic flow of western rivers could be controlled and harvested. As Wilkinson (1992:243) has written, "Dams create water." Individuals trying to implement this dream, however, ran into huge financial obstacles. It was impossible to take on water impoundment of any significant size, as Powell had recognized previously. Even western states with their small populations had limitations. The solution was federal monies to finance construction of large reclamation projects. By 1901, activists such as George W. Maxwell and the aptly named Congressional Representative Francis G. Newlands of Nevada had formulated a prospective national reclamation law. The act would federalize water control and provide a clear method for financing it and a wide scope of application. This bill failed, but the reclamation movement did not.

In President Theodore Roosevelt, federal reclamation found its staunchest supporter. He believed that the federal government should construct and maintain irrigation systems just as it did with other public works (Robinson 1979:16). Roosevelt was able to convince a skeptical Congress that western reclamation was not only practical but of extraordinary benefit to the nation. Writer Russell Martin (1999:30) quotes Roosevelt's stirring State of the Union speech in 1901, in which Roosevelt proclaimed that the western half of the United States would sustain a population greater than that of the whole country "if the waters that now run to waste were saved and used for irrigation." Reclamation of arid lands and their settlement would "enrich every portion of the country."

Perhaps the greatest stimulus to the federal reclamation crusade, however, came from the mighty Colorado River itself and the climatic events of the late nineteenth century. The wildest river in the West was tempestuous, varying in volume and flow with the vicissitudes of rainfall and snowpack. Cycles of climatic variability exacerbated the Colorado River's distinctive features, turning the wild river into a true outlaw. In his 1879 report, Powell had prophetically warned that periodic cycles of climatic variability would alternate between drought and flood, aridity and moisture. His ability to predict this in the absence of sophisticated stream-flow studies based on tree-ring analyses was nothing short of brilliant. Charitably debunking the myth that rain follows the plow, Powell said that climate is cyclic, and that any shift was likely to be ephemeral. One shift would likely be followed quickly by the opposite or compensating change. The extreme would be followed by a return to a mean condition or an oscillation in the opposite direction, and productive fields would be stricken by drought and return to desert (Powell 1983:76).

True to Powell's predictions, the last decades of the nineteenth century were characterized by wildly fluctuating variability in climate and the Colorado River's flow. The Colorado varied, Reisner (1986:122) has written, "psychotically between a few thousand cubic feet per second and a couple of hundred thousand, sometimes within a few days." Winter storms combining extended periods of rainfall with melting snow created the most damaging floods. Virtually all of the destructive floods since records have been kept took place between October and March (Hackbarth and Lancaster 1992:Table 10). Arizona residents of recent times can attest to the destructive power of winter floods. In 1983 and again in 1993, office buildings, homes, roads, bridges, barns, horses, and cattle were swept into the rushing waters of even small, normally dry streams such as the Rillito River in the Tucson area.

Tremendous floods were first recorded in the 1860s, but those of the 1890s and the first decade of the 1900s seemed to increase in ferocity, affecting not only the Colorado but also the Gila, Salt, and Verde Rivers and many of the tributary streams. Destruction of property and livestock was massive in these flood events. Irrigation canals were destroyed, bridges were swept away, cattle were drowned, and people were forced to flee to the rooftops, watching helplessly as bits of their homes and pieces of their lives drifted away with the current. The Walnut Creek Dam on the Hassayampa River near Prescott, built to supply water for the mines in this area, was breached in the 1890 flood. "Billions of gallons of water" swept down the riverbed at 20 miles per hour, and witnesses described the wave of water as 50 feet high. It took just one hour for the reservoir to empty. Estimates of people who died in this disaster range from 50 to 130 (Dobyns 1981:187–188; Tellman and others 1997:8).

Where once the river raged, now anglers find paradise. Photograph by Jefferson Reid.

To what extent these flood events were induced or worsened by human-caused environmental change remains controversial, but it probably played some role (Whittlesey 1998b). Destruction of beaver habitats caused water tables to decline; the *cienegas* eventually formed by beaver dams and wetland vegetation disappeared (Patten 1998:70–71). Overgrazing, woodcutting, and other human activities destroyed vegetation and increased runoff. Channel downcutting followed by lowered water tables further reduced riparian vegetation (Patten 1998:72). Swollen with runoff and unimpeded by vegetation and natural obstacles, the great river tore down its channel. It does not seem coincidental that the disastrous floods occurred during a drought period between 1891 and 1893. Drought must have reduced vegetative cover and induced watershed destruction. By contrast, some scientists cite geomorphological evidence indicating that the rivers have always flooded periodically and that ancient floods may have been even greater before records were kept.

Regardless of their causes, the flood events of the late nineteenth and early twentieth centuries created havoc for residents and farmers throughout Arizona. Some of the worst effects were felt along the lower reaches of the Colorado, where the outlaw river raged uncontrolled. A colony of apparently fearless farmers had established themselves in the Colorado valley near present-day Yuma, drawn by the vision of an enterprising irrigation engineer named Charles Rockwood. In 1892, he had became obsessed with transforming the desert along the lower reaches of the Colorado, where the river ran through a land "watered" by a scant two inches of rainfall. If that river could only be harnessed, Rockwood reasoned, the brutal desert would become green. His dreams fueled a flurry of settlements as farmers flocked to the promised land. Those dreams also spawned one of the greatest natural disasters of the Colorado desert, altering the landscape forever.

Rockwood's dreams were built on the solid observations of others. In 1856, government geologist William P. Blake had surveyed the Colorado desert for a railroad route. The Colorado River is like the Nile, he had observed, and like the Nile it could furnish water for perpetually rich, green fields. Yet Blake's report also cautioned that diversion of the Colorado might lead to uncontrolled flooding of the Salton Sink (Stevens 1988:9). This geological anomaly was essentially a valley beneath the level of the sea, which had been created by millennia of Colorado River silt forming an effective dam. At the lowest spot was the "shimmering, brine-encrusted" Salton Sink depression (Stevens 1988:7–8). Rockwood ignored Blake's warning with dire consequences.

In 1901, Rockwood and irrigation developer George Chaffey joined forces to cut a diversion channel into the valley once named the Valley of the Dead, which Rockwood had renamed optimistically and grandly as the Imperial Valley. Advertising brochures trumpeted the valley's rich farmland that could be purchased under the provisions of the Desert Land Act (Stevens 1988:11). "Bewitched by the siren song of bountiful harvests and soaring land values," thousands of prospective settlers flocked to the desert (Stevens 1988:12). Within eight months, there were two towns with 2,000 settlers, and 100,000 acres were ready for harvesting (Reisner 1986:122–123). At first, Rockwood appeared to be a visionary and a prophet who had transformed one of the greatest deserts in the world into America's salad bowl and fruit basket.

But the wildest river in the West did not meekly submit to Rockwood's will. By 1904, the artificial channel had silted up under the Colorado's heavy burden, and a bypass was required. Rockwood and Chaffey dug a new channel in Mexico where it would be free from U.S. government intervention. Once more, water began to flow to the fields around Brawley, Imperial, and Calexico. Disaster was looming, however. It arrived in 1905, when the spring floods came early, and a great surge of water from snowmelt and warm Pacific rain spilled out of the Gila River and into the Colorado, washing away the flimsy control gates and cutting new channels. Relentless on its way to the Salton Sink, the floodwaters washed away the farmers' soil. By summer, almost all of the river had escaped the main channel, and the Salton Sink had become the Salton Sea (Reisner 1986:123; Stevens 1988:14; Sykes 1937). Some geologists predicted that the river would carve out a canyon as much as a mile deep and several hundred miles long, destroying Yuma and eventually inundating southwestern Arizona and southeastern California (Stevens 1988:15).

The Cutback

"The cutback" was one of the most terrifying effects of the Colorado's rampage through the Imperial Valley in 1905. A waterfall developed at the point where the river poured into the Salton Sea. The sandy soil was too loose to withstand the force of the water, and it collapsed. Seeking to equalize its descent, the river began to cut back toward its highest point, which was the Mexican intake canal. "Like a ripsaw tearing through rotten wood, the Colorado cut back through the desert at the rate of more than a mile a day," wrote Joseph Stevens (1988:15). The river also cut deeper, so that the waterfall's height increased to 100 feet. A cloud of dust and spray marked the waterfall, and its roar could be heard miles away (Stevens 1988:15).

The Imperial Valley was saved that time by E. H. Harriman, owner of the Southern Pacific Railroad, who was pressured by President Theodore Roosevelt to stop the Colorado at all costs. But these events and their drastic consequences (and the equally terrifying events that followed) convinced Congress that federal reclamation was needed to tame the river. Heroic efforts were necessary to reduce its periodic flooding, stabilize the water supply, and decrease the silt load that continuously threatened to divert the river in the lower reaches. These goals were too

The Colorado River flooding in 1905. PHOTOGRAPH COURTESY ARIZONA HISTORICAL SOCIETY, TUCSON (AHS ACCESSION NO. MS 452, F. 528 A4-98).

optimistic, but too economically promising to be rejected. To do anything less than reclaim the river would have been unpatriotic. Representative Newlands modified his national reclamation bill slightly, to increase the size of the farms to 160 acres. Congress passed the bill on June 17, 1902, and President Roosevelt subsequently signed it into law.

The National Reclamation Act took large, federal water-control and water-diversion projects from dream to reality. Proceeds from public-land sales in 16 Western states and territories, including Arizona, were dedicated to a fund for financing storage and diversion projects. Control of the water, however, would remain with the West. Local users' associations would assume operation and maintenance responsibilities when half of the repayment obligations were met. The act thus solved the problem that had emerged earlier when private investors proved unattracted to irrigation works (Wilkinson 1992:247). In one brilliant stroke, federal water-control policy was established. So too was the uncompromising yet completely contradictory attitude toward the federal government that persists in the West today: "Get out and give us more money" (Wilkinson 1992:235).

The Reclamation Act authorized the Secretary of the Interior to administer the program but established no organization to carry out the work. In 1902, Secretary of the Interior Ethan Allen Hitchcock created the Reclamation Service within the Geological Survey for this purpose. The rationale for the separation of agencies lay in the existing Division of Hydrography, the branch of the Geological Survey that had studied western water resources for more than two decades. Frederick H. Newell, chief of the division, was appointed the first head of the Reclamation Service under the title of chief engineer.

Ironically, 1902 was the year that John Wesley Powell died, less than three months after the Reclamation Act was passed. Wilkinson (1992:247) has pointed out that the act realized Powell's vision in its entirety. But implementing the act to make the vision more than just a pipe dream was another story. Reclamation would not become the child of John Wesley Powell, Wilkinson has argued, or even of Elwood Mead. The actual workings of the reclamation program would be controlled by western water policy and law that had been set in place generations earlier.

The Early Reclamation Service and Theodore Roosevelt Dam

The ink was scarcely dry on the Reclamation Act when the agency appointed to execute it was put to task in Arizona. Theodore Roosevelt Dam, located on the Salt River about 75 miles northeast of Phoenix, was the first dam built by the Reclamation Service, and was in effect "a showcase effort for the new agency" (Rogge and others 1995:7). Whether by design or chance, Theodore Roosevelt Dam proved to be a monumental undertaking and a stunning achievement. Although the story of Roosevelt Dam is a tale of success, it also sheds light on the fledgling service's initial difficulties. The Reclamation Service manifested an ironic paradox during the first quarter-century of its operation. "Its public works were great achievements," according to Robinson (1979:19), "but on the whole the program's fundamental objectives went unfulfilled." The small farmers, the impoverished folk who had moved from eastern cities and were to benefit from federal water engineering in the West, did not reap the rewards. It was, rather, larger landowners who benefitted, fulfilling Powell's fears.

In the early 1900s, farmers in the Phoenix area were beginning to realize that the Salt River carried adequate flow only in about one out of every three years (Greenwald and Stein 1993:8). A tributary of the Gila, the Salt River was also fed largely by snowmelt, and was just as capricious. The vicious cycle of flood and drought meant that irrigation was a feast-or-famine proposition. Flood control was needed to prevent damaging floods, and some means of ensuring regularized and adequate flow in drought years was also necessary. Another factor made the involvement of the federal government attractive. Many of the early irrigation projects had included as much private as public land, often touching off a frenzy of land speculation (Worster 1985:171–172). In turn-of-the-twentieth-century Phoenix, intense and protracted battles over harnessing Salt River water had developed. The newly minted Reclamation Service was invited to resolve these water wars and develop the Phoenix valley, and the result was Theodore Roosevelt Dam (Worster 1985:172).

The dam would solve the Salt River valley's water problems. It would store sufficient water for the low-flow years and provide flood control during peak-flow years. A modest amount of hydroelectric power was a bonus. Best of all, federal monies would finance the enormous undertaking and federal oversight would end the squabbling over irrigation project construction and use of water. Theodore Roosevelt Dam was every Phoenix farmer's dream come true.

The massive, stone-block dam, which was originally called the "Tonto Basin Dam," was built at a location called "The Crossing" by early Arizona pioneers. The narrow gorge at the confluence of Salt River and Tonto Creek had been the only feasible place to ford the often treacherous Salt River. It was rugged, isolated country sandwiched between the towering Mazatzal Mountains and the Sierra

Ancha. There were no towns, no roads, and no facilities to house the construction workers. Western Apache from the San Carlos Reservation helped to build the dam, and their story is told in Chapter 6.

Construction began in 1905, the wettest year in memory (Sheridan 1995:210). On November 16, a warm rain melted snow in the mountains. The river rose 30 feet in 15 hours, slashing down the canyon and sweeping away the diversion dams that had been constructed to keep away the river. Floods barred construction from resuming until the following March. By the time the next floods surged in spring 1908, the south end of the dam was high enough to force the water over the northern end (Sheridan 1995:211).

The thick-arch, masonry dam was completed in 1911 and cost $10 million to build, an astronomical sum in early-twentieth-century dollars. When it was finished, the lake behind it impounded more than a million acre-feet of water and stretched almost 10 miles long and 2 miles wide (Rogge and others 1995:7). The Reclamation Service had "astounded the world with its ingenuity, resourcefulness, mastery over nature, and grace of design" (Worster 1985: 173). For many years, the dam was the biggest and tallest dam in the world. According to historian Thomas Sheridan (1995:211), President Roosevelt himself declared it one of the two greatest triumphs of his administration, the other being the Panama Canal.

Today the lake shines blue below the peaks, an unlikely combination of desert land and mountain water. In wet

Laboriously clearing land by mule team, 1905. PHOTOGRAPH COURTESY U.S. BUREAU OF RECLAMATION.

Building Theodore Roosevelt Dam

At the time of its construction, Roosevelt Dam was the largest masonry arch dam in the world. It was built in "cyclopean masonry," a Greco-Roman building style using huge, irregular stone blocks now invisible under its new coating of concrete. The completed dam stood 280 feet high. It was 184 wide at its base, 723 feet long at its crest, and 16 feet high. The original roadway across the top of the dam was designed to allow two Model-T Ford automobiles to pass abreast.

When President Theodore Roosevelt dedicated the dam named in his honor on March 18, 1911, the reservoir contained just over 526,000 acre-feet of water, less than half its eventual capacity. An 11-gun salute and the cheers of the hundreds attending the event greeted the car carrying Roosevelt. Standing below the flags of the United States and the Reclamation Service, Roosevelt said, "If there could be any monument which would appeal to any man, surely this is it. You could not have done anything which would have pleased and touched me more than to name this great dam, this reservoir site, after me, and I thank you from my heart for having done so" (U.S. Department of the Interior, Bureau of Reclamation 2003a).

For further information, please visit the U.S. Department of the Interior's Bureau of Reclamation Web site *at http://www.apo.lc.usbr.gov.*

What's an Acre-foot?

An acre-foot of water is the amount required to cover an acre of land with water one foot deep. It represents 325,851 gallons of water, or roughly the amount of water used by a family of four within a year. John Wesley Powell's Irrigation Survey, part of the U.S. Geological Survey, coined the term (Worster 2001:477). Acre-feet are usually measured by the millions (e.g., 1.5 million acre-feet). By any measure, that's a lot of water.

years, the lake nearly fills the valleys down which Salt River and Tonto Creek had flowed so unpredictably. Camping, boating, and recreational facilities allow Arizonans to use the water stored for Phoenix in ways the early cotton farmers and citrus growers could never have envisioned. When the dam was modified by the Bureau of Reclamation during the Central Arizona Project, the Tonto Basin was the locale of multiple archaeological projects that transformed our understanding of ancient Arizona. Salt River Project manages dam operations today.

While Theodore Roosevelt Dam was being completed, the Reclamation Service was undergoing its own alterations. In 1903, work commenced on the first of six approved projects. Newell, who was the Reclamation Service's chief engineer, astutely recognized that social and human conflicts as well as physical engineering challenges would have to be resolved if the agency was to succeed. The Reclamation Service broke away from the Geological Survey and became an independent agency in 1907. Newell was named director of the breakaway agency, and Arthur Powell Davis, nephew of John Wesley Powell, was appointed chief engineer. Davis had been working with the Geological Survey since 1882 and had been appointed head of its Division of Hydrography in 1896. He was, without question, "the world's leading expert on reclamation" (Stevens 1988:17).

Davis would make the conquest of the Colorado River a personal ambition. "The Colorado was in Davis' blood" (Stevens 1988:17), and like so many others, he dreamed of dams standing tall throughout the river's upper and lower reaches. It was a dream that would be only partially realized. As chief engineer, Davis developed an audacious plan, Stevens (1988:17) has written. He wanted to develop the entire Colorado River drainage, a monumental undertaking that would require comprehensive development, financial resources, and engineering beyond the capabilities of the individual farmer. Like his uncle, Davis recognized the necessity for cooperative development of the Colorado River, but he was convinced that the federal government rather than private irrigation districts should bear the burden (Stevens 1988:17).

Davis bided his time, collecting data and compiling information on potential dam sites. Meanwhile, despite the spectacular success of Theodore Roosevelt Dam, the Reclamation Service was not immediately successful. Its projects proved to be expensive and unworkable, and legislation and reorganization were proposed in an attempt to solve the problems. In 1910, Congress loaned the Reclamation Service $20 million to speed construction along and get water to settlers more quickly. The Warren Act of 1911 attempted to relieve the financial burden by providing for the sale of surplus water to irrigators. Despite these impediments, the Reclamation Act was directly responsible for the significant increase in homesteading that took place between 1900 and 1920. In 1910, 23 million acres were patented as a consequence of opening of western lands to settlement through irrigation (Wilkinson 1992:247–248). Entire communities, not individual farmers alone, benefitted from irrigation. Ranches, farms, equipment suppliers, businesses, and services flourished in irrigated areas.

Criticism of the service did not subside, however, and Newell was dismissed in 1914. Davis replaced him as director. The opportunity for which he longed had come at last. Under Davis's directorate of the Reclamation Service from 1914 to 1923, the agency built 100 dams and delivered irrigation water to more than three million acres in the West.

One irrigation feature that was not built—at least at that time—was the All-American Canal. The beleaguered farmers of the Imperial Valley had become further preoccupied with what they perceived as threats from the government of Mexico, through which flowed the newly cut channel then watering the valley. In 1919, they introduced a bill authorizing construction of a new canal that would run entirely through U.S. territory, hence the name. Davis opposed the bill, which was defeated. His opposition stemmed from his belief that the project should be undertaken only as part of the much grander program he had long envisioned (Stevens 1988:17).

Photograph by Jefferson Reid.

Congress had ordered the Reclamation Service to conduct an "exhaustive" survey of the lower Colorado Basin, and in late 1921, Davis reported the results to Secretary of the Interior Albert Fall. Not long afterward, "the Fall-Davis report" was submitted to Congress. The report recommended "a comprehensive development scheme to regulate the river, generate power, and irrigate the lower Colorado Valley" Robinson (1979:50). Davis maintained that the huge, multistate project should be federally sponsored.

The aftermath of World War I and the agricultural depression of the 1920s were affecting the reclamation program considerably. Davis was criticized for emphasizing engineering at the expense of financial solvency and accountability. Indebted farmers found repayment obligations impossible to meet in the postwar depression, and by 1922 only 9.5 percent of the $135 million invested in reclamation by the federal government had been repaid (Robinson 1979: 43). Davis became the scapegoat for the failure of federal irrigation, and he was fired in 1923, to a storm of protest among fellow engineers and those who worked with him at the agency. Secretary of the Interior Hubert Work appointed David W. Davis—no relation—to replace Arthur Davis as commissioner of the Bureau of Reclamation, as the Reclamation Service had been rechristened that year. Other men would see Arthur Powell Davis's dreams to fruition.

Before it could move forward, the agency had to be overhauled, and Secretary Work appointed a Committee of Special Advisors on Reclamation to study policy, operation, and application of arid-lands reclamation. The committee was particularly critical of the agency's failure to achieve its fundamental goal of making it possible for homesteaders to reclaim the public domain, and it highlighted four major reforms essential to success. Following publication of the committee's report in 1924, Secretary Work appointed Elwood Mead to be Commissioner of Reclamation and asked him to carry out the committee's recommendations. David W. Davis stepped down to become director of finance (Robinson 1979:44–45).

Elwood Mead was Bureau of Reclamation commissioner from 1924 until his death in 1936. Shortly after he assumed control of the agency, the Great Depression struck, and the bureau was attacked by those who favored reducing it drastically, if not eliminating it altogether. To save the agency, Mead turned to transforming the Bureau of Reclamation into a public-works organization contributing to economic recovery (Worster 1985:187). The stage was set for the grand, dam-building reclamation era.

Farming in Phoenix and the Struggle for Water

Drive through Phoenix today, and you will discover that the Valley of the Sun is a metropolitan complex of sprawling suburbs, fantastically stacked interchanges, and jammed rush-hour freeways. It is a big city with big buildings, planted incongruously where cotton fields and orange groves once stood. Phoenix is also an extraordinary paradox—one of the most arid North American deserts, where summer temperatures routinely top 105 degrees Fahrenheit and less than 10 inches of rain falls each year, is also "the greatest conjunction of arable land and flowing water in the Southwest" (Sheridan 1995:199). Three of the Colorado's major tributaries—the Verde, Salt, and Gila Rivers—converge in the Phoenix Basin where they are joined by smaller streams—the Santa Cruz, Hassayampa, and Agua Fria Rivers. Moreover, there were virtually no topographic obstacles to water diversion.

This vast, alluvial plain was a veritable garden in prehistory, transformed by Hohokam canals into an agricultural Eden. So it was in historical times as well. Akimel O'odham (Pima) farmers built large villages along the Gila River near its confluence with the Santa Cruz. The productivity of their fields, planted, watered, and tended by relatively simple techniques, was enormous. By some estimates, they raised as much as a million pounds of wheat each year, along with corn, cotton, melons, beans, and other crops (Nicolson 1974:109). Pima wheat fed Anglo-American soldiers, travelers, and stagecoach drivers; Pima hay fed their horses.

The Euroamerican settlers of the nineteenth century were quick to recognize the extraordinary if unlikely combination of resources in the Phoenix Basin and the advantages that would come from tapping its rivers. The struggle to control water and use it for farming defined the history of Phoenix, changed the physical landscape of the Valley of the Sun, and irrevocably altered the economy of Native American farmers.

Phoenix began as a military encampment—Camp McDowell along the Verde River on today's Fort McDowell Yavapai Indian Reservation. Civilians recognizing the financial benefit of supplying the soldiers and their horses began the first serious farming ventures, raising hay, wheat, and other produce. One was Jack Swilling, whom Sheridan (1995:199) has described as a Confederate deserter, violent drunk, stage robber, and morphine addict, perhaps not that unusual in the days of the wild, wild West. Swilling convinced a group of Wickenburg investors to form the Swilling Irrigating and Canal Company in 1867. Well aware of the money to be made from irrigated farming, Swilling was also keenly cognizant of Hohokam agricultural-engineering sophistication. The men dug out a prehistoric Hohokam canal on the north bank of the Salt River and christened it Swilling's Ditch. According to what is possibly

Vast Marshland

Ethnobiologist Amadeo Rea (1983:22) has told us that the confluences of the Santa Cruz, Salt, Agua Fria, Hassayampa, and Gila Rivers "contributed to a vast marshland the likes of which we can scarcely imagine now." Until the late 1800s, creeks flowed through marshes punctuated by springs and lagoons that the Akimel O'odham tapped using simple irrigation ditches. Reeds and grass waved under the blazing summer sun. The ditches were lined with sunflowers, and cottonwoods rose like massive, green clouds along the river's edges. An enormous, thick mesquite *bosque* called New York Thicket covered the confluence of the Gila and Santa Cruz Rivers (Rea 1983:33). Beavers built dams that impounded water and helped *cienegas* and marshes to form. Birds sang in the reeds, and insects buzzed and hummed. It was a magical, lush, glorious place filled with light and green, living things, where stories seemed to flow through the air like birdsong and wind. It has now utterly vanished.

George Webb, an Akimel O'odham elder, remembers what it was like in his book *A Pima Remembers* (1959:124):

> In the old days, on hot summer nights, a low mist would spread over the river and the sloughs. Then the sun would come up and the mist would disappear. . . .The red-wing blackbirds would sing in the trees and fly down to look for bugs along the ditches. Their song always means that there is water close by. . . .
>
> Now the river is an empty bed full of sand. . . .
>
> The dead trees stand there like white bones. The red-wing blackbirds have gone somewhere else.

an apocryphal tale, this event caused boosters to predict that a modern civilization would rise above the vanished Hohokam cities like a phoenix from the ashes, giving the town its name. In 1871, the ditch was irrigating 4,000 acres.

As Sheridan (1995:199) has pointed out, such joint-stock canal ventures along with communal enterprises by Mormon farmers expanded quickly after the Swilling prototype, some of which, in their zeal for a fast buck, were not unlike the real-estate speculators and developers who came later. New canals such as the Grand, Maricopa, and Salt River Valley (as Swilling's Ditch was rechristened) were built following lines of old Hohokam canals. Mormon settlers at the site of Camp Utah, which later became the town of Lehi, and at Nephi, Alma, Mesa, and Tempe began to carve out farming communities. They, too, cleaned out ancient Hohokam canals and began planting crops. Mormon historian James McClintock (1985:213) relates the fortuitous discovery of the prehistoric canal that would become the Mesa canal: "Nothing short of Providential was considered the finding of the canal, dug by a prehistoric people into the edge of the mesa."

In 1885, the Arizona Canal Company built a diversion dam below the confluence of the Salt and Verde Rivers. It was the most substantial diversion structure of its time (Zarbin 1984). Water flowed into the huge Arizona Canal—58 feet wide at the top—to land where no one had ever farmed before. Promoters claimed that 100,000 acres of "unproductive desert of no value for any purpose" would blossom under its waters (Sheridan 1995:200).

One of the most ambitious irrigation plans was hatched by investors of the Agua Fria Water and Land Company in 1888. Seeking to develop the water resources of the northern valley, the company envisioned storage dams, a main canal, and miles of distribution canals that would irrigate 160,000 acres. The project was plagued by financial problems, disastrous floods, and sheer bad luck. Despite the dedicated attempts of William Beardsley to keep it alive, the project languished for decades until the completion of Lake Pleasant Dam in 1927 (Whittlesey and others 1998:301).

A grandiose scheme to divert Verde River water had emerged as early as 1888. Its centerpiece was to be a dam and reservoir named Horseshoe for the shape of a bend in the Verde River. The reservoir would feed a 140-mile-long canal. Three other reservoirs on Cave Creek, New River, and the Agua Fria River were planned. Dam sites were also proposed on the Salt River, including the location where Theodore Roosevelt Dam would later be built (Whittlesey and others 1998:316). A. C. Sheldon formed the Rio Verde Canal Company to carry out this scheme. Like so many other joint ventures, this massive project was plagued by financial and legal problems, mismanagement, and competition with other water groups, including the Agua Fria Water and Land Company and the Salt River Valley Water Users' Association, later to become Salt River Project. Economic depression generated by the silver crisis of the 1890s was the final blow dooming the project to failure. But the eyes of Phoenix remained on the Verde River. Valley farmers and investors were fearful of the grand plans of the people living on the upper reaches of the Salt and Verde River. To Phoenix, that water was theirs by right, and without it, the valley would return to desert again (Merrill 1975). Phoenicians would continue to fight any attempts to divert water tooth and nail.

While the battles over rights to river water were ongoing, homesteads began to spring up like mushrooms on damp ground all over Arizona in the late 1800s and early 1900s. Lured by slick advertising and promises of paradisiacal country, hopeful farmers and ranchers from green, wooded midwestern states such as Ohio and Illinois flocked to the Valley of the Sun. Most probably had no idea what they were about to encounter. Homesteads without water were doomed to failure, and successful homesteads were those with rights to water, just as John Wesley Powell had predicted. One was the homestead of Francis "Frank" A. Young, who purchased the rights to land at the end of Grand Canal in 1886. The ranch, which was located along the Agua Fria and New Rivers, was flourishing in 1897 when Young died of typhoid fever at age 46. In his memoir, son Herbert V. Young chronicles growing up on this homestead. Water was sold by the "inch," Young tells us (1983:36)—measured by the size of the aperture through which it passed and equal to a small fraction of an acre-foot. Homesteads located at the end of the Grand Canal found themselves in a troublesome situation at times of low flow, when there was insufficient water to divide and distribute. When that happened, each rancher had to take the entire flow on a time basis. Water use was apportioned and regulated (if necessary, with pistols and shotguns) by the ditch boss or *zanjero.* Young notes dryly that "those located on the upper reaches of the canal made sure they weren't going to be the losers."

The astounding growth of the Phoenix valley was a boon for many Mexican and American settlers, but its effects on the Akimel O'odham farmers were deeply felt. Historian David DeJong (1992) has retold this sad story of betrayal and fear. Upstream farmers and miners began to divert the water in the Gila River that had once flowed to Pima fields and nourished bountiful harvests. Although a reservation for the Akimel O'odham had been established along the Gila River in 1859, it failed to protect their water rights. The mines that flourished along the upper Gila watershed in the 1870s consumed a great deal of the water that had flowed onto Pima lands, as did the canals tapping the Gila in places such as Florence, Adamsville, and Thatcher. These farmers built large, wasteful canals and did

Stealing Water from the Grand Canal

One morning, the water came down the Grand Canal, and it was the Youngs's turn to take the first 12 hours. Eight-year-old Herbert and his sister Fay were detailed to watch over the gates while their father was away to make sure that their wily neighbor did not divert the water for his own use. The children hid in bushes near the canal and watched the neighbor sneak to his gate and raise it, sending the Youngs's water into his own ditch. When the neighbor left, the children, this time armed with their father's loaded and cocked shotgun, closed the gate and waited to see if the neighbor would come back.

Sure enough, the neighbor returned, no doubt puzzled by the absence of illegal flow into his ditch. Watching him prepare to prop the gate open again, young Herbert felt "a feverish urge to act." As he has related the tale (Young 1983:93–94):

> I put a finger on the top trigger of the gun and pressed it down hard–so hard that my finger slipped and hit the other trigger too.
>
> That old gun sure made a noise. Two loud roars, in quick success, burst on the air.
>
> For a moment I was afraid. . . But. . . . The result of the double explosion was extremely satisfying.
>
> From Snider's throat came a harsh squawking sound. He leaped to his feet, took a flying leap off the band and, with giant strides, went crashing through the brush.

Young Herbert was chastised for touching his father's shotgun, his father and the neighbor had words, and it all turned out well in the end. "I never knew of Father having any more trouble with Snider. I was happy that he and Mother both seemed to forget that time I had disobeyed. They didn't always forget" (Young 1983:95).

Breaching of New Waddell Dam during a flood year. Photograph courtesy U.S. Bureau of Reclamation. Bob Knotts, photographer.

not return the used water to the river. The fields that had once fed American soldiers disappeared, and Native American friendliness turned to distrust. Enlarging the size of the reservation did little to allay the water shortage. By the early 1870s, the Pima were on the brink of starvation, and conflict was imminent. Many moved away from the river to settle in places where springs or seepage provided water.

Removing Indians from their homelands and consolidating the tribes in segregated territories was a mainstay of federal policy at that time, and this strategy was applied to the Pima "problem." But while the Pimas and Maricopas debated relocation to the Indian Territory in Oklahoma, a periodic cycle in Arizona's precipitation brought three times the normal amount of rain to Pima fields, and many lost interest in leaving their homeland. The abundant rain was short-lived, and drought years between 1875 and 1883 forced Pimas to resettle along the Salt River, where their presence alarmed non-Indian settlers.

The impasse continued. The government pressed for removal, and the Pima resisted. In 1879, President Hayes attempted to expand the existing reservation to include the Phoenix, Tempe, and Hayden's Ferry settlements. The resulting storm of protest caused him to rescind the order and establish a smaller reservation. This did little to appease Indian suffering, because under Arizona territorial law—based on the doctrine of prior appropriation—water rights were assigned to the upstream canals. There was nothing in territorial law to protect the water rights of the people who had been farming these lands for centuries.

At last, admitting the failure of the Indian removal policy, President Chester Arthur added lands south and west of the Gila River to the Pima-Maricopa Reservation in 1882 and in the following year issued an executive order doubling the size of the reservation. This action failed to address the Indians' longstanding problems. "It was more water, not land, that the Pimas and Maricopas needed" (DeJong 1992:391). Not until the San Carlos Irrigation project was created nearly 50 years later would the Pimas and Maricopas finally receive the water they needed to grow crops and sustain themselves in the Valley of the Sun.

Damming the Verde River

The marriage between farmers and the federal government was forged in floods (Sheridan 1995:203). The recurrent floods and cyclical drought events that plagued the Phoenix Basin and the farmlands on its borders during the 1890s had demonstrated the need for dams on the Salt River to prevent flooding and provide a reliable water supply in dry years. The history of joint-stock canals by Phoenix investors proved how risky such ventures could be, and territorial Arizona—it would not become a state until 1912—could not assume the cost of constructing a dam on the Salt River. With the passage of the National Reclamation Act, the federal government could assume the financial burden. The Salt River Valley Water Users' Association was incorporated in 1903 to furnish water, power, and drainage for about 5,000 individual landowners. With the fledgling Reclamation Service at the construction helm, Theodore Roosevelt Dam was built. Its completion in 1911 temporarily soothed the hostilities of valley residents (Worster 1985:173), who had been fighting for control of water among themselves and with the Indians for at least two decades. Phoenix began to hum—a desert metropolis in the making.

But Theodore Roosevelt Dam was not enough. In its first eight years of service, the Salt River overflowed the dam four times. Floods in April 1905 washed out the Arizona Dam owned by the Arizona Water Company, which had diverted water for canals on the north side of the Salt River. Serious losses to the farmers below this dam led the federal government to purchase the northside canal system and construct Granite Reef Diversion Dam. Located about four miles south of the Salt-Verde River confluence at a granite outcrop or "reef," the dam was constructed by the Bureau of Reclamation between 1906 and 1908. It is managed by Salt River Project today.

The Salt River Valley Water Users' Association built three additional dams downstream from Theodore Roosevelt Dam to grapple with the problem of Salt River flooding. These were, in order of their descent from upper to lower, Horse Mesa Dam (1927), Mormon Flat Dam (1926), and Stewart Mountain Dam (1930). The lakes behinds these dams (Apache, Canyon, and Saguaro Lakes) form a continuous chain almost 60 miles long and are havens today for fishermen, boaters, and recreational users.

Granite Reef Diversion Dam. PHOTOGRAPH COURTESY U.S. BUREAU OF RECLAMATION. JOE MADRIGAL, JR., PHOTOGRAPHER.

Bartlett Dam. Photograph courtesy U.S. Bureau of Reclamation. Joe Madrigal, Jr., photographer.

Although water-storage and flood-control needs were met by the concrete, thin-arch dams, their other purpose was to generate hydroelectric power, the sale of which would pay off federal loans for dam construction. These three dams, along with Theodore Roosevelt Dam, Granite Reef Diversion Dam, and two main canals (Arizona and South Canals), formed the original Salt River Project.

But what of the Verde River, one of Arizona's few perennial streams and the long-coveted tributary of the Salt River? In 1918, the old Rio Verde Canal Company plan was dusted off and revived as the Paradise-Verde Irrigation District, and surveys for dam sites began. The long-term competition over rights to the Verde River's waters simply would not die, however, and after Theodore Roosevelt Dam was completed and Salt River Project took control, construction projects languished once more. It was not until 1934 that Salt River Project was granted the right to form an irrigation district including all waters from the Verde River.

After decades of acrimonious conflict, financial collapses, and a considerable amount of scheming, Bartlett Dam, named after the engineer credited with discovering the appropriate dam site, was completed in 1939. It was built by the Bureau of Reclamation and funded jointly by Salt River Project and the U.S. Bureau of Indian Affairs. Bartlett was the last, multiple-arch dam built in central Arizona and, according to Rogge and Myers (1987:57), was the largest such dam at that time in the world. It cost a relatively paltry $2 million to build and was not designed to generate electricity.

Horseshoe Dam above Bartlett on the Verde River was completed in 1945 with financial backing from Phelps Dodge Corporation. Horseshoe was built to compensate for an interbasin transfer of Salt River Project water from the Verde River to the San Francisco–Blue River system, where copper mines in Morenci were gobbling water. This was also Arizona's wartime dam, built by the U.S. Defense Plant Corporation as an "emergency war measure" to help the copper mines support the war effort (Whittlesey and others 1998:319). The earthfill dam had no capacity to generate hydroelectric power. Salt River Project manages both dams today, using Horseshoe to replenish Bartlett Lake located downstream.

The Salt and Verde Rivers were almost totally controlled by the dams constructed between 1911 and 1946, reducing the possibility of flood damage and making it possible to water Phoenix farmland. Ironically, the agricultural industry that spawned the need to build dams on Arizona's major rivers began to diminish almost as soon as they were built. The market for cotton, which had flourished during World War I to provide materials for tires and airplane-wing coverings, declined. New industries, among them tourism, sprang up, and the manufacturing and service sectors grew at the expense of the greatest of water users, mining and agriculture. Today, housing developments, retirement communities, golf courses, and resorts sprawl across Phoenix and its margins where once cotton fields and citrus groves grew. Agrarian dreams faded and were replaced by urban dreams (Sheridan 1995).

Confident engineers would turn next to damming and storing the erratic, silt-laden, forceful flow of the much larger and more distant Colorado River and bringing it to Phoenix. Federal programs largely tamed the river, making it little more than a managed ditch, in Worster's (1985:211) words. The conquest of the Colorado River marked the emergence of the federal government as the most powerful authority in western water management (Worster 1985:211).

Water Wars and the Story of Hoover Dam

While overhaul of the reclamation agency was taking place in the early decades of the twentieth century, plans for developing the West by harnessing Colorado River water had begun to move forward quickly. In 1919, the states forming the Colorado River Basin organized the League of the Southwest to promote development of the river. Arizona and California had come to the joint realization that the unpredictable and temperamental Colorado River had to be impounded in its upriver canyons if it was going to be put to beneficial use—which at that time was presumed to be for agricultural purposes. The Fall-Davis report had advocated construction of a large dam in the vicinity of Boulder Canyon, its costs to be repaid through sale of hydroelectric power. Boulder was to be the first of the so-called "cash-register dams," designed to subsidize the irrigation component of the project (Wilkinson 1992:255).

Plans for Boulder Dam, today renamed Hoover Dam, instigated water wars between Arizona and California that would continue for decades. The dam would provide flood control, certainly, but by impounding water it would also provide the means to divert it to agricultural and municipal uses in California. Thousands were flocking to southern California, and its towns, businesses, ranches, farms, orchards, and vineyards were thirsty. All eyes were on Colorado River water. Only too aware of this fact, the Upper Basin states (Colorado, New Mexico, Utah, and Wyoming) opposed construction of Boulder Dam (Johnson 1977). The general sentiment was parochial—why should California (and Arizona and Nevada, as well) benefit from water rising hundreds of miles away in the mountains of the Upper Basin states? Whose water was it, anyway?

It was necessary, therefore, to develop legal means of preventing abuses and adjudicating use of the Colorado's water. The Colorado River Compact was organized for this purpose. The river was arbitrarily, rather than hydrologically or topographically, divided in two. Lee's Ferry at the mouth of Glen Canyon was the dividing point between the Upper and Lower Basins. The compact would spell out the rights of the Upper Basin and Lower Basin states. Each state named commissioners to negotiate the compact, and Herbert Hoover, who would later become president, represented the federal government (Johnson 1977:15). In 1921, Congress authorized creation of the compact and submitted it for approval in 1922.

According to the terms of the compact, each basin would receive 7.5 million acre-feet of water per year. Unfortunately, as several authors have pointed out, the Reclamation Service estimated the Colorado's annual flow at Lee's Ferry using poor techniques during a wet cycle. Extremely wet years between 1910 and 1922, when the compact was signed, led to an overestimate of the river's capacity. We have since learned from sophisticated tree-ring analyses that the average annual flow is far less than the original estimate of 17.5 million acre-feet—averaging between 13 and 14 million acre-feet annually. The decade spanning 1910–1920 was perhaps the most misleading upon which to base the river's average annual flow. John Wesley Powell, who had argued that the river's flow was cyclical, could have said "I told you so," had he been alive. Apparently, his earlier arguments had gone unheeded.

Decades of political battle would follow the seemingly innocuous compact. The squabbling was initiated when Arizona alone refused to ratify the compact and make it law. For years, Arizona and California would battle in and out of federal court over the states' share of the river water and the dams that would impound and distribute it. The Arizonans' slogan became "Save the Colorado River for Arizona," and campaigns on both sides of the issue were emotionally charged, politically motivated, and economically based (Johnson 1977). Arizona's governor, W. B. Hunt, opposed the compact because he believed that Arizona would soon cease to be a mining state and its needs for water and power would increase dramatically.

Six years of paralysis followed the 1922 compact. In 1928, Congress authorized Boulder Dam and the All-American Canal, although Arizona still refused to ratify the compact. The Boulder Canyon Project Act allocated the Lower Basin's share of water among the states. Arizona would receive 2.8 million acre-feet, California 4.4 million acre-feet, and Nevada 300,000 acre-feet. A separate and simultaneous act required that California would renounce forever any claim beyond the specified amount. Because Arizona's share was less than it wanted, the state continued to oppose the compact.

Arizona's fears were realized by the ominous Metropolitan Water District, which consisted of Los Angeles and 12 smaller cities in the greater metropolitan area. It was organized the same week that the Boulder Canyon Project Act was passed. Its mission was to develop a reliable water supply for the newly burgeoning cities of southern California. The district proposed to build a dam at Parker, about 150 miles below Boulder Dam, and to construct an aqueduct to carry water to metropolitan Los Angeles. The district would pay the greater part of the dam's cost if the United States agreed to deliver enough water from the reservoir behind Boulder Dam to fulfill its needs (Waters 1984:328). Not unexpectedly, Arizona opposed the proposed Parker Dam. Waters (1984:328) has described Arizona's resentments well: "California was not only grabbing all the hydroelectric power, but all the water of the river in order to build up her own cities and orange groves while Arizona remained an unpopulated, barren desert."

Parker Dam. Photograph by Jefferson Reid.

The battle between Arizona and California over Colorado River water continued to escalate. It was impossible to stop the California juggernaut of urban growth, however, and water was critical to population increase and development. By 1930, the debate had become incredibly acrimonious. In 1934, at the height of the imbroglio, Arizona Governor Benjamin B. Moeur called out the Arizona National Guard to halt construction of Parker Dam (Fradkin 1968:189). Secretary of the Interior Harold Ickes ordered dam construction halted while the Arizona-California dispute was settled in the courts. Parker Dam would eventually be built, Arizona's protests having been to no avail.

Boulder Dam, the first and greatest of the works on the Colorado River, was completed in 1935 under Mead's directorship of the Bureau of Reclamation. The dam has been called "the most significant American public works project of the twentieth century" (Robinson 1979:51)

Hoover Dam. Photograph by Jefferson Reid.

and was the first large, federal undertaking with multiple-purpose objectives. The motives for constructing the first of the great Bureau of Reclamation dams are unclear, however. According to Sykes (1937:34), Hoover Dam was to be built "primarily for the improvement of the Colorado as a navigable river." Control of the river's water was evidently the paramount objective. MacDougal optimistically wrote in the preface to Sykes's 1937 report (1937:iii) of the consequences of Boulder Dam. "The violent fluctuations in water volume . . . will cease in the lower river. The delta, therefore, enters a period of relative fixity. Channel changes will be very slight in the future." Sykes (1937:174) himself wrote,

> Flood hazard along the lower Colorado except for flash freshets originating in the still uncontrolled confluents of the Gila, will be practically eliminated by the vast storage capacity behind the Boulder Dam, and the controlled stream will undergo further settlement [of detrital matter] and additional clarification 155 miles farther down behind Parker Dam.

The wildest river in the West would be tamed, its waters running clear and controlled to the sea. Neither author mentioned that the monumental achievement was dedicated largely to generating electricity, which would be carried by towers marching across the horizon to Los Angeles.

Boulder Dam was not without its own share of controversy. Embroiled in the Arizona-California water war and the Parker Dam controversy, forces assembled in favor of and opposed to Boulder Dam. The Boulder Dam Association led those in favor of the dam. The coalition of farm groups and businesses included some of the West's most formidable businessmen, such as newspaper magnate William Randolph Hearst. Eastern legislators joined Arizona in the fight against the dam, along with the power lobby and Harry Chandler, publisher of the *Los Angeles Times*. Chandler feared that the All-American Canal would divert water at that time being used to irrigate a huge chunk of land he owned in Mexico south of the Imperial Valley (Stevens 1988:26–37).

Following sensational filibusters, obstructionist tactics, and multiple introductions of the enabling bill, the Boulder Canyon Project Act was passed on December 14, 1928, and signed into law a week later by President Coolidge. The final details of the six-state ratification of the Colorado River Compact (Arizona remaining obdurate and refusing to ratify) were worked out, and $165 million was authorized for construction of Boulder Dam and the All-American Canal. When the project was announced in 1930, Secretary of the Interior Ray L. Wilbur proudly stated the dam would be named after President Hoover. By choosing to honor Hoover, Wilbur touched off a partisan political battle that would last for 17 years (Stevens 1988:34).

Despite this inauspicious start, the Six Companies, which was an amalgam of groups that would subsequently become some of the world's largest corporations, began construction in 1931. The dam site was Black Canyon, a dark and forbidding chasm where Lieutenant Ives had wrecked his little iron boat decades earlier. The narrow gorge where the river separated Arizona and Nevada was selected over other potential sites because of geological

Sharing the Power

Ray L. Wilbur was Secretary of the Interior under President Hoover and as such, he was charged with the monumental task of apportioning Boulder Canyon Project Power. Competitive bidders were seeking more than three times the power the dam would generate, and Secretary Wilbur took seven months to pick through the political morass and make decisions (Stevens 1988:32).

Eventually, Wilbur gave the Metropolitan Water District the largest single share (36 percent) to pump water through the proposed 240-mile-long aqueduct. Other beneficiaries were Los Angeles, other southern California cities, and Southern California Edison. Arizona and Nevada were each given 18 percent of the power, but because neither state could then use that much, the excess was to be divided equally between Los Angeles and Southern California Edison until Arizona and Nevada could actually use it. Los Angeles and Edison would lease and operate the dam's powerhouse and along with the Metropolitan Water District would finance, build, and operate the transmission lines leading to the City of the Angels (Stevens 1988:32).

Pinto Polychrome bowl. PHOTOGRAPH BY JEFFERSON REID.

conditions—the strength and stability of rock formations and their hardness and permeability (Stevens 1988:19). Waters (1984:336) has listed some of the tremendous obstacles that faced the builders. Sheer, unbroken canyon walls had to be bridged and there was virtually nothing for initial footing, not even a sand bar. Around the dam site was a desolate desert environment that lacked housing, roads,

Designing a Dam

The Bureau of Reclamation hired English architect Gordon B. Kaufmann to consult on the design of Hoover Dam. Believing in the adage "form follows function," Kaufmann designed an edifice that would express the theme of power—human mastery over brute elements, power for the cities of southern California, the power of engineering technology to shape the land. It was a sweeping, concrete paean to power. Kaufmann created a design that emphasized the size of the dam, its clean lines, and its smooth, unbroken bulk. He stripped away the unnecessary decorative details that the federal engineers had built into the design, streamlined the powerhouse and outlet works, and created unadorned, monolithic concrete surfaces. The streamlined spillway piers he designed proved to be the most visually appealing of the dam's architectural elements (Stevens 1988:11).

and power. Perhaps worst of all, the builders had to face the terrific current of the silt-choked river. Frank T. Crowe, superintendent of construction for the Six Companies, was charged with solving these and many more problems

Erecting a dam the height of a 60-story building was no easy task. Fearless—crazy?—"high scalers" climbed down the canyon walls on ropes, working with jack hammers and dynamite to strip away loose rock. Two coffer dams isolated the construction site and protected it from flooding; four tunnels diverted the river's flow around the site. Around the site was nothing but naked rock that reflected heat like a blast furnace. Daytime temperatures reached 120 degrees Fahrenheit in the summer, and readings of 140 degrees Fahrenheit were recorded in the shafts of the diversion tunnels (Stevens 1988:63). According to the Hoover Dam Web site, between 96 and 112 men died during its construction. They were killed in falls off the high cliffs, heat prostration, blasting accidents, rock slides, tunnel cave-ins, breaking cables, and carbon-monoxide poisoning (Stevens 1988). Not one of them was buried under the never-ending stream of concrete, despite persistent urban legends that Hoover Dam was a sarcophagus (U.S. Department of the Interior, Bureau of Reclamation 2003b; Stevens 1988).

Harold Ickes was appointed Secretary of the Interior during the dam's construction. One of his first administrative acts was to announce that the dam rising in Black Canyon would be known as Boulder Dam. Stevens (1988:175) has suggested that this was a political act, "a mean-spirited attempt to shred the already tattered reputation of the former president."

Hoover Dam was completed in May 1935 one year ahead of schedule (Stevens 1988:252; Waters 1984:341–342). More than 5,200 workers were employed at the construction peak (Stevens 1988:227). The project earned between 20 and 35 percent profit, which was prorated among the consortium members (Stevens 1988:252). The dam had used 66 million tons of concrete, which according to Waters (1984:340) would have required 125 years to cool had the dam been solid. It was more concrete than the

Building Hoover Dam

Frank Waters (1984:339–340) has described the surreal world that was the construction site of Hoover Dam in 1932:

> One midnight. . . I stood on the bed of the river. The vast chasm seemed a slit through earth and time alike. The rank smell of Mesozoic ooze and primeval muck filled the air. Thousands of pale lights, likely newly lit stars, shone on the heights of the cliffs. Down below grunted and growled prehistoric monsters—great brute dinosaurs with massive bellies, with long necks like the brontosaurus, and with armored hides thick as those of the stegosaurus. They were steam shovels and cranes feeding on the muck, a ton at a gulp. . . . From the walls above shot beams of searchlights, playing over this vast subterranean arena. They revealed puny pygmies scurrying like ants from wall to wall. . . . And all this incessant, monstrous activity took place in silence, in jungle heat, and as if in the crepuscular darkness of a world taking shape before the dawn of man.

Bureau of Reclamation had used in the previous quarter-century of dam building. The daily equivalent of the mixing plant was a stream of concrete 20 feet wide, nearly 1 foot deep, and 1 mile long. The project had been completed in spite of torrid heat, horrific living conditions, labor strikes, floods, amoebic dysentery, the choking curse of ever-present dust clouds, the threat of delays, financial obstacles, and legal wrangling. Crowe had finished the job that would ensure the financial success of the Six Companies and his own reputation (Stevens 1988:195). Arizona's governor Moeur did not attend the dedication ceremony (Reisner 1986:257).

Lake Mead, the reservoir named after the Bureau of Reclamation commissioner who guided the work, impounded 31 million acre-feet of water, enough to irrigate 1.3 million acres of land in southern California, Mexico, and a small corner of Arizona. It was big enough to hold two full years of Colorado River flow. Providing abundant electricity, domestic water, and a controlled supply of irrigation water, Hoover Dam and its power plant turned the desert Southwest into boom country. It was a monument to the social, political, and financial factors that were turning reclamation dreams into reality—the centralized forces behind the Bureau of Reclamation, the emerging megalopolis of the Los Angeles metropolitan area, and the consortium of private contractors and financiers who built the dam (Worster 1985:211).

Frank Crowe went on to build more dams. After supervising several in California, he oversaw construction of northern California's Shasta Dam, the key structure in the Central Valley Project (Stevens 1988:253–254). He retired to a cattle ranch not far from Shasta Dam where he died in 1946. Crowe is remembered, Stevens (1988:254) has written, as the man who built Hoover Dam—and he had never hoped for anything more. The dam would also be remembered as a monument to President Hoover. In 1947, defying Ickes's mean-spirited name change, Congress renamed the dam permanently as Hoover Dam to honor the man who negotiated the compact that paved the way for its construction (Johnson 1977:50–51; Stevens 1988:34).

Work on the All-American Canal began in 1933. A dragline cut the channel; Imperial Dam was built to raise the river level 23 feet, and a series of desilting basins were built north of Yuma. In 1940, water coursed down the canal for the first time. The long-standing dream of Imperial Valley farmers—"an assured irrigation supply beyond the reach of Mexican officialdom" (Stevens 1988:258)—was realized at last. Parker Dam, the site of the acrimonious Arizona-California water wars, was also completed. Under Crowe's guidance, the dam was completed ahead of schedule in 1938. Today its reservoir, Lake Havasu, stores water for the Central Arizona Project and southern California cities. The gravity-arch dam also generates electricity. In 1941, water began to flow to Los Angeles along a 242-mile-long aqueduct. Los Angeles was no longer restrained by the availability of water. Its capacity to absorb ever more people and industries was virtually unimpeded (Harvey 1994:26). When World War II began, Colorado River water had begun to fuel industrial and agricultural expansion throughout southern California and transform the economy of the West (Harvey 1994:26–27).

Drowned Cities

The drowned settlements under Lake Mead—prehistoric pueblos such as Lost City, Mormon towns like St. Thomas—are symbols that can be interpreted in two ways, Frank Waters (1984:343) has written. On the one hand, they can be seen "as graves of men's fears of the great red river." But on the other hand, they can also be seen "as testimonials of its power to obliterate ultimately all the handiwork of man."

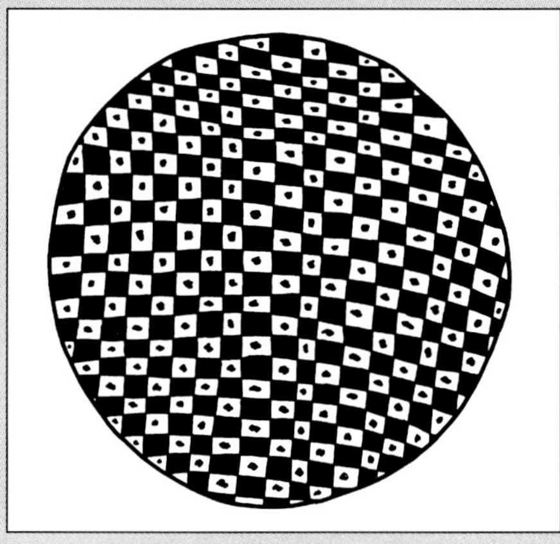

What Lies Below

Hoover Dam centers one of my earliest childhood memories. Driving east from California in the middle of the night (the only way to cross the desert in the days when air-conditioned cars were still rare), we crossed Hoover Dam. I recall that the night was moonless, and the dam was illuminated as if for a party. The narrow, ancient blacktop crossed the crest of the dam, and in those innocent days before terrorism and sabotage, no one prevented us from stopping to stretch our legs. My parents rousted me from fitful sleep to stand barefoot between the Art Deco columns and look down at the sweep of concrete. The water below was invisible, caught in the web of night. I remember the heat, still breathtaking at midnight. I recall the buzz of electricity flying invisibly along tangled wires to Los Angeles and the swarms of bugs circling the lights in suicidal frenzy.

More potent is the memory of fear. Scenes from every bad 1950s horror movie I had seen marched through my sleepy child's brain as I peered over the edge. Monsters were down there, I was convinced, plumped to gargantuan size by atomic energy. They lay curled in the black depths, ready to spring, drag me down with slimy tentacles, and devour me with huge white teeth. Scowling, I scuttled back to the car, flopped into the back seat, and covered my head with my pillow.

Monsters still swim in Lake Mead, perhaps. They are lulled to sleep by the hum of turbines and nest near the intake tunnels. When the dam is gone and the lake returned to desert once more, perhaps we will find their bones mixed with the batteries and oil cans, the styrofoam coolers and beer bottles. Archaeologists of the future will wonder. Maybe, just maybe, they will smile.

For further information, see: Philip L. Fradkin, A River No More: The Colorado River and the West *(University of Arizona Press, Tucson, 1968); Marc Reisner,* Cadillac Desert: The American West and Its Disappearing Water *(Penguin Books, New York, 1986); Joseph E. Stevens,* Hoover Dam: An American Adventure *(University of Oklahoma Press, Norman, 1988); Stephanie M. Whittlesey, Richard Ciolek-Torrello, and Jeffrey H. Altschul,* Vanishing River: Landscapes and Lives of the Lower Verde Valley: The Lower Verde Archaeological Project *(SRI Press, Tucson, 1998); Charles F. Wilkinson,* Crossing the Next Meridian: Land, Water, and the Future of the West *(Island Press, Washington, D.C., 1992); Donald Worster,* Rivers of Empire: Water, Aridity, and the Growth of the American West *(Oxford University Press, New York, 1985).*

The Story of the Central Arizona Project

3

Like a magic refrain the names of the many side canyons we saw during that trip go drifting through my mind: Forgotten, Twilight, Mystery, Music Temple, Hidden Passage, Labyrinth, Forbidden, Cathedral. If we should say them to our children, will they forgive us for having drowned them all in water?

—Ann Woodin, *Home is the Desert*

The Central Arizona Project is a huge, technologically sophisticated water-delivery system that carries Colorado River water across most of the state. It is a river of human-made rock, a concrete channel that brings flowing water to a region of little natural surface water—an audacious, gravity-defying phenomenon of twentieth-century engineering and federal dollars. A prehistoric Hohokam farmer who used wooden digging sticks, stone hoes, and baskets to carve out irrigation canals a millennium ago, whose canals were operated by hand and through the force of gravity alone, would probably stand speechless on the banks of its concrete-lined, chain-link-fenced, electrically powered canals. The system provides an average of 1.5 million acre-feet of water each year to Maricopa, Pinal, and Pima Counties. Although its primary purpose is to supply water to cities, industries, Indian communities, and farmers in lieu of pumping precious groundwater, the project also provides flood control, minor amounts of hydroelectric power, and recreational opportunities.

This cursory description of the Central Arizona Project belies its complexity, cost, and lengthy history. It was the outcome of decades of political maneuvering, litigation, and controversy over the best way to use Colorado River water, who would receive that water, and how much they would get. It is also a story of accommodation and compromise.

New Theodore Roosevelt Dam at dedication ceremony. Photograph courtesy U.S. Bureau of Reclamation. Joe Madrigal, Jr., photographer.

Engineering constraints were one part of a complicated situation that by law included the effects of the project on the cultural and natural environments. It was necessary to adjust to these requirements and often compromise on the aqueduct's location—sometimes losing huge, planned chunks of the system because of debates that emerged. And last, it is a story of change and growth. During the project's long history, the nation became aware of the importance of its natural and cultural resources and took steps to preserve them through law. The Bureau of Reclamation's philosophy and procedures adjusted to these changes, shifting attitudes and programs as it moved canal routes. Just as the river encapsulates the history and geography of the American West, the Central Arizona Project can be viewed as a shorthand version of western water history, economic growth, urban development, and competing, sometimes combatant philosophies. In the struggle to build this technological miracle we can see the greater confrontation between the emerging philosophies of conservation, environmental protection, and wilderness preservation versus long-held national ideals holding that America's resources should be used to the maximum and that its open spaces should be developed toward ever-growing national prosperity and opportunity.

The story of the Central Arizona Project is also deeply embedded in the larger history of the battle between Arizona and California over Colorado River water. We have laid much of the background for this tale in Chapter 2. The lesser controversies of where to build the dams that would divert the water, how to finance these diversions, how to deal with the upstream water works that threatened Arizona's share of the Colorado, and how to protect the project's environment are lesser players in the dramatic confrontation. The story is endlessly intriguing, a tale that pits colorful characters against the wildest river in the West.

In this chapter we look at the often contentious history of the Central Arizona Project from its beginning as an engineering dream to completed technological wonder. We will also learn how the project was built, constraints that affected project location, and how social, engineering, and economic problems were solved. We conclude with a brief review of Central Arizona Project archaeology to set the stage for the stories that follow in the *Midstream* section.

Envisioning the Central Arizona Project

The Central Arizona Project began as a dream. It is unclear who first envisioned diverting Colorado River water to central Arizona. Rich Johnson, who served as the executive director of the Central Arizona Project Association and later as executive director of the Arizona Interstate Stream Commission, has written (Johnson 1977:13) that "Nobody really knows who first dreamed of bringing water from the mainstream of the Colorado River into central Arizona. Whoever it was may have laughed at his own audacity." Whether this dreamer was an engineer with visions of grand dams that would stand as monumental testaments to technology or a politician who hoped to secure Arizona's economic future, he (history tells us he was probably male) was a bold individual with big dreams. Clearly the impetus for the project stemmed from the ongoing war between Arizona and California over Colorado River water. By the turn of the twentieth century, Los Angeles was becoming a dominant social and economic force in the West, doubling or tripling its population each decade (Wilkinson 1992:252). Its sole limitation on growth was water—the Los Angeles basin was essentially an arid plain with little fresh water that was bounded by the Pacific Ocean. Naturally, southern California turned its eyes to water sources outside the basin—the Owens River, the Colorado River, other distant streams.

By the 1920s, it had become clear that the burgeoning cities, orchards, and industries of southern California would

Parker Dam. PHOTOGRAPH BY JEFFERSON REID.

Parker Dam. Photograph by Jefferson Reid.

usurp sparsely populated Arizona's water unless steps were taken. Los Angeles was universally viewed as a rapacious, water-guzzling demon (Reisner 1986; Wilkinson 1992; Worster 1985). The Owens Valley scheme had convinced Arizonans that Los Angeles was not above subterfuge, fraud, and worse to achieve its ends (Marc Reisner [1986] has penned the intriguing tale in *Cadillac Desert*). California was "a water-thirsty vampire intent on sinking its fangs into the Copper State's jugular and sucking it dry" (Stevens 1988:26).

At that time, Arizona's needs for industrial, agricultural, and domestic water were relatively few compared to those of the southern California metropolitan area. But recall that the doctrine of prior appropriation dominated western water rights—Arizona was forced into a position of "use it or lose it." If California began to "borrow" Arizona's unused entitlement, which seemed likely, there was no guarantee that the water would be returned when the Copper State needed it, no matter how large the state had grown (Reisner 1986:257). Strong action was necessary to preserve water for future growth.

But who would pay for it? Reisner (1986:257) has pointed out the critical core of the issue: "Arizona was in no position to use its share of the river, because most of the people and most of the irrigated lands were in the central part of the state, nearly 200 miles away. Rich, urban Los Angeles had the money to build an aqueduct that long, but Arizona, still mostly agricultural, did not." Only a decade or so past statehood, Arizona was still a struggling political entity. For years, public opinion would shift between favoring a federally funded and a state-sponsored Central Arizona Project.

Arizona and California squared off. California insisted that impounded water in the reservoirs along the Salt River should be deducted from Arizona's share. Arizona resisted, of course; if California's reasoning prevailed, Arizona would be left with half a million acre-feet of water, hardly enough to support the population at that time, much less sustain growth. Audacious plans for bringing Colorado River water to Phoenix through a federally sponsored aqueduct were already being developed, and California vowed that if Arizona prevailed, California would block the Central Arizona Project forever. As this conflict developed, Arizona's governor Benjamin B. Moeur instigated a real battle over Parker Dam. In 1934, the Bureau of Reclamation was test drilling at the Parker Dam site. Moeur instructed the Arizona National Guard to block any attempt to place a structure on Arizona soil or in the riverbed, which would include the test drilling site where a barge was anchored in Arizona soil.

When the Bureau of Reclamation attempted to lay a trestle bridge to the Arizona shore, Governor Moeur declared the entire Arizona side of the river under martial law and sent out the Arizona National Guard. Although initially considered a joke—the advance guard was delivered via a Los Angeles Department of Water and Power motor launch—the incident quickly became a national embarrassment (Reisner 1986:258–259). Secretary of the Interior Harold L. Ickes ordered construction halted while the dispute was settled in the courts. To everyone's surprise,

The Arizona Navy

Arizona governor Benjamin B. Moeur was a colorful figure. A Tempe physician, the gruff, cigar-chewing, horseback-riding doctor once declared that he never billed a widow or a preacher (Goff 1983:264). Moeur was able to balance Arizona's books during the Great Depression, a not inconsiderable feat. Moeur is best remembered for mobilizing the Arizona National Guard against California to prevent construction of Parker Dam. Governor Moeur chartered the little steamboat *Nellie* and steamed her upriver to Parker, where the "Arizona Navy" remained obdurately anchored for months (Waters 1984:336).

the Supreme Court upheld Arizona's claims. The court ruled that Parker Dam was technically illegal because it had not been specifically authorized by Congress. Four months later, California succeeded in pushing a bill through Congress that did just that, leaving Arizona with no recourse other than to declare war on the United States (Reisner 1986:258–259).

According to Fradkin (1968:190), Governor Moeur had an ulterior motive. He offered to drop his opposition to Parker Dam if the Roosevelt administration approved the Gila Project, an ambitious irrigation scheme including the Wellton-Mohawk Project, which would prove to strain relations between the United States and Mexico. By the following May, the project was recommended to Congress for approval. We may never know the true story of Moeur's maneuvering to end the Arizona-California war.

While these battles were ongoing, plans proceeded quietly for a Colorado River aqueduct. As early as the 1920s, a version of the Central Arizona Project called the Arizona High Line Canal had emerged. The plan featured two dams—one at Glen Canyon and another at Bridge Canyon located at the lower end of the Grand Canyon. E. C. LaRue recommended the Bridge Canyon site in his 1922 study for the U.S. Department of the Interior. The Bridge Canyon Dam would produce the necessary electricity to finance the aqueduct and power its operation (Fradkin 1968:228). Phoenix businessmen also funded a survey of a possible route from the Bill Williams River near Parker into central Arizona (Johnson 1977:13). The survey staked out the general route of the Central Arizona Project's first segment—the Granite Reef Aqueduct, later renamed the Hayden-Rhodes Aqueduct. Soon plans expanded within the state to develop Colorado River water. The Arizona state legislature created the Colorado River Commission in 1938. The next year, the commission filed application with the Federal Power Commission for a preliminary permit to construct a dam at Bridge Canyon. In the same year, Arizona applied to the federal government for a contract to deliver Colorado River water from Lake Mead. By this action, Arizona admitted the authority of the government to allocate Colorado River water through delivery contracts (Johnson 1977:19).

With Parker and Hoover Dams completed and the All-American Canal carrying water by 1942, many politicians believed that California had gotten its piece of the liquid pie, and in 1944 the Arizona legislature finally ratified the Colorado River Compact. The state accepted the 2.8 million acre-feet allotted by the Boulder Canyon Project Act. Secretary of State Cordell Hull also formally promised Mexico the 1.5 million acre-feet of water previously set aside by the Colorado River Compact (Reisner 1986:259). Arizona immediately began agitating for a federal program to bring water to the state's interior. U.S. Senator Carl Hayden spearheaded this initiative, and he would follow it through to eventual completion many years later.

PHOTOGRAPH BY JEFFERSON REID.

The Bureau of Reclamation proceeded to study the feasibility of water-control projects throughout the entire West. In 1944, it released a study of irrigation and multiple-use projects that could be constructed after the war. The report included a plan to deliver water to irrigated lands in the Phoenix area by diverting water from the Colorado River. Planning for what would become the Central Arizona Project was in place, although nebulous (Johnson 1977:21).

The "Central Arizona diversion project," as it was then called, outlined three preliminary plans, some of which were audacious in the extreme. One called for constructing a 139-mile-long tunnel from the Grand Canyon to the Verde River near Camp Verde. A second plan proposed a 180-mile-long canal from a central-state reservoir to Granite Reef Dam in the Salt River valley. Tucson was added to the emerging Central Arizona Project plan at that time, although it did not use Colorado River water. Instead, the Tucson Aqueduct would convey water north from Charleston Dam on the San Pedro River (Morton 1996).

Arizona's desire for Colorado River water was fueled by demographic, social, and natural phenomena of the 1940s. First was the rapid growth of its central cities. Population was surging in Phoenix and Tucson, and would soar in the postwar years when veterans returned to the sunny deserts where many had trained. Second was the problem of groundwater pumping. Conditions in the Salt and Gila River valleys were ideal for such water development. The water table was shallow, water quality was good, and the alluvial aquifers were highly permeable. Farms in the Phoenix area, which were consuming the lion's share of Arizona water, pumped ancient groundwater at an alarming rate—1.5 million acre-feet in 1940 alone (Worster 1985:275). At first, groundwater pumping had a positive effect. It alleviated waterlogging that had developed in the early decades of the century, threatening irrigated fields. But in the 1940s, the rate of pumping was far exceeding the rate of recharge (Reisner 1986:260). It became harder to reach the underground water and more expensive to pump it. One of the worse effects was subsidence—sinking of the earth's surface caused by removal of underground water. The state was unable to agree on legislation that would curb unrestrained pumping.

A third factor was California's continued runaway growth and its usurpation of Arizona's water. California was using 5.2 million acre-feet, almost a million acre-feet above its allotted 4.4 million—with no end in sight. And last, it became clear by the 1940s that the estimates of the Colorado River's capacity made when the Colorado River Compact was signed in 1922 were based on faulty data. With the compact apportioning 7.5 million acre-feet to each basin, California using about 5 million, and the Mexico Water Treaty of 1945 guaranteeing 1.5 million acre-feet each year to Mexico, the Colorado was already falling short of its projected flow. The Bureau of Reclamation considered the Colorado to be a "deficit river," Fradkin (1968:188) has written, "as if nature were to blame for the faulty estimates." For Arizona, which was giving up surplus water to California, that deficit was a dismal prospect. Because of these factors, Arizona would be unable to meet projected needs unless other water-control projects were constructed and all of Arizona's entitlement was used. The Colorado River would be the Copper State's salvation.

In 1946, the U.S. Department of the Interior issued what was known as the "Blue Book," a comprehensive report on the Colorado River and guide for all subsequent water-control projects. Many of the proposed dam sites for the Central Arizona Project were included in this report. But echoing the claims made much earlier by John Wesley Powell (which had been ignored), Secretary of the Interior Oscar L. Chapman warned that there was not enough water available in the Colorado River system to expand existing projects, complete newly authorized ones, and develop all potential projects outlined in the "Blue Book" (Fradkin 1968:188). In the same year, the Central Arizona Project Association was organized. According to the Central Arizona Project Web site, this "unincorporated, private, nonprofit organization of civic-minded business and farm leaders" (Robinson 1979:39) was formed to educate the public and lobby for the project.

Aquatic Fault Lines

Heavy groundwater pumping affected central Arizona's water table, water quality, and even the earth's surface. In the early days, the water table was easy to tap; water could be found just below the ground. By the 1960s, farmers had to drill hundreds of feet to locate any water. What water could be found was salty, little more than concentrated brine. Subsidence was such a problem in central Arizona that drivers on the highway between Phoenix and Tucson had to watch cautiously for fissures in the asphalt that emerged when one block of land subsided next to another that did not (Reisner 1986:260)—fault lines created by shifting water, not earth.

One study estimated that since 1940, Tucson has withdrawn 9–11 percent of the groundwater beneath the Avra Valley and the Tucson Basin (Tobin 2001). The water table has dropped some 200 feet in parts of central Tucson. Unable to reach the water even with long tap roots, the mesquite trees across the basin are dying.

PHOTOGRAPH BY JEFFERSON REID.

In 1947, an alternative plan to develop the Central Arizona Project as an Arizona state enterprise emerged. Water would be brought from the reservoirs in Bridge Canyon and Glen Canyon; municipal power and irrigation districts would issue bonds to finance construction. This plan clearly ignored or denied the established role of the federal government in controlling the interstate and international Colorado River (Johnson 1977:25). Although the state legislature rejected this proposal, the idea would persist for many years.

The Bridge Canyon Dam was the key financial element of the Central Arizona Project. Its energy sales would finance repayment of project costs, and because of this, it was thought that California power interests would support the project. Arizona was also interested in the Glen Canyon dam site upstream of Lee's Ferry. The Bridge Canyon reservoir would be relatively small and have a short effective life span unless the river's silt load was checked by an upstream dam, which was Glen Canyon's function (Johnson 1977:23). Bridge Canyon would prove to be a sticking point that almost doomed the Central Arizona Project to failure.

In 1947, the Bureau of Reclamation had reduced the potential aqueduct routes to two choices—Bridge Canyon by gravity flow or Lake Havasu near Parker by means of pumping to lift the water. Whereas building the Bridge Canyon aqueduct would be more costly, operating the Parker route would be more expensive. The Parker route was recommended, and the Bridge Canyon Dam would provide the necessary hydroelectric power (Johnson 1977:26). Larry D. Morton, who served as the assistant area manager for the Bureau of Reclamation's Phoenix Area Office, has stated that the plan assumed 1.2 million acre-feet of water would be imported to central Arizona to be used on existing irrigated land, about 80,000 acre-feet would be used for domestic purposes in the Phoenix area, and Tucson would receive about 12,000 acre-feet from Charleston Reservoir on the San Pedro River (Morton 1996:42–43).

That year, Senators Ernest McFarland and Carl Hayden introduced the first Senate bill to authorize construction of the Central Arizona Project. Not surprisingly, California was resistant to this legislation; Arizona's hopes that Bridge Canyon Dam would soothe hostilities proved futile. "Antagonism between Arizona and California was at fever pitch" (Johnson 1977:32). The Arizona side of the story was presented to Congress through the Central Arizona Project Association in hearings on S. 1175 before the Subcommittee on Irrigation and Reclamation, a part of the Committee on Public Lands. Even while the bill was being introduced, there were continued warnings about the ability of the river to supply existing demands, much less meet the needs of new projects. "Anyone who knows the river and the river's history," said Congressman Wayne Aspinall, "knows that there is not sufficient water for the Central Arizona Project" (cited in Fradkin 1968:188).

But there was no real hope for authorization of the Central Arizona Project at that time (Johnson 1977:57). For years thereafter, Senator Hayden would get a federal Central Arizona Project bill through the U.S. Senate only to have the California delegation block it in the House of Representatives (Worster 1985:275). Hayden has often been called the "father" of the Central Arizona Project. Certainly the project owes much to his influence and political mastery, but the cadre of politicians and water-interest groups wrangling over the Colorado River water was also influential. As Chairman of the Senate Appropriations Committee, Hayden was able to underwrite urban development in Arizona, not only with the Central Arizona Project and other water-control projects but also with military bases. Hayden served Arizona from 1912 to 1969, first in the House and then in the Senate. President John F. Kennedy said of Hayden, "Every federal program which has contributed to western irrigation, power and reclamation bears Carl Hayden's mark" (cited in Fradkin 1968:250).

Congressional hearings and political maneuvers continued, and Arizona and California took up arms with emotional pleas. Arizona warned that, without the Central Arizona Project, business firms would suffer or dissolve, and more than 225,000 acres of farmland would revert to desert. California stressed that water was for the people, not to irrigate the Arizona desert in order to make a few land speculators rich at public expense (Johnson 1977:58, 73).

Support and planning for the project continued in state and federal contexts while attempts to push the authorizing legislation through Congress were ongoing. In 1948, a bill was introduced in the Arizona legislature to create the Arizona Interstate Stream Commission. The commission's purpose was to protect the state's rights to Colorado River water and advocate construction of the Central Arizona Project (Johnson 1977:41).

Recall that although Arizona had signed the 1922 Colorado River Compact, the Lower Basin states had been unable to agree on allocation of their share of the water, largely because of Arizona's opposition to what it saw as California's rapacious thirst. The Upper Basin states began negotiating allocation of their share among themselves. In 1948, the Upper Colorado River Basin Compact apportioned the 7.5 million acre-feet among the states. The compact gave the tiny corner of northeastern Arizona included in the Upper Basin a meagre 50,000 acre feet each year (Johnson 1977:47). Reisner (1986:259) has suggested that, when the Upper Basin compact was concluded, only two main issues involving the Colorado River remained unresolved—how much of its allocated 2.8 million acre-feet Arizona could take out of the river and whether California would invoke the doctrine of prior appropriation to deny Arizona most of that water.

Under Hayden's pressure, the Senate passed Central Arizona Project bills in 1950 and 1951, but they failed once more in the House of Representatives. California succeeded in getting a motion through the House Interior and Insular Affairs Committee to block the Central Arizona Project until the water was divided in the Lower Basin—which at that time, was about as likely as pigs flying or money growing on trees. In 1952, an angered and impatient Arizona filed suit in the Supreme Court to affirm its right to 2.8 million acre-feet of Colorado River water each year (Worster 1985:275). California, which was at that time using almost a million acre-feet over its allotment, maintained that the flow of the Salt, Verde, and Gila Rivers should be deducted from Arizona's share. *Arizona v. California* was to become one of the longest-running lawsuits in the annals of the Supreme Court, and California had a vested interest in the delay. Each year without resolution meant 300 billion gallons of additional water for the state (Reisner 1986:261).

Meanwhile, other impressive water-control projects were moving forward, and they would impact Arizona's plans. The Colorado River Storage Project, which included a series of dams, reservoirs, and power plants, was submitted to Congress in 1950. The project would subsidize irrigation in the Upper Basin through the sale of the electricity it generated. Its opponents emphasized the enormous cost of that electricity and the peculiarity of irrigating land that was utterly miserable and uninhabitable (Reisner 1986:140–143), as Powell had pointed out so many years before. The project appealed to almost everyone except Californians and environmentalists, who were horrified at the prospect of giant reservoirs in the West's magnificent river canyons (Martin 1999). The greatest battle would be waged against Echo Park Dam, which would have flooded the Green River and Yampa River canyons in Dinosaur National Monument. Glen Canyon Dam would be built instead as the tradeoff to protect this wilderness. This extraordinary story is told elsewhere in this book. Debate would continue for several years before the Colorado River Storage Project was finally approved.

At about the same time, more serious doubts were raised about the Colorado's estimated annual discharge. Hydrologist Raymond Hill observed in 1953 that the discharge at Lee's Ferry had averaged only 11.7 million acre-feet since 1930—substantially less than the 17.5 million acre-feet estimated in the 1922 compact (Reisner 1986:263). Plans proceeded for the Colorado River Storage Project and the Central Arizona Project nevertheless.

In 1955, Representative Stewart Udall again called for a modified Central Arizona Project as a state undertaking because the federal government was unable to reach a satisfactory outcome. The Arizona Interstate Stream Commission supported the modified undertaking as a state project if a means could be found to finance it. Moreover, the philosophy supporting the Central Arizona Project was shifting. "Because of our tremendous population growth with the attendant expansion of industry," said Wayne Akin, who was chairman of the commission, "the perspective of our problem has changed from one largely concerned with supplementary water for irrigation to one in which a very important fraction must be used for domestic and industrial purposes" (cited in Johnson 1977:103). The

Flaming Gorge Dam. PHOTOGRAPH BY JEFFERSON REID.

plan was presented to the state legislature where it encountered substantial opposition from Yuma irrigation interests. The bill was enacted, however, giving the Arizona Power Authority and the Arizona Interstate Stream Commission the authority necessary to proceed toward a state-built Central Arizona Project (Johnson 1977:105). Senator Hayden opposed the state project, and the stream commission gave a cool reception to a preliminary report proposing construction of dams in Bridge Canyon and Marble Canyon.

One year later, the trial of *Arizona v. California* commenced in the Supreme Court. Although Arizona argued that the Central Arizona Project was not an issue in the suit, many witnesses nevertheless offered testimony concerning the existing and impending water shortages in the state if the project was not constructed (Johnson 1977:112).

In 1956, after several years of public and congressional debate, President Eisenhower signed the legislation authorizing the Colorado River Storage Project into law. It authorized Curecanti Dam on the Gunnison River, Flaming Gorge Dam on the Green, Navajo Dam on the San Juan, and Glen Canyon Dam on the Colorado (Martin 1999:73). Glen Canyon was viewed as a solution to the Colorado River's erratic flow, which during dry years was insufficient to meet the requirements of the Upper Basin as well as obligations to the Lower Basin (Robinson 1979:85). Floyd E. Dominy became commissioner of the Bureau of Reclamation in 1959, and Glen Canyon Dam was built during his tenure. Echo Park had been deleted from the project by the intensive efforts of environmentalists led by David Brower of the Sierra Club. It was a hollow victory, however, for Lake Powell would inundate one of the West's most magnificent, wild river canyons.

In 1963, the Supreme Court handed down its opinion in the case of *Arizona v. California,* ending 12 years of court litigation over water rights (Reisner 1986:261). Surprising many, the Supreme Court upheld Arizona's claims. Arizona was allotted 2.8 million acre-feet of Colorado River water annually. The Salt-Verde-Gila watershed would be exclusively Arizona's and would not be counted against the state's entitlement. The battle had consumed a dozen years, $5 million, 50 lawyers, 340 witnesses, 25,000 pages of testimony bound in 43 volumes, and more than 4,000 exhibits (Fradkin 1968:250).

One difficulty marred the widespread joy. The Supreme Court ruled that if the river could not satisfy all the claims that were made on its water, the doctrine of prior appropriation would hold. Water rights predating the Colorado River Compact had to be satisfied before any other claims (Reisner 1986:261).

In 1963, Senator Hayden reintroduced the Central Arizona Project bill once again. It had become apparent that project water would be expensive water, essentially representing a river running uphill, and would require subsidies to farmers to ensure that they would use it. To supply hydroelectric power that could be sold to subsidize irrigation, the Bureau of Reclamation proposed to build the two dams in the Grand Canyon that had been on the drawing boards for decades. These were the only sites where reliable water fell a sufficient depth to fuel a power plant. The proposed Bridge Canyon Dam would flood part of one of the world's greatest natural wonders.

There was a more compelling reason that the Bureau of Reclamation wanted to build the Grand Canyon dams. These cash-register dams were the only way to finance importation of water to make up the shortfall in Colorado River water that had become all too apparent. In 1963, Commissioner Floyd Dominy and Secretary of the Interior Stewart Udall announced a monumental new water plan that in essence would replace the water then being diverted from the Colorado River and used by Los Angeles with water from California's Trinity River. The Colorado water would be pumped east instead of west as part of the Central Arizona Project. Bridge Canyon and Marble Canyon would provide the money.

Public opinion, however, was solidly against the Grand Canyon dams. Environmentalists marshaled their defenses against the dams as they had done to save Echo Park and Dinosaur National Monument. But the pressing need to build dams as a rescue measure for the diminishing Colorado River and dying irrigated lands in central Arizona took on even larger proportions. In 1965, hydrologist Randy Riter forwarded a confidential letter to Dominy revealing that "there is not enough water in the Colorado River to permit the Upper Basin to fully use its apportionment of 7.5 million acre-feet and still meet its compact obligations to deliver water at Lee's Ferry" (Reisner 1986: 263). The solution to this conundrum, Riter suggested, was to include in the Central Arizona Project bill an authorization to import 2.5 million acre-feet of water (Reisner 1986:264). Sale of hydroelectric power produced at Bridge Canyon and Marble Canyon could then be diverted to finance water importation (Reisner 1986:286).

Congressional wrangling over legislation authorizing the Central Arizona Project, part of the greater Colorado River Basin Project Act, continued throughout the mid-1960s. The bottleneck in Congress, Reisner (1986:294–295) has written, was not simply one of the Sierra Club battling the Bureau of Reclamation over the Grand Canyon dams. The biggest hurdle was California. What the state demanded as its price for acquiescence was to receive its full, 4.4-million–acre-foot-entitlement of Colorado River water before Arizona received its share. Central Arizona Project legislation was saddled with what became known as the California Guarantee. For its part, Arizona argued that the Copper State had entered dire straits. During and after the war years, Arizona agriculture had boomed, the state's population had increased vastly, and the costs of pumping groundwater had become prohibitive. If millions of acres of irrigated land providing food and fiber to the United States were to stay in production, the federal government needed to provide Colorado River water (Morton 1996:52).

By that time, Glen Canyon Dam had been completed and Lake Powell had risen behind it, flooding the incomparable canyons that had been traded to save Echo Park. The dam came to stand as a symbol of the emerging environmental movement (Martin 1999:280). The Marble Canyon and Bridge Canyon Dams were assuming a similar role as pivot points for angry environmentalists. It had become clear that, if the Central Arizona Project would ever be built, the dams would have to be jettisoned. The Bureau of Reclamation and many Washington politicians were being exposed to environmental awareness for the first time. Morton (1996:139) has described the emotions surrounding the fight over the dams. "Who are these elite Easterners who would have the audacity to oppose Reclamation's program?" they asked. The state of Arizona's congressional representatives were even more vociferous:

> it was their *birthright* to have CAP built, and they had just spent the preceding twelve years demonstrating before the Supreme Court that they had a God-given entitlement to the Colorado River. And what *was* this opposition that was materializing? What were these Wall Street bankers trying to do to Arizona, drive it to bankruptcy?

Concerns were also developing over the economic feasibility of hydroelectric power. There was considerable debate over the potential of nuclear, coal, and oil-shale energy versus water power. If alternative energies were projected to be much more economical in the future, why should a dam be built simply to generate expensive electricity (Morton 1996:141)?

Floyd Dominy remained steadfast in his determination to build both dams, however. It was not until Dominy left the country for his annual tour of overseas water projects early in 1967 that Stewart Udall announced an amended and streamlined Central Arizona Project. Martin (1999:282–283) has described this "lean and mean" plan. It did not make Colorado River delivery guarantees to the state of California, did not consider importing water from the Trinity River or the Pacific Northwest, and did not include either Marble Canyon or Bridge Canyon Dams. As a power alternative, Udall said, the administration favored forming a Bureau of Reclamation partnership with a consortium of private electrical utilities to construct a coal-fired power plant on the Navajo reservation. Just as the environmentalists had lost Glen Canyon to save Echo Park, they would save the Grand Canyon from being flooded only to have

Arizona's crystal-clear air polluted by coal emissions and its Native American lands affected. Much later, the Navajo Generating Station would be retrofitted with scrubbers to address the pollution issue.

The bill had limitations, but it was a politically expedient solution, and although Dominy would never admit that he had been bested by his opponents, jettisoning Bridge Canyon and Marble Canyon Dams had made the project move forward at last (Martin 1999:284). Morton (1996:45) has indicated that, in order to get the bill past California in the Senate and the House of Representatives, it had to contain political accommodations to that state. Therefore California received some assurance of water supply for Los Angeles and the Imperial Valley. New Mexico received authorization for Hooker Dam in the Gila River Wilderness. Other states also gained reauthorization for several projects, Everyone got something, or so it seemed.

In July 1968, the House and Senate agreed on a $1.3 billion Colorado River Basin Project bill that specifically prohibited future construction of any dams between Glen Canyon Dam and Hoover Dam. In September, the lame-duck president Lyndon B. Johnson signed the authorizing act for the Central Arizona Project into law (Fradkin 1968:251). Reisner (1986:290) has called this "the most expensive single authorization in history." With guests from the Colorado River Basin states attending, the U.S. Navy band playing, and the First Lady at his side, President Johnson signed S. 1004 into Public Law 90-537 (Johnson 1977:226). The Central Arizona Project was reality. It had been 100 years, almost to the day, since Powell and his crew of river runners had taken boats down the Colorado River for the first time.

BUILDING THE CENTRAL ARIZONA PROJECT

If the battle to authorize the Central Arizona Project was complex, time-consuming, and fraught with political accommodations, actually building the system was a far more complicated endeavor. The struggle had literally only begun when the project was authorized in 1968. Seventeen years would pass before the first water was delivered to the Harquahala Valley Irrigation District west of Phoenix. Building a project of such size and complexity was a many-layered task constrained at all levels by embedded financial, engineering, environmental, and social factors. The engineering considerations alone were monumental. The Central Arizona Project makes water run uphill, lifting it about 2,900 feet in elevation over its 336-mile traverse (Rogge 1983:105). To bring water that far uphill across rugged desert land requires routing around obstacles and pumping over elevation differences. There must be storage facilities to conserve water for times of low flow in the Colorado River and distribution systems to bring water to communities and agricultural areas. The system must be operated, which requires intakes, gates, and most of all, electricity. The canal and other facilities must also be protected, maintained, and repaired. For each segment of

Central Arizona Project canal (Hayden-Rhodes Aqueduct).
PHOTOGRAPH COURTESY U.S. BUREAU OF RECLAMATION. JOE MADRIGAL, JR., PHOTOGRAPHER.

the project, it was necessary to weigh the engineering and technological factors against social, environmental, and economic costs and choose among the most logical alternatives. In this section, we examine some of the issues that constrained construction.

As originally envisioned in 1968, the project included many pieces of a puzzle that had been on Reclamation drawing boards for decades. Colorado River water would be pumped from Lake Havasu up and then through the Buckskin Mountains in a tunnel. The prodigious amount of energy to accomplish this feat would be supplied not by the "cash-register" Bridge Canyon and Marble Canyon Dams but by the coal-fired Navajo Generating Station near Page, Arizona. Peabody Coal Company would strip-mine coal from Black Mesa on Hopi and Navajo lands and bring it to Page.

From the Buckskin Mountains tunnel, the water was conveyed to the open portions of what was then called the Granite Reef Aqueduct. The aqueduct would bring water to the proposed Orme Dam about 25 miles northeast of Phoenix near the confluence of the Salt and Verde Rivers.

Lake Powell looking toward Navajo Generating Station. Photograph by Jefferson Reid.

The Navajo Project

The coal-fired Navajo Project, which is the largest generating station in Arizona, consists of the Navajo Generating Station, 800 miles of 500 kilovolt transmission lines, and a railroad to move coal from Black Mesa to the generating station. Participants are Salt River Project, Los Angeles Dept. Of Water and Power, Arizona Public Service Co., Nevada Power Co., Tucson Electric Power Co., and the U.S. Bureau of Reclamation. The original investment was $926 million. More than $225 million was spent for environmental protection.

Two of the three transmission lines carry electricity into central and southern Arizona and the third provides power for other plant participants. Scrubbers to remove sulphur dioxide from the plant's emissions began to operate in 1997. They were added at a cost of $450 million.

It is the intent of the Navajo Generating Station participants to continue to make the plant an asset to the community of Page, the Navajo Nation, and the state of Arizona, by designing features which ensure environmental protection.

As Project manager, Salt River Project:

- conducts studies necessary to obtain a complete understanding of how any facility or activity may affect the environment, and takes appropriate action to protect the environment.
- installs necessary air pollution control equipment to meet state and federal statutes.
- saves any historic or archaeological materials for posterity.
- takes necessary steps to ensure there is no detrimental effect to the ecology of Lake Powell and area.
- builds into all units appropriate facilities for noise abatement and dust control.
- landscapes and designs all facilities so they will be compatible with the surrounding area.
- works harmoniously with all agencies and groups interested in environmental protection.

(Text from a litter bag obtained in the John Wesley Powell Museum, Page, provided by participants of the Navajo Generating Station).

Tunnel-boring machine used in Central Arizona Project construction (Buckskin Mountains tunnel). Photograph courtesy U.S. Bureau of Reclamation. Joe Madrigal, Jr., photographer.

Operating in conjunction with the Salt River Project storage system, the dam and reservoir would provide multiple services for the Phoenix metropolitan area. The Salt-Gila Aqueduct would be fed either by Granite Reef Aqueduct or Orme Reservoir and carry water to agricultural areas. Buttes Dam was proposed to be built on the Gila River downstream from Coolidge Dam, built much earlier by the Bureau of Indian Affairs. The Salt-Gila Aqueduct would link with the Tucson Aqueduct, which would convey water to that city. Tucson's water would be augmented by Charleston Dam and Reservoir on the San Pedro River; the San Pedro Aqueduct would carry water from the reservoir to the Tucson area.

Seven administrative and construction divisions cut the huge project into pieces of manageable size: Granite Reef, Orme, Salt-Gila, Gila River, Tucson, Indian Distribution, and Colorado River. Construction would be carried out by the Lower Colorado Region of the Bureau of Reclamation and largely coordinated from its Arizona Projects Office in Phoenix (now called the Phoenix Area Office).

Central Arizona Project office. Photograph by Stephanie Whittlesey.

This plan would be tinkered with considerably over the project's history for financial, social, and environmental considerations. Neither Orme nor Charleston Dams, for example, would ever be built. Even at the outset, however, the scope of the project had altered. Much had changed in the two decades since the 1940s, when the project was first envisioned, and the 1960s, when it was authorized at last. While legislative and political battles for the Central Arizona Project were ongoing, Arizona's population had soared. The city of Phoenix had expanded northward at a phenomenal rate, and housing developments now covered the aqueduct route the engineers had plotted through bare desert lands. It would have been too expensive to acquire the developed land now covering the original route. Rerouting the aqueduct, however, required pumping water uphill an additional 30 or 40 feet, which meant more electricity and more money (Morton 1996:91). Such problems were repeated throughout many segments of the project.

Water costs and quality were other problems. Would the soil lose its fertility or become waterlogged when project water was applied? How would the change from groundwater to river water affect productivity? Answering such questions required a team of soil scientists to conduct studies (Morton 1996:91–92). A vital issue involved estimating the differential costs of groundwater and Central Arizona Project water so that farmers would be able to use project water. Another was how to classify the lands that would be affected. A farmer using cheap groundwater might have gone bankrupt if project water was applied to his lands, so his property would be classified as uneconomic (Morton 1996:93). As initially envisioned, the project would bring water to new farms in central Arizona. But by the time the project was authorized, so many additional acres of land were in cultivation that only supplemental water could be delivered. It was decided that Central Arizona Project water would only be delivered to lands that had a history of irrigation in the 10 years prior to the date of authorization (Morton 1996:95).

One of the most important changes was to greatly enlarge the system's capacity. This was in direct response to the increased needs for agricultural, domestic, municipal, and industrial water deliveries—as much as fourfold increases from the 1940s. Consequently, engineers increased the capacity of the aqueduct from less than 2,000 cubic feet per second to about 3,000 cubic feet per second (Morton 1996:43). The rationale for this was simple, and again goes back to the California-Arizona debate. Because of the California Guarantee, Arizona would suffer any shortages in Colorado River supply, and this would affect the Central Arizona Project most of all. Morton (1996:228) has suggested that, under the worst set of circumstances, Arizona's entitlement would have to be reduced about a million acre-feet to satisfy the California Guarantee. In practical terms, this meant that the project would cut back its deliveries during times of shortages to ensure that the Lower Basin received its entitlement first. Good water management would enable Arizona to compile surplus water to offset such future shortfalls. To take the surpluses, a bigger diversion facility was necessary (Morton 1996:45).

In 1970, construction began on the power plant that would provide electricity to make Colorado River water flow uphill. Private groups cooperating in financing construction included Salt River Project, Los Angeles Department of Water and Power, Arizona Public Service Company, Nevada Power Company, and Tucson Gas and Electric Company (Rogge 1983:122). The Navajo Project includes the generating station at Page, the Southern Transmission System—a series of transmission lines beginning at Page and terminating at Westwing Substation in the Phoenix metropolitan area—and the Western Transmission System beginning at Page and terminating at McCullough Substation near Las Vegas (Morton 1996:282). Power would eventually be supplied to the pumping plants and check structures along the aqueducts via switchyards, substations, and tap stations. Although some electricity is generated by the Central Arizona Project, it is dwarfed by the amount of electricity the project uses. Planning for the rest of the Central Arizona Project went on with an advance from the state of Arizona through the Interstate Stream Commission, as there were no federal appropriations during fiscal years 1969 and 1970. Construction "limped along" (Morton 1996:223, 226).

In 1971, Congress appropriated $1.2 million to begin construction of the Central Arizona Project, but the U.S. Office of Management and Budget refused to release the money until a project-cost repayment contract was negotiated between the Secretary of the Interior and Arizona water users. In 1971, the Central Arizona Water Conservation

District was organized in Maricopa, Pinal, and Pima Counties to repay the federal government for the reimbursable costs of construction. Property taxes were levied in these counties for this purpose (Morton 1996:209). The conservation district would also manage and operate the Central Arizona Project. The Bureau of Reclamation transferred projects to the conservation district as they were completed.

At about this time, an extremely important new player entered the game and would alter project planning and construction enormously—federal legislation protecting natural and cultural resources. In 1969, one year after the project was finally authorized, Congress passed the **National Environmental Policy Act.** The act mandated that a federal agency (such as the Bureau of Reclamation) proposing an undertaking (like the Central Arizona Project) provide a detailed statement of the impacts of the action on the environment. There were several levels of impact analysis, but the most detailed was an **environmental impact statement.** Agencies were required to list beneficial and adverse environmental effects, alternatives to the proposed action, and other information for each project. Importantly, the act also mandated that agencies open the document to public commentary. In other words, the public needed to know the potential impacts of the project and what measures were to be taken to ameliorate them, and the public was given time to comment. (See the appendix for further information about the act and how it affects projects.)

The Bureau of Reclamation became responsible for preparing environmental impact statements. The Arizona Projects Office geared up to meet this demand by assembling archaeologists, biologists, water-quality specialists, and environmental specialists of many stripes. It was not an easy task, for no one was familiar with the process. As Morton (1996:216) has said, "We didn't know what an EIS looked like. Nobody else did either." Compliance with the act was the rationale for much Central Arizona Project archaeology. Environmental impacts would eventually doom Orme Dam and would affect the proposed routes of aqueducts and locations of dams.

The agency prepared a programmatic environmental impact statement for the entire project. The document, which Morton (1996:266) has described as "encyclopedic," allowed the Bureau of Reclamation to execute the master repayment contract. With this in place, construction funds were finally made available in 1973, and groundbreaking ceremonies were held. The following year, the first generating units of the Navajo Generating Station began producing power.

Specific environmental impact statements for each segment, such as the diversion system at Lake Havasu or the Salt-Gila Aqueduct, followed the programmatic document. Without this strategy, planning might have been stalled for years. Morton (1996:266) has suggested that it was a decision that served the Bureau of Reclamation well for a quarter-century. All potential environmental impacts were considered, not simply the obvious effects on plant and animal species: visual and noise effects, impacts to cultural resources and archaeological sites, impacts on existing settlements, effects on Native American cultural

Purpose of the National Environmental Policy Act of 1969

Section 2 (42 USC § 4321) reads as follows (U.S. Department of Energy 2003):

> The purposes of this Act are: To declare a national policy which will encourage productive and enjoyable harmony between man and his environment; to promote efforts which will prevent or eliminate damage to the environment and biosphere and stimulate the health and welfare of man; to enrich the understanding of the ecological systems and natural resources important to the Nation; and to establish a Council on Environmental Quality.

For further information, please visit the U.S. Department of Energy's Web site, *at http://tis.eh.doe.gov/nepa/.*

and religious practices, and so on. Environmental constraints in some cases determined the choice of an aqueduct route. When rerouting a project segment was not possible, mitigation measures were taken to eliminate or reduce potential effects.

Morton (1996:437–442) has described how environmental issues affected the Tucson Aqueduct. Two potential alignments were considered for Phase B, on the east side and west side of the Tucson Mountains. The west-side route was less costly in terms of impacts to cultural resources. The Brawley Wash area had not been settled as densely in prehistoric times as the Santa Cruz River valley. The east-side route would cross a number of small Mexican-American communities, and the residents were worried about effects on traditional lifestyles and relocation. There were also concerns about visibility of the canal from Interstate 10. For these reasons, the west-side alignment was chosen.

Other issues affected the Phase A alignment. It also had two potential routes on the east and west sides of the Picacho Mountains. The west-side route was less costly from an engineering standpoint but was home to desert tortoises. Through studies of tortoise habitat, the agency was able to determine that, if sufficient crossings were provided and the habitat areas were fenced, the tortoises would not be adversely affected. These mitigation measures enabled construction of the west-side route. Scarring left by construction of the west alignment on the flanks of the Picacho Mountains would be visible from Interstate 10. Not one of the proposed mitigation measures—artificial desert varnish, stains, paints—was effective, and the aqueduct is visible today, although perhaps not as visually unappealing as first thought.

At New Waddell Dam, the Bureau of Reclamation complied with Arizona state law protecting native plants. It initiated a major native-plant salvage program by which plants such as saguaro, barrel cactus, and others were retrieved from the area to be inundated and used in landscaping projects. Some plants were stockpiled for future agency use, and properly armed with state permits, the public was also allowed to salvage plants (Morton 1996:936).

A second critical piece of legislation affecting the Central Arizona Project was the **National Historic Preservation Act** (16 U.S.C. 470). Congress passed the act in 1966, acting on a study coordinated by Lady Bird Johnson that recommended a national historic-preservation program. The act set forth a national philosophy of preservation and protection of historic sites, buildings, and archaeological sites, making the federal government the lead player in American historic preservation. One of the act's most important provisions was to authorize the National Park

National Historic Preservation Act of 1966 (Public Law 102-575)

Section 1 (16 U.S.C. 470) of the National Historic Preservation Act of 1966, as amended through 2000, reads as follows:

(a) This Act may be cited as the "National Historic Preservation Act."

(b) The Congress finds and declares that–

(1) the spirit and direction of the Nation are founded upon and reflected in its historic heritage;

(2) the historical and cultural foundations of the Nation should be preserved as a living part of our community life and development in order to give a sense of orientation to the American people;

(3) historic properties significant to the Nation's heritage are being lost or substantially altered, often inadvertently, with increasing frequency;

(4) the preservation of this irreplaceable heritage is in the public interest so that its vital legacy of cultural, educational, aesthetic, inspirational, economic, and energy benefits will be maintained and enriched for future generations of Americans;

(5) in the face of ever-increasing extensions of urban centers, highways, and residential, commercial, and industrial developments, the present governmental and nongovernmental historic preservation programs and activities are inadequate to insure future generations a genuine opportunity to appreciate and enjoy the rich heritage of our Nation;

(6) the increased knowledge of our historic resources, the establishment of better means of identifying and administering them, and the encouragement of their preservation will improve the planning and execution of federal and federally assisted projects and will assist economic growth and development; and

(continued on following page)

National Historic Preservation Act of 1966 (cont.)

(7) although the major burdens of historic preservation have been borne and major efforts initiated by private agencies and individuals, and both should continue to play a vital role, it is nevertheless necessary and appropriate for the Federal Government to accelerate its historic preservation programs and activities, to give maximum encouragement to agencies and individuals undertaking preservation by private means, and to assist State and local governments and the National Trust for Historic Preservation in the United States to expand and accelerate their historic preservation programs and activities (National Park Service 2003).

The full text of the National Historic Preservation Act *can be found at the* National Park Service Web site *at http://www2.cr.nps.gov/laws/NHPA1966.htm.*

Service to maintain a **National Register of Historic Places.** The act specified in Section 106 that agencies consider the effects of their projects on properties included in the register (**historic properties**). In practical terms, this meant that, before construction began, archaeological sites listed in or eligible for listing in the National Register of Historic Places would be excavated to preserve information, thus mitigating adverse effects. Along with the National Environmental Policy Act, the National Historic Preservation Act would drive the bulk of Central Arizona Project archaeology. (See the appendix for additional information.)

Let's take a moment to recap the problems facing the Bureau of Reclamation. Before the project could be built, the agency was required to consider its effects on the natural and cultural environments. It was necessary to weigh the costs of mitigating adverse effects against the engineering costs of rerouting a project segment. The agency had to consider the different economic, demographic, and social conditions that had developed over two decades of wrangling. The effects of the project on soil and water conditions and the costs to consumers had to be considered. When construction finally began on a project segment, a new series of problems came into play. The Bureau of Reclamation contracted with many different construction companies, engineering firms, and other private organizations to build pieces of the project or supply materials. Often several contractors would be working on a single segment, such as the Tucson Aqueduct. Contractors' costs and schedules had to be monitored to keep the entire project on task. A virtual army of accountants kept track of the projects, and the Bureau of Reclamation's contracting officer supervised the entire process.

Under these monumental constraints, construction on the Central Arizona Project proceeded. The water tap was almost turned off permanently in 1977, however. The deleterious environmental effects and unsound economics of many proposed water-control projects were coming under fire. Back in 1973, 13 major environmental organizations issued a report calling for deauthorization of the most damaging and unsound projects. They issued a second report in 1977. In that year, President Jimmy Carter announced projected termination of appropriations for 19 authorized projects that he considered economically unfit, environmentally harmful, or technically unsound. The Central Arizona Project was among those targeted for substantial

Section 106 of the National Historic Preservation Act

The head of any Federal agency having direct or indirect jurisdiction over a proposed Federal or federally assisted undertaking in any State and the head of any Federal department or independent agency having authority to license any undertaking shall, prior to the approval of the expenditure of any Federal funds on the undertaking or prior to the issuance of any license, as the case may be, take into account the effect of the undertaking on any district, site, building, structure, or object that is included in or eligible for inclusion in the National Register. The head of any such Federal agency shall afford the Advisory Council on Historic Preservation established under Title II of this Act a reasonable opportunity to comment with regard to such undertaking (National Park Service 2003).

The full text of the National Historic Preservation Act *can be found on the* National Park Service Web site*, at http://www2.cr.nps.gov/laws/NHPA1966.htm.*

reevaluation and revision (Robinson 1979:94), or as others have stated more bluntly, the project was on Carter's "hit list." The ensuing storm of protest caused President Carter to revise his recommendations, and construction went on.

But the project was revised considerably, however, requiring further studies and more planning to come up with viable alternatives. Recommended modifications included eliminating Orme, Hooker, and Charleston Dams. Recall that Charleston Dam on the San Pedro River would have provided supplemental water for the Tucson area. Its elimination meant that alternatives would have to be found. Charleston Dam would have provided relatively expensive water, and a small amount at that; the eventual and more economical solution was to increase the canal height and move water all the way to Tucson through the Central Arizona Project system (Morton 1996:394–395). No further work was carried out on Charleston Dam after 1977. The Upper Gila Water Supply Study focused on alternatives to Hooker Dam. Located on the Gila River, the dam was to supply water to a portion of western New Mexico and provide flood protection along the Gila River in eastern Arizona. Hooker Dam remains authorized but has been deferred indefinitely. Buttes Dam was planned for the Gila River near Florence, about four miles upstream of the existing Ashurst-Hayden Diversion Dam. Although Buttes Dam remains an authorized part of the Central Arizona Project to provide water, flood and sediment control, and outdoor recreation, construction plans have also been deferred indefinitely.

Another outcome of the 1977 review of water projects affected Arizona directly. The Carter administration recommended that funding for the Central Arizona Project be contingent on a state groundwater management and conservation plan. The Central Arizona Water Conservation District also administers groundwater replenishment under this legislation. It can construct groundwater recharge projects and provide water credits when groundwater is not pumped. Groundwater replenishment is one way by which Arizona demonstrates to other Lower Basin states, California in particular, that it intends to use its full entitlement of Colorado River water and protect it from future use by other states (Morton 1996:660–664).

Orme Dam proved the most controversial part of the Central Arizona Project. The draft environmental impact statement filed in 1976 ignited unparalleled controversy. The dam was to be built at the confluence of the Verde and Salt Rivers on the Fort McDowell Reservation, home to one community of the Yavapai tribe and an area of dense prehistoric Hohokam settlement. The Orme controversy included disputes over the cost of the cultural-resource studies that would be necessary, impacts to endangered plant and animal species—nesting bald eagles in particular—and deleterious effects on the Yavapai community. The Fort McDowell community had not been consulted when plans for construction were generated. According to Khera and Mariella (1983:43), the reservoir would have inundated almost 65 percent of the reservation, including existing settlements and all of the fertile bottomlands then being farmed and used for other economic purposes. There were additional economic impacts to the community, because federal aid was withheld while dam construction was pending. The costs of cultural-resource studies were only a small part of the total controversy, but they were substantial—an estimated $25 million to mitigate the impacts of dam construction to archaeological sites (Rogge 1983:134).

According to Morton (1996:295), there were about 12,000 separate comments on the draft environmental impact statement for Orme Dam. Tongue in cheek, Morton has said that it had become obvious "that Orme Dam was not well thought of in some circles." At one public hearing, there were about 500 people with placards filling the hallways and room at the Phoenix Civic Center. Management asked them to leave because they were violating fire-safety rules (Morton 1996:317–318).

Many Phoenicians welcomed Orme Dam, however. The price of losing endangered species and the Yavapai's traditional homeland was viewed as a fair trade for stopping the periodic floods on the Salt River that washed away bridges, rerouted traffic, and played havoc with the orderly conduct of life in the Valley of the Sun (Reisner 1986:297). Despite their protests, the plan was rescinded in 1982 and replaced by an alternative plan the following year.

The outcry over Orme Dam sent shock waves throughout the Bureau of Reclamation. It had encountered controversy before—remember Echo Park and the Grand Canyon dams—but for the first time, there was federal legislation mandating that environmental and human effects be considered over purely engineering and technological concerns. The political and economic ramifications were widespread. Many in the agency were shocked at the vociferous opposition they encountered while trying to do their jobs and provide water for a thirsty state. Not surprisingly, some bitterness lingers today.

The controversy led to "an $11 million, 4-year search for a suitable alternative" to Orme Dam (Rogge 1983:134). The Central Arizona Water Control Study evaluated alternative plans to store water delivered by the Central Arizona Project and considered safety issues for existing dams on the Verde, Salt, and Gila Rivers (Rice and Lincoln 1998). In 1983, one of these plans, Plan 6, was identified as the agency action. The Orme Division of the Central Arizona Project was renamed the Regulatory Storage Division. Its purpose was to store and regulate water for the Central Arizona Project, taking water out of the Granite Reef Aqueduct and regulating it through the Salt-Gila Aqueduct. Modifications to Theodore Roosevelt Dam and construction of New Waddell Dam on the Agua Fria River would assume these functions in place of Orme Dam. In addition to water conservation, New Waddell Dam managed electricity from the Navajo Generating Station. Theodore Roosevelt Dam supplanted Orme Dam's flood-control benefits and stored surplus water. It would also provide recreational benefits to millions of Arizonans.

Plan 6 originally included building Cliff Dam on the Verde River. The dam was subsequently eliminated, but the remaining projects were completed. The Bureau of Reclamation also undertook Safety of Dams projects at Horseshoe and Bartlett Dams on the Verde River and Horse Mesa, Mormon Flat, and Stewart Mountain Dams on the Salt River. A final portion of Plan 6 was the Indian Distribution Division to deliver water for five central communities (Salt River Pima-Maricopa, Fort McDowell Yavapai, Gila River, Tohono O'odham Nation, and Ak-Chin Indian Community).

Plan 6 was adopted in 1984, and construction began on Phase A of the Tucson Aqueduct. By the time the project was actually built, technological capabilities had vastly improved, and the design was altered to take advantage of them. Central Arizona Project water was expensive water, involving pump lifts in several places. Morton (1996:231) has commented that when water is expensive, you don't want to waste it. The canals were designed to avoid water waste and also provide flexibility through in-line storage devices and automation. The project used a revolutionary approach—the entire system was controlled from a single, centralized place with a specially designed computer system.

How did the Bureau of Reclamation decide where to begin? This was not a simple question. Knowing that, depending on the vagaries of appropriations and many unknown factors, final construction would take decades to complete, the agency concentrated on those portions of the project that would provide immediate benefits, such as flood control. It also began with parts of the project that could be finished and then suspended without deteriorating or endangering the public, such as **siphons** that could be fenced off while the remainder of the project was completed (Morton 1996:235). Construction began on the diversion facilities and the Granite Reef Aqueduct. Morton (1996:385) recalls that the initial plan was then to begin the reservoir construction before returning to the rest of the aqueduct and distribution system. The controversy over

Paving the canal prism, Fannin-McFarland Aqueduct.
PHOTOGRAPH COURTESY U.S. BUREAU OF RECLAMATION.

Constructing the New River siphon, Hayden-Rhodes Aqueduct. Photograph courtesy U.S. Bureau of Reclamation. Joe Madrigal, Jr., photographer.

Orme Dam shifted this thinking, and construction turned to the portions of the other aqueducts that could be built and fenced off. Next, the concrete canal prism was built. Last to be constructed were the pumping plants, electronic control systems, telecommunications systems—anything likely to be more efficient as technology improved (Morton 1996:236).

This strategy was not without its downside (Morton 1996:491–497). Some of the siphons were built with huge, pre-stressed concrete pipes, which were larger than any pipes ever cast at that time. The contractor fabricated new equipment to build, transport, and lay the state-of-the-art pipes. Then the pipes were filled with groundwater, backfilled with some 20 feet of earth and rocks, and fenced for protection. Most were laid during the years between 1975 and 1978. Around 1989, after Colorado River water had been run through the pipes for four or five years, the Bureau of Reclamation discovered that the wire wrapped around the concrete to provide compressive strength had deteriorated. The pipes could literally explode, endangering human life and putting the operation out of service.

There were a number of theories to explain why this had happened. The wire may have been defective. The exterior mortar coating may have been damaged in backfilling or may have been mixed in the wrong ratios. Regardless, the pipes where the problem was greatest—the bigger pipes with greatest hydrostatic pressure—had to be replaced, and this added additional cost and time to the project.

The diversion facilities and Granite Reef (now named Hayden-Rhodes) Aqueduct were completed in 1985, and the first Colorado River water was pumped from Lake Havasu to the Harquahala Valley Irrigation District in western Arizona. Construction also began that year on New Waddell Dam, which was to replace Carl Pleasant Dam on the Agua Fria River. The pumping and generating plant and intake towers, which regulate water flow through the dam, were begun in 1988. Construction was completed in 1994 when the first stored water was released. The complex stores Colorado River water for the Central Arizona Project. It also provides flood protection, which the original dam did not. New facilities were also necessary, as the increased reservoir level would inundate existing facilities. The new dam added 7,000 surface acres to the lake and enhanced enjoyment of Lake Pleasant Regional Park. Its total cost has been estimated at $625 million.

Next, the remaining aqueducts (Fannin-McFarland and Tucson) were completed. The last projects to be undertaken were Safety of Dams Act modifications. Modifications to Bartlett Dam were completed in 1996. Studies conducted by the Bureau of Reclamation under the 1978 Safety of Dams Act had identified potential overtopping during times

Hayden-Rhodes Aqueduct. Photograph courtesy U.S. Bureau of Reclamation. Joe Madrigal, Jr., photographer.

of maximum flood, resulting in uncontrolled release of reservoir waters. To prevent this, the concrete, multiple-arch dam built in the 1930s was raised more than 21 feet, a parapet was built, the service spillway was modified, and a new auxiliary spillway was constructed. The dam is owned by the Bureau of Reclamation and operated by Salt River Project. Bartlett Dam regulates irrigation flow for Salt River Project. The reservoir, which is located within the Tonto National Forest, provides recreational opportunities and the U.S.D.A. Forest Service administers the boat launches and camping areas.

Safety of Dams Act modifications were also undertaken at Horseshoe Dam. Built in the 1940s, the dam was shown to be unsafe by modern engineering standards. The original rockfill-embankment dam was raised 8 feet, and a 4-foot parapet was constructed. An auxiliary spillway was also built. Originally designed to provide original water storage for the Salt River Project, the reservoir also provides recreational facilities that are managed by the U.S.D.A. Forest Service.

Safety issues for Theodore Roosevelt Dam in the Tonto Basin were even greater than for Bartlett and Horseshoe. If the dam failed during a flood—which studies predicted could happen, although it was considered unlikely—three dams on the Salt River downstream would also be threatened. If those dams failed, much of metropolitan Phoenix would be inundated, endangering lives and property. Modifications took place between 1989 and 1996, when the modified dam was rededicated. In addition to its flood-control functions, it provides supplemental storage that can potentially yield as much as 400,000 acre-feet of water each year. This water is sold to the cities of Phoenix, Glendale, Scottsdale, Mesa, Chandler, and Tempe (Morton 1996:303). Renovations used 444,000 cubic yards of concrete—enough to pave a two-lane road from Phoenix to Tucson. The quantity of reinforcing steel if laid end to end would be nearly 850 miles long, or the distance between Phoenix and Denver (Salt River Project 2003).

The Indian Distribution Division provides irrigation water to entitled tribes. By 1996, the Indian Distribution Division had expanded to 10 communities at 12 locations, including San Carlos Apache, Camp Verde Apache, Yavapai-Prescott, and Tonto Apache (Morton 1996:350–351). New problems were encountered in building the distribution systems. In addition to requirements for cultural and environmental impact studies, some systems encountered technological problems. The Santa Rosa Canal serves the Central Arizona Irrigation District, the Maricopa-Stanfield Irrigation District, and the Ak-Chin Indian Community. The 32-mile-long canal crosses the Santa Cruz River valley, an area affected by severe land subsidence from groundwater pumping. The canal engineers were forced to make predictions about future subsidence and take these into consideration in canal design to protect the agency's commitment to provide water to the Ak-Chin community in perpetuity (Morton 1996:626–630).

Central Arizona Project water arrived in Tucson in 1992. Not surprisingly, given the history of the Central Arizona Project, the final delivery of its water generated

Modifying Theodore Roosevelt Dam

Modifying Theodore Roosevelt Dam was a multimillion-dollar undertaking that required three separate, major contracts and several minor ones. Torno America built a lake tap and associated lined tunnels for $34 million. A $103.3 million contract was awarded to J. A. Jones Construction Co. to build a concrete overlay on the dam face, raise the height of the dam by 77 feet, construct new spillways, modify the power plant, and construct other facilities. The third contract to GEC Alsthom Electromechanical Corporation ($11 million) modified the turbine to handle increased pressures from raising the dam. Construction was set back in 1993 when record winter rainfall caused widespread flooding, overtopping the dam and causing a million dollars' damage.

Upgraded roads, recreational sites, and other facilities administered by the U.S.D.A. Forest Service provide enhanced public use of the lake. The Bureau of Reclamation also funded 55 percent of the cost to construct the new Theodore Roosevelt Lake Bridge. This is the longest two-lane, single-span, steel-arch bridge in North America. The award-winning bridge extends more than 1,000 feet across the lake.

The estimated cost of all activities was $430 million. Additional funding came from the Federal Highway Administration, Salt River Project, Arizona Department of Transportation, Maricopa County Flood District, and a coalition of six Phoenix-area cities (U.S. Department of the Interior, Bureau of Reclamation 2003c).

For further information, please visit the U.S. Department of the Interior's Bureau of Reclamation Web site *at http://www.apo.lc.usbr.gov.*

Pima lateral turnout, Fannin-McFarland Aqueduct. Photograph courtesy U.S. Bureau of Reclamation. Joe Madrigal, Jr., photographer

controversy. Recipients of the first water claimed that it dissolved ancient pipes, rusted water heaters and water softeners, and killed fish in aquariums and ponds. Although the water was of good quality when it left the treatment plant, it picked up deposits from old main pipes and plumbing in residences. The rusty brown water ruined clothes, was unpalatable, and was considered by many to be undrinkable. In the wake of the disastrous debut, a city ordinance banning direct delivery of Central Arizona Project water for at least five years was passed in 1995. The water-treatment plant was mothballed, and the canal was put into standby mode, with the exception of some water used to exercise the pumps and keep the system from deteriorating (Morton 1996:442). Although Tucson was required to pay a standby charge, it did not have to take delivery of water during this interim. According to Morton (1996:866), the problem could have been prevented by introducing additives to the water before it went into the mains. In 2001, a blend of groundwater and effectively treated project water began to be pumped into homes. It is expected that within three years more than 50 percent of Tucson's annual 45-billion-gallon Central Arizona Project allocation will be used (Tobin 2001).

The Central Arizona Project was a "political mirage for three generations of Arizonans. . . now a palpable mirage, as incongruous a spectacle as any on earth: a man-made river flowing uphill in a place of almost no rain" (Reisner 1986:293). The aqueduct and the river it diverts "are reduced to insignificance by the landscape through which they flow—a desert that seems too vast for the most heroic pretensions of mankind." The Central Arizona Project, which cost more than $4 billion, was probably one of the last truly grand projects of the Bureau of Reclamation—"It is the largest water resource development project Congress has ever authorized Reclamation to construct as a single venture" (Rogge 1983:103). Next, we will turn to the project as it looks today.

The Central Arizona Project Today

Today's Central Arizona Project—"canal" is a shorthand label for the system—is enormously complicated. It includes open, concrete-lined channels; underground tunnels; inverted siphons; and secondary systems—pumping plants, a share of the Navajo Generating Station, transmission lines, and many adjunct features.

Three major, interconnected aqueducts form the conveyance system. From west to east, these are the Hayden-Rhodes (originally called Granite Reef), Fannin-McFarland (originally called Salt-Gila), and Tucson Aqueducts. Each aqueduct has a different combination and number of features such as pumping plants, tunnels, siphons, **check structures**, and **turnouts,** depending on aqueduct length, the nature of the terrain it crosses, and how much water is conveyed. The canal narrows and capacity decreases along its length as water is delivered to users.

The canal begins at the Bill Williams Arm of Lake Havasu with the Hayden-Rhodes Aqueduct. This is the longest aqueduct of the system (190 miles) and covers the

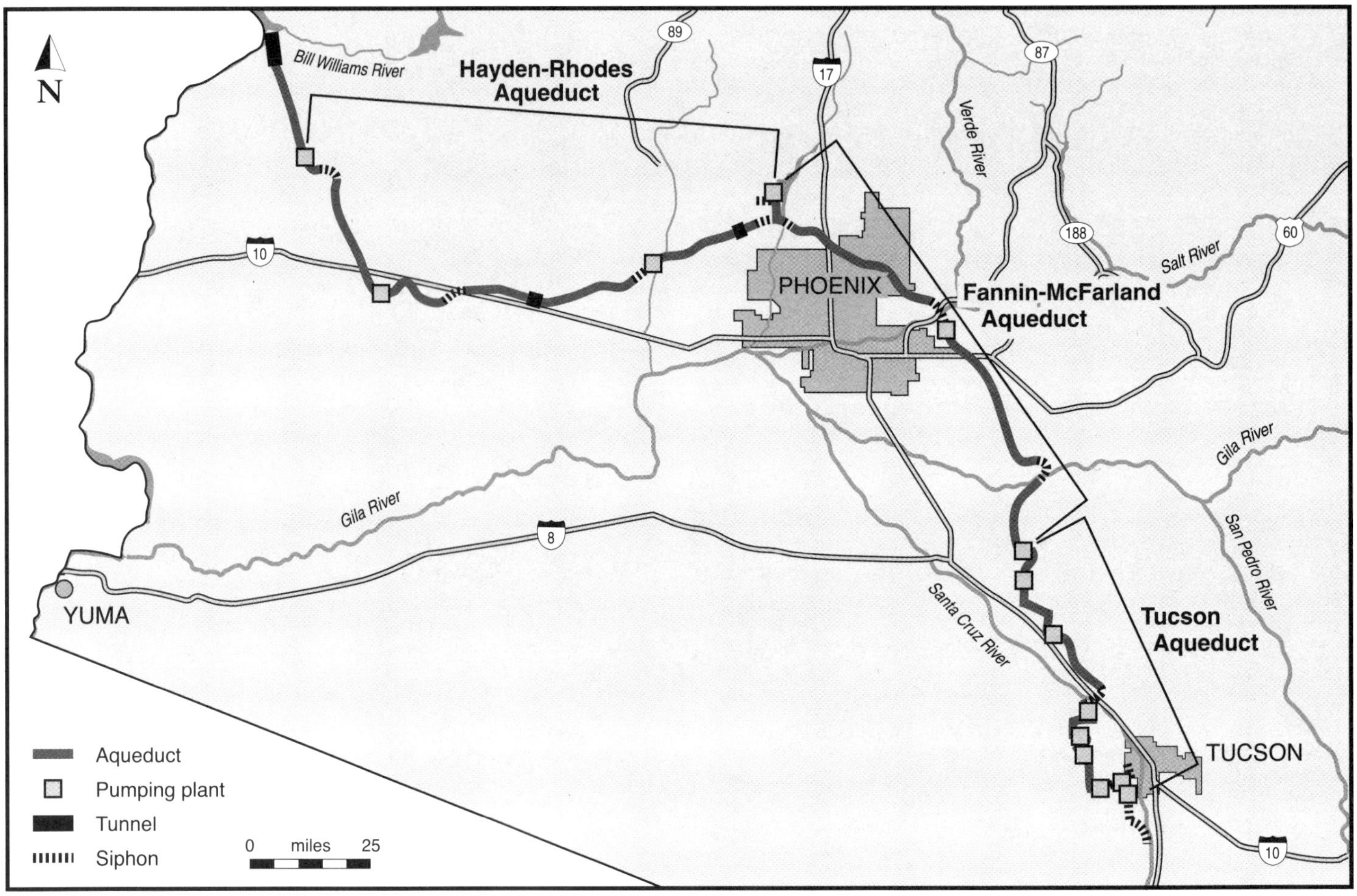

Features of the Central Arizona Project today.

most mountainous terrain, negotiating its way through the Buckskin Mountains, Bouse Hills, and the fringes of the Granite Wash Mountains. The Havasu Pumping Plant lifts Colorado River water 824 feet from the lake and into the first segment of the aqueduct, the Buckskin Mountains tunnel. There are three additional pumping plants that lift water about 1,200 feet over the aqueduct's length.

There are seven inverted siphons and two tunnels in the Hayden-Rhodes Aqueduct in addition to the Buckskin Mountains tunnel. Most of the aqueduct is a concrete-lined, open channel. Reach 1, a 17-mile-long, oversized section of canal between the Havasu and Bouse Hills Pumping Plants, acts as an in-line storage reservoir. With the exception of this reach, the canal averages 80 feet wide at the top and 24 feet wide at the bottom, has a typical water depth of about 16 feet, and has a capacity of 3,000 cubic feet per second.

Havasu Pumping Plant. PHOTOGRAPH BY JEFFERSON REID.

Typical check structure along Hayden-Rhodes Aqueduct, containing two gates. Photograph courtesy U.S. Bureau of Reclamation. Joe Madrigal, Jr., photographer.

Northwest of metropolitan Phoenix is the Waddell complex, consisting of the zoned earthfill New Waddell Dam on the Agua Fria River and its reservoir, Lake Pleasant; the Waddell Canal, and the Waddell Pumping and Generating Plant. The dam and reservoir provide seasonal storage for Colorado River water. The Waddell Canal, a reversible canal almost five miles long, connects from the reservoir to the main Central Arizona Project canal. During the summer or maintenance and repair of the Hayden-Rhodes aqueduct, water is released out of Lake Pleasant to Phoenix and Tucson customers, generating hydroelectric power. In the winter, when power costs are low, water is pumped uphill into the lake; the surplus can be sold to help repay construction costs. The reservoir provides as much as 2.2 million acre-feet of Colorado River water when it is available. If necessary, floodwaters can be released from the dam through the river-outlet works tunnel into the river immediately below the dam.

At the Salt River just west of its confluence with the Verde River, the Hayden-Rhodes Aqueduct terminates and the Fannin-McFarland Aqueduct begins. The Fannin-McFarland Aqueduct consists of 58 miles of open, concrete channel; one major pumping plant that lifts water a height of 86 feet; and one siphon that crosses under the Gila River. The aqueduct is about 80 feet wide at the top and 24 feet wide at the bottom, narrowing slightly at its terminal end. It averages about 16 feet deep, although the depth also decreases toward the terminus. Capacity decreases because of upstream water deliveries to the Phoenix area from the Hayden-Rhodes aqueduct and diversions along this segment to farmland south of Phoenix. The maximum capacity is 2,250 cubic feet per second.

The Tucson Aqueduct begins at the end of the Fannin-McFarland Aqueduct about five miles north of the Brady Pumping Plant and terminates southwest of Tucson where the canal ends. This aqueduct is 87 miles long and also passes through rugged terrain, including the Picacho Mountains, Twin Peaks, and Tucson Mountains. One siphon crosses beneath Interstate 10 northwest of Tucson. Nine pumping plants, the largest with a maximum lift of 397 feet, raise water along the aqueduct, which runs uphill toward Tucson. The canal is 69 feet wide at the top and 20 feet wide at the bottom, narrowing to only 52 and 12 feet respectively at its terminal end. The average water depth of 10–11 feet at the beginning of the aqueduct drops to about 9 feet at the end. Maximum capacity is 2,250 cubic feet per second, dropping to only 200 cubic feet per second at the terminus.

The Central Arizona Project includes other features as well as the aqueducts. There are diversion facilities such as those at Lake Havasu, and distribution systems, the largest of which is the Santa Rosa Canal. Road bridges, wildlife and cattle crossings, and earthen dikes to protect the canal were built. Overchutes and culverts divert local runoff. The entire canal is fenced to protect people and wildlife. The project is remotely operated from the project headquarters in north Phoenix by computer and a communications system that includes buried cables and microwave connections.

Central Arizona Project control room. Photograph courtesy U.S. Bureau of Reclamation.

Central Arizona Project Archaeology

We have seen that federal laws protecting environmental and cultural resources mandated that the Bureau of Reclamation find archaeological sites affected by the Central Arizona Project and take measures to mitigate adverse impacts, usually through excavation (see the appendix for a closer look at this process). The archaeological studies conducted before the Central Arizona Project was built were phenomenal in scope (Rogge 1983:103). Millions of dollars were spent on this massive undertaking. Over time there was a substantial increase in the scale of archaeological projects and a consequent increase in the size of contract awards (Rogge 1983; Whittlesey and others 1994:35–36). Central Arizona Project archaeology was big archaeology, Rogge (1983) has reminded us, as well as long-term archaeology. Both are unique in the world of **cultural resource management**.

As we have seen, federal legislation requires that cultural resources and archaeological sites be included during the planning stages of a project. This not only ensures that adverse effects will be avoided or minimized, but also that construction will be completed on time. As the scope of construction activities changed, so too did the archaeology. A number of archaeological studies were carried out for projects that were subsequently dropped from the roster. One of the first was an **archaeological survey** of the proposed Charleston Dam reservoir site, published in 1968. Archaeological surveys were also conducted for the proposed Buttes Dam and Reservoir on the Gila River near Florence, which was never built, although it remains on the Bureau of Reclamation's drawing table as an authorized project. The Central Arizona Water Control Study, which was initiated to determine alternatives to the scrapped Orme Dam, required surveys of potential dam and reservoir sites along the lower Verde River, such as the proposed Cliff Dam site. Along the way, all potential aqueduct alignments were surveyed for archaeological sites. This work provided invaluable contributions to our understanding of Arizona prehistory.

In the early years, while the kinks were being worked out of the national historic-preservation system, archaeological contracting for the Central Arizona Project was carried out through the National Park Service. Later, the Bureau of Reclamation acquired its own archaeological staff, and cultural resource studies were contracted directly between the agency and various consultants who performed such services (Rogge 1983). Organizations awarded contracts during the project's early history included Arizona State University, Arizona State Museum, Museum of Northern Arizona, and University of Nevada, Las Vegas. In the later years, private environmental and archaeological consulting firms conducted much more work, and contracts were awarded to Desert Archaeology, Inc., Statistical Research,

The Language of Cultural Resource Management

Cultural resource management has its own jargon. Use of acronyms pervades archaeological reports written after the late 1970s. Acronyms are used for the legislative acts (NHPA, NEPA); for agencies (SHPO, NPS); institutions carrying out archaeology (SRI, ASM); people involved in the work (COTR); and even for the discipline itself (CRM). Archaeologists speak in acronyms as well as write with them. Although they shorten a document, acronyms are emphatically not user friendly, making reports appear bureaucratic and divorced from the ancient people about which archaeologists write. For these reasons, I avoid acronyms in this book, spelling out even Central Arizona Project, typically abbreviated CAP, and the Bureau of Reclamation (BOR). "U.S." is usually dropped when it is obvious that we're talking about the United States and not other nations (Geological Survey instead of U.S.G.S., Bureau of Reclamation instead of U.S. Bureau of Reclamation, and so on).

Other jargon in this discipline requires some explanation. Many of these terms are highlighted in bold text and are defined in the Glossary. Others include: "data recovery (typically meaning excavation); "mitigation" (activities that will recover information to mitigate the effects of construction); and "impact" (effects on archaeological sites). "Cultural resources" and "historic properties" usually mean archaeological sites, although these also have specific definitions (see Glossary).

You will see archaeology spelled with and without the second "a." The latter is not a misspelling by hurried writers. It is the preferred spelling of federal agencies.

See the glossary for other jargon with which you may not be familiar.

Inc., Northland Research, Inc., Archaeological Research Services, Inc., Human Systems Research, Inc., Archaeological Consulting Services, and Dames & Moore.

The scope and character of archaeological projects also changed over the years. Many of the first surveys were perfunctory, and the reports were brief, cataloging the sites discovered and describing them in one or two sentences. Later, particularly after environmental-protection legislation, research programs were deliberately built into the design of archaeological projects with a subsequent increase in the quality of the work—and the length of the reports.

Central Arizona Project divisions structured archaeological work as well as construction and administration. The aqueducts were divided into phases and smaller reaches, and these segments usually also organized the archaeology. Most important to the stories told in this book is the tremendous environmental diversity of the Central Arizona Project. The Colorado River, which is the source of Central Arizona Project water, and the canal itself cross three physiographic provinces in the state of Arizona—the Colorado Plateau, mountain Transition Zone, and desert Basin and Range. These three provinces structure the stories that follow in subsequent chapters. Most of the canal lies within the Basin and Range province, and we will concentrate on the peoples of the Arizona deserts.

The first segment of the project connects us to the wildest river in the West, the Colorado River. Intake structures at Lake Havasu remove water that originates hundreds of miles away in the Rocky Mountains of Wyoming and Colorado and crosses hundreds of miles through the canyons of the Colorado Plateau. Lake Havasu and Lake Mead are a meeting ground for environmental diversity, where the Basin and Range province merges with the beginnings of the Colorado Plateau and the Transition Zone. Next, the Hayden-Rhodes Aqueduct angles the water across the Basin and Range province toward the central part of the state (refer to previous map). The Great Basin, Mojave, and Sonoran desert ecosystems merge along the aqueduct route.

The prehistory of this dry land punctuated by mountain ranges and intervening, arid valleys is poorly known. Sites were often small and ephemeral, typically representing artifact scatters with only **flaked stone tools**. Central Arizona Project archaeology (Brown and Stone 1982) discovered that this region represented a boundary zone between several prehistoric cultures—**Patayan**, Hohokam, perhaps others. Archaeologists found evidence that ancient people used the area seasonally to collect wild resources. They moved often and were linked with more permanent settlements along the rivers and streams. With the exception of a work camp for Granite Reef Diversion Dam near the eastern terminus of the aqueduct, historical occupation was rare. Although in this book we will not return to the archaeology of this region, Chapter 4 tells stories of the Colorado Plateau and the river providing Central Arizona Project water.

Granite Reef Archaeology

Archaeological studies along Granite Reef (now Hayden-Rhodes) Aqueduct were some of the earliest carried out during the Central Arizona Project. Initial studies included several surveys that located archaeological sites along the aqueduct alignments or investigated sites that would be impacted by particular features. Beginning in 1977, the Office of Cultural Resource Management at Arizona State University undertook a five-year data-recovery program as an "on call" contractor. The Bureau of Reclamation developed this innovative concept to reconcile the varying, sometimes conflicting requirements of project scheduling, compliance with federal and state laws, and research standards. Forty-six sites were investigated, including large artifact scatters, small artifact scatters, trail sites, discontinuous sites, and miscellaneous sites such as petroglyphs and rock rings (Brown and Stone 1982).

Next in the system is the New Waddell Dam complex, located northwest of metropolitan Phoenix. The complex lies in another prehistoric boundary area, which has been called the northern Hohokam periphery. Archaeologists once believed that the Hohokam occupied a "core" area in the Phoenix Basin and several "peripheral" areas away from it. Central Arizona Project archaeology was vital in changing this notion. Although they evidently were linked with Hohokam settlements in the Salt and Gila River valleys, the prehistoric people living in the New Waddell area developed their own unique cultural complex. They were evidently also joined by people of different cultural or ethnic affiliations, creating a culturally diverse zone. Sandwiched between the Mountain Transition Zone and the Basin and Range province and exhibiting environmental characteristics of both, the Waddell region was obviously attractive to many different folk.

Salado site (Schoolhouse Point Mound) in Tonto Basin near Theodore Roosevelt Lake during excavation sponsored by U.S. Bureau of Reclamation. PHOTOGRAPH COURTESY U.S. BUREAU OF RECLAMATION.

Archaeological Consulting Services undertook excavation for the New Waddell Dam project beginning in 1986. They worked at sites located in two areas along different drainages (Agua Fria and New Rivers), focusing their research on the ways in which ancient peoples used environmentally different zones. Archaeologists investigated 13 of 17 sites originally selected for study and excavated two more sites found during survey. The study found that agricultural techniques differed in the two areas as did the length and type of occupation. Archaeologists synthesized farming techniques and systems, defined a local ceramic tradition, and discovered that people of different cultures probably used the project area in prehistory. This work provided valuable information about a region traditionally considered "peripheral Hohokam" and altered archaeologists' views about such peripheral areas (Green 1989). Later studies would demonstrate that the region north of the Phoenix metropolitan area was wetter in prehistoric times than today and served as an agricultural area specializing in corn and agave cultivation.

The Fannin-McFarland Aqueduct begins in the Salt River valley, which in prehistory was the home of a dense prehistoric occupation (see previous map). This is the heart of the desert Basin and Range and the home territory of the Hohokam. The aqueduct leaves the valley and traverses Queen Creek as it heads toward modern Florence. Central Arizona Project archaeology along the Salt-Gila Aqueduct discovered evidence of sophisticated and diverse Hohokam farming strategies. We will visit this country, the archaeology carried out before the aqueduct was constructed, and its value to understanding the Hohokam in Chapter 5.

The Tucson Aqueduct segment of the Central Arizona Project crosses country that is often seen as culturally intermediate between the Hohokam culture of the Phoenix area and that of the Tucson Basin. The Santa Cruz Flats, an alluvial area at the confluence of the Santa Cruz River with the Gila River, was home to Archaic **period** people and later Hohokam who specialized in the manufacture of shell ornaments for trade. Later, large complexes including **platform mounds** were built near the Picacho Mountains. In historical times, the confluence area was the location of large villages occupied by the Akimel O'odham, or Pima, Indians. When the aqueduct reaches the Tucson Mountains, it crosses territory of the Tucson Basin Hohokam, who developed their own distinctive and vigorous culture. Chapter 5 discusses the Tucson Basin Hohokam along with other desert dwellers.

The most intensive archaeological investigations of the entire Central Arizona Project took place for the Regulatory Storage Division and associated Safety of Dams Act work. In the Tonto Basin, the Roosevelt Archaeology Project, which was carried out ahead of modifications to Theodore Roosevelt Dam, was so large that it was divided into several smaller projects involving four different archaeological organizations. The higher reservoir resulting from dam modifications inundated many archaeological sites, and associated construction-staging sites and other ground-disturbing activities impacted others. The Tonto Basin lies in the heart of the mountain Transition Zone and has environmental characteristics of that region and the Basin and Range province. It was home to diverse peoples in prehistory. It is also considered the heartland of the enigmatic Salado culture. Historical archaeology was carried out for the dam-construction camps housing the workers who struggled to build Theodore Roosevelt Dam. We discuss this region and its prehistory, focusing on the Salado culture, in Chapter 6. We also see how the Western Apache people contributed to building the dam and how Mormon farmers succeeded and sometimes failed in this arid country.

Safety of Dams Act work along the lower Verde River involved intensive data recovery at Hohokam and later sites. The Lower Verde Archaeological Project was a large excavation project including numerous sites located in the Horseshoe Reservoir and Bartlett Lake areas that contributed information to an area that was previously almost unknown. Historical archaeology of the construction camps associated with Bartlett and Horseshoe Dams provided a fascinating glimpse into Arizona's history.

What did we learn from Central Arizona Project archaeology? We collected an enormous quantity of new information. Reports totaling hundreds of thousands of pages of site and **archaeological feature** descriptions, artifact classification and analyses, maps, photographs, and computerized databases were generated. **Chronometric dates**, **paleobotanical remains**, **paleofaunal remains**, **material culture** or **material remains**, architectural information, and much more were retrieved from the soil and stones of central and southern Arizona. These data filled in many gaps in previous work, much of which was conducted before sophisticated analytic techniques such as **radiocarbon dating** were developed.

Project archaeology revolutionized our understanding of Arizona archaeology. We learned how people coped with living in desert regions throughout the millennia. Places such as the Tonto Basin, the Santa Cruz Flats region, and the Tucson Basin and its environs were poorly understood or dismissed as "peripheral" regions before the Central Arizona Project. As a consequence, we understand the processes by which people of differing cultural and

Scorpion Point Village near Horseshoe Reservoir, lower Verde River valley, during excavation sponsored by U.S. Bureau of Reclamation. Photograph courtesy U.S. Bureau of Reclamation. Joe Madrigal, Jr., photographer.

ethnic groups came to occupy desert lands, learned to adjust to life there, and sustained themselves through time. Several projects contributed a great deal to our understanding of lifeways during the Archaic period, particularly the poorly known earlier portions. It is not overstating the case to say that "CAP archaeology provided us with our first true understanding of the Hohokam, whose history before CAP was essentially limited to the report of a single, large site and a few scattered and small-scale studies" (Whittlesey and others 1994:43). If we add contributions concerning other prehistoric peoples and the historical-period native and nonnative peoples who followed them, what we know about the past through Central Arizona Project archaeology is truly impressive.

Research results were distributed in the professional community through publications, reports presented at scholarly meetings, and scientific symposia. The Bureau of Reclamation sponsored two research seminars concerning Central Arizona Project archaeology at the Amerind Foundation in Dragoon, Arizona, which resulted in two widely cited publications.

Publications sponsored by the U.S. Bureau of Reclamation.

Archaeologists were not the only beneficiaries of this research. The nonprofessional public interested in archaeology also benefited. Throughout the project's history, contractors offered site tours and lectures for the general public and coordinated events and exhibits for Arizona Archaeology Month. The book you are reading is another example of a public-outreach project sponsored by the Bureau of Reclamation. In this way, everyone benefits from federal archaeology and is able to participate in the programs that protect and preserve archaeological sites. It is everyone's heritage, not just the purview of the archaeologist alone.

Last, Central Arizona Project archaeology is a testament to federal legislation and the national policy of conservation and historic preservation that prompted it. As we move into the twenty-first century with its burgeoning population, development of unpopulated land, and demands upon natural resources, protecting our environment and its cultural resources has become even more important. This book tells a series of stories about life in the stone-dry land of desert Arizona, stories that encompass life from the Archaic period some 3,000 years ago to the building of Glen Canyon Dam. The central theme is water—how people prayed for it, symbolized it in their artwork, embedded it into their legends and creation stories, and learned to divert it and use it to grow crops. These stories say much about the human spirit and speak to our similarities more than they define our differences. There are many lessons woven into these stories, and we would be lesser individuals and a lesser nation had it not been for the enlightened policies supporting Central Arizona Project archaeology.

The Central Arizona Project was once envisioned as a means of watering an agricultural paradise in the desert. It now provides water primarily for the vastly developed cities of Phoenix and Tucson, where cotton fields and orange groves have given way to golf courses, housing developments, and winter resorts. The river of rocky canyons—the Colorado, the wildest river in the West—and the concrete canals wind through green fields and past communities basking in the desert sun, over places where the houses and farmlands of ancient peoples once stood, locales of songs and stories and legends. We turn now to these people and their stories.

Boating to Work

During the Roosevelt Archaeology project, archaeologists from Arizona State University found it necessary to get to work in an unusual way–by water taxi. One of the platform-mound sites they investigated was marooned on an island in the middle of Theodore Roosevelt Lake and could only be reached by boat. Each day, the project director ferried the crew, equipment, water, and lunches across in a blue pontoon boat. At least they didn't have to worry about traffic jams or parking tickets. They did have to make sure the boat was securely fastened, however, or they would have found themselves swimming home after work. It must have been a great way to spend the summer.

For further information, see: Advisory Council on Historic Preservation Web site *(http://www.achp.gov); Thomas F. King,* Cultural Resource Laws and Practice: An Introductory Guide *(Altamira Press, Walnut Creek, California, 1998);* National Park Service Web site *(http://www.nps.gov) (contains links to the National Register of Historic Places, the National Historic Preservation Act of 1966, and more).*

Midstream

Stories of the Colorado Plateau

4

Although recognized as an agent of erosion and sculptor of land forms, water, as essential to life, is taken entirely for granted where it is plentiful. But in arid regions such as Glen Canyon the distribution of water controls the distribution of living forms; hence, the ecology of the region can almost be reduced to a study of available water and its efficient use.

—Jesse Jennings, *Glen Canyon: An Archaeological Summary*

All around us was Indian land, the Indian land of our childhood dreams where past and future have no meaning and loneliness is nonexistent, for here one cannot be other than part of everything. Time is but a series of 'todays,' as limitless and tiny as the grains of sand beneath our feet, that progress as methodically as the stars above and as irrevocably as the rocks are worn away below.

—Ann Woodin, *Home is the Desert*

May 14, 2001

Imagining the Colorado Plateau

How to choose among the multiple images that define the Colorado Plateau? The land is slippery as slickrock, as hard to grasp as a cactus spine. It is as indefinable and evanescent as canyon light. One image is the Colorado Plateau as natural landscape. The general public evidently finds the Plateau's natural wonders irresistible and endlessly engaging, to judge by the hordes of tourists that Edward Abbey so loved to hate. The Grand Canyon gives its name to the state of Arizona and has become the quintessential symbol of the Colorado Plateau to millions of German, Japanese, French, and other international tourists. The carved spires, humanoid forms, and pristine isolation of the red rock country immortalized in Abbey's Desert Solitaire, *his "haunted monoliths*

San Francisco Peaks near Flagstaff, Arizona. Photograph by Jefferson Reid.

and goblin gulches"—Arches, Natural Bridges, Capitol Reef, Zion—these nationalized parks and places evoke the Colorado Plateau to many.

To others, the Colorado Plateau is synonymous with Native Americans, and this image has spurred a tourist industry of its own. Driving east on Arizona State Route 64 from the Grand Canyon toward Cameron, perhaps anticipating with relish the perfect Navajo taco at the trading post there, one encounters Chief Yellow Horse's fluorescent-yellow signs urging the consumer to stop and buy at reservation prices. The last sign has a pleading note—"NICE INDIANS BEHIND YOU," it reads. This scene is repeated at every overlook, each scenic vista, all the spots to stop and gawk at the natural wonders ahead or below. Under simple ramadas, groups of entrepreneurial Indians lay out their wares—incongruous, pastel ceramic pots; cheap, machine-made jewelry; the ubiquitous dream catchers—hoping to catch the eye and empty the pocket of the visitor who is unaware that these are not the best the nations can offer.

Native American arts and crafts for sale along State Route 64, Arizona. PHOTOGRAPH BY JEFFERSON REID.

Yet another image of the Colorado Plateau is archaeological. Many visitors choose images of the indigenous past as postcards from the Plateau—encounters with the ancient ones at Mesa Verde, Canyon de Chelly, or Tsegi Canyon. Tucked into great, melodious curves of rock, the walls of such places ring with the voices of those who are gone. Sit quietly, if it is possible to avoid the gaggles of tourists and their loquacious guides, and the lucky visitor of the right frame of mind and spirit can smell a hint of wood smoke on the breeze, catch the faint echoes of voices, jinglers on a dancer's kilt, stamping feet. The sweet-smoky taste of roasted fresh corn may linger in the mouth.

A final image of the Colorado Plateau is that of its technological wonders. Regardless of whether one agrees with the politics and policies that brought it to life, Glen Canyon Dam is a lovely thing, a heartbreaking, clean arch diving into an improbably azure lake. It nicely symbolizes the confrontation between engineered geometry and uncontrolled natural elements. Those of the Y-chromosome persuasion may see in such technological triumphs the ultimate symbol of the Colorado Plateau.

For me, however, the place that symbolizes the Plateau best is the overlook above the Goosenecks of the San Juan River in Utah. Coming back from a family vacation to Montana and Wyoming, at the end of days on the road that frayed tempers and unraveled tenuously achieved harmonies, we stopped there and found what can only be described as epiphany. The dirt road to the overlook led through a juniper- and sage-covered tableland that gave no hint of what was to come. We drove as far as we could, then parked the Explorer and walked south across the white rock, skirting crumpled trees that rose like tiny, ancient men stretching tired limbs to the morning sun. Soon the juniper and piñon gave way to bare rock, and the wind began to assault us. We came to the edge of the abyss, and the river lay before us, exposed and offering itself to the sky. Carved into the floor of the world, twisting and turning in seemingly aimless meanders, the river had neatly sliced through layer after layer of rock, revealing in its narrow, tightly walled canyons a stratigraphic past older than time.

We could hardly stand upright for the wind. Coming up off the flatlands below, it bludgeoned and chilled us, tugging at our hair and making our eyes water. The binoculars necessary to see what lay below and before us were shaky in our hands, and it felt like the naked stone itself was swaying with the wind. But oh—what a vision that was. Directly ahead, beyond the great looping river, lay the buttes and spires of Monument Valley, dust beginning to cloak their feet. Was this the essential image of the Plateau, Navajo sheep and their herders on scrawny ponies against a backdrop of towering red stone? To the southwest, capped by swirls of cloud, was sacred Navajo Mountain, femininely rounded, malely stout. I can remember seeing no

Goosenecks of the San Juan River. Photograph by Jefferson Reid.

postcards of that holy place. It felt as though we could see into forever and as if we could fly. If we lifted our arms and leaped up like kids do when an elevator begins to descend, the wind would bear us aloft, sweep us to the soaring space at the edge of the world through endless dreams of emptiness. I wondered vaguely if that nameless feeling was responsible for some of the many tourists deaths in the Grand Canyon over the years. My husband tells me that this syndrome is so common that psychologists even have a name for it, but neither of us knows it.

Perhaps the most striking thing about that panorama was the total absence of human modifications. No hint of the human presence could be detected—no pollution from the Navajo Generating Station, as the wind had taken care of that; no highways, no bridges, no houses. Certainly no cities, and even Lake Powell was undetectable, tucked into its rock basin behind and to the northwest of where we stood. Earlier that day, we had crossed over the bridge spanning the upper lake in a pelting rainstorm. It was as if the wind had scoured all signs of life from the bare bones of the earth; not even vegetation was visible. Except for the contrails of airplanes streaking the sky, it was possible to imagine that we were the only people on the planet, that no one had ever been there before us, that the technological wonders of the twentieth century were fitful chimeras, exhaustion-induced visions of the future.

Was this, I wondered, how the Spanish padres Escalante and Dominguez felt when they managed to cross Glen Canyon? Had they simply been too tired to care, or did they choose to leave all such details to God? Had John Wesley Powell experienced something similar when he gazed upon the land of naked rock, cliffs that could not be scaled, canyon walls that dwarfed the river below?

I wondered, because the emotion I encountered was not a feeling of mastery or power over nature, no awe of the limitless distances before me, no thrill of discovery. At base, it was simply fear. Fear of isolation, fear of being alone, fear of a land that is pitiless to our pitiful human forms. Edward Abbey (1968: 191) described this emotion well, and I can do no better than to borrow his words.

> *Alone in the silence, I understand for a moment the dread which many feel in the presence of primeval desert, the unconscious fear which compels them to tame, alter or destroy what they cannot understand, to reduce the wild and prehuman to human dimensions. Anything rather than confront directly the antehuman, that other world which frightens not through danger or hostility but in something far worse—its implacable indifference.*

Abbey knew well that the Colorado Plateau is not a warm-and-fuzzy place, a Walt Disney world where baby deer gambol and bear cubs play with bunnies. There is death here as well as life, and those humans who managed to survive and thrive here understood that well. Love this land and respect it, but never, ever forget that it can kill.

AT FIRST GLANCE, it is difficult to see how any farming people could prosper in northeastern Arizona's mesa and canyon lands. Much of it is bone-clean country swept by wind and carved by water. Pinnacles of nude sandstone rise from an immense sweep of sparse vegetation, and narrow gorges cut through the living rock like knives. The eye is drawn inevitably to the sky, where massed clouds all too infrequently pour life-giving water upon the parched land. The apparent isolation and barrenness of the Colorado Plateau are deceiving, because the land was exploited, farmed, and inhabited for thousands of years. The record of this interaction can be seen in thousands of prehistoric and historical-period archaeological sites dotting the canyon country.

Vermilion Cliffs. PHOTOGRAPH COURTESY ARIZONA HISTORICAL SOCIETY, TUCSON (AHS ACCESSION NO. 44938).

Land of Rock

The landscape everywhere, away from the river, is of rock—cliffs of rock, tables of rock, plateaus of rock, terraces of rock, crags of rock—ten thousand strangely carved forms; rocks everywhere, and no vegetation, no soil, no sand.

When thinking of these rocks one must not conceive of piles of boulders. . . but of a whole land of naked rock, with giant forms carved on it; cathedral-shaped buttes, towering hundreds or thousands of feet, cliffs that cannot be scaled, and canyon walls that shrink the river into insignificance, with vast, hollow domes and tall pinnacles and shafts set on the verge overhead; and all highly colored. . . bare, and often polished.

—*John Wesley Powell,* The Exploration of the Colorado River and Its Canyons

"Park Avenue" at Arches National Park, Utah, named for the architectural forms of the standing rock. PHOTOGRAPH BY JEFFERSON REID.

To understand the paradox of abundant life in a stone-dry land, we need to look beyond the obvious features of the physical landscape—the scientific history of stones, plants, animals, all the things that can be seen, touched, smelled—and even farther than the character and history of its people. We must examine how people perceived the land and interacted with it. Over time, the Colorado Plateau's inhabitants created a landscape potent with meaning and rich with symbol, a landscape that simultaneously taught them how to live and recorded the history of their interactions. The ancient inhabitants of the land; the historical Navajo, Hopi, and Pai peoples; the Mormons who sought refuge and an earthly farming paradise; and the many people of all nations who come to visit today—all have created landscapes where the earth tells stories, teaches lessons, and supports life itself. Each living group has created a different Colorado Plateau by imbuing the land with meaning, because "Meaning depends less on the scene's physical geography than on the ideas through which it can be viewed and imagined" (Pyne 1998:xiii).

Stephen Pyne has illustrated these points in his book *How the Canyon Became Grand: A Short History* (1998). He describes how shifting meanings and ideologies have shaped the Grand Canyon as a *landscape,* not simply a place. In the early years of Euroamerican discovery, explorers such as Lieutenant Ives viewed the canyon as an impediment to travel, a worthless region that could not be crossed. Such dismal assessments of the Grand Canyon scarcely seem plausible; today, literally millions of visitors throng there. Later explorers and scientists such as John Wesley Powell saw the canyon country as an unknown land to be conquered, and its discovered geography became an edifice to newly reconstructed cultural values of art, science, literature, and national philosophy. The locals who clung precariously to a living in the canyon country viewed it as a simple resource-extraction zone, ignoring its sublimities in favor of more practical ideologies. Still later, the Grand Canyon became a vehicle for the common individual to become intrepid explorer, and through the medium of tourism the canyon was emblematic of the national motto "See America First." Last, the Grand Canyon entered and helped define what Pyne (1998:139) has labeled "the white-water age of postwar environmentalism." Through all this, the physical realities of the canyon remained the same. Only its meanings changed.

The ancient **puebloan** farmer raised corn, beans, and squash on the canyon floors by manipulating scarce water in inventive ways. Later, Mormon farmers found northern Arizona to be so rich in farmland and water that it became known as Utah's Dixie and yielded cotton abundantly. In the twentieth century, Bureau of Reclamation engineers dammed the Colorado River to create a huge artificial lake and recreational paradise. The single constant in these changing perceptions is water, the most precious commodity in an arid land. In this chapter, we tell stories of water as it shaped human lives in this etched and painted land of stone and sky, concentrating our tales on the Arizona section of the Plateau.

The Colorado River is our metaphorical pathway on this journey. Into the river, "[w]ater spills from seven states, traveling from hundreds and thousands of miles away" (Childs 2000:263). "It is a pilgrimage with pathways set deeply into the land where every rock leans toward the river. It is not wind or fire or humans or gods, but water that defines this land." Water will define our journey across the Colorado Plateau and will be the medium for telling our stories. We begin, therefore, with the land and its water.

THE LAND, WATER, AND LIVING THINGS

The Colorado Plateau is a vast landscape of stone, sky, and paradox. In this sweeping panorama of color and form, the ironies of the desert Southwest are most apparent. Consider these, for example. Although today best described as a high-elevation desert where water is scarce, the Plateau was largely shaped by water. Over unimaginable sequences of time, water created the layered crimson, purple, and russet geologic strata forming the land. Water and its companion wind cut immense canyons into the ancient rock and shaped it into improbable spires, buttes, and mesas. Consider the irony of pioneer explorers standing on the rim of the Grand Canyon and thirsting, even as a mile below them, torrents of muddy water coursed down the canyon, as inaccessible as the stars. And most ironic, canyons once shaped by wind and water now lie drowned beneath the turquoise waters of Lake Powell, where houseboats currently float.

Visit Lake Powell, and the paradox seems entirely artificial, a product of good scriptwriting and special effects. One notices the light first. In summer, it pours down with almost unbearable intensity. Without sunglasses, it is painful; stay in it too long, and the skin crisps. Stone rising abruptly from the lake is striped in candy-cane colors reminiscent of Neapolitan ice cream—strawberry pink, chocolate brown, vanilla white. In the summer of 2002 when we last visited, the water level had dropped to astonishingly low levels, exposing rock as white as the eroded bones of beached sea mammals.

Wahweap Marina, Lake Powell, Arizona. PHOTOGRAPH BY JEFFERSON REID.

The water was intensely colored, turquoise and teal fading to azure in the shallows. Hundreds of vehicles jammed the parking lots; the smells of diesel exhaust and sunscreen, and the noise of motors and exhaust pipes filled the air. The towers of the Navajo Generating Station rose above the lake, their smoke staining the horizon with a faint brown haze. As we left, we saw the greatest paradox of all—a huge houseboat on a trailer, seeming to glide on its own through a shallow sea of saltbush and snakeweed.

Renting Boats on Lake Powell

A brochure describing the recreational opportunities of Lake Powell gives the following figures for renting water craft (daily rate, except for houseboats, for which the brochure provides the 3-day rate).

Boat Rentals:
14' Fishing/Utility $72–120
18' Run-About $139–232
21' Deck Boat $174–290

Personal Water Craft: $60–228

House Boats:
36' Standard Class $577–961
52' Captain Class $1,084–1,807
59' Admiral Class $1,716–2,860

The pursuit of watery fun evidently does not come cheap.

Grand Teton Mountains, Wyoming. Photograph by Jefferson Reid.

What is the Colorado Plateau? The geographic definition—the northern drainage basin of the Colorado River, exclusive of the Gila River—scarcely does it justice. The Plateau covers more than 130,000 square miles in the Four Corners states of Arizona, Utah, Colorado, and New Mexico, extending northward into Wyoming. On the north, the plateau is bounded by an extension of the Green River, and the Rocky Mountains mark its eastern limit. On the western edge, fault lines slope to demarcate the Plateau from the adjoining Basin and Range province. It is convenient to identify the Plateau's western boundary as the point where the Colorado River turns abruptly to flow south toward the Gulf of California. In Arizona, the Colorado Plateau physiographic province encompasses the area north of the Mogollon Rim. Through it winds the Colorado River, and the Plateau lies tilted in a northeasterly direction against the stream.

The Plateau's size and the diversity of geological processes that shaped it have resulted in a region of unparalleled topographic variability and extraordinary natural beauty. Popular images of the Plateau—the red spires of Monument Valley, scenic Canyon de Chelly, the twists and meanders of the San Juan River in southern Utah—belie the scenic diversity of snow-capped mountains, blue mesas, tropical canyons. "The Colorado Plateau," trumpets a recent map and guide to its public lands, "hosts the greatest and most diverse collection of national parks and public lands on earth!" (Time Traveler Maps 1999). Many of these public areas celebrate the peoples who forged their history on this landscape.

Geology and Earth History

Many geologists have described the plateau country, beginning with Powell's explorations of the "plateau province." Karl Grove Gilbert, who joined the Powell survey in 1874, delineated the region in impressively scientific geological terms. Geologist Clarence Dutton, another to join the Powell survey, was perhaps the most eloquent profiler of the canyon country. It is unclear which of these learned gentlemen first used the singular label "Colorado Plateau." Although the label correctly reflects the great river-drainage system that bears the same name, the region is not so much a single, uplifted plateau as a mosaic of smaller ones (House 1994). The composite plateaus have shifted upward and downward along major breaks in the earth's crust, forming a sort of "grand staircase" from south to north. Each individual plateau differs in elevation from its neighbors and heads in different directions. In the remainder of this chapter, "Plateau" serves as an abbreviation for the Colorado Plateau.

The simple geographic label gives no hint of the Colorado Plateau's physical diversity or its grand, sometimes forbidding beauty. Its scenery seems unreal, constructed of cardboard, a cheap, painted imitation found on an old-time movie set. As Dutton wrote, "Surely no imagination can construct out of its own material any picture having the remotest resemblance to the Grand Canyon" (cited in McNamee 1993:111). It is a land at once ancient and new, bearing evidence of its sedimented history in layered and sculpted stone and in the homes of the many peoples who have wrested a living there, rising from and sometimes indistinguishable from the stone itself. Pipes bring water from desert reservoirs held back by dams of human-made stone, flowing to cities once thought impossible to build. "Everything is alive, dynamic with constant change. Even the stones breathe; water is electric; the air is luminous with the memory of belching volcanoes" (Waters 1984:14).

Elevations on this highest plateau in North America average around 5,000 feet above sea level. This is an inverted country, an upside-down land. Instead of mountains reaching to the sky—although it has some of those as well—the Colorado Plateau is cut by chasms that look down into eons of geologic and human history. The Grand Canyon, greatest of all canyons, effectively divides the Colorado Plateau in two. C. Gregory Crampton (1972:2), who carried out the historical-archaeological studies for the Glen Canyon Project, has called the Grand Canyon a "masterpiece of land sculpture 279 miles long." There are lesser canyons, such as the Little Colorado River canyon where the river falls in cocoa-colored torrents at Grand Falls, and hundreds of smaller, unnamed gorges.

The canyons of the Plateau are more than geological lessons. The "most colorful land in the world" (Crampton 1972:2) has defied adequate description since Europeans first took pen to paper. The Grand Canyon in particular is so far beyond knowing that "There are no concrete notions founded in experience upon which a conception of these color effects and optical delusions can be constructed and made intelligible" (Clarence Dutton, cited in McNamee 1993:109). We feel so insignificant in comparison that we may feel fright, even terror, when we look upon the Grand Canyon for the first time.

The "plateau" rubric implies a flat tableland, but great topographic relief actually characterizes the country. Mountain ranges punctuate the Plateau, and some reach extraordinary heights. The San Francisco Peaks near Flagstaff, for example, crest at 12,655 feet above sea level atop Mount Humphreys, which is the highest point in Arizona. These snow-capped peaks, so high they are above the tree line, are sacred to the Hopi people and are one of the four mountains that define the Navajo sacred landscape. Elsewhere there is desert land, ironically lying in the shadow of spectacular mountain ranges. In his summary of Glen Canyon archaeology, Jesse Jennings (1998) encapsulates these topographic zones into four major environments—lowlands or canyon country, uplands or mountains, slickrock and dunes, and the riverine zone.

How did this land come to be? Its geologic history can be read like a textbook in pages of stone (Chronic 1988:6). The sedimentary formations that constitute the land's exposed underbelly were laid down by wind and water. Shallow seas covered the region during the Permian period some 200 million years ago, much earlier during the Mississippian period, and so on back in time. The sedimentary formations were laid down in the peaceful Paleozoic era, when there was no mountain building or vulcanism, only the slow

In the Canyon

Ann Woodin, writing of Glen Canyon before it was flooded (1964:150–151):

> This is a place of texture: the slippery shining surface of the river, the sandstone walls, the feathery fringes of the willows and tamarisks, the smooth pebbles scattered on sand bars, the dried cracked mud. It is a place of color: burnished copper and gold, sand beige and pink, metallic black patches of shadow, soft greens. It is a place of form: flowing curves in slit side canyons, sweeps of domes and cave lips, pools of water in pockets, scraggly limbs of a dead sycamore. It is a place of reflections: bits of smooth water everywhere imprisoning pieces of sky, of cliff, of green leaves.

Grand Canyon from the South Rim. Photograph by Jefferson Reid.

accumulation of sediments across an almost-horizontal surface (Chronic 1988:24). Now-solidified formations such as the Kaibab and Redwall Limestone—the latter first named by Powell—these rocks contain evidence of their watery origin in the form of billions of shells and skeletons of sea creatures, most of them microscopic in size. Zion Canyon and Rainbow Bridge at Lake Powell were sculpted from this formation. Some deposits, such as the Hermit and Supai Shale in the Grand Canyon, are little more than hardened mud still retaining impressions of plant leaves and stems.

Eroded arch at Bryce Canyon National Park, Utah. PHOTOGRAPH BY JEFFERSON REID.

Other deposits—the Navajo Formation and Coconino Sandstone, for example—were deposited by wind. The Plateau was a great Sahara during Mesozoic times (age of dinosaurs), millions of years after the retreat of the Permian sea that deposited the Kaibab limestone. Dunes advanced across the older floodplains, covering and distorting the soft river muds (Chronic 1988:26). Some formations bear witness to this origin in the form of petrified dunes that in their stony ripples even hint at the direction of the prevailing wind. Navajo Sandstone is one of the greatest dune-sand formations on earth, and it is about 1,400 feet thick in the vicinity of Page. The Vermilion Cliffs, which the visitor must skirt on the way to the North Rim of the Grand Canyon, is a massive, looming composition of Navajo Sandstone. The land was shaped by and now bears the evidence of tremendous transformations of the earth's surface from sea to desert and back again through processes of mountain building and continental drift, movements of the earth's crust, and erosion on a truly planetary scale.

The Plateau has resisted the forces that built mountains and distorted the surrounding land (Chronic 1988:1). Reasons for the Plateau's geological stability are poorly understood but may relate to the region's thick crust and relatively cool character. The crust under the Plateau is thicker than under surrounding areas (Chronic 1988:13), making it more resistant to distortion. Many of its uplifted rocks still lie in the horizontal position in which they formed, the "layer cake" of geological strata undisturbed by the uplifting, stretching, compressing, and faulting that has elsewhere twisted and deformed the land.

Some plateaus are outlined by **faults** and folds, marking points where the earth's crust has shifted and bent. The Laramide **Orogeny** uplifted the entire Plateau. The uplifts taper gently on the western edges and tend to plunge abruptly on the east, forming **monoclines** or step-like bends in horizontal rock layers. Waterpocket Fold, which extends through Utah's Capitol Reef National Park and Grand Staircase–Escalante National Monument, and Echo Cliffs in northeastern Arizona are two spectacular monoclines. Between the monoclines are basins or areas of downfolded rocks.

The land has been eroded by the same processes that work on stone today—wind and water, and to a lesser extent, freeze-and-thaw cycles—such that the original layer cake has

Colored Shadows

The colored shadows that fall from the full moon are music heard and held in the feather of a red-shafted flicker. The flicker flies. A fire burns. Love is as varied as the spectrum red. Break my heart with the desert's silence. My tongue aches and swells, touches the roof of my mouth. I begin clicking my tongue like the call blackbirds make when they fear they are alone on the river.

—*Terry Tempest Williams,* Red: Passion and Patience in the Desert been altered and in some places removed entirely. Erosion has shaped the soft sandstone, cutting it like a knife in some places and in others creating soft hollows, graceful curves, hidden alcoves, and arches. Monument Valley testifies to these processes. Here the hard De Chelly Sandstone rests on the soft Organ Rock Shale. The shale forms slopes like antebellum hoop skirts at the feet of harder-rock spires that once were cliffs created during the Laramide Orogeny (Chronic 1988).

Sunset Crater. Photograph by Jefferson Reid.

The canyons were cut by the inexorable, abrasive process of rivers flowing downhill and carrying considerable gritty material—virtual liquid sandpaper. Unlike lands receiving greater rainfall, in a dry land a river's downward-cutting action takes place much faster than the erosion of the canyon sides. This is why so many of the plateau's canyons are narrow and deep. In some places, erosion has created the eerie formations called badlands—denuded, colorful hills; the weird, capped spires called hoodoos; sharp ridges and pinnacles. Arizona's Painted Desert is one of the most spectacular and intriguing of such badlands.

Here and there is evidence of an entirely different geologic process—vulcanism. Volcanic flows mark the eastern, western, and southern margins of the plateau and in some places have interrupted river channels. The San Francisco Peaks near Flagstaff are perhaps the most compelling of the volcanic mountains. The peaks represents a composite, or stratovolcano, where **magma** has burst through to the surface; it was built by alternating layers of ash and lava over a period of about 1.5 million years (Chronic 1988:27; House 1994). It last erupted about 400,000 years ago, long before people came to inhabit the Plateau. Numerous cinder cones skirt the peaks and form a 2,300-square-mile volcanic field. Sunset Crater, named in 1885 for its rosy color by Powell, is perhaps the most famous and most recent remnant of an ancient volcano. When Sunset Crater Volcano erupted around A.D. 1064, people of the prehistoric **Sinagua culture,** Ancestral Puebloan, and other people witnessed the incredible and awe-inspiring event. In fact, the eruption of Sunset Crater Volcano was originally dated by the prehistoric pottery and houses underlying the ash and cinders. Elsewhere on the Plateau, molten magma squeezed up along fissures and faults to create domed laccoliths such as Navajo Mountain (Chronic1988:27).

In Navajo County, organic-rich, dark shales leaking into porous and permeable sandstone form oil and natural gas fields. These deposits have been exploited—often illegally and

Painted Desert in Petrified Forest National Park, Arizona. Photograph by Jefferson Reid.

unethically on Navajo Nation lands—since the 1920s (Baars 1995). Because coal forms in the decaying plants of ancient swamps, the sedimentary strata of northeastern Arizona also yield this mineral. Most coal occurs within structural basins, such as the San Juan Basin, where Cretaceous rocks have not been removed by erosion. The extensive coal deposit on Black Mesa southwest of Monument Valley was used by the prehistoric Hopi to fire their brilliant yellow ware pottery and today is strip-mined and transported to the Navajo Generating Station at Page. Although a source of mineral royalty revenue to the Navajo Nation, coal mining and use on the Plateau have created serious environmental concerns and cultural controversies (Baars 1995).

Monument Valley. PHOTOGRAPH BY JEFFERSON REID.

Water

The mighty Colorado River dominates the hydrology of the Colorado Plateau, but other watercourses are few. Much of this land yields so little water that it even gave a name to one of its prehistoric native cultures. Spanish explorers traveled from Hopi country to the San Francisco Peaks, which they called Sierra Sin Agua, or mountains without water—foreshadowing the label given to the Sinagua inhabitants of the San Francisco volcanic fields and the Verde Valley. Writer, environmentalist, and iconoclast Edward Abbey (1968:171) wrote of the paradox of water on the plateau. "It is a strange fact that in the canyon country the closer you get to the river which is the living artery of the entire area, the drier, more barren, less habitable the land becomes." Watercourses that could provide irrigation water are scarce and dry during much of the year, containing water only after summer storms or springmelt.

The Little Colorado River is one of the larger streams on the plateau. Rising in the White Mountains in Arizona's mountain Transition Zone, it flows north and west to join the Colorado near the Grand Canyon. In spring and late summer, the Little Colorado pours over a cliff in a waterfall of liquid mud at Grand Falls. The falls are higher than Niagara Falls and at times carry more water. Although the waters of the Little Colorado River can be harnessed for farming, it is a singularly risky business, as Mormon settlers discovered in the nineteenth century.

Much of the Plateau's water comes from springs and seeps, which are distinguished by rate of flow. A spring produces a liter of water in less than a minute, whereas a seep takes longer, sometimes days, to produce that much water (Childs 2000:87). "Spring lines" along the cliffs where porous sandstone meets impermeable shale are green, living seams drinking from the groundwater seeping to the surface. Seepage may enlarge the spring-line alcove, and pools may develop below dripping springs. Sometimes spring lines flower into virtual hanging gardens on the steep rock faces. Maidenhair ferns, moss, and monkey flower flourish at such rare water sources. Those who are thirsty must be careful, however, for some springs and seeps are poisoned water,

Grand Falls of the Little Colorado River. PHOTOGRAPH BY JEFFERSON REID.

bitter and alkaline, sometimes stinking of brimstone and laced with arsenic.

Each day, about 400 million gallons of water spill from rocks into the Grand Canyon. Different sources of springwater define the North and South Rims of the Grand Canyon (Childs 2000:97, 99). On the north, where large underground volumes are flushed out of the Kaibab Plateau, the taste of springs does not alter much. The angles of the rock formations send water hurtling rapidly, literally exploding from the faces of cliffs. It is young water, with few minerals. On the south, water tastes different at almost every canyon. This water is old, high in mineral content, and emerges from the rock slowly. Most of the water used by people in the Grand Canyon comes from Roaring Springs in the main canyon (Childs 2000:99).

Water hides in many places. Water pockets—secret places where the stone has been hollowed to hold water—are found scattered across expanses of sandstone. The older a water pocket is, the deeper it becomes, as the water it holds further erodes the soft sandstone (Childs 2000:49). Some water pockets are tiny, and others are big enough to swim in. Each of these watering places is a miniature ecosystem teeming with life: crustaceans called ostracods the size of dill seeds; water fleas of the genus *Daphnia;* fairy shrimp *(Chirocephalus salinus);* the crustacean species *Triops,* "a creature an inch or so long, looking like a cross between a horseshoe crab, a trilobite, and a catfish. It is the oldest living animal on the planet, perfectly matching fossils from 180 million years ago, each part of its anatomy unchanged since then" (Childs 2000:47). Dragonflies and other insects swoop and dart over the water; toads and frogs find a home, and larger creatures are drawn to the hidden source of life.

Rivers, springs, seeps, and water pockets are precious resources in a land with little water, and humans have learned to recognize water by using all of the senses. The signal marker of water is often the trembling green of cottonwoods. The rushing, bubbling, or tinkling sound of water running over stone is unmistakable. Like wildlife drawn to springs, it is possible to smell water, even if only by the herbal scent of the plants that grow beside it. Like the ancients before them, modern, educated, literate travelers have been awed by the divinity of springs—"the leafy god, the desert's liquid eye" (Abbey 1968:176). It is little wonder that springs were holy places imbued with legends. Today, offerings are still left at springs. One spring near Flagstaff is surrounded by bushes decorated with loops of bright ribbon and strings of white shell beads, even though the water is caught in a pipe and cannot be seen, heard, or tasted. The spring and its spirits remain holy and respected.

Hopi Respect for Water

"Every drop of water was precious, and there was never enough," writes Helen Sekaquaptewa, a Hopi who grew up at the Third Mesa village of Oraibi. "From infancy we were taught to drink sparingly; even then, there were times when we were always thirsty. You never asked for a drink when visiting a neighbor's house but went home to drink from your own water. . . . There was concern about the future of the village. Were the water supply to diminish and the population increase, what would become of the people?" (Sekaquaptewa 1969:21–22).

Spring pool at Keyhole Sink near Flagstaff, Arizona. Note petroglyphs on rock. PHOTOGRAPH BY STEPHANIE WHITTLESEY.

Petroglyphs mark water at Keyhole Sink. PHOTOGRAPH BY STEPHANIE WHITTLESEY.

Lockett Meadow and lake on the slopes of the San Francisco Peaks. PHOTOGRAPH BY STEPHANIE WHITTLESEY.

Water can also inspire fear. There are two easy ways to die in desert lands, Childs (2000) tells us: thirst and drowning. This is especially true of the canyon country. Floods such as those which carved the canyons still pour down in dangerous torrents. Slot canyons hold enormous appeal. In Antelope Canyon, mysterious, swirling rock faces molded by water fashion narrow passageways and larger rooms. Light falls like water from above, illuminating secret chambers. The beauty of such seductive, secret places can be fatal. Although the Navajo Nation requires tourists to be accompanied by Navajo guides, they have been swept away and drowned in flash floods that cannot be anticipated or even heard as they descend. Perhaps for this reason, the Havasupai avoid the interior depths of the canyon they inhabit. They believe that the dead reside in the lower gorges, and as Childs (2000:249) has pointed out, they are probably right.

Death by Drowning

Flash floods can devastate the canyon country of the Colorado Plateau, as Craig Childs (2000:217) has described. One flood in Havasu Canyon happened so quickly, he has told us, that a helicopter was needed to fly ahead of the flood and warn hikers to seek high ground away from this event of "focused rage." At the Colorado River, the flood pounded into rafting equipment. "Two fully loaded twenty-two-foot snout boats, three eighteen-foot Canyon rafts, and several other large boats were hurled end over end. Deck canoes, kayaks, and trees blew out like confetti. Every rope, metal D-ring, and chock holding the boats to the rock snapped."

Childs (2000:217) goes on to write that two days after the Havasu flood, twelve people were struck by a flash flood in Antelope Canyon. Only one person, the hiking guide, survived. "He was thrown onto a ledge, mud packed beneath his eyelids, completely naked. When he was found, he was delirious, asking over and over why he had lived and the others had not." (Childs 2000:217). The other eleven hikers drowned, and the bodies of the last two were never found.

Climate and Vegetation

The Plateau's climate varies as much as its topography. Precipitation averages little more than 10 inches a year—surprisingly, about the same as Tucson. The great barrier of California's Sierra Nevada prevents moist Pacific Ocean air from reaching the Plateau during much of the year. Precipitation is biseasonal, falling in summer when moist air comes from the south and in winter, when it arrives from the northeast. More precipitation occurs at higher elevations where snow falls regularly, sometimes accumulating in great drifts. At 7,000 feet in Flagstaff, for example, the average is some 100 inches—about the same as Buffalo, New York—and snow has been recorded in all months of the year (once, so the story goes, forcing cancellation of the annual Fourth of July parade). At the higher elevations, daytime temperatures seldom exceed 90 degrees Fahrenheit in summer, and winter temperatures can fall into single digits overnight.

Some parts of the Plateau are extremely hot and dry, especially the valleys in the lees of the great uplifts. At lower elevations, desert temperatures of 100 degrees Fahrenheit and more prevail, particularly in the canyon bottoms; temperatures of more than 120 degrees Fahrenheit have been recorded at Phantom Ranch in the bottom of the

Grand Canyon. Winters are correspondingly warmer than at higher elevations, and snow almost never falls.

Relentless winds blow, irritating the Plateau's human inhabitants and further drying the climate. Spring is especially windy, and the combination of wind, mud generated by melting snow, and the remnants of winter snow and ice can make this season uncomfortable.

Elevational differences and variability in rainfall support diverse vegetation. In much of the region, the combination of high elevation and little precipitation creates a bleak landscape covered by tough, bunching grasses and little else. Although there are many different ecological zones, more richly vegetated areas tend to be limited in distribution and extent. Much of the Plateau is covered with juniper and piñon; brushy growths of cliff rose, ephedra or Mormon tea, evergreen oaks, mountain mahogany, and spiny yucca clothe the rocky slopes and canyons. The flatter basins, interrupted by eroded pinnacles and mesas, are sparsely vegetated and primarily support Navajo sheep and goats. Cottonwoods and willows line the banks of washes and secondary streams. Dense growth of aspen and conifers—pine, spruce, fir—carpets the mountain slopes. Alpine meadows and arctic vegetation characterize the highest elevations. The trees become thin and stunted, eventually dropping out altogether on Mount Humphreys.

Trees turned to stone at Petrified Forest National Park, Arizona. Photograph by Jefferson Reid.

The deeper canyons are not unlike southern Arizona's "sky islands," although inverted. They provide distinctive and varied kinds of plant and animal life. Naturalists are fond of using the Grand Canyon as a measure of the remarkable life-zone changes that the variability in elevation creates. The canyon illustrates well why the Plateau teems with such diverse plant and animal life. The Grand Canyon "is the most revealing single page of earth's history anywhere open on the face of the globe" (Krutch 1989:17). Naturalist Joseph Wood Krutch tells us that to go down 800 feet in the canyon is equivalent to traveling southward nearly 500 land miles. As one hikes down into the canyon, it becomes noticeably warmer. In summer, the canyon bottom about a mile below the rim is tropically hot, and desert vegetation prevails. The Plateau's cactus cannot match the variety and abundance of the desert, however.

The Land No One Knew

The Colorado Plateau has always been remote, inhospitable to travel, and a formidable obstacle to settlement. It is a land best traversed on foot or on the backs of mules or horses. Modern forms of transportation—wagons, automobiles, and the railroad—have fared poorly when pitted against the Plateau's chasms. We can see this in the travails of Mormon pioneers. In 1879, families from southwestern Utah were called to settle along the San Juan River. The established routes necessitated detours to the north or south, both fraught with hazards. The Mormons chose to take the direct route straight through the canyonlands.

Riding the Plateau on Horseback

Mary-Russell Ferrell Colton was the talented, artist wife of Harold S. Colton. Together they founded the Museum of Northern Arizona, one of three private archaeological research institutions in Arizona. Before they moved permanently to Flagstaff, the Coltons spent summers traveling in the Colorado Plateau region, visiting archaeological sites and Indian villages. Consider a trip the Coltons took in 1913. From Canyon de Chelly, which the Coltons explored on horseback, they traveled to the Hubbell trading post at Ganado in northeastern Arizona where they camped for several days. From there the Coltons rode to the Hopi mesas and then returned to Gallup. At Gallup they boarded a train for the Grand Canyon. Mary-Russell wrote of these experiences to her mother, a passage that hints at her own stamina as well as the tremendous energy traveling at that time required. This passage is from Richard and Sherry Mangum's *One Woman's West: The Life of Mary-Russell Ferrell Colton* (1997:30):

> Riding for a month has caused me to lose flesh, & when I return you will be surprised to find that you have a hipless daughter. It takes eight pins to hold me together now & I feel myself rapidly coming to "galluses" for my skirts hang in great pleats about me. . . . I am solid muscle from head to heel & have been enjoying good health all summer. I can be in the saddle from dawn to dark, ride forty-five miles a day, without feeling tired.

Historical Lee's Ferry. PHOTOGRAPH COURTESY ARIZONA HISTORICAL SOCIETY, TUCSON (AHS ACCESSION NO. PC 182, BOX 1, F.12 A).

To cross the Colorado River in Glen Canyon, the party enlarged a crack in the canyon wall with dynamite, picks, and hammers. They picked a shelf into the rock wall wide enough for the inside wheels of a wagon. Then they literally tacked a "road" built of log stringers, brush, and poles onto the side of the canyon—a cantilevered, precarious support clinging to the cliff face. The wagons descended more than a thousand feet to the river in less than three-quarters of a mile, their speed checked by teams of men with ropes. At the river, the Mormons built an oar-powered ferry to cross the river two wagons at a time. It took the settlers six weeks to cross the relatively insignificant distance from rim to canyon bottom—and then they had to repeat the task to climb up the other side. The Hole-in-the-Rock wrought by the Mormon party can still be seen today rising above the waters of Lake Powell.

In the twentieth century, automobiles fared little better in the sandy washes—perhaps even worse. Modern

Crossing the Washes

In 1923, Harold Colton and Frank Baxter of the Museum of Northern Arizona published a guidebook for the adventurous motorist that included the following instructions.

(1) A car should be equipped with (a) chains, (b) a good jack, (c) a good pump, (d) a shovel, (e) a small axe or hatchet, (f) a stout tow line, (g) cans of gas, oil and water.

(2) If stuck in heavy dry sand, as in some dry washes, do not try to drive the car through with jerks, as a broken axle or ring gear may result. . . .

(3) When a sandy wash in the Hopi Reservation is running, use particular caution. (a) if possible, get local advice and aid before attempting to cross; it may save your car. . . . It is sometimes a wise precaution to employ Indians with a team to tow the car across. . . (b) If local advice is unobtainable, wade across, testing for holes and quicksand. (c) Do not attempt to cross if the water is over the hubs of the car. (d) If the banks are quakey but the bottom hard, cut brush may make the banks passable. . . . If a car stops in running water on a sandy bottom, it begins to sink at once. The authors have known cars to sink out of sight.

(4) If stuck in a muddy chuck hole or small arroyo, do not try to get out by filling the hole with rocks and sticks and jerking the motor. On the other hand, (a) if possible, dig a trench draining the hole, (b) jack up the car using the floor boards. . . (c) put on chains. . . . It is better to spend twenty minutes in preparatory work than to wait several days for a new part.

archaeologists, geologists, explorers, and engineers found one of the best ways of crossing the canyons to be the oldest. Many times they enlarged and used the precarious handholds and footholds that the ancient peoples had carved centuries earlier.

A Bureau of Reclamation geological report on the Glen Canyon region gave good reasons why the land was uninhabited except for a few Navajo families. "Travel over land is difficult and slow," the report read. "Water is scarce and only a very scant desert growth, developed on the scattered patches of blowsand and alluvium, covers the otherwise continuous rock exposure. The entire area is a vast expanse of wasteland" (cited in Martin 1999:83).

Music Temple

Naturalist Ann Woodin, her herpetologist husband, and several colleagues made a trip down the Colorado River through Glen Canyon before it was flooded by the waters of Lake Powell. She wrote of this trip (Woodin 1964:156):

> Across the river is Music Temple, an enormous amphitheater carved out of the sandstone that magnifies and nourishes sound. Chiseled in the cliff one can read the name POWELL. In August of 1869 this indomitable one-armed geologist-explorer with a party of eight others made the first trip down the Colorado through the Grand Canyon, a feat of endurance and courage that ranks with the greatest.

The rock formation for which Mexican Hat was named. Photograph by Jefferson Reid.

The Colorado Plateau changes people. Values shift, and survival value dictates whether something is important or not. Trivial worries pale against life-or-death contests with the elements and the land's creatures. A profound change affects the newcomer to the desert Southwest, and many writers have tried to capture this phenomenon. "A perpetual glamour envelops the landscape," Dutton wrote (cited in McNamee 1993:111). Some newcomers, finding themselves locked in battle with the land, attempted to apply notions that worked in other lands to the new country—and failing, they grew to hate the land. Others learned to accept the land on its own terms, with affection and respect. Novelist Willa Cather captures the essence of this transformation. In her novel, *The Song of the Lark* (Cather 1915:299–300), one of her characters, summering in Walnut Canyon near Flagstaff, muses:

> All her life she had been hurrying and sputtering, as if she had been born behind time and had been trying to catch up. Now, she reflected . . . it was as if she were waiting for something to catch up with her. She had got to a place where she was out of the stream of meaningless activity and undirected effort. . . . And now her power to think seemed converted into a power of sustained sensation. She could become a mere receptacle for heat, or become a color, like the bright lizards that darted about on the hot stones outside her door; or she could become a continuous repetition of sound, like the cicadas.

People of the Plateau

Many different people have lived on the Colorado Plateau throughout the centuries, despite its unforgiving nature. They developed innovative means to use its scarce water and often sparse resources in forging a successful way of life. Intensive human occupation began in Archaic times, although even earlier, **Paleoindians** had hunted and sojourned there briefly. The earliest-documented expression of an Archaic lifeway anywhere on the Colorado Plateau was found in Glen Canyon (Geib 1996b). Settlement progressed to the golden era of the Anasazi or Ancestral Pueblo people, who dominated the plateau country in prehistoric times and mastered its environmental challenges. Later, people who spoke Numic languages, such as the Southern Paiute and Southern Ute, moved into the region. Yuman-speaking Havasupai and Hualapai came to live in the Grand Canyon region, and the Athapaskan-speaking Navajo moved from central Canada to occupy northeastern Arizona alongside the Hopi. In historical times, people of diverse ethnic groups and religious affinities staked new claims to the old land. We will look more closely at three of these groups—ancient puebloans, Hopi, and Navajo.

Ancestral Pueblo People (Anasazi) of Northeastern Arizona

The Anasazi occupied a vast stretch of the Colorado Plateau in the Four Corners region and northern Nevada. The label "Anasazi" is controversial and glosses over a great deal of linguistic and ethnic diversity that no doubt characterized them (as well as other prehistoric folk of the Southwest, such as the Hohokam and **Mogollon cultures**). Moreover, ethnic diversity is a difficult subject for archaeologists, who cannot reconstruct ancient languages and must rely on the artifacts that are preserved in sites to differentiate among ancient cultures. The reader should keep in mind that we are discussing cultural generalities and that reality was much more complicated.

Archaeologists group the prehistoric culture into Eastern and Western Anasazi, a division corresponding broadly with the distinction between today's Eastern and Western **Pueblo** peoples. The Western Anasazi (Hisatsinom) lived in northeastern Arizona and southeastern Utah. Some of the most spectacular of their homes are found in Canyon de Chelly and Navajo National Monument in northeastern Arizona. Canyon de Chelly is a name of Spanish derivation. The Hopi name is Koyongtupa, meaning "turkey canyon." Many ruins are found in the canyon bottom and tucked into alcoves in the cliff faces. Navajo National Monument contains two spectacular cliff ruins, which despite their Navajo names are not Navajo in origin: Betatakin, called Kawestima by the Hopi, and Keet Siel, or Talastima in Hopi.

Keet Siel Cliff Ruin. PHOTOGRAPH BY JEFFERSON REID

The Eastern Anasazi dwelled in northern New Mexico and southern Colorado. Their most famous dwelling places are found in Mesa Verde National Park in Colorado and Chaco Culture National Historic Park and Aztec Ruins National Monument in New Mexico. It is difficult to discuss the Anasazi of northeastern Arizona without bringing in Chaco culture, but this topic is too complicated for our purposes here. Suffice it to say that Chaco culture was

Cliff Palace, Mesa Verde National Park. PHOTOGRAPH BY JEFFERSON REID.

characterized by an expansion into areas that were far from Chaco Canyon, including Mesa Verde and the San Juan River drainage. Chacoan sites outside of the canyon, called outliers, are found in many areas. One of the most famous is Aztec Ruins National Monument located near Farmington, New Mexico. Several outliers are found in northeastern Arizona; some archaeologists think that Wupatki Pueblo, one of the many ruins in Wupatki National Monument, was not built by the Sinagua but was an outpost constructed by people of Chaco Canyon. Archaeologists further subdivide Western and Eastern Anasazi into several distinct, regional branches based on lifeways and material culture. In this chapter, we restrict our stories to the Western Anasazi.

Much is known about these ancient puebloans. The first professional archaeologists, including famous scholars of the American Southwest such as A. V. Kidder, did pioneering work at cliff sites of the Four Corners region. For years thereafter, the region was the locale of intensive excavation. In addition to its wonderful climate and inspiring sites, the excellent preservation, tree-ring-dateable wood, and living Pueblo peoples made the Colorado Plateau an archaeological paradise.

The prehistoric people of the Plateau were master farmers who did much more than eke out a bare existence

Labeling Ancient Peoples

The ancient people of the Southwest that archaeologists study left no written records. We do not know what languages they spoke or what they called themselves in their native tongue. Archaeological cultures have therefore been labeled by archaeologists, and these labels have been a source of controversy. The ancient people of the Colorado Plateau were originally called the Anasazi, which is a Navajo word usually translated as "enemy ancestor." Many native peoples consider this term offensive, because the pueblo sites were not occupied by Navajo people, and it is equivalent to calling one's own forebears "ancient enemies."

There is no easy solution to this problem. Scholars such as Walters and Rogers (2001) have pointed out that the word Anasazi is not Navajo, but an English word with English meanings. Although derived from a Navajo word, there are no implications for the Navajo in any of the standard usages of the word Anasazi. A kinder translation of the word would be "those non-Navajos who lived beside the Navajos but not among them many generations ago," but even that would be controversial (Walters and Rogers 2001:324).

The Hopi call the prehistoric people of the Four Corners region the Hisatsinom, a word literally translating as "people of long ago" and meaning "ancestral." Other Puebloan groups speaking different languages have objected to Hisatsinom. Many substitute the more politically appropriate label "Ancestral Puebloan people" for Anasazi, and this term has been accepted by the National Park Service.

Ancestral Pueblo is also a problematic label, in that other prehistoric peoples such as the Mogollon contributed to the biological and cultural heritage of living Pueblo people along with the Anasazi or Hisatsinom. Walters and Rogers (2001:323) have pointed out that ancient pueblo peoples also contributed to the gene pool of present-day Navajo people.

It is helpful to remember that archaeologists once invested tremendous energy in classifying ancient cultures and that the discipline is burdened with jargon and labels. Archaeologists use standard terms to communicate among themselves and with the public. Anasazi is an accepted archaeological term like Basket Maker or Mogollon, and most nonarchaeologists recognize the word Anasazi and know what it means.

Some Indian people believe that there are more important issues affecting relationships between Native Americans and non-Indians than how ancient cultures are labeled (Ellis 1997:15). Certainly one task for the future is to develop archaeological terms that everyone can use without offense and that are scientifically accurate as well.

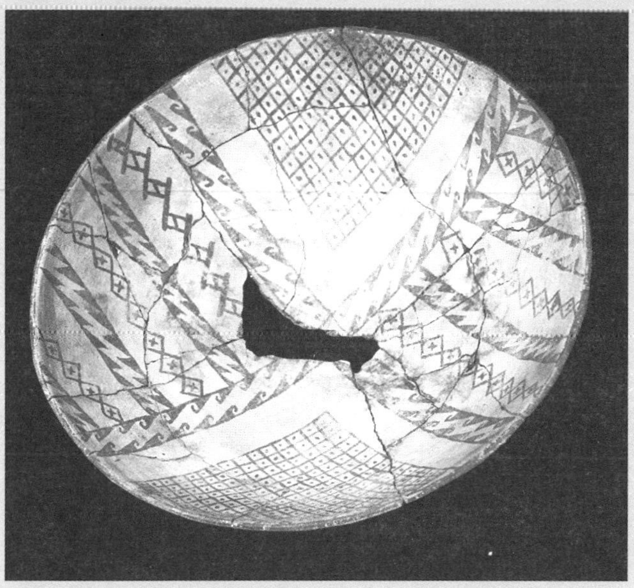

Black-on-white bowl. Photograph courtesy U.S. Bureau of Reclamation.

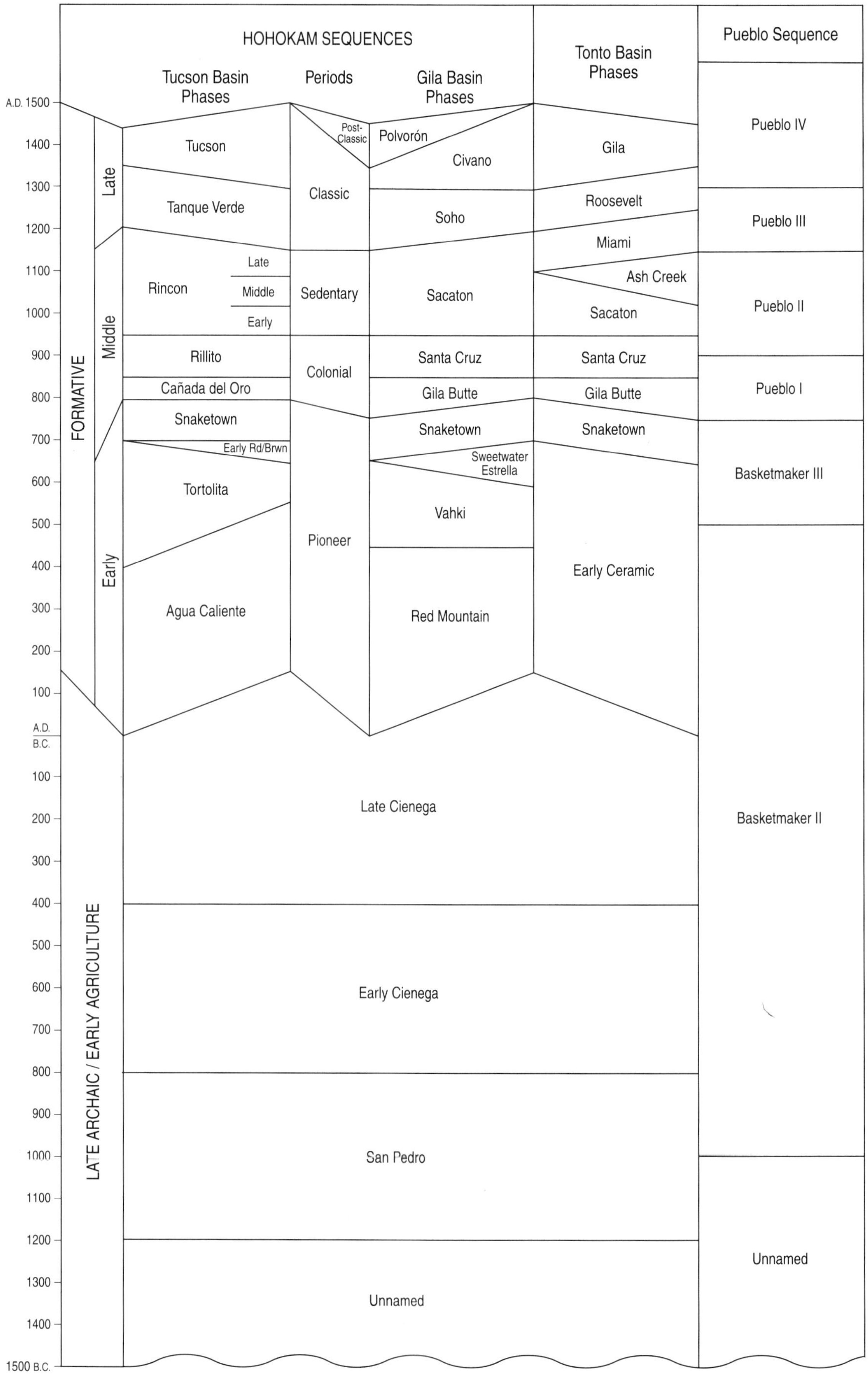

Comparison of chronologies for Hohokam, Tonto Basin Salado, and Puebloans of the Colorado Plateau.

in the slickrock canyons and juniper-covered mesas. Their farming technology was highly specialized for the unique conditions of the Plateau environment, and on this base the people built a culture rich in symbolism, oral history, religious meaning, and aesthetic arts that has endured to this day (Reid and Whittlesey 1997).

The earliest people were called the Basket Makers because, like other early farming peoples of the Southwest during the Archaic period, they did not make pottery. Many early Basket Maker sites are located in dry caves that preserved perishable materials, including textiles, cordage, human hair, wooden objects, and a variety of baskets, giving archaeologists a richly detailed picture of their lives. Later Basket Maker people depended heavily on corn agriculture and lived in pit-house villages located in sheltered caves or on the mesa tops. It is unclear whether the Basket Makers were descended from local people. Archaeologist R. G. Matson (1991) thinks that **Cochise culture** people from southern Arizona migrated northward to the Plateau and brought corn agriculture with them. By late Basket Maker II times (500 B.C.–A.D. 600), the people had begun to make gray-brown pottery. Most houses were what archaeologists call true pit houses, structures using a relatively deep excavation as the lower portion of the house walls and placing the wall-support posts on the exterior rather than inside the house pit. In Basket Maker III times (A.D. 600–800), the people began to paint gray designs on gray **plain ware pottery** made with the **coil-and-scrape technique** and covered some pots with **fugitive** red **pigment.**

Multiple ethnic groups lived in northeastern Arizona in Basket Maker and early Pueblo times. On the basis of basketry construction and rock-art styles, archaeologist Phil Geib (1996b) concluded that the Colorado River represented a boundary between groups living in the Glen Canyon area. North of the river, he believes, the population was nascent Fremont rather than Anasazi, who lived south of the river. The former culture, first named by archaeologists working along the Fremont River in south-central Utah, is an ambiguous and poorly understood cultural manifestation found in the Great Basin between A.D. 500 and 1350. Archaeologists believe that the Fremont peoples did not take up farming until long after populations living to the south had begun growing cultivated crops—probably not until the beginning of the Christian era—and farming was a notion borrowed from other peoples (Bischoff and others 2000). The Fremont are perhaps best known for their unique style of rock art. Competition among the Fremont, Basket Maker, and other cultural groups for scarce resources may have spurred the transition to farming in the Glen Canyon region.

The Horned Gods

Edward Abbey expresses the awe many people experience when they view petroglyphs, particularly the impressive figures that have been attributed to the Fremont culture of southern Utah.

> While many of the pictures may have had for their makers a religious or ceremonial significance, others look like apparitions out of bad dreams. In this category belong the semihuman and superhuman beings with horned heads, immensely broad shoulders, short limbs and massive bodies that taper down to attenuated legs. Some of them have no legs at all, but seem to rise ghostlike out of nothing, floating on air. These are sinister and supernatural figures, gods from the underworld perhaps, who hover in space, or dance, or stand solidly planted on two feet carrying weapons–a club or sword. Most are faceless but some stare back at you with large, hollow, disquieting eyes. Demonic shapes, they might have meant protection and benevolence to their creators and a threat to strangers:
>
> Beware, traveler. You are approaching the land of the horned gods.
>
> —Edward Abbey, *Desert Solitaire*

Black-on-white lobed pitcher and jar. PHOTOGRAPH COURTESY U.S. BUREAU OF RECLAMATION. BOB KNOTTS, PHOTOGRAPHER.

A transitional time between Basket Maker and Pueblo followed, and by A.D. 800, the Anasazi were living in small, aboveground **pueblos** built of masonry blocks. They began to make painted, black-on-white **bichrome** pottery and continued to use gray pottery for cooking and storage. Pueblos tended to be linear or U-shaped in layout, and **jacal** rooms were often combined with masonry rooms. Circular,

Artist's conception of Fremont petroglyphs. DRAWING BY LOIS KAIN.

As master dry farmers, the ancient puebloans cultivated corn, cotton, beans, and squash using rainfall alone, supplemented wherever possible with simple diversion features. Diverse wild-plant and animal resources could be found in the canyons, on mountain slopes, and on mesa tops. The people collected and ate cactus and yucca fruit, grass seeds, piñon nuts, juniper berries, grapes, cattail, and green weedy plants—essentially any available, edible plant resource. They hunted deer, antelope, rabbits, and other game and raised turkeys. Turkeys were one of only two domesticated animals in the Southwest; the other was the dog, serving as best friend, garbage disposal, and alarm system. The birds were seldom eaten but were raised for their downy feathers. Woven, soft feather blankets were traded widely, but we do not know what the ancient puebloans received in return.

underground **kivas** were usually located in front of the living and storage rooms. Small pueblos were scattered wherever conditions made farming possible. There were a few larger villages and some with big or **great kivas.** Toward the end of this time, influences from Chaco Canyon began to appear in northeastern Arizona.

Between A.D. 1150 and 1300, villages had grown much larger, evolving into compact pueblos with two or more stories and rooms entered through roof hatchways. This time was marked by the collapse of Chaco culture in Chaco Canyon and reorganization of their settlements elsewhere on the Colorado Plateau. A warmer and drier climate may have been responsible. The people managed to get along well under comparatively crowded conditions, and dry-farming techniques had been perfected. The spectacular **cliff dwellings** that can be visited in Canyon de Chelly and Navajo National Monument were built during this time. Archaeological lore suggests that the spectacular cliff dwellings were built in the canyons for security and defense. Perhaps it was fear that kept such communities together, as Abbey (1968:178) speculated:

> Every child . . . would have learned, along with his language and games, the legends of old battles and massacres, flights and migrations. He would be taught that the danger of attack was always present, that in any hour of the day or night, from up or down the canyon or over the rim, the Enemy might appear—cruel, devious, hungry, terrible.

The ancient puebloans also built less spectacular hamlets in the smaller side canyons and on the mesa tops. Every spring and stream would have a community nearby, raised from the rock like plants from water.

In the latter part of the A.D. 1200s, environmental conditions deteriorated in some parts of the Plateau. The time of the worst conditions has been labeled the Great Drought, and it lasted from A.D. 1276 to 1299 in some areas. Drought, erosion, and lowered water tables made farming difficult and risky. Although not all archaeologists agree that drought drove people away, it is undeniable that there were widespread population movements at that time. It is difficult to believe that, faced with worsening environmental conditions, the people would not have sought better places, whether on the Plateau or in more distant areas (Reid and Whittlesey 1997). We know that Anasazi people from northeastern Arizona abandoned their

Tusayan Ruin

Tusayan Ruin is a delightful, masonry room-block village on the South Rim of the Grand Canyon within Grand Canyon National Park. The little ruin was excavated in 1930 by Emil W. Haury of the Gila Pueblo Archaeological Foundation as his first project for that institution. The ruin consists of a U-shaped pueblo of four or five living rooms, associated store rooms, and two circular kivas. A small museum offers a glimpse of lifeways during Pueblo III times (Reid and Whittlesey 1997:191).

homes to live among the Mogollon people of the Point of Pines region in east-central Arizona, a trek of some 240 miles (Haury 1958). From there, they traveled another 100 miles to the south toward present-day Safford in southeastern Arizona (Woodson 1995), building settlements along the San Pedro River valley as they went (Di Peso 1958). Some people evidently also traveled to the Tonto Basin of central Arizona.

The people had abandoned much of the plateau by A.D. 1300, concentrating in a few especially favorable places. Large villages were built at the Hopi mesas and along the Little Colorado River in the Winslow area. Cotton grown on the river's floodplain was an important commercial commodity. The **katsina** cult emerged, and the Hopi way began to consolidate in accord with the prophecies embodied in Hopi migration legends. This era ended when Spanish explorers discovered the Hopi pueblos in 1540.

Hopi pueblo and woman. Photograph courtesy Arizona Historical Society, Tucson (AHS Accession No. PC 196, Box 57, F. 891).

Today's Native Peoples

Although they live side by side, and the small Hopi reservation is completely surrounded by the larger Navajo Nation, the language, lifeways, and history of these peoples could not be more different. The Hopi are the probable descendants of the prehistoric puebloan peoples who occupied northeastern Arizona and whom they call Hisatsinom, whereas most scholars believe that the Navajo are relative newcomers. Next, we will look at the lifeways and histories of these contemporary residents of the Colorado Plateau.

Hopi Anthropologists group the Hopi with Zuni, Acoma, and Laguna as the Western Pueblos on the basis of broad cultural similarities, although languages differ. Hopi is part of the large Uto-Aztecan language group that includes such diverse languages as Nahuatl, Shoshone, and Piman. Today the Hopi occupy three mesas on the fringes of Black Mesa, named from east to west First, Second, and Third Mesa. First Mesa includes Hano, a Tewa-speaking community assimilated into the Hopi way, Sichomovi, and the ancient village of Walpi. Shungopavi, Mishongnovi, and Sipaulovi are on Second Mesa. On Third Mesa are Hotevilla, Kykotsmovi ("K Town" or New Oraibi), Bacabi, and Oraibi. The modern Hopi reservation centers on these mesas. Moenkopi near Tuba City is an outpost community, a small island of Hopi people in Navajo Nation land. Anthropologist John Connelly (1979) has said that it is misleading to speak of Hopi as a "tribe." Traditionally, each village was an independent entity, with its own dialect, political organization, and economic foundation. The villages on a mesa were more closely linked than those on different mesas, however. There was no political mechanism unifying the Hopi as a tribe (Griffin-Pierce 2000:93).

The Hopi have largely adopted modern construction methods and materials, but many buildings built in the ancient way—rectangular, sandstone blocks stacked together with mud mortar and chinking—are still occupied. Hopi villages look strikingly like those of the ancestors and seem to grow out of the rock itself. Room blocks conforming to the shape of the mesa tops are built around open plaza areas where the impressive *katsina* dances take place. Hopi kivas are underground and rectangular; ladders reaching toward the sky define their locations. Walking through a Hopi village today is like being transported back in time. The present fades; the weight of time and history are palpable. To the Hopi, these mesas always have been and will always be their home.

Until recent times, the Hopi lifeway was predicated on dry farming, and like the ancient puebloans, they perfected techniques for making the high, arid land yield abundantly. Fields were located along washes below the mesas, and each village had its own land. The richly textured Hopi religious life focuses on bringing rain to the fields and peace to the people. The *katsinam* are central to spiritual life and bring clouds and rain. These ancestral spirits spend half the year with the Hopi and the other half in the subterranean world.

Gray Mesas, Gray Pueblos

Some people are repelled rather than attracted by the Southwest. The novelist D. H. Lawrence was one. Although dismal, his description of the Hopi country conveys a sense of blended human and natural landscapes and the vast emptiness and silence of the Colorado Plateau. In his book, *Mornings in Mexico* (1982:141–142), he wrote that the Hopi reservation

> consists of a square track of greyish, unappetising desert, out of which rise three tall arid mesas, broken off in ragged, pallid rock. On the top of the mesas perch the ragged, broken, greyish pueblos, identical with the mesas on which they stand.
>
> The nearest village, Walpi, stands in half-ruin high, high on a narrow rock-top where no leaf of life ever was tender. It is all dry, utterly grey, utterly pallid, stone and dust. . . . Below it all the stark light of the dry Arizona sun. . . .
>
> Odd patches of corn blew in the strong desert wind, like dark-green women with fringed shawls blowing and fluttering, not far from the foot of the great, grey, up-piled mesa.

Pueblo of Old Oraibi. PHOTOGRAPH COURTESY ARIZONA HISTORICAL SOCIETY, TUCSON (AHS ACCESSION NO. PC 196, BOX 37, F. 602, NO. 12).

Kinship was vital to traditional Hopi life, and a system of ranked lineages and clans functioned to regulate marriage, religious life, and economic activities. In this matrilineal society, women owned the fields, houses, and other property. Weaving of cotton textiles was an important craft, supplemented in early historical times by silversmithing, pottery making, and crafting of **kachina dolls**. Today's kachinas vary—old-style, blocky figures; artistically carved and painted figures; tall, graceful sculptures that follow the curved form of the cottonwood root. Painted Hopi pottery was revived largely by Jesse Walter Fewkes's excavation of Sitkyatki Pueblo in the late 1800s. The most famous Hopi potter is Nampeyo, a Hopi-Tewa woman from the village of Hano on First Mesa who incorporated ancient Sitkyatki designs into her pottery. Women also produced tightly woven, colorful plaques and shallow baskets decorated with vegetal dyes. Baskets are still used in ceremonies and are the centerpiece of the Basket Dance.

The ceremonial calendar is organized around solar events that divide the year into summer and winter seasons, and most religious events are conducted by men's societies. These societies crosscut kinship groups, although clans in theory "own" a particular ceremony. Ceremonies include private performances in the kivas and one or two days of public dances held in the plazas. Distribution of food and other gifts and interludes during which clowns perform punctuate the public performances.

The Hopi language survives despite pressure to speak English. Emory Sekaquaptewa, a Hopi linguist and professor at the University of Arizona, created a monumental Hopi dictionary, which, along with associated teaching programs in the schools, has been his lifelong project.

Navajo Unlike the Hopi farmers, the Navajo in historical times were a pastoral people who made their living by herding sheep and goats, weaving, and carrying out some farming. Called in their own language Diné (also spelled Dineh), meaning "the people," the Navajo are linguistically and culturally distinct from other native peoples of the U.S. Southwest except their close relatives, the Apache peoples. Today the Navajo are the most populous Indian nation in the Southwest and one of the largest tribes in the United

Navajo man on horseback. Photograph courtesy Arizona Historical Society, Tucson (AHS Accession No. 81711).

States. The Navajo speak a southern Athapaskan language, one of a large linguistic group including the related Apache languages. Most scholars believe that the Navajo and Apache peoples moved southward from subarctic, central Canada possibly as late as the A.D. 1500s, perhaps earlier, but definitely after the ancient puebloans had abandoned the Four Corners region. Coming into contact with the modern Pueblo peoples of New Mexico, the Navajo borrowed and reworked elements of Pueblo culture into their own lifeways.

After about 1700, the Navajo quickly adopted European domesticated animals to become herders and skilled weavers of wool blankets and garments. The horse increased mobility, making it easier to herd the livestock and travel about the country. The Navajo farmed a little, but in early historical times it was sheep that were the primary source of the Navajo family's identity, welfare, and status. Whereas corn is the metaphor of Hopi life, "sheep are life to the Navajo" (Griffin-Pierce 2000:321). Anthropologists Henry Dobyns and Thomas Euler (1972:14–15) have pointed out that women were central to the adoption of sheepherding and thus to the economy. The combination of traditional hunting and gathering, farming, raiding, and herding provided the people with an economic base unparalleled among other indigenous peoples. Silverwork was an important craft and source of supplemental income. Unlike the Hopi, the Navajo were indifferent potters.

The traditional home is the hogan, or *hooghan,* literally meaning "place home," of two types—the older, forked-stick hogan and the larger, eight-sided hogan. Hogans are built in time-honored ways according to the dictates of holy beings. Now built of wood, tar paper, and other modern materials, in earlier times the larger hogans were sometimes built of stone blocks. Women own the hogans and pass them to their daughters, and a man lives at his wife's home. A typical Navajo extended family consists of maternal grandparents and parents, their unmarried children, and their married daughters with husbands and children. Several such extended families usually live in a particular locality, forming an "outfit" or land-use community. Clan identity remains important to these matrilineally organized people.

The ceremonial system copes with the uncertainties of the universe and restores it to order. Carefully performed rituals that include chants, prayers, and dry paintings (sand paintings) bring dangerous things under control, exorcize evil, cure the sick, and bless new endeavors with the assistance of the benevolent Holy People. As among the Western Apache, the girl's puberty ceremonial, or *kinaaldá,* is particularly significant.

Open conflict and unfair treatment punctuated interactions between Navajo and Euroamericans as with other indigenous peoples of the Southwest. The Navajo found Euroamerican settlements a tempting target for economic raiding, particularly for horses and other livestock. In the 1860s, the tribe was nearly destroyed by Colonel Christopher "Kit" Carson and his U.S. Army troops. Convinced that the Navajo were responsible for violence against settlers, Carson burned Navajo farms and hogans and slaughtered their livestock. Fleeing, the Navajo took refuge in secret places such as Canyon de Chelly. The Indians were forced to undertake the "Long Walk," a 300-mile, forced march to Fort Sumner at Bosque Redondo on the Pecos River in eastern New Mexico, where they were imprisoned for four dreadful years. After the Navajo Treaty of 1868, which established the initial boundaries of the Navajo reservation in Arizona, the Navajos were allowed to go home again.

Another trauma was the stock-reduction program of the 1930s. When scientists in the U.S. Soil Conservation Service diagnosed the Navajo Reservation as seriously overgrazed, sheep were slaughtered, and no amount of cash could compensate for the deeply felt sense of loss. In the late 1930s, a tribal council with elected representatives was organized, and administrative offices were established

The Diné Creation Story

In the beginning there was the First World, the Black World or the Running-Pitch World. The earth's surface was barren. In the east, blackness and whiteness rose up. Where they joined together, First Man came into being. In the west, yellowness and blueness rose up. Where they joined together, First Woman came into being. First Man and First Woman created Water Monster and other beings from their own skin. There were four houses at the north, south, east, and west directions containing jars filled with precious water. The beings living there grew the first plants—corn, tobacco, watermelon, pumpkins, squash, beans, cotton, gourds, muskmelons—and gave some of their seeds to First Man and First Woman. But the gods living at the corners of the earth lacked seeds and became angry and jealous. Eventually Black God created a huge flood by smashing all the water jars. First Man and First Woman floated safely away on a large reed and passed through a hole in the sky into the Second World or Blue World.

The Second World was not yet lit by sun or moon and was bathed in luminous blue light. First Man and First Woman created the mountains, fixed day and night, and made the first people who were placed on four mountains. First Man had brought all the seeds from the First World and he planted everything that grows. He raised four animals who became the rulers of the earth. At first there was harmony, but the world was small and crowded, and some of the people became witches. Another great flood was brought forth, and the people climbed a huge reed to the Third World or Yellow World, taking all the seeds and animals with them.

In the Third World, there was no sun or moon, only the four great mountains. In this world, Water Monster lived in a house below the surface of a river. Coyote caught the children of Water Monster while they were swimming. Water Monster was consumed with grief and anger and sent out another great flood. The people escaped on a reed into the present world, which was the Fourth or White World.

A Navajo cornfield along State Route 89, northeastern Arizona, looking toward the Echo Cliffs. PHOTOGRAPH BY JEFFERSON REID.

In the present world, First Man made the Sun, Moon, Stars, Sky, and Earth. Sky Father and Earth Mother smoked tobacco to bring about the rest of creation. First Man caused four sacred plants to grow on the surface of Earth Mother: tobacco, corn, beans, and squash. The people prospered, their families grew large, and they spread across the earth. But then some of them began to do bad things, and the women gave birth to horrible monsters who killed the people. The infant Changing Woman was found in the clouds on top of Spruce Mountain. She rapidly grew up to become a woman who changes with the seasons and later gave birth to twin boys, Monster Slayer and Born For Water, whose father was the Sun. Monster Slayer killed the monsters and made the world safe again. From her skin, Changing Woman created the Navajo clans.

Some versions of the creation story identify the place of emergence into the Fourth World as the southern Colorado mountains near Silverton. This place has some of the most ancient rocks on the continent. The songs that recount the story tell of the creation of humans and mountains, of all life; of the prehistoric monsters whose footprints are still embedded in rock. They tell it in great singing poetry, literally the voices of the rocks themselves.

There are many versions of the Navajo creation story, and all of the following offer variations of this story—Trudy Griffin-Pierce, Native Peoples of the Southwest *(University of New Mexico Press, Albuquerque, 2000); Aileen O'Bryan,* Navaho Indian Myths *(Dover Publications, New York, 1993, Retitled republication of* The Dine: Origin Myths of the Navajo Indians. *Smithsonian Bureau of American Ethnology Bulletin 163. U.S. Government Printing Office, Washington, D.C. 1956); Frank Waters,* The Colorado *(Ohio University Press/Swallow Press, Athens, Ohio, 1984); and Paul G. Zolbrod,* Dine Bahane, The Navajo Creation Story *(University of New Mexico Press, Albuquerque, 1984).*

Bosque Redondo

People are their own histories. Each of us carries history in our bodies, in the memories of blood and bone, tissue and nerve cells. We carry history in words, in the spoken stories that tell of a past of which we may not even be aware. Navajo writer Nasdijj (2000:61) frames the ghostly memory of his own past, writing of the Bosque Redondo and the Long Walk. "Alone at night when the wind kicks up out here on the mesa of the Bosque Redondo, you can hear the singing voices of ghosts. The Bosque Redondo is a past that runs like blood through a river of my dreams."

Navajo rock art in Canyon de Chelly. Photograph by Stephanie Whittlesey.

at Window Rock. Today the Navajo Nation covers more than 25,300 square miles in Arizona, New Mexico, and Utah. Energy resources, economic development, land disputes, and Indian gaming are important contemporary issues.

Stories of Water and Life in Northeastern Arizona

We have met some of the people who lived on the Colorado Plateau in northeastern Arizona—the ancient ones, the Anasazi or Ancestral Pueblo peoples; the Hopi; and the Navajo, or Diné. Now we turn to the recounting of stories of their lives in this striking but difficult country. Each people developed different ways of making a living and coping with the dangers and advantages of the Plateau environment, but to each, water was critical and a focus of religious life, economy, and social organization. We will discover ways in which the ancient ones used scarce land and precious water to farm Glen Canyon long before it was drowned beneath the waters of Lake Powell. We will learn how the Hopi farmed in a land of little rain, creating a spiritual landscape imbued with the essence of water and an agricultural landscape teeming with water's benefits to the people. We will view the Navajo cultural landscape, where the stones are dense with stories and mountains raise water-bearing clouds. Last, we will hear the story of twentieth-century Anglo-Americans building one of the greatest of the West's dams and creating a huge, artificial lake that shimmers like a mirage in a region where almost no surface water exists.

The Ancient Ones Farm Glen Canyon

Picture a tourist from some well-watered, midwestern state standing at Yaki Point on the South Rim of the Grand Canyon. As he looks down at Unkar Delta and then back to the interpretive sign at the edge describing Anasazi farm sites below, it is easy to see his confusion. He knows corn, and he almost assuredly thinks that corn could never have been grown on that sandy delta a mile below. If the tourist stopped to consider, he might think that the Anasazi were pushed into such an agriculturally marginal area because of population pressure or other stresses. This was likely not the case. Archaeologist Jesse Jennings (1998:99) has written that "the Anasazi actually specialized in gardening in 'marginal' areas, and that by understanding water and its conservation and use . . . extended their domain into areas where neither then nor now is gardening truly feasible." The ability to exploit and thrive on limited water—not their spectacular cliff dwellings, their great towns, or their beautiful arts and crafts—was the crowning achievement of the ancient puebloans. They thrived in the waterless canyon country by virtue of technology and culturally derived notions about the relationships between people and land. Religion and landscape formed a seamless symbiosis that sustained life and spirit.

The archaeology of Glen Canyon tells this matchless story. When the Bureau of Reclamation built the dam, the canyon and its archaeological treasures were flooded. Before that happened, archaeologists salvaged what they could. Their research gave us a glimpse into the lives of the ancient people. A recent return to Glen Canyon spurred by potential leasing of the recreation area for energy-resource exploration (Geib 1996b) provided an opportunity that is rare in contract archaeology—to return to a place and further study its archaeology with new methods and

Rock Houses

What did they have, these people who built rock houses in the hidden canyons? In her poem, "A Divide," Ann Weiler Walka answers —"gardens, each other, smoothed and painted clay, stars, stone, stories."

Photograph by Stephanie Whittlesey.

theories. Although not part of the Central Arizona Project or its archaeology, the Glen Canyon work was funded by the Bureau of Reclamation and has been instrumental in our understanding of ancient life on the Colorado Plateau.

By A.D. 1000, the canyon and its environs were occupied by several different cultural groups, including the Fremont culture and the Kayenta, Mesa Verde, and Virgin branches of the Anasazi. Efficient use of water determined whether these groups succeeded or failed. This is the paramount lesson of Glen Canyon archaeology.

In his summary of the research, Jennings (1998) pointed out that, although the uplands around the canyon were subject to less rigorous climatic conditions than the canyon bottoms, they were also more poorly watered. The canyon bottoms had a more dependable supply of water, but they were also difficult to access, provided little land on which to build, and were subject to flooding. The environmental dichotomy between canyons and uplands gave rise to the notion that the canyons were used seasonally by people whose permanent homes were on the surrounding mesa tops. They traveled to the canyon bottoms in summer to farm small patches of land and collect wild resources.

The archaeological data seemed to support this theory. Pueblo sites in the canyons were small, lacked the kivas usually found only in permanent habitation sites, and were invariably located near well-watered, alluvial soils. Jennings also offered an alternate theory: that disastrous floods after the Anasazi abandoned the area swept away evidence of the villages and fields that once occupied the canyon floor.

Subsequent research by Phil Geib and his colleagues (Geib 1996b) indicated that the flooding theory was inade-

Grand Canyon and Colorado River. Photograph by Jefferson Reid.

Glen Canyon Archaeology

The Glen Canyon Archaeological Project was part of the Upper Colorado River Basin Archaeological Salvage Project, which was undertaken when construction of four dams in the Upper Basin was authorized in 1956. The Bureau of Reclamation funded the project through the National Park Service. The agency contracted with the Museum of Northern Arizona and the University of Utah for survey and excavation in the canyon area to be occupied by Lake Powell and the adjoining uplands.

Jesse D. Jennings was the project leader. The Museum of Northern Arizona took responsibility for the 74 miles of the San Juan River canyon that the reservoir would inundate, its adjoining side canyons, and 69 miles along the left bank of the Colorado River between its confluence with the San Juan River and the canyon's terminus at Lee's Ferry. The museum also conducted geological studies. Alexander J. Lindsay, Jr. was field director for the Museum of Northern Arizona.

The University of Utah took responsibility for the 130 miles of upper Glen Canyon and its tributaries, the right bank of the Colorado River and side canyons below the San Juan confluence, and ecological and historical studies. C. Gregory Crampton headed the historical studies.

Some 800 miles of rock-walled canyon were investigated by boat and on foot during seven seasons of fieldwork between 1957 and 1963. More than 2,000 sites were identified, and dozens of sites were excavated during this massive archaeological undertaking. Don Fowler (1998:xiv–xv) has written of the logistical nightmare that the starkly beautiful canyon presented to archaeologists.

> In many places, to get from one canyon rim to the opposite rim directly across the river–a linear distance of a mile or less–required a vehicle trip of 400 to 500 miles or more, if there were any roads at all on the other side. Wooden boats and World War II surplus rubber rafts [popularly called "baloney boats"] provided transport on the river proper, but they could only be launched, or hauled out at two points that were 160 river miles apart. Access to the upper reaches of the side canyons was primarily from the canyons' heads, via jeep, on horse- or mule-back, or on foot.

Some of the project's findings seem dated now. Today's archaeologists have more sophisticated methods than those available when the salvage work was undertaken, and they recognize that many more sites should have been investigated. Nonetheless, the Glen Canyon Project provided a priceless glimpse into archaeological sites drowned forever below Lake Powell.

The opportunity to fill some of the gaps in the Glen Canyon Archaeological Project research came in the 1980s, when the National Park Service sponsored a five-year survey and excavation project in the Glen Canyon National Recreation Area. Between 1984 and 1989, Northern Arizona University conducted research to identify the densities and types of cultural resources in the recreation area and evaluate their eligibility for listing in the National Register of Historic Places. Known as the Glen Canyon Archaeological Investigation, this project carried out survey, limited testing, and collection that contributed new information toward resolving some of the unanswered questions of the earlier project (Geib 1996b). During its five-year span, the project surveyed almost 19,000 acres, recorded 489 sites, and tested 20 of these.

quate. Although some canyons were subject to site loss through flooding, many were not. These archaeologists believed that few Pueblo II groups (those living in the time between A.D. 1000 and 1150) established permanent residences in the canyons. Instead, they used the lowlands on a logistical basis throughout the year, with some families establishing temporary residences in prime agricultural settings that they would occupy during the growing season.

Trails—if they can be called that, as they were nothing more than precarious footholds and handholds carved into the living rock—connected the canyon bottom with the mesa tops. It is quite clear, as Jennings observed, that the canyon dwellers were not restricted to the canyons. In fact, they could move more easily through the canyon country than later travelers in wheeled vehicles. **Petroglyphs** pecked on the canyon walls may have marked trails, water sources, and fields, or they may have been a form of communication among the canyon's occupants.

The ancient ones surely would have mapped the vital sources of water, if only in their memories. They would have known where holes in the slick sandstone held rainwater after a summer storm, the springs and seeps coming straight from the barren rock, the seemingly dry streambed where it was possible to dig down and find water. They would have known all the sources of clear, sweet water hidden in unexpected places, for water was the key to survival. Such places no doubt anchored the people's travels across the rocky, bare land. In dry places between water sources, they may have hidden **ceramic** containers of sweet water as the Hopi did much later.

The canyon bottoms offered an ideal farming situation with deep, easily tilled, fine-grained alluvium that was periodically enriched by flooding. A variety of sources—seeps, groundwater, floodwater, runoff—provided an abundant water supply. The ancient pueblo farmers sowed many small, scattered farm plots to take advantage of different water sources, a strategy that ensured that at least some of the fields would produce a crop. At these low elevations, the climate was warmer and the growing season was longer than on the mesa tops. These advantages were offset by the fact that there were few canyon oases, and each one had only a small amount of tillable acreage.

The ancient puebloans located terraced fields, some of which were protected with stone retaining walls, on the larger sandbars along the Colorado River and in side canyons. These terraces were artificial, in that the soil behind the walls was evidently brought in. This was a way to create arable land where it was in short supply. Terracing has a price, however. Labor is required to build terraces, and they must be maintained, or runoff leads to rapid erosion and gullying.

Although the ancient puebloans were highly proficient at dry farming, the archaeology of Glen Canyon demonstrated that simple water-control technology was also used to enhance farming. Many centuries before the Bureau of Reclamation built Glen Canyon Dam, Anasazi farmers were also building dams. The deep canyons made it impossible to use the extensive, gravity-driven, canal irrigation techniques so well developed by the Hohokam, however. At a place called Creeping Dune, archaeologists excavated an unusual, double-walled masonry dam that caught water spilling off the Chinle shale. The U-shaped dam included a notched slab that regulated water flow; a stone-lined ditch system led from the dam to the fields.

Along Beaver Creek, archaeologists found a field area and features to control and disperse water. A stone-lined ditch carried water to fields on the upper portions of an alluvial fan; terraces and linear borders spread the water and kept it from flowing too quickly, eroding the soil, and washing away the young plants. Near Castle Creek, an earthen aqueduct conveyed water across a shallow depression, making it possible to irrigate a field cut off from other water sources.

The characteristics of different types of bedrock influenced farming techniques and determined where the people lived. Farm sites and homes were located near outcrops of Navajo, Kayenta, and Wingate Formation stone, where soils tended to be more fertile and drainage was better. The porous sandstone yielded seeps and springs of sweet drinking water.

Analysis of **coprolites** from Glen Canyon sites showed that the people's diet was focused on squash, corn, and wild plant foods, in that order. They also grew beans. Cotton

Time and Space

Time and space. In the desert there is space. Space is the twin sister of time. If we have open space then we have open time to breathe, to dream, to dare, to play, to pray to move freely, so freely, in a world our minds have forgotten, but our bodies remember. Time and space. This partnership is holy. In these redrock canyons, time creates space—an arch, an eye, this blue eye of sky.

—*Terry Tempest Williams,*
Red: Passion and Patience in the Desert

Ancient Pueblo storage structures tucked in a cliff overhang. Photograph courtesy Arizona Historical Society, Tucson (AHS Accession No. PC 29, Box 1, F. 12 C).

was an important economic mainstay that could be grown most easily in the lowland fields because the plants need considerable water and warm temperatures.

Numerous storage sites or granaries were tucked into sandstone alcoves throughout the Glen Canyon region at living and farming sites and were also located as isolated features. Many were oval or circular, slab-lined cists built wholly or partially underground. They had clay floors, mortar between the slab joints, and roofs made of sticks, mortar, and slabs. The larger storage structures had domed roofs and irregular masonry walls above ground level. Geib (1996a) has proposed that these capacious storage features, holding as much as 3.5 cubic meters of food and crop seed, indicate a relatively mobile population putting up stores for protection and scattering their supplies among many different storage facilities to reduce risk of loss. Storage features were often located in places that are difficult to access, further indicating a concern with security.

Dependence on corn as the dietary mainstay exacted a high price on health. Corn is not a particularly nutritious food, being deficient in calcium, iron, certain amino acids, and vitamins. It also contains a substance in the hulls called phytate or phytic acid that actually leaches iron from the human system (for example, Snow 1990). Populations subsisting heavily on corn, such as the ancient puebloans of Glen Canyon, have an increased incidence of iron-deficiency anemia and associated bone abnormalities and tooth loss. Poor nutrition led to other health problems, including high maternal and infant mortality and an increased incidence of infectious diseases.

In addition to shaping the land and flow of water through construction of farming features, the ancient puebloans modified their environment in many ways. Jennings (1998) has pointed out that the tributary canyons were small, closed ecosystems that were susceptible to minor changes in the ecological balance. The people introduced new cultivated and semicultivated species, altered the natural distribution of plants by intentionally or unintentionally encouraging their growth, and depleted wild species. Certain plants colonized farm plots after the fields were abandoned. These changes in turn affected how the people used the land.

Such shifts are documented elsewhere among the Anasazi. Archaeologist Timothy Kohler (2000) has suggested that to clear fields the Ancestral Pueblo people of south-western Colorado burned the piñon-juniper cover on mesa tops. Repeated burning encouraged the growth of fire-resistant junipers and decreased the piñon trees that provided food and construction wood. Long-term cultivation also eventually depleted the thin soils that were relatively slow to be replenished. It was not a successful strategy over the long run. We do not know if the people of Glen Canyon practiced this farming strategy, but if they did, it surely would have impacted the long-term fertility of mesa-top fields.

For many centuries, the ancient puebloans maintained the delicate balance between their needs and the environment's ability to supply them. We do not know to what extent the disturbance of this balance through environmental, technological, cultural, or social causes may have been responsible for abandonment of the region, but we suspect that it must have played a part. One mechanism for coping with environmental stresses is through technology. The ancient people obviously discovered ways to maximize the limited arable soil in the canyon bottoms and use every available drop of water. A second mechanism is social in nature. Water-control features are more easily built, used, and maintained when there are many people to help. Increased cooperation evidently helped to make water control more effective among the Anasazi.

Perhaps this alone explains the evolution of the compact, pueblo lifestyle and the presumed importance of kinship and family relationships to the ancient ones. Geib (1996a) has pointed out that, although the Glen Canyon farmers did well in the canyon bottoms, living there meant social isolation. Because of the scattered nature of the farming areas, communities were small and dispersed. The cooperative strategy may have held the seeds of its own destruction. Large, aggregated groups would have impacted the land much more than small, scattered communities and would have further depleted resources.

Palatki Cliff Ruin. PHOTOGRAPH BY STEPHANIE WHITTLESEY.

A third way to maintain the balance between people and land is ideological and religious in nature. Ideas about the respectful use of the land and its resources permeate the beliefs of many historically known Native Americans, and the ancient puebloans of Glen Canyon probably had similar values. One of the most vital aspects of this ideology is seen in the *katsina* cult. This religious orientation of modern pueblo peoples is most strongly developed at the Hopi pueblos, at Zuni, and at Acoma. The *katsinam* are ancestors who serve as messengers between the people and the gods; they are also rainmakers who come as clouds to the villages that summon them. The *katsinam* have many duties, but the chief function is to bring rain to the fields. People must behave properly so that the gods will be pleased and send them bountiful harvests, as in the Hopi covenant with Maasaw. The dancer who dons a *katsina* mask is transformed into that spirit, taking the prayers of the village people for rain, healing, and fertility to the gods. The religion thus gives puebloan people a sense of mastery over what can be a capricious, unforgiving environment.

It is not surprising, given the reliance of the ancient puebloans on rainfall, that archaeologists believe the *katsina* cult developed in prehistoric times, giving the people the same sense of control over the environment as among the modern Pueblos. Most archaeologists agree that masked human figures and bird symbolism indicate that the cult was present in prehistoric times (Adams 1991). Other designs and objects associated with the cult include terraced designs or so-called cloud symbols, animals and insects associated with rain and water (frogs, tadpoles, dragonflies), raw cotton, and cotton textiles. Pueblos were oriented around central plazas that provided the stage for *katsina* dance performances (Adams 1991). Because the cult is thought to be an integrative mechanism bringing diverse elements of pueblo culture together, it is often associated with large villages that may have housed people of different origins.

Archaeologists dispute when and where the *katsina* cult arose. It may have originated in areas where different, displaced populations congregated after much of the Colorado Plateau was abandoned in the late A.D. 1200s. We do not yet understand why the cult was accepted in some areas and not in others. All agree that the cult arose in prehistory and that the modern version we see so impressively displayed at Hopi pueblos is the culmination of centuries of humanity's spiritual adaptation to the harsh excesses of the Colorado Plateau.

The ancient peoples' ingenuity in conserving and using all of the precious water and farmland that was available to them is striking. Optimal use of and a natural balance among resources continued for three or four centuries in Glen Canyon. The Glen Canyon Archaeological Project provided us with abundant data and a number of new questions to ask, and the story is far from being completely told.

Hopi Farming and Ideology

The Hopi, like the Hisatsinom before them, are master dry farmers of the Colorado Plateau. These people work "agricultural miracles in an environment which is today regarded as unfavorable for cultivation of crops without irrigation" (Jennings 1998:100). Hopi farming methods in early historical times at the village of Oraibi on Third Mesa provide models for understanding the ways in which the ancestral peoples accomplished feats of mastery over inhospitable land and little rain. Many traditional techniques are still used today.

The dissected escarpments of Black Mesa are drained by ephemeral washes that collect rainwater after summer storms and empty onto alluvial fans. Prevailing winds blow sand against the mesa bases and onto the fields. Rainfall is scant, only about 8–10 inches each year, and Hopi farmers learned how to make the most of it. They developed strains of cultivated plants specially adapted to the harsh growing conditions and learned how to coax them into yielding abundantly.

Farming a dry land: Hopi farmer in the arid Plateau landscape. Photograph courtesy Arizona Historical Society, Tucson (AHS Accession No. 74392).

Water, more than anything else, determined a field's productivity. Ethnographer Jerrold Levy (1992) has described the two kinds of fields. The best farmlands, the *nayavasa* or "good fields," were found on the large, alluvial plain at the mouth of Oraibi Wash, where they received abundant water and were periodically enriched by flooding. Rainwater rushing down the wash overflowed onto the fields and renewed the soil with deposits of silt after rainstorms. The next-best lands were on the smaller alluvial fans of the tributaries running into Oraibi Wash and were fed by runoff from Black Mesa. Called *pisavasa* (sand fields) for the layer of sand overlying them, they received substantially less water than the other fields. Many of the better *pisavasa* farms were watered by runoff from the mesas. In wetter years, there was enough moisture to germinate seeds and water young plants. The least productive lands were found high on the slopes alongside washes or in the sand dunes where there was little runoff and only moisture from rainfall reached the plants.

Fields on the higher portions of the Oraibi Wash floodplain received ample water directly, even in dry years; fields on the lower portions could be watered by digging ditches. "Through every large field, especially those devoted to raising corn," wrote ethnographer Mischa Titiev (1992:182), "there runs the shallow, rather narrow bed of an ephemeral stream whose precious overflow is retained by judicious damming and artificial banking."

Most fields, especially those receiving more water, were owned communally by clans. Fields of poorer quality were set aside for farmers who did not have access to clan lands, and people were free to establish farms in other locations. Corn and cotton, flanked by beans, melons, squash, and gourds, grew in the clan fields. Beyond the fields were peach orchards; at some villages, peaches were grown on the mesa tops. Chile peppers, onions, and other vegetables grew in irrigated gardens watered by springs. Many of these plants were introduced by Europeans and were not available to the Hisatsinom.

Cotton plants adapted to the cool climate and short growing season were raised in the best-watered fields, including those at Moenkopi. This village began as a farming colony of Old Oraibi. After the breakup of the village in the early 1900s, many of Old Oraibi's former residents moved permanently to Moenkopi. Its residents still maintain ties to Third Mesa. Moenkopi offers an interesting analogy to the upland-lowland dichotomy seen at Glen Canyon. It is a low-elevation area with rich farmland and irrigation canals coming from spring-fed streams, and cotton and sweet corn can easily be grown there.

Hopi fields were cleared in February, and the ground was broken with simple wooden tools. Corn was the focus of Hopi farming. The Hopi cultivated 24 varieties of corn categorized by color, the most familiar of which is blue corn (Whiting 1939). The first planting was made in April to ensure that some corn would be mature in time for the Home-going, or Niman, ceremony in July. The main planting was usually in mid-May after all danger of frost was past. Some 10–20 seeds were planted in each hole with a digging stick that scarcely disturbed the soil. Simple features helped Hopi farmers. Embankments and ditches spread flood-waters to fields on the alluvial fans. The features were renewed each year because they washed away in summer storms. Brush windbreaks held down by stones helped to keep sand from piling up on the fields and retarded erosion. Farming was a male purview, although the women would help as needed. Planting was carried out individually or by work parties.

The growing corn sprang up like a bush. Fields were tended throughout the summer to coax the corn into higher yields. The plots were weeded, and the soil was loosened and mounded around the base of the stalks to conserve moisture. Griffin-Pierce (2000:94–95) has reminded us that planting and caring for crops on the arid Plateau was more than just work; it was an act of faith. "Even the planting stick is a sacred object, a physical symbol of the faith and prayer it takes to raise corn and other crops" (Griffin-Pierce 2000:95).

Harvest began in the fall (earlier at Moenkopi) and was a time of great happiness if the crops yielded abundantly. Sweet corn maturing early in September, a favorite food, was baked in pits among the fields. The main harvest began in October when the rest of the corn was picked, husked, and stored by color. Corn was stacked like cordwood in store rooms at the rear of the houses.

Finely ground cornmeal was the basis of most traditional foods, and in past times women devoted hours each day to its preparation. Essential pieces of equipment in traditional homes included several **metates** of differing coarsenesses and the *piki* oven. *Piki,* a paper-thin, rolled, crackling bread of blue cornmeal and ashes baked on an oiled stone, was an essential food that continues to be made today. No Hopi man, it is said, will marry a girl unless she is skilled at making *piki.*

The Cloud People Bring Rain

Robert Boissiere (1986:127–128) tells this story of rain and Hopi cornfields. One summer he was working with his friend Leslie Kayawena of Shipaulovi on Second Mesa in Leslie's cornfields. The fields were dry, needing rain. The drought had been with them for months. Robert had brought his bow and arrows, hoping to catch a rabbit unawares. Robert notices Leslie is praying:

> Reaching for his cornmeal, he sprayed the earth, gently. He turned himself toward me and he said: "Shoot one of your arrows so the sun brings rain." I could see he believed in my magic more than I did.
> Leslie knew better.
>
> I cocked the arrow on the bowstring of my sixty-pound aluminum steel bow,
> and aiming straight at the sun,
> I let the arrow fly.
> Disappearing from sight, the fleeting arrow
> must have reached its sacred destination:
> it never came to earth again.
>
> Without a word we picked up our hoes and started to push the sand against the corn plants—
> but not for long.
> Answering the Hopi prayer, the Cloud People sent us rain. It came down, drenching, at last, the corn and melons so blessed.
> We kept on working.
> The earth smelled good, the Hopi Sun God had been good to us. Leslie believed the magical power of the Hopi activated motion
> to bring rain;
> now I believed it too.
> The Cloud People, the Catsinas, the God of Heaven and Earth
> had favored us. . .
> It had rained on the parched Earth of the Hopis.

(Robert Boissiere, "The Rainmaker"*)*

Then and now, Hopi beliefs, cosmology, and ceremonies are structured around the intimate and integral connections among corn, life, and rain—what Reid and Whittlesey (1997:98) have termed a "philosophical union of the ideological and ecological domains of daily life focused on corn." Corn is not only a source of sustenance but a metaphor for life. Its life cycle from seed to harvest parallels the path of human life. Rain is the source of all life, and through the combination of rain with earth and its transformation into corn, the blessings of the *katsinam* become the essence of human bodies. The dual universe—this world and the world of the spirits—are transformations of one another.

Ceremonies are focused on bringing rain, sprouting plants, and ensuring abundant harvests. Ritual performances and objects center on corn, clouds, and rain. The most sacred clan objects are ears of corn kept with reverence, and holy cornmeal and water are integral to virtually every ceremony. Tobacco is smoked ceremonially to simulate the clouds that bring rain. At the Powamu ceremony in early spring, beans and corn are planted in the kivas to ensure good harvests. Even Hopi names have meaning in relation to corn. Many of those who left Oraibi during the nineteenth-century conflict were members of the Crow clan. The western raven, or crow, is despised by the Hopi because it ravages the corn crop (Levy 1992).

The Hopi have created a cultural landscape dominated by water. The Pacific Ocean, Colorado River, rain, underground aquifers, and springs all exist in a sustained relationship that demonstrates the universal, life-sustaining force of water. "*Paahu,* 'natural water' or 'spring,' is absolutely central in Hopi social and environmental thought. Indeed, the identity of the term points to the significance springs hold. Springs are the prototypical water sources" (Whiteley 1998:192). Springs supply drinking water and water for livestock and irrigate the terraced gardens. The wet environments surrounding springs are oases in an otherwise arid land, and with their rich plant and animal life, they represent the ideal model of life and growth—abundant, diverse, charged with water. Originally "planted" by deities, springs are dynamic demonstrations of the process that produces and sustains life.

Springs, water, and rain are focal themes in religious belief, paraphernalia, and rites. Water symbols and metaphors are found in ritual costumes, kiva iconography, mythological narratives, and personal names. Water is represented by insects, plants, and animals that inhabit springs. Springs are memorialized in clan tradition as important points along migration routes. According to Whiteley (1998:192–193), water symbolism in songs serves to:

> call the cloud chiefs from the varicolored directions to bear their fructifying essence back into the cycle of human, animal, and vegetal life. That essence—as clouds, rain, and other water forms—manifests the spirits of the dead. . . . The waters of the earth (where the Kachina spirits live) are, then, transubstantiated human life.

The spirits of the dead return as *katsinam,* or cloud people, and it is the cloud people who bring the rain—the distilled essence of the spirits. At death a cloud "mask" is placed over the deceased's face. "Now you are no longer a Hopi," it is said. "You are changed, you are a *katsina,* a cloud."

Springs and groundwater are also homes for the deity Paalölöqangw, "Plumed Water-Snake." Ceremonies such as the Snake Dance appeal to this powerful patron of water sources on earth and in the heavens. The Flute ceremony is specifically devoted to "the consecration and regeneration of major springs, and the Lenmongwi, head of the Flute society, dives, in an archetypcal gesture, to the bottom of a particularly sacred spring to plant prayer sticks for Paalölöqangw" (Whiteley 1998:193).

Resources such as water, clay, reeds, and spruce branches are gathered and taken back for use in village ceremonies. Used in this manner, they will draw in the life-giving power of the springs themselves (Whiteley 1998:193). "Springwater properly placed in one's field," wrote Whiteley (1998:195), "mud from spring bottoms as body plaster in Kachina costumes, painted tadpoles or dragonflies on Katchina *friends* [masks]. . . . All sympathetically entice the rain." Because springs attract the rain and snow, every spring is a place of worship and a shrine. Prayer sticks are planted, blessings of cornmeal are scattered, and prayers are offered there. At the winter-solstice ceremonies, feathered prayer sticks are placed over major springs near each village as protection and supplication. Offerings may also be made in the course of daily activities, as people pass by the sacred places.

"In short," Whiteley (1998:196) wrote, "springs are key in Hopi social life, cultural values, and the conceptualization of the landscape—all of which form the grounds of deeper religious thought and action." The environment is populated by intentional, spiritual entities that are part of the same moral system that encompasses human beings. As one Hopi put it, "We pray for rain so that all the animals, birds, insects, and other life-forms will have enough to drink, too" (Whiteley 1998:196–197).

But at Hopi, as elsewhere in the Southwest, the sacred water is diminishing. The springs are drying up; water seldom flows in Moenkopi Wash, and irrigation-dependent

The Serpent in the Spring

At the spring, where women and children waited to fill the water jars, gossiping and laughing, the young Hopi woman Polingaysi was warned to be quiet, keep her eyes to herself. "Do you want to be charmed by Water Serpent?" her mother chided. The snake might make a girl or woman pregnant simply by breathing on her. Across from where the women collected water, in a mossy place where the water seeped, was a submerged pottery vessel. In a niche above fluttered a feather prayer stick. The pot was a "transplanter," placed by the priest of the rainmakers and sacred. The priest would plant these pots, filled with sweet, holy water, at failing springs to make them live again (Qoyawayma 1964:58–59; 138–139).

A snake on the rock marks water. PHOTOGRAPH BY STEPHANIE WHITTLESEY.

fields are in jeopardy. Hopi believe that Peabody Coal Company has caused this by impounding upstream water and pumping the aquifer for slurry. It has become a contentious issue between the Hopi and Peabody, which claims that it is tapping an aquifer that does not feed springs. Regardless, drying of the springs is a source of deep anxiety for the Hopi. Their moral philosophy follows a covenant entered into with the deity Maasaw, charging people to take care of the earth and its resources. If the covenant is broken, catastrophe and cataclysm will ensue. Whiteley (1998:204) has related a legend telling of a time "when Paalölöqangw, the water serpent deity, would turn over and lash his tail deep within the waters of the earth, and all land-life would tumble back down to the bottom of the ocean." The future cataclysm can be directly related to the drying up of groundwater, which is intimately linked with the spirits of the dead.

We can see in Hopi life the culmination of centuries of Western Pueblo peoples living on the Colorado Plateau. In that time, they experimented with plants and methods for cultivating them, nurtured the plants that survived the harsh growing conditions, and discovered ways to prepare foods that nourished the body and fed the soul. We also see a unique and seamless blending of religion, cosmology, and ideology with economy and ecology—a fusion that ensured Hopi survival and has made them one of the Southwest's most admired native peoples.

Navajo Sacred Geography

The Navajo conceive the natural world differently than the Hopi and link it to human endeavors through religion and story in different ways. Whereas the Hopi (and we presume also the ancient puebloans) visualized their lives and their world in terms of farming, cultivated crops, and the natural elements that raise the growing plants to maturity, the Navajo viewed their world from the perspective of a mobile people who farmed only sporadically. Nevertheless, water was a crucial feature of their spiritual geography. The Navajo world is an extraordinary lesson in cultural landscape, according to McPherson (1992:11):

> The earth is not just a series of dramatically poised topographic features that incite the wonder of man or beckon for exploitation, but is rather a living, breathing entity in an animate universe. The land with its water, plants, and animals is a spiritual creation put into motion by the gods in their wisdom. These elements are here to help, teach and protect through an integrated system of beliefs that spell out man's relationship to man, nature, and the supernatural.

The Navajo say that the whole land is sacred (Kelley and Francis 1994:1). Kelley and Francis (1994:2) (one of whom is an ethnographer and the other a Navajo) have written that the land "is a physical link between people of the present and their past." Storied places form a text in the larger, living narrative of the land. Holy places are where the essence of the immortals—moisture, earth, air, and light—came together.

Sacred geography is focused on water, for moisture is the essence of the Holy People (Kelley and Francis 1994:203). Four sacred rivers are inhabited by holy beings who answer prayers and provide protection—the Rio

Navajo Respect for Water

People show respect to the huge moisture-bearing air masses that sweep in from the southwest, with rain, thunder, and lightning, and to even the smallest spring. These people see water in its various forms as not only controlled by, but outer forms of, immortals who can hear and respond to human prayers and other ceremonial acts performed season after season, year upon year, century after century, to keep the cycle going. Because people have experienced long droughts when the hydrological cycle seemed to have stopped, they believe their acts, performed pure-heartedly, are necessary to keep it going.

—*Klara Kelley and Harris Francis,* Navajo Sacred Places

Grande, San Juan, Colorado, and Little Colorado Rivers. The most important of these is the San Juan, and the confluence of the San Juan and Colorado Rivers was particularly significant. The Navajo say that these rivers made love at the base of Navajo Mountain. Lake Powell, which Walka (2002:40) calls a "featureless plain," now drowns the canyon confluence of these sacred rivers.

San Juan River near Mexican Hat. Photograph by Jefferson Reid.

As among the Hopi, "Springs are symbols of life and are gifts of the Holy People," according to Kelley and Francis (1994:203), "as one expects in dry country where springs are rare." The land's capacity to yield abundantly is evident at springs. The rain ceremony focuses on springs, and springwater is a basic need in many other ceremonies.

Mountaintops are sacred because the dawn's first rays strike them, and they gather rain for the land (Kelley and Francis 1994:45). At the heart of spiritual geography are four sacred mountains assigned to the cardinal directions that delimit the boundaries of the Navajo world. These mountains are Sisnaajinii (Blanca Peak) in Colorado (east); Tsoodził (Mount Taylor) in New Mexico (south); Dook'o'oosłíí (San Francisco Peaks) near Flagstaff, Arizona (west); and Dibé Ntsaa (Hesperus Peak), also in Colorado (north).

Talking God and Calling God assumed guardianship of the mountains, giving them songs and placing supernaturals within them to gather the clouds and answer prayers. Each mountain is associated with a color and a "jewel," such as obsidian. Each mountain has human personalities and qualities and embodies important Navajo values—healing the sick, protecting the people and their property, and ensuring tranquility. Soil from the sacred mountains is collected for the earth bundle used in healing and protection. Mountains must not be climbed unless done in the proper way with ceremony and prayer.

Other mountains also have spiritual significance. The dark-blue bulk of Navajo Mountain stands stark against the lighter sky above Lake Powell. Anglos know it as a laccolithic dome formed when imploding gasses beneath the earth's surface pushed magma upward and folded it into a dome. To Navajos, this mountain is the head of Earth Woman. Holy beings shaped the mountain with soil carried upward from another world. Monster Slayer, the son of Changing Woman and the Sun, lived for a while atop the mountain where he fought a life-and-death battle and was victorious (Walka 2002:59).

Rock formations hold special importance, and as with mountains, people are cautioned not to climb on them for fear of offending the holy beings. The monoliths of Monument Valley are thought to be water containers, and important rainmaking and healing ceremonies take place there. The graceful arch of Rainbow Bridge is now lapped by the waters of Lake Powell and accessible only by boat. This rainbow turned to stone blessed the union of two sacred rivers and the births of the water children Rain and Cloud. Stones "are rich in experience and dense with wisdom" (Walka 1993:5).

Archaeological ruins teach lessons and history. The Navajo consider the ancient ones to be part of their history (Kelley and Francis 1994). They believe that the cliff dwellers strayed from correct behavior, transgressed sacred laws, and abused the power given to them by the holy beings, causing their ultimate destruction. The ruins serve as a constant reminder that nothing can survive unless it is vested with holy power, behaves properly, and lives in harmony.

To the Navajo, the entire world is a storehouse of history, tales, and teachings that help a person to understand the realities of life and live successfully and harmoniously. As McPherson (1992:69) has written, "everything has a spirit, is male or female, controls power, teaches a lesson, deserves respect, and has its place." All life is "a metaphor in which one reenacts the spiritual through the physical" (McPherson 1992:75). When the tenets of proper behavior are not followed, prayers fail and disaster strikes. Spiritual geography thus keeps the world functioning and ensures the Navajo an enduring place in the landscape they have created. Water in its precious forms is central to this spiritual geography and sacred landscape.

Chant

I will walk in places where good Dark Clouds keep coming.
I will walk in places where good Male Rain keeps falling.
I will walk in places where good benevolent Lightning keeps flashing.
I will walk in places where good Black Fog is moving.
I will walk in places where good Female Rain keeps falling.
I will walk in places where good Rainbows float about.
I will walk in places where good Thunders are rolling.
I will walk in places where I hear the Water Bird. . . .
In places like these I walk.
I will walk in places where every kind of Plant is growing.
I will walk in places where all sorts of Flowers are blooming.
I will walk among Dew and Pollen.
Pollen and Dew will touch my feet.
They will reach my legs. . .

—*Karl Luckert,* Coyoteway: A Navajo Holyway Healing Ceremonial

THE STORY OF GLEN CANYON DAM AND LAKE POWELL

The story of Glen Canyon Dam is complicated and multilayered, a tale of political squabbles, conflicting values, and clashes over the most beneficial ways to use the canyonlands and its water. It is not an easy story to tell. Since the dam was completed in 1963, "the canyon has inspired paeans, laments, and diatribes, a remarkable body of literature—the literature of the lost" (Farmer 1999:xiv). There are actually three, intertwined stories—the local story, which explains the region's history; the story of the emerging American conservation movement in the 1950s; and the history of federal reclamation (Farmer 1999). We have explored the last of these in Chapters 2 and 3. Here, we delve deeper. According to Russell Martin (1999:6), who has written most compellingly about the history of Glen Canyon Dam and Lake Powell, it is a story "that winds like a red river in Glen Canyon, a story that stands like a dam."

Glen Canyon Dam and Lake Powell reflect how and why the Southwest's rivers were conquered and harnessed in the twentieth century. This story stands in stark contrast to the humble water-control technologies of Hopi, Navajo, and ancestral peoples. It is tempting to conclude that, whereas those peoples had a deep, religious connection to the land from which to create their spiritual geographies, twentieth-century Anglo-Americans did not. Looking more closely, we can see that the dam also stands for twentieth-century values. Its history marks the tale of confrontation between two opposing philosophies—the transformation of the West for the collective good and the preservation of wild, open spaces untouched by technology as a legacy for the future.

The story begins at Echo Park inside Dinosaur National Monument on the Colorado-Utah border. Long after John Wesley Powell's party camped there, a remarkable paleontological discovery was made downstream from Echo Park near the town of Vernal, Utah—a quarry containing the remains of some 400 Jurassic dinosaurs. In 1915, President Woodrow Wilson established a monument to protect the bone bed under the authority of the 1906 **Antiquities Act**. About two decades later, presidential proclamation established a greatly enlarged Dinosaur National Monument including vast stretches of scenic landscape along the Green and Yampa Rivers. The National Park Service obtained a spectacular new monument in a remote corner of the American West, but there was a price, according to historian Mark Harvey (1994). The proclamation contained clauses that made the monument subject to the construction

The Green River in Dinosaur National Monument, looking toward Echo Park and Steamboat Rock, where John Wesley Powell's expedition camped in 1869. Photograph by Jefferson Reid.

of future dams and power plants inside its boundaries (Harvey 1994:20–21). The tale of Glen Canyon Dam hangs on this point.

The next player to enter the controversy was the Bureau of Reclamation. In 1949, after the 1948 water-allocation compact among the Upper Basin states, the agency issued a planning report suggesting several potential dams and storage reservoirs that included one in Glen Canyon and another at Echo Park. As urban and industrial growth sprouted in the Upper Basin during World War II, the Bureau of Reclamation responded with the massive Colorado River Storage Project. The proposal included two huge, power-producing dams and storage reservoirs to be built at Echo Park and Glen Canyon, another dam at Split Mountain along the Green River inside Dinosaur National Monument, additional storage reservoirs, and 12 irrigation projects in four states.

The Upper Basin had been devastated by industrial slump, years of drought, and depression, which ravaged an already precarious agricultural base. Historian Robert Athearn has noted that "western agriculture was carried out under marginal conditions, and when all of the . . . negatives were present the additional blows of drought and dust spelled the difference between a momentary defeat and absolute disaster" (cited in Harvey 1994:25).

Reclamation's ambitious Colorado River Storage Project coincided perfectly with Utah's Central Utah Project, which was designed to bring water to Salt Lake City and the Bonneville Basin. At that time, Colorado River water was fueling the tremendous growth of southern California. It was feared that, unless storage projects such as the Central Utah and Colorado River Storage Project were implemented, the Upper-Basin states would lose their own share of water while meeting delivery requirements to the Lower Basin mandated by the Colorado River Compact.

Then the third player entered the game—the emerging national conservation movement. Although Echo Park Dam was a symbol of the Upper Basin's aspirations, to conservation forces it was a different kind of symbol—representing the American wilderness, "at once magnificently beautiful as well as in danger of disappearing under development pressure" (Harvey 1994:5).

The strident battle between conservationists who saw the Echo Park Dam as a threat to America's national parks and dam builders and their supporters occupied six years in the 1950s and became the best-known conservation issue of the decade (Harvey 1994:53). The core issue was the preservation and protection of the National Park system. Arguments for and against the dam sites, filibusters, and heated debates raged in newspapers, congressional committee meetings, and Senate hearings. According to Harvey (1994), opponents of Echo Park Dam developed three strategies, including promotion of Dinosaur National Monument's scenic beauty and recreation potential, development of political partnerships, and proposing alternative dam sites. A controversy over evaporation rates and the amount of water that would be lost by the proposed reservoirs took center stage. David Brower of the Sierra Club appeared before the Senate, challenging the Bureau of Reclamation's estimates and calculations. This appearance "has since become a famous episode in the annals of American environmental history, taking on almost legendary proportions" (Harvey 1994:191).

When the dust settled, a tradeoff was forged. It was largely based on the fact that, despite its awesome beauty, Glen Canyon was not part of the National Park system. Echo Park was abandoned, Glen Canyon Dam would be built in its stead, and Split Mountain was jettisoned. The battle ended when final provisos were placed into the proposed legislation to ensure that no dam would be built inside a national park or monument and that adequate measures would be taken to protect Rainbow Bridge in Glen Canyon. In March 1956, the legislation was approved, and it was signed into law by President Eisenhower the following month. Construction began in October of that year.

In hindsight, this tradeoff would be considered a bittersweet success. Glen Canyon Dam lay outside the basic agenda of the conservationists, whose campaign was to affirm and protect the integrity of the National Park system, but its glorious beauty was virtually unknown and would become apparent only after construction began on the dam. The Sierra Club book, *The Place No One Knew,* would become a memorial to the sacrificed Glen Canyon, and the canyon "became a touchstone for environmental action along the Colorado River and Plateau for the next generation. It steeled wilderness activists against any further dams along the Colorado River" (Harvey 1994:299).

Glen Canyon Dam and Lake Powell, looking toward city of Page, Arizona. PHOTOGRAPH BY JEFFERSON REID.

According to Martin (1999), the contract for the dam was at that time the largest nondefense contract ever entered into by the United States. The prime contractor was Merritt-Chapman & Scott. Multiple, separate contracts were let for construction of the power plant, roads, infrastructure for the support city of Page, and some of the integral materials. First to be built were necessary roads, cableways, and the bridge across the canyon. The bridge was completed in 1958 and dedicated in 1959. Tunnels and cofferdams to divert the river around the dam site were built next. The keyways—notches that would prevent the dam from moving downstream—were blasted out of the rock. Soon 5,000 people lived in the spanking-new town of Page, where only a few short years before the only inhabitants had been the Navajo family of Manson Yazzie and their sheep. The city was named for John Chatfield Page, the Bureau of Reclamation commissioner who served between 1937 and 1943 after Elwood Mead's death in 1936.

The concrete-block dam was an engineering compromise between a gravity structure of pyramidal shape to direct the water load vertically down to the dam's foundation and an arch dam arcing concavely into the water load and transferring it into the abutments in the canyon walls. The first concrete was poured in 1960. The story of dam construction is compelling in itself, marked by dramatic labor strikes, rival publicity campaigns by conservationists and the dam supporters, and fiscal losses (Martin 1999).

Aggregate composing the bulk of the concrete mass was mined from Wahweap Creek and processed on site. The American Cement Company hauled cement from a limestone quarry and mill near Clarkdale (a $10 million contract). Pozzolan—crushed pumice that would improve the concrete's set as it cured—was removed from a deposit near Flagstaff and crushed in nearby mills by the J. G. Shotwell company (a $2.5 million contract). The scars from pumice mining can still be seen today along U.S. 89. Martin's (1999:195) description of the quantities of these materials and the effort required to move them is breathtaking.

Chilling was necessary to allow the concrete to cure without cracking. The materials that went into the mixture and the concrete blocks themselves were cooled, the latter by means of cooling pipes laced into the structure. Lewis

Refrigeration of Seattle built a refrigeration plant composed of 18 ammonia compressors, 8 condensers, 10 chillers, and 22 ice-making machines.

Making Concrete

Making the concrete used to build Glen Canyon Dam was not an easy task. Incredible effort was required to mine or fabricate the ingredients, haul them to the dam site, and mix them. The standard batch of concrete was four cubic yards. It contained about $5\frac{1}{2}$ tons of aggregate, $1\frac{1}{2}$ tons of sand, 200 pounds of flaked ice, 500 pounds of water, 750 pounds of cement, 375 pounds of pozzolan, and 32 ounces of an additive to minimize air bubbles. One batch filled a space about the size of a king-sized bed (Martin 1999:199). Russell Martin (1999:195) has described the process of hauling the materials to the dam:

> Beginning early in 1960, and for almost four years thereafter, a truck hauling pozzolan delivered a load to the dam site every two hours on average. Every *forty minutes,* day and night, seemingly endlessly, in the heat and sometimes the heavy snow, one of a constantly moving fleet of White Autocar diesels pulling tandem trailers filled with 28 tons of bulk cement from the Clarkdale plant pulled onto the government scales. . . each load a mere 142 barrels, meaning that 21,500 round-trips totaling 376 miles each ultimately were required to bring enough cement to Glen Canyon to make the mud.

Glen Canyon Dam. Photograph by Jefferson Reid.

Slowly, the dam rose, truckload by truckload, block by block. The diversion tunnels were filled, and water began to rise behind the dam in 1963. Electricity was first generated in 1964. Eight penstocks pull water to the hydraulic turbines, each weighing 45.75 tons. Together, the eight generators can produce 1,296,000 kilowatts. The power is sold to Arizona, Colorado, Utah, Wyoming, New Mexico, and Nevada. The power plant produces 5 billion kilowatt-hours of electricity each year, enough to supply the needs of about 400,000 households.

Glen Canyon Dam and the Navajo Generating Station make Page a real center of western power. The modern city of about 7,000 residents is a landscape paean to the dam and the lake, the wonders of technology that fuel the engines of its modern economy. A tiny museum dedicated to John Wesley Powell in downtown Page is a perfect union of ironies, commemorating the river that once was, while simultaneously celebrating Lake Powell and its watery pursuits.

City of Page, Arizona, looking toward Glen Canyon Dam and Lake Powell. Photograph by Jefferson Reid.

The Glen Canyon National Recreation Area was established in 1972 and is operated by the National Park Service. At maximum capacity of 3,700 feet, the lake impounds 27 million acre feet of water, encompasses 252 square miles of surface area, and creates 1,960 miles of shoreline—longer, according to Martin (1999:314 315), than the Pacific coastline from Seattle to San Diego. Ironically, one of the least populated places in the Southwest—a place widely popularized as one that "nobody knew"—now hosts more than 3 million visitors each year. The recreation area ranks among the 20 most popular places administered by the National Park Service. The Carl B. Hayden Visitor Center overlooking Glen Canyon Dam and bridge receives about a million visitors annually.

Was it worth it? This is a question that only history can address adequately. It was a costly project, without doubt. In addition to its monetary cost, 18 men were killed, and there were 365 serious injuries during construction. Although Merritt-Chapman & Scott built one of the word's great dams and finished the job just six months after the original completion date, they absorbed a loss, it was widely believed, of as much as $20 million on the project.

Efforts to convert Dinosaur National Monument into a national park failed. The Bureau of Reclamation lost credibility, and consequently, many of its future projects were closely scrutinized. Perhaps most sadly, two technical reports released by the U.S. Geological Survey in 1959 concluded that Glen Canyon Dam was unnecessary to regulate the river and was wasteful of precious water, shaking to the core the environmentalists who had supported the tradeoff for Echo Park Dam.

Bureau of Reclamation Commissioner Floyd Dominy, the "tough, ferociously disciplined, indomitable" leader who browbeat Glen Canyon to completion, was fired by the newly inaugurated President Richard M. Nixon (Reisner 1986:250–251). He retired to his cattle ranch in the Shenandoah Valley, and although he was occasionally hired in a lucrative consulting position, he would build no more dams.

More serious than these consequences were the dam's environmental effects, which are severe and ongoing. Effects include lowered water temperature, reduction in sediment load, destruction of beaches, increased severity of rapids, invasion of nonnative plants such as tamarisk, and loss of or reduction in plant and animal species. The lake destroyed animal, fish, and bird habitats, drowned the impressive natural scenery of Glen Canyon, and submerged its archaeological sites. In the 1980s, the Submerged Cultural Resources Unit of the National Park Service conducted dives to check on the condition of Glen Canyon's archaeological ruins. The conclusion was that most were devastated. Constant use of Lake Powell has created an enormous amount of garbage and pollution. More than a hundred truckloads of trash and a thousand batteries were dumped into the lake near the marinas between 1981 and 1990 (Farmer 1999:177).

Even the sacred landscape has suffered. Provisions for protecting sacred Rainbow Bridge that were originally built into the Colorado River Storage Project were suspended by Congress, and no barrier dams were built to keep the waters of Lake Powell away from the bridge. Reisner (1986:248) has written that Dominy received a special exemption from the federal law prohibiting significant

Human Sanitation

"If you are camping within one-quarter mile of Lake Powell, you are required to possess and utilize a human sanitation device (portable toilet), that does not use plastic bags to contain the waste."

"It is illegal to have a boat on Lake Powell that can discharge sewage overboard."

—*Glen Canyon National Recreation Area Newsletter*
July 2002

Rainbow Bridge

Carved out of Navajo Sandstone by the work of water and wind, frost and storm, the great arch called Rainbow Bridge is one of the Southwest's most scenic places. Professional scientists first visited Nonnezoshie, as it is called in Navajo, in 1909. The heartbreakingly beautiful arch spans 275 feet and soars 290 feet high. The crest is 42 feet thick and 33 feet wide. The Navajo say that Rainbow Bridge consists of two holy beings—one male, one female—stretched together across the canyon. In concert with holy beings of Navajo Mountain and the confluence of the Colorado and San Juan Rivers, from their union come the rain people, rainbows, clouds, and moisture to bless Navajo land.

Today tourists can take an all-day or half-day boat tour to Rainbow Bridge. Through the National Park Service's preservation efforts, trumpets the Lake Powell brochure, "you'll feel as though it was just discovered yesterday." Adults pay $69 and upwards, children $49 and more, for this experience.

Rainbow Bridge has become a symbol of the clash between cultures. To the Navajo, Rainbow Bridge is a holy place that must be treated with respect. Anglos view it as a natural wonder, a recreational spot among the many surrounding Lake Powell, and a prime place to play. Indians sued the National Park Service under the American Indian Religious Freedom Act to block access to the bridge, which was being defiled by tourists, boats, graffiti, garbage, and rude behavior. They lost the court battle. To stop the National Park Service from restricting access to Rainbow Bridge, which it had done at times when Navajo ceremonies were being held there, a group of Anglo-Americans countersued the National Park Service. Personal watercraft are banned from the bridge area today.

Time will tell whether Rainbow Bridge will be able to connect these disparate viewpoints and bridge the gulf between cultures, or if it will continue to symbolize the division between them.

human intrusions in national monuments. Today, steadily increasing numbers of visitors to the bridge trample vegetation and cover the sacred stone with graffiti. The Glen Canyon National Recreation Area newsletter pleads, "you can help the National Park Service by staying on the trails and showing respect for this sacred place."

Because the dam was constructed before the National Environmental Policy Act of 1969, no studies were made of its effects on the environment until after the fact. In 1989, the Bureau of Reclamation was directed to prepare an environmental impact statement on the operation of Glen Canyon Dam. After the draft was submitted and public hearings were held, the Secretary of the Interior and the bureau signed an agreement stating that the dam would be operated in a more environmentally sensitive manner. The government pledged to monitor flow from the dam, reduce daily fluctuations, and carry out periodic flood releases meant to help restore the downstream ecosystem, beaches, and native fish habitat. Park management recently conducted an environmental impact study on personal watercraft to ensure compliance with the National Environmental Policy Act. Personal watercraft were banned everywhere on the lake on September 15, 2002. The Bureau of Reclamation continues to pursue and pay for studies of the dam's environmental effects and various mitigation measures.

Personal watercraft. Photograph by Jefferson Reid.

There were broader consequences as well. The debate over Echo Park and Glen Canyon Dams represented the first great clash between water developers and preservationists, Harvey (1994:292–293) has written, and it established a major theme of environmental conflict in the West for the next two generations and more. The conflict pitted two philosophies. One was the managed use of natural resources such as water, rangelands, and forests for the public good, which had become woven into the fabric of the West in the early decades of the twentieth century. The other was the interest in wilderness, conservation, and associated values that emerged nationally in the postwar decades. Resentment against so-called environmentalists remains strong in much of the West even in this millennium and was evident in the rampant accusations following the Southwest's wildfires in summer 2002. The conflict gave a new dimension to the old colonialism that had tied the West to the elite, wealthy industrialists of the East (Limerick 1987). Perhaps most significant, the Colorado River became the battleground for the forces that clashed over development of the West and its preservation.

There are many who continue to mourn the loss of Glen Canyon and its priceless scenic and cultural treasures. They believe that the recreational opportunities, the

Wallace Stegner

Wallace Stegner, prolific writer, biographer of John Wesley Powell, and most ardent of dam haters, has written of Glen Canyon and Lake Powell (cited in Farmer 1999:171):

> Lake Powell is beautiful. It isn't Glen Canyon, but it is something in itself. The contact of deep blue water and uncompromising stone is bizarre and somehow exciting. . . . And yet, vast and beautiful as it is, open now to anyone with a boat or the money to rent one. . . it strikes me, even in my exhilaration, with the consciousness of loss. In gaining the lovely and usable, we have given up the incomparable.

Chief Yellow Horse's advertisement. Photograph by Jefferson Reid.

undeniable scenic beauty of Lake Powell, and the power supplied by the dam are not fair compensation for the loss of wilderness. In the 1990s, the Sierra Club began promoting the idea that Glen Canyon Dam should be destroyed and Lake Powell drained, a notion first raised years earlier by Edward Abbey in his novel *The Monkeywrench Gang*. To date, there has been little support for this project. At the John Wesley Powell Museum, the visitor can purchase a license plate that reads "Another Dam Friend of Lake Powell" for only eight dollars. Whether the drive to drain Lake Powell will gain momentum is impossible to predict. The advocates of draining the lake are opposed by many who want to keep it just as it is. Few people today remember Glen Canyon as it was or the earlier controversy surrounding the dam and the lake. To them, it has always been there, not as a mirage but as palpable, living water.

Colorado River near Moab, Utah. PHOTOGRAPH BY JEFFERSON REID.

In Moab, Utah, a modern mecca for trail bikers and river runners, I spoke with a woman who ran an antique shop along the town's main street. She had grown up in Glen Canyon at a place called White Canyon, now under Lake Powell. Each year her family holds a reunion on the lake to remember and celebrate. This woman preferred to leave her own history flooded along with the traces of so many other human lifetimes. She claimed that the people who want to drain Lake Powell are not thinking carefully. The previously submerged rock would look terrible when dried, nothing like the original polished walls of the canyon. Then there would be the problem of all that garbage—refrigerators, bicycles, trash, perhaps even a missing person or two—everything dumped in the lake for the past half-century. No, she said sadly with a shake of her head. Better to leave it the way it is.

Perhaps the river itself will provide a solution. A local joke asks how long it will take for Lake Powell to fill completely with sediment, making dismantling the dam a moot issue. The answer? "Optimists say 300 years, pessimists say 400 years." Regardless of the time it takes, the lake is doomed. Glen Canyon Dam, built in part as a sediment trap, is doing its job well. By some estimates, it removes as much as 90 percent of the water's sediment

Draining Lake Powell

Some environmentalists and wilderness advocates have begun a grass-roots movement to dynamite Glen Canyon Dam and drain Lake Powell, realizing Edward Abbey's fantastical vision at last. What would we gain if we drained the lake? Author Ann Weiler Walka (2002:49) answers:

> mud, red mud slicked over black; mud-plastered ruins, mud-encased trash; rusted gas tanks, pontoons, batteries; battered jet skis; toilet seats, toilet tanks, toilet contents; beer cans and oil cans; the remains of hikers, cows, cottonwoods; heavy metals; radioactive wastes. The detritus of a high-tech society and locals with no trash collection service, of built environments and un-built ones, borne downstream and piled up in Eden.

Edward Abbey

It is impossible to read about Glen Canyon and Lake Powell without encountering Edward Abbey. He is a central figure in the body of literature that has been constructed around the dam and its consequences. Edward Abbey was the pivotal figure in and spiritual leader of the conservationist, monkey-wrenching, anti-dam crusade of the 1960s and has often been compared to Henry David Thoreau. Abbey's experience with the Colorado Plateau was concrete and life changing. He served three summers as a ranger at Arches National Monument near Moab, several others as a fire lookout near Grand Canyon, and in 1967, he worked as a National Park Service ranger at Glen Canyon. He floated down the river through Glen Canyon for the first and only time in 1959. Some of these experiences are detailed in the memoir *Desert Solitaire,* a moving and mystical account of his confrontation with the slickrock country that became the bible of the environmental movement.

Abbey was a radical, outspoken critic of technology and government—a Luddite and an anarchist (his master's thesis in philosophy, presented to the faculty of the University of New Mexico, was titled *Anarchism and the Morality of Violence*). In his novels, essays, lectures, and voluminous, peppery letters to editors of newspapers and magazines, Abbey praised wilderness, preached revolution, and urged active resistance against those who were destroying the West and its waters. Like the man himself, characters in Abbey's Monkey Wrench gang are gleeful saboteurs who blow up machines and dams in defense of the earth. Jack Loeffler (1996:38) has written that "Through his great talent for writing, he himself became a vehicle and launched a relentless attack against those who would inordinately prosper at the expense of wilderness." Abbey's targets included cows and ranchers, developers, and government agencies such as the Bureau of Reclamation and the Bureau of Land Management, which he called the Bureau of Livestock and Mining. He was a revolutionary and an ecowarrior who inspired the radical *Earth First!* environmental group.

Abbey believed that a writer must also be a critic of the society in which he or she lives (Urrea 1996:45). He was thoroughly outrageous, a trickster who urged Americans to stem the tide of immigrants from Mexico and Latin America before the West was transformed into another manifestation of the Third World. He was much married with a voracious appreciation for femininity and an attitude toward women that can be most kindly regarded as patriarchal. "Abbey, the cur. The contemptible mongrel hillbilly. The hairy lone wolf, *Canis lupus amorus lunaticum*" (Hepworth 1996:118). Many have also labeled him a patriot and an American. His biographer James Cahalan (2001) claims Abbey was a living myth, who constructed a deep cocoon of half-truths and fictions about himself as protective camouflage. Edward Abbey was nothing if not complex—"as diverse and slippery as the slickrock country he writes about and as predictable as a flashflood" (Solheim and Levin 1996:139).

Abbey died in 1989 and was buried as he had lived—illegally and with much irreverence and joy—in the desert he so loved to the west of Tucson, or so the story goes. In the years since his death, Abbey has become a mythical culture hero of epic proportions. I wish I had known him.

Several biographies of Abbey are available. I think the best is Cahalan's Edward Abbey: A Life *(University of Arizona Press, 2001). I also like the collection of remembrances by friends and fellow writers—*Resist Much, Obey Little: Remembering Ed Abbey *(edited by James R. Hepworth and Gregory McNamee, Sierra Club Books, 1996).*

load. Eventually the lake will fill, although not in our lifetimes. It may overtop and cut through the soft sandstone around the dam, leaving a concrete monolith. Today, standing on the bridge and looking down into the seamless, sweetly curving arc of Glen Canyon Dam, one wonders if the spirits of the ancient ones linger still in the sandstone crevices and alcoves of Glen Canyon. And one wonders as well what they might think.

The Heart of the Matter

The old river sliced down through our stratiform
hearts, revealing the lenses of delight—
cool desert nights, skin on skin, bright-eyed babies—
and wind-blown, crosswise layers of loss,
all the things that can never be again.

Closer to base level she dropped our night
dreads and dead ends, our heavy metals
onto her bed of mud and cobbles.

An August flood would surely break the snarls apart,
dilute the poisons, swirl the detritus downriver,
wrack and feast for ravens or noon-fire,
or the next thunderbuster.

Ah but this river is damned.
We are stuck, stranded.

How then will our breath bodies float free?
How will they come back as rain?

Glen Canyon Dam

(Ann Weiler Walka, "The Heart of the Matter")

For further reading see: Donald L. Baars, Navajo Country: A Geology and Natural History of the Four Corners Region *(University of New Mexico Press, Albuquerque, 1995); Halka Chronic,* Pages of Stone: Grand Canyon and the Plateau Country: Geology of Western National Parks & Monuments *(The Mountaineers, Seattle, 1988); Jared Farmer,* Glen Canyon Dammed: Inventing Lake Powell and the Canyon Country *(University of Arizona Press, Tucson, 1999); Phil R. Geib,* Glen Canyon Revisited *(Anthropological Papers of the University of Utah Press No. 119, Salt Lake City, 1996); Trudy Griffin-Pierce,* Native Peoples of the Southwest *(University of New Mexico Press, Albuquerque, 2000); Laura Gilpin,* The Enduring Navaho *(University of Texas Press, Austin, 1968); Dorothy A. House,* "Landscapes of the Colorado Plateau" *(Plateau Magazine, Vol. 65, No. 3, Museum of Northern Arizona, Flagstaff, 1994); Jesse D. Jennings,* Glen Canyon: An Archaeological Summary *(University of Utah Press, Salt Lake City, 1998); Joseph Wood Krutch,* Grand Canyon: Today and All its Yesterdays *(University of Arizona Press, Tucson, 1989); Stephen H. Lekson,* The Chaco Meridian: Centers of Political Power in the Ancient Southwest *(Altamira Press, Walnut Creek, California, 1999); Russell Martin,* A Story that Stands Like a Dam: Glen Canyon and the Struggle for the Soul of the West *(University of Utah Press, Salt Lake City, 1999); Robert S. McPherson,* Sacred Land: Sacred View: Navajo Perceptions of the Four Corners Region *(Brigham Young University, Salt Lake City, 1992); Jefferson Reid and Stephanie Whittlesey,* The Archaeology of Ancient Arizona *(University of Arizona Press, Tucson, 1997); U.S. Department of the Interior, Bureau of Reclamation,* Glen Canyon Dam *(booklet available at the Carl B. Hayden Visitor Center, Page, Arizona).*

Red Mountain

Red Mountain is an eroded, volcanic cinder cone northwest of Flagstaff, Arizona that is a popular hiking destination. The trail leads gradually uphill into the cone's core through a weirdly sculpted, almost lunar landscape. Hiking Red Mountain is an evocative, out-of-the-world experience that defies adequate description and demands more poetic interpretation.

Water and fire join in the vermilion pyramid before me,
Its stratiform heart sliced and thin sectioned, bleeding
    glassy stone and burnt cinders.
Time was, steam erupted from the crater.
    Evaporating and reforming,
    It returned to earth on the wind.
Now it manifests in the cold pour of rain and hail's bonecracking pound.
Time and again, frost splintered the mountain's smoking cinnabar bones, and
    thunderstorms sculpted its molten shoulders and limbs.
Lightning cracked open its crimson skull and exposed it to the sky.

This mountain smokes and glitters still.
Spirit-clouds drape its head, and
    obsidian glimmers in the ebony-sand ripples,
    black pearls under water.
Rainwater cups in the alizarin basin, trickling down to join
    the antique water flowing above
    the molten core of the planet.

Haunted by semiotics, I draw closer to
    this perfect elemental union,
    seeking a matchless topographic prayer.
My pockets stuffed with the goddess's tears,
I walk toward the rainy mountain,
And into the heart of fire.

Flagstaff, Arizona

Stories of the Desert

5

Looking out over the pure sweep of seamless desert, I am surprised to realize that the easy landscapes stifle me—closed walls of forests, ceilings of boughs, neat-trimmed lawns, and ruffled curtains of trees hide the soft horizons. I prefer the absences and the big empties, where the wind ricochets from sand grain to mountain. I prefer the crystalline dryness and an unadulterated sky strewn from horizon to horizon with stars. I prefer the raw edges and the unfinished hems of the desert landscape.

Desert is where I want to be when there are no more questions to ask.

—Ann Zwinger, *The Mysterious Lands*

June 5, 2001
Another Day in the Sonoran Desert

On the day I began writing the final pages of this book—two days before Independence Day 2001—the temperature in Tucson reached a record-breaking 111 degrees Fahrenheit. Walk outside on such a day, and the heat sears your face as if you were peeking into an oven to check a cake, although in this heat you cannot bear even the thought of baking. Simply stand outside, doing nothing, and sweat pours down your face. Turn on the tap, and the cold water pours out at what feels like body temperature.

Power lines crossing Interstate 10 sagged from their great, crackling burden feeding the city's air conditioners, swimming-pool pumps and filters, and refrigerator-freezers. Drooping, the lines tangled with an 18-wheeler barreling down the highway and lost, snapping and pulling down power poles. Whipping about, breathing fire like the Quetzalcoatl of legend, the electrified snakes ignited a brush fire and then lay twisted, their mischief complete, on the burning-hot asphalt. Traffic backed up for five miles behind the mess.

View of city of Tucson, Arizona, from Gates Pass in the Tucson Mountains.
Photograph by Jefferson Reid.

On that day, three more Mexican citizens lost their lives to the desert's scorching heat. Trying to cross Organ Pipe Cactus National Monument where the temperature reached 114 degrees Fahrenheit, they lost too much body water to sustain life. Unlike most who perish in the blast furnace who are typically undocumented aliens, these were drug smugglers returning from south of the border. The Border Patrol listed the casualties to date—23 deaths from heat exhaustion and dehydration in the Tucson sector and another 22 in the Yuma sector, including 14 who died in a single horrifying episode. Humanitarians now leave water and medical kits stashed in the desert for these people—people who are so desperate to live in the States that they will pay thousands of dollars to human coyotes and risk their lives crossing the desert in summer. Anything, they believe, is better than what they have.

PHOTOGRAPH BY JEFFERSON REID.

It was so hot that rabbits dug holes in the backyard dirt, still damp after watering the lawn, and stretched out on their bellies, trying to cool off. I counted six cottonttails on that afternoon. The following summer, we will give up on watering the lawn, and the rabbits will cease to visit. Indoors, the cats who live there safe from hungry canine coyotes were doing the same thing. They stretched out on any cool, horizontal surface like elegant fur scarves, legs dangling off the edges of polished furniture. In such heat, even cats must dream of water.

That afternoon fitful storms feeding on the moist air from the south boiled up over the city, small and impotent hurricanes of wind and jagged lightning. They dropped measurable rainfall in some parts of the city, but not on our home. There was only the smell of rain—the delicious scent of creosote—and a few hot drops. When the storms faded, muttering and growling, they left behind piles of dry leaves that backed up on the patio like drifts of beach flotsam.

Our home is equipped with an optimistically named device called an evaporative cooler, less kindly called a swamp box or swamp cooler. To be more precise, we have three of them. The device uses water pumped through shredded aspen pads and delivered as cooled air by means of a fan. Actually, the contraption works pretty well in the dry days of summer. When the humidity climbs during the July monsoon, an evaporative cooler is worthless. That night, I lay awash in sweat, turning and twisting under a ceiling fan in a tangled mess of damp sheets, dreaming of air conditioning. It was so hot that day that electrical transformers flamed out all over the city, leaving entire neighborhoods in darkness when night fell. People sat out of doors, lighting the blackness with candles or battery-powered lanterns and sweated it out. Many fled to the cool comfort of a Holiday Inn or Motel 6. Fleetingly I wished I'd had that excuse. All the electric motors in the house were humming, struggling to cool our misery. I shuddered to contemplate the electric bill.

I awoke three times in the night, wrenched out of disturbed and transitory sleep by peculiar dreams. I couldn't call them nightmares, as they were not so much frightening as weird. Every one was about water. Bodies of water. Dams bursting and pouring down dry riverbeds. Boats cresting the tidal bore. I had obviously been reading far too much about the Colorado River. The second time I woke, I noted that mosquitoes had fed on the exposed parts of my body. I fervently hoped that they did not carry dengue fever, which some mosquitoes in Tucson are said to do.

When I went to bed at 10:30, the thermometer on the patio read 95 degrees Fahrenheit. The third time I woke it was 4:30 in the morning and nearer to 80 degrees Fahrenheit. I felt cool at last. The mosquitoes were sated, and I thought I could probably be able to fall back to sleep. But the dawn had broken, and it was already light outside. Some bird with which I was unfamiliar had begun to call. Desert, desert, he said. Then a Gila woodpecker assaulted the metal sides of the swamp box on the roof above me, sounding like an automatic rifle. I gave up at last and trudged off to make coffee. The sun rose into the sky and began its daily siege. I sat with the rich smell of roasted coffee filling the kitchen, thinking. It was another day in the Sonoran Desert, and none of our technological advancements, none of the mastery over nature in which we pride ourselves, could conquer this land of little rain. Not then, not tomorrow, not ever. The desert will always win.

Life and Death

Charles Bowden (1986:143) writes of the desert's paradox:

> The desert fires my appetite for life and here I know this fact: the desert is where I want to die, where I do not fear death, do not even consider it. Here death is like breathing. Here death simply is.

One experiences the desert through all of the senses, and those who live in desert lands know it by the scarce but transformative presence of water. Sight—the eye drinks in the glorious, tumbled masses of clouds that presage the rain, and the spirit longs to see them rise over the mountain peaks, knowing the long, dry months will end at last. We literally lean toward them, impatient in our eagerness (Childs 2000:161). Smell—the indefinable, pungent scent of creosote damp with early morning dew or drenched in a summer thunderstorm defines the desert's aura. "The desert smells like rain," say the Tohono O'odham, the Desert People (Nabhan 1982:5). Hearing—we welcome the startling peals of thunder, for it means the sweet rain will follow, and sometimes, the *culebra de agua*—the great windstorm, the serpent in the cloud. Touch—we feel the wind on our skin and lifting our hair—the breath of the ocean, the essence of rain bestowed through the benevolence of I'itoi, our Elder Brother.

To understand the desert requires that we go beyond the senses, however, to apprehend it in our hearts and emotions. The desert forges respect and sometimes fear, for people die in this land. They perish from thirst, from heat exhaustion, sometimes from starvation. "Death here is the norm, not life," Waters (1984:93) has written. "And the land gives the same impression." Even the sky is a desert, one that is "infused with the vast, hot smell of dust" (Nasdijj 2000:27). The desert can be cruel, and it cannot be swayed or appeased. One can learn to love the desert just the same, marking its thorny heart as home. In its secret watering places, the desert also holds life.

Newcomers to the desert country—there are many of them, and their numbers are growing—often appreciate the land in terms of freedom from shoveling snow and the opportunity to play endless winter golf; as a place to grow citrus trees in the backyard and sit year-round by the pool. They also live insulated from the land, moving from air-conditioned house to air-conditioned car to air-conditioned mall, never feeling the searing blast of raw desert air. But it was the ancient desert, the land of little rain and fiery sun, that obsessed humans and drove them to build canals and dams and aqueducts to conquer it and make it habitable. In this chapter, we tell stories of this ancient, implacable desert, not the moderated, controlled, pumped, and electrically powered desert of today. As Bowden (1986:146) has pointed out, the ancient desert is real, but it has no meaning to those who populate the modern desert oases. The desert landscape is a kind of bad memory, "a nightmare world where people once lived off the land and thus had to live with land." Politicians, farmers, engineers, miners, ranchers, retirees, college students—"none of these people believed in the desert or lived in the desert or heard the rasping whispers of the landscape stretching just beyond their safe city streets or neat furrows" (Bowden 1986:137). In this chapter, we will connect the desert's past and present residents, tracing the course of living lines of water and greenery through the centuries.

Two geographic concepts give our desert stories context. The first is the Basin and Range physiographic province. This is the southernmost province through which the Colorado River flows on its way to the sea. The second is the Sonoran Desert, one of four North American deserts that crosscut the Basin and Range province. The Central Arizona Project is a phenomenon created by the need to bring water to desert land, and it encompasses more territory in the Basin and Range province and the Sonoran Desert than in either the Colorado Plateau or the mountain Transition Zone. This is a land of contrasts and paradoxes, a place of implausible contradiction where scarcity and excess coexist. The rain falls too much, or not enough; the cactus repels at the same time that it yields luscious fruit. The land is also remarkable for its physical and biological diversity. Distinctive, rich plant and animal communities have taken hold in the mountains, *bajadas*, river valleys, basin floors, and the coast—places which people in their ingenuity have colonized, farmed, and used for millennia. Through centuries of experimentation and inevitable failures, the people of the desert, past and present alike, have forged a surpassing compromise with this land of contrasts. It all begins with Basin and Range topography, and this is where our story unfolds.

LAND, WATER, AND LIVING THINGS

The Basin and Range province contrasts with the Colorado Plateau in many ways. Instead of softly shaped pinnacles and mesas of flowing, red stone, the desert is pale and craggy, sharp as the spiky tips of agave plants. Black, volcanic mountains punctuate the clean, light expanses of sandy plains. Plants cling to the rocks precariously, and the light is blindingly brilliant. Most mountains are not softened by pine and juniper or rounded by erosion through unimaginable epochs of time. The Basin and Range province does not resemble the stereotypical desert of windswept, bare sand. Only in the westernmost parts of Sonora and Arizona do expanses of dunes recall the desert's cinematic image. We can look primarily to geological processes to explain these contrasts.

Narrow mountain ranges and intervening alluvial valleys define the province and provide its label. The province extends from eastern California into Nevada and encompasses Arizona south of the Mogollon Rim. The Colorado Plateau and the Sierra Madre Occidental in Mexico form a huge island separating the western part of the province from its eastern extension into New Mexico, Texas, and northern Mexico (Scarborough 2000). Elevations range from sea level to mountain peak and are responsible for the Sonoran Desert's unusual biological diversity.

Desert

We remember why we love the desert; it is our tactile response to light, to silence, and to stillness.

Hand on stone—patience.

Hand on water—music.

Hand raised to the wind—Is this the birthplace of inspiration?

—*Terry Tempest Williams,* Red: Passion and Patience in the Desert

The Basin and Range physical landscape began to form some 15 million years ago. Unable to resist tectonic movement, the earth's hot, fluid crust was uplifted, tilted, and rotated to create abruptly rising mountains. Scarborough (2000:75) has described this process as "a giant geo-taffy pull." The granitic "metamorphic-core-complex" mountains were further shaped by continuous faulting. By about 8 million years ago, the Basin and Range province stabilized (Scarborough 2000). Erosion then began to fill the intermontane basins with sediment, which eventually covered much of the **mountain pediment**, leaving remnants we recognize as today's ranges. Erosion of the pediment and rising slopes created much of the alluvium in the intermontane basins. As much as 5,000 feet of sediment fills the valleys (Scarborough 2000:77).

The mountain ranges rising above the basin floors—bare, patient, and often shaped into fantastic, ragged forms—trend from northwest to southeast. They range

Basin and Range topography. PHOTOGRAPH BY JEFFERSON REID.

from 3,000 to nearly 10,000 feet above sea level, although most are between 3,000 and 5,000 feet high. These mountains created enormous technological challenges for the engineers who built the Central Arizona Project. The Hayden-Rhodes Aqueduct must cross through or skirt the Bouse Hills and Buckskin, Granite Wash, Harquahala, Big Horn, and Hieroglyphic Mountains. The Superstition, Picacho, Tortolita, Waterman, and Tucson Mountains constrained the location of the Fannin-McFarland and Tucson Aqueducts.

Most mountains are geologically old ranges formed of granitic rocks, although there are also some young, volcanic mountains. The Tucson Mountains, for example, are the remnants of an ancient volcanic caldera. Some sedimentary deposits occur in the Basin and Range province, but far less than the vast expanses of sandstone and limestone on the Colorado Plateau.

Tucson Mountains. Photograph by Jefferson Reid.

Varied landforms distinguish the province: alluvial fans, stream terraces that developed as rivers cut their way across rock and sand, floodplains along the rivers and washes, desert pavement, lava flows and cinder cones, sand-dune fields. One of the latter is the Gran Desierto of extreme northwestern Sonora, a sand sea covering 2,200 square miles and the largest area of active sand dunes in North America (Kresan 1997).

West of the Tucson Aqueduct and south of the Gila River is a huge stretch of dry land called the Papaguería, homeland of the Papago, after the former name of the O'odham people who live there. The region extends west to the Colorado River and encompasses the Barry M. Goldwater Air Force Range, which was established in the 1940s for training U.S. Air Force pilots and bombers; Cabeza Prieta National Wildlife Refuge; and Organ Pipe Cactus National Monument. Historically, the Papaguería was home to two groups of the O'odham people, the Hia-C'ed O'odham, formerly called the Sand Papago, and the Tohono O'odham, once known as the Papago.

Aridity, steep landforms, and lack of vegetative cover are desert features that precluded the development of deep, rich soils in most areas. Much of the desert is covered with a thin mantle of soil, and some areas, such as exposed bedrock and drifting sand dunes, lack it entirely. Relatively shallow, coarse soils cover the upper *bajadas,* increasing in depth on the lower *bajadas.* Most desert soils lack moisture and humus and have a sandy texture; they may be highly alkaline. A hardpan or caliche formation—a rock-like deposit of cemented calcium carbonate—occurs below the surface of many desert soils, lurking to present an unwelcome discovery to modern-day gardeners. Soil also affects vegetation. Creosote, for example, is often found on shallow soils lacking clay and high in calcium content. Where clay content is higher, cactus and bursage dominate (McAuliffe 2000). "Red," writes Williams (2001:139), "is the color of water in the desert"—the red of iron-rich soil washed into desert streams in flood, the red of blood, the red of sunset hues.

Deeper, finer soils developed in the intermontane basins and the floodplains along the river courses. These soils can and did support intensive farming in prehistoric and historical times—but to be productive, desert soils require water. This, of course, was the original rationale for damming desert streams and building canals. With enough water, desert soils yield abundantly, especially those that are periodically enriched by slopewash or flooding. Because of the richer soils and availability of water, desert dwellers concentrated in the river valleys throughout prehistory and history. These same desert valleys were the locale for many later water-control projects, including those built by the Bureau of Reclamation.

Desert Water

Because water is the key to survival in this land, all life has developed strategies to conserve and use it. Although the word "desert" implies little water, it is there nonetheless, for different water sources mark and web the desert surface. Rivers are first, the lifeblood of the land. Today's rivers have been dammed, diverted, and lined with concrete. Most carry no water except after heavy storms or when spring snows melt. But when the West was still wild, water flowed in the now-dry riverbeds, at least some of the time. With their aquatic habitats and riparian woodland borders, rivers were one of the most important zones of human habitation and use.

Water is Life

In Spanish, desert dwellers say, *sin agua, no hay vida*—without water, there is no life.

The Gila River is one of the Colorado's major tributaries and the most important drainage system in the Basin and Range province. Some say that this river "has a history as long, as dramatic, and as significant as any in America" (Corle 1951:Foreword). The Gila has been christened many times—El Río del Nombre de Jesus, Río Azul, Río de los Apostoles (Waters 1984:151). Xila, said to be a Spanish rendering of a Yuman-language name (Corle 1951:9), was the one that stuck. By the time James Ohio Pattie penned his recollections in the 1820s, it was known as the Gila, or "Helay" as Pattie spelled it.

Gila River near Safford, Arizona. PHOTOGRAPH BY STEPHANIE WHITTLESEY.

The Gila rises in the icy Mogollon Mountains of western New Mexico. It crosses 600 miles of Arizona territory on its way to join the Colorado River, traversing the entire state. On the way, the Gila crosses Transition Zone mountains and some of the most arid parts of the Basin and Range province—spanning on a small scale the Southwest's remarkable repertoire of physiographic and environmental diversity.

This river, too, has been dammed—"We owe the river honor," Gregory McNamee (1994:7) has written. "Instead, we continue to destroy it." The Gila River is controlled by Coolidge Dam, which holds back San Carlos Lake in the Mountain Transition Zone. The reservoir began silting up immediately after the dam was built in the 1930s, and erosion entrenched the river channel. Other dams on the Gila River are downstream in the desert Basin and Range country.

Paradoxically, the desert basin surrounding Phoenix is well watered by rivers. By a quirk of topography, all of Arizona's major streams—the Gila, Santa Cruz, Verde, Salt, Hassayampa, and Agua Fria, all except the Colorado, Little Colorado, and San Pedro Rivers—meet and flow together there (Sheridan 1995). Before the dams, some of these rivers carried water during most seasons and in most years, but others did not. Peculiar geological circumstances forced water to the surface only along the middle stretches of the Santa Cruz River. Elsewhere, the river ran underground. This water could often be reached by digging wells or waterholes (*pozos*) in the riverbeds.

Santa Cruz River. PHOTOGRAPH BY JEFFERSON REID.

Next in importance are the many secondary watercourses draining the higher slopes. These run with ephemeral water after summer storms, water that fades as quickly as it comes. There are too many to list them all, but some of the major washes include Cunningham, Bouse and Centennial Washes along the Hayden-Rhodes Aqueduct; Queen Creek near Florence; McClellan, Durham, and Los Robles Washes around the Picacho Mountains; and Brawley Wash near the Tucson Mountains. We will return to some of these places later in the chapter.

To Childs (2000:171), the desert is a dry map of floods. "The desire of water is scribed across the desert like graffiti, until all that is left of the desert is water." As it flows, water moving across the land leaves indisputable traces that can be read like the pages of book. Imbrication, or the particular way water stacks objects in a downstream direction; polished curves in stone; the webbed network of drainages—these are some of the clues that tell us where water has passed and how it moved. Coyote, Mohawk, San Cristobal, Growler, Sauceda, Sand Tank, Vekol, Santa Rosa Washes—these names speak of moving water in the O'odham people's native home.

Floods rushing down the watercourses keep the riparian forests along desert rivers alive. Because the streams are not perennial, plants rely on groundwater that is recharged by floods. Cataclysm therefore brings life (Childs 2000:138). It has meant life to humans as well. Floodwater rushing in the streams could be diverted and conveyed to fields by simple ditches. Archaeological and anthropological studies tell us that this was one of the desert farmer's most important strategies. Floodwater is extremely high in nutrients, a rich soup like liquid compost. Analysis of the water's content has shown that the floating detritus is the richest part of the floodwater, containing more than 50 times as much nitrogen (Nabhan 1982:128). Tohono O'odham farmers knew this, locating their fields ingeniously so as to receive the nutrient benefit of rushing floods. Each flood brought a new surge of crop growth (Nabhan 1982:128).

A third source of desert water is rare, often hidden—springs, *cienegas,* and natural waterholes. Springs located along fault lines and driven by artesian flow have become literal oases in the desert, what Nabhan (1982:90) has called "watermarks." Sweet water and luxuriant vegetation thick with birds define these places. Perhaps the most famous is Quitobaquito Springs in Organ Pipe Cactus National Monument. Called in O'odham 'A'al vaipia, "little spring or little water," this spring with its fresh water and shade has welcomed travelers for centuries. Tohono O'odham used its water to raise squash, watermelon, medicinal plants, beans, wild greens, and fruit trees (Nabhan 1982). According to geologist Peter Kresan (1997), radiocarbon analyses indicate that the springs, which emerge from the granite of the surrounding hills, are less than 2,000 years old. A city oasis is Agua Caliente Springs in eastern Tucson. Now an urban park, it also has a long history of use by many different peoples.

Charcos are clay-bottomed, natural depressions that hold rainwater intermittently. Mexican and Tohono O'odham ranchers sometimes enlarge and dam them to make *represos* (stock tanks). Whereas water flowing in washes often disappears where it hits the sandy wastes, it hides high in rocky places (Childs 2000:28). *Tinajas* are aligned along watercourses instead of scattered randomly like the water pockets of the Colorado Plateau (Childs 2000). *Tinajas* helped early travelers cross the deserts and still succor its animal denizens. *Tinajas* are evanescent, entirely natural, steadfast against human interference. Attempts to enlarge or improve them usually fail, changing the quality of the water or causing it to disappear entirely.

The Gulf of California is the last desert water source, although no one can drink it. The sandy beach abutting a deep-blue sea presents a backdrop against which curious cactus and stark mountains rise in inexplicable contrast. As we saw in Chapter 1, tidal wetlands, salt flats, and marshes once marked the Colorado River delta, with its braided riverbed and its sandy islands. *Pozos* supplied fresh water along the coast. In prehistoric and historical times alike, people traveled to the Gulf to collect salt and seashells, to hunt and fish in this rich ecological zone. Even desert peoples dream of the sea, the source of all rain.

The Desert Smells Like Rain

Even before the clouds become visible, the other sensory nerves are affected. The odor of wet dirt precedes the rain. It is an aroma so strong for some that it wakes them from sleep. People like to breathe deeply of this wet dirt smell. It is the smell not only of dirt but of the dry bark of mesquite and other acacias. It is the smell of the fine dust that must settle on all the needles and spines of saguaro and all manner of cactus, the dust that settles on the fine leaves of the ocotillo and other leafed plants. It is all of those things that give off an aroma only when mixed with rain. It is all breathed in deeply.

[The women] would remark about the *si s-wa 'us u:wi* (it smells like wetness).

Ofelia Zepeda, Ocean Power: Poems from the Desert

The Sonoran Desert

Within the Basin and Range physiographic province is the Sonoran Desert, the greatest of North America's desert ecosystems. A desert is defined by climate and biological communities, and it is important to remember that living communities are supported by the desert climate. In other words, a desert would not be a desert if more rain fell, and its living residents would not survive.

Defining a Desert

Ecologist Mark Dimmit (2000a:10) has provided a good definition of a desert:

> A desert is a biological community in which most of the indigenous plants and animals are adapted to chronic aridity and periodic, extreme droughts, and in which these conditions are necessary to maintain the community's structure.

PHOTOGRAPH BY JEFFERSON REID.

The Sonoran Desert occupies most of southern Arizona and consequently encompasses the majority of the Central Arizona Project. A north-south line between Arizona east of Tucson and Guaymas, Sonora bounds the desert on the east. The Chihuahuan Desert lies beyond this line. To the northeast, the Sonoran Desert (like the Basin and Range physiographic province) is limited by the Mogollon Rim. In the west, the desert extends to the central mountains of California and Baja California. This vast region, covering about 120,000 square miles, includes Baja California, the arid portions of southwestern Arizona, parts of southeastern California, and northwestern Sonora. In the sections that follow, we focus on the Sonoran Desert when we describe climate, plants, and animals.

Climate

By definition, aridity stamps this land as a desert. The Sonoran Desert averages between 3 and 15 inches of precipitation each year. Most places receive less than 10 inches—indeed, this is the threshold ecologists typically use to define a desert—and much of the desert garners considerably less. We can blame the encircling mountain ranges and prevailing winds. The Cascade Mountains and Sierra Nevada create a rain shadow that dries moist air coming from the Pacific Ocean. Most storms fail to generate enough force or sufficient moisture to reach the Sonoran Desert without losing their precious cargo as they cross the mountain ranges. Moist air that makes it that far arrives on the back of strong, westerly winds (Ingram 2000).

Rain falls in a biseasonal winter-summer pattern. The seasonal changes in wind systems that bring wet and dry periods to the desert are called the monsoon. In the summer, moist-air masses collide with superheated air rising over the desert, generating intense storms. Although it was once thought that summer storms originated in the Gulf of Mexico, meteorologists now believe that most moisture derives from the Gulf of California and the Pacific Ocean. The circular movement of winds across the desert, which cause storms to arrive from a southeasterly direction, gave rise to the Gulf of Mexico theory (Ingram 2000:43). The biggest summer storms come from convective complexes that arise over Sonora and move into southern Arizona.

Summer rainfall is highly localized. Rain may fall torrentially in one place and leave the land a quarter-mile away as dry as dust. Summer-monsoon thunderstorms are brief, violent, and spectacular, punctuated by crashing thunder, blue-hot lightning, and are often accompanied by destructive hail and windstorms. So-called microbursts—intense, highly localized wind and rain storms resembling tornados in miniature—can do tremendous damage, tearing off roofs and splintering mobile homes. In the southern desert, storms inevitably occur in the afternoon and taper off in the evening hours. Typically, enormous cumulus masses begin building over the mountains around noon and spill their precious cargo by the middle of the afternoon. Farther north, rain is often a late-night phenomenon, as storms built over the Mogollon Rim are blown down into the Phoenix area.

Chubasco

Sonoran tradition holds that the summer monsoon—*chubasco* in local Spanish—begins on the Feast Day of San Juan, June 24. In times past, Tucson families would celebrate the rains with picnics on the banks of the Santa Cruz River. The traditional feast-day treats always included watermelon (*sandía*).

So-called "flash floods" are common in the desert summer. Rain falling in the mountains rushes down bare slopes, collects in washes, and floods downhill along normally dry watercourses. Washes running after storms are hazards for unwary motorists, trapping "both the ignorant and those who have grown contemptuously familiar" (Krutch 1951: 70–71). Every summer, automobiles are washed away when drivers ignore the warning signs and instead of waiting prudently for the water to subside—which it usually does rather quickly—try to drive through a flooded wash. Inevitably, some marooned driver must be rescued by helicopter, giving rise to the "stupid motorist" law that makes the driver responsible for the rescue costs. Some have even drowned in the raging floodwaters.

Winter brings an entirely different kind of rainfall. Cyclonic storms from the Pacific Coast usually bring cloudy skies and strong winds to the Sonoran Desert. Only the most powerful storms created by low pressure and accompanied by sufficient moist air bring significant winter precipitation (Ingram 2000). Winter's rains are typically prolonged, widespread, and gentle. Sonorans call them *las equipatas*, "little packages" of rain (Ingram 2000:45). These storms tend to last for several days, and when the airflow pattern is established, it tends to persist, bringing several successive storms (Ingram 2000). Snow falls only rarely—some desert stations have never recorded snowfall—and it does not last for long.

Winter rain is more important than summer rain for maintaining desert ecosystems. Soft, gentle, soaking into the ground, it is the winter rain that keeps away drought. When winter is wet, the desert puts on an amazing show of colorful bloom in spring, and the benefits last into the summer. When cyclical La Niña events bring changes to ocean currents and air-circulation patterns, winter drought is often the result. The Tohono O'odham knew this, too. They planted their desert wheat in January or February. A Tohono O'odham farmer explained this to naturalist Gary Nabhan (1982:7). "It grows good on just the *rain*water from the sky. It would not do good with water from the *ground*, so that's why we plant it when those soft winter rains come to take care of it." Strangely, only rainwater has this effect. Experiments have shown that the same amount of groundwater artificially applied to the desert does not produce the same results (Nabhan 1982).

El Niño and La Niña

El Niño and La Niña are cyclical, global weather patterns that characterize the winter season. El Niño was named in Spanish for the Christ child because it often arrives in December. Mrill Ingram (2000) explains El Niño and La Niña. El Niño increases the likelihood and severity of winter storms. During El Niño, warm water collects in the western Pacific as trade winds weaken, keeping ocean water from circulating and raising water temperature. Warm water drifts eastward, causing changes in atmospheric pressure and trade winds, which reinforces changes in ocean temperature. The jet stream shifts to the south and powerful Pacific storms form farther to the east. The net result is that strong storms and moisture are carried to the southwestern United States and northern Mexico.

La Niña is the opposite pattern, and drought is the typical result. Unusually cold ocean temperatures reverse the mutually reinforcing effects of winds, ocean temperatures, and resulting storm events. Storms are weaker and carry less moisture.

Sometimes the desert suffers from a surfeit of water, one of its many paradoxes. Virtually all of the destructive desert floods since records have been kept have taken place between October and March. Widespread, soaking winter storms cover much of the desert watershed—unlike the highly localized, summer monsoon—and drop quantities of rain and snow in the mountains. When the shallow, drenched soil cannot absorb further moisture, it washes away and is funneled into the riverbeds. This sometimes happens when tropical cyclones originate in the north Pacific Ocean, usually in the fall (Ingram 2000:45). Some of the worst desert floods have been tropical-cyclone events.

Those who lived through Arizona's floods of 1983 or 1993 can fully comprehend the power of water in the desert. Rivers overflowed and spread into low-lying areas, submerging homes and turning formerly dry property into

Desert Floods: Human-caused or Mirage?

An ongoing debate is whether destructive floods are a long-term pattern in the Southwest or if they are the product of recent human activities. On the one hand, stream-flow reconstructions based on tree-ring studies indicate that tremendous floods extended back into prehistoric times and even further. The A.D. 1300s were a time of particularly marked high precipitation and flood events. On the other hand, some scholars believe that human activities around the turn of the twentieth century exacerbated the destructive effects of floods. Overgrazing by cattle and sheep, the eradication of the beaver population, and woodcutting destroyed vegetative cover and irrevocably damaged the watershed, increasing erosion and contributing to flooding.

Longhorn cattle. PHOTOGRAPH BY JEFFERSON REID.

Although dams, the soil cementing of river banks, and the artificial diversions of natural channels have been widely used to control flooding, floods can still occur in the winter when the reservoirs are full to capacity and heavy storms drench the mountain ranges of the desert watershed. Moreover, runoff can actually be increased in cities, where acres of roads, pavements, parking lots, and other covered surfaces cannot absorb water. Ingram (2000:49) has suggested that flood control can worsen the effects of storms by increasing the speed with which floodwaters move as well as the amount of water.

Regardless of their causes, floods can be devastating. According to Ingram (2000:45), more than 1,300 homes were destroyed or severely damaged during the 1983 flood, the bridge over the Gila River on Interstate 10 between Phoenix and Tucson was washed out, and nine people drowned.

lakes. Houses, office buildings, corrals, stables, horses, cattle, automobiles, bridges, roads, and more were literally swept away as torrents of water undercut the river banks, causing collapse.

Spring and fall tend to be the driest months of the desert year. Little rain falls after the monsoon ceases in August until the winter storm pattern sets in, and there is a similarly dry interval in the spring before the monsoon begins again. May and June are typically the driest months—in two years of every three, no rain falls at all in May. As we have seen, the fall dry season is sometimes broken by tropical-cyclone storms.

Within this general pattern, there is considerable variability according to latitude, landform, and elevation. The gradient of total annual rainfall declines from east to west; whereas Tucson benefits from 10 to 12 inches of rain each year, Yuma receives less than 4 inches, and virtually no rain falls in some places. The Gran Desierto, for example, is one of the most arid regions on earth. According to Kresan (1997), no measurable precipitation was recorded there for a 34-month period between 1969 and 1972.

There is a similar gradient from north to south. Many areas of Sonora receive more moisture relative to the desert north of the border. South of Tucson, summer rainfall is also greater than winter precipitation. Elevation creates additional variation. Mountain ranges receive more precipitation than valley floors as a consequence of the orographic effect of moist-air masses rising above the peaks. Rain shadows create drier areas on the lee side of the mountains.

Summers are long and hot in the desert and were so even before city construction and pavement created urban heat islands where temperature is artificially increased. Like rainfall, temperatures vary with elevation and also generally decline from west to east, but variability is much less marked than with rainfall. Maximum daily temperatures commonly exceed 100 degrees Fahrenheit between the months of April and October. According to biologist Richard Felger and colleagues (1997:414), the highest temperature ever recorded in the Sonoran Desert was 134 degrees Fahrenheit. It literally takes the breath away to contemplate such heat. In the winter, daytime temperatures commonly are mild, between 60 and 75 degrees Fahrenheit, but nighttime temperatures may dip below freezing in the coldest months of December and January. The mountains are colder than the valley floors, of course. Thus it is possible for Tucson to attract snow-weary winter visitors to bask in its sun and mild temperatures when just a few miles to the north, Mount Lemmon in the Santa Catalina Mountains supports a ski area.

The long interval without frost in the desert region creates another paradox—there is a long, frost-free growing season coupled with a dearth of water for farming. Phoenix has more than 300 frost-free days each year and Tucson about 250 days. Throughout the modern irrigated areas of the Sonoran Desert, the growing season is long enough to plant and harvest two crops each year. Some archaeologists think that prehistoric farmers might have similarly benefited from the long growing season.

Plant and Animal Life

The Sonoran Desert is marked by biological diversity, defying the common perception that deserts are wastelands where no living creatures can exist. Ecologists divide global habitats into a few basic, widely spread classes that are identified by dominant plant life-forms, called biomes. Remarkably, all of the world's biomes occur in the Sonoran Desert region (Dimmitt 2000a:4). The Sonoran Desert comprises seven divisions based on characteristic vegetation, first defined by Shreve (1951). Two of these, the Lower Colorado River Valley and the Arizona Upland divisions, are found in Arizona.

The former borders the lower course of the Colorado River and the uppermost reaches of the Gulf of California. The driest and hottest of the Sonoran Desert divisions, it is distinguished by sparse, monotonous vegetation that has adapted to little rain and high temperatures. Creosote *(Larrea divaricata),* white bursage *(Ambrosian dumosa),* and burro bush *(Franseria dumosa)* are the dominant plants on the low-lying, sandy plains. Mesquite (*Prosopis* spp.) and ironwood *(Olneya tesota)* live along the ephemeral watercourses and take advantage of every possible drop of water. Columnar cacti such as saguaro are rare in this division.

Greater precipitation means far richer vegetation in the Arizona Upland division, in which much of the Central Arizona Project occurs. In this division, which occupies the highest and coldest parts of the Sonoran Desert, large shrubs and trees combine with an amazing display of cactus to create what has been called an "arborescent desert" (Dimmitt 2000a:14). **Leguminous** trees—ironwood, several species of mesquite *(Prosopis),* littleleaf or foothills palo verde *(Cercidium microphyllum),* blue palo verde *(Cercidium floridum)*—occupy the rocky *bajada* slopes. Cacti of incredible diversity in size, shape, and color include saguaro *(Carnegiea gigantea),* barrel cactus (*Ferocactus* and *Echinocactus* spp.), cholla (*Cylindropuntia* spp.), and prickly pear (*Opuntia* spp.), among many others (Dimmitt 2000b). The *bajadas* are one of the desert's richest ecological zones for human uses, yielding edible bean pods, buds and fruits of cactus, and the seeds of many different plants.

The mountains of the Arizona Upland division are "sky islands"—likened by ecologists to oceanic islands, where mountain-adapted plants and animals are isolated by miles of hot desert instead of saltwater sea. Species that would perish in the hot, dry sands of the basin floors live on the mountain slopes. The oak woodlands found on lower mountain slopes were an important source of resources not available to residents of lower elevations, although the Hohokam did not exploit this zone as often as their predecessors, the Archaic people, and later historical-period folk.

A vital but limited ecological zone is the riparian border found along desert streams. Desert watercourses harbor a rich community of plant species found nowhere else—pure stands of mesquite called *bosques,* rare deciduous trees (cottonwood *[Populus fremotii],* ash *[Fraxinus velutina],* willow [*Salix* spp.]), the tangled undergrowth of many species, and at the edges where the water slows and in marshy areas, water plants such as cattail and sedge. Birds and animals of surpassing diversity were drawn to such linear oases, and people followed. Paradoxically, the desert people were also river people, populating the riparian edges of desert streams and farming the floodplains.

The plants of the desert are at once familiar and alien. Many are desert-adapted varieties of familiar species, but others are outlandish. The tall and stately columnar cacti most readily evoke the desert—saguaro *(Carnegiea gigantea),* organpipe cactus *(Lemaireocereus thurberi),* and the huge, multiple-armed Sonoran *cardón (Pachycereus pringlei),* largest of the desert cactus. The boojum *(Idria columnaris),* a plant resembling an enormous, inverted carrot, is as bizarre looking as its Lewis Carroll name suggests. It lives in Baja California and the coastal desert of Sonora.

Boojum cactus. Photograph by Jefferson Reid.

Krutch (1951:64) remarked that the boojum "is a far more improbable looking tree than the giraffe is as an animal."

Desert plants have learned to conserve moisture through evolution and adaptation. "Almost every plant," Krutch wrote in *The Desert Year* (1951:56), "has modified itself in some visible way and announces to the most casual beholder that moisture is precious." Many plants, not only cactus, bear wicked hooks, thorns, and barbs—trees, shrubs, even herbaceous plants. The common names bear witness to the prickly nature of desert plants so dangerous to the unwary—crucifixion thorn, fishhook cactus, catclaw acacia, prickly pear. Even the innocuous, yellow-flowered *Martynia* plant develops long, hooked pods that must have inspired its evocative name, devil's claw. This plant is the primary basket-making material of the O'odham. Its peculiar claws are dried and split to provide the black color used in designs. On such plants, thorns are not simply protective devices but leafy adaptations to aridity that conserve moisture.

The Machinations of Living Things

Roger Dunbier has written in *The Sonoran Desert: Its Geography, Economy, and People* (1968:45):

> The infinitely changing size and composition of desert plant associations mirrors [the] ability of vegetative forms to exist and prosper under adverse soil and climatic conditions.
>
> A solitary walk in the desert should never fail to impress the thoughtful observer of the numberless subtle machinations of living things pitted against compelling forces of inanimate nature.

Long tap roots on plants such as mesquite enable the trees to access the higher water table along desert streams. Thickened stems, succulent pads or leaves, and pulpy interiors preserve a high ratio of mass to surface, reduce evaporation, and enable plants to store water almost indefinitely. The saguaro, barrel cactus, and the paddle-shaped prickly pear are examples of this mechanism in action. The saguaro's shallow roots, which form a network spreading for yards around the plant, can take up enormous quantities of water after summer downpours. The plant

Prickly pear cactus. PHOTOGRAPH BY STEPHANIE WHITTLESEY.

can store the water for as long as a year. The saguaro pays a price for this adaptative mechanism. Its shallow roots make the plant susceptible to toppling over in windstorms, a problem that is exacerbated by the tremendous weight of the water-heavy cactus. In plants without leaves, chlorophyll is concentrated in stems and bodies, as in the green bark of palo verde trees and the columns and pads of cactus.

Another strategy is simply to lie low and wait. Seeds may overwinter, awaiting rain to germinate and burst into bloom in the spring. Many desert plants put forth small leaves and blossoms only after rains and then quickly resume their typical barren state. The ocotillo *(Fouquieria splendens)* is one such plant. Its long, slender, thorny branches—much used by O'odham and Mexican peoples for building shelters, shades, and living fences—are bare most of the time, bursting forth with fresh, green leaves after the briefest of rains. For the ocotillo, there are many springtimes (Krutch 1951:211).

There is paradox in desert plants. Driving through the desert on a late-spring or early summer evening, one may catch the faint but exotic perfume of blooming plants that are scarcely visible by day and well armored to boot. Night-blooming cereus or queen of the night *(Peniocereus greggii)*—a cactus with long, spindly arms, a huge, bulbous root, and gorgeous white blooms—and devil's claw are among the most beautifully perfumed plants of the desert. Tohono Chul Park in Tucson holds special events allowing the public to see the brief, gorgeous blossoming of its queen-of-the-night cactus—a spectacular, once-in-a-lifetime opportunity. The exotic lushness of desert flowers contrasts strongly with their thorns, hooks, and barbs, their wizened leaves and spindly stems. When the winter rains have been sufficient, the brown, seemingly bare desert appears to bloom overnight, bursting forth in a riot of color and scent (Waters 1984:92).

Like plants, the animals of the Sonoran Desert must conserve moisture. Life literally goes underground to escape the blistering heat and await the rains. Creatures seek crevices in stone, the shade of trees and jumbled rocks, ledges on north-facing hills. They dig dens and burrows in the cool dirt, damp after rare rains. Some animals are never active during the day, others only in the winter or in the cooler dusk and dawn hours (Siminiski 2000). Desert dwellers have developed odd mechanisms to conserve precious moisture in their bodies. Some animals drink very little, if at all, acquiring moisture from the vegetation they eat. Others have developed unusual appendages, systems, and behaviors. Vultures, for example, urinate on their own legs to cool the body by evaporation (Siminiski 2000). Insects have developed mechanisms to locate sources of desert water. The predacious backswimmer (Notonectidae family)

Desert Torches

Joseph Wood Krutch (1951:211) writes of the ocotillo in spring:

> Nevertheless, it knows somehow when the one authentic spring has come and, whether it be at the moment leafy or leafless, a tapering cluster of buds forms at the very tip of nearly every branch and soon expands into a four- or five-inch cone of waxy scarlet blossoms. Over many a bare slope otherwise almost completely destitute of bright color, hundreds of these little flames are waved gently back and forth in the breeze until it is hard to not believe, literally, the inevitable description–hundreds of torches mysteriously burning across the desert as far as sight can reach.

Ocotillo. PHOTOGRAPH BY JEFFERSON REID.

The Body's Need for Water

Naturalist Ann Zwinger (1989:116–117) has written eloquently about the human body's physiological need for water and what happens when water is lost:

> No amount of training, no amount of acclimation, alters the amount of water that is needed to replace water lost in perspiration. Because the body can neither store water nor reduce its need, water supply is critical. . . .
>
> Paradoxically, even with ample water available, it is difficult to drink and recover the amount lost immediately, because thirst becomes satiated before one's intake equals water loss. A person, voluntarily, drinks only a third to half of what is needed for replacement. . . .
>
> . . . If water loss from sweating is not replaced, sweat glands extract water from blood plasma, and body temperature rises. . . .
>
> At 2 percent loss of body weight due to loss of body water, thirst for some may already be fierce, accompanied by anorexia, flushed skin, and increased pulse rate. Small increments of debit have large symptoms: at 4 percent the mouth and throat go dry; by 8 percent the tongue feels swollen, salivary functions cease, and speech becomes difficult. At 10 percent the ability to cooperate, or even operate, disappears. At 12 percent loss, circulation becomes so impaired that an explosive heat rise deep in the body is imminent and deep body temperature rises dangerously fast. Death follows. . . . When liquid is available, recovery can be nearly complete an hour after drinking.

captures insects living in pools, which it locates by seeking polarized, ultraviolet light reflected from smooth bodies of water (Childs 2000:68).

The Sonoran Desert's animal life is as rich as its plants and equally distinctive. Pronghorn, deer, bighorn sheep, ring-tailed cats or coatimundi, bobcats, the Mexican gray wolf, and farther south in earlier times, jaguars, are less familiar desert denizens than coyote, jackrabbit, cottontail, the pig-like javelina, and Gambel's quail. Birds are particularly varied, as desert streams serve as migration routes for many species. From hummingbirds to hawks, the desert is alive with the language of birds and the sound of wings. Native fishes inhabiting the Colorado River and other desert streams include squawfish *(Ptychocheilus lucius),* chub (*Gila* spp.), and suckers *(Xyrauchen texanus).* Along the coast, many species of fish, marine animals and birds, and shellfish offer another diverse set of resources.

SONORAN DESERT PEOPLES

The Sonoran Desert's human occupants evoke yet another paradox. "Desert," meaning uninhabited place, does not apply to a land that has hosted many people of diverse cultures. We might attribute the desert's mixed population to its geographic position, situated between the Colorado Plateau–Transition Zone country to the north and Mexico. Perhaps the Sonoran Desert's singular landscape and rich resources lured people. Today, the desert is home to an astonishing diversity of peoples drawn to its climate and unique character. In historical times, many Native American groups lived in the desert, traveled through it, or used it as a resource zone—the O'odham peoples profiled in this chapter, Yaqui or Yoemé, Maricopa, Chiricahua Apache, and Western Apache. People of African, Chinese, and Mexican descent lived and worked alongside those of European background. In prehistoric times, cultures labeled by archaeologists as **Trincheras,** Salado, and Patayan coexisted with the primary prehistoric culture, the Hohokam. Still earlier, Archaic peoples of different cultural traditions and perhaps languages occupied the desert.

To profile all of these peoples would require more space than we have in this book. Instead, we will focus on the ancient Native Americans that we learned so much about from Central Arizona Project archaeology—the Hohokam and the Archaic peoples. We will also meet the O'odham. Although distinct in their lifeways, subsistence practices, religious beliefs, and social organization, all the Sonoran Desert's residents shared characteristics that enabled them to forge a successful life in this capricious, unpredictable, sublime land. To master the desert requires flexibility, ingenuity, fortitude, and perhaps most importantly, affection. It is impossible to hate the desert and live there with equanimity.

Desert Home

[The desert is] a hard-mind place, not a soft-skin place, and concealed in its openness. You cannot stroke it as you would a meadow, you cannot dissemble, nor are there corners in which to hide. . . . In its qualities of severity and reserve, in its harmony of line and color, in its abstraction of design, lies an uncompromising formality. No other scene achieves this to such a degree. Once met on its own terms it evokes a curious tranquility and composure.

No, the desert cannot be fought successfully, and to join it one must come to know it, and to know it one must walk in it.

—*Ann Woodin,* Home is the Desert

Archaic Culture

Archaeologists do not know with certainty when people first came to inhabit the Sonoran Desert. Native American peoples often react with amusement and skepticism when asked how long they have been in their homelands. "We have always been here," they will answer. We know that intrepid, Paleoindian big-game hunters of the Clovis tradition tracked their prey across the Sonoran Desert some 10,000 to 12,000 years ago, but we know little of these people or their lifeways. Our first good glimpse of ancient life in the desert comes from the campsites of the Archaic people.

At the end of the Pleistocene, a dramatic shift in climate signaled the extinction of numerous animal species—mammoths, dire wolves, horses, camels, many others. Cold winds no longer blew icily off the glaciers that had covered most of Canada, and Arizona's climate became more like that of today. New vegetation and animals were established. These changes meant the end of the big-game-hunting lifestyle. People lived by hunting smaller game and collecting a great variety of wild-plant foods—

The O'odham Creation Story

Two Akimel O'odham (Pima) men, Juan Smith and William Allison, told this version of the creation story to archaeologist Julian Hayden. The telling took place over several spring nights in 1935 during excavations at Snaketown on the Gila River Indian Reservation. The full text of several versions of the story can be found in Bahr and others (1994:52).

In the beginning there was no earth and no heaven, only darkness. God made the first being, who was made of light, and another being, Earth Doctor (Jewed Ma:kai). Earth Doctor sang a song to make the earth and heavens come together. From their union came Siuuhu (The Drinker or Drink-it-all-up). (In Tohono O'odham versions of the creation story, Siuuhu is named I'itoi or Elder Brother.) Together, Earth Doctor and Siuuhu made the first man and woman from clay, breathing life into them. From them came all the O'odham peoples.

God, Earth Doctor, and Siuuhu worked together to create the dawn, the sun, the moon, the rain, and clouds, and all the foods for the people to live on. Each of these creations were made with songs. First man killed a deer and first woman cooked grass seeds for supper. God, Earth Doctor, and Siuuhu made the stars and the Milky Way. Earth Doctor made a buzzard (Nui) from light. Buzzard created the mountains.

Earth Doctor and Siuuhu sang:

The land is still now
And on it everything seems to be all right
Everything is made perfect.

The mountains were shaking
But now they are still
And on them everything is perfect.

seeds of grasses, nuts and berries, fruits of cactus and yucca, beans from leguminous trees such as mesquite. Although the people fabricated a rich variety of tools and equipment from perishable materials, wood, and stone, they did not make pottery. For this reason, the Archaic is also sometimes called a "**preceramic**" culture. The time, the lifeways, and the people are collectively called the Archaic. During the Archaic period, farming and domesticated plants would become critical to life in the Sonoran Desert.

In southeastern Arizona, Archaic period sites have been known since the 1920s. It was not until 1941 that E. B. "Ted" Sayles of Gila Pueblo Archaeological Foundation in collaboration with Ernst Antevs defined the culture and gave it a name—the Cochise culture. The name and its definition were destined to change several times. Archaic sites were explored sporadically in subsequent years, but it was largely thought that southern Arizona was an empty niche, virtually uninhabited until Hohokam farmers arrived (Doyel 1984). Central Arizona Project archaeology in the Picacho Reservoir area of south-central Arizona put this notion to rest. In the 1990s, our understanding increased exponentially with a virtual explosion of contract-sponsored work.

The lifestyle of Archaic peoples was dictated by necessity and emphasis. Hunting took second place to gathering, and the contribution of women to the economy increased significantly from earlier times when the hunt was vital. Archaic people followed a seasonal round of movement dictated by the ripening of wild plants, seasonal variability in game, and later, by the needs of farming. Their shelters, equipment, tools, and indeed all material goods were geared to this mobile lifestyle and to the plant foods they ate. They fabricated baskets, cordage and nets, items of hide and wood, and used wild gourds. Stone tools were adapted for hunting small game and grinding the seeds of wild plants. They did not make or use pottery—the essential equipment of the settled village farmer—and their houses were relatively ephemeral structures of perishable construction. Long familiarity with plant gathering provided Archaic women with the knowledge that would eventually allow them to adopt plant cultivation. For thousands of years, this lifeway remained essentially unchanged.

Although other nomenclature and classificatory systems are used, most archaeologists divide the Archaic period into three intervals—Early (about 10,500–6,800 years ago), Middle (6,800–3,500 years ago), and Late Archaic (3,500–1,650 years ago) (Whittlesey and others 1994). Because farming and cultivated plants appeared during the Late Archaic period, this portion of the sequence is sometimes labeled the Early Agricultural period (Mabry and others 1997). The Cochise culture label is little used today. Note that the Archaic period of southern Arizona corresponds to the Basket Maker II period of the Colorado Plateau. (See chronology chart in Chapter 4.)

Southern Arizona was evidently sparsely settled during the Early Archaic period. By the Middle Archaic period, campsites were built on the slopes of the Santa Catalina and Santa Rita Mountains in the Tucson area, at Ventana Cave in the Papaguería, near Picacho Reservoir, and in the Santa Cruz Flats (Whittlesey and others 1994). Pits, hearths, and tools indicate that people camped while they collected and processed wild foods, sheltering in perishable structures that left no traces for archaeologists to find.

By Late Archaic times, the trajectory toward settled life and farming was nearly complete. It was a time of rapid and unprecedented change. Substantial architecture, storage facilities, cultivated plants, and more permanently occupied settlements were among the innovations characterizing Late Archaic times. Many more people lived in southern Arizona and northern Sonora in Late Archaic times than in earlier periods. Their settlements were also larger and more widespread. These shifts may imply that people migrated into the area. Many different environmental zones were used, including the *bajadas,* floodplains along rivers and secondary streams, and mountain slopes.

Some settlements, such as the Santa Cruz Bend site in the Tucson area (Mabry and others 1997), were extremely large and contained hundreds of pit structures built of brush, poles, and mud, although all were probably not occupied at the same time. The structures were relatively small, shallow, and circular. Most contained deep, bell-shaped storage pits. Along with the absence of interior hearths, this suggests that structures were specialized for storage purposes rather than habitation. Corn, squash, cotton, and tobacco were cultivated; later, beans would be added to the domesticated-plant list. A wide range of wild plants continued to be used, however, and hunting remained important.

Overview of the Santa Cruz Bend site near Tucson, Arizona.
PHOTOGRAPH BY STEPHANIE WHITTLESEY.

Archaeologists have speculated that the seasonal round and the emphasis on seed-bearing plants preconditioned Archaic peoples to accept cultivated plants enthusiastically when they were introduced. It took little additional effort to plant seeds of corn and squash and tend the growing crops, and these tasks could be incorporated into the seasonal round. Domesticated plants apparently came from what is today Mexico. There is no evidence that native peoples of the Southwest independently domesticated crops. Once cultivated foods became a dietary mainstay, there was a reciprocal effect on residential stability and population increase. In this way, Archaic peoples became committed to farming over the course of hundreds of years.

As recently as 1982, it was thought that domesticated plants, settled village life, and pottery appeared simultaneously as a complex of traits. We now know this to be untrue. There is good evidence that relatively permanent habitation preceded the arrival of corn, and pottery did not appear until long after corn was introduced to the Southwest.

Archaic people understood that clay could be mixed with water and fired to produce a stone-hard object. They made beads, figurines, and crude "ceramics." Archaic "pottery" was nothing more than poorly made and fired mud that could not have functioned adequately for cooking or storage. These containers, some containing organic materials and decorated with rough, incised designs, appeared around 200 B.C., and perhaps earlier. By A.D. 1 or so, true, functional pottery containers had appeared. The uniform appearance and characteristics of these containers, regardless of where they were found, suggests that ceramic technology was received from a single source rather than arising through experimentation. Archaeologists think that, as with domesticated plants, the cultures of Mexico were the likely source of pottery-container technology.

With the appearance of pottery vessels, the Archaic or preceramic period came to a close. Archaeologists label the initial pottery-making period the Early Formative or Early Ceramic period. Most of the earliest pottery vessels were neckless jars used to store shelled corn and other foodstuffs, indicating the close relationship between farming and pottery-container technology. The next few centuries were characterized by increasing sedentism, dependence on corn agriculture, and architectural development. Perhaps as early as A.D. 650, one of the Southwest's most sophisticated and artistically refined prehistoric peoples appeared in the desert valleys along the Santa Cruz, Gila, and Salt Rivers. These were the Hohokam, the masters of the Sonoran Desert.

Hohokam

They are enigmatic, their origins obscured and their relationships to the ancestors ambiguous. They are unique, and in many ways distinctive from their contemporary neighbors. They chose the deserts of southern Arizona as their home, mastered the technology necessary to transform the desert into a farming paradise, and flourished there for centuries. They are the Hohokam of southern Arizona, and the material evidence for their presence appeared rapidly.

The Hohokam were "discovered" and defined by archaeologists from the Gila Pueblo Archaeological Foundation in the 1930s. Piling into a Pierce-Arrow touring car especially outfitted for archaeological fieldwork, archaeologists surveyed the deserts and adjoining country for traces of the culture they named after the characteristic red-on-buff painted pottery. They found no traces in the places they surveyed, however, except in the middle Gila River valley (Reid and Whittlesey 1997:81). Shortly thereafter, the preeminent southwestern archaeologist Emil W. Haury excavated at the Roosevelt 9:6 site in the Tonto Basin and defined the culture named for an O'odham word. Later excavations at Snaketown in the Gila River valley established the validity of the culture,

Gila Pueblo Archaeological Foundation

In 1928, Harold S. Gladwin and Winifred MacCurdy Gladwin established Gila Pueblo Archaeological Foundation, a private institution for archaeological research. Gladwin was not formally educated or trained in archaeology, but instead was a stockbroker who came to archaeology as an avocation and made it his life's work. Gila Pueblo was a Salado ruin in Sixshooter Canyon just outside the mining town of Globe in central Arizona. The Gladwins purchased the ruin, excavated it, and built Gila Pueblo on the ruins. The building was constructed to resemble a prehistoric pueblo with adobe walls and multiple stories, and the prehistoric ruin's stones were used in its construction. The archaeologists Gladwin assembled lived and worked at the modern Gila Pueblo where Mrs. Gladwin grew irises and other flowers in her gardens.

Gladwin had worked for the Southwest Museum in Los Angeles, taking on a project near Casa Grande National Monument where his interest in the Hohokam culture was sparked by finding evidence for two distinctive cultures, one stratigraphically above and therefore more recent than the other. He set the staff of Gila Pueblo onto the trail of the Hohokam, or the red-on-buff culture as it was then known for the colors of its painted pottery. While tracing the spoor of the Hohokam, they discovered a large site along the Gila River—Snaketown. From this work would come the landmark publication on the Hohokam culture that stood for decades as the definitive work on the desert farmers.

The same polychrome pottery found in the Gila River valley was also found in the Tonto Basin. Gila Pueblo archaeologists began investigating this area and would define a puebloan culture they called the Salado. While surveying, archaeologist Emil Haury found plain brown pottery that was different from other known wares. He would return to the sites in western New Mexico where this pottery was found and from this work define the Mogollon culture. Gila Pueblo archaeologists also defined the Cochise culture of southeastern Arizona in addition to Mogollon, Salado, and Hohokam.

Gila Pueblo Archaeological Foundation was an extraordinarily productive enterprise that was crucial to early southwestern archaeology and prehistory. It was dissolved in 1951 and its collections donated to the Arizona State Museum. The buildings at Gila Pueblo served as a National Park Service facility for years. Today, the Gladwins' Gila Pueblo still stands, now housing a local community college. Nothing like it has come along in southwestern archaeology since, and nothing probably ever will.

Gila Pueblo as it looks today. Photograph by Stephanie Whittlesey.

its sophistication, and the wonderful artistry and skill of its craftspeople. For years, Snaketown would remain the standard by which the Hohokam would be judged. It was not until the advent of contract archaeology in the 1970s that many more Hohokam sites were excavated and our understanding increased dramatically. We now know that Hohokam people settled river valleys and desert areas away from the rivers as well as the Gila River valley.

Who, then, were the Hohokam? Some of southwestern archaeology's best minds have grappled with this question, and it is not easily answered. There are two basic theories. First, they may have been descended from Archaic and Early Formative peoples who had occupied the Sonoran Desert for thousands of years. Second, they may have been immigrant people who moved northward from what is today Mexico to establish themselves in the desert valleys.

There is no question that southern Arizona was settled during the Late Archaic period, and some places, such as Ventana Cave southwest of Tucson where Haury also excavated, exhibited an unbroken sequence of occupation for thousands of years. This is not necessarily proof of ethnic, cultural, or linguistic continuity, however. The second theory was more readily accepted when it was thought that southern Arizona was uninhabited prior to the Hohokam's arrival. Many aspects of Hohokam material culture and lifeways are similar to those of **Mesoamerica**, giving credence to the migration theory. Hohokam ceramic figurines; stone sculpture; exotic ceramic vessel forms such as tripod vessels, effigies, and **censers;** ceremonial facilities (**ball courts** and **platform mounds**); and sophisticated canal irrigation are features resembling those of their neighbors to the south. Essentially, we do not know the answer.

The Hohokam lifestyle was predicated upon innovative adjustment to the Sonoran Desert. Wholly dependent on corn agriculture, they were farmers first and foremost, although they also relied heavily on wild-plant foods, particularly mesquite and cactus. The Hohokam of the Phoenix Basin were the Southwest's premier irrigators. They depended on irrigation farming to a much greater extent than the people living in the Tucson area, because the Salt and Gila Rivers were permanent streams in contrast to the Santa Cruz River. Even in ancient times, the Santa Cruz had only intermittent surface flow. The canal systems along the Salt and Gila Rivers were many miles in length and irrigated thousands of acres of land—fields of corn, beans, cotton, squash, tobacco, other crops. According to archaeologist William Doolittle (1990), the Hohokam canal system was larger in scale than all other prehistoric systems in North America, including Mexico. Canal systems persisted over generations, not unlike Hohokam villages themselves. The Phoenix area along the permanent rivers was the center of Hohokam culture, and large, continuously occupied settlements such as Snaketown were built there.

In the desert areas away from the rivers, Hohokam farmers relied on floodwater and rainfall to water their crops and developed ingenious ways to collect, divert, and use water. Hunting was the least important aspect of subsistence. So-called "garden hunting" kept rabbits and other pests out of the cornfields and only secondarily provided meat.

Snaketown

Gila Pueblo Archaeological Foundation surveys in the late 1920s and early 1930s demonstrated that the Hohokam culture was limited to southern Arizona and concentrated in the middle Gila River valley. In the latter place they discovered an enormous site covering one square mile and containing some 60 mounds. It was called "the Place of the Snakes" by the O'odham families who lived there. Snaketown would become the first intensively excavated and most famous Hohokam site. It was excavated in 1934 and 1935 by Emil W. Haury, Julian Hayden and his father Irwin, E. B. "Ted" Sayles, and Erik K. Reed—all legendary names in southwestern archaeology—among others. The monumental report of this work was the standard by which the Hohokam would be known for many years. Haury returned to Snaketown in the 1960s to excavate another portion of the site.

Hohokam painted vessels with typical geometric motifs.
PHOTOGRAPH BY WILLIAM L. DEAVER.

Hohokam Houses

Dwellings were dome-roofed or flat-roofed constructions of poles, grass thatch, and mud, usually rectangular with rounded corners. They were typically "houses in pits," constructed by placing the side walls inside the house pit, rather than true pit houses that placed the side supports on the outside. Covered entries provided access, and the hearth was invariably located in front of the entry. Each house was occupied by a household. Pairs or clusters of pit houses facing a common outdoor space, called courtyard groups, were occupied by extended families.

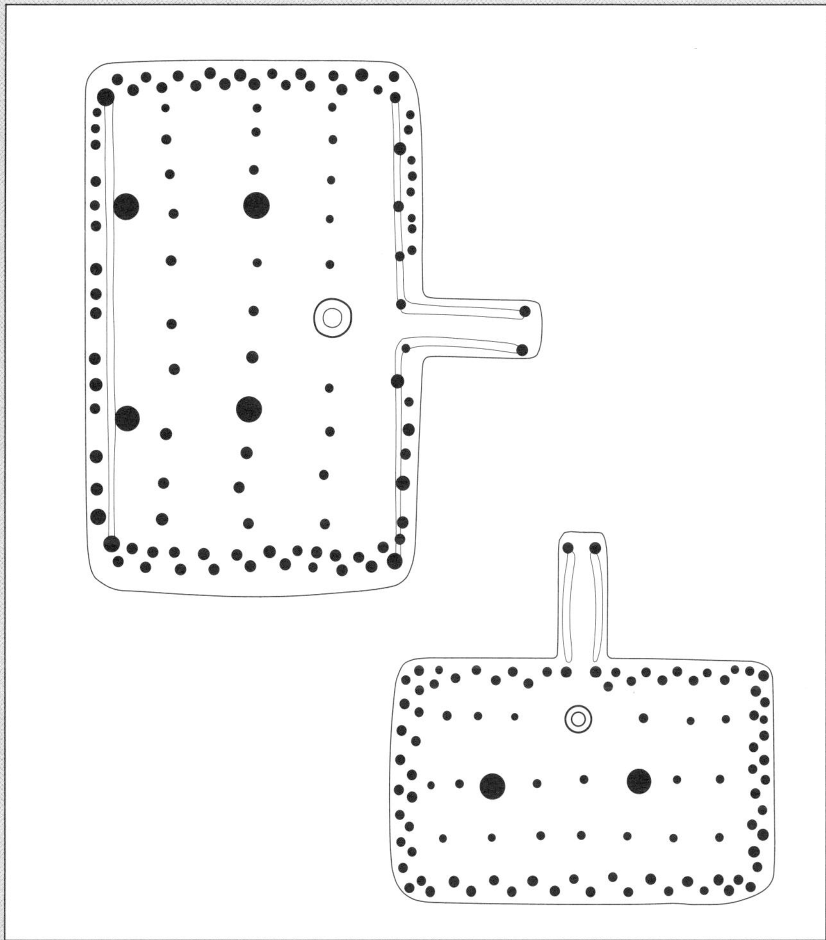

Idealized drawings of Hohokam pit houses with four-post (left) and two-post (right) roof supports.

Material culture and settlement patterns reflect the great emphasis on corn and on settled village life. People lived year-round in villages, although smaller settlements, field houses, and campsites were used for specific purposes, such as when tending and harvesting crops or collecting wild plants.

Material culture was distinctive and diverse. Pottery vessels were constructed by coiling and were smoothed with a wooden paddle and a stone or ceramic anvil. They were painted with a variety of human, animal, and geometric forms; plain ware vessels were **tempered** with micaceous **schist** that gave them a shiny, glittering appearance. It appears likely that red-on-buff painted vessels and schist-tempered vessels were made in only a limited number of locations in the Phoenix area and were transported to settlements elsewhere through trade or population movement.

Archaeologists know the Hohokam for their carved and etched shell ornaments shaped as birds, frogs, lizards, and geometric forms—all exotic, masterfully executed, and beautiful. Marine shell was obtained from the Gulf of California and fashioned with great skill into a variety of bracelets, beads, and pendants. Central Arizona Project

Unpainted Hohokam pottery vessels. PHOTOGRAPH COURTESY U.S. BUREAU OF RECLAMATION.

archaeology demonstrated that entire villages were devoted to making shell jewelry; house floors yielded shell-working tools, shell debitage, and thick deposits of dust that accumulated from grinding the shells (Howard 1993). Hohokam shell ornaments were as widely distributed as their pottery.

Unlike other prehistoric peoples of the Southwest who buried their dead, the Hohokam treated their deceased with a complex mortuary ritual centering on cremation, at least until the Classic period. The cremation ritual

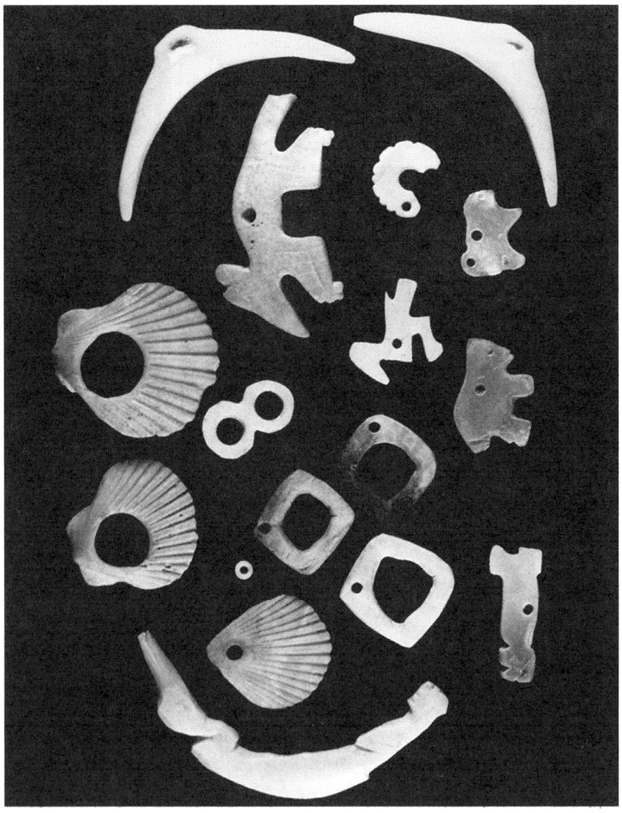

Hohokam shell ornaments. PHOTOGRAPH COURTESY U.S. BUREAU OF RECLAMATION.

evidently involved several steps. The dead were often cremated in special areas devoted to this purpose. The body was placed on a wooden platform and burned along with offerings. The remains were then either buried in place (primary cremation) or moved to another location (secondary cremation). Secondary cremations were typically placed in jars and covered with an inverted bowl. At many sites, cremation cemeteries formed spatially discrete areas associated with groups of households, indicating the importance of kinship and ancestors. There was much variability in mortuary practices, however.

Ball courts were first used during the Colonial period (refer to chronology chart in Chapter 4). These were ceremonial facilities where sacred games were carried out, although they may have served other functions as well. The elliptical, embanked constructions were made of earth. Although variable in orientation, courts were typically oriented either north-south or east-west (Wilcox 1991). Most courts had three markers, one in the center and one at each end. Most ball courts were abandoned during the Sedentary period and ceased to be used in the Classic period.

Desert areas outside of the Phoenix Basin area, thought to be the core of Hohokam settlement, were also occupied. The Tucson Basin was the locale for a vigorous and distinctive tradition, characterized by its own painted pottery, lifeways, and history. The Papaguería, the Gila Bend area, desert valleys and foothills in central Arizona north of Phoenix, and the San Pedro River valley were other places where the Hohokam settled. Outposts were established in more distant places, including the Tonto Basin, Flagstaff, and along the Verde River. It was once thought that these areas were settled by colonization, as the label "Colonial" indicates. Archaeologists also considered such areas as "peripheries" that were linked to the core via economic, political, and social relationships. Current information suggests a more complicated picture of settlement.

Differences among the areas in material culture and lifeways indicated that local populations participated in an overarching ritual, social, and cultural system, although they adapted it to their own needs. Haury (1950) used the environment to explain such differences, dividing the Hohokam into two branches—the River Hohokam along the rivers and the Desert Hohokam of the desert valleys and foothills away from the riverine zones. Other explanations for the differences among regional Hohokam groups focus on organizational variables.

The Classic period beginning around A.D. 1150 or 1200 ushered in new lifeways, organization, and material culture across the desert region (see chronology chart in Chapter 4). (Archaeologists often label the time preceding this interval as the "pre-Classic period" without distinguishing specific **phases**.) Ball courts were abandoned and replaced by platform mounds. New techniques, shapes, and designs appeared alongside traditional pottery forms.

Salado painted pottery (Tonto Polychrome jar). PHOTOGRAPH BY JEFFERSON REID.

Inhumation burial became more important or supplanted cremation burial entirely. Instead of pit houses, people lived in rectangular, aboveground houses of **adobe** construction, and settlements were often surrounded by adobe **compound** walls. In many places, population shifted rapidly and remarkably. Existing settlements were abandoned or their locations shifted, and new settlements were established in previously unoccupied areas—sometimes, it seems, almost literally overnight (S. Fish and others 1992).

Surface adobe houses at the Dairy site near Tucson, Arizona. Photograph by Stephanie Whittlesey.

The causes and processes responsible for these sweeping changes are highly controversial. Archaeologists from the Gila Pueblo Archaeological Foundation thought that a migration of puebloan people they called the Salado was responsible. Later, other scholars developed the notion of change within Hohokam culture itself. Today, some archaeologists are reverting to the original explanation—migration—although the migrating populations are viewed differently. Ancestral Puebloans fleeing the Colorado Plateau during the Great Drought traveled into the mountain region, to the Tonto Basin, along the San Pedro River, and into the Safford area. Some of these displaced peoples may have moved into the Phoenix and Tucson Basins and surrounding areas where they built homes, made pottery, and buried their dead in their accustomed ways. The Hohokam may have reorganized as their lifeways changed, possibly embracing a new ideology and religion. More work is necessary before archaeologists will fully understand this important time of transition.

By A.D. 1450 or 1500, much of the desert had been abandoned. The people appear to have concentrated around the Picacho Mountains and along the Gila River, but there was little occupation along the Salt River. In the latest phase of occupation, called the Polvorón phase in the Phoenix area, there was a return to pit-house construction, an apparent decline in population density, and other shifts that appear to mark small, impoverished, and possibly struggling groups. There remains a tremendous gap in our knowledge from this time until the first Spanish explorers and priests arrived in the Southwest. This is one of many reasons why it is so difficult to understand the fate of the Hohokam and their relationship to the historical-period native peoples of southern Arizona, to whom we turn next.

O'odham

When the first Spanish missionaries arrived in what would become Arizona in the late 1600s, they found a land populated by an industrious and generous native people. Although they were known by many different names, the Spanish called them the Pima, and their land in Arizona and Sonora was the Pimería Alta. In their own language, the Indians called themselves O'odham—simply meaning "the people."

Anthropologist Edward Spicer (1962) has estimated that as many as 30,000 Piman speakers may have been living in the Pimería Alta when Padre Kino made his famous missionary quests on horseback. The Piman language is part of the Uto-Aztecan family that includes Hopi and Tepehuan, the latter spoken by people who occupy Mexico as far south as modern Guadalajara. Piman speakers on both sides of the international border shared cultural as well as linguistic similarities.

The Spanish thought of the O'odham peoples in terms of four subdivisions—"Pimas," "Soba Pimas," "Sobaípuri" or "Soba y Jipuris" living along the San Pedro and Santa Cruz Rivers, and "Pimas Gileños" residing along the Gila River. These groups probably corresponded to dialects among Piman speakers. Anthropologist Bernard Fontana (1983) suggested that there were many different Piman-speaking groups in northern Sonora and Arizona, each living independently and with its own distinctive dialect.

Padre Kino

Eusebio Francisco Kino was a Jesuit priest of Italian descent who worked among the O'odham peoples of northern Sonora and southern Arizona. Today fondly called the "padre on horseback," Kino (the Hispanicized spelling of his original surname) arrived in the New World in 1687 already a seasoned missionary. He was soon assigned to work among the Pimas Altas, the northerly O'odham.

Kino was a tireless explorer and trailblazer, a rancher and cattleman, a teacher, and an inquisitive scientist as well as a missionary. He rode vast distances on horseback—once as far as Mexico City, an amazing 1,200-mile journey—throughout Baja California, Sonora, and Arizona. On the way he met with the native inhabitants, baptized converts, and distributed livestock, seeds, and European goods. Kino established missions in Sonora and Arizona, perhaps the most famous of which is San Xavier del Bac in today's Tucson—although the White Dove of the Desert church that now stands there was actually built later by Franciscan missionaries.

Kino left breeding stock (horses, mules, sheep, goats, and cattle) at O'odham villages, transforming the local economy to include raising livestock. He was one of the first Europeans to view the Gulf of California from Pinacate Peak, make the death-defying El Camino del Diablo crossing into California, and see the ruined Casa Grande along the Gila River.

He died in Magdalena, Sonora on March 15, 1711, as Father Charles W. Polzer (1982:19) has written, "as he had lived—in peace and poverty, and on the brink of something greater."

Facade of Mission San Xavier del Bac. PHOTOGRAPH BY JEFFERSON REID.

Biographies of Padre Kino include: Charles Polzer's Kino Guide II: His Missions and Monuments *(Southwestern Mission Research Center, Tucson, 1982), and Herbert Bolton's* The Rim of Christendom *(Russell and Russell, New York, reprinted 1960).*

These groups were absorbed into O'odham communities or became extinct through time (Rea 1997).

The O'odham made distinctions among themselves primarily on the basis of lifestyle and territory. The Akimel O'odham, or River People, lived along the Gila River; Fontana (1983) has called these people the "One Villagers" because they occupied a single village throughout the year. Today these people are generally known as the Gila River Pima.

The Tohono O'odham were the Desert People who lived away from the rivers. Fontana (1983) has called these people "Two Villagers," because they shifted their village locations between summer farming settlements and winter encampments. They were once known as the Papago; today this name is considered inappropriate. Some say that the name "Papago" can be traced to the Tohono O'odham diet, which was largely based on tepary beans. The O'odham word for tepary is *bawĭ* or *pawĭ*. When the Spanish applied their version of the word to the O'odham, it became something like the Papavi Kuá'adam, or "Tepary Eaters." Fontana (1989:38) thinks this is a possible but "highly improbable" source for the word "Papago."

The Hia-C'ed O'odham, or the "Sand Root Eaters," were the "No Villagers," once called the Sand Papago.

The Milky Way Appears

Regardless of whether it was the ultimate source of the name "Papago," the tepary bean is vital to the Tohono O'odham. The tepary bean was created and given to the people even before corn, so the story goes. The Tohono O'odham creation story as told to anthropologists Saxton and Saxton (1973:20–23) relates how the white bean became the child of the Desert People.

> Long ago, it is said, there was a little old man who hated his daughter's child. . . . He scolded his grandson and always beat the child for his faults.
>
> So, one day, he again beat his grandson, and the boy went out and slipped away. . . . The old man waited for him but he didn't come. [The old man] looked for him and couldn't find him. Then he felt very bad and went around grieving.
>
> The child had gone away and lay down up above [in the heavens]. From there he saw his grandfather going around looking for him. So he said, "I think I'll go see my grandmother and give him something. That will make him happy so he won't be doing something uselessly." So he came down.
>
> He sat down by his grandfather and said, "I am going to give you something. Take care of it, and when it multiplies, eat it and be filled and think of me. When you want to see me, go out at night and you will see me. I will be all across the sky above."
>
> When he had said this, he gave him some seed and said, "Plant it right by your head where you sleep and keep watching it so nothing will take it. It will come up and blossom and bear beans. When it gets dry, its seed will be scattered. Gather them all up[,] . . . bury them four together and watch them . . . . When they ripen, pull them up and pile them [,] . . . [t]hen get a stick to beat them with. The seed will be removed. . . . [T]ake them in your hands and throw them up, and [the wind] will blow away the stalks and leave the seed . . . . When you have planted four times it will increase enough. Then you will eat and be full from me. You will be alive and happy from me, your grandchild, who is the white bean."
>
> So that is why the white bean is the child of the Desert People. It is born here and grows here and endures dryness. When it doesn't rain enough, the white bean still comes up. The Milky Way is said to be the white bean. He lives clear across the sky. Beans grow in abundance and we see them scattered across the sky.
>
> —*Traditional Tohono O'odham story*

Living in the driest part of the western Papaguería, they were the most mobile and least agricultural of the O'odham peoples—although to some extent this may be a stereotype that has been conditioned by changing environments and shifting traditional territories.

Were the O'odham descended from the Hohokam? This is not an easy question to answer. The most widely accepted theory, one entertained by anthropologists, archaeologists, and some O'odham, is that they were related. Both groups shared irrigation farming, pit-house dwellings, and pottery made with paddle-and-anvil technology. The chief problem with the Hohokam-O'odham continuity hypothesis, Rea (1997) has noted, is that the

Tohono O'odham woman and dwelling near Mission San Xavier del Bac in 1899. Photograph courtesy Arizona Historical Society, Tucson (AHS Accession No. 13666).

theory only considers southern Arizona. Pima and Tepehuan languages are continuous along a 900-mile-long corridor extending south into Mexico, suggesting cultural continuity and a shared history. Who were the prehistoric ancestors of the Tepehuan speakers in Mexico? No archaeological remains identified as Hohokam have ever been found there.

The O'odham creation story as recorded by archaeologist Julian Hayden at Snaketown in the 1930s (Bahr and others 1994) relates another possibility—that the Hohokam of the Classic period and the O'odham were contemporary peoples who battled with each other. O'odham ancestors came from below the earth to struggle with the Hohokam. The O'odham emerged from this battle victorious, destroying as many as 10 settlements ruled by powerful chieftains with magical powers, known as *siivañi*.

Linguistic and bioarchaeological evidence appears to support the theory that the O'odham were relatively late immigrants into Arizona and Sonora. There is little time depth in the Pima language, suggesting that the O'odham came to an area that had only recently been abandoned by prehistoric peoples. **Physical anthropologist** Christy Turner (1993) compared skeletal traits, particularly dentition characteristics, among prehistoric and living peoples. He found differences among modern O'odham, pre-Classic Hohokam, and Classic period Hohokam sufficient to indicate no ancestral-descendant relationship between Hohokam and O'odham. (His findings also provide no proof of continuity between pre-Classic and Classic period Hohokam.)

This would also confirm what some of the Akimel O'odham say. According to Rea (1997), the people disasso-

The Conquest of the Hohokam

In the O'odham creation story as told by Bahr and others (1994), Siuuhu has brought the Wooshkam, the ancestors of the O'odham, from the underworld. They battled with the Hohokam chiefs, the *siiwañi*, who lived in the adobe great houses along the Gila River. The *siiwañ* of the Casa Blanca, a ruin located near the Pima settlement of that name not far from the archaeological site of Snaketown, was a master of moisture. The *siiwañ* controlled the night, mist, fog, and mirage. He commanded four different kinds of fog to surround the *vahki* (clay house) so the Wooshkam could not see it. A Wooshkam medicine man saw that the chief's hands had been tied by a snake, however, and he could do nothing. The medicine man sang (Bahr and others 1994:247):

Vahki is built of clay
In it I saw
A medicine man.
He is afraid of me
He is staying in there
The vahki is made of clay.

The Wooshkam and the Hohokam inside the *vahki* fought for four days. The Hohokam shot arrows through holes made in the adobe-clay walls of the great house and people died. But the chief's powers could not prevail against the O'odham people's command of light and heat. The *vahki* fell down, and that was the end of the *siiwañ*.

The medicine man worked over the *siiwañ's* body to make sure he was dead. He found that the *siiwañ's* power was waning, his understandings were gone, and the rainbow-colored things that he had used in his medicine were only shining dimly. The medicine man sang (Bahr and others 1994:249):

I am holding my hand
And with my cane
I have destroyed the understanding
Of this medicine man
And the stones that he used
Are now coming out in black colors.

The Wooshkam went on to defeat the Hohokam who were living at Pueblo Grande in the Phoenix area and in other great clay houses whose abandoned ruins can still be seen today.

Casa Grande National Monument, Arizona. Great house (under protective shade) surrounded by adobe buildings and compound walls. PHOTOGRAPH BY STEPHANIE WHITTLESEY.

ciated themselves from the builders of the big house at Casa Grande National Monument and other great ruins. O'odham traditions provided rather specific calendrical dates that placed their arrival some 350 years ago, long after prehistoric peoples abandoned the desert. Rea thinks that the Arizona O'odham should be viewed as the northernmost representatives of a cultural group who came from the desert or thorn-forest lowlands of northwestern Mexico.

Rea's scenario contradicts the findings of linguistic anthropologists Jane Hill and David Shaul, however. They found that the center of maximum linguistic diversity in the Piman and Tepehuan languages is in the north; they also found evidence of borrowing with Yuman languages in the first millennium A.D. (Shaul and Hill 1998). This would support the notion of a desert people of considerable antiquity who became the O'odham people of history. Shaul and Hill (1998) concluded that what archaeologists know as Hohokam was a multiethnic complex consisting of the linguistic ancestors of Piman, Tepehuan, Yuman, and surprisingly, Zuni speakers. (A connection between Zuni and the Hohokam was originally suggested by Frank Hamilton Cushing, an eccentric character who dug in the ruins of Los Muertos and Pueblo Grande in the 1880s; see Reid and Whittlesey [1997:13].) Discovering the truth about the relationship between the O'odham and Hohokam will take much more study, and indeed we may never know.

The Tohono O'odham were farmers who moved their farm sites and residences throughout the year. The summer field villages were located near the mouths of arroyos where water rushing downslope could be diverted onto the fields, a style of farming called *ak-chin* (arroyo mouth) cultivation. In the winter they moved to well villages with reliable water. Tohono O'odham worked in Akimel O'odham fields in exchange for food. Some Tohono O'odham may have maintained summer field villages along the Gila River.

The Hia-C'ed O'odham obtained drinking water from springs and natural tanks, or *tinajas*. They lived in the driest part of the Sonoran Desert where there was little water for crops, and it was available only in a few locations. They cultivated tepary beans, corn, and squash in floodwater-farming fields at the best-watered locations. Seeking many different wild plant and animal foods, they ranged across a huge territory stretching from the Gila River to Seri country in Mexico and from the Colorado River midway across the desert. They traveled to the coast for fish and other marine life. One of the names for the Hia-C'ed, "Sand Root Eaters," derives from the delicacy upon which they depended before American supermarket foods replaced their traditional diet. This was the bulbous, underground part of a vascular plant they call *hia tadk*, "dune root." The parasitic plant attaches itself to the roots of desert shrubs. Sand root is sweet and nutritious.

The Akimel O'odham depended on farming more than the other O'odham. Their villages along the middle stretch of the Gila River were clusters of individual dwellings loosely arranged into large villages, a type of residence referred to as the *ranchería* lifestyle. The homes were located on the terraces above the river, and the irrigated fields were on the lower terraces to keep the dwellings from flooding. Fields were separated by brush fences, and irrigation ditches brought water from the river and *cienegas*. In their riverine oasis, the Akimel O'odham cultivated wheat, corn, barley, beans, melons, peas, and many other crops.

Reliance on wild foods was inversely related to dependence on farming. The Akimel O'odham relied on these foods least, primarily resorting to them in times of drought, whereas wild foods were the mainstay of the Hia-C'ed

Rain Song

Anthropologists Saxton and Saxton (1973:335–336) relate the following song that was sung during the saguaro wine ceremony:

> Drink what we have prepared, my relatives, and be revived, be elated—begin from the east side to draw the east closer. A beautifully shining ancient house stands there in the east, wrapped in white clouds. Start there and be kind to us, mixed within, speaking softly within, lightning moving very zigzag, roaring beautifully, pattering rain and moving along. Although the earth is wide, the clouds are braced across it and will come, though far away. They are hung on the heads of the mountains standing there, and will come. They will leave the earth soaked everywhere, even the highest hills. The water will gently flood the little washes, wherever they are. The driftwood is stopped crossways where the trees are standing. The sound of rushing water echoes down the valleys. It will leave the earth well moistened. After that various kinds of seed will sprout. All over the land, greet one another, my relatives.

—*Traditional Tohono O'odham song*

Sandfood

Ethnobotanist Gary Paul Nabhan (1985:51–59) relates tales about the curious, delicious food called sand root. Colonel Andrew Belcher Gray wrote one of the earliest English descriptions. In 1854, Gray surveyed a route to San Diego for the Texas Western Railroad. One evening he traveled into the dunes on the Sonoran side of the Gulf of California. Gray's O'odham guide dismounted from his horse and began digging with his hands. "At first," Gray wrote, "I could not perceive his object, but shortly discovered that he had pulled out of the sand a vegetable-looking substance, which was shaped somewhat like a mushroom. He showed great eagerness to obtain more, and made a sign that it was good to eat." Later Gray knew the truth of this, discovering that the plant, which had been roasted over hot coals, tasted like "the sweet potato, but more delicate." This edible part of this plant (botanical name *Pholisma sonorae)* is a subterranean flower stalk that rises to open on the surface of the sand.

Today, the O'odham recall that there was plenty of rain in the old days, and the desert yielded lots of food. Sand root was sweet and could be eaten raw. Today the plants are very bitter, the Indians say. They don't taste the same at all.

Sand-root plants are endangered by dune buggies and off-road vehicles. Despite this, Nabhan says that it is still possible to find sand root in the dunes that lie between the Colorado River delta and the Sierra Pinacate lava fields.

> Walk toward the soft shape on the horizon, dunes like hips of women sleeping on their sides. Wander through the tracks of sidewinders, lizards, windswept bushes, and beetles. Look down at your toes. There it is, like another moon coming up through the sand: sandfood, reflecting back at you.

O'odham diet. Mesquite, saguaro, and other cactus were important wild-plant foods and were prepared in a variety of ways. Wild greens, seeds of grasses, and many other plants completed the native diet, which was healthy and nourishing. The transition from native-plant foods to the modern diet, rich in processed wheat flour, sugar, and lard, has been responsible for a high rate of obesity and diabetes among the O'odham (Nabhan 1982). The wild foods were good foods, the O'odham say—full of strength, nourishing the body, delicious. Nothing else tastes like the gruel made from the seeds of wild plants (Underhill 1979:37).

Traditional dwellings were pole-and-thatch houses. The dome-shaped, round house, or *ki,* was not unlike the Hohokam pit house. In good weather, most activities were carried out outdoors under brush shades or ramadas *(vatto).* An arrow weed cooking enclosure and a menstruation hut completed the everyday buildings. Hia-C'ed O'odham shelters were less substantial given their mobile ways.

Men cleared, planted, and irrigated the fields, which were then harvested by women. Women were charged with gathering the wild-plant foods and preparing them. Families were patrilineal and extended, with the wife usually moving into her husband's home. When villages grew too large, they would split into several smaller settlements that maintained close social and ceremonial ties with the original village.

Social organization was egalitarian and oriented to specific tasks. There were few offices of authority. The village crier (*tobdam*) announced the work of the day—a rabbit drive, cleaning the ditches, repairing the dam. Among the Akimel O'odham, the ditch boss (*huis* or *shuudagĭ ñuukuddam,* "water caretaker") was charged with irrigation tasks. He organized the village to build brush dams across the river and maintain the irrigation ditches, and he distributed water to the fields.

Although primarily known for their excellent basketry made of willow and devil's claw pods, the O'odham also created well-made pottery—painted red-on-buff and red-on-brown **ollas**, highly polished red ware, and manure-tempered water ollas with black cores. The manure particles burned out during **firing**, leaving a porous paste that evaporated slowly and kept the water cool and sweet. Virtually every household in territorial Tucson—Mexican, O'odham, and Anglo—kept a Tohono O'odham water jar in the courtyard. Making these jars was a cottage industry for the women until European containers, ice, and refrigeration made water ollas obsolete.

Although the O'odham were not a particularly warlike people, they were fierce defenders against the raids of the Apache people, who were considered enemies. O'odham scouts and troops aided the U.S. Army in its fight to contain Apache aggression. In times of war there was a war leader (*chukud namkam,* "great horned owl meeter"). The O'odham maintained amicable relations with most other neighbors, including the Seri, Cocopah, and Opata.

The O'odham were greatly affected by Euroamerican intrusions. Spanish missionary and military efforts in the late 1600s sought to concentrate people into settlements, a policy called *reducción.* The strategy buffered the Spanish against Apache forays by providing a tempting and concentrated source of horses, mules, cattle, tack, weapons, and foodstuffs away from Spanish settlements. It also increased the spread of contagion and the effects of diseases to which the native peoples had little resistance. As the O'odham living in the concentrated settlements died from the effects of disease and war, they were replaced by people from the desert margins. Many O'odham dialect groups lost their identity as a result. Some groups died out entirely, and others were submerged and disappeared.

Today, the O'odham peoples live on several reservations in southern Arizona, and many also reside in Sonora south of the international border. Tohono O'odham occupy more than 2.7 million acres of land in Pinal and Pima Counties. The main Tohono O'odham Reservation is located west of Tucson and extends to the Barry M. Goldwater Range. There are several smaller communities. The Akimel O'odham reside on 372,000 acres in Maricopa and Pinal Counties on the Salt River Pima-Maricopa Reservation, which they share with Maricopa (Xalchildom Pii-pash) people, and on the Gila River Indian Community. They continue to depend on an agricultural economy, raising cotton, wheat, alfalfa, barley, citrus, vegetables, and other crops. Although the Hia-C'ed O'odham were declared extinct in the early 1900s and consequently denied rights to their traditional lands, approximately 1,300 individuals today identify themselves with this group. There is no reservation set aside for their use; the Barry M. Goldwater Range, Organ Pipe Cactus National Monument, and the Cabeza Prieta National Wildlife Refuge occupy virtually all of traditional Hia-C'ed O'odham territory in the United States.

Stories of Water and Life in the Sonoran Desert

Imagine this scenario—you wake up early one summer morning to a changed world, and are not really sure what happened or how. The sun shines into the east-facing open doorway of a dirt-floored hut where you have been sleeping on woven matting with a light blanket of hand-spun cotton. The light has awakened you instead of your alarm clock. Puzzled, you get up, stretching a little stiffly after the night on the hard ground. You see no kitchen, no range, no microwave. Indeed, the lack of appliances of any sort suggests that there may be no electricity whatsoever in

Mission San Xavier del Bac ("the White Dove of the Desert") on the San Xavier Indian Reservation near Tucson, Arizona. Photograph by Jefferson Reid.

this place where you have awakened in confusion. There is only a shallow, scooped-out clay hearth. You must stir the cold ashes and get the fire going. What will you eat to break your fast? Apparently not the eggs, cereal, or toasted bagel with cream cheese to which you are accustomed.

You sigh, your empty stomach grumbling in protest, and wander outdoors. The desert waits, prickly and a little dangerous looking in the morning sun that is beginning to become disturbingly warm. What will you eat? Where will you find it? And how will you prepare it? Most critical, where will you find water? Perhaps in that pottery vessel over in the corner, you hope. Your mouth was dry when you awoke, and the sensation only increases as the sun climbs. You are beginning to think you could be in trouble. Evidently it's going to be a long, hard, hot, possibly hungry and thirsty day.

For thousands of years, the people who lived in the Sonoran Desert faced this situation daily. They solved the problems of supporting themselves with ingenuity and learned to make a living in the hot and dry land where the water is scarce and the plants are armed and dangerous. And although they spent a considerable time each day in the quest for food and in making the tools, equipment, and shelter they needed, there was time for much more—for songs, dances, and stories; for raising families; for travel, friendship, and exchange. In respecting the desert, its plant and animal dwellers, and the spirits of rain and sky, the desert people coexisted and worked together with their land in mutually beneficial ways. The people did much more than simply "adapt" to their environment, a quaint notion that archaeologists have borrowed from cultural ecology. They created their landscape in song and story, they gave it respect with ceremony, and altered the face and quality of the environment that they had created.

In this section, we explore the different ways in which Archaic, Hohokam, and Tohono O'odham peoples lived in the desert. These stories teach the single most important lesson about life in the desert—without water, it would not exist. The benison from the sky, falling gently and softly in the winter, rushing in foamy torrents down an arroyo after a summer thunderstorm; the wide, placid waters of an archaic desert river; the hidden eye of the gods in springs and *cienegas*—water meant life. These tales also reveal the indomitable human spirit as well as the richness of the seemingly inhospitable desert land.

Centering Life on Water: The Archaic Lifestyle

For the greater portion of human history in the Sonoran Desert, people lived without cultivated plants and farming. The success of Archaic peoples in the desert underscores how bountiful this region can be even without sophisticated technology. Water focused Archaic life, even though they did not use it to farm until relatively late in their history. Water made possible the seasonal round of Archaic life exploiting the abundance of the land. As so many have learned painfully, it is fatal to cross the desert without water. Water sources anchored the people's movements between springs and *tinajas* spread along trails like beads on a string. Plants grow more abundantly near the rare sources of water, and many are not found outside these habitats. Animals are drawn to these places as well. People followed, for the plants and game as much as for the water. Even when the Archaic people did not farm, it was the rains that brought forth the bounty of the desert. We have seen that winter's gentle, mild rains germinated seeds in the spring and made wild-plant crops flourish in late spring and early summer. Later, when the people learned to farm cultivated crops, rainfall and summer's thunderstorms became even more vital.

Two Central Arizona Project archaeological studies illustrate these points and help us to understand how Archaic people lived in the desert and used its water. The Picacho Reservoir Archaic Project demonstrated how the Santa Cruz Flats area was used intermittently during the Middle Archaic period by at least two different groups. The later Coffee Camp site excavated during the Tator Hills Archaeological Project told the story of a people who continued the traditional hunting-and-gathering lifestyle even though many of their neighbors had begun to grow cultivated plants.

Episodic Use of Sand Dune Sites at Picacho Reservoir The Picacho Reservoir Archaic Project reveals the lifestyle of a Sonoran Desert people who did not farm but derived a livelihood from the desert's wild bounty. Their story illustrates how Archaic peoples structured their movements and activities around water—secret water hidden in unexpected places like diamonds in the sand.

Picacho Reservoir is located west of the Picacho Mountains, north of Tucson, and about six miles from the small town of Eloy. The reservoir lies in a natural depression at the confluence of McClellan and Brady Washes and has been enlarged and stabilized over the past century. Today it is fed by the Florence–Casa Grande Canal. The area was crossed by the Phase A alignment of the Tucson Aqueduct. Most of the sites investigated by Arizona State University during this project dated to the Middle Archaic period.

Archaeological sites were located in two distinct ecological zones. A few special-purpose sites, including five stone-quarrying sites, were situated on the lower *bajada*

The Picacho Reservoir Archaic Project

The Tucson Aqueduct is the final leg of the Central Arizona Project. It begins where the Fannin-McFarland Aqueduct ends and finishes 87 miles to the south just southwest of Tucson. The aqueduct was built in different reaches, which also structured the archaeology. Reach 1, which skirted the Picacho Mountains, crossed a number of archaeological sites that dated to the Archaic period.

Construction of Reach 1 of the Tucson Aqueduct was projected to impact 21 archaeological sites. Arizona State University conducted the Picacho Reservoir Archaic Project between 1983 and 1986 to mitigate these impacts. Surface collection, geologic trenching, and feature excavation were carried out. The report that resulted from this work (Bayham and others 1986) considered foraging strategies, mobility, patterns in flaked stone tool production, and game procurement. The project was particularly important because few other Central Arizona Project archaeological studies had included Archaic period sites. The report gives us a fascinating glimpse into life among the sand dunes millennia ago.

of the Picacho Mountains where saguaro, palo verde, and other cactus flourished. Most excavated sites were found in an unexpected setting—an area of vegetation-stabilized sand dunes at a lower elevation south of Picacho Reservoir where creosote and bursage were the dominant plants.

The Santa Cruz Flats, a place where the Santa Cruz River and several ephemeral washes join to form a delta-fan area, is located just west of the dune field. Dunes were deposited by wind eroding the alluvial plains of the flats beginning at least 4,300 years ago and continuing through the Middle Archaic and Late Archaic periods. The five-foot-deep sand deposits were subsequently modified by wind to form parabolic dunes or "blow outs." Filling with water after rainstorms, these natural depressions formed pools, and this explains why people were drawn to the dunes. Although most pools were temporary, eventually evaporating completely, they nonetheless provided precious water. Some pools may have been more permanent—ancient pollen indicating a possible *cienega* was found at one site. The green margins of pools were thick with vegetation and attracted game.

Drawn to the water and resources, people camped intermittently in the dune area throughout the Middle and Late Archaic periods. Clusters of fire-cracked rock, hearths, roasting features, and pits indicated that food was prepared and cooked at campsites such as the Buried Dune site. People stayed long enough or returned enough times to generate considerable food waste and other refuse that they deposited in **middens** that the archaeologists later excavated. Although the same kinds of features were found at the dune sites and the *bajada* sites, suggesting that similar activities took place, the dune sites were typically larger and contained more features. The rainwater pools evidently allowed people to camp there for longer periods.

When archaeologists Frank Bayham and Donald Morris (1986) compared the archaeological record with evidence for the ancient environment, they found a striking correlation. Episodic use of the Picacho Reservoir area took place during times when temperatures were higher and there was more rainfall. The area was not used when it was colder and less rain fell. Rainfall drew the Middle Archaic people to Picacho, and when it decreased, they left.

Stone tools for grinding small seeds of wild plants are common at Archaic sites. **Ground stone tools** found at Picacho Reservoir were primarily small, one-handed **manos** and flat, slab metates. They were easy to store and could be securely cached at places to which the people planned to return. The small hand stones were relatively portable and may have accompanied the people on their travels. Remains of ancient plants found at the sites indicated that the people were collecting, processing, and eating cactus and the seeds of grasses and weedy annual plants such as tansy mustard. There were no mesquite beans, a staple of the Hohokam diet, in this collection of ancient plant remains. Archaeologists found no stone mortars or pestles, which are tools usually used to prepare mesquite beans. Ancient pollen demonstrated that mesquite was growing in the area when it was occupied, however. Evidently the hunter-gatherers living in the Picacho Reservoir area chose not to make use of this plant or had not discovered it was a good foodstuff.

Archaeologists compared flaked stone artifacts and animal bone collected from two of the larger dune-field sites, the Buried Dune and Arroyo sites, and the results were again unexpected. People living in each camp carried out disparate activities, stayed for different intervals of

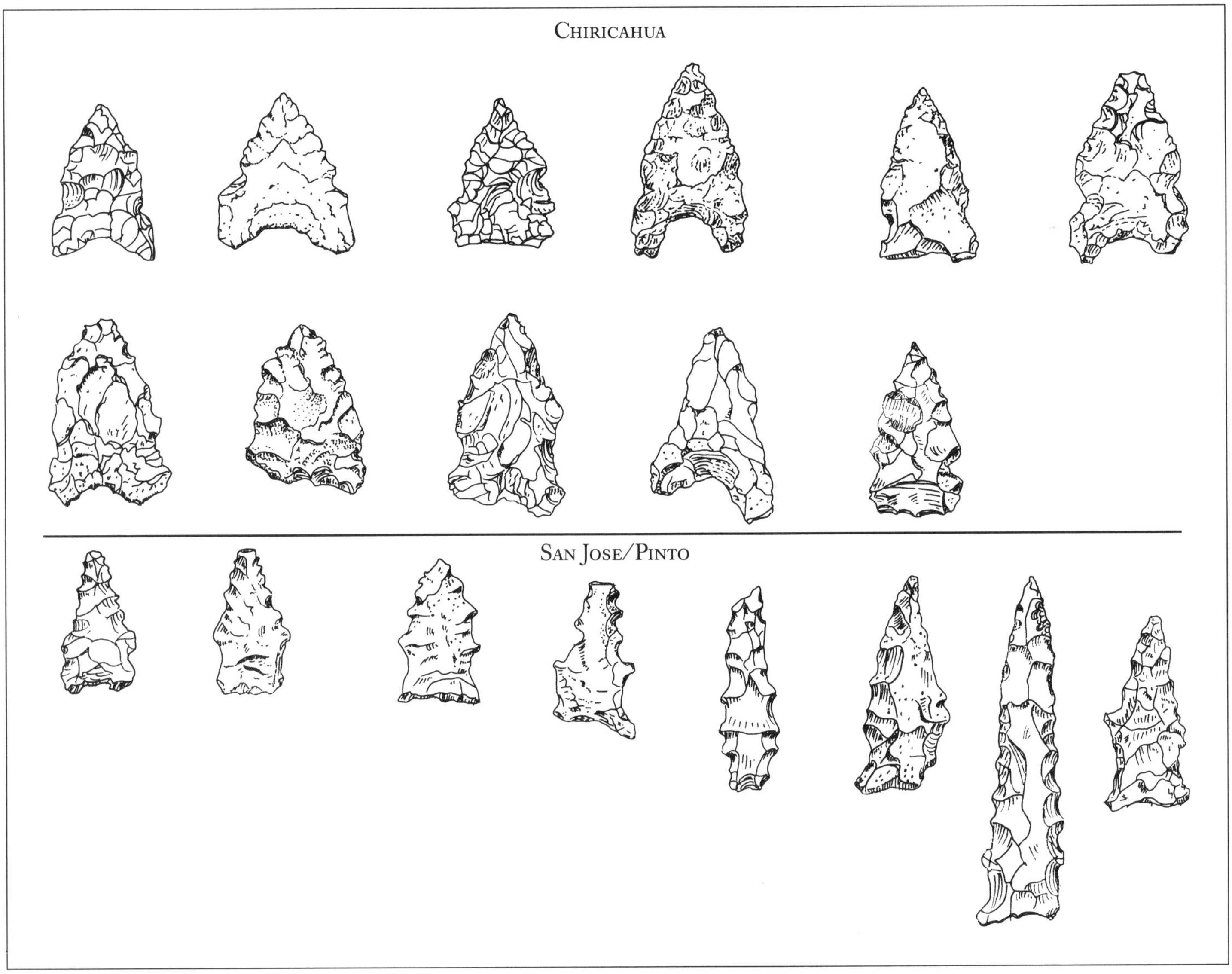

Archaic projectile points: Chiricahua style (top) and San Jose/Pinto style (bottom).

time, and made distinctive kinds of tools. Because the sites were found in the same environmental setting, were located near to one another, and dated to the same time, it is likely that the two groups had different cultural, linguistic, or ethnic affiliations.

The Arroyo site was used during the summer and fall months as a residential base from which people moved to collect resources and hunt. Pollen remains provided insight into why this location was particularly attractive to ancient hunters and gatherers. Evidence of cattail and other plants preferring a riparian habitat suggested that a *cienega* was probably present in Middle Archaic times. Flaked stone tools indicated that people made and refurbished stone tools such as arrow points, worked wood, and processed wild plants while camping at the Arroyo site. They used little obsidian to make their tools, preferring the locally available, diverse stones, such as felsite. The obsidian they used did not come from distant sources. The people hunted with **projectile points** archaeologists label as the Chiricahua style. Animal bone was abundant, and many different species were represented, confirming the importance of hunting. Together, this information indicated that the Arroyo site residents were local people with a relatively restricted territory from which they obtained resources.

The Buried Dune site contrasted in many ways. It was apparently occupied for a shorter period, and people did not carry out as many different kinds of activities. Flaked stone tools provided evidence that scraping and chopping tasks, perhaps related to woodworking or preparing plants for cooking, were most common. Stone materials were not diverse; there was considerable obsidian, and it came from distant sources. People hunted with the projectile point style called San Jose (see projectile point illustration). Animal bone was not abundant, and fewer species were found than at the Arroyo site. This information suggested that people camped at the site for specific purposes and for short periods during the winter and early spring, temporarily leaving their residential base camp located elsewhere. The people appear to have traveled widely in southeastern Arizona, southwestern New Mexico, and northeastern Sonora.

We turn now to a later Archaic time to see how people coped with the Sonoran Desert at that time. Surprises await at the Coffee Camp site, as well.

Stability without Farming: The Coffee Camp Site

By the Late Archaic period, the people of the Sonoran Desert had learned about domesticated plants such as corn and how to grow them in desert environments. Archaeologists have emphasized the importance of farming and how it affected other aspects of lifestyle, such as permanence and size of settlements. We often think that farming was a revolution that caused a complete change in lifeways. Evidence from the Tator Hills Archaeological Project demonstrated that not all Late Archaic people farmed, even though many had committed to an agricultural lifestyle. Continuing their hunting and gathering ways, the people nevertheless built large settlements that were occupied for much of the year and contained possible ritual structures.

The Tator Hills Archaeological Project

One portion of the Central Arizona Irrigation and Drainage District, a part of the Central Arizona Project irrigation and distribution system, would impact prehistoric archaeological sites. Northland Research conducted the Tator Hills Archaeological Project between 1987 and 1993 to mitigate the effects of construction on the sites. Archaeologists investigated two Archaic period campsites and one Hohokam resource-procurement locale during this project (Halbirt and Henderson 1993).

The project area was located along Greene Wash in the Santa Cruz Flats and southwest of the Picacho Reservoir sites. Coffee Camp was a Late Archaic site used intermittently between 300 B.C. and A.D. 100 with evidence for less intensive earlier and later occupations. Excavation revealed more than 350 subsurface features, most of them pits used for cooking, caching artifacts, and storing foodstuffs. Artifact caches contained grinding tools (manos, metates, and pestles) and one flint-knapping kit. Archaeologists also found burial features, four pit houses, a midden, and living surfaces (Halbirt and Henderson 1993). Three of the pit houses were small, shallow, circular structures, and two of these contained hearths.

The fourth structure was much larger and probably served a special purpose. It contained an unusual collection of artifacts—a figurine, a bone tube, shell artifacts that may have been gaming pieces, a wand or baton of **phyllite**, and some crude ceramic **sherds**. The structure was the only one with mud plaster on the roof. A pair of mule deer antler racks had evidently been resting on the roof. The size of the structure and its unusual artifacts suggest that it may have served ritual purposes for a larger group of people than individual families.

Large communal or ceremonial structure at the Santa Cruz Bend site. Photograph by Stephanie Whittlesey.

Whereas contemporaneous sites in the Tucson Basin and elsewhere typically yielded abundant evidence for corn and other cultigens, archaeologists did not find any remains of cultivated plants at Coffee Camp. This is unlikely to have

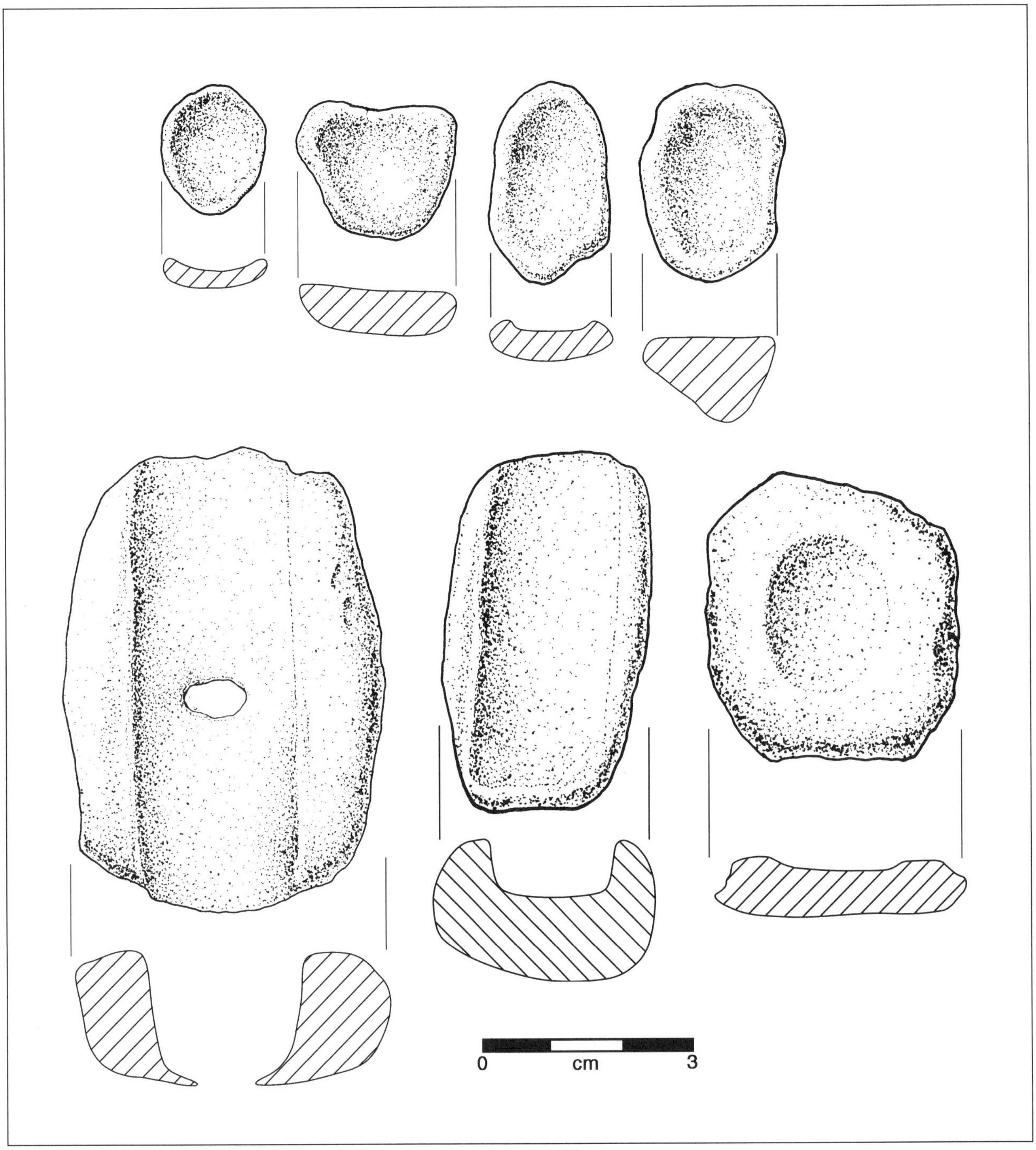

Basin metates (top row, bottom row, right) and trough metates (bottom row, left and center).

been a product of archaeological techniques or preservation, because many samples were taken, revealing the remains of other plants. Moreover, the metates were the flat-surfaced slab and shallow basin types, not the deeper trough metates that archaeologists traditionally associate with grinding corn.

The wild plants that were collected, processed, and eaten at Coffee Camp were not unlike those found in the Picacho Reservoir area, with two important differences. The kinds of plants were more numerous, and there was evidence that mesquite was used, such as stone mortars and pestles for grinding the beans.

Coffee Camp also gives a glimpse of a major acquisition of the terminal Late Archaic period—fired-ceramic containers. The ceramic sherds may have represented fragments of crude vessels or unintentionally fired, clay linings for containers made of basketry. Most of the sherds were found in the large pit structure, suggesting that their function might have been ritualistic rather than purely domestic. These patterns have since been replicated elsewhere, indicating that the development of fired-ceramic containers may have been closely linked to ritual behaviors, perhaps to prayers for rain.

Water

"The water from the sink is no good for making pottery.
It just ruins it," my children's Acoma grandmother would say.
Thereafter, she sent the kids to replace the full bowls of rainwater
that had filled since it began to rain.
Her son said that when he was a child, the rain smelled
and tasted so good—he and other kids played outside,
laughing and running around—and they stopped once in a while to lick
the cool adobe walls. The sides of the smooth houses were
fragrant and nurturing. From atop the mesa at Acoma Pueblo,
it is possible to see almost seventy miles in each direction.

(Luci Tapahonso, "Dust Precedes the Rain")

Several kinds of evidence indicated that Coffee Camp was used intermittently or seasonally, although for longer periods than the Picacho Reservoir sites. Caches of tools were probably left behind as "insurance," as archaeologist Carl Halbirt and his colleagues (1993) have suggested—safely stored until needed at some time in the future. Caching behavior does not suggest permanence, but rather the opposite—caching protects gear while people are away from home and is therefore a probable indicator of seasonal or periodic abandonment. The Coffee Camp residents stashed stone tools that were too heavy to be moved, such as large metates, in such caches. The emphasis on storage may also suggest seasonal use. Archaeologist Kathleen Henderson (1993) thinks that the different kinds of processing and storage pit features indicated that people were emphasizing the preparation of foodstuffs for preservation rather than immediate consumption. Together, the information indicated that the campsite was seasonally occupied, although people remained there for relatively long periods before departing to another locale. Later, they would return, knowing they would find safe caches of food and tools waiting for them.

These interpretations were supported by geological deposits and paleobotanical data, which provided a picture of periodic occupation and abandonment during the spring and early summer, perhaps in conjunction with flooding of the Santa Cruz River or Greene Wash. Features were constructed and used, the settlement was abandoned, and the features were buried by a flood event. The locale was subsequently reoccupied, and new features were built. The vertical depth of features and deposits (nearly seven feet) indicated that this process took place repeatedly over a long time.

Water drew people to this location year after year, century after century. Coffee Camp was located on the floodplain, which offered water, game, and abundant mesquite, weedy plants, and grasses. Archaic people could camp there for several months, wandering onto the *bajadas* to hunt and to collect resources such as cactus.

The people of Coffee Camp may never have farmed. It is also possible that their farm sites were located elsewhere, and that Coffee Camp was simply a special-purpose camp devoted to collecting wild resources. The location of the site in an area that could be farmed suggests the former possibility. In addition, farmers typically take agricultural produce with them when they go on journeys or undertake specific tasks. If the Coffee Camp residents had domesticated plants and knew how to grow them, it is likely that cultivated-plant remains would have been found there.

We cannot know what was sacred to the people of Coffee Camp or what sorts of ceremonies and beliefs helped them to cope with the rigors of desert life. It is likely, given the scarcity of water in the desert, that they prayed for rain—rain to fill the pools in the dunes, to bring forth the mesquite and clothe the hills with sweet grass.

Pit structure at Santa Cruz Bend site with deep, interior storage pits.
Photograph by Stephanie Whittlesey.

Hunting rituals may also have been important, as suggested by the antlers gracing the big house. Whatever their prayers, they were successful, for the residents of Coffee Camp lived well and returned time and again to their camp along the stream. The Hohokam, who came to occupy the Sonoran Desert after the Archaic peoples, discovered new ways to make the desert blossom. We turn now to these outstandingly successful farmers.

Hohokam Farmers

Influenced by our twenty-first-century American pride, many of us probably believe that the Sonoran Desert was not a productive place to live and work until modern technology transformed it with great dams, pumping plants, tunnels, and miles of concrete channels. This was not the case. Long before the Central Arizona Project brought water to thirsty desert cities and farmlands, Hohokam farmers were building canals and transforming the desert. It is striking, even stunning, that the desert and the Hohokam's use of it were intertwined and inseparable. Their agricultural technology was predicated on the nature of the land and its water; it would not have been necessary or fruitful in another place. The desert made the Hohokam an extraordinarily successful prehistoric culture, and the Hohokam in turn altered the desert to make it yield abundantly.

Farming technology was the means by which the Hohokam achieved this transformation. No other prehistoric people of the Southwest were as skilled in controlling water for agricultural uses. Where they lived away from the river, they also developed ingenious ways to harvest and store water. In the process, the Hohokam modified the desert. They built dams, canals and ditches, rock-pile fields, headgates, terraces, and other features to control soil erosion, divert water, and transport it to the fields. The end result was an intricate agricultural landscape that was green and bountiful, not a sere desert but a watery and fertile place. Hohokam modifications changed the quality of the soil itself; prehistoric fields can still be recognized by sampling the soil and analyzing its chemistry. Archaeologists think that Hohokam religion, ideology, and ceremonies centered on water, bringing rain, and ensuring fertility of the fields. Water and the creatures that inhabit it were pervasive in Hohokam art and symbolism. In this section, we will use a Central Arizona

The Name "Hohokam"

Because, like other prehistoric southwestern Indians, the Hohokam did not leave behind a written record, we do not know what language they spoke or what they may have called themselves in that language.

Archaeologists of Gila Pueblo Archaeological Foundation labeled the Hohokam culture after the O'odham word *huhugam.* This expression is usually translated as "those who have gone before," "those who are finished," or "all used up." According to ethnobiologist Amadeo Rea, who has worked with the Pima people, the word Hohokam (more properly spelled *huhugam*) is the plural of *hugam,* which is the polite way of referring to a person who is deceased to avoid using the dead person's name in the presence of relatives or friends.

Agricultural fields along the lower Verde River.

Project example to illustrate the remarkable farming technology of the Hohokam and their agricultural landscape. We will also consider the sacred landscape, belief systems, and rituals that benefited Hohokam farmers in their life in the Sonoran Desert.

Farming the Desert The diversity of Hohokam farming and water-control techniques was remarkable. They built reservoirs to store water and dug wells to tap the water table. They constructed rock-pile fields to conserve rainwater, dammed and diverted floodwater onto farming plots, and irrigated fields with canals that drew water from the rivers. Using different fields and various techniques, the Hohokam had a unique strategy to buffer themselves against risk. We use the findings of the Salt-Gila Aqueduct Project, one of the larger Central Arizona Project archaeological studies, to illustrate these points. Although the Hohokam success story was repeated in many areas across the Sonoran Desert, the Salt-Gila Aqueduct Project is particularly useful because the project's research focused on understanding the ancient environment and how the Hohokam used it.

Recall that the Salt-Gila Aqueduct, now named the Fannin-McFarland Aqueduct, is the second segment of the Central Arizona Project. It begins just west of the confluence of the Salt and Verde Rivers south of the Fort McDowell and Salt River Indian Reservations and near the modern community of Mesa. The aqueduct travels to the Gila River near Florence and then southward to Picacho Reservoir to join the Tucson Aqueduct segment. South of Apache Junction, the aqueduct corridor crosses a series of desert washes including Siphon Draw and one larger stream, Queen Creek. Today an intermittent stream that carries water only after major storms, the creek flows southwest out of the Superstition Mountains. One cluster of sites was found along Queen Creek. Near Florence, the corridor crosses the Gila River, and a second group of sites was found there.

The aqueduct corridor therefore represented many of the land and water features of the Sonoran Desert, from dry terraces to intermittent streams to permanent rivers. Project sites demonstrated the farming technologies the Hohokam used to exploit this variety of landforms and water. On the dry terraces above the river, they used dry farming depend-

The Salt-Gila Aqueduct Project

The Salt-Gila Aqueduct is the middle segment of the Central Arizona Project canal. It begins at the Salt-Gila Pumping Plant located south of the Salt River at the base of the Usery Mountains and northeast of the city of Mesa, and it ends near Picacho. The Salt-Gila Aqueduct was renamed the Fannin-McFarland Aqueduct when construction was finished.

Archaeologists from the Arizona State Museum investigated 45 sites along a 58-mile-long transect of the proposed corridor between 1980 and 1984. Many different kinds of sites spanning a great portion of the Hohokam cultural sequence were investigated. Project research focused on understanding the past environment, subsistence, and farming methods through various archaeological and analytical techniques. The project corridor spanned two distinct topographic and hydrological areas, which required different solutions to the problem of making a living in the desert.

The nine-volume technical report of this work (Teague and Crown 1984) contains descriptive site reports, specific analyses of material culture and ecological data, and synthetic chapters. Almost $2 million were spent on the archaeology of the Salt-Gila Aqueduct Project.

Central Arizona Project canal (Fannin-McFarland Aqueduct). PHOTOGRAPH COURTESY U.S. BUREAU OF RECLAMATION. JOE MADRIGAL, JR., PHOTOGRAPHER.

ing on rainfall alone. On the lower *bajadas,* floodwater or runoff farming was used to harvest water flowing in washes after summer storms. Canals took water from Queen Creek and the Gila River. One of the most important findings of the Salt-Gila Aqueduct Project was that different kinds of farming strategies were used selectively in the two environmental zones (Crown 1984a, 1984c). Along Queen Creek, which is bordered by flat, open areas covered with relatively deep alluvium, the Hohokam farmed primarily by irrigation. They used more diverse strategies along the Gila River—irrigation, floodwater farming without canals, and dry farming. These techniques were not necessarily limited to a particular zone, however. Dry farming was practiced along the Gila River, for example. Technical mastery of water-control and water-conservation features made it possible for the Hohokam to seemingly disregard the constraints of an environment that could be capricious, even hostile.

We look at floodwater farming and dry farming first. Away from the rivers as well as in many areas where irrigation farming was also possible, the Hohokam used farming techniques that relied on floodwater or rainfall alone. The Salt-Gila Aqueduct Project identified 23 separate areas along the Gila River with evidence for floodwater and dry farming (Crown 1984b)—field systems containing rock piles, check dams, cleared areas, and terraces. Two areas bordered by rock alignments were readily identified as fields.

Rock features such as check dams and terraces, which originally were made of brush as well as rocks, captured the runoff flowing downslope after summer storms, slowed its speed and force, and spread the water gradually over the fields where it could soak the ground around the growing plants. The Tohono O'odham used similar techniques in historical times, as we will see in a following section. Many of the crops grown in the irrigated fields, including corn, could also be cultivated in floodwater fields.

The Hohokam planted crops needing little water on the shallow, rocky soil of the higher Pleistocene terraces bordering the river. Unsuitable for either irrigation or floodwater farming, the terraces were used to grow agave, one of the Hohokam's most important crops. Agave was planted in huge rock-pile fields sometimes measuring thousands of acres. Rocks piled around the bases of the growing agave plants conserved moisture from rainfall, retarded soil erosion, and protected the young plants from predators (Fish and others 1985).

Tabular stone knives used to harvest the plants were found discarded in the fields. Huge roasting areas—mounded accumulations of fire-cracked rock, ash, and charcoal—in the rock-pile fields were used to prepare the tender hearts of agave. We know this because the charred remains of agave plants were found in the roasting areas. Roasted agave hearts yield a nutritious, sweet, and palatable food that may also have been fermented to make alcoholic beverages.

What of irrigated farming? Today, the Gila River and Queen Creek carry water only after summer thunderstorms or winter rains; how was irrigated farming possible? Recall, however, that the Salt and the Gila Rivers have been dammed upstream. In prehistory, these watercourses carried permanent water in most years. Many different studies have shown that a thousand or so years ago, there was also more water in the intermittent streams such as Queen Creek. Remains of ancient plants and animals collected during the Salt-Gila Aqueduct Project demonstrated that parts of southern Arizona were wetter in times past and enough water flowed in the Gila River and Queen Creek to sustain farming.

A thick mesquite *bosque* and stands of cottonwood trees bordered the Gila River. Remains of plants living in wet ground, such as cattail, indicated marshy areas along the river's margins. Mesquite, cottonwood, and other riparian vegetation also grew along Queen Creek. Bones of creatures that need permanent water to live and breed, such as the Colorado River toad, or Sonoran Desert toad *(Bufo alvarius),* and the Sonoran mud turtle (*Kinosternon* sp.), were found at several sites along the Gila River. There were many different animal species, suggesting to faunal analyst Christine Szuter (1984) that a varied animal population occupied the environment, which was much

Relict stand of agave plants (century plants or mescal), perhaps the remnants of ancient cultivation by Hohokam farmers. PHOTOGRAPH BY STEPHANIE WHITTLESEY.

Bringing Back the Rain

Many Tohono O'odham perceive that the rain is dying. It no longer falls gently in winter to nourish the wheat or thunderously in the summer to rush down the washes and flood the fields. "What do you do when the rain is dying?," asked ethnobiologist Gary Nabhan (1982:48) of some elderly Tohono O'odham farmers.

> "Only one way—to do that—" the old man replied with a grin.
> "You got to know the right old songs—"
> "Then you just got to dance to bring down that rain!"

The old men lifted their feet, shuffling in the dry desert dust, laughing.

Photograph by Stephanie Whittlesey.

more diverse than today. This information suggests the presence of a permanently wet, riverine habitat.

The riparian forest along the river, along with beaver dams and thick ground cover, currently nonexistent, evidently halted erosion and slowed the floodwaters. Paleobotanist Charles Miksicek (1984) found few pieces of nonlocal wood charcoal in **flotation** samples, indicating that the Gila River flooded little during the period of Hohokam occupation. Such floods would have swept driftwood from pine and other nonlocal trees into the desert. This gives support to the notion that eradication of beavers, introduction of grazing animals, woodcutting, and other processes in historical times altered the desert environment to increase the frequency and intensity of floods.

The Salt-Gila Aqueduct Project discovered canal-irrigation systems along Queen Creek and the Gila River that relied on this water-rich environment. Archaeologists identified 19 individual canals in the Queen Creek area by examining aerial photographs, looking at differential vegetation patterns, and excavating the area itself (Crown 1984b). There were two types—main canals, which took water from the stream, and distribution canals, which took water to lateral canals that emptied directly onto crops. Topography allowed main canals to be built along both sides of Queen Creek, and distribution canals could be placed on both sides of the main canals. No lateral canals were found.

Canals grouped into four main systems north and south of Queen Creek. Most canals were relatively shallow and U-shaped. The main canals were 10–13 feet wide and the distribution canals 1–10 feet wide. Main canals sloped at some 13–16 feet per each half-mile, a gradient that is somewhat steeper than optimal but useable nonetheless. Canals contained evidence that they had been periodically cleaned and exhibited some scouring that could indicate flooding. The original courses of some canals had been altered, but overall there was little evidence for remodeling and reengineering over time. The capacity of the canals was quite large in relation to the amount of land that could be irrigated. This evidently permitted the rushing flow of Queen Creek after a summer storm to be used to its maximum extent and helped to retard overflow.

Irrigation technology along the Gila River was more sophisticated than along Queen Creek. Canals were larger and longer, their gradients were more gradual, and they irrigated more land. Canals were constructed on both sides of the Gila River. Unlike Queen Creek, high terraces along the river meant that fields could not be located on both sides of the canals.

Irrigated fields were located at some distance from the residences. Fields were identified by the pollen of weedy plants that spring up in disturbed areas—spiderling (*Boerhaavia* spp.), Arizona poppy (*Kallstroemia* spp.), globemallow (*Sphaeralcea* spp.), and evening primose

Hohokam petroglyph. Photograph by Jefferson Reid.

(Onagraceae family) (Fish 1984). The pollen from these plants is not well dispersed by wind and tends to fall where the plants bloom. Agricultural weeds were more common and abundant in pollen samples from irrigated fields and canals than those collected from dry-farmed fields. Field houses where the people stayed while tending their crops were located near canals. Petroglyphs pecked into boulders may have marked field boundaries.

Crops requiring considerable water—corn, beans, squash, tobacco, cotton—were grown in the irrigated fields. More corn and cotton were recovered from the Gila River sites than the Queen Creek sites. Evidently there was plenty of water in the Gila River, and Hohokam farmers took advantage of this abundance.

Archaeologist and **palynologist** Suzanne Fish (1984) noted that irrigated fields represented a unique habitat supplying more than cultivated crops. They were a rich, varied, and predictable source of wild foods the Hohokam made by removing nonedible plants and encouraging those with edible seeds and leaves. The fields also created a lush habitat for animals, and the so-called "garden hunting" of rabbits and other creatures not only provided a source of meat but simultaneously rid the fields of pests.

In some areas along the aqueduct corridor, such as Siphon Draw, no farming features were found, although large habitation sites were located nearby. Archaeologists assumed that floodwater or runoff farming was carried out using brush dams, leaving no traces in the archaeological record. Flat land along Siphon Draw could have been watered by such means.

Drinking water was collected and stored in reservoirs near the villages. Such features seem to have been necessary for year-round living in the desert, for the Tohono O'odham who occupied the desert after the Hohokam constructed similar reservoirs. Salt-Gila Project reservoirs were large (46 to about 100 feet long), horseshoe-shaped or elliptical, earthen constructions that contained thousands of gallons of water. The features were originally wells to tap the water table that were subsequently expanded. Alternating deposits of gravel and coarse sand along with laminated, water-lain silts and manganese-dioxide stains suggested a water-storage function (Crown 1984c). Lacking outlets, the reservoirs were evidently not used in farming, although they could have been used for "pot irrigation"—carrying water by hand to kitchen gardens close to home.

By combining different kinds of water-control technology, the Hohokam created a redundant agricultural landscape. The same kinds of plants were grown in the irrigated and floodwater fields, although yields may have been lower in the latter because of less abundant, less regular water. Some cultivated crops were better suited for one type of farming strategy than another. The high water requirements of most cotton strains meant that cotton was best cultivated in irrigated fields, whereas the succulent agave plants did very well in the rocky fields watered only by rain. This combination of farming strategies, field localities, and crops helped to minimize risk by ensuring that at least some fields would yield a good crop—an excellent strategy in a land where rainfall is sporadic, unpredictable, and often either too scant or too heavy.

The agricultural landscape of ancient times must have looked very different than the thorny, scrubby desert of today. We can imagine a mosaic of green and well-watered fields along the Gila Rivers, secondary streams such as Queen Creek, and at the bases of alluvial fans. Lush vegetation marked the courses of irrigation ditches and the margins of reservoirs. Red-winged blackbirds sang among the cattails. Agricultural weeds with economic uses flourished in the fields, and sunflowers raised their golden heads. When it was time to water the fields, farmers would open headgates or move diversion weirs to let water into the main canals. When the skies opened and water poured down the *bajada* slopes, everyone would scramble to make sure that the brush-and-stone check dams functioned properly to divert the water onto the *ak-chin* fields. Extensive fields of gray-green, prickly agave plants grew in rock piles on the terraces and *bajada* slopes. When harvest time arrived, we can imagine smoke rising from the fields as huge fires were kindled to heat stones and roast agave hearts.

Many farmers probably walked to the fields each day, but the Hohokam also built field houses in fields that were far from the village. Families camped in these temporary shelters while tending the growing crops and later harvesting them. We do not know exactly how division of farming labor was apportioned, but we can guess that, as among most historically described farming peoples, both men and women contributed. Children probably practiced their shooting and trapping skills on the rabbits and other rodents inhabiting the fields, and even the littlest could help by throwing stones at the ravens.

Today, few traces of this landscape remain. The bed of the Gila River is dry, and only rarely does water flow in Queen Creek. The desert has reclaimed the fields. Archaeologists must use a variety of analytical techniques to locate fields and canals, identify the plants that were grown, and determine what the ancient environment was like. Practical avenues for coping with the Sonoran Desert were clearly successful. Perhaps equally vital were spiritual mechanisms.

Prayers, songs, and rituals called down water from the clouds and filled the irrigation canals. We look now at these aspects of Hohokam life.

Growing up on Queen Creek

Carlotta Silvas Martin grew up in Superior, Arizona, a mining town not far from Globe, in the early decades of the twentieth century. She recalls (Martin 1992:206) what the streams were like then:

> My early childhood years were spent playing in Queen Creek near my grandmother's home. It was so pretty—a green oasis shaded by huge cottonwood trees that made my playground a cool haven. Clean, clear water ran in the creek all the time. Sometimes, after a heavy rainstorm, the creek would flood as high as the bridge and then miraculously turn into a trickle the very next day. But now it's dirty, and there are no trees.

Ritual and Belief: The Sacred Landscape and Water

Many scholars believe that the Hohokam traveled from somewhere in modern-day Mexico to settle in the valleys of the Salt, Gila, and Santa Cruz Rivers. As such, the Hohokam shared a world view common to other ancient Mesoamerican cultures (Preucel 1996). Water was central to this religious system and permeated ideology and imagery. In this section, we examine parallels between Mesoamerican and Hohokam religion using findings of the Central Arizona Project, other studies, and comparisons with the literature of ancient Mexico. The reader should be forewarned that we will flirt with speculation, for in discussing this topic we are dealing with aspects of ancient life that are the most difficult for the archaeologist to reconstruct. Moreover, as folklorist James Griffith (1992:9) has cautioned, those of us who are steeped in European traditions may find it difficult to grasp the sophisticated Mesoamerican religions, which were the product of centuries of philosophical speculation and ritual practice.

In ancient Mesoamerica, a pantheon of deities governed a cosmos that was divided into several vertical and horizontal dimensions. Themes of ancestor veneration, sacrifice, rebirth, and renewal structured the mythological and religious events of the cosmos and human interactions with deities, spirits, and the dead. Directionalism, duality, and a suite of cosmological, plant, animal, and elemental metaphors characterized cosmology. This complex was translated into the sacred landscape of Mesoamerica. All life was a metaphor in which the spiritual was reenacted through the physical (McPherson 1992:75).

The most important Mesoamerican deities represented gods and goddesses of powerful, vital natural forces such as wind and rain. In these guises, they became patrons of agriculture and corn. Gods of rain and lightning included the Maya Chac and the Nahuatl Tlaloc. The Tlaloc cult was one of the oldest identifiable rain cults, appearing as early as 800 to 300 B.C. (Weaver 1981:106). Tlaloc and his female counterpart Chalchihuitlicue governed the Tlaloque, who were spirits of mountains and powerful weather phenomena (Miller and Taube 1993:166–167). Another wind-rain spirit was Quetzalcoatl. This ancient deity and mythical culture-hero appeared by the A.D. 400s in central Mexico (Miller and Taube 1993:141). The feathered serpent was one of his guises. Quetzalcoatl brought corn to the people, and in his fertility aspect as the bird-masked wind god Ehecatl, Quetzalcoatl was said to be the wind that swept the path for the gods who brought rain (Bierhorst 1974; Markman and Markman 1992:194, 229). The quincunx, or equal-armed cross, was associated with Quetzalcoatl (his "cross of fire") and Tlaloc (Markman and Markman 1992:81, 163; Séjourné 1976).

A third important god was the fire god, who went by several names. Fire-god imagery included the brazier, the fire serpent, Xiuhcoatl, and the quincunx. The fire god was intimately connected with the house and household and was invoked in household shrines.

The structure of the cosmos was repeated in the everyday world and mirrored in numerology, the sacred landscape, art, and ritual performances. Vertical space was divided into three segments (the upperworld or heaven, the middleworld or earth's surface, and the underworld). Horizontal space was divided into four segments representing the cardinal directions (Preucel 1996:125). Duality of opposites, such as fire and water, was another key structural concept (Miller and Taube 1993:81). The Nahuatl glyph "burning water"—two streams of water and fire uniting—was emblematic of the dynamic harmony between water and fire. The symbol was often associated with Quetzalcoatl (Séjourné 1976).

Informed speculation suggests the Hohokam maintained a strikingly similar religious complex with shared cosmology and a suite of elemental deities. Directionalism and duality appear to have structured Hohokam cosmology and iconography, and can be seen in buildings, material culture, and village organization. The larger villages were organized with respect to north-south and east-west axes and were also centripetally organized outward from the core or center, conceptually representing a circle within a square, or the reverse—an arrangement not unlike the quincunx. This arrangement can be seen at Water World, a site excavated during the Tucson Aqueduct Project, Phase B (Czaplicki and Ravesloot 1989). An open "plaza" area lacking houses and other features formed the village core. Clusters of pit houses, some of which had associated trash areas and cremations, were arranged around the plaza. Outdoor cooking facilities and other specialized activity areas tended to be located on the perimeter of house groups. A ball court was located east of the plaza. Two small cremation areas were located at opposite sides of the village.

Hohokam painted pottery was often decorated with four lines partitioning the design into four quarters (Haury 1937, 1976). This may reflect the division of the cosmos into four quarters (Doyel 1991:244; Kelley 1966) and suggests a clear parallel with the Mesoamerican quincunx. The cardinal directions were likely also associated with colors and elements, as among many Mesoamerican peoples and modern Puebloans of the American Southwest.

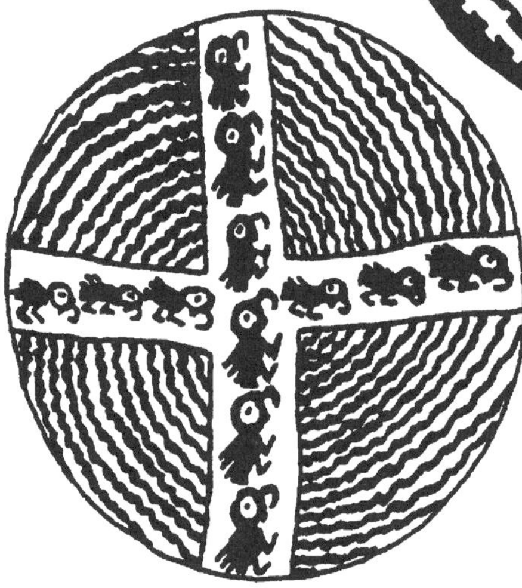

Quartered design layouts on interiors of Hohokam painted bowls.

Tucson Aqueduct Project, Phase B

For construction and administrative purposes, the Tucson Aqueduct portion of the Central Arizona Project was divided into two phases, Phase A (northern segment) and Phase B (southern segment). Following overviews and surveys to locate cultural resources within the aqueduct corridor, the Arizona State Museum conducted data recovery at 13 sites along the Phase B segment in 1986 and 1987.

Tucson Aqueduct. PHOTOGRAPH COURTESY U.S. BUREAU OF RECLAMATION. JOE MADRIGAL, JR., PHOTOGRAPHER.

Excavation was carried out at two large sites dating to the Rillito phase of the Colonial period (between about A.D. 850 and 950), Water World and Fastimes. The project also investigated a small, late Pioneer–early Colonial period farmstead dating between about A.D. 700–850 called Hawk's Nest; four sites where raw materials for stone tools were quarried; two farmstead or field-house sites; and four small sites that were used for special, limited purposes.

The five-volume report was published between 1988 and 1989. This project was particularly important because before the project, the Pioneer and Colonial periods in the Tucson area were poorly understood. The project also provided an excellent cross section of site types, information on farming strategies and resource procurement, and geomorphological studies that contributed to understanding agriculture and settlement patterns along Brawley Wash.

Turning to religious themes, we find that ancestor veneration was central in Mesoamerican religion (Wilcox and Sternberg 1983:80), and mortuary ritual was elaborate. Funerary practices integrated the spirits of the dead with natural forces, transforming them and placing the ancestors in a vital position to ensure the fertility of fields, the abundance of crops, and the beneficent character of natural forces (Schaafsma 1999:184). Because fire was viewed as a purifier, the dead were cremated to prepare them for rebirth (Markman and Markman 1992:196–197; Séjourné 1976:101, 108).

Many aspects of Hohokam material culture, architecture, and settlement patterns also indicate a concern with family and the ancestors. Courtyard groups often persisted in the same place for many years. Households and kinship groups were evidently closely connected to a parcel of land for generations. Cemeteries were usually located adjacent to house clusters, suggesting that the deceased members of a kinship or descent group continued to occupy in death the place where they had lived in life. Some cremation practices, such as division of the remains into multiple lots for burial, may reflect ancestor veneration (Whittlesey 1998c:616).

Land, ancestors, and family were clearly linked and pervaded Hohokam symbolism. Earth symbolism permeated domestic architecture (Schroeder 1979). Hohokam houses, which were excavated into the earth and required the resident to step down in order to enter, may have represented the symbolic place of emergence from the underworld. Centered on a hearth and perhaps the site of household shrines and family rituals, the house was a perfect composite symbol of home, family, hearth, and land. Ceremonial architecture also reflected earth symbolism. Ball courts, which had earthen berms, and platform mounds, which were constructed with earth fill, reflected this emphasis on the land. Snakes may have mediated between the Hohokam and the underworld, as they do today for the Hopi people (Preucel 1996:126).

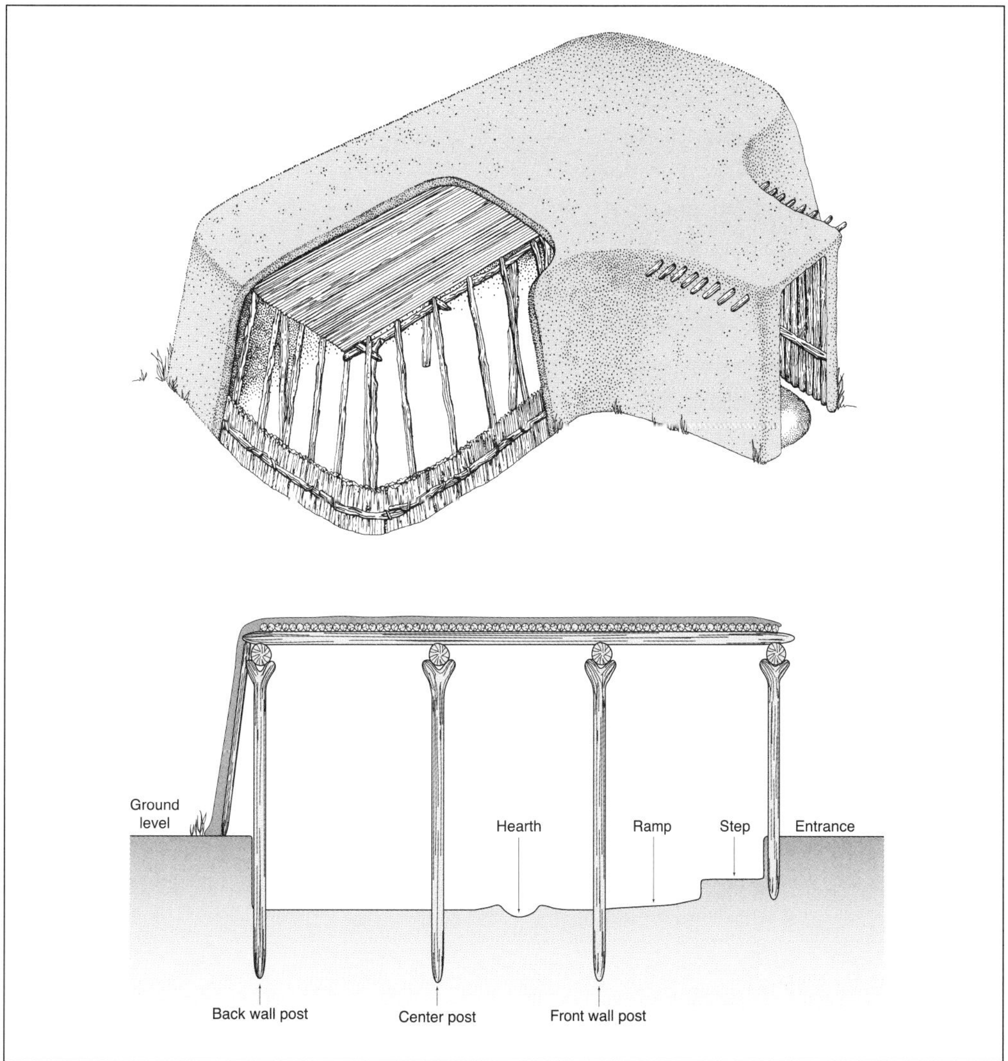

Artist's reconstruction of a Hohokam pit house showing roof construction method. Cross section shows roof-support posts.

Another vital religious theme in Mesoamerica was the act of sacrifice to achieve balance and harmony and to repay the gods for life (Miller and Taube 1993:30). Material objects and living peoples were sacrificed, monuments were defaced, and altars, sculptures, and temples were torn down to achieve these ends, often during termination and purification rituals. Fire and water played a central role in such rites (Miller and Taube 1993:87, 164). Themes of sacrifice, cremation, and transformation reenacted the myth of Quetzalcoatl, who sacrificed himself by fire and was reborn (Bierhorst 1974; Sahagún 1946; Séjourné 1976).

Transformation, purification, and termination rituals focusing on fire and destruction may have been equally important to the Hohokam. Fire was used to purify the dead, prepare them for burial and rebirth, and purify offerings and ritual objects. It may have been used in magical performances. Palettes of schist and stone censers (often bearing images of serpents) were used to burn minerals during ritual performances, creating brightly colored flames with symbolic meaning (Haury 1976:288–289; Hawley 1965). Termination rituals may also have been practiced. Burned houses, many of which contain floor assemblages, are common at Hohokam sites. Some archaeologists (for example, Huntington [1986]) have suggested that the residences of the deceased were burned during mortuary rites. When heads of lineages or households died, however, effectively ending the existence of those groups, the deceased's houses may have been burned in a termination ritual. Such rituals may have been used to mark cosmological events or points in calendrical cycles.

Hohokam mortuary practices may reflect the Quetzalcoatl myth. Burning of the dead, their houses, personal belongings, and offerings may have been designed to transform and purify the deceased and prepare them for rebirth as in the Quetzalcoatl story (Séjourné 1976). Deliberate destruction of ceramic vessels and other offerings by smashing and burning accompanied the cremation rite (Haury 1976:164–166). Incense may have been burned during the rite, symbolizing the elements of air and fire, and the incense burner may have represented the fire god's brazier.

Caches of deliberately destroyed, burned, and broken objects—ceramic vessels, censers, palettes, effigy vessels of stone and clay, shell, clay figurines, and other objects—have been found at the largest Hohokam settlements, such as Snaketown (Haury 1976). Such offerings may have substituted for the human sacrifice so common in Mesoamerica, and parallels with renewal ceremonies seem inescapable.

The ball game played an important role in Mesoamerican ritual. It ensured the proper functioning of the universe through sacrifice and transformation and was a vehicle for reenacting important myths (Cohodas 1991; Lincoln 1990:166; Preucel 1996:126). It was also a public ritual linked to the solar calendar and to agricultural rejuvenation, reenacting the descent, transformation, and regeneration of the sun god and moon goddess through the annual cycle of equinoxes and solstices (Cohodas 1991:269).

The ball court was one of the most obvious elements of the Hohokam sacred landscape, and the ball game evidently played a central role in the agricultural year and in water control. In Mesoamerica, sacred waters were thought to flow to the crops from a hole in the center of the ball

Dancing figures on Hohokam Buff Ware cauldron.

Ball court at Water World site. PHOTOGRAPH COURTESY U.S. BUREAU OF RECLAMAT
JOE MADRIGAL, JR., PHOTOGRAPHER.

Hohokam Buff Ware pottery.

court (Schaafsma 1999:170). Observing that ball courts were consistently located along riverine systems and that the largest courts were associated with confluences of two or more streams, I have previously proposed (Whittlesey 1998c:622) that the ball game was used in some way to control and distribute irrigation water. Archaeologist Stephen Lansing (1991) has described how ritual features were used in Bali to govern water allocation. Balinese water temples, which were located at several strategic points within irrigation systems and managed by their resident priests, not only controlled the timing and distribution of water by setting irrigation schedules, but were in some indefinable and mysterious way linked with the health and abundance of crops. When the water-temple system was replaced with modern farming methods, water shortages and outbreaks of pests and diseases ensued. Crop production dropped dramatically as a consequence. When the traditional water temples were restored, so was the health of the agricultural system. Ritual thus served the practical role of maintaining crop health and preventing such afflictions.

Wilcox (1991; Wilcox and Sternberg 1983; Wilcox and others 1981:143, 208) has suggested that Hohokam ball courts were associated with a cycle of annual, calendrically based rituals and festivals as in Mesoamerica. These rites, possibly supervised by a priest, may have governed the distribution of irrigation water in a manner similar to the Balinese water temples. Magical rites may also have been used when canals were built, refurbished, or cleaned.

Orientation of ball courts in the cardinal directions reflects directional symbolism. The court at Water World was one of the north-south oriented courts, with its long axis headed east of north (Ravesloot and Czaplicki 1989). It was surrounded by cremations and roasting pits, suggesting that mortuary rituals and community food preparation (feasting?) were carried out along with the ball-court ceremonies. It is striking that the court was located east of the plaza. This is the preferred location of I-shaped ball courts among prehistoric Mexican cultures (Cohodas 1991:254).

What of imagery and symbolism related to the religious-ritual complex? In Mesoamerica, rain, corn, clouds, and lightning were blended images. Water was both a means of ceremonial purification and the symbolic opposition to fire. Lightning was considered a powerful manifestation of fertilizing and generative energy. For example, corn was thought to have originated when lightning split open a rock containing hidden corn kernels (Miller and Taube 1993:106). Symbols associated with water, rain, and agricultural fertility included earth, clouds, lightning, serpents, shells, corn, and the color blue. These symbols often appeared on representations of Tlaloc and Quetzalcoatl and were used as offerings to these gods (Markman and Markman 1992:255, 259; Miller and Taube 1993; Thompson 1970:252). Serpent deities associated with rain were considered to exist in the sacred multiple of four, or as four-in-one, and were often associated with separate colors and directions (Miller and Taube 1993:150).

Water and mountains were closely linked. Mountains were universally viewed as generators of clouds and sources of springs, lakes, and streams (Markman and Markman 1992:202). As an artificial sacred space, the pyramid symbolized the natural mountain (Markman and Markman 1992:413). Mountain peaks and pyramids were therefore locales for Tlaloc ceremonies and sacrifices associated with renewal and reciprocity at the beginning of the rainy season (Sahagún 1953; Townsend 1992). Mountains were also seen as homes and meeting places of ancestors and deities, who were thought to dwell in watery domains that could be accessed by caves and springs. Mountains were associated with cardinal directions and colors.

Caves, mirrors, ceramic vessels, and water were connected in complex ways. Caves represented springs and sources of water (Sullivan 1974), symbolized entrances to the underworld (Townsend 1992:178), and were the origin places for many Mesoamerican peoples, therefore symbolizing creation and life itself. Caves were concealed within mountains, thus connecting metaphors of birth, origin, and water. Because of their bright, reflective surfaces, mirrors were compared to shining pools of water. Mirrors also represented caves and were considered passageways for the supernatural (Miller and Taube 1993:115). Ceramic containers were intimately associated with water, rain, and the rain gods. Pottery vessels were iconographic representations of containers holding the clouds that produce rain (Schaafsma 1999:168).

As an agricultural people deeply committed to corn cultivation, the Hohokam probably adopted a rain-fertility cult early in their history. The Tlaloc and Quetzalcoatl cults of Mesoamerica were sufficiently ancient to have provided inspiration. Of all the symbols used in Hohokam art, water was probably the most vital. Water made life possible by nourishing plants, animals, and bringing the crops to bountiful harvests. As irrigation farmers, water was particularly vital to the Hohokam. The redundant use of moisture symbols throughout Hohokam iconography suggests more than fortuitous connections with a rain cult, such as the Tlaloc cult (Schaafsma 1999) or that associated with Quetzalcoatl.

Consistent bird and serpent imagery implies a Quetzalcoatl motif. We can imagine a connection among snakes and water, rain, and lightning, as in Mesoamerica. When translated into Hohokam imagery, the serpent may have been simultaneously a metaphor for rain and lightning. The sinuous winding of rivers and irrigation canals through fields may have been likened to a water serpent in a complicated and layered metaphor. Today, Sonoran folk dialect refers to irrigation canals and snakes by the same name, *alicante* (Griffith 1992:5).

Rattlesnake in bush. PHOTOGRAPH BY STEPHANIE WHITTLESEY.

The Origin of Irrigation

There is an intricate and fascinating connection among water, canals, and snakes among desert peoples that may have begun with the Hohokam. In the O'odham creation stories, there is a tale called "The Origin of Irrigation" (Bahr and others 1994:124). The people noticed a decrease in rainfall and began to build a canal, but when it was completed, water would not flow through it. The people asked several medicine men to attempt the task, and the last and most powerful magician succeeded. He accomplished this by pulling a hair from his head and putting it in the water. He sang a song, and the hair became a snake and moved (Bahr and others 1994:132). The magician sang:

> There lie the canals
> And in the midst of those
> I stand
> Making water-hair snakes.

In this way, irrigation canals were first made and irrigation farming was created—through magic.

Hohokam bowl (Rillito Red-on-brown) with bird and serpent imagery. PHOTOGRAPH BY WILLIAM L. DEAVER.

Water was symbolized in reflective items such as pyrite mirrors, in the shiny surfaces of schist-tempered pottery (which may also have represented stars), and the birds and animals associated with water that were endlessly repeated in Hohokam pottery designs, stone censers and bowls, and shell ornaments (Kelley 1993:238). Water-filled

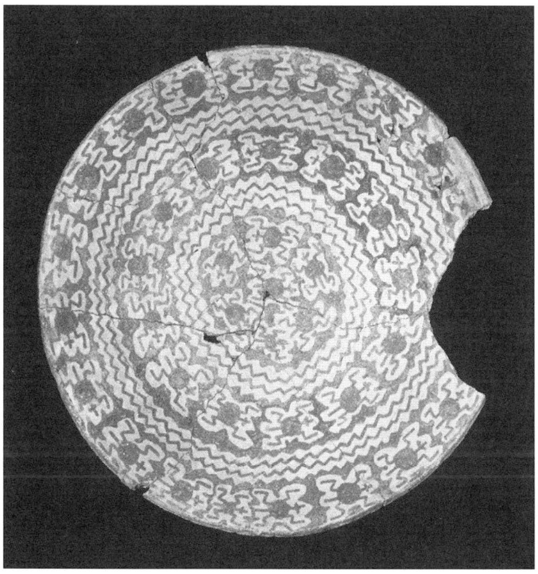

Hohokam bowl (Rillito Red-on-brown) with turtle or tortoise designs. Photograph by William L. Deaver.

ceramic containers would serve as redundant symbols of moisture, the underworld, and springs (Whittlesey 1998d: 442). As symbols of entrances to the underworld, water-filled containers may have also functioned to link the cult of rain to the ancestors. Among Hopi and other Puebloan peoples and perhaps among the Hohokam as well, ancestors were represented as clouds that bring rain to their descendants on earth. Stepped elements probably representing clouds were pervasive in Hohokam art, particularly on

Hohokam jar (Rillito Red-on-brown) with rainbird motifs. Photograph by William L. Deaver.

painted pottery. Marine shell ornaments may have been the core symbol of Hohokam identity. Ornaments were often carved to represent water birds, little frogs with legs tucked next to their bodies ready to leap, and other animals symbolic of water.

Desert Toads

The Sonoran spadefoot toad *(Scaphiopus couchii)* spends its life burrowed into the ground, emerging only after summer's first storms. Toads sing, court, and mate in ephemeral pools of rainwater. The loud, curiously sheeplike voices of the spadefoot toads chorus around the puddled water on summer nights. Perhaps they sing, Edward Abbey (1968:125) has suggested, "out of spontaneous love and joy, a contrapuntal choral celebration of the coolness and wetness after weeks of desert fire."

Joseph Wood Krutch (1951:75) came upon a choir of spadefoot toads one summer evening. Some were sitting gravely around the edge in contemplative poses; others were swimming about happily. Krutch has described the voice of one toad as the most heartfelt sound he had ever heard. "The plaintiveness was gone, past wrongs were forgotten. He was hailing the wetness as a cock hails the first light of dawn."

The toad's voice heralds the monsoon, the coming of the rain that will fill the streambeds and potholes, the canals and the pools, rain that will puddle in the fields and water the parched corn. Which came first, one might ask? Did the rain bring the toads, or did the toads call down the rain onto the land?

Hohokam sacred geography, as in Mesoamerica, appears to have been centered on mountains, springs, and caves as important landscape metaphors for rain and water. Mesoamerican landscape metaphors and symbols translated well in the arid environment of the Southwest, where caves containing pools of water and *tinajas* are often found in mountain settings (Schaafsma 1999:179). Significant topographic features, such as Gila Butte, were metaphors for rain in the natural world. This highly visible, twin hill near Snaketown, where much of the micaceous schist used to temper Hohokam plain ware pottery was quarried, was probably an important landmark with sacred significance. Platform mounds were the mountains' counterpart in the built environment, and ritual performances were carried out on some of them. Mountain peaks may also have served as locales for ceremonies. Springs in southern Arizona were typically marked with petroglyphs (Wallace and Holmlund 1986), and caves served as locations for more elaborate offerings. Red Cave in southeastern Arizona was a cave shrine with a pool of water where sherd disks and other offerings were left (Ferg and Mead 1993).

Figurines were evidently an important part of the Hohokam ritual complex, as they were in Mesoamerica. Human figurines, many of which were female, occasionally depicted as pregnant, reflected the perfect joining of the elements earth, water, and fire. The Hohokam figurine was therefore a union of opposites, such as that symbolized by the Nahuatl burning water symbol associated with Quetzalcoatl. The sedimentary clay from which figurines were made was taken from a riverbed, canal, well, spring, or other water source (Neitzel 1991; Thomas and King 1985). This fine, light clay was unlike the heavier, brown clay used to make pottery containers. Figurines were fired in fabrication, used in cremation rituals, and sometimes destroyed by burning.

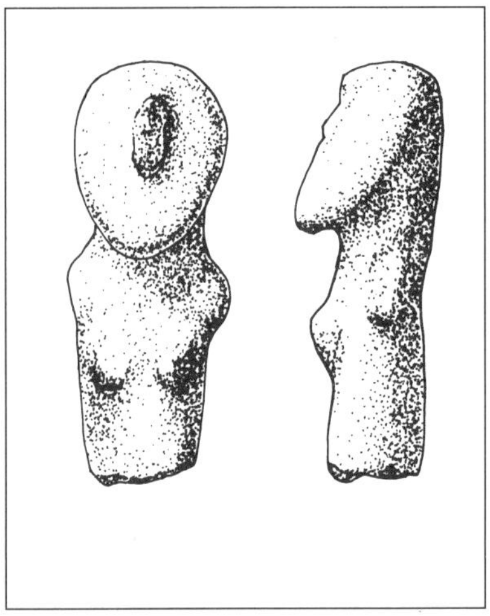

Hohokam figurine.

Figurines may have been "clay prayers"—offerings to bring rain and to increase the fertility of fields, crops, and women, who may have had an important role in farming, as they do among many peoples. Figurines may have been left as offerings at springs, in irrigation canals, or in reservoirs. The linking of water, fertility, ancestors, and farming through female figurines made of water-borne clay is particularly striking. The objects may also have represented ancestors (Wilcox and Sternberg 1983:229). Some male Hohokam figurines (Haury 1976:Figure 13.15e, 13.16) imply a connection with the ball game (Ekholm 1991:242). Last, at least some modeled-clay figurines (Gladwin and others 1937:Plate CXCVIa; Haury 1976:Figure 13.13) may have been representations of gods, perhaps the ancient god of fire who carried a brazier on his head (Markman and Markman 1992:Image 13).

Hallucinogenic substances, such as datura (sacred datura or jimson weed, *Datura meteloides*), and alcoholic beverages may have been consumed during Hohokam rituals. Datura seeds have been found in archaeological sites, and some ceramic containers were shaped like datura seedpods. Large ceramic containers with eroded interiors may have been containers for corn beer or other alcoholic beverages (Simon 1997). By drinking such beverages, the Hohokam would have been reinforcing the real and symbolic links among cultivated crops, farming, fluids, and ritual. In the following section, we will see how the O'odham used saguaro wine to bring the rain.

Lest all of this sound too speculative, many peoples living in the desert Southwest today share a suite of beliefs, symbols, and rituals similar to those we have inferred for the Hohokam. This may suggest that a fundamental religious system derived from Mesoamerica had ancient roots in the American Southwest. We have seen in Chapter 4 that the Hopi associated snakes with water and specifically springs (Griffith 1992; Whiteley 1998). The Water Serpent is believed to have come from the red land to the south and is the patron of the Water Corn Clan, which also derived from that land (Griffith 1992:11). The priests in charge of irrigation at some New Mexico pueblos pray and make offerings to the water serpent (Parsons 1939). Snakes also symbolize water to the O'odham and Mexican peoples.

Recall also that the Navajo associate mountain peaks with water, clouds, and rain, just as Mesoamerican peoples associated mountains with Tlaloc. Mountain peaks are also sacred to the Western Apache and associated with spirits called *ga'an,* as we will see in the next chapter. The O'odham Wi' Kita ceremony, used to bring rain, included many symbolic images that seem to have been derived from antique Mesoamerican practices. Dancers wore strings of shell and blue-glass beads and shell pendants on deerskin girdles. Sacred cornmeal was sprinkled on four little piles of sand (mountains?) and into four holes made at the cardinal points of the ceremonial ground. Dancers paraded a white cloth symbolizing clouds as a means of bringing rain (Fontana 1989). It is intriguing that the Tohono O'odham tell a Quetzalcoatl-like myth of death and rebirth about I'itoi, Elder Brother (Underhill 1993).

The living and ancient peoples of the Southwest, like those of Mesoamerica, recognized the importance of water to life and farming, deified the spirits of rain and wind, incorporated ceremonies to bring the rain into their religious practices, and symbolized water in their artwork. The sacred and secular built environments were organized to reflect crucial beliefs, and cosmology related to water and may have had vital functions in controlling water and maintaining the health of the fields and land. Next, we turn to the O'odham people to see how they accomplished these tasks.

Culebra: The Desert Water Snake

In southern Arizona, O'odham and Mexican legends link water and snakes in a relationship embedded deep in prehistory, perhaps going all the way back to ancient Mesoamerican theology and cosmology. Every water source is thought to have a harmless serpent-god that watches over it, called *la corúa* in Spanish and *nehbig* in the O'odham language. According to folklorist James Griffith (1992:5), the word *corúa* derives from a Yaqui word meaning "snake," and its roots lie in the Uto-Aztecan language, in which the word *co* means "snake." The same word appears in the Aztec word Quetzalcoatl, the name of the great, feathered-serpent deity commanding the winds and water.

Should the serpent-god of a spring die, the spring in which it lived would dry up. If the serpent's fangs were removed and hidden, it would be unable to find them and would kill itself, and the spring would dry up. Therefore, it was important to protect the serpent so as to protect the spring. Mexican and O'odham children alike were enjoined to keep out of the irrigation ditches lest the *corúa* get them. The serpent legend may have served to protect precious water resources from human tampering.

The legend of La Llorona may serve the same purpose of protecting water sources. This famous Wailing Woman haunts watercourses all over Mexico and the Southwest. Doomed to wander in eternity searching for her children, whom she drowned so that she could run off with a man, La Lorona collects living children for her own purposes (Griffith 1992:125).

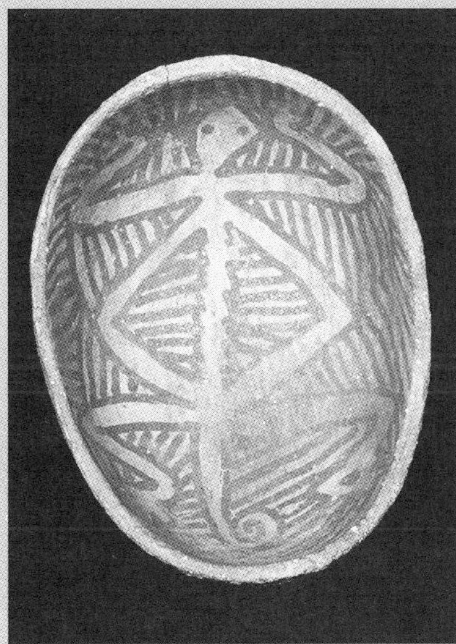

Other serpents dwell in the heart of the summer thunderstorms, bringing rain in great, black, undulating curtains of water, sometimes leaving floods and destruction in their wakes. This serpent is called *culebra* or *culebra de agua* in Spanish.

Tohono O'odham: Bringing Down the Clouds

Centuries ago, the Spanish priest Pedro Font penned his opinion of the land occupied by the Tohono O'odham—the Desert People—writing that "in all this land of Papaguería which was passed through, I did not see a single thing worthy of praise." He was looking at the Sonoran Desert with European eyes, for the Desert People above all others knew that the desert could sustain those who understood it. The Tohono O'odham were able to "wrest a subsistence from so reluctant and forbidding an environment" (Castetter and Bell 1942:37), coaxing it to yield food, beverages, materials for crafts, and medicine. They also fashioned fulfilling lives rich in songs, dense in stories, and resonant with laughter. Moreover, Tohono O'odham lifeways help us to understand how the Hohokam farmed away from the rivers and provide models for arid-land living throughout the world.

Life in the desert is conditioned by the scarcity of water. Water, not land, constrained farming, for a field without water is useless. Fields with good soils and water were in scarce supply, and the people developed a biseasonal pattern to adjust to this scarcity. In winter, the

Pulling Down the Clouds

Ñ-ku 'ibadkaj 'ant 'an ols g cewagĭ.
With my harvesting stick I will hook the clouds.
'Ant o 'i-waññ'io k o 'i-hudiññ g cewagĭ.
With my harvesting stick I will pull down the clouds.
Ñ-ku 'ibadkaj 'ant o 'i-siho g cewagĭ.
With my harvesting stick I will stir the clouds.

(Ofelia Zepeda, "Pulling Down the Clouds")

Tohono O'odham lived in "well" villages at higher elevations with permanent water sources. In summer, they moved down to their field villages in the open, desert country.

Castetter and Bell (1942) reported that Tohono O'odham women once spent more time fetching water than gathering food. Even at the well villages, it was sometimes necessary to travel 3–4 miles, perhaps as much as 10 miles, for water. One informant reported that as a boy he made a daily trip of 15 miles on horseback to obtain water, carrying two ollas holding about three gallons each. Sometimes an olla had to remain under a dripping spring for as much as an hour until it filled, and the women waited patiently in line for their turn. At times the water supply at the winter villages could only be obtained by digging through the bottoms of sandy washes on the mountain slopes—and then it was often a trifling amount. At the summer villages, the people hollowed depressions into the soil to catch and hold rainwater and sometimes built dikes and ditches for this purpose. If we extend this pattern back into prehistory, which seems plausible in the absence of evidence for substantial change in water sources or climate, the Hohokam may have had to travel just as far to obtain potable water.

Although the Tohono O'odham irrigated wherever it was possible to do so, it was their mastery of floodwater farming that ensured their survival in the land of little rain. Their proficiency with floodwater farming in the Sonoran Desert, where only a few inches of rain falls each year, is nothing short of remarkable. Some geographers and economists insist that dry farming is not possible in the Tohono O'odham homeland. The miracle began in May, when the land and the people waited for the saguaro fruits to turn crimson. This month was called in O'odham the "painful moon" or "hunger-hurting moon" *(ko'ohk macat),* for the stored fruits of last year's harvest were gone. In the "black-seeds moon" (early June), the seeds of certain plants were ripe and black, and hope rose. The people greeted the ripening of saguaro fruit in the saguaro-harvest or rainy moon (late June and July) with laughter, and they prepared for the ceremony to call down the clouds. Anthropologist Ruth Underhill (1965:244) wrote of this time, "the sense of joyous expectation was such as

Tohono O'odham woman drawing water at a well near Mission San Xavier del Bac, early twentieth century. PHOTOGRAPH COURTESY ARIZONA HISTORICAL SOCIETY, TUCSON (AHS ACCESSION NO. 15255).

I have not seen since I was a child awaiting Christmas." The rains will come, the earth will be moist. Soon it will be time to plant.

To be certain that drinking water was available, Tohono O'odham families moved to the field villages only after the rains had begun. Natural pools along the washes could retain water as late as October or November, when the people returned to the well villages. Farming plots were invariably located in the broad apron of alluvial soil at the mouth of washes—the *ak-chin,* or arroyo mouth. Many villages throughout the Papaguería were called Ak Chin for these arroyo-mouth fields. The torrent of muddy water rushing down after a rain would lose its momentum and spread out over the level fields, sometimes to a depth of two or three inches. The people would hurry to plant while the soil was moist. Every suitable plot of ground was used, and the *ak-chin* fields were often small. By farming many small fields scattered across the land, the Tohono O'odham coped with the sporadic and uneven spatial distribution of rain and reduced the risk of crop failure.

A thick growth of weeds or large mesquite or palo verde trees indicated a good soil. The siting of fields was

The Saguaro Wine Ceremony

Saguaros, the well-known symbol of the Sonoran Desert and Arizona's state flower, march along the rocky *bajada* slopes and raise their arms to the sky. In May, creamy white, exotic blooms appear on the tips of the branches, followed in June by crimson fruit that splits open and is often mistaken for flowers. The fig-like fruit was an important part of the Tohono O'odham diet and the focus of a crucial ceremony. Preparing saguaro wine and drinking it pulled the rain clouds down from the sky and brought the vital moisture to the earth so the people could plant. Anthropologist Ruth Underhill wrote of this magic in her book *Singing for Power.* "It is the duty of every man to drink his fill of this liquor; drink to a saturation, even as the rain-soaked earth is saturated" (Underhill 1993:22). Every man must learn to drink respectfully and bring the rain.

Every family had a grove where they camped to pick the fruits, pulling them down with long tongs made from saguaro ribs. The fruit was boiled and sieved to extract the juice, leaving the empty shells lying on the ground with their red side showing to summon the rain.

The families brought their ollas full of bright-red juice to the council house, where an elder supervised the fermentation. At night the people danced around the rain house. The old men would lie awake under the stars, singing the drinking songs. Until morning they sang of rain and the animals who are its harbingers. When the wine was ready, neighboring villages were invited, and all partook of the *nawait.* With much singing and many ceremonial speeches, the people drank. The object of the drinking was to vomit the wine on the ground, an act that brought the rain. People said with pleasure, "Look—he is throwing up the clouds" This was also a time when, as Underhill (1993:25) delicately puts it, a woman can have her pick of the men. "Love has no laws tonight." When all the liquor had been consumed and the people were "beautifully drunk," lightning and wind came bearing the rain. The storm unleashed, the desert bloomed with shining water. Now the planting could begin.

Photograph by Jefferson Reid.

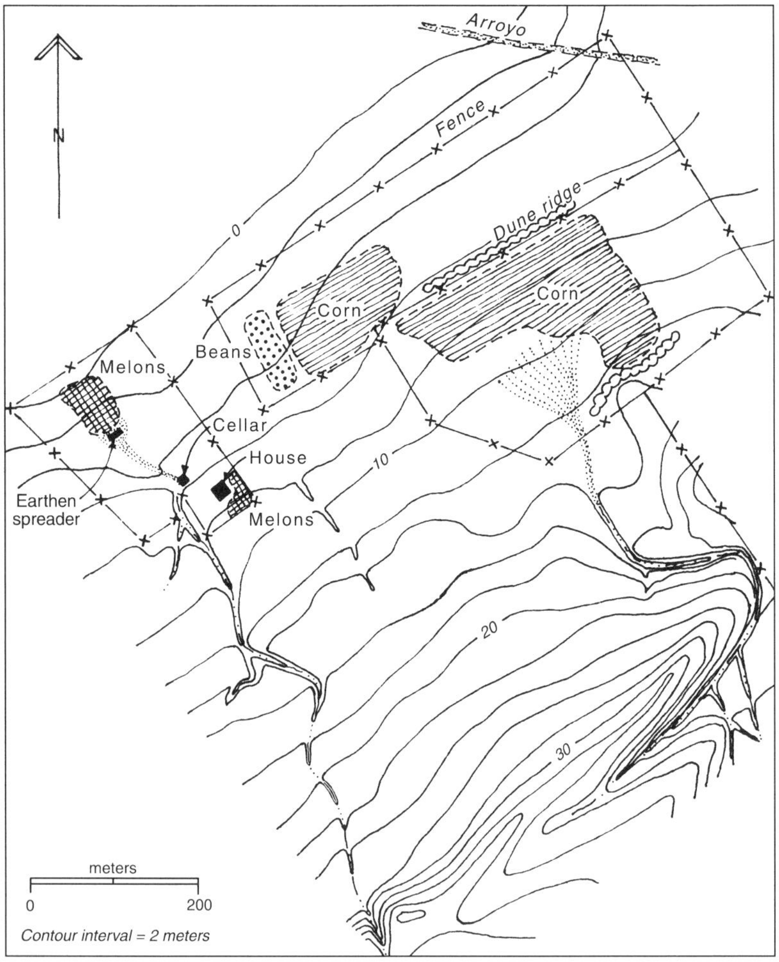

Location of Hopi ak-chin *fields in relation to arroyo mouth (after Waters 1989:Figure 3.8).*

tricky, for they had to be located where they would receive sufficient water but not enough to wash the crops away, although sometimes this disaster was unavoidable. Clearing new ground or preparing existing plots by removing weeds and brush was men's work. Before the Spanish brought metal implements and draft animals, the people planted and weeded, constructed ditches, and dug water holes with simple digging sticks and hoes made of ironwood or mesquite. Fields were leveled by hand, the people carrying the dirt in baskets to low-lying areas. Large, extended-family groups farmed the same fields for generations.

In years when the rains were late, there was trouble. It was sometimes possible to plant a crop as late as August (the "short-planting" or "late-planting moon") if the ground was still moist, but there was the risk that the crops might not mature before the first frost. If that happened, the people would have to subsist entirely on wild foods, because there would be insufficient time for crops to mature before the cold frosts came. The Akimel O'odham, with their more secure supply of water from the Gila River and a slightly warmer climate, were usually able to plant twice, but the people of the higher, drier, and colder desert typically made a single planting each year.

The first crop to be planted was always corn. Seeds were planted in rows of small hills, using the digging stick to loosen the dirt and dig a hole. A man could plant about a half-acre of corn or tepary beans each day with this method. Fields usually contained mixed crops, a strategy that may have helped to buffer risk.

Of the substantial storms that rain on the desert, typically no more than five or six are sufficient to stimulate plant growth. O'odham informants told Castetter and Bell (1942) that crops required two floodings to produce, three floodings to provide a good yield. Farmers built low embankments, small brush dams, and shallow ditches to collect, divert, and distribute the water. In modern times, they also built earthen and brush dams across the washes. By these simple but effective means, it was possible to harvest surface runoff from several square miles and concentrate it on a single field (Nabhan and others 1980). If several fields were located at an arroyo mouth, the men might built a single large ditch with smaller lateral ditches to each field. Ditches were built and maintained cooperatively by all the men using the water.

Ak-Chin Farming

Charles Bowden (1986:141) writes of the system called *ak-chin* farming, an agricultural way of life that has now almost entirely disappeared:

> No irrigation produces this crop. No well gushes forth the buried hydrologic treasure of the earth. This is something the Papagos called *ak chin,* floodwater farming where human beings cast down seeds after the rain and hope the plants grow and flourish before the desert winds dry out the soil. For centuries and centuries this was the nature of farming in much of the Southwest. Now such practices have been vanquished and made foolish by the agribusiness dreams that drain the American and Mexican ground of the region. The field is a living fossil, a garden planted in the manner of people long gone from most of the land.

A Tohono O'odham hay field at San Xavier Indian Reservation near Tucson, Arizona. PHOTOGRAPH BY JEFFERSON REID.

The diet was based on the tasty and nutritious tepary bean *(Phaseolus acutifolius)*. Each person ate as much as 300 grams of beans each day, perhaps the highest consumption among North American native peoples (Nabhan and others 1980). Teparies grow extremely well on arid lands with floodwater farming. These hardy plants provide a satisfactory yield with only two floodings. More water actually seems to produce leafy growth at the expense of the protein-rich bean pods. Analyses of the nutrient content of beans demonstrated that floodwater-fed teparies were more nutritious than those grown in irrigated fields (Nabhan and other 1980).

In two rounds of the moon—between 9 and 10 weeks—the corn would be ready. October ("frost moon") was the harvest season. Harvesting was women's work, and families shared the labor, receiving some of the produce in return. Corn was usually harvested first and was considered ready when the stalks and husks were thoroughly dry, although some of the ears might still be green. Teparies were harvested next, and pumpkins last, for it was thought that a little frost would not hurt them. Cotton and gourds were usually harvested after all the food crops had been stored.

The farmer rises before sunrise, works without stopping until noon and rests during the hottest part of the day, returning to the fields and toiling until dark. Working slowly by necessity in the heat and glaring sun, the farmer's work must be ceaseless if the family is to have enough to eat. Everything must be taken care of, the people say. Take nothing for granted. It is farming without fertilizer, pumped groundwater, insecticides, or herbicides, a system that relies on faith rather than technology—a way of growing food that has all but vanished (Bowden 1977:28).

Beliefs and ceremonies focused on rain. The ocean, or the "outspread water," retains powerful significance. The wind blows over the water, bringing the clouds from which the rain falls on the desert—a sophisticated understanding of meteorology for a people who lived with so little water (Bowden 1977:8). But the ocean will yield its blessing only if the people give it gifts, and the people must also take back the "white corn," the kernels of salt the ocean creates. One of the most arduous means of obtaining the ocean's power and blessings came through a pilgrimage to fetch salt from the Gulf of California, crossing miles of waterless desert in a journey that took four days. "The salt journey has seemed to them difficult enough and the sight of the ocean amazing enough to bring a man into contact with the supernatural" (Underhill 1993:111).

Ocean Power

This poem, Tohono O'odham linguist and poet Ofelia Zepeda wrote, "is about two O'odham men who came too close to the ocean as they were being deported back to Mexico from Arizona" (Zepeda 1995:83–84). This excerpt tells of how men might feel when encountering the ocean without the proper spiritual preparation.

. . . .

We do not belong here,
this place with the sky too endless.
This place with the water too endless.
This place with the air too thick and heavy to breathe.
This place with the roll and roar of thunder always playing to your ears.

We are not ready to be here.
We are not prepared in the old way.
We have no medicine.
We have not sat and had our minds walk through the image
of coming to this ocean.
We are not ready.
We have not put our minds to what it is we want to give the ocean.
We do not have cornmeal, feathers, nor do we have songs and prayers ready.
We have not thought what we will ask from the ocean.

. . . .

(Ofelia Zepeda, "Ocean Power")

A priest led the men and boys to the sea, a race of endurance wrapped about with song, ritual prohibitions, and special language. Arriving, they walked into the waves—a frightening prospect for people who have never seen water more than three feet deep—to bring out a blessing. When the salt was gathered, they walked into the water, strewing cornmeal on the waves.

At home, the salt was purified. With singing, fasting, and tobacco smoke, the boys who completed this journey for the first time awaited their visions. No matter what he might see, each boy emerged a "ripe" man. By his journey to the sea, each person helped to bring rain. O'odham elders believe that rainfall has decreased in recent years because people no longer make the salt journey as often as in the past (Joseph and others 1949:74).

Proper ceremony and song are necessary to bring up the corn. The farmer speaks gently to his seeds as he plants them, instructing them to grow tall and nourish his children

Corn Songs

Coming together in the blue evening, the Tohono O'odham farmer sings to his crops. Let them spring up in the fields, growing green and high. Let the corn tassels tremble and the green leaves shake in the breeze. In the fields there will be much sweet corn. The magic tobacco will bloom and the white and red beans will be like the stars of the Milky Way. The bees and the crickets know. The dragonflies and the hummingbirds know. Ruth Murray Underhill (1993:44) relates this Tohono O'odham song:

The corn comes up;
It comes up green;
Here upon our fields
White tassels unfold.

The corn comes up;
It comes up green;
Here upon our fields
Green leaves blow in the breeze.
. . . .

The wind smooths well the ground.
Yonder the wind runs
Upon our fields.
The corn leaves tremble.

An Experiment in Traditional Technology

The enormous difficulties of making a living in the desert were brought home forcefully when I was a graduate student at the University of Arizona in Tucson. For my student project in a class in traditional technology, I prepared a traditional O'odham meal using desert foods and old-time equipment that I made myself. What a lesson that was! My pottery jar for saguaro syrup, arduously made from clay I collected along the Santa Cruz River, was misshapen and weighed about five pounds. The basket of beargrass and willow was laughably crude. I had no better luck with the foodstuffs. It took hours to grind the mesquite beans, and the bread made from it was bitter and unpalatable. I learned only later than one is supposed to use the fresh bean pods before the seeds mature and dry out or just grind the pods alone, discarding the seeds. Ethnobiologist Amadeo Rea (1997) confirms this. None of the O'odham he interviewed remembered using the seeds, just the pulpy pods.

My lesson? To use desert foods successfully and make functional tools requires more than just hard work. It requires *knowledge*—knowledge that I completely lacked as an Anglo-American without O'odham family to teach me. I had learned from books, from anthropologists and biologists, how to make O'odham foods and equipment. People were the missing factor in my education. There is more to survival in desert land than water and labor. Survival requires language, stories, family, and love.

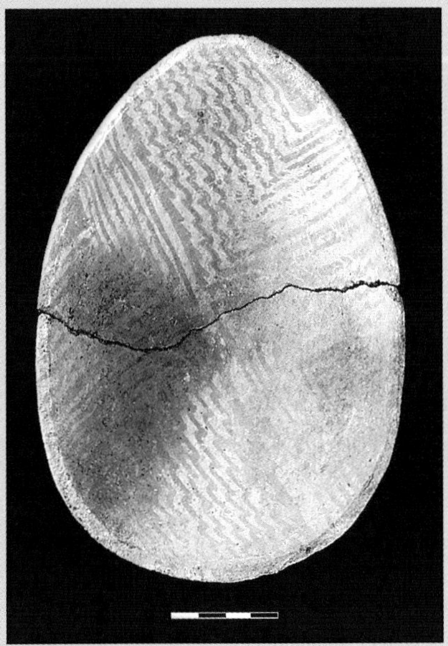

and friends. While the young plants are growing, the farmer sings to them, night after night. There are songs for knee-high corn, for waist-high corn, for corn with tassels forming. Sometimes the men get together and sing all night for the corn, squash, beans, and the wild things (Underhill 1993:43). Simple effigies of natural materials are planted in the fields to make the crops flourish.

"It is important to listen to people who have been in the desert," Childs (2000:34) has written. "To ask for too much water is to invite disaster. Only in a place like this would you bow your head and humbly request just the water you need and no more. Only here would you walk away from water when thirsty." This lesson is brought home with great power in the story of the sacrifice of the children, an event still memorialized at the Children's Shrine near Santa Rosa. The story begins in a time of famine and drought. A man went out to look for rabbits and found a badger instead. He chased the animal into a hole, intending to kill it, although it is forbidden to even touch a badger. As the man prodded the hole, a burst of wind shot out as if a seal had been broken, followed by rushing water that would not stop. Water poured from the hole, inundating villages and destroying the land. In desperation, the village headmen called for the shamans, the medicine doctors, or *makai,* to stop the water. Four times they tried, first putting water birds and then a sea turtle into the hole, to no avail. At last they sacrificed their most valuable possession—their children. Four children, two boys and two girls, were dressed and ceremonially painted. Dancing around the hole, they slowly sank into the ground. When they were gone, the roaring flow of water stopped. The water drained back into the earth, and rocks were piled over the hole. (Versions of this story are related by Childs [2000]; Griffith [1992]; Nabhan [1982]; and Saxton and Saxton [1973].)

The shrine lies on level ground in the floodplain, and many visit it each year. It is a pile of rocks surrounded by a five-foot-tall fence of ocotillo branches that is renewed every four years in a four-day ceremony. Four sets of ocotillo branches placed in the cardinal directions and hung with feathers encircle the cairn. The rock pile is decorated with all manner of offerings, mostly made by children for children: plastic toys, beads, costume jewelry, crepe-paper flowers, coins and dollar bills, teddy bears, traditional O'odham baskets, pens and pencils, a miniature tea set, medals, shells and coral, barrettes, ripe fruit. These gifts tell us that "Drought is ordinary here, dealt with adeptly, no need to make great sacrifices" (Childs 2000:181). What is terrifying in the desert is not drought, but flood—too much water, requiring the gravest sacrifices of all. Remember the flood, the shrine whispers. Remember the children who died to stop it.

For further information, see: Edward F. Castetter and Willis H. Bell, Pima and Papago Indian Agriculture *(University of New Mexico Press, Albuquerque, 1942);* Dry Borders *(Journal of the Southwest Vol. 39, Nos. 3–4, 1997); Suzanne K. Fish, Paul R. Fish, Charles H. Miksicek, and John H. Madsen,* Prehistoric Agave Cultivation in Southern Arizona *(Desert Plants 7:102–112, 1985); Bernard L. Fontana,* Of Earth and Little Rain *(University of Arizona Press, Tucson, 1989); Joseph Wood Krutch,* The Desert Year *(University of Arizona Press, Tucson, 1951); Gary Paul Nabhan,* Gathering the Desert *(University of Arizona Press, Tucson, 1985) and* The Desert Smells Like Rain: A Naturalist in O'odham Country *(University of Arizona Press, Tucson, 1982); Amadeo M. Rea,* At the Desert's Green Edge: An Ethnobotany of the Gila River Pima *(University of Arizona Press, Tucson, 1997); Jefferson Reid and Stephanie Whittlesey,* The Archaeology of Ancient Arizona *(University of Arizona Press, Tucson, 1997); Ruth Murray Underhill,* Singing for Power: The Song Magic of the Papago Indians of Southern Arizona *(University of Arizona Press, Tucson, 1993); George Webb,* A Pima Remembers *(University of Arizona Press, Tucson, 1959); Stephanie M. Whittlesey, Richard Ciolek-Torrello, and Matthew A. Sterner,* Southern Arizona: The Last 12,000 Years *(Statistical Research Technical Series 48, Tucson, 1994).*

Stories from the Mountain Transition Zone

6

Across the landscape of time, we see the ebb and flow, adjustment and readjustment, of populations on small and grand scales. The Southwest did not do it all on its own, and cannot be understood in isolation from obviously related events to the south. Neither did or can the Salado.

—Richard Lange, *Proceedings of the Second Salado Conference, Globe, AZ*

June 5, 2001
In the Hall of The Mountain Spirits

It was the Fourth of July in the White Mountains of east-central Arizona, and we were climbing the sacred peak of the Western Apache known to Anglos as Mount Baldy. I do not know its Apache name. Apache friends had agreed to take the University of Arizona Archaeological Field School there, for Mount Baldy is off-limits to non-Apache people unless accompanied by a tribal member. It is one of the few places in Arizona not subjected to an endless parade of tourists clad in goofy hats and sloganed t-shirts, snapping photos and pulling the kids back from the edge, all of them teetering on the brink of something too enormous to comprehend.

We drove the trucks as far up the road as we dared, stopping often to drag fallen trees and other debris out of the way. No highway maintenance crews work on that road. When we began hiking to the summit, it was still summer, the noon air smelling of pine resin driven from the bark by sun and heat. But as we climbed higher, the temperature dropped. Soon we were straggled out along the slope, the older and chubbier of us, myself among them, fighting age and altitude. We crossed a saddle and snow began to appear.

View toward Theodore Roosevelt Lake at Tonto National Monument, Arizona. Photograph by Jefferson Reid.

Old snow, to be certain, and lying mostly in the shade of trees, but snow nonetheless.

Somehow all of us managed to reach the top. It's 11,403 feet above sea level there, well above the tree line—hence the Anglo name, especially apropos in the winter when covered with snow—and the wind struck our exposed body parts like frozen vapor. Many of us, coming as we had from the relative lowland altitude of 6,000 feet, had chosen to wear shorts, and were beginning to regret it. The wind howled and shrieked, threatening to blow us away. I imagined that I could see it, a palpable presence ripping at our bodies. The ambient temperature, I estimated, was around freezing, but maybe I'm exaggerating for effect.

Field school students atop Mt. Baldy. PHOTOGRAPH BY JEFFERSON REID.

Standing on the summit and struggling to stand upright in the buffeting wind, we looked wondering in a 360-degree circle at the land all around, although haze made it difficult to pierce the distances. To the east, we could see all the way to the Gila Mountains in New Mexico, where the waters of the Gila River head. Our Apache host claimed he could locate Mount Graham far to the south. Most of us could see the Mazatzal Mountains and the Sierra Ancha. To the west was the mountain heartland we had left that morning, where range after range of canyon-cut mountains climb all the way to the Mogollon Rim. The San Francisco Peaks, sacred mountains to Hopi, Navajo, and many other indigenous peoples, rose to the northwest. Snow would still be lying on its north slopes. Due north of where we stood was the Colorado Plateau, clad as always in seasonless brown and tan hues. The Little Colorado River valley was clearly visible to the northeast.

The land before us was layered with the stratigraphic levels of the past. The people archaeologists call the Mogollon once were the masters of the mountains, somehow managing to farm these cold if well-watered lands. Next came the Western Apache, to whom the mountains were home, source of sustenance, refuge, and spiritual bulwark. Mormon farmers followed, seeking a spiritual and earthly refuge in the high, cold rim country. After them were the dam builders, the engineers of the twentieth century who erected mighty dams to check the flow of rivers in the mountain basins. Last to arrive were the archaeologists, whose saga of discovering the ancient Mogollon and Salado peoples unfolded in the mountain valleys not far from where we stood freezing and gazing into the distance.

View from the summit of Mt. Baldy. PHOTOGRAPH BY JEFFERSON REID.

Nothing in that place spoke of water except the dirty snow lying purple in the shade. The Little Colorado River winding toward the great red river seemed as distant as the moon. The erosive power of wind and water must be at work, I knew, inexorably grinding down the peak on which we stood, but we had crossed no streamlets, seen no signs of springs. Surely this mountaintop would ring with storms, and its stones would be melted by lightning in summer. There was little to indicate the presence of such powerful forces on that day, except the twisted and stunted forms of trees everlastingly blasted by wind and the weight of snow.

Those who had come before us knew differently. The ground was weighted with evidence of a human presence, gifts left for the mountain spirits—piles of potsherds, gleaming in rich, painted-earth colors; pieces of turquoise, reflecting tones of sky and water. Here and there, a bit of marine shell. A corncob or two. They were offerings left by people who respected the mountain's power and the invisible forces of nature. Symbols of water—pieces of white shell from the sea, stone the color of ocean and river water. The sweet corn that rainwater nourishes. Ceramic bowls, round as Edward Abbey's leafy eye of the god, cupping water and sacred cornmeal even as the stone holds the sacred spring. Mogollon and Western Apache alike had prayed to the mountain spirits in this storied place where the holy people dwell.

This mountain is the house of storms and spirits, home of clouds and rain. Perhaps the wettest place in central Arizona, Mount Baldy is drenched with summer rain, pounded with hail, blanketed with many feet of snow in winter. The ancient ones knew that gods and spirits, heroes of mythic proportions, live in this place. It is the home of the ga'an, *the mountain spirits, the benevolent protectors of life and bringers of rain. Wreathed by clouds that generate the storms, the mountain holds water in its innermost depths. Tlaloc speaks, and the clouds send lightning bolts hurtling*

Mountain spirits (Western Apache ga'an *dancers).* Photograph courtesy Arizona Historical Society, Tucson (AHS Accession No. 65199).

to break the water jars inside the mountain. Rain falls, the green corn trembles in the wind. Pools of water shine among the cornfields.

It was not my holy place, but I felt the mountain's power nevertheless. I had brought no gift for the mountain spirits. None of us had. Later, an Apache friend would tell us that the powerful and icy wind blew so hard that day because we had not brought an offering for the mountain. A pine bough is left as a mark of respect, regardless of one's ethnicity or beliefs. Magic and mystery breathe from the stones in that place, older than time itself. Tread here with care, the mountain seemed to say, for this is where the ga'an *dwell. This is the home of thunder, the source of all water. Speak softly. Do not linger long, and when you leave, go with reverence.*

IT IS ASTONISHING, difficult to comprehend—you stand high on a mountain, where the highway has flattened out briefly on its steep drop off the Mogollon Rim. You have pulled over to take in the incomparable view. Mountain ranges stretch as far as you can see, rolling in successive green, purple, and blue waves as they recede. These are not the ancient, subtly rolling hills of the eastern United States. These are young mountains, thrust up from the earth by incomprehensible geologic forces and sharply etched by time. They are the mountains of the Arizona Transition Zone, one of the most rugged pieces of territory in the Southwest.

The Central Arizona Project canal skirts the mountain Transition Zone on its journey across the state. But as we saw in Chapter 3, much of the Plan 6 work took place in the Tonto Basin, one of the largest intermontane basins in the Transition Zone. Many archaeological sites were impacted, and the largest and most extensive Central Arizona Project excavations took place there. The stories told in this chapter focus on this rugged area northeast of Phoenix.

As the name suggests, the Transition Zone is sandwiched between the Colorado Plateau and the Basin and Range province. Although it shares characteristics of both, it is a unique and compelling environment. The most obvious feature of the Transition Zone, which is also called the central highlands and the central mountain region, is its rugged character. Its dissected mountains and high elevations have shaped other topographic features, plant and animal life, and even the climate. The mountains have also dictated human uses of the land. To understand the land and its people, one must first understand the mountains.

Moreover, the Transition Zone, and the Tonto Basin in particular, shared a peculiarly cosmopolitan character over the course of human occupation. Despite its constraints, the mountains also presented many advantages, and these drew different peoples. Prehistoric Hohokam and ancient puebloans joined the indigenous **Mogollon** and Salado inhabitants, creating a multicultural population that has proved extraordinarily difficult for archaeologists to interpret. After about A.D. 1700, the Western Apache called the mountains their home and remain there today. A stream of different nonindigenous peoples arrived in historical times to mine and farm the land, raise cattle, and build dams. Each group left their imprint upon the land and imbued it with stories, some of which we will tell in the following pages.

The Name "Mogollon"

The name Mogollon dates back to the 1700s. Don Juan Ignacio Flores de Mogollón was a Spanish Colonial period governor who administered lands in what is today New Mexico between 1712 and 1715. The Mogollon Mountains In New Mexico and the mining ghost town of Mogollon bear Don Juan's name. In the 1930s, archaeologist Emil W. Haury excavated sites in this spectacular corner of New Mexico, one of which he named Mogollon Village. In 1936, Haury wrote a monograph about the ancient people who had lived there—*The Mogollon Culture of Southwestern New Mexico.*

In his catalog of Arizona place names, Will Barnes (1988) has given us no clue how places in Arizona also came to be called Mogollon. In Arizona, the name has been applied to the mountain region of central Arizona and was an early label for Fort Apache (Barnes 1988:282). The great escarpment of the Mogollon Rim was popularized in the novels of Zane Grey, who called it the Tonto Rim after another of its common names. Today the word is generally pronounced "muggy-own" rather than the more elegant Spanish pronunciation. Mogollon is also the name of a western band and a brand of microbrewery beer.

Land, Water, and Living Things

The West is a rough land, and the mountain Transition Zone is rougher still—not a place for the timid to settle, travel, or farm. Obstacles are topographic—highly dissected terrain blocking travel and communication; climatic—a short growing season, heavy snowfall, killing frosts; and psychological—isolation and danger. Whereas the Colorado Plateau's steep canyons blocked occupation, in the Transition Zone the great mountains barred travel and settlement. It was least difficult to settle where climatic advantages and diverse resources coincided with expanses of arable soil and abundant water—places called "islands of resource advantage" (Whittlesey and others 2000:243). The Tonto Basin was one such advantageous area.

The northern boundary of the Transition Zone is the Mogollon Rim or Escarpment, a critical topographic feature that has shaped the physical and natural environments. The escarpment trends from northwest to southeast across the state. An often-dramatic, uplifted feature in the west, the rim traces an almost imperceptible track along its southeastern margins to end in the volcanic fields of the White Mountains. Above the rim is the Colorado Plateau. On its southern boundary, the extensive bedrock exposures of the Transition Zone interface with the alluvial desert basins of the Basin and Range province, and the mountains take on some arid-lands features. Because of its central geographic and structural position, geologist H. Wesley Peirce (1985) has labeled the Transition Zone "Arizona's backbone."

Living at the Q Ranch

Glenn R. "Slim" Ellison was born into a well-known Arizona ranching family in 1891. His grandfather, Jesse W. Ellison, came to mountainous central Arizona in 1885 and built a prosperous cattle ranch. Slim worked as a cowboy, camp cook, trail driver, homestead rancher, and in other occupations throughout the mountain country of central Arizona. His memoir, *Cowboys under the Mogollon Rim,* tells of growing up in the Wild West in the early years of the twentieth century. In 1932, when Gila Pueblo Archaeological Foundation archaeologists excavated Canyon Creek Ruin, Slim packed Emil W. Haury into and out of the ruin on mules. He also packed another revered archaeologist, Byron Cummings of the University of Arizona, and his students on one of Cummings's famous field trips.

Ellison (1968:45) has described life at "the Q," the Q Ranch owned by Jesse Ellison, located northeast of Tonto Basin and east of Young, Arizona:

> The Injuns would pack in four or five ton of corn and sell it to the Q and trade at the trading post the Q had. Bein 100 mile from the railroad, they couldn't git freight in over the Mogollon rim except between May 15 and October 15. No county kept up roads, and nobody had trucks like now. What was freighted in in October had to do till next May. The Q also had a post office then, called Ellison. The mail was packed horseback from Payson to Pleasant Valley, then to the Q, generally at nite. The contractor couldn't always git there till the next day, so when they had some important mail due, Grandad would send a cowboy to meet the Pleasant Valley mail and bring the Q mail on that nite.

Watering horses at the Q Ranch. Photograph courtesy Arizona Historical Society, Tucson (AHS Accession No. 22766).

The mountains of east-central Arizona. PHOTOGRAPH BY STEPHANIE WHITTLESEY.

This land is extremely different from the Colorado Plateau. Instead of colorful mesas and buttes, deeply carved canyons, and sandstone sculpture, mountains dominate the Transition Zone. Only a few sculpted formations, such as Tonto Natural Bridge near Payson, relieve the terrain. Geological processes are responsible. Whereas largely undisturbed, sedimentary strata define the Plateau, faulting and episodes of volcanic activity produced the mountain zone and distorted the original strata. The land has not been softened by the inexorable processes of erosion over time. The Transition Zone also contrasts with the Basin and Range province, where mountains simply punctuate broad, low expanses. Instead, mountains are the major physical feature of the Transition Zone—implacable, looming, unavoidable presences.

Mountains, Geology, and Soils

The mountain ranges defining the Transition Zone generally trend from northwest to southeast across the state. Some of the most prominent ranges are the Sierra Ancha and Mazatzal Mountains in the heart of the zone, Juniper and Bradshaw Mountains near Prescott, White Mountains at the boundary between the Transition Zone and the

The Serpent and the Stone

Tonto Natural Bridge is located along the East Verde River near Payson, just a few miles below the imposing Mogollon Rim. The bridge is a great, mossy arch above Pine Creek. The Apache tell a story, so Gregory McNamee has written (1994:50), of Tonto Natural Bridge in which, like other rare places where polished stone holds the sweet pour of water, a serpent is linked with the precious liquid. In ancient times, so the story goes, there was a deep, clear lake shimmering high in the mountains. In its depths lived an enormous guardian serpent. A solid wall of travertine stone formed on the lakeshore. One day there was a huge flood, which broke through the travertine and carved a great arch. The serpent was swept down into the Salt River, into the Gila River, and along the Colorado River all the way to the Gulf of California. The serpent presumably dwells there still, sharing the ocean with the other sea creatures.

Today Pine Creek pours over the bridge in a lacy veil into the plunge pool below. The water has carved an immense, echoing cavern where the stones are slick with moss and polished by the passage of water and human feet. It is a holy place, shining with mystery and magic. Even the visitors who come to Tonto Natural Bridge State Park seem subdued, awed by stone reminders of flood's passage and a serpent's travails.

Tonto Natural Bridge. PHOTOGRAPH BY JEFFERSON REID.

Transition Zone vista. Photograph by Jefferson Reid.

people went from time to time for rituals and ceremonies.

According to geologist George Davis and colleagues (1981), the Transition Zone represents the structural geology of the Colorado Plateau that has been transformed by faulting characteristic of the Basin and Range province. The land graphically reflects these processes. The mountains were produced by orogenic processes and downward block faulting, and their sharp slopes feature steep stream gradients and bedrock exposures. Average elevations in the Transition Zone are intermediate between the extremes of the physiographic provinces on either side.

The Mogollon Rim is a monocline extending for about 300 miles. It was produced about 30 million years ago by folding and buckling of the earth's crust as the Pacific Plate and the North American Continental Plate moved. Evidence of geologically recent volcanic activity is abundant along both sides of the rim.

In the Southwest, geologic structure—the arrangement and geometric shapes of rock masses—rises toward the south and culminates in the Transition Zone. As a result, the Transition Zone displays some of Arizona's oldest rocks. Later deposits, such as the sedimentary sequences so clearly apparent in the Grand Canyon, have been eroded

Colorado Plateau, Black Hills and Mingus Mountains near the Verde Valley, Blue and San Francisco Mountains near the New Mexico border, and Gila and Natanes Mountains near the southern border of the zone. The region's highest peaks are Mount Baldy (11,403 feet above sea level) and Mount Ord (11,357 feet) in the White Mountains. Chediski Peak (7,460 feet) and another Mount Ord in the Mazatzal Mountains (7,128 feet) are two of the next highest peaks.

We can give these elevations meaning by comparison with the ancient mountains of the East. Mount Mitchell in North Carolina has an elevation of 6,684 feet—less than 300 feet higher than the Transition Zone town of Show Low in east-central Arizona (Reid and Whittlesey 1997:133). Asheville, North Carolina, located at the edge of the Appalachian Mountains and nicknamed "Sky City," is substantially lower in elevation (1,985 feet) than Globe, Arizona (4,400 feet), which is located on the edge of the Tonto Basin and is one of the Transition Zone's lower areas. In comparison to the Rocky Mountains where the Colorado River rises, however, many of Arizona's mountains pale.

Lying between and paralleling the mountain ranges are alluvial basins filled with materials eroded from the slopes. The Tonto Basin and the Payson Basin are two of the largest intermontane basins. Because many basins contain through-flowing streams, occupation centered there. People did not live year-round above the 7,000-foot level where farming was impossible. The highest peaks, where the clouds and the spirits gathered, served as locales where

Mountain vista from atop Chediski Peak. Photograph by Jefferson Reid.

away. Amazingly, there is a minimum difference of more than 11,000 vertical feet between Precambrian rock in the Paradise Valley of the northeastern Phoenix area and the same rocks on Mazatzal Peak—a horizontal distance of about 40 miles! Faulting and other processes created this tremendous vertical distance separating the same strata.

One of the most important faults is the impressive Canyon Creek Fault, which runs along the western slope of the Sierra Ancha and north of the Salt River. More than 30 million years ago, the land west of the fault was raised several thousand feet, promoting canyon-cutting erosion on the western side and defining the ancestral edge of the Sierra Ancha. Later, the western block was dropped several thousand feet to its present position, promoting a younger cycle of canyon cutting that culminated in the topography of the modern Salt River Canyon. Alcoves and overhangs hollowed into the escarpment provided sheltered places in which prehistoric people built their homes.

The Transition Zone is rich in mineral deposits—limestone, salt, asbestos, schist, uranium, argillite, steatite, zinc, gold, silver, copper, and mercury—some of which yield high-grade ore. Prehistoric people came to the mountains to mine salt, minerals for paint, and stone for making tools and ornaments. Much later, Anglo-American miners were drawn by the promise of riches, flocking to the Globe-Miami mining district, Jerome overlooking the Verde Valley, and the Prescott area. The land bears the scars. Vast piles of yellow tailings mark places where copper was wrested from the earth. Driving past a smelter at night,

---

View from the Mogollon Rim near Payson, Arizona. PHOTOGRAPH BY JEFFERSON REID.

Filaree

Marguerite Noble based the autobiographical Arizona novel *Filaree* on her mother's life. The novel realistically and often graphically describes a woman's life in turn-of-the-twentieth century, territorial Arizona. Filaree Ranch was located in the Tonto Basin. Filaree (botanical name *Erodium cicutarium*), also called heronbill or alfilaria, is an invasive, introduced (nonnative or exotic) plant. It produces long fruits supposedly resembling a heron's head and bill. When dried, the fruits split into seeds with corkscrew tails that burrow into the fur of passing animals and ensure transportation. There is no known traditional use for this plant (Rea 1997:225). In wet springs, the lacy, low-growing filaree transformed the desolate Tonto Basin landscape into a green and purple quilt (Noble 1979:43):

> She looked at the filaree covering the yard. The rains had come generously at last, and it had responded. The land everywhere was layered with the plant and stippled with its blossoms, as if quilted in a green-and-purple fabric—a fabric fastened by the giant pins of the saguaro cactus.

Salt River Canyon northeast of Globe, Arizona. Photograph by Jefferson Reid.

one may encounter the spectacle of fiery, molten rock pouring down tailings piles like a volcano spewing lava. Mine openings appear like black eyes against the hills, and ancient headworks crumble in the sun.

In contrast to the zone's mineral wealth, soils that can be farmed are limited in extent and easily eroded. Although some are fertile, many are rocky and cobbley or have a high clay content, making them unattractive for farming. Many soils that were farmed in prehistory tend to be derived from diabase bedrock. These are correlated with the larger pueblos of the mountain zone. The land testifies to the many failures of later farming attempts by Anglo-Americans. Ruined buildings, ramshackle fences, rusty wire, and abandoned machinery pockmark old farmlands.

The bare facts of geology cannot do justice to the spectacular scenery or give a coherent impression of its wildness and inaccessibility. Peirce (1985) has pointed out that, although the Transition Zone only encompasses 16 percent of Arizona's total acreage, it contains almost 30 percent of its wilderness areas. Most of it is remote, difficult to travel through, and even harder to farm. This did not stop the indomitable people who sought the mountains as refuge, homeland, and resource zone, however.

Walnut Gulch

Walnut Gulch in Tonto Basin was named for the huge, black walnut trees that towered above a creek flowing into a narrow canyon. It was a seductive setting, one that lured settlers with the promise of water and forage. Marguerite Noble (1979:96) tells of her encounter with a vanished rancher's wife in her novel *Filaree:*

> A quarter of a century earlier a family had settled here. They had long since been "starved out" and had moved on, leaving scattered ruins as a reminder of their striving. The Mesa ranchers referred to Walnut Gulch as "the Old Role Place" after the family which "couldn't last out the drouth." . . .
>
> Now the man rode the hills; his wife stayed alone in the abandoned homestead. She encountered the presence of the Role woman everywhere, in the loneliness, in the box nailed to the tree for an outside cupboard, in the river rocks lining the pathway, in the gnarled plantings of vines and bushes. In these mournful remnants, Melissa could sense the frustrations she must have endured, the agony of defeat.

Rivers and Streams

Peirce (1985) has called the Transition Zone "the surface-water province of Arizona." He was referring to the reservoirs behind the region's dams, because Arizona has no natural lakes. Today, except in the highest mountain valleys and in times of dramatic rainfall, most of the mountain's rivers and streams are dry—a legacy of periodic fluctuations in precipitation coupled with the technological manipulation of mountain waters in the twentieth century.

Although the Gila River is the major drainage of the Basin and Range province, its tributaries drain the mountains. The Gila watershed drains an area somewhat larger than the states of Kentucky and West Virginia (Corle 1951:12). Before modern technological interventions, according to McNamee (1994:29), the Gila drainage system provided 3–4 million acre-feet of water each year. Coolidge Dam is the Gila's major control feature and was built in 1930 by the Bureau of Indian Affairs. The reservoir filled in so slowly that, according to McNamee (1994:150–151), Will Rogers said at its dedication ceremony, "If this was my lake, I'd mow it." From east to west, the Gila's major tributaries are the San Francisco, Blue, San Simon, San Carlos, San Pedro, Santa Cruz, Salt, Agua Fria, and Hassayampa Rivers. The Salt, which joins the Gila just west of the Phoenix metropolis, is the largest tributary and the major stream crossing the Tonto Basin.

Another important stream is the Little Colorado. Heading in the Transition Zone, it receives the benefit of runoff from the Mogollon Rim's windward escarpment, particularly during the summer monsoons and spring snowmelt season. Many smaller streams cross the mountains and were important connecting routes. Clear Creek, Cherry Creek, Cibecue Creek, White River, Ash Creek, Sycamore Creek, Oak Creek, Canyon Creek—most of these watercourses run from north to south. Other water sources include springs, *cienegas,* and seeps. The water table is relatively high in some areas and can often be accessed with simple, walk-in wells. People built their homes and farms near these water sources.

The Hassayampa's Water

"A legend so old that its origins are lost," writes Gregory McNamee (1993:54), "is that no one who has drunk from the Hassayampa River in west-central Arizona will ever tell the truth again." Mary Austin, in her book *Land of Journeys' Ending,* writes that "This is a river inconsiderable except that its waters have a virtue by which, after having drunk them, you see the world all rainbow-colored, as all poets and most Arizonians see it" (Austin 1985).

Climate

Historian James Byrkit (1992:304) has written that the "rim's influences dramatically illustrate the causal relationships between Southwest landforms and the region's climate and human activities." The Mogollon Rim's most dramatic effect is orographic. In the summer, moisture-laden, warm-air masses originate to the west and south and are blown toward the rim. The warm air rises and meets the drier and colder air above the rim. The moist air condenses, releasing most of its burden on the southwestern or windward side. In the winter, a similar orographic effect ensures more snowfall along the rim than above it. By this process, the Mogollon Rim casts a rain shadow over thousands of square miles of northern Arizona and western New Mexico. In part, the Mogollon Rim creates the aridity of the Colorado Plateau.

The White Mountains, with the highest elevations in the Transition Zone, receive the state's most abundant precipitation—in some places, more than 40 inches each year. Heavy, summer-monsoon rains and winter snowmelt drain into the Black, White, Verde, Little Colorado, and Salt Rivers. The relatively high precipitation of the mountains is offset by greater cold, such that farmers must plan the spring planting carefully to avoid killing frosts.

Much of the Transition Zone receives substantially less precipitation than the White Mountains, although more than either most of the desert Basin and Range or the Colorado Plateau. Some portions are effectively deserts, with high mean annual temperatures and less rainfall than the rest of the zone. In these regions, the longer, warmer growing season is offset by less precipitation than in the colder, more mountainous areas. Regardless of where the Transition-Zone farmer planted crops, there were advantages and constraints that had to be carefully balanced to bring in a good harvest.

Plant and Animal Life

Much of the Transition Zone is rich in wild-plant resources that provided food, construction materials, medicine, and materials for crafts. Familiar resources were available to people who moved into the area from elsewhere—cactus fruit and mesquite beans for the Hohokam, piñon nuts for the Plateau dwellers. The diversity of landforms and vegetation was one reason that the mountains were so attractive to different peoples.

As elsewhere in Arizona, vegetation varies with elevation because precipitation and temperature vary. Some plant species are limited by available moisture, others by extremes of temperature. Ponderosa or western yellow pine forests occupy the higher elevations (above 6,000 feet). Some of the most extensive stands of ponderosa in the West are found in the Transition Zone, particularly the lands occupied by and adjacent to the White Mountain Apache Reservation. These forests suffered tremendous losses in the terrible Rodeo-Chediski fires of summer 2002. Years of sustained drought had dried the forest to a moisture percentage lower than that of kiln-dried lumber, and when strong winds fanned the fire, it moved miles in a few hours' time. Nearly 500 homes were lost, and $28 million in damages were sustained. Firefighters spent $43 million to stop the fire (Pimental 2002). Priceless wilderness, areas of great scenic beauty, and places of extraordinary cultural value were destroyed. Foresters estimate it will take decades, if not centuries, for recovery.

Photograph by Jefferson Reid.

Desert scrub populates the lower elevations (below 3,500 feet). Chaparral and piñon-juniper-oak woodland dominate the intermediate elevations. These zones contain yucca, sotol, beargrass, mesquite, acacia, cactus of many species, manzanita, and other economically useful, shrubby plants. Stands of agave, an important succulent plant that was used by prehistoric people and the Western Apache, grows well on the gentler slopes at intermediate elevations.

The mountains can be a hunter's paradise. The Transition Zone contains some of the best bear habitat in the western United States, as archaeologists working at the University of Arizona Archaeological Field School at Grasshopper discovered. Young bears occasionally made themselves at home in the cabins, looking for food and company. Elk and deer populate the higher and intermediate elevations, respectively, and pronghorn can be found in the grassier parts of the region, although not as abundantly as on the Colorado Plateau.

Although rich and diverse, the mountain region's resources are also scattered and often unpredictable from year to year. This made it necessary for people who successfully lived in the mountains to maintain a flexible lifestyle with considerable mobility. They "were essentially a mountain people," Reid and Whittlesey (1999:8) wrote of the Western Apache, "moving from one chain to another, following the ridges." Like the Apache, the Mogollon also moved through the mountains "like the wind."

Lush mountain meadow on the Fort Apache Indian Reservation, Arizona, following a wet winter. Photograph by Stephanie Whittlesey.

A Closer Look at Tonto Basin

The scenic, if ruggedly inhospitable, Tonto Basin offers much of the natural diversity of the Transition Zone. The blue waters of Theodore Roosevelt Lake, now a bass-fishing mecca, hide the drowned channels of Salt River and Tonto Creek. These streams watered the Tonto Basin before the dam. Precipitation is relatively abundant, too—more than most of desert Arizona can boast. The basin contains the largest expanse of arable alluvium below the Mogollon Rim. Little wonder that it proved extremely attractive to farmers. With water and diverse resources characteristic of desert as well as mountains, the Tonto Basin proved a particularly alluring destination for diverse peoples from the beginning of its human history to the end of the prehistoric period.

Theodore Roosevelt Lake. PHOTOGRAPH BY STEPHANIE WHITTLESEY.

The Tonto Basin is literally ringed with mountains. On its west side are the Mazatzal Mountains, where Mazatzal Peak rises to 7,888 feet above sea level. South of the Mazatzals is the Four Peaks Wilderness, where mountains sacred to the Yavapai Indians overlook the Phoenix Basin (Khera and Mariella 1983:40). East of the basin are the Sierra Ancha, where Aztec Peak reaches to 7,694 feet. South are the Superstition and Pinal Mountains. To the north, the Sierra Ancha and Mazatzal Mountains narrow, separating the Tonto and Payson Basins. Water divides the basin into two parts. The upper basin consists of the middle reaches of Tonto Creek and Rye Creek; the lower basin represents the middle reach of Tonto Creek eastward.

The Salt River running through the Tonto Basin is borne of mountains. Black River and White River join on Western Apache land southwest of modern Whiteriver to form the Salt. The river then flows into the Tonto Basin from the east. The river heads in some of Arizona's most productive watershed, and about three-fourths of its annual flow derives from melting snowpack. During summer storms, the mountains' bare bedrock and steep stream gradients increase surface runoff greatly. Consequently, the Salt is a capricious river, with runoff varying extremely from year to year. This high-energy depositional environment has produced a coarse-grained floodplain with little deep soil development. The river carries considerable sediment—although not as much as the Colorado, which used to be virtually liquid rock—and is high in dissolved salts, giving

Bourke's Tonto Basin

John G. Bourke was a captain with the U.S. Third Cavalry who accompanied famed Apache campaigner General George W. Crook on forays throughout Arizona. His depiction of the Tonto Basin (Bourke 1971:145) faithfully captures its dissected, stark terrain, abundant water, and natural beauty:

> The course of those who were to accompany General Crook was nearly due west, along the rim of what is called the Mogollon Mountain or plateau, a range of very large size and great elevation, covered on its summits with a forest of large pine-trees. It is a strange upheaval, a strange freak of nature, a mountain canted up on one side; one rides along the edge and looks down two and three thousand feet into what is termed the "Tonto Basin," a weird scene of grandeur and rugged beauty. The "Basin" is a basin only in the sense that it is all lower than the ranges enclosing it—the Mogollon, the Matitzal [Mazatzals] and the Sierra Ancha—but its whole triangular area is so cut up by ravines, arroyos, small stream beds and hills of very good height, that it may safely be pronounced one of the roughest spots on the globe. It is plentifully watered by the affluents of the Rio Verde and its East Fork, and by the Tonto and the Little Tonto.

the river its name. These salts posed problems for farmers using river water to irrigate crops.

Salt banks along the Salt River in east-central Arizona. Photograph by Jefferson Reid.

Disastrous floods have long plagued the Salt River. Geological analyses demonstrate that such floods began in prehistory, but they were exacerbated in historical times by human-induced environmental degradation (Whittlesey 1998c). Canal irrigation was extremely hazardous along this fierce and unpredictable river (Welch 1992:164). Its periodic floods and unpredictable nature were among the reasons for seeking to dam the river in the early twentieth century. For now, the Salt River is tamed, controlled by a series of dams downstream from the first and largest, Theodore Roosevelt Dam.

Tonto Creek is the major secondary stream in the basin, flowing into the Salt from the north. Many smaller streams draining the slopes of the Mazatzal Mountains and the Sierra Ancha join Tonto Creek—Slate Creek, Rye Creek, Greenback Creek, Deer Creek, and Salome Creek among them. Theodore Roosevelt Dam, which was built at the confluence of Tonto Creek and Salt River, now holds back the waters of Theodore Roosevelt Lake. At capacity, the lake holds about 1.4 million acre-feet of water and covers some 17,000 acres. The confluence of Tonto Creek with Salt River, where the dam stands, is a geographic point dividing the lake. The Tonto Arm is the portion northwest of the confluence, and the Salt Arm is the portion to the east.

Photograph by Jefferson Reid.

Below the dam, the Salt River winds toward the Phoenix Basin through a narrow, steep canyon between the Four Peaks Wilderness and the Superstition Mountains. The dizzying road that follows the river, the Apache Trail, is a not-to-be-missed journey through remarkably rugged terrain. The road was built by Apache laborers while the dam was under construction. The Apache Trail links the downstream recreational areas on the Salt River.

The Tonto Basin is a relatively wet desert. It receives between 15 and 17 inches of precipitation each year, and its annual temperature averages between a low of about 54 degrees Fahrenheit and a high of about 81 degrees Fahrenheit. Although this is more rainfall than Tucson's average of 10–12 inches, the temperature varies minimally from Tucson's low and high averages of 53 and 83 degrees Fahrenheit, respectively. In the summer, there can be no question that the Tonto Basin is a desert despite the mountains that surround it. It is just plain hot, and although today relief can be found on the lake waters, this luxury was unknown to the residents of the past. A long growing season coupled with abundant water were boons to farmers (Welch 1994b). Rainfall is irregular and unpredictable, however, largely due to a complex air-circulation pattern created by the basin's rugged topography (Welch 1994b).

At a Tonto Basin Cemetery

In her novel *Filaree,* Marguerite Noble (1979:120) poignantly describes an old cemetery.

> The cemetery that served The Mesa folk was a forsaken spot on a hillside. The wagon stopped outside the sagging barbed wire enclosure. The filaree that ordinarily covered the graveyard had turned brown from the heat. A splintered cross listed. Melissa discerned the weathered marking: "Our Mother. 1869–1898." Twenty-nine years old. Women died early here. Work, births, deprivation, loneliness sapped their life; only death relieved them.

Grave of Al Sieber, chief of Apache Scouts, near Globe, Arizona. PHOTOGRAPH BY JEFFERSON REID.

Many upland wild plants and animals could be found with an easy walk from the valley floor—juniper, oak, and piñon with edible nuts and berries; pine and fir for construction wood; agave; and a variety of game animals. In the valley, desert plants grew abundantly—saguaro, prickly pear, and cholla cactus; mesquite, palo verde, and other leguminous trees; grasses; many weedy and shrubby plants—staples of the prehistoric Hohokam diet. We must be cautious, however, in thinking that the Tonto Basin is nothing more than an extension of the Phoenix Basin, although some archaeologists have made this mistake. It shared desert characteristics with the Phoenix area, to be sure, but the mountains were near, rising tall and dominating the physical landscape. Mountain resources were important, too, and their use resulted in a lifestyle that borrowed from the Hohokam pattern but was not a simple copy.

Irrigation was the most effective solution to balance the Tonto Basin's constraints and advantages, despite irrigation's risks (Welch 1994a, 1994b). So it was in historical times. An early assessment of the basin's environmental potential (Forbes 1916) concluded that irrigation was vital for farming. Small tracts of land with water were more desirable than large tracts without it. Nonetheless, historical records suggest that the Tonto Basin was difficult to farm successfully, regardless of field locations, field size, or availability of water, and people living in the basin were first and foremost stockmen rather than farmers. We can assume prehistoric farmers would also have found cultivation a risky proposition, although highly rewarding in good years.

Next, we look at some of the farmers who chose to take advantage of the Transition Zone's advantages weighed against its considerable risks.

PEOPLE OF THE MOUNTAINS

In this section we profile some of the people of the Arizona mountains. We look at the controversial culture called the Salado, a group that many archaeologists think was an amalgam of different prehistoric peoples. We also meet two of the Transition Zone's historical-period peoples, the Western Apache and members of the Church of Jesus Christ of Latter-day Saints, more commonly called Mormons. Regardless of religious affiliation or the time in which they lived, whether they possessed sophisticated technology or only simple means of water control, the mountain peoples shared the ability to survive and sometimes thrive in a region that was one of the most challenging in Arizona.

The Controversial Story of Salado

Defining Salado was a major objective of Central Arizona Project archaeological studies in the Tonto Basin. "Here was a chance to answer the question of what, really, was Salado," archaeologist Jeffrey Dean (2000:xv) has written. This was not an easy task, however, because "Tonto Basin Salado is a thing of shreds and patches. . . . The only constant about Salado is its inconsistency" (Lekson 1992:336). Probably more ink has been spilled over the Salado culture and more research dollars spent on it than any other archaeological entity in the Southwest. Archaeologists have struggled with the mystery of Salado for more than 60 years. They have described Salado as everything from a mortuary cult to a characteristic assemblage of material culture, and assigned the cultural affinity of Salado to Hohokam, Mogollon, Anasazi, Sinagua, none of these, and all of these. Clearly all of these characterizations cannot simultaneously be true.

Dean warns in the introduction to *Salado,* a book summarizing the Roosevelt archaeological studies, that readers searching for a consensual definition of Salado will be disappointed. "Salado remains as murky a concept after the Roosevelt Archaeology Project and the seminar as it was before" (Dean 2000:8). In part, this is because we are coming to understand that Salado was not one people or culture, but the outcome of population movements that brought different peoples together. Their differing subsistence and economic strategies, shifting political alliances, and diverse religious affiliations mingled in the Tonto Basin. In this place, at least, "Salado" is best understood as "an overarching label for a cultural melting pot where peoples of many different cultures met and merged" (Reid and Whittlesey 1997:230).

We begin with the story of how archaeologists came to define the Salado culture, a tale that reveals much about archaeology as a science. Fellow archaeologist Jefferson Reid and I (Reid and Whittlesey 1997:230) have observed that we "have come full circle in our understanding of the Salado Culture," and that "Salado stands as a testament to the intractability of the often mute past and the difficulties encountered when we attempt to make it speak." Ideas that originated in the 1930s held sway until the 1970s, when prevailing notions were dramatically revamped. The earlier ideas were resurrected in the 1980s and taken up wholeheartedly in the 1990s.

Discovering Salado: Changing Paradigms By the 1930s, archaeologists working in the Phoenix and Tonto Basins had found red, black, and white **polychrome** pottery in **stratigraphic** contexts above Hohokam red-on-buff ceramics, indicating that the polychrome pottery had been produced later. In the Tonto Basin, this pottery was associated with aboveground, masonry architecture unlike Hohokam pit houses. At one of these masonry ruins near Globe, Harold and Winifred Gladwin erected the buildings of the Gila Pueblo Archaeological Foundation. Archaeologists associated with this private archaeological institution were the first to formally name and describe the Salado culture, which they labeled in Spanish for the Río Salado, the Salt River.

At that time, migration was a popular explanation for culture change. It was thought that the Hohokam abandoned the Tonto Basin during the Sedentary period around A.D. 950, leaving the area open to colonization by the Salado (refer to chronology chart in Chapter 4). Gila Pueblo archaeologists suggested that the Salado had moved into the Tonto Basin from the Little Colorado River area via the mountain country below the Mogollon Rim. They labeled the time of the immigrants' arrival in the Tonto Basin and the new traits they brought as the Roosevelt phase and dated it around A.D. 1150 or 1200. Around A.D. 1300, the Gladwins believed, another migration of Anasazi people initiated the Gila phase. Subsequent research would push both phases forward in time. Last, archaeologists hypothesized that the Salado moved farther south into the Phoenix area, where they built the adobe houses of the Hohokam Classic period and left their polychrome pottery on the ruins of earlier sites. This theory would be elaborated in Haury's 1945 dissertation on the Classic period ruins of Los Muertos.

This early work established ideas about the Salado that would persist for several decades. One of the most important was the intimate connection between the histories of Salado and Hohokam; it was not possible to consider one without the other. These notions held sway until the 1970s, but in the interim, surprisingly little work was done in the Tonto Basin to refute or support the Salado theory and ideas about its relationship to Hohokam. There simply was not enough information from the Tonto Basin, the supposed "heartland" of Salado culture.

The seeds of a new perspective on Salado were planted by archaeologist William Wasley in 1966. He thought that the striking changes of the Classic period resulted from indigenous pre-Classic period Hohokam developments along with a liberal dose of influence from Mexican cultures. In the 1970s, these ideas were enthusiastically adopted and expanded upon by archaeologists in the emerging field of cultural resource management, which was energetically building a database of newly investigated Hohokam sites.

Plan 6 was the chosen construction alternative for the Central Arizona Project after Orme Dam was deleted. The plan included modifications to Theodore Roosevelt Dam. The Bureau of Reclamation planned to increase the capacity of the reservoir behind the dam, in part to provide better control of the Salt River's flow and to reduce flood danger to metropolitan Phoenix. The archaeological sites of the Tonto Basin were severely affected by the proposed modifications. Many sites would be inundated by the higher lake level. It was also necessary to build a bridge over the lake, reroute roads, build access roads, and clear staging sites for construction. In addition, Tonto National Forest planned to build several new campgrounds and other recreational facilities. To offset the loss of information that these impacts would cause, the Bureau of Reclamation designed the massive Roosevelt Archaeology Project.

The Roosevelt Archaeology Project

According to Bureau of Reclamation archaeologist Kathryn Pedrick (1992:2), a suite of sites were chosen for study based on three criteria: how representative they were of the range of archaeological sites in the Tonto Basin, the likelihood that they would be directly impacted, and their capacity to be investigated as complexes of sites. Initially, 140 sites were selected for investigation.

No single contractor could reasonably investigate all of these sites, many of which were large village and platform-mound sites. The Bureau of Reclamation chose to divide up the pie into smaller pieces that narrowed the research by focusing on specific themes. The result was three project subdivisions on which contractors bid competitively.

The Roosevelt Rural Sites Study was awarded to Statistical Research, Inc., to investigate small, so-called "rural sites"—field houses, agricultural areas, small pit-house and compound sites—located on both sides of the Salt Arm and on the west side of Tonto Creek. This project was also charged with investigating the past environment and farming practices. Sites dating to the pre-Classic and Classic periods were excavated as well as agricultural field areas.

Desert Archaeology, Inc., conducted the Roosevelt Community Development Study. The group was tasked with investigating the origin and development of platform mounds and communities along the right bank of the Salt River. This project assessed a variety of earlier sites dating from about A.D. 400 to 1000 in addition to platform mounds and studied Tonto Basin demography and population movement. Excavated sites included the Meddler Point site—a large site complex consisting of a platform mound and residential areas that dated to several different periods—Griffin Wash, Pyramid Point, Saguaro Muerto, and the Eagle Ridge sites.

The largest project was the Roosevelt Platform Mound Study, which was conducted by Arizona State University's Office of Cultural Resource Management in the Department of Anthropology. This project focused almost entirely on Classic period sites, investigating five platform-mound complexes and villages on both sides of the Salt and Tonto Arms. Archaeologists were supposed to synthesize all of the Roosevelt Archaeology Project studies into a final summary and synthesis. Platform-mound sites included Bass Point, Pinto Point, Cline Terrace, and Schoolhouse Point, some of which had large residential areas.

In addition, SWCA, Inc., carried out a large survey of upland areas adjoining the Tonto Basin. A group of sites on the northern side of the Tonto Basin discovered during this survey was added to the Roosevelt Platform Mound Study.

The Roosevelt Archaeology Project was the largest of all Central Arizona Project archaeological studies and lasted eight years. The archaeology cost $8 million. Results are presented in an enormous set of descriptive volumes produced by the contractors participating in the project. Along the way, contractors and the Bureau of Reclamation hosted a number of events to allow the public to view the work and made numerous presentations to professional and popular audiences. In May 1995, the Bureau of Reclamation funded a New World Study Seminar at the Amerind Foundation in Dragoon, Arizona, to conclude the Roosevelt Archaeology Project and to discuss and synthesize its research. The resulting book, *Salado* (Dean 2000), is a compilation of multiple-authored papers and the capstone to the huge archaeological undertaking that was the Roosevelt Archaeology Project. Some of its most intriguing stories are told in the pages of this book.

Tonto National Forest

Tonto National Forest represents a huge chunk of central Arizona territory. Its 2.9 million acres stretch from south of the Superstition Mountains northward to the Mogollon Rim and are bounded on the west by the Agua Fria River and on the east by the Fort Apache and San Carlos Indian Reservations. Will Barnes (1988:447) has reported the name's supposed origin—Spanish explorers gave the name "tonto," which means "fool" or "stupid" in Spanish, to the Western Apache people who populated the region. (He also observes that this seems unlikely, given that the Tonto Apache were neither fools nor stupid.)

Tonto National Forest was established by presidential proclamation in 1905. Because it encompasses many of the project areas investigated during Central Arizona Project archaeology, Tonto National Forest was the land-managing agency for a number of projects, including the Roosevelt Archaeology Project. It is headquartered in Phoenix with six district offices in Carefree, Globe, Mesa, Payson, Young, and Tonto Basin.

At the same time, new theoretical developments were radically restructuring the discipline of archaeology, making migration models seem old-fashioned and looking to the environment as a source of cultural differentiation and change. The result of these developments was the idea that Salado was nothing more than Classic period Hohokam.

The "continuity" hypothesis was rapidly accepted to explain Salado in Arizona. Tonto National Forest archaeologists applied it to the Tonto Basin. The continuity theory was appealing, new, and different. Viable causes for dramatic, internal changes were sorely lacking, however, and did not explain the Salado phenomenon found in other regions, such as New Mexico and Chihuahua, which had no Hohokam occupation. The theory was accepted essentially without rigorous scientific testing.

A few archaeologists disagreed with the continuity theory. For example, J. Jefferson Reid and I (1982) developed a notion of Salado as the product of multiple cultures meeting and interacting, of which Hohokam was only one. Our ideas were based on a large contract project that crossed the uplands on the flanks of the Tonto Basin and years of experience in the Mogollon Pueblo culture of east-central Arizona. Meanwhile, archaeologists continued to explore Salado with pen and paper. They organized conferences, wrote papers, and squabbled, often politely.

Such was the state of affairs when the Roosevelt Archaeology Project began. It was an exciting opportunity to resolve the controversy with the shovel and trowel, as Haury had always maintained it should be done. When the dust settled, the ideas had come full circle. With much new data in hand, many archaeologists concluded that the Salado culture represented people of several different cultural or ethnic affiliations, with some settlements representing immigrants from above the Mogollon Rim. It was déjà vu all over again, one might say.

New data were also collected that helped to revise ideas about the time before the Salado arrived in the Tonto Basin. We begin our discussion of Salado by exploring this time.

Before Salado One of the first discoveries made by archaeologists who worked on the Roosevelt Community Development Study was that, long before the first Hohokam colonists arrived in the Tonto Basin, the area was occupied by small groups of farmers. By A.D. 300, perhaps even earlier, people who made and used ceramic containers were farming the basin (refer to chronology chart in Chapter 4). These people were probably descended from the Archaic people who had inhabited the area previously. We know them from the Eagle Ridge site, which was perched on the terrace above the Salt Arm, where the river would have flowed in prehistory. An estimated 30–60 pit-house dwellings were occupied over the course of the settlement's history.

Early ceramic-period house at the Eagle Ridge site, Tonto Basin. Note "bean" shape. Photograph by Stephanie Whittlesey.

The Eagle Ridge farmers grew corn, beans, and cotton. We do not know the exact techniques they used, because Theodore Roosevelt Lake has inundated the field areas and any irrigation ditches. Because cotton is difficult to grow with rainfall alone, it is likely that the farmers irrigated from the river or captured floodwater runoff. The residents also collected a variety of wild-plant foods from the riverine environment and lowlands near the river and hunted game (Van West and others 2000). It was a good place to make a living, and hence Hohokam and Western Apache people would return to the place along the river in the following centuries.

Eagle Ridge demonstrated that the Tonto Basin was occupied before the Hohokam. It also told us that the early farmers differed little from those living in contemporary settlements elsewhere in Arizona. Intriguingly, in their architecture, ceramics, and general lifeways, they were much like what has been called the Early Pit house period Mogollon in other parts of the Southwest. Whatever we choose to call it—some archaeologists prefer to call it the "Central Arizona Tradition" rather than Mogollon (Elson and others 1992)—this local population would continue to thrive and develop into the ceramic period. A unique, local cultural tradition had emerged, one that had probably begun in Late Archaic times and that was heavily stamped by the Mogollon, perhaps by means of constant movement and contact among peoples.

Sometime around A.D. 850, the first of the Hohokam farmers arrived. They did not have to travel far, as the Tonto Basin is only about 60 air miles from the heart of the Phoenix Basin. Why did the Hohokam move into the Tonto Basin? It was once thought that the Colonial period (refer to chronology chart in Chapter 4) witnessed an expansion from the Phoenix Basin, the Hohokam bringing their religion, political organization, and lifeways to other regions. Some archaeologists suggested that the so-called "peripheral" zones, such as the Tonto Basin, were colonized to provide economic support and resources for the burgeoning population of the Phoenix Basin, where the environment may have been deteriorating. One of the more fanciful reconstructions suggested that the Hohokam military directed this operation (Wood and McAllister 1980). Another idea was that the Hohokam sought new frontiers for trading enterprises. None of these explanations is completely satisfactory, and indeed we may never know.

Regardless of the reasons that brought them there, the Hohokam found the Tonto Basin an attractive and hospitable place. There were familiar resources, such as mesquite and saguaro cactus. The climate was similar to that of their homeland, and they could use traditional water-control and farming methods. The small size of Hohokam settlements excavated to date indicates that there was no tremendous wave of immigrants, however, but a rather small-scale movement of family groups.

The newly arrived immigrants established homes that were virtually indistinguishable from Phoenix Basin Hohokam settlements in architecture and organization. At the Hedge Apple site excavated as part of the Roosevelt Community Development Study, several lines of evidence indicated that the Hohokam occupied the settlement seasonally and repeatedly. Archaeologists concluded that Hohokam pottery and other items found at the site were brought there by the immigrants rather than through trade (Elson and others 2000). This site was very much like the hamlet, Roosevelt 9:6, that Haury had excavated some six decades earlier. We can imagine a hopeful little colony of farmers building their homes in the traditional way on the terrace above the river, looking to family and prayers to help them through hard times. What pressures brought them to settle so far away from home?

Despite this indisputable Hohokam presence, no ball courts have yet been found in the Tonto Basin. Ball courts may once have been present, but have not been detected, have been destroyed by pothunters, or have been inundated by the lake. If ball courts were absent in prehistory, this suggests that the colonists were not completely integrated into the Hohokam cultural and religious system or remained dependent upon larger settlements in the Phoenix area for their religious needs. The latter notion correlates with evidence for seasonal, repeated occupation at the Hedge Apple site. In other words, the colonists may have repeatedly traveled back and forth between the Tonto Basin and the Phoenix area for subsistence and religious purposes.

At the same time, the indigenous population, who perhaps were descended from the people who lived at Eagle Ridge, continued to occupy the upper Tonto Basin. This tradition was represented at the Deer Creek and Ushklish sites, which had architecture, ceramics, and burials that were unlike those of the Hohokam (Elson and others 1992). We do not know whether a similar population also occupied the lower Tonto Basin, because no sites like Deer Creek have been excavated there. It is possible that the two populations—Hohokam and the local, indigenous group more closely resembling Mogollon—occupied different parts of the Tonto Basin. Perhaps there was a cultural boundary or frontier zone where the indigenous occupants blocked Hohokam efforts at colonization. Regardless of the cause, Hohokam settlements with a full array of organizational and material characteristics such as those found at Hedge Apple are not known in the upper basin.

The situation appears to have remained stable throughout the Sedentary period, and there is no evidence that the basin was abandoned. In fact, the salubrious, moist climatic conditions of the Sedentary period fostered expansion into areas that had previously been marginal for farming (Van West and others 2000). But this quiet, rural way of life would shortly change in dramatic fashion.

At some time during the A.D. 1000s, people living in the Tonto Basin stopped interacting with the Hohokam of the Phoenix area, at least as measured by nonperishable goods such as ceramics. This is a controversial topic and one subject to multiple interpretations. It seems likely that Hohokam organization and culture in the heartland region was altered. There were abrupt changes in Hohokam culture, economy, and social organization in much of central Arizona during the A.D. 1000s. Whatever its causes, Hohokam culture had changed dramatically by the close of the eleventh century, and repercussions were evidently felt across a broad area.

In the years between A.D. 1100 and 1250, pit-house architecture was replaced by a variety of aboveground masonry constructions—cobble-and-adobe masonry reinforced by posts, **jacal** rooms with cobble footings, and other architectural forms. Plain ware ceramics and a pottery type called Salado Red—a red-**slipped**, **obliterated-corrugated** ware—were dominant. We know little about this transitional time, largely because of the scarcity of excavated sites. Soon, with the appearance of polychrome pottery, the Salado era began.

Salado: Enigmatic People of the Tonto Basin

During the Roosevelt phase between about A.D. 1250 and 1350, extraordinary developments began to take place in the Tonto Basin. The population surged, and subsistence and settlement practices that had remained stable for hundreds of years changed. Platform mounds representing a new ritual and religious organization appeared. Inevitably, there was also conflict. The end product was the phenomenon called Salado (refer to chronology chart in Chapter 4).

Archaeologists link these shifts in part to regional climatic and demographic processes. In the closing years of the thirteenth century, some parts of the Colorado

Lower Ruin, Tonto National Monument. Photograph by Jefferson Reid.

Plateau experienced lowered water tables, erosion, reduced precipitation, and marked variation in rainfall. People living on the Plateau needed to farm to live, and in some areas, they needed to move to farm. Lured by its abundant rainfall, resource diversity, and arable land, some displaced populations sought refuge in the Tonto Basin. Their original homeland is unknown. Some hailed from the Transition Zone above and below the Mogollon Rim—perhaps the Silver Creek drainage, the upper Little Colorado River valley, and the area immediately below the rim. If so, "Salado culture is in fact the product of immigrant groups from the Mogollon Rim," Adams (2000:269) has stated—a notion replicating the ideas posed by archaeologists from the Gila Pueblo Archaeological Foundation almost 70 years earlier.

The stage for immigration had been set long before Salado. Mogollon and Ancestral Pueblo people had lived together in the mountain Transition Zone, intermarried, and moved back and forth seasonally between Plateau and mountains (Reid 1989; Reid and Whittlesey 1999). The indigenous people of the Tonto Basin were accustomed to sharing their territory with Hohokam immigrants (Reid 1982, 1989; Whittlesey and others 2000; Whittlesey and Reid 1982).

Puebloan immigrants brought their own style of architecture to the Tonto Basin. Using familiar techniques, they built coursed and chinked stone masonry wherever suitable building materials were available and used cobbles set into adobe where it was not. They organized their living space in the pueblo style of contiguous, compact rooms. Instead of the local cottonwood and mesquite favored by the Hohokam to build their pit-house dwellings, the immigrants used high-elevation trees, such as fir and ponderosa pine. The newcomers also made and used new kinds of ceramics and imported polychrome pottery from the Mogollon Rim area. They cultivated plants that the Hohokam had not emphasized, such as cotton and agave, and their food preferences differed (Elson and others 2000).

At the same time, people began to occupy the uplands flanking the Tonto Basin. Cliff dwellings were built at Tonto National Monument and in the nearby Sierra Ancha, and formerly scattered populations came together to create the first village-sized residential areas in the basin (Van West and others 2000). Although striking, these processes of expansion and population increase must be assessed on a relative scale. There was no enormous wave of immigrants and no tremendous local population growth. Estimates of resident populations at two Tonto Basin platform-mound sites range from fewer than 67 people (Lindauer 1995:435) to no more than 150 people (Craig 1995:235). Nevertheless,

Tonto National Monument

Tonto National Monument is a group of well-preserved cliff dwellings overlooking Theodore Roosevelt Lake northwest of Globe, Arizona. A steep, paved trail to the Lower Ruin is self-guided. The Upper Ruin is closed to visitors during much of the year. The monument was established by President Theodore Roosevelt in 1907, one of the first such monuments to be established.

Many of the masonry and adobe rooms have T-shaped doorways like those of Ancestral Pueblo cliff dwellings. Preservation in the cliff ruin was excellent, and sandals, woven cotton textiles, basketry, infant cradleboards, clothing, and a variety of foodstuffs were found. The ruin and museum provide a good introduction to the people and archaeology of the Tonto Basin.

Upper Ruin, Tonto National Monument. PHOTOGRAPH COURTESY U.S. BUREAU OF RECLAMATION.

we can assume that there must have been some competition for good farmland and that the existing fields were stretched to the maximum of their ability to produce.

Dean (2000:13) wrote, "Clearly, the presence of ethnically distinct immigrants and indigenes together in the same community would have created unprecedented, complicated, and fragile social arrangements to define and maintain relationships between the groups and to preserve the communities against the strong fissive pressures inherent in such situations." To cope with such stresses, the relatively large, ethnically diverse communities may have looked to the religious organization associated with platform mounds.

Platform mounds were built in the Tonto Basin with impressive rapidity, almost all of them appearing around A.D. 1280. Mounds had different construction histories and forms, however, and served different functions. Some were built all at once in a single construction episode, whereas others evidently grew by accretion over time (Elson and others 2000; Rice and others 1998). Some mounds may have been signaling or viewing towers, others may have served as locales for ritual performances, and still others used as elevated places for constructing residences. Archaeologist Stephen Lekson (1992:335) has cautioned that some platform mounds may actually be collapsed pueblos.

Where did the platform-mound concept originate? The traditional viewpoint has been that the mounds were inspired by the Hohokam, for platform mounds appeared in the Phoenix and Tucson Basins and other Hohokam regions during the Classic period. The fact that mounds evidently appeared earlier in the Phoenix area supported this notion (Doelle and others 1995). Had the Hohokam of this area brought the platform-mound idea to the Tonto Basin, they surely would have directed construction and use toward similar ends. They did not, however (Doelle and others 1995). Platform mounds in the Tonto Basin were incorporated into existing communities in various ways, not all of which were religious in nature. This was also true of other Hohokam regions, such as the Papaguería. It seems plausible, therefore, that the platform-mound concept originated elsewhere, from a single source outside Arizona, and was adopted in distinct ways by people living in many different areas. Potential sources, as suggested by Doyel (1992:348) and other scholars, could be the organizationally complex cultures of Mesoamerica, perhaps Chihuahua. Other archaeologists would argue this point.

Cline Terrace Platform Mound site near Theodore Roosevelt Lake during excavation sponsored by U.S. Bureau of Reclamation.
Photograph courtesy U.S. Bureau of Reclamation. Bob Knotts, photographer.

The platform-mound organization evidently was not completely successful in achieving peace and integrating diverse communities. Archaeologists found evidence for conflict in the form of burned settlements and injuries to people. Male skeletons discovered at a compound site excavated by Statistical Research were sprawled on a room floor and exhibited wounds sustained around the time of death (Turner and others 1994). In the face of conflict, people may have built the cliff dwellings of the Sierra Ancha and Tonto National Monument largely for the increased security such inaccessible places offered.

There were further changes to settlement and organization during the Gila phase between A.D. 1350 or so and 1450. Population estimates, although subject to different interpretations, suggest that the total number of Gila phase rooms could not have accommodated the Roosevelt phase population (Elson and others 2000:186–187). Some of the original immigrants may have returned to their Plateau and mountain homes or moved elsewhere. Burial practices suggest that the people who remained behind were culturally distinct from those who left (Ravesloot and Regan 2000). The platform-mound ceremonial organization was evidently dismantled; most mounds ceased to be used, and the remaining ones were used as residences rather than ritual structures. Those who remained in the Tonto Basin clustered together in a few, relatively large settlements.

Why did they come together in this fashion? Perhaps the people relocated at places that were most favorable to farming, such as the terraces overlooking the Salt River. Or perhaps the conflicts of preceding times continued, spurring a desire to protect people and food stores in easily defended villages.

Have we answered the question, "who were the Salado?" Probably not, for as Dean has pointed out, the problem has not been resolved despite the millions of dollars that have been spent in search of the answer. We have come closer to an understanding of who the Salado were, and it seems likely that they were not a single people but a mixed population. The two centuries of the Salado culture was, in the words of archaeologist Thomas Lincoln (2000:25), a "very complex time, ripe with population movement, environmental disruption, economic expansion, religious institutionalism, and intense political interaction." It was a regional Southwest phenomenon, not something that can be understood only within the context of the Tonto Basin. If we consider Salado in these terms, we can come to grips with it in an intellectually healthy and even exhilarating fashion.

We turn now to the Native American people who occupied the mountain Transition Zone and the Tonto Basin during the historical period—the Western Apache.

Western Apache

The Apache are one of the Southwest's most enigmatic peoples. The names of their great leaders are household words synonymous with courage and defiance. Just as the red sandstone buttes, snowy mountain peaks, and desert sands depict the Wild West of our imagination, nothing evokes its people and social values more readily than the Apache. As is the case so often in the American West, reality is far more complex and difficult to grasp.

Even as the Mogollon were the primary residents of the mountain Transition Zone in ancient times, the Apache were its historical-period occupants, making a difficult land their home. The Apache were a mountain people throughout their history. Mountains defined their traditional territories and provided food and shelter. In

Eskiminzin

In her novel *Enju: The Life and Struggle of an Apache Chief from the Little Running Water,* Sinclair Browning offers this description of the Aravaipa Apache chief Eskiminzin (Browning 1982:14).

> He wore a long buckskin shirt streaked with grease and decorated with signs of lightning and sun. . . . Around his neck he had a string of sacred relics, medicine to the Apache: fragments of lightning-struck wood, pieces of bone, and a pierced silver coin. A sash, ornamented with power signs, hung loosely about his waist. The signs would help him invoke power should he need to use it. Dangling from a buckskin thong was a silver cross, more medicine. . . . Eskiminzin's mid-thigh buckskin moccasins had queer pointed toes and were tied to his waist by long thin strips of leather. Straight, shoulder-length hair hung in two thick braids, woven with more bones and beads and silver rings. A piece of red flannel was tied securely across his forehead, to keep his hair back and to offer the wearer good luck.

times of conflict, mountains were the Apache's refuge. Moving swiftly and unseen, these mounted warriors were able to elude their pursuers long after other native peoples had surrendered to reservation life. Today as yesterday, mountains mark the Apache sacred landscape and offer a spiritual bulwark.

In many ways, the Apache are unlike the village farmers of the Southwest. Their traditional lifeways and their means of making a living were distinctive. In prereservation times, the Apache were highly mobile, a lifeway resulting from their subsistence base. They made their living through hunting, collecting wild-plant foods, raiding, and some farming. The Apache moved across vast distances during the course of a year in search of ripening wild crops, game, and stores to raid. "Once I moved about like the wind," said Geronimo at his surrender (Roberts 1993). Whereas the Hopi lived year-round in solid stone houses and depended upon corn, the Apache were casual farmers who stayed at their farms only long enough to bring in a crop and then moved on. Facilitated by their reliance on the horse, this way of life brought the Apache into frequent, often violent contact with more settled Native American farming peoples and Euroamericans. The history of relations among Apache, other indigenous peoples, and Euroamericans is a sad and bloody chapter in the chronicle of the American West.

Western Apache woman in camp below Tonto National Monument in 1902. Note dwelling (gowa) *and baskets.* Photograph courtesy Arizona Historical Society, Tucson (AHS Accession No. 62744).

The Apache call themselves Ndeh, also spelled Nde and Indeh, which means "the people." Anthropologist John Swanton (1952:327) relates what is possibly an apocryphal story, that the name "Apache" derives from the Zuni word *apachu,* meaning "enemy"—the Zuni name for the Navajo. The Apache are linguistically and culturally distinct from other indigenous peoples of the Southwest except the Navajo, to whom they are closely related. The Apachean languages fall into the southernmost division of the Athapaskan language family, which includes Navajo. Athapaskan languages incorporate Northern Athapaskan, found throughout a wide area of western Canada and interior Alaska, and Pacific Coastal Athapaskan.

The Athapaskans were relatively recent immigrants into the Southwest. Most scholars agree that Southern Athapaskan speakers moved southward from central Canada sometime around A.D. 1500, if not earlier. No one knows what sparked such a migration. Anthropologists also know comparatively little about the separation of the Navajo and the Apache as distinctive cultural groups, although it was quite recent in historical and archaeological terms.

Anthropologists group the Apache peoples according to territorial, linguistic, and cultural differences. The largest grouping was the tribe or division that was further subdivided into smaller groups and bands. Two Apache groups whose traditional territories were based in Arizona are the Western Apache, who ranged throughout central Arizona, and the Chiricahua Apache, who occupied the mountain strongholds of southeastern Arizona.

Debate surrounds the timing of the Apache's entry into Arizona. Coronado's chroniclers labeled the mountain Transition Zone a *despoblado,* or uninhabited area. If the Apache had already colonized the mountains by the time of the Spanish *entrada,* they must have been well hidden and infinitely cautious. In the late 1600s, the land lying north of the Gila River as far as the Hopi and Zuni pueblos was "Apachería," or Apache land. By 1700, the Western Apache had successfully claimed an extensive territory stretching south from the Mogollon Rim across the Natanes Plateau to the Gila River (Basso 1983:465).

Archaeologist Michael Graves (1982:211) has observed that the Apache colonized much of Arizona rapidly. Evidently they "had found a remarkably resilient and dynamic way of adapting to a range of uninhabited, local environments." To the question, How did they do it? Graves answers that the Western Apache maintained a generalized subsistence strategy in what must have been a relatively uncertain natural environment. Moreover, it was a strategy that probably sustained the people in their original homeland. Anthropologist Richard Perry (1991:158) has pointed out there were more similarities between Arizona and the Subarctic-Canadian Rockies regions than there were differences. A mobile people accustomed to relying on a wide variety of wild resources could adjust rapidly to new situations. By taking up some plant cultivation and learning to use the horse, the Western Apache lifeway was complete.

Anthropologist Grenville Goodwin (1969), who lived among and studied the Western Apache, divided them into territorial units called groups, bands, local groups, and family clusters. The largest unit was the group, and there were five—Cibecue, White Mountain, San Carlos, Northern Tonto, and Southern Tonto. Groups were divided into bands that occupied specific territories. The Northern Tonto group occupied the country north of the Mogollon Rim and Verde River as far as Flagstaff. The Tonto Basin was the home territory of the Southern Tonto, who ranged along the eastern edge of the Mazatzal Mountains on both sides of the Mogollon Rim. The San Carlos group traveled around modern Globe and Miami as well as points east and south. The Cibecue Apache ranged throughout the extremely rugged country east of the Sierra Ancha, today's Fort Apache Indian Reservation. The extensive home territory of the White Mountain Apache lay east and south of the Cibecue Apache in the White, Blue, and Gila Mountains.

Tonto Apache country near Sedona, Arizona. PHOTOGRAPH BY STEPHANIE WHITTLESEY.

Martha Summerhayes Sees the Tonto Basin

Shortly after Mrs. Summerhayes joined her husband John W. "Jack" Summerhayes in Cheyenne, Wyoming, the U.S. 8th Infantry with which he served was ordered to Arizona. Mrs. Summerhayes called Arizona "that dreaded and unknown land." Among other Arizona camps, Lieutenant Summerhayes was stationed at Fort Apache (then called Camp Apache) in the heart of the mountains and Western Apache territory.

In 1874, Martha Summerhayes trekked with her husband and a detachment of his regiment across the mountains from Camp Verde to Camp Apache. They were the first to travel by wagon train on Crook's Trail, the infamous "road" built by General George W. Crook during the Apache wars. Mrs. Summerhayes noted that for miles and miles the "road" was nothing but a clearing. Her description (Summerhayes 1979:67) of the vista spread before her from a mountain overlooking the Tonto Basin—likely the Mogollon Rim itself—gives an idea of the spectacular scenery and the travail of traveling through the mountain country.

> The scenery was wild and grand; in fact, beyond all that I had ever dreamed of; more than that, it seemed so untrod, so fresh, somehow, and I do not suppose that even now, in the day of railroads and tourists, many people have had the view of the Tonto Basin which we had one day from the top of the Mogollon range.
>
> I remember thinking, as we alighted from our ambulances and stood looking over the Basin, "Surely I have never seen anything to compare with this—but oh! would any sane human being voluntarily go through with what I have endured on this journey, in order to look upon this wonderful scene?"

The Western Apache regularly moved through an enormous homeland covering about 90,000 square miles. The diverse wild-plant and animal resources of the mountains fostered a mixed economy. Each group maintained a slightly different balance among gathering, hunting, raiding, and farming, and this flexible economy also shifted throughout the year and from year to year depending on resource availability and abundance. The extent to which groups relied on the horse also affected their economy and the size of their traditional territory (Basso 1983).

Wild-plant foods were the mainstay of the diet. The Apache moved their camps often throughout the course of the year as different wild crops became available. Mescal or agave was the most important food plant. The tender stalk was roasted, and the crown was dug up, trimmed, and baked in underground pit ovens near the growing areas, just as the Hohokam had processed mescal in their Sonoran Desert home. The baked mescal was sun dried and stored, supplying sweet and nutritious food for many months. Mescal also provided a fermented drink, fibers for sewing, and a stalk for lance shafts and musical instruments. In the summer and fall, the Apache collected the fruits of saguaro, other cactus, and yucca; mesquite beans; acorns; piñon nuts; and juniper berries. The people moved to particularly rich stands as the resources ripened. From their secure winter camps, often located in lower, warmer elevations, they made raiding forays and hunting expeditions. Raiding continued into the early spring months, when food shortages were common. It was an unfettered existence, as cyclical and natural as the solar year. It is easy to see how curtailment of the traditional lifestyle and enforced sedentism on reservations would have been profoundly disturbing.

Sampling Mescal

Beginning in 1825, the father-and-son team of Sylvester and James Ohio Pattie began an exploration and beaver-trapping expedition that would lead them along the Gila River into Arizona. On the way they traveled through Apache territory—lands of the Chiricahua, White Mountain, and San Carlos Apache. In his *Personal Narrative*, first published in 1831, James Ohio Pattie (1984:54–64) related several encounters with the Apache.

At the mouth of the San Carlos River, they saw a small group of startled Indians who fled swiftly, leaving behind rabbit-skin robes and a small child. The Patties bound the child so it would not stray and left. When they returned to the Indian camp, they found the child gone and in its place a large dressed buckskin, "an article, which we greatly needed for moccasins, of which some of us were in pressing want."

Several times, when the provisions were exhausted, the horses so weary and lame they could scarcely go on, and the men weak from hunger and fatigue, the Patties availed themselves of Apache foodstuffs. One time they found mush prepared from grass seeds, which the men devoured. They ate the bread made of "mosquito" (mesquite) beans left behind at an Apache camp. Another time they frightened a group of Apache with whom they exchanged fire, and the Indians fled. Returning to the Apache camp to look for food, the hungry men found a mescal pit.

> At no great distance from their camp, we observed a mound of fresh earth, in appearance like one of our coal kilns. . . . We opened the mound, and found it to contain a sort of vegetable that had the appearance of herbage, which seemed to be baking in the ground, to prepare it for eating. I afterwards ascertained, that it was a vegetable, called by the Spanish, mascal [sic]. . . . The Indians prepare it in this way, so as to make a kind of whisky of it, tasting like crab-apple cider. The vegetable grows in great abundance on these mountains.

"Hunger knows no laws," wrote Pattie, and they found the mescal "sufficient to sustain life." And Pattie also observed that the "language of kindness is a universal one." Equally universal is hunger.

Mescal (agave) growing atop Spotted Mountain on Fort Apache Indian Reservation, Arizona. PHOTOGRAPH BY JEFFERSON REID.

As a whole, the Western Apache depended on farming more than the other Apache tribes, but groups differed greatly in their dependence on cultivated plants. Whereas the Northern Tonto were perhaps the most insouciant farmers, the Cibecue Apache were the most heavily dependent on farming. Yet even among the latter group, Goodwin (1969) estimated that in the prereservation economy, agricultural products formed a maximum of only about 25 percent of the food consumed each year.

Farming was incorporated into the seasonal round of gathering and hunting. In the late spring, people left their winter camps for farm sites located along streams in the mountain valleys. The farms are analogous to the base camps of the Subarctic Athapaskans near salmon rivers or caribou-drive sites (Perry 1991:156). The people usually stayed at the farm sites until their corn plants were off to a good start in July. In the summer, families would drift away to cactus and mesquite camps in the low-desert regions, returning periodically to check on the maturing corn. September and October was harvest time, and after the crop was brought in, the Apache moved to upland areas to gather juniper berries and piñon nuts and to hunt.

Raiding was an integral part of Apache economy. It was a purely economic activity that was distinguished from war, which was an enterprise involving revenge for a kinsman's death (Basso 1971:4). Raiding parties traveled over enormous distances, venturing as far south as the Gulf of California and as far north as the Navajo country. O'odham, Mexican, and American farms in southern Arizona and northern Sonora were the frequent target of Apache raids (Goodwin 1969:93). Raiding brought livestock—horses, mules, cattle. Because horses and mules were often killed and eaten during raids, the animals represented a highly transportable food source which enabled the Apache to extend their raiding activities even farther. Raiding also brought food, hides, blankets, clothing, saddles, bridles, firearms, and metal to fashion knives and arrow points.

Apache ceremonialism was based on the acquisition and manipulation of supernatural power *(di yih)*. There were complicated rituals for curing, protecting against illness, ensuring success in hunting and warfare, and marking life-cycle events. Perhaps the most important of the latter ceremonies was the girl's puberty ceremonial, or Sunrise Dance *(nai'es)*, which lasted four days and involved ritual songs and dances, social dancing, and food redistribution. The puberty ceremony emphasizes the importance of femaleness in Western Apache social organization and sacred belief.

Customs persist: Twentieth-century White Mountain Apache Sunrise Dance (nai'es) *on Fort Apache Indian Reservation, Arizona.*
PHOTOGRAPH BY STEPHANIE WHITTLESEY.

The *ga'an*, or mountain spirits, are supernatural beings who dwell in mountains, caves, and underground. They bring goodness and benefits to the Apache people. Crown Dancers, named for the elaborate, wooden headdresses they wear, impersonate the mountain spirits much as Hopi dancers represent the *katsinam*. There is a general aversion

Mountain Spirits

The *ga'an* are benevolent mountain spirits—personifications of abstract, positive associations with mountains as refuge and source of livelihood (Perry 1993:70). The *ga'an* are closely linked with farming, rain, and mountains. In some Western Apache traditions, it is said that the *ga'an* gave agriculture to a young Apache woman in a time of starvation (Perry 1991:157). Masked impersonators of the *ga'an* appear at the girl's puberty ceremony (*nai'es* or Sunrise Dance). They wear tall, crown-like wooden headdresses that give them the name "Crown Dancers." The dancers carry wooden sword-like objects, and one carries a bullroarer to chase away evil. Dressed in fringed buckskin kilts with jingling bells on their belts and ankles, painted with clay, dipping and swaying with the beat of the drum, the *ga'an* dancers are impressive in the firelight. Once heard, the sound of bells and the eerie *whoosh* of the bullroarer as a full moon rises over the mountains will never be forgotten.

to the dead and a dread of ghosts, and people take pains to guard against the potential effects they caused—beliefs with deep roots in ancient Athapaskan ideology (Griffin-Pierce 2000:369). The high mountain peaks had sacred meanings; many were considered holy places and ceremonies took place there.

Apache social organization was built on small, highly mobile, autonomous groups that lacked any overall political structure. Bands were composed of 3–12 local groups, which were the basis of Western Apache society. The local group consisted of extended families who chose to live together because of social, economic, or kinship ties. Each family cluster typically included four to five households. Each household, also called a *gowa* or "camp," lived in its own residence, but the entire cluster acted together to carry out tasks above the household level.

Clans were important in social relationships and had numerous functions, from regulating marriage to affecting the inheritance of chieftainships. As with other aspects of Apache organization, clans were matrilineal—a person's membership in a clan was the same as his or her mother's group. The Apache believe that many clans originated to the north of today's home territory (Goodwin 1969; Perry 1991). Women enjoyed considerable status and influence in Apache life. Their contribution to subsistence was vital. Women owned the dwellings and passed property from mother to daughter; residence was matrilocal. That is, when a man married, he went to live with his wife's family.

The traditional dwelling was a dome-shaped, pole-and-brush structure, the *gowa,* or wickiup. The structures required little labor to build and used locally available materials, a necessity for people on the move. Many activities took place in open-sided brush arbors or ramadas, which are still used by traditional Apache who live in modern houses.

As would be expected for such a mobile people, containers and tools made of basketry, wood, and fiber were used for most domestic purposes, and ceramics were less important. Coated with pitch, baskets could serve as water containers. Arrow points were made of stone and metal and from bottle glass when available. The Apache were inveterate collectors and recyclers, often reusing items collected from prehistoric sites (Whittlesey and Benaron 1998).

Mobility and raiding brought the Apache into constant conflict with Euroamericans. As population increased in the nineteenth century, the Apache found it increasingly hard to live by their traditional, mobile ways. Raiding increased, and soldiers and settlers destroyed Apache farms and camps. Treachery and deceit marked the interactions between Apache and Americans. Supposed "peace parleys" between the Apache and American settlers and the U.S. Army sometimes ended in bloodshed and death. Bounties on Apache scalps led to further depredations on innocent people. In the 1860s, hostilities deepened not only with the United States but also with Mexico.

Following the Camp Grant Massacre, General George Crook was installed as the head of the Department of Arizona for the U.S. Army. His campaign against the Apache and Yavapai was based on a sweeping offensive assisted by Indian scouts coupled with destruction of winter food supplies. Crook surrounded the Tonto Basin, driving

The Camp Grant Massacre

Camp Grant, located on the San Pedro River at its junction with Aravaipa Creek, was a place where the Western Apache people came to receive rations, clothing, and protection from lawless settlers in exchange for their promise of peaceful behavior. It was also the site of one of the most shameful chapters in the history of Apache-American relations. Chief Eskiminzin had established a settlement of about 500 Aravaipai and Pinal Apaches near Camp Grant—too close to Tucson, which blamed all depredations in southern Arizona on the Camp Grant Apache. In April 1871, 6 Anglos, 48 Mexicans, and 94 Tohono O'odham Indians from San Xavier del Bac attacked the Aravaipa Apache camp, mutilating and killing more than one hundred Apache, mostly women and children, and capturing 27 children.

The Tucson settlers considered the incident justifiable homicide. Not so the U.S. military, which ordered the perpetrators to be brought to trial or the territory would be placed under martial law. The sham trial lasted five days. After deliberating for 19 minutes, the jury brought in a verdict of not guilty for each of the hundred-odd defendants. The Camp Grant Massacre and its aftermath left all Apache people wary of claims of peace, and it was a stunning indictment of federal Indian policy. As Sheridan (1995:81) has pointed out, however, the massacre was not an aberration but "the culmination of two centuries of conflict on the Arizona frontier."

Sinclair Browning's Enju: The Life and Struggle of an Apache Chief from the Little Running Water *(Northland Press, Flagstaff, 1982) is a fictionalized but factual account of the Camp Grant Massacre.*

the Apache ahead of his army and killing those who would not surrender. Starvation and weakness eventually took their toll, and by 1872 Crook's campaign began to succeed.

Four Apache reservations, including the White Mountain and San Carlos Reservations, were hurriedly established between 1871 and 1872 as part of the federal government's "peace policy" (Basso 1983:480; Kelly 1953:23). In 1875, many Western Apache were forced to move to the newly established reservation at San Carlos. Today, most Western Apache in Arizona still live on the White Mountain and San Carlos Reservations, where their economy is focused on cattle and timber. The White Mountain Apache Tribe owns and operates the Hon Dah Casino and Resort south of Pinetop, Arizona, and the Sunrise Ski Resort; the San Carlos Apache operate the Apache Gold Casino and Resort.

Apache Gold Casino and Resort, Arizona. PHOTOGRAPH BY STEPHANIE WHITTLESEY.

The Mormons

Perhaps the best known of the West's historical-period farming peoples are the members of the Church of Jesus Christ of Latter-day Saints, commonly known as Mormons. The Mormon way of life, which blended religious beliefs, community values, and subsistence practices in a seamless fusion, enabled them to succeed in farming the arid West, so different from the well-watered midwestern states from which they fled.

Mormon history begins on the East Coast. By 1830, the Saints had formed a tightly knit group in New York under the leadership of Joseph Smith, who was believed to be a prophet of God. The religion he created was not new but a reworking of the old. True Christianity had become factionalized and corrupted, Smith believed. The Church of Jesus Christ of Latter-day Saints restored its lost unity (Limerick 1987:281). Soon Mormon colonies were established in several midwestern states, including Ohio, Missouri, and Illinois.

Mormon social and political organization differed in profound ways from mainstream American society of that time and proved threatening. They maintained their own militia, for example, which was actually larger than the state of Illinois's own (Bischoff and others 2000:79). Such practices fostered resentment among non-Mormon neighbors in the Midwest, and persecution was inevitable.

The governor of the state of Illinois began a virtual war of extermination on Mormons, largely over the issue of plural marriages. "The absence of a racial difference could not keep white people from throughly hating each other," historian Patricia Limerick (1987:281) has written. Joseph Smith was murdered by a lynch mob in Nauvoo, Illinois, in 1844. Forced to flee their homes in the Midwest, the Mormons began to consider a move west under the leadership of Brigham Young, who had emerged to take Smith's position in the church.

In 1846, the Mormons camped for the winter in Iowa. Their agreement with the federal government permitted them to camp on Indian lands in exchange for 500 Mormon volunteer soldiers. Known as the Mormon Battalion, these volunteer troops would later march to the Gila River during the war with Mexico. While in Iowa, the decision was made to settle near the Rocky Mountains.

Led by Brigham Young himself, an advance guard ventured from the Winter Quarters to find a new home. Illness, extraordinary travel difficulties, and chance combined to locate them near what is now Salt Lake City. In Utah, the Mormons believed they could escape persecution and would be rewarded for their endurance with a refuge and a homeland, a Zion in the West (Limerick 1987:283).

From Salt Lake City, the Mormons radiated to found colonies in Arizona, Nevada, and many other places throughout the West. The federal government's war on the Mormons prompted many of these colonies. Mormon theocratic organization conflicted with the political and secular organization of the territorial government. The people obeyed only church leaders, convincing the federal government that Utah was in virtual rebellion. In 1857, the U.S. Army moved in "an extraordinary case of the U.S. Army deployed against a church primarily composed of U.S. citizens" (Limerick 1987:284–285). When this war was over, the battle over polygamy commenced. Many chose to flee Utah, repeating the pattern that had brought them there initially.

Although the church called for the wave of immigrants trekking to Arizona, different personal reasons motivated those taking up the call (Peterson 1973). Some went because of the drought that swept the country in 1878 and 1879. Others felt the pressures caused by the growing population and scarce land in Utah. Still others, such as John D. Lee, who operated the ferry crossing the Colorado River, were effectively exiled (Peterson 1973:47–48).

Lee's Ferry became the conduit for Mormons colonizing Arizona territory. The Little Colorado River valley was one of the first targets, along with the Arizona Strip and the southeastern corner of Nevada. When John Wesley Powell and his men came down the Colorado River for the first time, Mormons trying to grow cotton along the Muddy River pulled the boats from the river and fed melons to the starving men (Worster 2001:281). By 1876, communities had been established at Sunset Crossing, Obed, Brigham City, and St. Joseph. From there, people moved up the Silver Creek drainage into the country spanning the mountains and the plateau—a landscape marked by rolling hills, distant snowy peaks, and piñon-juniper-ponderosa pine woodlands. Small communities in this area—Snowflake, Taylor, Shumway, Pinedale, Show Low, Lakeside, Pinetop, Forestdale, Springerville, Eagar, and Greer—were settled.

The push to settle Arizona territory continued southward. In the upper Tonto Basin and surrounding areas, deep in the rugged mountain country described so well by Marguerite Noble in her novel *Filaree,* Mormons founded little farming communities at Payson, Rye Creek, Pleasant Valley, Pine, and Strawberry. Colonies were established during the 1870s and 1880s in the Salt River valley at Lehi, Tempe, and Mesa under the direction of Daniel Jones and other leaders. In southeastern Arizona along the San Pedro River, the Saints built homes and farms at St. David and Pomerene, where artesian wells irrigated the fields. Prosperous farming communities developed in the Gila River valley at Safford and Thatcher. These southern Arizona settlements would serve as staging centers for the Mormon drive into Mexico when attacks on their beliefs and values drove them to seek refuge once more from gentile economic interference and political oppression. Everywhere they settled, the Mormons built ditches with spirit level and straight edge, mules and Fresno scrapers, occasionally reusing Hohokam canals, and began to plant the land.

By the 1880s, the church had begun to discourage immigration from the East Coast, Midwest, Scandinavia, and Europe. Many Mormon communities thrived and survive to this day, although some are now highly urbanized communities in the Phoenix metropolitan area. Cotton fields and irrigation ditches have given way to shopping malls, office buildings, and fast-food restaurants.

In the Malpais

Traveling from Fort Apache to Camp Verde in 1874, Lieutenant Summerhayes's detachment went to Holbrook, crossed the Little Colorado River at Sunset Crossing, then went southwest by means of Stoneman Lake to the Verde Valley. Much of this journey was across the torturous lava beds called "malapais," pronounced "malapie" *(malpais)*. Mrs. Summerhayes (1979:107, 121–122) wrote of the mountain crossing and the Mormon settlements along the way. The lack of water took its toll on animals and people:

> The road was lined with dry bones, and skulls of oxen, white and bleached in the sun, lying on the bare rocks.
>
> Indeed, at every stage of the road we had seen evidences of hard travel, exhausted cattle, anxious teamsters, hunger and thirst, despair, starvation, and death.

All of the ranches in the Silver Creek area were located at springs or creeks, she wrote. Stoneman Lake was astonishing not only for its beauty but also for its water. Mrs. Summerhayes (1979:121) wrote:

> Ponds and lakes were unheard of. They did not seem to exist in that drear land of arid wastes. We never heard of water except that of the Colorado or the Gila or the tanks and basins, and irrigation ditches of the settlers. But here was a real Italian lake, a lake as blue as the skies above us. We feasted our eyes and our very souls upon it.

Corn, Ritual, and Risk

Three different cultures give us three views over time of the ways in which people adjusted their farming strategies to the mountains—a place of great abundance, yet often also tremendous risk—and of the importance of water in their lives and cultures. These are the prehistoric Salado, the Western Apache of the historical period, and Mormon

The Great Emptiness

[Melissa] wanted again to see the distant jagged peaks, the endless sky, to touch again the broad flat earth cut by Tonto Creek, to walk in the country she had pushed from her thoughts for so many years. . . .

In Roosevelt the stage crawled along the narrow one-way road leading over the dam that held the waters of Salt River and Tonto Creek. It passed the shimmering lake, then continued up, up and on, to the beginning of The Mesa country.

. . .The Mesa had always been an unpredictable land, a land of change, contrast, and surprise. . . . Melissa recalled the miles of dried grasses whipped by the wind, a landscape desolate and scarred. The memory pained her. *Dear God, what emptiness it was.*

—*Marguerite Noble,* Filaree

Tonto Creek. PHOTOGRAPH BY JEFFERSON REID.

farmers of the nineteenth century. We will also see what happened when Western Apache laborers incorporated wage work into their traditional lifeways to help build Theodore Roosevelt Dam.

These stories are marked by their differences. We will discover that there is no single best way to live in the mountains, that people's choices were determined largely by cultural and ideological values, and that each group created a unique cultural landscape.

Salado Farmers in the Tonto Basin

We have seen that people of diverse cultures moved into the Tonto Basin to take advantage of its rich alluvial soils, abundant rainfall, and permanent streams. As we might guess, not all of these people used the same farming strategies or grew the same crops. Moreover, agricultural methods changed over time to adjust to changing climate, political conditions, and population size. In the same way, social and cultural values shifted, and spiritual means of ensuring farming success also changed. In the multicultural population that was Salado, we see a group constantly altering technology, social organization, and religion to survive environmental vicissitudes. Corn remained central to subsistence and ritual throughout these changes, as did the Saladoan's reliance on spiritual as well as practical means to reduce risk. We examine the practical side of life in the Tonto Basin first, looking at Salado farming strategies and crops.

Water, Farmland, and Crops Tonto Basin farmers took advantage of one of the area's greatest benefits, its abundant and diverse water sources. Water was available as rainfall, snowmelt, runoff from spring floods and summer thunderstorms; it was found in the often torrential Salt River and in the typically peaceful flow of Tonto Creek. By using all of these sources, depending on how much rain fell each year, Tonto Basin farmers maintained a flexible strategy that reduced the risks associated with farming in the mountain Transition Zone. Although irrigation was a good strategy for balancing the basin's advantages and constraints, it may not have been the best method at all times and in all places. Irrigation is labor intensive, requiring considerable work to prepare the ditches and fields for cultivation. Individual farmers and small groups may have had difficulty marshaling enough people to do the job. Moreover, irrigation is inherently risky. Young and mature crops can be washed away when summer thunderstorms pour down on the fields (Welch 1994b). Archaeologists Carla Van West and Jeffrey Altschul (1994:415) have explained how farmers chose

A Hard Thing

"It is a hard thing to live freely in the wild," the Navajo writer who goes by the name Nasdijj (2000:27) has stated. "It is a thing of enormous, breathtaking contradiction. There is not a shred of romance in it."

whether to irrigate their crops or use a different technique, depending on rainfall and their ability to predict it.

When late-winter and spring precipitation was sufficient to germinate crops, and summer rains were abundant enough to keep crops well watered, nonirrigated farming would usually succeed. If winter and spring were unusually wet, farmers could anticipate that early spring floods would wash out irrigation canals and damage fields, and would stay with farming techniques that harvest water and divert it to the fields. By contrast, if the winter and spring were dry, farmers would turn to irrigation and would let fields that relied on rainfall alone lie fallow. Each strategy had its own risks, and these varied from year to year.

An ideal place to farm: rich floodplain along Theodore Roosevelt Lake. Photograph by Stephanie Whittlesey.

Using soil-moisture indexes and reconstructions of Salt River stream flow, Van West and Altschul (1994) found that the probability of farming success with different techniques varied a great deal. Precipitation fluctuated rather remarkably over the course of time. In wet years, nonirrigated farming would have been more successful, and in dry years, irrigation would have been the better technique. In other words, there was no single best strategy; farmers had to be creative and flexible, adjusting their methods to the conditions that prevailed in a particular year. In the long run, this would have been successful, because combining different methods reduced the risks associated with any one technique and increased the likelihood of bringing in a good harvest. Combined strategies were probably used throughout most of Tonto Basin's history; only in the Gila phase would irrigation agriculture have been difficult, forcing farmers to turn to other strategies (Van West and Altschul 1994:425).

Each farming strategy used different field locations. Irrigation requires field areas where canals can bring water by gravity, whereas floodwater farming must locate fields where runoff will water them. Dry farming has no such constraints. Studying soils, landforms, and water, geoarchaeologist Michael Waters (1998) found three areas where fields could have been located.

Terrace 1, the floodplain along the Salt River, could have been farmed by irrigation or what has been called floodwater-inundation or flood-recession farming (Welch 1994a:249). In wet seasons, the streams overflowed their banks, providing sufficient moisture to germinate and water crops. Waters (1998) believes that farming in this locale would have been a risky proposition for ancient farmers, however. Soils were not well suited for growing crops, and fields would have been highly vulnerable to floods. Waters thinks that only supplemental crops, not those on which the people depended for food, would have been grown in the floodplain. Cotton may have been one such crop.

Waters concluded that Terrace 2, located above the Tonto Creek and Salt River streambeds, was the most favorable place for farming because of its good soils, water availability, and location about six feet above the floodplain. It would have been fairly easy to bring water onto this surface using simple irrigation technology—diverting water from the stream by means of a gate, moving it by gravity flow through canals or ditches, and directing it onto the fields with secondary ditches or impoundments (Waters 1998:32). Welch (1994b) and Waters agree that land along Tonto Creek could be farmed more easily with irrigation than land along the Salt River, because Tonto Creek had a wider floodplain, better soils, and a more gentle gradient. Today, Theodore Roosevelt Lake gives the illusion that the valley along the Salt River was wide, but in prehistory it had a narrower, more rugged profile than Tonto Creek.

Most of Terrace 3 had been eroded before the Salaldo occupation began. Terrace 3, where it existed, and the higher Pleistocene terraces had limitations. It was not possible to bring irrigation water to these areas, and the soils were poor. The Salado therefore built their residential settlements on the higher terraces. This maximized the valuable and limited farmland of Terrace 2 and kept the residences safe from flooding. To date, archaeologists have found only field houses and processing facilities on Terrace 2, with the exception of a single site—indirect evidence that most Salado fields were located in this area. Some farming was possible on the higher terraces. Small gardens could have been watered by hand. In historical times, the Hopi carried water to such waterless gardens in ceramic containers, giving them the name "pot gardens." Dry-farming fields were also located on the high terraces and the *bajada* slopes. Rock-pile fields nurtured agave plants in such settings throughout the Sonoran Desert.

Farming was also carried out along secondary watercourses. Water flowing in these ephemeral streams after storms was directed onto and spread out over the fields by simple diversion dams, rock alignments, and brush impoundments (Welch 1994a). Archaeologists have found such systems throughout the Tonto Basin. Many such fields would be necessary, because each provided much less acreage than the larger arable plots on the lower terraces above the river.

Some archaeologists have proposed there were "irrigation districts" in the Tonto Basin—unique sets of topographic and hydrological constraints that limited where irrigation could be used (Wood 2000; Wood and others 1992). Eight districts have been identified, four along Salt River and four along Tonto Creek. Each district was affected by one or more water or land constraints with deleterious effects on farming, such as susceptibility to flash floods or erosion and limited arable land. In some districts, fields could have been located only on one side of the river; in others, the streambed, floodplain, and terrace areas were too narrow to accommodate a canal and fields. Flash floods were a particular danger. Small drainages intersecting canals would have periodically washed them away and necessitated constant repair.

View from the Eagle Ridge site along the Salt River, Tonto Basin. PHOTOGRAPH BY STEPHANIE WHITTLESEY.

How much land could have been farmed in these districts? This is not an easy question to answer, and the published estimates clash. Waters (1998:39) estimated relatively small areas that could be farmed with irrigation, whereas Wood's (2000) estimates were many times larger. Even with the smaller estimates, there was enough farmland to feed the Salado. A study by archaeologist Douglas Craig (1995) suggested that residents of the Meddler Point Platform Mound had sufficient land to maintain a two-year supply of corn using canal irrigation. In fact, Craig has suggested that it was necessary to increase the labor force to dig irrigation canals, clean and maintain them, and allocate water to the fields. This need alone may explain why small communities grouped into a few large settlements late in Tonto Basin prehistory.

Regardless of the actual acreage farmed, prehistoric irrigation systems in the Tonto Basin were much smaller than those of the Phoenix Basin. The Salt and Gila River valleys did not suffer from the severe land and water constraints that restricted irrigation in the Tonto Basin. It may not be surprising that conflict emerged in the latter area, where a growing population was competing for a limited amount of land that could be farmed.

What crops did the Salado farmer grow? We must remember that there were different peoples living in the Tonto Basin, and each group had a distinctive diet. As a whole, however, the Salado diet differed from the Hohokam diet. The Salado did not consistently collect and consume the wild plants of the Sonoran Desert. Instead, they were farmers first and foremost. Plant remains obtained from flotation analysis led paleobotanist Phil Dering (1998:96) to conclude that "Tonto Basin farmers did not rely on Sonoran Desert plant resources to the same degree as the Hohokam; the staple plant foods were agricultural products." Moreover, they relied predominantly on corn, which represented as much as three-fourths of the diet. The importance of corn to the Salado peoples recalls its significance to the Hopi and the Hisatsinom before them.

It is intriguing that the staple wild-plant foods of the pre-Classic Hohokam—mesquite and saguaro—were less common than cultivated plants, although mesquite and saguaro grow abundantly in the Tonto Basin. The scarcity of these plants in the archaeological record suggests dietary practices that probably reflect cultural differences between Hohokam and Salado.

Other cultivated plants were agave, cotton, squash, and beans; archaeologists found agave to be the most frequently cultivated plant after corn. Salado farmers grew four kinds of beans: jack beans (*Canavalia* spp.), common beans,

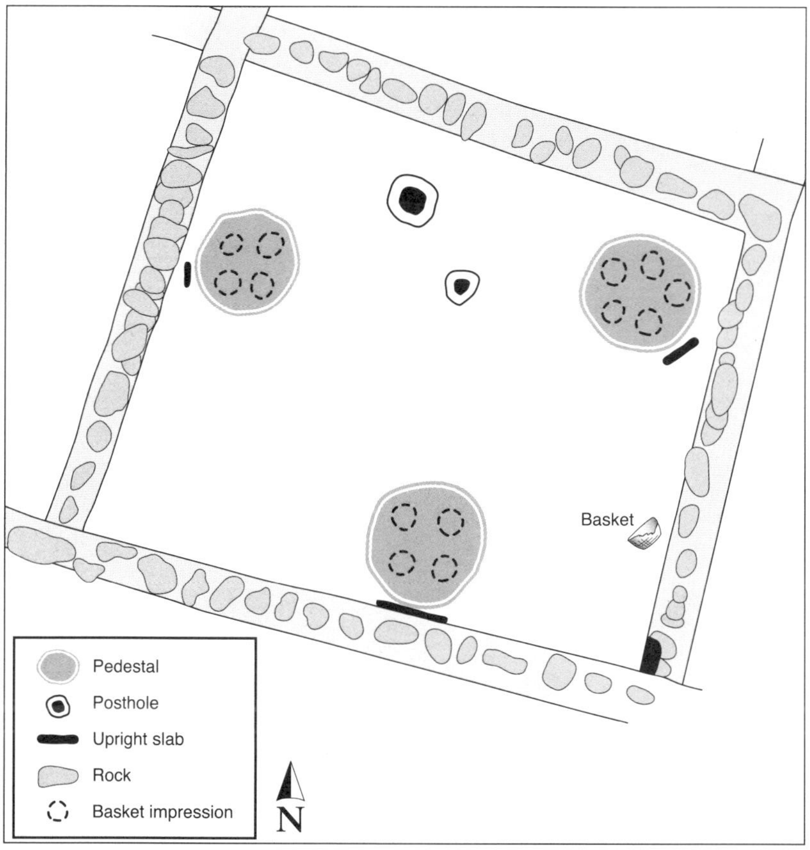

Idealized Salado room showing location of granary bases, or pedestals.

These were general patterns; what of possible ethnic differences among Salado farmers? Dietary differences reinforced conclusions derived from architecture, ceramics, and other classes of information asserting that at least some of the people living in the Tonto Basin after A.D. 1250 were immigrants from northern regions. There was a distinction between sites with room-block architecture—clusters of contiguous rooms not unlike the pueblos of the north and thought to represent the homes of puebloan immigrants—and platform-mound sites. Residents of the room-block sites emphasized farming, particularly corn. At the Griffin Wash site, for example, archaeologists found abundant pollen of corn and agricultural weeds. Mustard, an edible plant whose seeds and greens were eaten, was found at many other residential sites but was conspicuously absent at Griffin Wash. These people also cultivated much agave and perhaps even specialized in growing this crop (Elson and others 2000:179; Miksicek 1995).

Corn was also stored and prepared in distinct ways by residents of room-block sites and was likely central to religious beliefs and practices as among the Hopi. Corn was apparently stored in the husk rather than as shelled kernels and was processed intensively by grinding with

teparies, and limas (*Phaseolus* spp.). They cultivated three kinds of squash (*Cucurbita moschata*, *C. pepo* [pumpkin], and *C. mixta*). Less important cultivated plants were bottle gourd *(Lagenaria siceraria)* and amaranth, which was used for dye, medicine, and food.

This is not to say that Salado people did not collect wild plants for many different purposes. Trees such as acacia, mesquite, oak, palo verde, juniper, walnut, and piñon provided wood for construction and fuel, edible nuts, beans, and berries. The fruits of desert hackberry and the stems of Mormon tea (*Ephedra* sp.) were used to make beverages; the seeds of grasses (little barley *[Hordeum pusillum]*, panic grass, Sacaton grass) and weedy plants inhabiting fields and disturbed ground (spiderling [*Boerhaavia* sp.], mustard, evening primrose) were ground into flour and eaten as gruels or breads, and the greens were stewed. The fruits of yucca, sotol, and cactus (saguaro, barrel, cholla, hedgehog, fishhook, prickly pear) were eaten, and many wild plants had uses as medicine, dye, and craft materials.

Site AZ V:5:16/15a, the Pinto Point Mound. Photograph courtesy U.S. Bureau of Reclamation. Joe Madrigal, Jr., photographer.

mano and metate (Fish 1998). Corn pollen may have been used ritually, as among modern puebloan peoples, to consecrate objects, in rituals, and as a blessing.

Another important plant for the pueblo immigrants was cotton. The room-block portions of the Griffin Wash site yielded extremely high quantities of cotton remains, in sufficient amounts to suggest that their growers specialized in this crop as well as agave (Elson and others 2000:179; Miksicek 1995). Cotton was found much less frequently at other sites occupied at the same time.

Did these puebloan immigrants find that the best farmland had already been taken, and were they forced to make use of less fertile or poorly watered fields? Some archaeologists think so. Based upon the fact that the room-block communities were located on the peripheries of settlements, Elson and colleagues (2000:176) believe that "intrusive groups did not have ready access to prime agricultural land. . . . Immigrant groups were permitted to construct nearby settlements in areas of lower irrigation potential." This interesting theory is unsubstantiated by the facts. Although agave—found so abundantly at Griffin Wash—is a drought-tolerant crop that is usually grown with rainfall alone, corn and especially cotton have high water requirements. It is unlikely that cotton could have been grown in the Tonto Basin without irrigation. The abundance of corn and cotton suggests that the Griffin Wash residents not only had access to high-quality land that could be irrigated, but that they had enough of this land to grow surplus cotton and corn.

Inside Tonto Basin Granaries Practical and spiritual means for farming the desert were evidently successful for the people of Tonto Basin, at least for much of their tenure there. Archaeologists found capacious storage facilities at many sites. Moreover, some of the platform-mound sites seem to have been elaborate structures for storing and protecting agricultural surpluses. These were mounds that served primarily as residences or combined residential and ceremonial functions.

A unique storage facility found in the Tonto Basin (and also in Chihuahua, some Salado sites in New Mexico, and perhaps elsewhere) is the granary. These were dome- or beehive-shaped facilities made of perishable materials and covered with adobe mud. The domed structure was placed on a stone pedestal of cobbles set into the ground. These granaries were built inside rooms and in open areas. Typically, archaeologists found only the cobble pedestals, the perishable materials having disintegrated with time. The outer adobe-mud covering was preserved in a few cases. Impressions left in the mud indicated that granaries were constructed of coarsely woven plant materials—reeds, willow twigs, arrowweed, corn stalks—and the mud-adobe plaster over some granaries appeared to have been covered with cloth (Lindauer 1996). Granaries were probably semipermanent facilities that were emptied, burned, and rebuilt with each new harvest, a procedure that would kill insects harboring in the granaries and protect the new stores.

Fallen gypsum-masonry wall of tower-like room at Cline Terrace Platform Mound site in Tonto Basin. PHOTOGRAPH BY STEPHANIE WHITTLESEY.

Archaeologists discovered many granaries at the Cline Terrace and Schoolhouse Point Mound sites. Cline Terrace, which was located along Tonto Creek, had unique architectural features. It was surrounded by a massive cobble-masonry wall enclosing elevated areas, an elevated tower-like room, and unusual, narrow, L-shaped rooms. Portions of the walls, including the elevated areas, were faced with shaped and chinked slab masonry of white gypsum (Jacobs 1997). Many of the elevated rooms were devoted to storage and food preparation, containing granary pedestals, storage vessels, and hearths (Dering 1997). Some of the ground-level rooms also contained storage vessels, and granary pedestals were found in unroofed plazas. The Cline Terrace granaries contained corn, cattail, and cactus pollen, sometimes stored separately (Fish 1997).

So many granaries and rooms devoted to storage were found at the Schoolhouse Point site that archaeologists called it "The Place of the Storehouses." Most of the granaries were found in ground-level storerooms at the center of the mound, which may have increased their security (Lindauer 1996). Rooms and plazas held granary pedestals, slab-lined storage pits, and storage vessels. Storage vessels and granaries contained shelled corn kernels and beans, and perhaps also cotton, little barley, and wild plants (Dering 1996). Archaeologist Owen Lindauer calculated that the excavated granaries could have stored enough surplus food to last from 1.4 to 2 years. To the Salado residents of the Tonto Basin, this was treasure indeed—food to last through the winter and seed next year's crop, the material sign of answered prayers.

Cobble pedestal or base of Salado granary underlying a fallen gypsum-masonry wall at Cline Terrace Platform Mound site.
Photograph by Stephanie Whittlesey.

Ritual, Risk, and Cotton We have seen that Salado farming practices were risky and depended heavily upon the ability to predict rain from season to season and year to year. How would people predict rain and reduce risk? Knowledge, of course, was vital, and we can imagine that the elders, with their store of farming and ritual knowledge, would guide the people through the agricultural year. Scattering many fields in different places and using different farming methods was a highly practical means of reducing risk. So was storing foodstuffs in granaries. Puebloan peoples who depended heavily on corn preferred to keep a two-year supply on hand to reduce the risk of hunger. If rainfall was insufficient to bring in a crop, this surplus would buffer the people against starvation and enable them to plant another crop.

Prayer, however, may have been more important to the ancient Saladoans than any other means of reducing risk. Sacred means of predicting the rain and calling it down from the sky, ritual methods for keeping track of the solar cycle and agricultural year, ceremonies, sacred dances, and offerings—no doubt the Salado peoples required this buffer as much as the Hopi of historical times. In the platform mounds of the Tonto Basin, we see a perfect blending of secular and sacred mechanisms for coping with scarcity and maintaining the ideal food surplus.

Although we cannot be sure, it seems likely that water was the central focus of religious belief and practices. Salado fields were farmed by harvesting the waters of Tonto Creek, Salt River, and ephemeral streams. Rainfall was critical, for when it did not fall the fields would wither and die, leaving the children hungry. Canal irrigation depended on rain, too, for rain and melting snow filled the rivers from which the irrigation ditches flowed. Prayers for rain probably focused Salado religion, and platform mounds—at least some of them—were sacred spaces where these prayers and ceremonies were carried out.

Much of Salado religion, cosmology, and sacred landscape may have been adapted from the beliefs of ancient Mexican peoples. We saw in Chapter 5 that many living and ancient southwestern peoples borrowed much of their religious practice from extremely old Mesoamerican rain cults, such as those devoted to Tlaloc and Quetzalcoatl. As agricultural peoples with a long history of cultivation, the Salado would have benefited from a cult devoted to deities of rain, water, and wind; to agricultural fertility; and to corn. Such cults were closely associated with mountains, ceramic containers, and richly detailed water imagery. In Mexico, Tlaloc provided the regularly timed rainfall necessary to sustain life, and the deity accomplished this by means of mountains (Markman and Markman 1992:202). It does not seem improbable that platform mounds in the Tonto Basin, as artificial mountains, served as locales for religious performances related to a rain cult.

Some platform mounds evidently served a highly specific, ritual function and were not places where people resided. We know this because the rooms at such mounds lacked features common to residential rooms, such as hearths, granaries, and storage vessels. Meddler Point Mound was one such platform mound. Craig (1995:245) has argued that the mound was a special-purpose religious facility serving the residents of nearby residential compounds.

The cardinal orientation and rectangular shape of platform mounds symbolized the important cardinal directions and the four-part division of the cosmos. Mounds were probably considered to be sacred pathways linking the middle and upper worlds and mediating between the important dualities of earth and heaven. Rituals were likely focused on bringing rain to the crops and calling for abundant harvests. Prayers were made to keep the rivers

Water in the Mountain

Ancient Mesoamerican peoples had a complex set of beliefs and symbols linking the rain gods, mountains, and containers of water. Mountains were described as containers of water, or "vessels," where water was stored in the dry season to be released in the rainy season. In the oral traditions describing Tlaloc's home, four jars containing beneficent rain, mildew, drought, and destructive rain were said to stand in the four corners of his patio (Peterson 1959:131). Tlaloc's spiritual assistants, the Tlaloque, dispensed or withheld beneficial and destructive rain from these containers.

Mountains generated the clouds that bring rain. From them flowed springs, lakes, and streams. The ancestors, who could mediate with the gods and bring rain, were thought to dwell in mountains.

Pottery vessels assumed an important symbolic role relating to water among ancient Mesoamerican peoples. These containers made of earth and holding water were viewed as symbols of springs and caves, the natural contexts where water is held within the earth. In their symbolic role, pottery vessels were iconographic representations of containers holding the clouds that produce rain (Schaafsma 1999:168).

Similar beliefs and symbols are found in many Native American cultures of the U.S. Southwest. In the Diné creation story, the First World held four houses at the north, south, east, and west directions containing jars filled with precious water. The beings living in these houses grew the first plants—corn, tobacco, squash, and more. In later worlds, four mountains were placed in the four directions. Tohono O'odham stories tell of beautiful, shining, ancient houses placed in the four directions, each wrapped in clouds. From them comes the wind and rain. Cloud Man lives in the mountains and carries water. I'itoi, Elder Brother and creator of the Tohono O'odham, lives in a cave on Baboquivari Peak southwest of Tucson. Elder Brother has left I'itoi Ki, I'itoi's House, to live among the people in times of trouble.

We can see in the platform mounds of the Tonto Basin the symbolic representations of mountains holding life-giving water. In the myths and beliefs of later native peoples, we also glimpse the importance of sacred mountains, water, and ceramic containers that may be a heritage of ancient Mesoamerican beliefs.

Interior of Salado bowl (Pinto Polychrome) showing design with stepped elements or "cloud symbols."
DRAWING BY STEPHANIE WHITTLESEY.

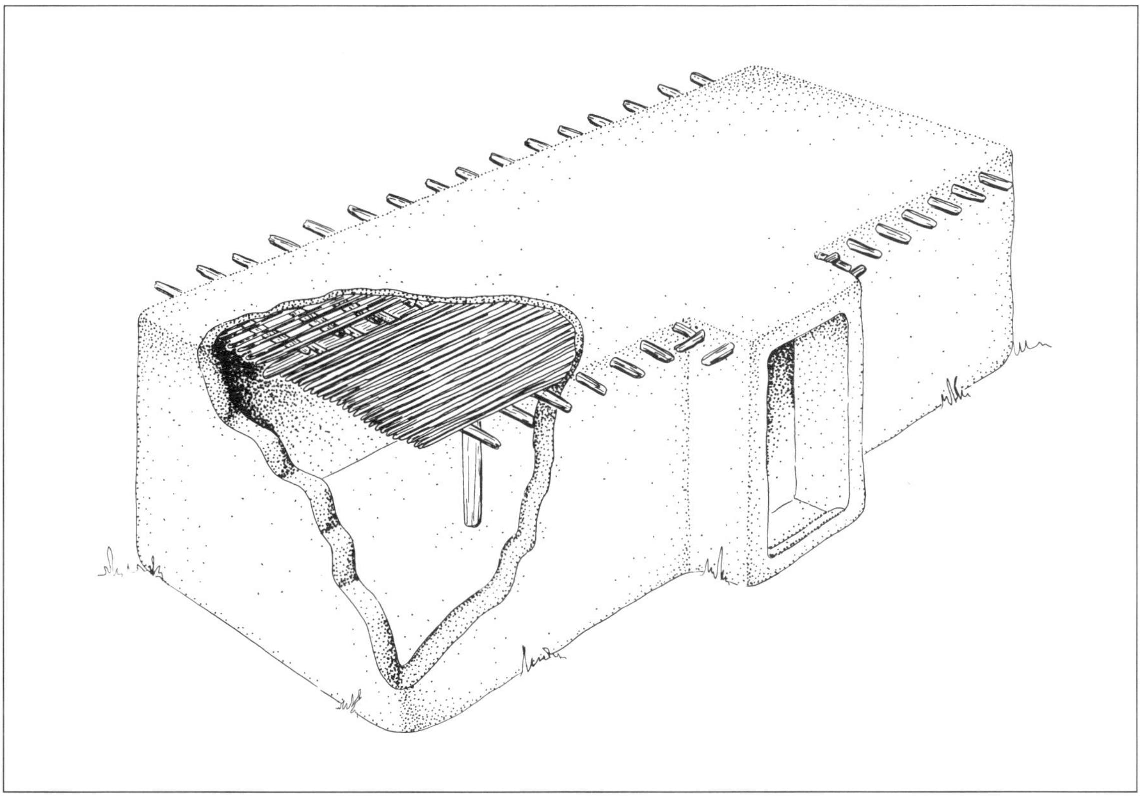

Artist's conception of an aboveground Salado room built of adobe showing roof construction and supports.

and creeks from flooding and washing out the canals and diversion dams. Bring us enough water, the Salado must have prayed, but not too much. We can picture the colorful ceremonies that must have taken place atop the mound, as priests led the people in prayers and rituals designed to bring the rain that nourished the growing crops and sustained life in the Tonto Basin.

Cotton may have played a role in this ritual system. Cotton has a central symbolic role in Pueblo religion. Among the Hopi today, cotton textiles woven in kivas are worn by *katsina* dancers and by newlyweds as ceremonial wedding costumes. Because it symbolizes rain clouds, raw, unspun cotton is used in ritual paraphernalia. It is placed over the face of the deceased at burial and decorates prayer feathers. Cotton may have played a similar symbolic role among the puebloans of the Tonto Basin.

In cotton, we may see yet another link between the religious practices of the Southwest and Mesoamerica. Intriguingly, the Salado of Tonto Basin and the ancient peoples of Mesoamerica were united by similar cotton textiles.

Salado petroglyph, perhaps depicting the sun, in Tonto Basin.
Photograph courtesy U.S. Bureau of Reclamation.

Going to the Underworld

Robert Boissiere (1986:98) tells this story of preparing the desert dweller for the journey to the Underworld:

. . . .

> After the four ritual days,
> there is a new home for the Underworld-bound Hopi.
> Religious, reverently, the mask of wild cotton is made
> that the cloud people will recognize him.

According to archaeologist and textile specialist Lynn Teague (1992:304):

> The fabrics of the Saladoan people are representative of a broader textile tradition that appeared after A.D. 1100 below the Mogollon Rim as far south as Casas Grandes and the Río Sonora. It represents a fusion of technical approaches found earlier in the central Southwest with the addition of significant influence from both the west coast expressions of Mesoamerican culture and also from the simpler cultures of inland northern Mexico.

It is possible that the unity in textile designs reflects the spread of the Salado culture or its religious underpinnings from Mesoamerica (Adams 2000:269).

The puebloan immigrants of the Tonto Basin may have used cotton in religious and secular ways more often than other residents. More cotton seeds were found at sites with room-block architecture than elsewhere (Dering 1998), suggesting that the residents may have focused on growing cotton and processing it.

Some archaeologists have suggested that cotton was the reason people moved into the Tonto Basin (Adams 2000; Lindauer 2000:233; Van West and others 2000). The crop could tolerate the saline waters of the Salt River and would flourish in the basin's warm climate and long growing season (Van West and others 2000:40–41, 53). Adams (2000) has taken the argument one step further to propose that cotton was grown for exchange with people living on the Colorado Plateau in return for ceramics and other goods, which are invisible in the archaeological record.

Although there is no doubt that cotton was an important cultivated plant with economic, ritual, and food uses or that it was grown by the Tonto Basin Salado, it will take much further study to demonstrate that it was a specialized crop grown for exchange. Irrigation necessary to grow cotton in the Tonto Basin is a risky business, as we have seen. It is also unclear whether the relatively limited amount of farmland in the Tonto Basin could have supported intensive cotton farming as well as food crops. Faced with a choice, the farmer would probably have chosen corn to feed the family rather than cotton to trade (Levy 1992:46). And last, people on the Colorado Plateau grew their own cotton in many different locations, ranging from the well-watered, warm bottomlands of Canyon de Chelly in northeastern Arizona (Teague 1998:24–25) to the cold, arid Colorado Plateau near Flagstaff (Kamp 1998).

The Salado's spiritual bulwarks against the lean times and their highly practical, flexible farming strategies served them well for many decades. When the end came, it seems to have come from climatic events that were too severe to withstand. According to Carla Van West and colleagues (2000), the period between A.D. 1350 to 1450 was characterized by extreme variability in stream flow with concomitant effects on farming. There were two intervals of high precipitation and probable floods, one between A.D. 1356 and 1359 and a second between A.D. 1380 and 1384. Floods during these times would have destroyed irrigation canals. The flood years were also characterized by lowered water tables, which reduced ground cover and resulted in greatly increased erosion. Rich soil would have washed away as

Pictograph near Canyon Creek Pueblo with textile design. PHOTOGRAPH BY STEPHANIE WHITTLESEY.

water poured unimpeded down the slopes and streams, destroying valuable irrigated farmland.

In dry years, farmers would have had to cope with little water, perhaps finding it difficult to grow corn and cotton. Irrigation canals would have been stranded high and dry without water. Farmers along the Salt River may have had to cope with increased salinity as well. The soils of irrigated fields would have grown progressively more alkaline without copious fresh water to wash out the accumulated salts. Salt-intolerant crops such as beans and corn would have been difficult to grow.

When the food stores were exhausted, great changes may have been necessary for Tonto Basin farmers to survive. They might have changed their diet to include cultigens that could be grown without irrigation, such as agave, or increased their consumption of wild-plant foods. Eventually, the Salado abandoned the Tonto Basin for places more favorable to farming. Weeds choked the fields and canals, and their homes gradually fell into decay, leaving only stones and stories behind. Sometime afterward, the Western Apache came to occupy the same land. We turn to their stories next.

Western Apache Farming

Because of the richness of their homeland, farming was not as central to Western Apache subsistence as it was among the Hopi or O'odham peoples. Anthropologist Winfred Buskirk (1986:227) has suggested that "the very abundance of environmental possibilities in the Western Apache habitat led the Apache to follow them all instead of concentrating on one." Farming was considered a luxury rather than a necessity (Goodwin 1969). The seasonal round into which agriculture was seamlessly fused created a mixed suite of social and religious values. On the one hand, the Apache concentrated on the acquisition of personal power that would ensure the success of hunting, raiding, and gathering. On the other hand, they celebrated, petitioned, and prayed to the rain that nourishes the corn.

When we look at Western Apache farming, we see a highly mobile group adopting agriculture without changing the basics of their lifestyle. Corn was viewed as a gift that augmented nature's abundance, and it was incorporated into their religion and culture in ways that reinforced existing ideology and ideals. It did not transform subsistence, which anthropologists often assume to be the case. The path to settled, village agricultural life, such as that characterizing the Hopi, may have been artificially attenuated by the conflicts of the nineteenth century and the reservation system, but nevertheless the transformation seems unlikely to have taken place among the Apache.

The Western Apache's vital connection with their homeland created a cultural landscape rich in stories—the physical landscape transformed by experience into a landscape of the mind. Anthropologist Keith Basso (1996:127) relates how a Cibecue Apache man described the importance of place:

> Wisdom sits in places. It's like water that never dries up. You need to drink water to stay alive, don't you? Well, you also need to drink from places. You must remember everything about them. You must learn their names. You must remember what happened at them long ago. . . . You will walk a long way and live a long time. You will be wise. People will respect you.

Place-names are central to Apache geography. Descriptive of the natural landscape, naming rocks and water, mountains and trees, place-names do much more. They evoke history, the time when the ancestors first settled the country and sought good places to hunt, farm, and live (Basso 1996). They also suggest more recent history, reflecting stories of clans and local groups and individuals. Speaking the place-name evokes the events that happened there in the past, serving as a mnemonic to retell the story and at the same time reinforcing self-identity. Place becomes a means to reconstruct the past. By contrast, Euroamerican history is, in Griffin-Pierce's (2000:393) words, "geographically adrift" and cannot evoke the past in the same way.

Sacred geography focuses on mountains, the center of identity, morality, and ritual (Whittlesey 1998b:715). Mountains figure prominently in cosmology as among the Navajo; sacred peaks are associated with directions, colors, and jewels (obsidian or black jet, turquoise, shell, and red stone). The *ga'an* are mountain spirits. They are also associated with agriculture, and tales relate how the Apache once lived in close proximity with the *ga'an* and benefited from their expertise before the Apache learned how to farm (Goodwin 1969:64). It is tempting to see the *ga'an* as Apache versions of the ancient Tlaloque of Mesoamerica, the spirits who lived on mountains and dispensed rain from Tlaloc's jars. It is likely that the Apache saw mountains as generators of clouds and rain as did the Navajo. When the Apache were forced from their mountain homes, their strong cultural and spiritual values associated with mountains were displaced as well, engendering a loss of identity. According to Porter (1986:256), Chiricahua Apache exiled to Florida pined for snow and high, barren peaks. They disliked living alongside the water, saying that they "were a people who had been born and raised in the high mountains." Mountains remain sacred locales today, as the conflict over building telescopes on Mount Graham indicates.

Mountains and water shared significance in sacred geography. From Spanish Colonial times onward, observers have noted the importance of water to the Western Apache. According to McNamee (1994:49), a Spanish Colonial writer once remarked of the Apache that "Water is what they worship most, to which they offer small painted sticks and feathers and yellow powder made of flowers." Springs and streams had sacred meaning and were remembered in traditional stories. In some versions of the creation story, agriculture originated with a man who traveled down a river in a hollow log aided by his pet turkey (Griffin-Pierce 2000:369). Places were often named for sources of water—seeps, springs, bogs, and seasonal pools located at the bases of canyon walls (Basso 1996). In this way, water, life, and farming were linked in mythology and spiritual geography and were translated into the everyday world of physical landscape.

Modern Apache cornfield and field house on Fort Apache Indian Reservation, Arizona. PHOTOGRAPH BY STEPHANIE WHITTLESEY.

The White River near Fort Apache, Arizona. PHOTOGRAPH BY JEFFERSON REID.

Social organization and farming were also linked by means of place-names. The Apache say that their clan lines go through the women because it is the women who plant the corn (Basso 1996:21). Archaeologist John Welch (1994c:114) has suggested that clans served as a means to maintain descent-group ties to the most agriculturally important localities. "Where agriculture was less important, so too were clans." The Apache's clan names are in essence the names of clan places, and many were named for the locales where Apache clans first began to farm. The Apache considered their farm sites to be permanent locations to which notions of land tenure, ownership, and trespass applied (Goodwin 1969:150). This is readily understood in a country where there were many hunting and gathering sites that people inhabited temporarily, but few good farming sites, which were hard to come by and difficult to prepare for planting (Goodwin 1969:150).

In Apache farming practices, we can see how concepts of spiritual geography, natural elements, and place are integrated. We look first at the practical facets of farming and the agricultural landscape. Water determined the location of Western Apache fields; vegetation cover and terrain were secondary factors. The amount of available water had to be just right, neither too much nor too little. Most farms were located along broad valleys bordering major streams, such as Tonto, Fossil, Oak, Pinal, Cibecue, Carrizo, and Forestdale Creeks. Along the Gila and Salt Rivers, the threat of losing ditches and fields to flooding was constant, and the Apache always chose to farm along smaller streams when possible (Whittlesey 1998b:713). Some farm plots were situated at small springs or seeps. At farm sites located in broad, alluvial valleys enriched by periodic flooding, the soil was seldom depleted of nutrients.

Families usually owned from two to six farm plots. Seeding many small plots in different areas ensured that at least some fields would be safe from predators and produce a crop. The amount of land cultivated was sufficient to feed the family for a year; there was no desire to grow more than that or to acquire larger farms. Men and women could own fields, but when a field was owned by a man, its produce was the property of his wife.

The agricultural year and farming tasks were structured around water. The agricultural year began in the late spring, when even dry arroyos became freshets running with snowmelt. Chiefs exhorted their local groups to go to the farm sites when it was time to plant. "You should go to your farms. Build up your ditch and dam well, and put in your corn carefully" (Goodwin 1969:156). Cleaning and repairing the irrigation system, or building new ditches if necessary, were the first tasks.

Next, fields were cleared. The men burned off grass, removed small stones, and broke the ground with a digging stick. Then the women irrigated the fields and pulled weeds. Planting took place between March and July, depending on elevation. A strategy that distributed risk was to stagger planting times. The corn was soaked before planting in irregular rows of hills. Preparing the fields and planting were group enterprises that distributed labor. Relatives and neighbors often helped, although brothers and husbands were obligated to their wives' families. Assistance was given reciprocally, with the understanding that families would take turns working each other's fields.

The Apache planted the same crops that had nourished southwestern people for millennia—corn, beans, and squash. These plants were usually grown in separate fields. The Apache supplemented the major crops with sunflowers, tobacco, and gourds and encouraged edible and useful weeds such as devil's claw, lambsquarters, and wild grape to grow in the fields.

Controlling water helped the Apache to grow crops in the mountains, where early frosts and cool temperatures made farming a risky proposition. Headgates and lateral gates made of bear grass or grama grass weighted with rocks controlled ditches running to the fields from streams or springs. Main ditches and dams used for irrigation were owned and maintained jointly by everyone who used them. Men known as "ditch bosses"—elders with a storehouse of agricultural and ritual knowledge—notified the people when repair work was needed. At times, these elders would make the first ceremonial planting and perform rituals to hasten the ripening of the crop. Ditches leading to individual fields were the responsibility of the field owners, and thus irrigation was largely women's work. Most of the time, ditches conveyed the precious resource in orderly fashion, each family receiving its share in turn. The ditch boss stepped in to allocate irrigation water and arbitrate disputes as necessary.

Occasionally, runoff was used to irrigate fields. Dams diverted rainfall running down a hillside or flowing in an arroyo after a storm, and ditches conveyed it to fields. White Mountain Apache farmers built substantial dams of willow and juniper poles, brush, grass, and gravel for this purpose. Other farming methods were once more common. For example, the farmers of San Carlos planted in the damp soil along the river bottom (Goodwin 1969:31). The severe droughts of the late nineteenth century made this an extremely risky practice. By contrast, the Tonto Apache never irrigated their fields.

Families usually stayed at the farm sites only until the corn was six to eight inches high, usually early in July. After that, only a few people were left to tend the growing crops—usually old people or captives in prereservation times (Goodwin 1969:156). The rest of the people moved away, because summer was the time when saguaro fruit, acorns, and mesquite beans were harvested.

Turkey Gives Corn to the People

Many years ago, Apache elder Anna Price told the following tale to ethnographer Grenville Goodwin (1994:61–62):

> Turkey made the food for our people. That was long ago when all the animals talked like people. A boy and his sister were living together. They were talking to one another about how they had no food. Turkey overheard them talking and came to that place. . . .
>
> . . . Turkey said to the boy and girl, "I have four kinds of corn seeds here for you. This is a good place to plant so you might as well plant your seeds." The boy and girl started to work on the planting. They cut digging sticks and with these made holes. In the holes they planted all their corn seeds. They planted all their corn in one day. The next day it had already come up and was about a foot and a half high. Then the girl said, "We still have some more seeds here to plant;" these were squash seeds. They planted these. . . .
>
> The squash plants had young squash on them, and the corn was grown tall and had ears on and tassels. . . . That is the way our corn grows and ripens now.

In September, farm crops were beginning to ripen, and chiefs or headmen urged the people to return to the farm sites and gather in the harvest. Harvesting was women's work and was also a cooperative endeavor. Buskirk (1986:39) estimated that in the early 1890s, a farm plot three-fourths of an acre in size yielded 3,700 ears of corn. After the harvest, green ears of corn were pit baked and dried. Crops were stored in baskets, pottery vessels, or wrapped in bear grass. Storage caches were constructed in caves or in the ground. Seed corn was stored separately from corn destined to be consumed, and different corn colors were also stored apart. The people stayed at the farms until all the crops had been stored away, usually by the end of October (Goodwin 1969:157).

Cultural and social values supported farming, and in turn farming metaphors imbued Western Apache stories and beliefs. The people honored corn with rituals and prayer; they petitioned the rain to fall perfectly—neither too much nor not enough. To ensure a bountiful harvest, rituals accompanied planting, irrigating, cultivating, and harvesting corn. At planting time, the people prayed and sang to the *ga'an* and the mythical Corn People residing in each farming locality (Buskirk 1986:68). Medicine men carried out rain-making ceremonies and prayed for protection against flood and hail. Prayer feathers and talismans were planted in fields for protection. When the corn tassels formed, a woman with ceremonial knowledge sang for the emerging corn (Buskirk 1986:70). When the corn ears began to turn white, tradition demanded that the people stay out of the fields for four days. There was pollen all around, and it was thought that snakes were gathering pollen at that time (Goodwin 1994:71)—yet another connection between snakes and farming. The first harvest act was to select ceremonial stalks and female ears for the first or "leader" seed (Buskirk 1986:61–63, 71). The people piled up the corn in four mountains atop the first ears, as they had been instructed by Turkey in the old stories (Goodwin 1994:71).

Women and their role in agriculture are affirmed in the traditional puberty ceremonial. Changing Woman, who is the supernatural being impersonated during this rite, controls the fertility and fruition of plants. Four times the celebrant grinds corn, which is then cooked and shared.

Basso (1996:13) has pointed out that Western Apache place-names indicate recent transformations in the environment. Many evoke wet places that no longer exist—springs that have dried, for example. In the Apache mind, there is no question that the land was once wetter and greener when the ancestors arrived than it is today. The reason for this, they explain, is that Water has been disrespected. Perhaps the people were greedy, taking more water than they needed, or were wasteful of it. Perhaps they "ceased doing everything correctly, neglecting in haste or forgetfulness to give repeated thanks to Water for giving of itself" (Basso 1996:16–17). The solution is simple, the Apache say—pray to Water, that it may not go away everywhere and for good. Pray that Water takes pity. Make amends, and the water will come back.

Corn Mountains

Turkey tells the Apache how to harvest their corn in this tale told to Grenville Goodwin (1994:71):

> Before you pile corn ears up, place four ears of corn on the ground, each one placed so that it points to one of the four directions and all butts pointing to a common center. Now pile your corn on top of these four ears. When you start husking, the first ear that you husk, throw it up so high (about four feet and a half) saying, "Let our pile of corn be so high." When you have done it all, pile your corn up to see how much you have. It will be as high sometimes as you have thrown the first ear.

The Apache Workmen at Theodore Roosevelt Dam

It was an unlikely place for the largest artificial lake in the world, pooling behind a dam that would cost millions of dollars to build—a narrow canyon at the confluence of Salt River and Tonto Creek. Yet in that place would rise not only a massive dam—at that time the highest in the world, designed to be the showpiece for the fledgling Reclamation Service—but also an ephemeral city, a boomtown of more than 2,000 people that would disappear when the dam was completed in 1911 and the waters of the lake rose. Many different people came to this place to raise the dam and build the roads, including the Western Apache. Their story is told here.

Building Theodore Roosevelt Dam was a monumental task. Archaeologist A. E. "Gene" Rogge and his colleagues (1995) tell of its history and the stories of the men (and a few women) who labored there. In the early 1900s, the town of Phoenix was only 60 miles from the construction site but linked to it by impossibly primitive trails through the Salt River Canyon and by convoluted railroad connections spanning hundreds of miles. Infrastructure was needed for dam construction along with support facilities to house and feed its builders. Beginning in 1903, a complicated web of features seemed to spring from bare ground—a diversion dam, quarries, a 19-mile-long canal to bring water for generating hydroelectric power, a cement plant, logging camps, sawmills, hundreds of miles of roads, telephone lines, office buildings, and the village of Roosevelt, where Euroamerican construction workers would be housed.

Deterred by the remote location, isolation, and difficult conditions, workers were hard to find and skilled labor even harder. The Texas contractor who built the dam recruited laborers of many ethnic and racial backgrounds—Italian stonemasons, Mexican and African-American laborers, "Anglo hoboes recruited from farms and freight cars" (Worster 1985:172), and many Western Apache workers from the nearby San Carlos Reservation. The Apache's contribution to the dam remained unknown until historical-archaeological studies were carried out for the Central Arizona Project. Rogge and colleagues have written (1995:10) that:

> histories of Roosevelt Dam generally mention that Apaches labored on the new roads needed for dam construction, but the descriptions of their contributions invariably seem vague and insubstantial, casting them as bit players on the grand stage of the history of Roosevelt Dam. Although State Route 88 has been named the Apache Trail, few realize that Apache laborers actually built the road.

The Apache way of life had been irrevocably altered by the conflicts of the late nineteenth century. Geronimo had surrendered, ending the Apache Wars at last. Many Chiricahua Apache had been imprisoned in a mountainless home far from the center of their cultural and spiritual geography. "The sense of spiritual dislocation," Griffin-Pierce (2000:363) wrote, "must have been profound and unrelenting." No longer able to follow their traditional subsistence round and having their raiding curtailed, the people became accustomed to handouts of nontraditional foods rationed by the Office of Indian Affairs. The fabric of Apache life began to unravel. In the early years of the twentieth century, the Office of Indian Affairs adopted a policy of integrating Indians into the work force as laborers. "Our first duty to the Indian," the Indian commissioner proclaimed in 1906, "is to get him off the reservation and to teach him to work" (quoted in Rogge and others 1995:136).

Raising Arizona's Dams

As part of the archaeological research for Central Arizona Project Plan 6, Dames & Moore carried out historical archaeology for the construction camps occupied while Theodore Roosevelt Dam and several other dams on the Salt and Verde Rivers were built. Research historians and a crew of about a dozen archaeologists dug into the past to reveal the hidden history of the camps. In 1986 and 1987, 58 archaeological sites at Roosevelt, Bartlett, Horseshoe, Waddell, and three other dams in central Arizona were investigated. About 144,000 items were collected—glass, nails, tin cans, ceramics, and much more. The researchers dug through boxes of dusty records—files, stacks of paper, school and tax records—as well as dirt. Their research revealed a picture of daily life, danger, and discrimination among peoples who are often considered among history's forgotten.

"We used historical archaeology to reveal the grit and smell, the taste and texture, and the danger and discrimination that were part of the lives of the people who raised these dams. In a real sense, the hands of such laborers built the West we inhabit," wrote archaeologist Gene Rogge and colleagues (1995:14).

However it may have happened, many Apache laborers were hired to work on Theodore Roosevelt Dam. Rogge and colleagues (1995:136) estimated that as many as 1,500 Apache workmen and their families lived in camps near the construction site, virtually depopulating the San Carlos Reservation of its able-bodied workers. These people were historically invisible—only a fraction of those living in the construction area were counted in the 1910 census, and their fragile, ephemeral camps were undocumented. Most of the photographs taken at that time were staged, showing the fictionalized, romantic illusion of the Native American and rarely showing the Apache at work. Historical archaeology put them back into the picture.

Apache laborers and their families lived separate lives at the Roosevelt construction city. Housing, labor, and entertainment were separated by ethnicity. Unlike the Euroamerican bosses and workers who lived mostly as bachelors in government housing and tent camps, the Apache workers brought their families to live with them in segregated camps. They built traditional wickiups of poles and brush near Roosevelt, on hillsides, along the power canal, and along the roads leading to the mining town of Globe. The remains of the wickiup sites were indicated only by subtle, cleared areas, sometimes ringed with rocks.

Archaeologists of Dames & Moore documented almost 150 wickiup locations among five Apache camps near Roosevelt, grouped into clusters varying from 6 to 87 wickiups per camp. These camps and the artifacts recovered from them, along with historical records, provided the basis for reconstructing Apache life in the Roosevelt construction camps.

The Apache laborers worked together in crews to build the roads. They were valued for their skill in dry masonry—laying and fitting rocks without mortar to construct road embankments in the rugged Tonto Basin environs. The most famous of these roads is the Apache Trail, the sinuous, steep, torturous road extending along the Salt River from Roosevelt to Mesa. It cost half a million dollars to build (Rogge and others 1995:144).

A typical work crew consisted of four to five teamsters and another six to eight men with shovels, each of whom was paid $2.50 per day. Only a few Apache were employed as subforemen on these work crews; they received $3.50 to $4.00 each day. The wages of Apache laborers and subforemen were equivalent to those paid to non-Apache workers.

Roosevelt boasted restaurants and numerous entertainments—an ice-cream parlor, a bowling alley, saloons, hot springs, tennis courts, and a pool hall. Dances, horse races, and sports events were held. The Apaches participated in few of these entertainments. Even the baseball teams were rigidly defined by racial and ethnic composition.

Archaeologists were surprised by the extent to which Apache lifeways in the Roosevelt construction camps adhered to tradition. Social structure and camp organization, religious practices, domestic life, and even foods and cooking equipment conformed to time-honored Apache ways. The camps were organized along traditional family lines. The *gota* were clusters of traditional *gowa* representing extended families. The largest of the camps housed about 20 of these families. The Apache extended-family organization affected the work schedule at Roosevelt. Men would work only as long as they needed to and would frequently take lengthy absences to deal with family or clan obligations (Rogge and others 1995:136).

The Apache conducted the puberty ceremonial, or *nai'es,* for young women coming of age, held traditional dances, and treated the dead with Apache rites. During the mortuary ceremony, the deceased's property was burned or otherwise destroyed. There were several reasons for this practice that revolved around the Apache's deep respect for and avoidance of death and ghosts. The deceased's wickiup and possessions were burned, and those objects that would not burn were destroyed in some fashion. An axe or knife was used to slash buckets and washbasins or punch holes in the bottoms. This was done to prevent anyone from using them, which would attract the unwelcome attention of the dead.

In their camps, Apache women cooked customary foods over open fires. In this aspect of daily life, it is difficult to separate what may have been traditional preferences from the poverty and ethnic discrimination the Apache suffered. Whereas the boarding houses in Roosevelt fed the Euroamerican workers lavishly with fresh vegetables, meat, fruit, and pies, the Apache consumed a bland, heavy diet based on bread, coffee, and meat. The women baked ash bread, a tortilla-like bread made of flour, water, and baking powder, on a wire grill over the fire. A traditional beverage was *tulapai,* a mildly alcoholic beer made from sprouted, ground, and fermented corn. The range of food containers was limited, and few nonstaple food, medicine, and beverage containers were found in the Apache camps.

Apache Respect for the Dead

Anthropologist Richard J. Perry lived and worked among the San Carlos Apache for many years. He writes about the ways in which the Apache beliefs concerning death and the dead reinforced lifeways and social organization in prereservation times (Perry 1991:161–162):

> The feeling of dread associated with the scene of death, the destruction of the [deceased's] dwelling, and the abandonment of the [death] site all tended to ensure that groups would not become "locked into" any particular locality but would continue to cover wide territories. By the same token, strictures against mentioning the name of the deceased effectively prevented any deep genealogically based structures that might have led to more rigid social units.

Few, if any, Euroamerican cooking utensils were found. Traditional Apache material culture had evidently not been replaced by twentieth-century containers and kitchenware. Whether the Apache could have afforded such items is doubtful. Instead, various discarded items were recycled to serve domestic needs. The Apache twisted wire together to make grills for baking ash bread. They poked holes in the bottoms of large, metal cans or lard buckets and attached handles to make strainers for the cooked, ground corn used in *tulapai*. The Apache made drinking cups with handles by bending back and folding the lids of tin cans. They reused five-gallon oil and blasting-powder cans as storage containers and recycled empty canvas cement bags as tarps to cover *gowa*. The Apache reused almost every item in some way. One can readily see the women poking through the refuse dumps looking for useful items—and at the same time affecting the distribution of garbage that historical archaeologists would later study.

Roosevelt was an isolated, hot, and deadly place. "Tunneling, blasting, cutting rock, mixing concrete, and grading roads, all the work of building Theodore Roosevelt Dam, used human muscle rather than heavy machinery" (Rogge and others 1995:89). That labor took its toll on human life. Two dozen workers lost their lives in construction accidents, about one every four months. Disease—typhoid, smallpox, a variety of less serious illnesses—spread through the crowded camps. Alcohol took a great toll. In the early 1900s, the Apache were suffering from deterioration of their traditional culture. One of its most damaging effects was excessive alcohol consumption. At Roosevelt, suicide, murder, and accidents were directly related to alcohol abuse among Apache and non-Apache alike. With Prohibition impending, alcohol was banned within a dry zone surrounding the dam site, forcing laborers to drink patent medicines, bootleg liquor, or visit saloons outside the dry boundary. One of these saloons was closed after an Apache died from drinking wood alcohol sold to him there (Rogge and others 1995:108).

Al Sieber's death is perhaps the best known of accidental deaths at Roosevelt. Sieber had been chief of scouts at San Carlos for 20 years beginning in 1871. Under General Crook, he led Apache scouts to locate Indian resisters, including Geronimo. At Roosevelt, Sieber was valued for his ability to communicate with and supervise the Apache workmen. When the accident happened, he was working as the foreman of an Apache crew using dynamite to build the wagon road along Tonto Creek. In his early sixties and limping from old rifle wounds, Sieber was attempting to move a precariously balanced boulder and was crushed when the stone dislodged and he was unable to get out of its path. A monument paid for by the Apache work crew commemorates his death (Rogge and others 1995:117).

Memorial to Al Sieber along Arizona State Route 188 at Theodore Roosevelt Lake. Photograph by Jefferson Reid.

Life at Roosevelt was clearly hard, and some of the Apache laborers were evidently believers in Daagodighá, a messianic cult or revitalization movement. Its followers believed that they would be "raised up to the sky" at the appointed time, when the earth would be purged of evil and the believers would return to a rejuvenated world of peace and plenty (Rogge and others 1995:25).

When President Theodore Roosevelt dedicated the dam that bears his name in 1911, he shook hands with several of the 30 Apache workers who had come to the ceremony, thanked them for their efforts, and presented them with awards. A banner reading "Apaches Helped Build Roosevelt Dam" graced the dedication (Rogge and others 1995:132). It is likely that building Theodore Roosevelt Dam was beneficial for the most part. Working for wages at Roosevelt was incorporated into the traditional round. An unexpected benefit was that the Apache workers and their families could live somewhat more freely and in a traditional manner in the Roosevelt camps than on the reservation. On the reservation, they were forced to cut their hair and wear western garb instead of their traditional dress; children were required to go to school. An order by the San Carlos agent to round up school-age children at the Roosevelt camps was rescinded, and the children were permitted to stay with their families.

When Theodore Roosevelt Dam was completed, Phoenix began its phenomenal growth toward a desert metropolis. When construction was over, "the Apaches, Mexicans, and hoboes went elsewhere looking for jobs. And the Salt River valley farmlands, now with an ample, assured supply of water and worth far more on the market than before, remained in the same old hands" (Worster 1985:173). The Apache, never among the Southwest's most prolific farmers, returned to the San Carlos Reservation where they were able to farm even less than before, as the water they had helped to impound flowed to other people's farms.

Bellotas

Rosalía Salazar Whelan (Martin 1992:157–158) recalled meeting Apache who came to her father's ranch in Aravaipa Canyon to pick *bellotas* (acorns):

> The Apache Indians used to come down from the San Carlos Reservation every summer during the bellota season. They'd stop at the house to visit my father. They called him "El Paisano"; they were very fond of him. Whole troops of them would come on horseback, and the minute they arrived they would go to the milpa to cut hay for their horses. . . . They'd tether them on long ropes and then feed them. They'd also help themselves to the produce in the garden, especially the corn. How they loved the corn! They roasted it on the open fire.

Paradise in the Desert: The Story of Mormon Farming

According to Mormon historian James McClintock (1985:2), one of the foundations of the Church of Jesus Christ of Latter-day Saints is the belief that "its membership shall live by, upon and through the products of the soil." Nowhere was this belief more sorely tested than in Arizona. In this section, we look at Mormon farming in the Transition Zone and the nearby Little Colorado River valley—places where strength, faith, and determination were pitted against a capricious and often fierce natural world. Historian Charles Peterson (1973:177) has pointed out that this struggle was repeated in many places across the Southwest. The process of taming desert streams "dominated the lives of those who stayed as it dictated the departure of many who left."

Southwestern Utah and northwestern Arizona were settled by pioneers from Salt Lake City in the 1850s. Joseph Smith believed that colonization was directed by God, a manifestation of His will that the Mormon kingdom would no longer be limited to a narrow refuge in some Zion but would spread over the two American continents (Peterson 1973:5). Great excitement had greeted the discovery that cotton could be grown along the Muddy and Virgin Rivers, and the cotton-producing region became known as Utah's "Dixie" (Lavender 1984). A series of severe rainstorms and floods proved how harsh the land could be, and nascent towns, dams, ditches, and fields disappeared under torrents of raging water. Indian raiders devastated the stock that supplemented the farmers' incomes. Worst still was the national depression of the 1870s that severely impacted stock raising (Lavender 1984). Spurred by these and other events, exploring parties were sent to Arizona in the quest for better lands. The upper and lower Little Colorado River valley and the Silver Creek drainage were settled. Settlers also pushed into the intermontane basins, such as the Tonto Basin and Payson Basin. Eventually, Mormon settlers colonized the Salt River valley, where metropolitan Phoenix would spring up, and portions of southeastern Arizona.

Colonists took the treacherous route from Kanab, Utah, to Lee's Ferry across the Colorado River, and then on to Moenkopi and the Little Colorado River valley. The initial explorers returned disappointing reports about the barren land and its streams. They described the Little Colorado River as a "loathsome little stream. . . . As disgusting a stream as there is on the continent" (Peterson 1973:12). It was also "a treacherous stream at best, with a broad channel that wanders at will through the alluvial country that melts like sugar or salt at the touch of water" (McClintock 1985:141). Lot Smith called it a "strange country, belonging to a people whose land the rivers have spoiled" (cited in McClintock 1985:142).

The country's disadvantages were not necessarily a wholesale deterrent to settlement, for Mormons believed themselves to be as persecuted in their potential farmlands as in other aspects of life. Church leader George Cannon, quoted by Peterson (1973:9), wrote that "The worst places in the land we can probably get, and we must develop them. If we were to find a good country how long would it be before the wicked would want it and seek to strip us of our possessions?" By that time, Mormons had already suffered decades of persecution in the East and Midwest, and their sufferings had been likened to the crucifixion of Christ. "Certainly, the Little Colorado River left an indelible mark upon the colony that depended upon it" (Peterson 1973:177).

Thank God for Deserts

Mormon leader George Q. Cannon penned the following passage in his discourses (cited in Peterson 1973:9):

> If there be deserts in Arizona, thank God for the deserts. If there be wilderness there, thank God for the wilderness. . . . When we go hence to extend our borders we must not expect to find a land of orange or lemon groves, a land where walnut trees and hard timber abound; where bees are wild and turkeys can be had for the shooting. . . . But if we find a little oasis in the desert where a few can settle, thank God for the oasis.

To Brigham Young, settling the Little Colorado region was not a question of the nature of the land or water but of fortitude and obedience (Peterson 1973:9). The middle Little Colorado River, with its perennial flow and broad, alluvial valley, was a natural target for Mormon colonization. Although the Little Colorado carries less water than many of the Southwest's streams, the volume along its arable middle stretches was a treasure in that waterless land lying on the boundary of the Transition Zone and the Colorado Plateau. Moreover, the settlers had little choice. The better land, including the likely farmland higher in the Silver Creek drainage, had already been taken by Indian or nonnative settlers (Peterson 1973:17). The Little Colorado region would become more attractive by necessity as it became apparent that Young's mind was firmly made up. The horrifying constraints imposed by the river and the climate would not be felt until the settlers had battled with the river again and again.

The land along the Little Colorado River receives only 8–10 inches of rainfall each year and is further desiccated by the fierce southwesterly winds that give Winslow the "dubious distinction as the windiest town in Arizona" (Welch and Ciolek-Torrello 1994:75). The soil is alkaline, quicksand makes the riverbed treacherous, and the river is subject to unpredictable and destructive variations in flow much like the Salt River (Welch 1992, 1994b). Floods would repeatedly wash out the Mormon dams.

The settler's first objective was to control the water. "Water for irrigation and a means to control the floods . . . were the first concerns of the settlers. . . . Unless the river could be controlled, the colony would not survive" (Ferg and others 1988:12). This task would not be easily achieved, however. Water development was more than a matter of persistence, as Peterson (1973:19) has pointed out. It "was also a question of sustaining life, and only by the most determined effort and by heavy subsidy were the settlers able to do so."

Early water development focused on diverting, impounding, and transporting water. Water was sometimes diverted from the streambed by rock walls into which headgates were built. Diversion dams were more common. Initial expectations that small dams would suffice proved dismally incorrect, and larger dams or repeated rebuilding were necessary (Peterson 1973:177–178). Working together, men of the camps began to build dams and ditches. Enterprise and will proved insufficient means to success, however. McClintock (1985:141–142) chronicles the struggle of the St. Joseph settlers to build dams, a tale that also reflects on the intransigence of the Little Colorado River. The first dam was a combined effort of two communities, cost $5,000, and required 960 days to complete. Although wide and thick, it was only 12 feet high, and a month after it was completed, it was washed down river in the first summer flood. In the spring of 1877, a second dam was built one and one-half miles upstream. It also washed away. Two years later, they tried a third dam site at LeRoux Wash just west of modern Holbrook, with the same result. More attempts followed; a dam built in 1882 remained in use until 1892, but had to be repaired almost every year. In 1894, it was estimated that the community of 15 families had lost $50,000 on dam-building efforts, making St. Joseph "the leading community in pain, determination and unflinching courage in dealing with the elements around them" (McClintock 1985:142).

Little Colorado River in flood. PHOTOGRAPH BY JEFFERSON REID.

After the early years, settlers attempted to impound water in reservoirs to supplement natural stream flow when irrigation needs were great (Peterson 1973:179). Unfortunately, upstream reservoirs were often breached, sweeping away dams on the lower stretches of the river near St. Joseph and Woodruff (Peterson 1973:179).

Last, the settlers built irrigating ditches. Like the first dams, these were relatively small constructions, rarely being more than six feet wide or deep. Despite their size, they often ran considerable distances and required labor and money to construct and maintain. Difficult conditions included the "sugary" character of the sandy soil, which gobbled up water in the ditches; volcanic deposits that drained water from ditches; and gully washers that filled them with sediment. Ditch cleaning was a job the colonists knew all too well (Peterson 1973:180).

All of the settlements along the Little Colorado River struggled to maintain the water supply and to control the stream. How many times, McClintock (1985:141) wondered, "each of the poor struggling communities had to rally back on the sands of the river bed to build up anew the structure of gravel and brush that must be depended upon, if bread were to be secured from the land." Moreover, production tended to be inversely correlated with the effort put into water control. In 1876, only one of the Little Colorado settlements produced a crop, and it was said to be little more than 75 bushels of grain and a few melons (Peterson 1973:19). Land, by contrast, required little labor investment to clear and plow. Despite this, Little Colorado colonists submitted to sharp restrictions on acreage. Most did not develop large personal landholdings, but rather submitted to church interests and authority (Peterson 1973:161).

Spiritual means bolstered Mormon confidence in the wake of repeated failures and inspired them to build again (Leone 1979). In the Little Colorado River valley, where floods washed out dams with depressing regularity, the Mormons heard sermons from the leadership telling them that the failure of their dams was God's way of testing them for their mettle and determination.

Yet the bulk of the work was accomplished by more practical means. Church organization helped to build and repair dams when individual efforts failed and local coffers were empty. Day-to-day canal and dam construction and maintenance were placed into the hands of the local community, however. The community elected a supervisor to oversee allocation of water and construction of waterworks. Economic as well as ideological value was attached to volunteer labor, and such labor was a form of paying tithes. For example, each of the brethren was called upon to donate one day of labor to the Woodruff dam, which had been breached periodically (McClintock 1985:162).

A Study in Postponed Defeat

The first dam at Woodruff was built in 1877. In all, the community built 13 dams, 11 of which were lost to the flooding river. One was cut voluntarily, and one was still surviving in the 1970s when Peterson (1973) wrote his story of farming in the Little Colorado River valley. First hammered by floods that swept away dams number two through eight, the community enjoyed a respite between 1886 and 1890, when meteorological changes gave the people hope that they had conquered the river. In 1890, it all began once more. The twelfth dam, a masonry structure built with church assistance, was destroyed in 1915. The thirteenth dam was completed in 1919.

Communal enterprises under local church supervision were the first attempt by the lower river settlements to keep mercantile profits within the community and distribute any surplus to best advantage. The Arizona Cooperative Mercantile Institution was an umbrella organization for Mormon-led businesses. With its freighting operations, livestock, and wool industry, the group eventually became sufficiently solvent to provide supplies to Mormon towns and buffer them from the incursions of gentile business (McGuire 1980). Abruzzi (1989) has argued that the joint enterprises were not initially successful because they competed directly with agriculture for labor and financial resources. A tithe-based redistribution system begun in 1882 was more successful. As long as some of the regional community's members had productive years, the effects of environmental variability and destructive impacts could be eased, ensuring that all of the constituent settlements were successful (Welch and Ciolek-Torrello 1994). One factor in the ultimate success of the Little Colorado region's Mormon communities was diversification, according to anthropologist Thomas McGuire (1980). Along with cooperative efforts and redistribution, a diversified economic strategy helped ameliorate the constraints of high-altitude farming along the Mogollon Rim.

Water control was not the only activity occupying the Little Colorado colonists. Ranches and a sawmill were established to support the four valley villages, and an Indian mission was founded at Moenkopi, a farming colony of Oraibi (Peterson 1973:21). Settlements soon expanded along Silver Creek on unclaimed land or tracts sold by earlier Mexican and American settlers. A third area of colonization was the upper Little Colorado River region.

Along the Mogollon Rim, Mormon settlement and economy proceeded along different lines than in the river valley, and this diversified, regional strategy was responsible for the ultimate success of the rim communities (Abruzzi 1989). Collection and redistribution of resources throughout the larger Little Colorado region buffered shortfalls among individual settlements.

The Mormons watered their stock from mountain streams, springs, and stock tanks they constructed. They directed much of the water to their irrigated farms (McGuire 1980:50). Natural and prehistoric water-control systems often showed the way. Near what would become the town of Payson, for example, settlers took advantage of a beaver dam to begin an irrigation canal (McClintock 1985:174). Mormon settlers along the rim aggressively pursued water rights. They often purchased unsurveyed and unrecorded water rights from the original squatters, instigating decades of legal wrangling.

PHOTOGRAPH BY STEPHANIE WHITTLESEY.

Mormon settlers also apportioned land through the church. Each new arrival at the settlement of Snowflake was given rights to a town lot on which to build and two farm plots of 10 acres each. According to McGuire (1980:41), these holdings were inadequate to support growing families, and the farmers would seek other means to survive.

The experiences of Hans Hansen may be typical of such homesteaders. After an unsuccessful attempt at dry farming near Show Low, Hansen desperately needed arable land that could be irrigated. In 1893, he purchased the rights of an earlier homestead at Woodland. There he built a ditch to irrigate his fields, cultivated vegetables, and raised chickens, hogs, and milk cows (McGuire 1980:52). Soon additional families bought other lots near Hansen and renamed the area Lakeside. They cleared farms, built irrigation ditches, and dammed a spring-fed creek to form Rainbow Lake (Schuck 1978).

As in the lower Little Colorado River valley, many of the rim communities suffered financially and economically in attempts to build irrigation systems. The settlers at St. Johns conceived the idea of building a dam across the river to create a reservoir for irrigation water. The church provided $5,000, and an irrigation company was formed. The dam was completed at a cost of $200,000 (an enormous sum in early 1900s dollars) and the reservoir filled. In 1915, the dam washed away, eight people were killed, and hundreds of acres of downstream farmland were flooded (McClintock 1985:183).

Mormons soon realized that the livestock industry was best suited to the rugged land of the Arizona mountain belt. It was largely untouched by the vicissitudes of drought and unstable markets and became increasingly attractive around the turn of the twentieth century. At 7,000 feet above sea level, survival demanded diversification. The communities soon broke with church doctrine regarding interaction with gentiles and the value of self-sufficient agriculture and entered the regional economy, becoming masons, sawyers, cowboys, sheepherders, and freighters.

Soon after settlements were founded along the Little Colorado River, exploration of the area to the southwest began. The first explorations were made in 1876, and reports were unfavorable. The upper Tonto Basin was settled in 1878 (McClintock 1985:174). Mormon settlement never gained a foothold in the Tonto Basin proper, although small settlements were founded at Pine, Strawberry, along the East Verde River, and in Pleasant Valley. Most of the land holdings were small, and the water supply was irregular (McClintock 1985:176). The paramount obstacle to settlement was the Western Apache (McClintock 1985:175). Remote and plagued by frequent Apache raiding, many of the small towns never prospered.

The nature of the land and its water created even greater obstacles, as Welch (1994b) has pointed out. There was little land suitable for irrigated farming, and of necessity the farms were small. In 1891, only 800 acres in small patches and strips along Salt River and Tonto Creek were irrigated by small ditches. In 1902, a survey of the proposed reservoir site for Theodore Roosevelt Dam showed only about 740 acres of cultivated land that would be submerged. Those few settlers who attempted to file irrigation claims in the Tonto Basin focused on Tonto Creek rather than Salt River. Despite the booming, hungry mining communities in Globe and Miami, commercial farming never blossomed. Welch and Ciolek-Torrello (1994) admit that to some degree, the failure of Mormon settlement in Tonto Basin is an anomaly. "Abandonment of all Tonto Basin settlements was authorized at a meeting of President Woodruff with the heads of the Arizona Stakes, held at Albuquerque August 14, 1890" (McClintock 1985:176). The Mormons moved on to better agricultural conditions elsewhere.

For further information, see: Winfred Buskirk, The Western Apache: Living with the Land before 1950 *(University of Oklahoma Press, Norman, 1986); Grenville Goodwin,* The Social Organization of the Western Apache *(University of Chicago Press, Chicago, 1969); James H. McClintock,* Mormon Settlement in Arizona *(University of Arizona Press, Tucson, 1985); Richard J. Perry,* Western Apache Heritage: People of the Mountain Corridor *(University of Texas Press, Austin, 1991) and* Apache Reservation: Indigenous Peoples and the American State *(University of Texas Press, Austin, 1993); Charles S. Peterson,* Take Up Your Mission: Mormon Colonizing along the Little Colorado River, 1870–1900 *(University of Arizona Press, Tucson, 1973); Jefferson Reid and Stephanie Whittlesey,* The Archaeology of Ancient Arizona *(University of Arizona Press, Tucson, 1997), and* Grasshopper Pueblo: A Story of Archaeology and Ancient Life *(University of Arizona Press, Tucson, 1999); A. E. Rogge, D. Lorne McWatters, Melissa Keane, and Richard P. Emanuel,* Raising Arizona's Dams: Daily Life, Danger, and Discrimination in the Dam Construction Camps of Central Arizona, 1890s–1940s *(University of Arizona Press, Tucson, 1995).*

Sandstorm

In the monsoon season, desert sandstorms may boil up across the agricultural landscape of central Arizona. Blinded by sand and dust, unwary motorists on the interstate highways are sometimes caught in multiple vehicle accidents. A sandstorm is a frightening, claustrophobic experience that reminds us of human fragility in the face of elemental forces.

The sky is a vast, ochre dome
Clamping down on unseen horizons.
The air boils with flotsam:
    Topsoil, chips of bone, runaway dreams.
    Powdered corpses, torn blossoms, and
    the haunted pieces of broken hearts.
Grit grates under the eyelids and blots our tears.
Be still, and attempt to breathe.

Curtains of sand hide feathered serpents. Their lashing
    tails send whirlwinds churning. They leave clawed
    footprints in the shrieking, twisting air.
Their charred, bitter breath burns up our illusions.
Our throats choke on the ashes of dried promises.

This desert is damned.
Its rivers are plugged with spoiled visions. Streams cra-
    dle emptiness and the dust of our sins.
Scant, chemical rain evaporates,
    trailing faint virga of hope.
    Teasing,
    cruel,
The culebra de agua brings flattened fields, drowned
    corn.

Knock us to our knees, serpent. Remind us of
Forgotten duties, obligations abandoned
For arrogant ambitions and unholy lusts.
    Teach us to pray.
Caught in its coils, we could do little but seek
earth's forgiveness.

Trapped in the windstorm of decay, the taste of smoke
    lingers on lips
That long for the blessing of water.

Slackwater

A Landscape View of Water

In a Stone-Dry Land

7

Where did rivers come from and where did they go, was always his beginning point. Rivers changed their course over time, and that history made him curious. Rivers washed away dirt and uncovered a past when strange forms of life swam the waters and walked the earth. The land was constantly in motion, presenting a different face to its inhabitants from year to year.

—Donald Worster, *A River Running West: The Life of John Wesley Powell*

Archaeology inherits the earth; most places contain the debris and cradle the memory of innumerable past events.

—David Lowenthal, *The Past is a Foreign Country*

***Midstream* recounted stories** of life in a stone-dry land. We have seen some of the ingenious ways people have used to live in desert Arizona for thousands of years. Sometimes highly practical, often spiritual, these techniques molded the raw material of desert land and water into a rich, nourishing context for life. Although sharing an environment that presented similar challenges and offered similar advantages, each people solved the problem of desert living in different, often distinctive ways. In this section, we step back to take a larger view of desert living and make comparisons, focusing on the substance most vital to desert life—water. We will look at some of the approaches that sustained people in their adjustment to a land of little rain and rivers of rock. We will also examine the ideas that were not so viable, that impacted the environment, fueled the runaway growth of the twentieth century, and had other negative consequences.

In our discussion, we take advantage of archaeology's unique perspective—tremendous time depth and diachronic viewpoint—to make our

Central Arizona Project canal. Photograph courtesy U.S. Bureau of Reclamation.

comparisons and give them contextual meaning. We use the overarching cultural-landscapes approach introduced in the prologue to structure this discussion. This chapter seeks to engage readers in topics to which they may have given only cursory attention—particularly the ability of humankind to effect alterations to the land, both good and bad, and our infinite capacity to change.

The prehistoric Hohokam, the Church of Jesus Christ of Latter-day Saints, and the Bureau of Reclamation can be seen as three different points along a continuum of water control and desert living, and we will use these groups as our examples. Each group had its own set of techniques and mechanisms for controlling and using water. They also developed unique social relationships, political arrangements, and patterns of power. Most important, culture, beliefs, and perception created the distinctive structural and organizational armature of each group and in turn shaped a cultural landscape—the physical and biological environments transformed by human thought and action.

Little Colorado River at Grand Falls. PHOTOGRAPH BY JEFFERSON REID.

In this chapter, we will look at the ways in which the environment shaped these three societies and how they created an environment that was not wholly natural but the product of their interactions with it. In other words, we will examine how perceptions, ideologies, and religious beliefs created cultural landscapes. Next, we will look at the different

Alone in the Desert

Eva Antonia Wilbur-Cruce (Martin 1992:183) describes her relationship to the land when she was growing up near Arivaca, southern Arizona, during the earlier part of the twentieth century:

> There were times when I would go up to the water hole and be so tired and sick. It was so hot. I would get under an oak tree where one branch had fallen and lay across it. I pressed hard against the tree and could feel something along my arms—a thumping. . . . I felt some sort of nutrition coming from the tree. It gave me a lift; it gave me the stamina that I didn't have. I couldn't go anywhere or do anything but look at the blue distance. It spoke, and the wind sang and moaned. I learned to listen to the silence. When you are not alone, you sit and hear, but you don't pay attention to what you hear. When we are alone, ah, that's when we listen, and that's when we hear. We hear the wind sing and nature pulsate.

Cathedral Rock and Oak Creek near Sedona, Arizona. PHOTOGRAPH BY STEPHANIE WHITTLESEY.

ways land and water were used according to cultural perceptions. We will examine important issues in water use, such as the scale of water-control systems and the group or institution controlling water. Last, we will discuss the consequences of people interacting with their environments. How successful was the humanized environment in sustaining life and culture over the long term? Decision making regarding the ways to modify and use the land and its water sometimes had damaging consequences, and we will consider those as well. In our comparisons, we will learn a great deal about life in this stone-dry land.

Hohokam

The prehistoric cultures we have examined in this book—Ancestral Pueblo, Salado, and Hohokam—and historical-period Native Americans, including O'odham, Hopi, Navajo, and Western Apache, are the least complicated along the continuum of water-control technology. Worster (1985) would call them "local subsistence farmers." In these kinds of societies, "[t]here is no centralized seat of command, no stratification of people into social and economic classes, no large accumulations of private wealth, no elaborate division of labor, no state" (Worster 1985:32). Water control is small in scale and interferes minimally with the natural flow of streams. Control is maintained within the community, and organization is loose and unconsolidated, generally executed along kinship and family lines. The products of farming remain within the community, and consumption is largely personal and direct, although certain foodstuffs may be exchanged out of the community. Perhaps most significant, ideology and religion often determine the ways people used land and water. Spiritual values support and maintain subsistence, water control, and land use in these societies. This does not mean that either water control or social organization is simplistic. We must be careful not to judge other cultures in terms of our own technology and organization.

The Hohokam represent this level of water-control technology well, for from the beginning of archaeological studies, it was understood that Hohokam culture, territory, and lifeways were shaped by water. Haury (1976:354) wrote:

> the natural surroundings determined what the people *could* do. . . . [M]an's responses to the opportunities provided by physical resources of the earth became functions of culture through the application of the technology available to them. To a point, the natural surroundings determined Hohokam behavior, but it was their attitude, will, and skills that decided the effective use of the habitat. . . . [T]hrough the centuries there were refinements in water management, increases in canal mileage, and expansion of acreage brought under cultivation.

Haury thought that the key barrier to cultural progress was the aridity of the Sonoran Desert, which he called "a parched land." The Hohokam solved this problem "by taking the water from the river and putting it where it was needed" (Haury 1976:354). Away from the river, they developed inventive methods to capture and divert floodwater and to conserve precious moisture from rainfall.

Values and Ideology

Perhaps the lack of evidence for political complexity among the Hohokam, a topic we discuss at the end of this section, can be attributed to the dominance of spiritual means for controlling water, coping with scarcity, and distributing the bounty of the land. We have seen that the Hohokam developed a rich, multifaceted cultural context that included ideological, religious, and ceremonial means to control and use water. Their beliefs apparently centered on deities and spirits dwelling in mountains and caves who brought beneficial and destructive rain. The sacred landscape reconstructed the cosmos and symbolized important phenomena related to water, such as mountains. Hohokam ceremonials reenacted mythological events and perhaps controlled the distribution of irrigation water. Their prayers no doubt petitioned the gods for rain to fill the irrigation canals and wash over the fields and asked that floods not destroy their canals and villages. In combination with the Hohokam's highly efficient and flexible water-control technology, their religious system evidently functioned effectively. Together, technology and spiritual beliefs helped the Hohokam adjust to environmental vicissitudes—too much rain or not enough, damaging floods, droughts that withered the wild plants and crops, insects that devoured the ripening corn—for centuries.

Scale and Form of Control

Although the physical size of irrigation-canal networks and the labor required in construction were impressive, the system nevertheless was moderately scaled. The Hohokam lacked metal tools, impermeable materials with which to line canals, methods of pumping water, and domesticated animals to pull digging tools and lift water. These deficiencies constrained the size and location of canal systems and made them subject to the effects of seepage, erosion, and sedimentation. Hohokam canals were physically limited by terrain and slope; they could not duplicate the Central Arizona Project feat of making water run uphill for hundreds of miles.

I'itoi's Cave

The Baboquivari Mountains southwest of Tucson form the eastern border of the Tohono O'odham Indian Reservation. Towering high above the range is Baboquivari Peak, a sharp, triangular spire of rock that, at 7,730 feet above sea level, can be seen everywhere in Tohono O'odham land. I'itoi's Cave, home of Elder Brother, lies on the flanks of Baboquivari Peak. I'itoi was one of the first three beings that were created and helped the Tohono O'odham to emerge from the underworld into the present world. In the past, I'itoi has left his cave to help the people in times of trouble.

Tohono O'odham and others visit the cave and leave offerings. When Gary Nabhan visited in the 1980s, he found rosary beads, shoelaces, and chains hanging from the ceiling and a jar of saguaro cactus syrup and a green frog effigy on the cave floor. Medallions, bullets, chewing gum, and cigarettes were tucked into niches in the cave walls. The visitors were standing in the cool, damp air of sanctuary that was saying, Nabhan (1982:21) writes: "There is always something hidden in this world, that you can't just realize from the outside. You need to make contact with it now and then, to nod your head in knowing, to receive its blessing."

There were limits on how big the system could grow. As archaeologist W. Bruce Masse (1991:214) has expressed it:

> the Hohokam lacked certain critical engineering features, including permanent dam structures, drop structures, the general use of artificial linings to retard water seepage, and apparently a conception of the use of drainage canals. . . . These omissions prevented the Hohokam from achieving the level of sophistication necessary to deal successfully with various environmental hazards such as field waterlogging and salinization and the destructive effects of catastrophic river flooding.

Control evidently was not centralized but was distributed among the villages sharing river water. In the Phoenix Basin, so-called irrigation communities contained one to five platform-mound villages and other settlements along a

PHOTOGRAPH BY JEFFERSON REID.

single canal system (Gregory 1991). Within an irrigation community, platform mounds were regularly spaced at three-mile intervals—the first was located three miles from the canal intake, the second six miles, and so on. Evidently each canal irrigated the fields of several villages, and the upstream irrigation communities shared water equitably with those downstream. At the canal intake, a diversion weir or headgate sent water from the river into a main canal and thence into secondary canals. The smaller feeder canals, the laterals that distributed water to fields, and the fields were located downstream, often extending for many miles along the main canal.

Although the regular spacing of irrigation communities (and other aspects of Hohokam land use as well) imply that concepts of land tenure existed, we have no evidence that land or water was commodified or privately owned. Each village may have controlled canal maintenance, distributed water, and settled disputes under the supervision of a resident priest or headman, not unlike the Western Apache and Tohono O'odham "ditch bosses." A connection with spiritual control of irrigation water is certainly implied by the presence of regularly spaced platform mounds in light of their presumed religious and ceremonial functions and water-in-the-mountain symbolism.

Manufactured housing along the lower Colorado River near Parker, Arizona. PHOTOGRAPH BY JEFFERSON REID.

Consequences

The success of Hohokam irrigation systems does not mean that their prayers were always successful or that they did not alter the physical landscape. They were unable to achieve complete domination of land and water, despite their masterful irrigation technology, and were not immune to the effects of their land modifications on the natural environment. When these effects coincided with cyclical shifts in climate and environment, the outcome could be disastrous. The actual situation conflicts with a widespread perception, which Shepard Krech (1999) has called the myth of "the ecological Indian," that Native Americans were conservationists who consistently preserved and maintained their environments. The myth derives in large part from nineteenth-century philosophy depicting Native Americans as "noble savages"—authentic, primitive, romantic, mystical. Indians were viewed as having more spiritual and more harmonious relationships with their environment than Europeans (see discussion in Comer [1999:37]). The myth persists today and is responsible for drawing many tourists, especially Europeans nourished on the novels of Karl May and other romantic western writers, to the American Southwest. The consequences of Native Americans' interactions with the land appear minimal in comparison to those created by modern technological interventions only because prehistoric technologies were simple and populations remained comparatively small.

When we look more closely at interactions between the Hohokam and their environment, we discover numerous intentional and unintended consequences of farming practices and other interactions with the land. Farming altered the land, its plant cover, and animal inhabitants. Some changes were minor, even beneficial. Seepage from irrigation ditches favored abundant plant growth, including mesquite, upon which the Hohokam depended heavily (Fish and Nabhan 1991:46). Agricultural weeds with useful properties colonized the fields and margins of the ditches, providing a lush habitat for animals serving as a convenient source of protein (Fish 1989; Szuter 1988). Suspended silt in floodwater and irrigation water enriched the field soils, which was particularly important because desert soils are relatively shallow and lacking in organic materials (Redman 1999:148). We do not know if the Hohokam burned fields to remove trees and brush, but many Native Americans did (Dobyns 1981), and there is some evidence that the Hohokam did as well (Bohrer 1971; Miksicek 1984). Burning fields could have altered soil chemistry to an unknown degree, potentially enriching it.

Other effects were more dramatic and potentially negative. Clearing land to make fields and to build houses altered vegetative cover to the extent that the preferred habitats of rabbit species were altered. In paleofaunal collections, archaeologists have observed a shift over time in percentages of rabbits—from cottontails, which prefer densely vegetated habitats, to jackrabbits, which like open areas. The shift suggests increasingly open land over time in the vicinity of Hohokam settlements (Redman 1999:151; Szuter 1991). It seems likely, however, that the Hohokam spared mesquite *bosques* in the vicinity of their villages because they depended on the plant for food (Redman 1999:151). This meant that other sources of fuel, such as driftwood or dead wood, and construction wood were necessary. Over time, it is likely that nearby wood sources were depleted, and the daily trek for wood would have grown ever longer. Moreover, clearing vegetation would have increased the volume and velocity of runoff, thus increasing the likelihood of soil erosion (Redman 1999:155).

Large pueblo ruin along the lower Verde River. PHOTOGRAPH COURTESY U.S. BUREAU OF RECLAMATION. JOE MADRIGAL, JR., PHOTOGRAPHER.

Irrigation and floodwater farming may have had deleterious effects in the long run. Archaeologists have pointed to the effects of irrigation on soils and the susceptibility of canals to flooding and other damages. An insidious problem for Hohokam farmers would have been salinization, an accumulation of salts in the soil at or near its surface. In irrigated fields, evaporation concentrates salts in the surface water sinking into the soil. Capillary action can bring this excessively salty water to the root zone of crop plants (Redman 1999). Throughout the world in past and present times, salinization of irrigated fields has been a perennial and often unsolvable problem. It would have been a particularly acute problem for Hohokam farmers, because desert river water contains salts even before it has been concentrated through irrigation.

Salinization can be reduced by leaching the fields with enough water to flush out the salts, much as indoor gardeners do with potted plants. This solution would have been difficult in dry years. Another remedy is to lower the water table through digging wells. A third solution is to leave the fields fallow. Growing salt-tolerant crops such as little barley *(Hordeum pusillum)* and reducing plantings of salt-intolerant crops (beans, corn) was another potential strategy (Redman 1999).

Waterlogging of irrigated fields is another likely problem that Hohokam farmers faced, especially those living in the Phoenix area. Before groundwater pumping in the twentieth century, the water table was high there. Hohokam irrigation would have further raised the water table. Draining the land was a solution that the Hohokam may have found difficult or impossible to employ, and there is no solid evidence that they attempted it. Flooding to leach fields of salts may have further increased waterlogging.

The process of irrigation itself had consequences, and coping with these effects was labor intensive. Irrigation canals required continuous maintenance to keep them operational. Archaeologists know from the stratigraphic profiles of excavated canals that they were periodically resurfaced, cleaned, scoured by flooding, and moved in the course of their use lives. Sediment constantly built up in the canal bottoms, requiring the farmers to continually remove the silt to prevent weeds from choking the canal. Water moved slowly in the earth-lined or unlined canals; moisture seeped through and was wasted. Resurfacing the canals was often necessary. Irrigation canals were also highly susceptible to flood damage. Floods swept away diversion weirs and canal headgates, pouring over canal banks onto the fields, drowning plants, and eroding fields located in the floodplain. This problem affected Mexican-American farmers along the Gila River and Aravaipa Creek in the early twentieth century. The streams grew wider through time, washing away fields and good arable land (Martin 1992:45, 150).

Canals that crossed secondary watercourses were particularly subject to flood damage, as a historical example dramatically indicates. The Velasco Ditch at Fort McDowell, located near the confluence of the Verde and Salt Rivers, was used in the early twentieth century. During rainstorms, each arroyo crossing the ditch washed away the embankments and filled the ditch with sand. Berms constructed in a futile attempt to prevent this from happening were washed away in every flood (Hackbarth and Lancaster 1992:429). Hohokam

Working in the Fields

Rosalía Salazar Whelan (Martin 1992:156) recalls what farming was like in Aravaipa Canyon in the early twentieth century:

> Another job that the men did was clean the dams and **acequias.** When the river flooded, the acequias filled with debris and mud. It was heavy, dirty work with a shovel. They also detasseled and picked the corn. Because the corn plants are very tall, we [girls] couldn't reach them. But we helped wherever we *could* reach. After the corn was harvested, it was dried and stored. Whenever we had the chance to sit down, we would remove the kernels from the cob, little by little. *El negocio nunca se acaba.* (The work is never done.)

A river of rock—the Santa Cruz River south of Tucson, Arizona. PHOTOGRAPH BY JEFFERSON REID.

canals, which were similar to the Velasco Ditch in construction, would have been affected in the same way.

Entrenchment, or the process by which a stream cuts downward by erosion, would also have affected irrigation systems. According to hydrologist Barbara Tellman and her colleagues (1997:46), the Verde River had been deepened so much by entrenchment that by 1913 farmers were unable to divert water to fields that were stranded without water far above the riverbed. Hohokam canal systems depending on simple gravity flow would have been particularly vulnerable to entrenchment.

Floodwater farming had its own inherent problems. Anthropologist Richard Ford (1999:78) has described how historical-period Zuni fields were altered through time. Sediment gradually accumulated behind dams used to divert water onto arroyo-mouth fields. The eventual result was level, instead of sloping, fields onto which only rainfall, not floodwater, was directed. The Zuni found it necessary to move field areas when this happened and begin the process anew. Hohokam farmers using the *ak-chin* method might have faced a similar progressive alteration of fields.

Ak-chin farming also had the potential to create significant erosion. Geomorphological studies during the Tucson Aqueduct, Phase B Project (Waters 1989) demonstrated that major settlements were situated near the distal ends of arroyo fans where *ak-chin* fields were located. Through time, erosion and headcutting affected runoff, making it necessary to abandon existing fields and locate new ones in more favorable places. "The loss of gully-mouth fields undoubtedly played a role in the abandonment and relocation of some Hohokam settlements" (Czaplicki 1989:17).

Nature often won the Hohokam's battles with the environment. No doubt there was a reciprocal effect among environment, climatic fluctuations, land modifications, and the solutions Hohokam farmers developed to cope with land-use problems. For example, increased bank erosion and overflow during flood episodes might have followed in the wake of intensive land clearing and destruction of vegetative cover. This may have prompted Hohokam farmers to further modify water-control features and perhaps necessitated moving field locations. It is likely that by such processes Hohokam irrigation altered stream-flow patterns to some extent. Such changes have been documented in historical times. The San Simon River was drastically incised during the floods of 1890, and Olmstead (1919) blames the entrenchment on digging of the Solomonville drainage ditch. Similar problems occurred along the Santa Cruz River channel around the turn of the twentieth century (Schwalen and Shaw 1957).

The Hohokam's mixed subsistence and farming strategies likely allowed them to transcend most of these impacts, although perhaps not the worst. The potentially greater productivity of irrigated fields was offset by the vulnerability of fields and canals to erosion, flooding, waterlogging, and salinization. By locating many fields in other farming contexts—floodwater fields along ephemeral streams, *ak-chin* fields at the mouths of arroyos, dry fields on the higher terraces—the Hohokam reduced their dependence on irrigation. Wild-plant foods provided an excellent bulwark against hunger when the fields were soggy or the canals washed out.

We can see the success of this strategy in the long-term stability of Hohokam farming settlements. Hohokam villages in the Avra Valley along Brawley Wash excavated during the Tucson Aqueduct, Phase B Project were

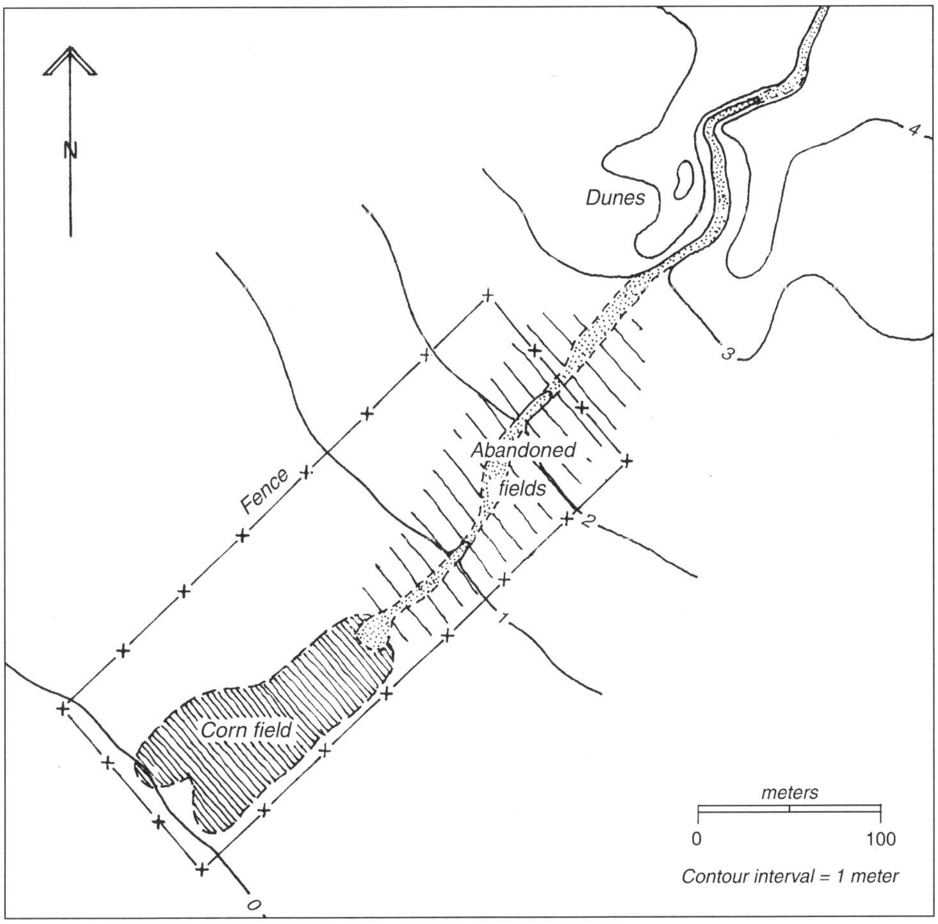

Drawing of an ak-chin field affected by erosion (after Waters 1989:Figure 3.9).

consistently located on the lower *bajadas* where floodwater farming was possible. (Waters 1989:104). Archaeologists found high percentages of agricultural-weed pollen at one of these sites—in fact, among the highest in the Tucson Basin (Fish 1989:247). Corn, cotton, and squash pollen were ubiquitous. The site was located in an area where multiple tributaries of Brawley Wash joined the main drainage to create a large, cumulative watershed. Canals may have been diverted from Brawley Wash, adding floodwater irrigation to the suite of farming possibilities. Few differences were found in the overall distributions of cultivated and wild-plant resources through time, meaning that farming remained successful over the long term.

How lasting were the effects of Hohokam land and water modifications? This is a difficult question to answer. We know that some changes in soil chemistry remain for centuries, for archaeologists can still identify Hohokam fields by altered concentrations of particular elements and minerals. We do not know how long the effects of salt accumulation may have lasted, or how long it would have taken fallow fields to return to their former condition. However permanent these effects may have been, they were apparently not serious enough to affect the Akimel and Tohono O'odham farmers who lived and farmed in many of the same places several hundred years after the Hohokam abandoned them. The productivity of Akimel O'odham fields along the Gila River was remarkable.

PHOTOGRAPH BY JEFFERSON REID.

Throughout pre-Classic times, a fortuitous combination of climate, a diversified economic base, varied farming techniques, and good management helped the Hohokam to survive in their Sonoran Desert home. Paleobotanical and paleofaunal evidence indicates a wetter environment than today's and one that the Hohokam seem not to have significantly altered, judging by their long-term success. In most parts of Hohokam country, population remained relatively low and was dispersed among *ranchería* settlements. The system was self-adjusting, keeping population in line with the ability of the land to support it. The successful strategy persisted until the Classic period, when the effects of climate and land modifications exceeded the Hohokam farmer's ability to adjust.

Disastrous floods have been implicated in the demise of the Classic period Hohokam culture. The Classic period was a time of extreme fluctuation and unpredictability in rainfall. Alternating dry and wet years began around A.D. 1248 and continued until the end of the thirteenth century. The production of crops "would have been a highly uncertain enterprise" at that time (Van West and Altschul 1994: 431). Two decades of high precipitation followed and then three decades of little rainfall. In the 1350s, drought and flooding episodes alternated almost yearly. Extreme flood events in the mid-1300s were separated by less than 25 years. It makes sense that, faced with such extreme conditions, the Hohokam would have abandoned their riverine villages and moved elsewhere (Nials and others 1989). Indeed this seems to have happened in much of Hohokam country; there is little archaeological evidence for occupation after about A.D. 1350, and settlements that remained were small and simple. The Hohokam's mastery of the desert was simply "a prolonged illusion. The desert was master, and the Hohokam were never quite able to throw off the shackles of their environmental bondage" (Masse 1991:222).

The sophistication of Hohokam water-control technology is clear, but its effects on social, political, and economic organization have been debated for decades and remain poorly understood. The controversial scholar Karl Wittfogel believed that irrigation had tremendous consequences and resulted in the development of what he called "hydraulic states." He proposed in *Oriental Despotism: A Comparative Study of Social Power* (Wittfogel 1957) that irrigation's outcome was always repressive use of power. Some archaeologists think that, because the Hohokam used irrigation technology as sophisticated as any in the New World north of Peru, a similar "hydraulic state" must have developed. The Mesoamerican cast of much Hohokam material culture, architecture, and economy gave further support to this notion. Certainly the land and water potential were sufficient to support a large population, and a large labor force would have been necessary to construct, maintain, and operate the canal systems. Archaeologists have estimated that sufficient water was available to irrigate more than 17,000 hectares of land and perhaps as much as 26,000 hectares along the Salt River alone (Nials and others 1989). Fish and Fish (1991:157) suggested that almost 3,500 person-years of labor would have been required to construct the main Classic period canals along the Salt River. This translates into almost 420 years, if 100 men gave one month of service annually (Fish and Fish 1991:157).

Another facet of Hohokam farming that gave rise to the notion of political complexity was the arrangement of their irrigation systems. The spiderweb organization meant that several downstream communities relied on a single source of water (Redman 1999). Centralized control of the main canal, with its ability to send water to downstream fields, would have given those who achieved it a great deal of political power and economic clout.

There is no clear evidence, however, that the Hohokam followed a political trajectory toward complexity. Archaeologists have evidence for relatively large populations, extensive irrigation systems, elaborate religious organization, craft specialization, a communal labor force, and fine arts and crafts. There was no political dominance, militaristic organization, warfare, or human sacrifice, however, as far as can be determined, although these certainly characterized Mesoamerican societies (Fish and Fish 1991:169). In short, the Hohokam remain enigmatic.

Battling Over the Water

Herbert Young (1983) recalls the irrigation canal systems of the later portions of the nineteenth century in the Phoenix area. Impermanent dams made of rocks, poles, and brush took water from rivers into the canals. Wooden headgates were used to divert water from the canal into ditches leading to the fields. Irrigation water was uncertain, even if a farmer held rights to canal water. A farmer living at the end of a canal was at a disadvantage, as people living higher up the canal would attempt to appropriate as much water for themselves as possible. There were times when insufficient water flowed in the canals for diversion, in which case it was necessary to allocate the entire flow on a temporal basis—say, 12 hours for one farmer and the next 12 for an adjacent farmer. This was a basis for dispute, as the flow would often dwindle long before the allocated time was up.

Ditch bosses, or *zanjeros,* pronounced "sankerro" locally, were appointed to allocate water and settle disputes. The *zanjero* would notify farmers as to how long water would be diverted to the fields. Disputes were often acrimonious and not that uncommonly settled by means of firearms and deputy's badges.

Farming Zion: Mormons in the Nineteenth Century

Members of the Church of Jesus Christ of Latter-day Saints built an irrigation society that was highly successful, at least in some places. Called to Arizona, Mormons colonized its desert river valleys and mountain basins. Like the Hohokam before them, Mormon society was founded on control of water. Although they took the bee and its hive as a symbol of their industry, a more appropriate one would have been the beaver, Worster (1985:77) has written, "for control over water became the ecological basis of their society." Mormon society resembled in many ways the structural and organizational category that Worster (1985) has labeled the "agrarian state." Such states characterized much of the preindustrial, prehistoric world, including the agricultural societies of China, Egypt, Mesopotamia, and India. The characteristics of agrarian states, according to Worster (1985), include a bureaucratic organization to design, administer, and control the water system; a redistributive economy; hierarchical social organization; and often standing armies and an imperialist philosophy. The state, often theocratically organized, provided dependable water supplies, built and maintained irrigation works, and distributed and controlled water. In return, water users paid tribute to the state in the form of money or crops. Mormon society shared many of these social and political characteristics, with the church serving as the overarching bureaucratic organization.

Where they succeeded—the Mormons can claim the first commercially successful use of irrigation in the United States—it was often by virtue of the unique features of Mormon society. Hierarchy and group discipline enabled them to maximize water resources and freed them from petty squabbles over water rights. Religiously sanctioned accumulation and distribution of capital helped to support and maintain irrigation works and provided a cushion of security in times of failure. Where the Mormons failed, it was because the desert environment could not be effectively altered by Mormon beliefs, social organization, and technology.

Values and Ideology

We have seen that religious beliefs and teachings permeated secular life. Government was theocratic, and church leaders wielded substantial power in nonreligious activities and decisions. Mormon society was communal, in contrast to the strongly independent character valued by gentile (non-Mormon) American society. Private ownership was restricted, tithing was mandatory, and surplus goods were given to the church for redistribution. Cooperative economic efforts were the rule rather than the exception. Moreover, Mormons set themselves apart from American government. Although many of these features contributed to their success as an irrigation society, they also fostered persecution and isolation.

The Mormon state was nothing less than imperial in its ideals (Worster 2001:263). Brigham Young envisioned a church empire stretching from Utah to Los Angeles, which he intended to be the Mormon seaport. Colonists from across the nation and many foreign countries would help the Mormons maintain their independence against the competing, secular American empire. Utah's Dixie was settled as part of the plan to open a corridor to the sea via the Colorado River, an idea that Young and other church authorities had entertained since Lieutenant Ives steamed up Black Canyon (Crampton 1972:107). In 1873, Young was even planning to build his own railroad, linking with the new Atlantic & Pacific line south of Salt Lake City (Worster 2001:273). The Saints' expansion was bolstered by the authority of scripture and the moral right to take possession of new lands in the name of God.

The Mormons proceeded with the confidence that, not only had God picked out a part of the desert for their homeland, he would ensure that they thrived in it. Mormons sought a refuge from the evils of the world in the desert valleys of Zion; these beliefs fostered separation and isolation from the rest of American society. It was an agrarian and antiurban philosophy modeled in part on the prevailing agrarian lifestyle of the West and in part on an Old Testament view of pastoral and agricultural life (Peterson 1973:155). The geographic isolation that resulted from failing to embrace mainstream industrial and commercial enterprises, such as mining, reflected the church's efforts to hold the world at arm's length (Peterson 1973:156). These beliefs drove the Saints to deliberately choose remote, often desolate places.

These beliefs and values affected how Mormons viewed the land and its water. Nature was given to the Saints by divine right as a reward for labor and faith and for enduring persecution. They practiced the gospel of desert conquest by divine sanction, and they believed that they were destined to make their living from the soil. The land was imbued with a spirituality that the rest of America did not sense.

Personal watercraft for rent on Lake Havasu. PHOTOGRAPH BY JEFFERSON REID.

These beliefs did not prevent the Mormons from battling the land or overusing it, however. The environment was an adversary, and their relationship with it was militant and militaristic. Whereas Native Americans believed that water, land, living creatures, and cultivated plants were given to them by benevolent spiritual beings for their own use—provided they used these benisons wisely and thankfully—Mormons believed that they were on earth to master nature. Essentially, Mormons were at war with nature, and they considered themselves an army of God that would unquestioningly rebuild dams again and again. These earthly labors were directly linked with spiritual salvation. The Saints explained the disastrous events that often befell them as a way of God's testing them, and they transformed defeat into another chance to show their worthiness to be God's chosen (Leone 1979). Persecution and failure helped to knit together their emerging Mormon ethnic group (Limerick 1987).

Gentile and Mormon Americans shared the belief that they could dominate the land, but these views were founded on vastly different value systems. Non-Mormon Ameri-

This Vast Worthless Area

Daniel Webster, arguing against the lands ceded to the United States by the Treaty of Guadalupe Hidalgo after the Mexican War, asked (McNamee 1994:83):

> What do we want with this vast worthless area—this region of savages and wild beasts, of shifting sands and whirlwinds of dust, of cactus and prairie dogs? To what use could we ever hope to put those great deserts and endless mountain ranges?

Colorado River in Rocky Mountain National Park, Colorado. Photograph by Jefferson Reid.

cans cast their faith in technology and in the standards of evidence and truth set up by nineteenth-century science (Worster 2001:291). Mormon doctrine was essentially closed to, or immune from, such standards. Whereas the gentile believed that rain followed the plow, the Mormon put faith in God to provide land and water in abundance. The idea that land and water could be owned by individuals who could maintain exclusive rights of use was foreign to Native American belief systems and also to those of the Church of Jesus Christ of Latter-day Saints. Mormons recognized that land and water resources were to be used by all for the common good.

In many respects, the principles that Mormon farmers used to divide land and allocate water differed from mainstream, gentile society. These principles were also better suited to the realities of the desert West beyond the hundredth meridian than the arbitrary rules that had been invented in the East. Jefferson's Land Ordinance of 1785 had established a survey dividing land into uniform, square townships and ranges. John Wesley Powell had seen that this "simple, rational geometry" did not fit the "messy, complicated terrain" of the arid West (Worster 2001:42). Consistent with Powell's notion, Mormons ignored the township and range system. Wherever there was water, they planted a community. Moving outward from this core, they established farms in 10-acre increments according to the needs and abilities of families. Farming was the objective, and lands that could be farmed and watered, such as the cotton-growing valleys of the Virgin and Muddy Rivers and the Little Colorado River valley, were sought. These pioneers "were interested in the productive capability of the land and not in the beauties of the landscape" (Crampton 1972:106). Clusters of settlements sprang up like mushrooms wherever farming was possible (Bischoff and others 2000), often in lonely, stark, dangerous places.

Moreover, Mormons created "a set of water rights that had no precedent in the East" (Worster 2001:351). The Saints apportioned water among all those who owned farmland, and water rights inhered in land ownership (Worster 2001:352). Powell had used a similar model for his 1879 treatise on western land and water rights. By 1898, there were 41 self-governing irrigation districts in Utah (Worster 1985:79). Mormons also appointed livestock pasturage and maintained it communally. Instead of establishing isolated ranches as other Americans were doing, the Mormons developed village herds that were grazed under joint supervision (Worster 2001:352).

Ranching at Pipe Spring

Pipe Spring near Kanab, Utah, was a settlement where the Mormon belief in irrigated farming gave way to the practical exigencies of an arid land. In 1863, Utah's Washington County issued a land certificate to James M. Whitmore that gave him title to a 160-acre town site. The land surrounded a flowing spring of sweet, cold water sacred to the Paiute peoples. It was enough water on which to base a good ranch, gardens, and a life. Pipe Spring was a stockman's paradise, not a farmer's Eden (Lavender 1984). By 1865, Whitmore had hauled timber, built corrals and fences, planted 1,000 grapevines, put in apple and peach trees, and was milking 50 cows. No would-be farmers followed Whitmore, however. Perhaps they had already learned that the spring was insufficient for farming.

Later, Mormon and gentile settlers purchased land from Whitmore's widow to establish a communal ranching venture, the Canaan Cooperative Stock Company, at Pipe Spring. To protect against Indian raids, they built a virtual fortress, which became known as Winsor Castle after the foreman of the operation. The two-story block structure completely enclosed the precious spring. Protecting the water and using it were paramount to the ranchers. The women created an extensive dairy operation at Pipe Spring, using the flowing spring water to make cheese and butter in the cool, damp stone building. There would never be any extensive farms at Pipe Spring. In 1872, the soil was so sandy and porous that only 15 acres of farmland could be irrigated (Lavender 1984:11, 21–22).

Today, the summer sun beats down on the gardens at Pipe Spring National Monument, wilting the squash and tomato plants. Water still gushes cold and sweet from the spring and into a pool shaded by huge trees where ducks float and dip. A couple of ancient, pet longhorn cows in search of handouts greeted us, their warm, grassy breath soft on our hands. The butter churns are stilled, and the telegraph wires no longer buzz with warnings of antipolygamist lawmen. The water still flows, but the Mormon way of life at Pipe Spring has vanished.

Pipe Spring National Monument, Arizona. PHOTOGRAPH BY JEFFERSON REID.

Scale and Form of Control

In several respects, Mormon water control differed little from Hohokam or O'odham methods in scale, materials, and labor. Canal systems were similar in size, length, materials, and diversion features. Water-control features were built communally and by hand. Wherever they moved, such as to the Little Colorado River valley, Mormons built dams of earth, brush, and rock to divert water and constructed simple, unlined community ditches. Careful organization and maintenance was required to keep the dams in working order and to ensure that each user received the agreed-upon amount of water (Worster 2001:352).

Mormons did have advantages over the Hohokam in wheeled vehicles, metal tools, and horsepower. Fresno scrapers drawn by horses or mules, shovels, and wagons made the task of constructing and repairing irrigation ditches less onerous. A picture taken in 1915 of Akimel O'odham farmers repairing a diversion weir at a canal intake on the Gila River (Haury 1976:148–149) shows how these tools were used. At least 50 men used 21 two-horse wagons to carry brush for lining the intake. With such technological advantages, Mormons could build, maintain, and repair irrigation canals more rapidly than the Hohokam, tasks they evidently undertook repeatedly as dams and ditches washed out.

Centralized control of water may have been the feature of Mormon farming that was most distinct from the Hohokam. Control of water was theocratic, vested in the church. The Saints looked to the church, its bishops, and its president for guidance concerning where to live and how to divide up the land and water. The church provided the overarching bureaucratic organization and the funds necessary to build irrigation works, allocate irrigation water, and distribute farm products. The best lands and water rights usually went to those who were well up the ladder of church hierarchy, however, and the rest of the community received land by lot (Worster 2001:351). Tribute was paid in the form of tithing, ensuring that the church received the benefits of the community's labor. The ultimate effect of these principles and the organization they fostered was to keep land and water control in church hands and out of the jurisdiction of territorial governors and legal systems, which proved threatening to emerging state governments (Worster 1985:78). By contrast, although archaeologists continue to debate the Hohokam's relative political complexity, most agree that there was no centralized labor force to construct canals, no single oversight of water allocation, no agency to adjudicate disputes (for example, see Masse [1991:218]). There was no capital accumulation to fund irrigation works or repair them.

Consequences

Mormon cultural geography prevented them from facing the realities of environmental hardships. Irrigation allowed the Saints to grow the same crops and raise the same livestock as in the eastern farms from which they fled (Jackson 1994). In Utah, Mormons reestablished their cultural landscape around the Great Salt Lake, ignoring that it was "an arid land, a fragile land, a dependent land" (Jackson 1994:143). The philosophy was carried to other Mormon outposts farmed through irrigation technology. By putting their faith in God and the church, the Saints could ignore the real and palpable conditions of their new country. To Mormons "bent upon extending the kingdom of God in the wilderness, a few acres and a little water spelled opportunity" (Crampton 1972:106).

Mormon beliefs and values did not induce them to conserve land and resources better than their gentile neighbors. Because they had been given dominion over nature, the Saints were permitted to consume resources—wood, water, grasslands—as needed. They overstocked the range, depleted streams, destroyed riparian habitat, and assaulted indigenous peoples and their resources. When these human effects coincided with drought, the effects could be devastating. In 1881, Clarence Dutton visited the Pipe Spring region near Kanab, Utah. He found it denuded compared to when he had visited in 1871. There was not a single blade of grass to be seen, and the bare land was covered with the bleached bones of horses and cattle (Worster 2001:353–354). Overgrazing by the Pipe Spring cattle contributed greatly to this problem (Lavender 1984:30).

The Mormon's irrigated farms in the Phoenix area were also subject to waterlogging, as the Hohokam fields must have been. Over two decades in the early 1900s, according to Krech (1999:59–60), irrigation raised the

Water in a Parched Land

U.S. Army wife Martha Summerhayes's description of coping in desert Arizona in 1874 underscores the importance of water in a parched land. She writes (Summerhayes 1979:53) that:

> I had my own canteen hung up in the ambulance, but the water in it got very warm and I learned to take but a swallow at a time, as it could not be refilled until we reached the next spring—and there is always some uncertainty in Arizona as to whether the spring or basin has gone dry. So water was precious, and we could not afford to waste a drop.

Photograph by Jefferson Reid.

Dry Bones

Sharlot Hall describes a drought year in Arizona:

The fence posts blister in the burning sun
And wisps of wind like hungry hunting dogs
Sniff the dry corn that rattles and falls down
Like dead bones gnawed and left long time ago.
Dry bones are plenty on the water trails
Where long before the sun comes up the dust
Swings in the air like low-hung graying haze
And staggering cows creep slowly in to drink—
Hides taut and sere and hair like bleached-out grass.

(Sharlot Hall, "Dry Bones")

Longhorn steer. PHOTOGRAPH BY JEFFERSON REID.

water table in the Salt River valley some 40 feet. Groundwater pumping in the Phoenix area was initially begun to alleviate the problem of saturated fields. The relative simplicity and small scale of Mormon irrigation systems prevented environmental effects from being more disastrous, as did the size of individual communities.

It is too great a task to evaluate here the success of the Mormon farmers who settled in Arizona during the nineteenth century. On the one hand, they succeeded in acquiring clear title to land in places such as the Little Colorado River valley, winning a land base for their communities. On the other hand, their success was illusory, for the Saints were unable to consolidate the necessary economic and political control demanded by their agrarian isolationism (Peterson 1973:175).

The Little Colorado River settlements were essentially "the last physical frontier of the Mormon kingdom" (Peterson 1973:175). After these places were settled in the 1870s, the necessary geographic isolation would seldom combine with the agrarian requirements of land and water. When they did forge a limited accommodation, it would be at the expense of Mormon unity and the nonconforming practice of polygamy (Peterson 1973:241). The Saints eventually confronted the world.

One of the most intriguing parts of the Mormon story is how they exemplified the western philosophy so prominent in mainstream nineteenth-century America—the myth of the West as Zion and refuge. Wallace Stegner called this the "geography of hope" (Comer 1999:44). Western lands would serve all the needs that could not be met in the urban, secular, crowded East. In short, the West was a brimming container of human optimism. This persistent trope in western history was an Anglo-American affectation, for as Comer (1999:45) has pointed out, one person's geography of hope was often the end of hope for another. We will return to this myth in the epilogue.

In their cooperative communities, the Mormons provided a proven method for coping with the exigencies of the desert West. The essential lessons they taught were simple—be prepared to work together and be prepared to change. Although founded on a vastly different belief system, the Hohokam had used a similar cooperative and flexible strategy that was equally successful. Rugged individualism had no place in the desert Southwest, despite the romantic fictions that imbue the imagined West.

Farmer in hay field in the Salt River Valley around the turn of the twentieth century. PHOTOGRAPH COURTESY ARIZONA HISTORICAL SOCIETY, TUCSON (AHS ACCESSION NO. 5789).

Twentieth-Century Water Control and the U.S. Bureau of Reclamation

Last, we turn to the U.S. Bureau of Reclamation and the water-control works of the twentieth century, the most technologically sophisticated water-control system we will examine in this chapter. Worster (1985) has described the social and political framework of twentieth-century water control in terms of "the modern capitalist state." He labeled the American West as "a modern *hydraulic society,* which is to say, a social order based on the intensive, large-scale manipulation of water and its products in an arid setting" (Worster 1985:7).

Values and Ideology

Many of us have never considered the cultural values of our own times. Because most do not don masks to dance in the village plazas and bring rain and no longer make our living by tilling the soil, it is easy to think that we lack a consistent set of culturally defined values toward the environment and a coherent cultural landscape. We do not. In this section, we explore some of these values, beliefs, and the resulting cultural landscape of our own times.

A suite of ideological concepts supporting an expansionist, imperial national philosophy threads through western water-control history like canals in irrigated fields. Most of the cultural ideals, values, and ideological concepts underlying modern water control can be traced to the nineteenth century. The driving force behind federal water control in the West was cultural imperialism, the belief that the destiny of the American nation was to expand from coast to coast. This doctrine saturated nineteenth-century philosophy and economic policy and the early Bureau of Reclamation's ideology. A legacy of this philosophy was that Americans viewed their self-identity as based on expansion and colonization (Smith 1970). Many believed that American democracy was best served through expansion of the nation. Irrigation became linked to this belief system. It came to be regarded as the flowering of American democratic ideals and institutions (Worster 1985:114, 120).

Moreover, expansion and wealth were linked. The land in its abundance provided the raw material for progress, economic expansion, and acquisition of personal and national wealth. The Bureau of Reclamation adopted this national philosophy, which was symbolized effectively by the agency's original slogan—"Our Rivers: Total Use for Greater Wealth." The Colorado River had to be controlled for the common good and economic benefits. "Unharnessed it tore through deserts, flooded fields, and ravaged villages. It drained the water from the mountains and plains, rushed it through sun-baked thirsty lands and dumped it into the Pacific Ocean—a treasure lost forever" (Fradkin 1968:244). This philosophy drove construction of the Central Arizona Project, which was originally designed to bring irrigation water for the greater economic good of the arid Copper State.

This ideology was foreign to both Native Americans and Mormons. Native American peoples sanctioned resources as gifts from the deities and the spirits, not as a source of wealth. The Western Apache, for example, apparently were not driven "by the land hunger so characteristic of many Anglo-Americans or by the desire to possess or use more than enough to meet the needs of the family" (Buskirk 1986:41). Land and water were used for the common good of the community. They were not commodities that could be manipulated for the accumulation of personal, private wealth. Although theocratic Mormons shared many attitudes with mainstream American society in the late nineteenth century, church doctrine and control prevented the ideology from being translated into accumulation of personal wealth. Mormons did not strive to accumulate large personal landholdings, but submitted to church directives regarding acreage to be farmed (Peterson 1973:161). Whereas Mormons justified taking resources by evoking God's will and divine right, capitalistic gentile Americans simply took them.

Like the Mormons, nineteenth-century Anglo-America did not view its relationship with nature as symbiotic and mutually reinforcing. Instead, nature and humans were essentially at war. As Worster (1985:5) has expressed it, western society was dependent on "a sharply alienating, intensely managerial relationship with nature." This attitude was European in derivation and can be traced to the Judeo Christian tradition of subduing the earth as set forth in Genesis (Worster 1985:56). The theme is well illustrated by the title of irrigation booster Smythe's 1899 book—*The Conquest of Arid America.* John Widtsoe, who served with Bureau of Reclamation commissioner Elwood Mead on the advisory group appointed by President Coolidge to study federal reclamation organization, policies, and projects, expressed the philosophy well (cited in Worster 1985:188):

> The destiny of man is to possess the whole earth; and the destiny of the earth is to be subject to man. There can be no full conquest of the earth, and no real satisfaction to humanity, if large portions of the earth remain beyond his highest control. . . . By the vision of its statesmen and by its marvelous power of accomplishment [America] has made use of the country west of the hundredth meridian

> which lies under a low rainfall. The nation is now one country: not two strips of country, with a desert between. . . . And all the world will be helped by the conquest. It is an imperial problem which as it is solved will satisfy a world-wide need.

The war in the West of the late nineteenth and early twentieth centuries was against aridity and scarcity. Writers and speakers of that time focused on subduing and conquering the wild rivers rather than living with them harmoniously. The Colorado was the wildest river in the West, and it had to be tamed, subjected, and controlled if people were to make use of it. Irrigation was commonly defended in the late nineteenth century as the epitome of rational, scientific agriculture, by which irrigation promoters meant it would control the forces of nature (Worster 1985:114). The ideology of conquest of nature was foreign to Native Americans, who viewed their relationship with the environment and its plant and animal inhabitants as one of community and mutual respect.

In this philosophy, people and nature were conceptualized as existing in a dichotomous and exclusive relationship. Humans were outside nature, not a part of it, and thus were able to control it without consequences to themselves. This viewpoint was new to the late-nineteenth-century nation. Dichotomous thinking separating people from the environment had no place in the cultural landscapes of Native American peoples. As we have seen in many examples throughout the previous chapters, nature and people were considered as forming one universe, along with deities, spiritual entities, cosmological phenomena, living things, and natural forces.

Few people questioned the motives or benefits of the imperialist ideology and the concepts that supported it. Powell might have pointed out that we were building irrigation works far greater than the ability of the land to sustain them, drawing far greater numbers of people than had ever lived in the West before. Some naysayers, even within the Bureau of Reclamation, wondered about the ability of the Colorado River to sustain projects of enormous scope. Such questioning was based on the natural facts of the river's flow, precipitation, and other scientific facts, however. No one seemed to be asking whether "the West should in fact be growing crops and building up its population, that it should be cut up into private property, that its water or any other resource should be exploited to its maximum economic potential" (Worster 1985:92). The ideology was simply accepted, and in the nineteenth-century West, which was still largely agrarian, underpopulated, and rural, it may have been appropriate or at least consistent with the facts of the environment at that time. The philosophy that nature's resources should be used for economic benefit still underwrites Arizona's land-use and water-use policies, although neither the human nor the natural environments resemble those of the nineteenth century.

Time turns trees to stone. PHOTOGRAPH BY JEFFERSON REID.

Commodification was an inevitable consequence of the nonnative Americans' dichotomous, alienating, and managerial view of humans and the environment. Water, land, and resources were conceived as abstract commodities that could be owned, bought, and sold. Decisions about environmental resources were based on western principles of private property and ownership and were guaranteed by the U.S. Constitution. The binding glue of mainstream American society was love for exclusive property (Ambrose 1996:32), and this drove the development of land and water policy. Keiter (1998:24) has pointed out that land and water laws developed in the nineteenth century were directed toward making the West's land and abundant resources available for the taking by those first in time. They were justification of appropriation, a form of "tolerated trespass." Commodification and private-property rights resulted in protracted, intense, and expensive battles among water users, federal agencies, legislators, and states over the right to use water. When commodification of land and water confronted Native American notions of territory, which for the most part did not conceive space as a discrete, geopolitical entity, conflict was inevitable, and it was often bloody (Whittlesey 1998b).

Commodification and managerial philosophy promoted a pseudoscientific approach to the land and water

The Land

Rosalía Salazar Whelan (Martin 1992:169) describes what happened to her family's land in Aravaipa Canyon:

> I sold my parcel to my sister Lucía, and her children still own that. They're going to hang on to it because that is where their roots are; they don't intend to ever let it go. They might not have anything else, but they have the land.

characteristics of the West and allowed those who wanted to develop the West to don some rather peculiar cultural blinders. For example, in 1882 L. P. Brockett claimed in his enormous guide to *Our Western Empire or the New West beyond the Mississippi* that the Great American Desert was a myth. Arizona Territory had plenty of water, he maintained, and the river valleys were made for irrigated agriculture (Bowden 1977:81). Moreover, Arizona could not be overgrazed. Cattle actually enriched the soil, Brockett claimed. Native grasses would grow stronger and richer after a few years' pasturage (Bowden 1977:82). Another booster was Patrick Hamilton, who argued in a book titled *Resources of Arizona,* written in 1884 and commissioned by the Arizona legislature, that groundwater was a treasure as great as the gold and silver in the rocky hills. Moreover, it was an inexhaustible treasure, one that the "cunning of man" would use to make "the barren waste smile with verdure" (Bowden 1977: 82). As we have seen in previous chapters, it was thought that any deficiencies in land and water would be remedied by ranching and farming. Rain followed the plow, and all settlers had to do was farm and the rains would come.

Scale and Form of Control

In terms of scope and advanced technology, the irrigation works of the last century were far bigger than anything that had come before. "For the Americans the problem in the arid West. . . was not any shortage of resources, but rather a failure by earlier inhabitants in the area of technique. What was needed was know-how" (Bowden 1977:82). Technology and science had become intertwined by the time the Reclamation Act set the grand dam-building era into motion, providing the necessary know-how to fix the West's problems. Although the notion that science would serve in the conquest of the West and its rivers had been born with Powell, if not earlier (Worster 2001:297), it flowered into full bloom with the technological advancements of the late nineteenth and early twentieth centuries. Science offered practical insight, salvation, better ways to inhabit the land and use its resources. It was science in the service of the farmer. Science would also remedy nature's deficiencies. No competent engineer would have left so much land without water, created rivers that flowed through canyons so deep that the water was inaccessible, or designed rivers that depended upon the vagaries of fickle rainfall and snow. Technology and science triumphed over these natural deficiencies (Worster 1985:154).

The Bureau of Reclamation supplied technological know-how in abundance, providing new machinery, materials, and energy sources, offering better engineering

Oak Creek. PHOTOGRAPH BY STEPHANIE WHITTLESEY.

designs and capabilities. Bigger dams were built than had ever been dreamed of by Mormon settlers in the Little Colorado River valley, and they would last for decades, if not centuries, rather than a season or a year. Canals were bigger, longer, impermeable, far vaster than the simple, gravity-driven ditches of Hohokam and O'odham farmers.

As in ideology and scale, the form of control in the modern system differs from everything that had gone before. Truly massive amounts of money were necessary to construct and maintain the systems. Capital accumulation on such a grand scale was far beyond the capabilities of individuals, communities, churches, and states. It could only be provided by the federal government. Capital to finance public water-control projects derived from public coffers through taxes and the federal largesse (White 1991). The great dams of the Colorado River, beginning with Hoover Dam, were designed, located, financed, and supported by the federal government. This was also true of the other dams on Arizona's streams and certainly of the Central Arizona Project, which from its inception was far too big for the state to construct, although there were attempts to do so. In this way, modern water control is driven and supported by an industrial, capitalist superstructure (Worster 1985:123).

Control of the huge system is centralized and political rather than theocratic and also lies with the federal government. Instead of a priest deciding where to locate a canal and allocating irrigation water or a church bishop sending out a call for a new dam on the Little Colorado River, the federal government had authority to identify the projects worth undertaking, construct them, and control the distribution of water. Rather than a Western Apache ditch boss or a Mexican *zanjero* settling disputes among water users, the federal courts adjudicated conflicting claims. The federal government called the shots concerning the Colorado River from the beginning. It negotiated the original compact of 1922, litigated the disputes between California and Arizona over allocation of the Colorado's water, and intervened consistently over the subsequent years. Historian Richard White (1991:383) has pointed out that the development of the Colorado River marked the emergence of the federal government as the most powerful authority over the Colorado and other interstate and navigable streams. The 1963 Supreme Court decision gave the secretary of the interior the authority to allocate water among the states and among users within states (White 1991:554). Today, users of Central Arizona Project water are assuming its control, operations, and distribution, but ownership remains with the federal government.

Scholars loosely labeled the "new western historians" take the role of the federal government as the major theme in western history. Limerick (1987) believes that the West was a stage on which the struggle for an increasing role of the federal government in many aspects of modern life was played out. The resulting dependence and resentment have been major issues in contemporary politics (Limerick 1987:28). As a number of writers have underscored, the West has always been marked by a fierce dedication to freedom, independence, and self-reliance. Westerners are ferocious advocates of private-property rights and deeply hostile to regulation of any kind. "In the imagination of modern America," writes White (1991:57), "the West has come to stand for independence, self-reliance, and individualism." Westerners see themselves as coming from a lineage of pioneers who "conquered a wilderness and transformed the land; they spring from a people who carved out their own destiny and remained beholden to no one."

There is an inherent duality in this ideology, however. Federal money has been always been one of the West's principal resources. The American West is not so much a creation of individuals or states but of the federal government (White 1991:57). Westerners depend on federal goodwill in many ways: "from Indian reservations to national parks, from grazing permits on the public lands to reclamation and hydroelectric projects, from defense contracts to shale oil subsidies, federal resources had become vital supplements to local economies" (Limerick 1987:138).

Moreover, the federal government bails us out when we get ourselves into trouble, particularly when we settle in places where we have no business being. "Pioneers intruded into Indian territory," Limerick and Travis (2002) have written. "When they got themselves into a mess, the Army arrived to protect them and remove the Indians. Farmers tried to grow crops in places with low rainfall, and the U.S. Bureau of Reclamation built the dams and reservoirs that filled in for the rain." In essence, the federal government provides a buffer against the many serious risks of the western environment. Federal disaster relief after floods, fires, and other natural disasters—promoted, if not caused, by dense population in the West's dangerous places—is another form of the federal bailout.

Westerners resent the government that largely makes life in the West possible, however, as Bernard DeVoto initially emphasized (Fradkin 1968:83). Westerners treat the federal government as a scratchy wool shirt—necessary to keep us warm, but incredibly irritating nonetheless (White 1991:57). Some westerners pretended that federal dependency did not exist; others battled the federal government, refusing to pay grazing fees on Forest Service land, for example (White 1991:408). Most westerners have preferred complaining while clinging to the federal handout. Subsidized Central Arizona Project water is one of the most delicious ironies of this kind. Irrigation farmers not only depend on water that they literally cannot afford, but on water that is heavily subsidized by the federal government (White 1991:523). In this way, many conservative farmers have become in essence an embodiment of the welfare state that they decry (Reisner 1986:301).

As a consequence of this oddly contradictory ideology, blaming nature for refusing to cooperate and blaming the federal government for failing to fix nature's errors have been two common pastimes in the West. Because it was the government's responsibility to control nature, aggrieved westerners could point to the federal government as a convenient scapegoat when the government failed to do so. It was a theme of victimization, in essence, that precluded westerners from taking responsibility for their own role in courting misfortune. "Western risk-taking has often relied on this backup plan," Limerick and Travis (2002) write. "We get into a pinch and the government rushes to get us out of it. Nature presents challenges that are at once dangerous and appealing, but human ingenuity and government funding quickly drain the danger and leave only their appeal." A challenge we face in the future is resolving these contradictions and figuring out new ways to inhabit the West that do not put us at tremendous risk or have negative consequences on its resources.

Consequences

We have seen that the beliefs of Native Americans in the unity of the natural and human worlds and the spiritual investment of Mormons in farming did not prevent consequences to the environment. It was largely the small scale of water-control systems and human populations along with natural checks on growth that kept societies in relative balance with available resources, at least most of the time. By virtue of scale and technology, the consequences of water control in the twentieth century are greater than any before. Commodification of natural resources, the inevitable outcome of nineteenth- and twentieth-century ideology, has all too often led to abuses of land and water. "We abuse land because we regard it as a commodity belonging to us," explained Leopold (1949:vii). One of the most immediate consequences was overuse of resources. Bowden (1977:82) has pointed out that the curious nineteenth-century beliefs about the West and its resources had rapid and dire consequences. Because the land was not really arid, water could be used with complete abandon. Cattle could be grazed without thought to numbers or consequences to rangeland. Technology allowed us to accumulate resources on a huge scale, permitting many more people to settle and farm in desert Arizona than was possible with systems of smaller scale. Technology would permit us to use "inexhaustible" resources to the point of exhaustion.

Natural and cultural processes also contribute to an atmosphere of waste. Evaporation from reservoirs is a tremendous problem in the arid West, with its low humidity. Some estimates place the total annual water loss through evaporation as high as that of the entire Colorado River's annual flow (Wilkinson 1992:260). Seepage, consumption by phreatophytes, and other natural processes further increase waste. Western water users are profligate, and water conservation is minimal. Water consumption in the West, much of it due to irrigation, is three times greater than that of the eastern states (Wilkinson 1992:260). Per capita water consumption is nearly one-and-one-half times as much as that of the East Coast. Moreover, much potable water goes to lawns and golf courses, and mining and industrial uses, although urban areas have begun to use reclaimed water for recreational and landscaping purposes. Unrestrained water development has contributed to waste by creating the illusion that water supplies are abundant and there is no need for conservation.

Starr Pass golf course and housing development near Tucson, Arizona. PHOTOGRAPH BY JEFFERSON REID.

Modern water control has achieved a remarkable transformation of the environment. The dream of dominating nature's waters has largely been fulfilled. The Colorado River is no longer a natural stream, a living creature of fierce beauty and uncontrollable temper. It is completely

Water Magic

There is magic when water opens
the walls of rock
like they are shells,
when it reaches the end of its journey
and finds itself waking
in another strange place.

Tonight when I speak of water,
I don't mean the big oceans
rocking themselves, but water
moving place to place
underground, small veins
finding their way to sunlight
where they rupture.

(Linda Hogan, "Water Rising")

managed, varying not with natural fluctuations in precipitation but with controlled releases from its many dams. Sophisticated mathematical algorithms and computer modeling have enabled the Bureau of Reclamation to predict and manage the Colorado River's hydraulics (Morton 1996:125–126). The Colorado is effectively controlled by its operators, who monitor changes in velocity, volume, and demands and make minute adjustments in response (Morton 1996:126–127). Hidden, linked to the outside world with sophisticated telecommunications, the river's operators make the water flow. Stand on one of the great dams and you can literally hear it hum, moving the water along with electricity instead of prayers.

A quick tour through the state's desert lands tells the truth about environmental alteration. Near Yuma, acres of irrigated farmland produce vegetables, hay, and melons in a desert where less than four inches of rain falls each year, where Hia-C'ed O'odham farmers struggled to bring in a basic subsistence crop. Cotton fields stretch across the Santa Cruz Flats where Archaic hunter-gatherers had huddled around pools of water hidden in the sand dunes. Riparian forests that once bordered desert rivers have largely vanished. Combined with effects of livestock grazing, vegetation has been changed and erosion increased (Bahre 1991; Cooke and Reeves 1976). Wetlands and *cienegas* have been destroyed (Carothers and others 1974; Hendrickson and Minckley 1984). Glen Canyon and other desert canyons have been filled with water. Groundwater has been seriously depleted, and the land tells the tale, sinking and collapsing into itself.

The environment has been so seriously altered that in many cases it is no longer natural. The loss of biological habitat has been pronounced and is nowhere more readily seen than in the drying of the Colorado's delta at the Gulf of California. Large water diversions have created dry rivers; no water flows in most of Arizona's streams except during major storms. The contrast between a living river and a modern, concrete-lined canal tells this tale without words. A canal is unlike a river in almost every respect. It is not an ecosystem; it is barren, fenced to keep out all living beings, and flows through a world to which it has no relationship (Worster 1985:5). The Central Arizona Project canal even defies the laws of gravity and nature by forcing water to flow uphill. In this new guise, nature is largely unrecognizable.

Moreover, the purposes of the environment have shifted. Whereas land and water once were the foundation of subsistence, the means of life itself, they have become commodified and commercialized, tools for making money. Lake Mead, Lake Havasu, Lake Powell, and Theodore Roosevelt Lake provide a reservoir of water used for irrigation, generating hydroelectric power, and municipal uses. They also represent water that has been commodified for commercial, recreational uses. Water skiers, jet skis, houseboats, and fishing boats float above the drowned settlements of Mormon farmers, the fields and ditches of Anasazi farmers—all of the empty, silent ruins of the past.

Rafting the Colorado River near Lee's Ferry, northeastern Arizona.
PHOTOGRAPH BY JEFFERSON REID.

City of Tucson, Arizona, looking toward the Santa Catalina Mountains. Photograph by Jefferson Reid.

The Bureau of Reclamation, like many other agencies and the nation itself, was slow to come to grips with issues of environmental alteration, degradation, and habitat loss. In the 1960s and 1970s, environmental improvement meant greater opportunities for hunting, fishing, and recreation rather than protecting species or habitats (Morton 1996:944). Today, the Bureau of Reclamation is taking steps to operate the Colorado River in an environmentally sensitive manner and funds additional studies of environmental impacts.

One of the most important consequences of modern water control has been demographic. The availability of water where little once existed has enabled cities to flourish in impossible places and allowed the population to soar beyond the natural capacity of the land. Lured by the promise of an unending supply of renewable water, development interests have capitalized on the big water and energy projects. Look at the Phoenix metropolitan area today, and it is easy to see the result. Massive water-control projects, runaway growth, and population increase on a vast, geometric scale have perpetuated the process of systematic dismantling of the western environment that began with the arrival of Europeans on the continent (Flores 1998b:59). The scale of twentieth-century irrigation works—bigger and technologically advanced—tipped the population-resource balance so tenuously achieved in earlier centuries. The natural system that operated for many thousands of years to keep population in balance with resources was utterly swept away by twentieth-century technology.

Writing on the Wall

Charles Bowden (1977:138) has written:

> It is not a revelation to learn that cheap energy makes societies boom, that groundwater in arid regions has negligible recharge, that humans tend to use as much of anything as they can lay hands on. We can ignore these facts and pump, mine, and combust with abandon, or we can recognize these facts and attempt to construct a sustainable society. There will be no painless answers, nor were there any in the past.

One of the most serious consequences of modern water control has been the impact on Arizona's indigenous peoples. In the nineteenth century, the West's native peoples were as much an obstacle to American empire and expansion as the scarcity of water. The contest for property and profit was accompanied by a battle for cultural dominance, and Native Americans were as much subject to Anglo-American domination of water rights as other kinds of technological, political, and social domination. Appropriation of Native American water rights and other policies swept away the human obstacle even as the river washed away flimsy dams (Worster 1985:115). Sadly, realizing the American dream all too often meant the end of hope for Indian tribes. Fradkin (1968:155) has pointed out that historically, the Colorado River has been a white man's river and more than that, a U.S. river. Small Indian and Mexican farmers lost their farmlands even as the rivers were controlled to water the fields of Euroamerican farmers. Today, this picture is changing, although change has been a long time coming. Legal battles have restored water rights to Indian tribes, and they are receiving their share of water distributed

Spring pool at Palatki Ruin near Sedona, Arizona. PHOTOGRAPH BY STEPHANIE WHITTLESEY.

through Bureau of Reclamation systems. The federal government assumed a large role in the distribution of water to Native Americans as in other aspects of modern water control. The government intervened during the Supreme Court battle between Arizona and California over Colorado River water to ensure that the eventual decision protected the water rights of Indians on the 25-odd reservations in the Lower Basin (White 1991:554).

CONCLUSION

John Wesley Powell would not recognize the land that today is watered by the Central Arizona Project. What he encountered as an unknown land, a desert in both senses of the dictionary definition, has been replaced by metropolis—urban centers, agribusiness operations, seas of retirement communities and mobile-home parks, laser-leveled fields, artificial oceans, international airports, stadiums with retractable roofs, water parks, stacked concrete highways, golf courses, resorts, casinos, enormous desert lakes, and every conceivable recreational attraction for residents and tourists. Water supports the toys of a nation heavily invested in leisure activities rather than the simple mechanisms of subsistence farmers.

What was once a wild, uncontrollable, free river—anthropomorphized as fierce, uncompromising—a river that was essentially useless, laden with silt, prone to excesses of flooding or drying up to nothing, a river that would not obey and remain uncomplainingly within its banks—has become an industrial artifact. It is a monument to the technological mastery of dam and reservoir, concrete and canal, pipeline and aqueduct, pumping plant and siphon, triumphing over the natural contours of land and the limits of topography and hydrography. As the struggle to build the Central Arizona Project ended, it became evident that the highly debated, adjudicated, politicized, and controlled Colorado River water would not be used to irrigate farmland but to flow into Arizona's homes, businesses, and industries.

The Central Arizona Project was designed to last for a century of service (Morton 1996:608). If we take 1985 as

A Pima Remembers

The Pimas are a very humble people who like to farm. Perhaps they have been too humble. They are intelligent in their own way, and many of them have had a good education. But the pace of progress is a little hard on them. I have heard several white men say that the pace of what is called progress today is almost too much for *them.*

Think how it must seem to a simple Pima who remembers the Gila River when it was a running stream.

George Webb, *A Pima Remembers*

its birth date, we can count on the Central Arizona Project performing its water-delivery functions until 2085. To reach that milestone, we will need to alter much of our ideology as well as improve our technology. The Arizona of 2085 will probably be much different than today's Copper State, and the needs of its people and industries will likely be radically changed. The epilogue looks at some of the ways we can meet the challenges of the future.

For further information, see: Patricia Nelson Limerick, The Legacy of Conquest: The Unbroken Past of the American West *(W. W. Norton and Company, New York, 1987); Barbara Tellman, Richard Yarde, and Mary G. Wallace,* Arizona's Changing Rivers: How People Have Affected the Rivers *(Issue Paper No. 19, Water Resources Research Center, College of Agriculture, University of Arizona, Tucson, 1997); Richard White,* "It's Your Misfortune and None of My Own:" A New History of the American West *(University of Oklahoma Press, Norman, 1991).*

Epilogue: Where the River Meets the Sea

Epilogue

We remember our rivers, even if we do not honor them.

—Gary Holthaus, *Wide Skies: Finding a Home in the West*

Though it is dry, we are here, we say, because we love the West, especially its landscape. But if we love the West, we will beware of anyone who proposes to bring us an endless supply of bountiful water and will do everything we can to thwart the plan. If such a person were successful, it would mean the end of the West as we know it. That person brings us not a happy life in the West; he or she would bring us Ohio.

—Gary Holthaus, *Wide Skies: Finding a Home in the West*

Our voyage down the mythical Colorado River, our journey through the landscapes and waters of time, is at an end. Along the way we have heard many stories, tales that tell fundamental truths about life in a stone-dry land. Among all we have learned, two truths appear most salient. First, water lies at the heart of the desert, as paradoxical as this may seem. "Water or the lack of it," Gary Holthaus (1997:26) has written, "rivers or their absence, are among the defining characteristics of the West." Through time, the desert was shaped by water or by the lack of water. Water laid down the structural bones of the Colorado Plateau, eroded it, and reformed it as desert dunes. Water continues to shape the land, carving it into sculptural forms and sending its raw materials hurtling to the sea in the waters of the Colorado River. The desert Basin and Range country is a map of water, telling us where it has passed and how it has moved.

So necessary that it has become valued more than any other treasure, water defines desert life. Water has shaped our values, spiritual lives, and subsistence, forming the structure of life itself. Not technology alone, but

The Colorado River near Parker, Arizona. Photograph by Jefferson Reid.

also ideology, religion, and secular values have determined how land and water have been used and have shaped the resulting cultural landscape. The ancient land that is now Arizona shares with other western lands the fact of little rain. Since humans first began to inhabit this land, they have coped with the scarcity of water. The irony and paradox of the desert Southwest is that, although rain is often deficient, sometimes we suffer from a surfeit, and an excess of water has often created havoc and destruction. This was as true for nineteenth-century Arizonans as it was for the Hohokam of long ago. Little wonder, then, that so much effort has been expended on controlling water, that "it has been and is the focus of intense argument and debate, and sometimes the cause of violent confrontation and death" (Holthaus 1997:26).

Historical water-driven mill near Sedona, Arizona. PHOTOGRAPH BY STEPHANIE WHITTLESEY.

A second truth is that each human group has adjusted to these facts of desert life in ingenious, innovative ways. Archaic, Hisatsinom, Hohokam, Hopi, Navajo, O'odham, Western Apache, Mormon, and twentieth-century Arizonans—each group viewed their piece of western land differently. Each group's perceptions of land and water, beliefs, and interactions with the natural environment created a distinctive, humanized landscape that supported life and gave it meaning. Each developed a suite of spiritual, technological, and social ways to live with the land. Often their adjustments were effective and successful; sometimes they proved dysfunctional and negative, affecting land and water profoundly.

Through time, our general way of coping with the environment and its excesses and gifts has changed remarkably, as traditional knowledge has been replaced by technology. By necessity, traditional peoples were intimately familiar with the land, its resources, and its sources of water. They knew where they could find rainwater pooled in bare-rock *tinajas* or sand dunes, where the green-bordered springs were located, where it was possible to dig through a dry riverbed and find hidden water underground. When they became farmers, people invented some imaginative mechanisms to capture rainfall and the liquid wealth of rivers and direct it upon their fields. People developed an understanding of stream flow, knowing when the riverbeds would have water and when they would be dry. All this took place in a land where, according to John Wesley Powell, it is not possible to farm by rainfall alone.

Religion, ritual, and a richly textured sacred landscape supplemented traditional environmental knowledge. The people developed spiritual and calendrical methods to predict the cycle of the agricultural year and seasonal fluctuations in rainfall. Religious beliefs and ideology were more than a spiritual bulwark. Religion was an effective and eminently satisfying means of controlling an uncertain and unpredictable natural world, helping many ancient and modern Arizonans to cope with scarcity and the effects of environmental excess.

Much of this traditional knowledge and the long-held spiritual connections with land and water have vanished along with traditional farming methods and water-control technology. The Tohono O'odham once farmed thousands of acres by floodwater methods. Today this method is nothing but a memory in most villages (Bowden 1977:28). Mexican farmers in the late nineteenth and early twentieth centuries raised corn, chiles, melons, beans, lentils—the great bulk of their food. They milked cows, which were grazed on their own land, and made homemade cheese. Hay cut from their *milpas* fed the horses drawing the wagons and plows. The women made jam from saguaro fruit they gathered, stewed wild greens, and patted out hot, delicious tortillas by hand. The men butchered the animals, cut wood to fuel the stoves, and hauled drinking water (Bowden 1986:60–61; Martin 1992). Even the medicines they used came from the land and traditional knowledge. Herbal remedies from the *curanderas* cured all sorts of illnesses, and the midwives, or *parteras,* ushered babies into the world.

The Arizona in which these farmers lived and their self-sufficient way of life have gone. Tortillas come from the El Grande Tortilla Factory, and the women no longer dry *carne seca* by hand and make the old-style quesadillas. Drugs come from the pharmacy, and obstetricians deliver the babies. Alone in the desert, we rely on coolers and bottled water, six-packs of beer and soda, air-conditioning in our vehicles, and sunscreen to protect our skin. Most of us have no idea where to find water in the desert, and when circumstances make this necessary, we often die in the attempt.

The old way of life was certainly different, but it is difficult to make the value-laden judgment that it was better than the way we live today. We must be cautious not to color the past with rosy tones simply because it has gone. In times past, people's ways of living with the land and using its resources were not always successful, and their actions did not always have beneficial effects. Sometimes the rain did not fall, and the land failed to produce crops. The people were hungry and turned to whatever foods they could find to keep starvation at bay. Even in good years, nutrition was often poor. Life was short, infant mortality was high, and deficiency diseases such as anemia were common. There were also times when the residues of farming practices and daily living were harmful, altering the land, changing the soil, and affecting the distributions of plants and animals. This was true in the ancient past as today. Geographers such as Martyn Bowden (1992) believe that Native Americans had a far greater impact on the environment than is commonly believed. The lushness of the North American continent and the diversity of its animal species as recorded by early European explorers reflected a land that was ecologically rebounding, Bowden thinks. European-introduced diseases had decimated Indian populations, permitting the land to recover from overhunting, woodcutting, vegetation clearing, and other human activities by the time early explorers recorded their impressions.

Water and stone. Photograph by Stephanie Whittlesey.

Depending upon the scale of farming systems, the sophistication of technology, and the size and extent of human populations, environmental effects were sometimes transitory and sometimes, we fear, will be permanent. When the Hohokam people left, for whatever reasons, their farmland eventually returned to a condition approximating its original. The canals filled with washed-in silt when the rain thundered down on the desert. The salty fields became fertile once more. The technological revolution of the industrial age tipped the balance forever, allowing population and environmental effects to increase. It is easy to see that much more than a few centuries of abandonment would be needed to return the Colorado River to its pre-nineteenth-century state, if indeed that is what we wanted to do. Moreover, technology has also increased the deleterious effects upon our resources. Hohokam farmers did not have to cope with the effects of chemicals tainting their groundwater supply or agricultural fertilizers and pesticides in used irrigation water.

It remains to be seen whether we have succeeded in controlling the rivers at last by virtue of our modern technology, finalizing the nineteenth-century dream of dominating the earth. In times past, when humans were pitted in an adversarial relationship with Arizona's rivers, the rivers always won. Neither technology nor ideology and spiritual values were enough to defeat the environment. Hohokam farmers lost canals in flood years, forcing the abandonment of entire villages when the floods came too often and too high. Mormons rebuilt dams on the Little Colorado River year after year, as floodwaters tore down the sandy valley and ripped out the flimsy brush, rock, and earthen constructions built by religious hands with church money. Whereas Mexican farmers once cultivated lush fields along the San Pedro River between Benson and Winkelman, today the river has washed away fields and houses (Martin 1992:45).

Some early-twentieth-century constructions failed despite advanced technology. The Power Canal built between 1904 and 1906 to supply electricity for constructing Theodore Roosevelt Dam was "the largest, longest, and most technically advanced water control feature ever used in the Tonto Basin" (Welch 1992:165). Despite its advanced design, flow to the penstocks was interrupted by floods at least 10 times. The canal filled with some 200,000 cubic yards of silt, necessitating a massive renovation project. Although the canal was designed to withstand Salt River flows of up to 150,000 cubic feet per second, the floods of February 1937 put it out of service. It remained out of service during most of the period between 1937 and 1952, when it was permanently retired (Welch 1992:165). The greatest technological wonders, the enormous dams built with federal monies, were not immune. The Salt River overtopped Theodore Roosevelt Dam several times during its first years of service, flooding the Phoenix area.

Even today, sometimes the rivers still win. During the floods of winter 1993, dams throughout Arizona were breached as reservoirs filled to capacity and overtopped. Lakes were choked with driftwood swept downstream by the floodwaters. Safety modifications to Arizona's dams completed since that time may have solved this problem, but the proof will be in the next great flood event.

Throughout this book we have observed the boundless human capacity for changing perceptions and beliefs. As our attitudes and values have changed, so have our means of adjusting to the scarcity and excess of desert water. To consider the future of water in the West, in the mythical Arizona of 2085 after the Central Arizona Project has fulfilled its century of usefulness, we need to look more closely at our own cultural knowledge and perspectives. It is not true that the land has lost spiritual meaning or that we adjust to our environments solely in technological terms. It is true that meanings have changed. How can we alter perspectives and values to meet our future needs? In answering this question, we may want to examine a persistent theme that has marked the history of the American West, the state of Arizona, and our water-control and water-use policies. Since the nineteenth century, the West and its resources have been linked to the idea of salvation. The West represented a mystical and mythical Eden where those who toiled by the sweat of their brow would be rewarded by earthly and spiritual gifts—a land of milk and honey for the chosen ones.

Salvation was on the one hand economic, highly practical, and physical. The unlimited opportunity of the West, once its aridity had been resolved with irrigation technology, offered Americans a chance that was no longer available in the industrial East and the populated Midwest. Obtaining a farm was the key to achieving independence, becoming self-sufficient, and accumulating wealth, and it was the paramount goal of most people moving out West. Western states and territories viewed irrigated agriculture as the cornerstone of development for the economic benefit of private landowners and the public alike. This ideology of an aspiring middle class—the West as a desert paradise—was promoted to immigrants eager to buy into a dream.

An Unprofitable Land

Edward Abbey (1968:29), writing of Arches National Monument:

> Despite the great variety of living things to be found here, most of the surface of the land, at least three-quarters of it, is sand or sandstone, naked, monolithic, austere and unadorned as the sculpture of the moon. It is undoubtedly a desert place, clean, pure, totally useless, quite unprofitable.

Wilderness of rocks: Bryce Canyon National Park. PHOTOGRAPH BY JEFFERSON REID.

On the other hand, the geography of hope was also one of spiritual salvation. "The Romantic Age and America's cultural need had already made the primeval continent into a metaphor for the Divine, if not actually God, as then the best and freshest example of His handiwork" (Flores 1998b: 62). Many believed that in the West, fresh air, open spaces, and a spiritual connection with nature would resolve the social and economic ills of the urban, industrial East. It would be the salvation of the soul as well as the body. The philosophy is seen clearly in the western novels of Zane Grey, in which the morally ill of the urban East find new hope and new lives in the rough-and-tumble West, emerging better people for the confrontation. We have seen that this trope pervaded Mormon as well as gentile value systems. For the Saints, the West was literally a physical sanctuary as well as a spiritual refuge. It was to be a safe harbor from the legal and political storms that had buffeted Mormons in the East and Midwest, a place to escape the persecution that had dogged them for decades. The ideology of West as salvation was closely intertwined with other persistent myths—Native Americans as proud conservators of the western landscape, the wide open spaces celebrated by western writers, the cowboy hero (Comer 1999), and wilderness. Wilderness—"the West-That-Was"—has long been emblematic of spiritual salvation and "worshiped as the holiest of the holies" (Flores 1998b:62).

This view was always problematic, as many have underscored. The geography of hope required an environment of abundance that was easily accessible to private enterprise. By the beginning of the twentieth century in the West, such places were becoming scarcer and the case could be made, so Worster (1985) has argued, that they never existed. The psuedoscientific notions of the nineteenth century promoted the West as a place of abundant natural resources when this was clearly not the case. The ideology fit nicely with claims of the irrigation boosters that the West could be remade into a garden, if there were only enough water. Today, however, we know that there are no pristine environments of abundance, and the situation is rapidly growing worse. *National Geographic* (National Geographic Society 2002) has estimated that more than half of earth's accessible fresh water is already used, and many of its greatest watersheds suffer from pollution, political conflict, and overexploitation.

The idea that the American West was virgin wilderness until nineteenth-century people arrived to despoil it was also imaginary. This falsehood was an extension of the belief that humans and nature were separate phenomena, things apart. Because people had not shaped the West into a landscape that was familiar to western Europeans and Anglo-Americans, White (1991:57) has argued, they concluded that humans had not shaped the land at all. This, of course, was not true. For as long as humans have populated it, the West has never been a wilderness untrammeled by the human touch. For thousands of years it hosted human populations who burned grasslands and forests, hunted animals, cut wood, dug ditches and wells, built houses, harvested wild plants, altered animal habitats, created trails and roads, built dams, grew domesticated plants and raised a few domesticated animals, erected platform mounds, affected the soil, constructed reservoirs and canals, extirpated species, altered the course of rivers, built their own landscapes, and changed the very genetic structure of life. Pretending that this did not happen has allowed us to ignore the consequences of our actions on the land, other living creatures, and our own kind. Flores (1998b:62) has written that "the garden does not have to be free of the human touch to still be a garden." More significantly, a garden by definition is not a garden without the human touch.

Pipe Spring National Monument. Photograph by Jefferson Reid.

The values and beliefs that supported the notion of the West as economic and spiritual salvation had begun to change even as the great dams of the twentieth century rose in the remote canyons of the West's rivers, the reservoirs filled, and the canals began to flow. The Jeffersonian ideal of the small, independent farmer and the notion that the American West held an immensity of land awaiting the farmer's hand to transform it began to fade by the time the concrete blocks were poured in Hoover Dam. The small subsistence farm had long been the practical and efficient solution for coping with the environmental constraints of the desert West. Small farmers succeeded in much of prehistoric and early-historical-period Arizona by virtue of maintaining the precarious balance between population size and resources.

Today, however, both the independent-farming way of life and small populations are largely gone, replaced by other ways of making a living and by large urban centers. Even before the Central Arizona Project was begun, Bureau of Reclamation engineers were wondering how the tremendous changes following on the heels of Arizona's urbanization were going to affect the project. Who would take the water? How many people should they plan for? To what degree would urban growth displace agriculture? Would it replace agriculture? (Morton 1996:99).

Water in a barren land: Hayden-Rhodes Aqueduct. PHOTOGRAPH COURTESY U.S. BUREAU OF RECLAMATION. JOE MADRIGAL, JR., PHOTOGRAPHER.

Ironically, large water-control projects once designed to help the small farmer actually fueled the growth of agribusiness. White (1991:484) has pointed out that during the New Deal, the Bureau of Reclamation broke away from its older mandate to irrigate small farms and embarked on huge projects that benefited agribusiness and industry. Hoover Dam, for example, was a multipurpose project that was fitted into the larger design of controlling the entire Colorado River. The water in the All-American Canal flowed to large farms, the "field factories" of California and Arizona. White (1991:484) tells us that by 1938, the canal was capable of carrying a flow equal to that of the Potomac River and opened up an additional million acres of desert land. Repayment obligations, the lack of legal or political obstacles to leasing, and other factors promoted the consolidation of farms. The small Indian and Hispanic farmer was often dealt out of the game (Wilkinson 1992:248).

Paradoxically, the water used by agribusiness is highly subsidized by the federal government. Subsidies for irrigation-project water have been substantial. The irrigation districts served by the All-American Canal, for example, promised to repay without interest the total cost of the canal over a period of 40 years. Such interest-free loans "represented a massive subsidy to the private growers that the canal served" (White 1991:484). A 1980 federal study found that the subsidies for Bureau of Reclamation water ranged from \$58 per acre to a high of \$1,787 per acre in California's Wellton-Mohawk District. This meant that the federal government absorbed 57 percent to 97 percent of the cost of the projects (White 1991:523).

How to solve the problems that face western water users? There is no easy answer to this question, but there is an element of urgency to finding answers. We live in an impoverished West, a land that has been systematically dismantled by its inhabitants over the centuries (Flores 1998b:59). It is a West whose aquifers have been pumped dry to sustain growth far beyond the capacity of the land to support it. Two issues are most pressing for western water users. The first is the problem of astronomical population growth. In the past, among traditional societies and even among nineteenth-century farmers, there were limits on growth, self-adjusting mechanisms that constrained population to stay within the capacity of the land to support people. Twentieth- and twenty-first-century technology and the change in our economic foundation have altered this balance irrevocably. Although the opening of arid lands to settlement was an immediate and important benefit of reclamation in the West, today too many people are demanding too much from the land. Somehow we need to find a way of bringing growth into balance with the ability of the land and water to support the population.

Sonoran Desert landscape. Photograph by Jefferson Reid.

We can predict that whatever trajectory Arizona will take in the future, the trend will be toward higher population and greater urbanization. According to *National Geographic,* the Colorado Basin's urban areas are growing at an annual rate of 2.1 percent (National Geographic Society 2002). The Arizona of 2085 is likely to be big—more people, bigger cities. The population of Pima County alone reached 900,000 in fall 2002, and its annual growth rate of 2 to 3 percent outstrips that of the Colorado Basin as a whole (Cañizo 2002). Population density is less than in Phoenix, however—2,500 per square mile versus Phoenix's 2,782 (Cañizo 2002). Population growth has become an invidious problem—clogging city streets and freeways, packing schoolrooms, turning desert land into developments, and using resources at an alarming rate—all made possible by a supply of relatively cheap, safe, clean water. This is a worldwide problem. Many experts see population, consumption, and technology as the primary source of environmental impacts on a global scale. We will have to discover ways to supply enough water for Arizona's large and growing population to consume and ways to provide it that do not adversely impact and destroy the environment.

Stegner (1981:3) has asked some hard questions relating to water and the West. Who gets it when the pinch comes? "Do the new cities get it on the argument of the greatest good for the greatest number? Does agriculture get it on the basis of priority and contract? Do the power plants with their coal slurry lines get it? When an irrigation civilization, precariously floated on a few inches of water, begins to crumble, what crumbles first?" We may find it necessary to choose between irrigating Yuma's farms or providing water to our burgeoning cities. We may also have to consider a moratorium on growth. Santa Fe is a western city that has contemplated such restrictions. As recently reported, some city council members have sought to completely halt new construction. As a compromise, the council ruled in September 2002 that new construction could proceed only if its effects were offset by forcing builders to replace old, water-wasting toilets in existing homes, hotels, and businesses with new, water-efficient toilets (Jehl 2002). The new rules speak to "the kinds of hard choices and questions surfacing in communities across the West, where water supplies are stretched to the limit by population growth and drought" (Jehl 2002).

A second major problem facing the West is drought. We have now experienced several consecutive years of low precipitation and La Niña–induced dry winters. Whether created by burning fossil fuels or representing a natural cycle of change, global warming also is real with unknown

Central Arizona Project canal in metropolitan Phoenix area. Photograph courtesy U.S. Bureau of Reclamation. Joe Madrigal, Jr., photographer.

effects on North American weather patterns. The Colorado River upon which we depend is fed by melting snow; what will happen if there are extended periods when snowfall is less than normal? Stegner (1981) has pointed out that the two-year drought of 1977–1978 came near to destroying the stock industry in large portions of the U.S. Southwest; what will happen if we get a drought that lasts a quarter of a century? We know from the tree-ring record that droughts of such magnitude have occurred before; it is likely that they will come again. On the one hand, it is true that the tremendous storage capacity of the West's reservoirs serves as a buffer for times of drought. There are 50 million acre-feet of water in Lake Mead and Lake Powell alone (Morton 1996:128). Moreover, the Bureau of Reclamation gives Lake Powell a half-millennium life expectancy (Farmer 1999:200). On the other hand, no one knows how well this buffer will operate in times of extended drought. The problem may be particularly serious because the capability of water use in the Lower Basin exceeds the basin's entitlement (Morton 1996:473), and California consistently uses more than its allocation.

Rocky Mountain snowmelt feeds the Colorado River. PHOTOGRAPH BY JEFFERSON REID.

One solution that keeps resurfacing is to restore the West to its original state. Some wilderness advocates urge a militant solution—blow up the dams, let the rivers rage wild and free. Farmer (1999:183) has called such propositions "semicredible, semiludicrous," largely because restoring the West and its rivers would require much more than simply tearing down Floyd Dominy's dams. It would also require dismantling the treaties, laws, legal precedents, and policies governing the use of the Colorado River, other western rivers, groundwater sources, and land (Farmer 1999:183). The economies of water-dependent cities and families would be devastated. In the town of Page alone, tourists visiting Lake Powell generate $455 million each year; the Navajo Nation employs more than 1,000 tribal members at the Navajo Generating Station (Farmer 1999: 185). Most residents of Page and the Navajo Nation do not favor blowing up Glen Canyon Dam.

Of course, the rivers may win in the end, despite our technology, science, and hopes. In eons past, the Colorado

Hard Facts

Wallace Stegner (1981:3) reminds us of some of the hard facts of desert living:

> But meantime we do exactly what Powell warned us against doing. We refuse to listen either to the land or to history, both of which, if we listened, would say to us that this is a land of little rain, of severely restricted water supply. And therefore it is a land that must be settled and lived in with respect for facts, by a limited number of people with a limited amount of agriculture and industry.
>
> It says that to us, but we do not hear it, for we are Americans with a tradition of imposing ourselves on nature. Eventually, though, we will hear, and it won't take geological time.

Warning sign. PHOTOGRAPH BY JEFFERSON REID.

River has fought its way through obstacles far greater than Glen Canyon Dam. Just as we do not understand how extended drought will affect our water supplies, we also do not know what will happen if the 500-year flood comes. Arizona's cities have been destroyed before; it could happen again. Nature may win even without a flood. Perhaps someday we will confront absolute failure, a final and dreaded inability to meet the demands of the population for water and food. Like the ancient ones of Glen Canyon, the Salado of Tonto Basin, the Hohokam of the desert rivers, we may have to pack up and leave for good. "Their whole environment was altered," Martin (1981:13) has written, "as ours may be if we go too far. Thrown out of uneasy balance, we too may then have to leave."

Although a less naive solution to western water problems is to alter our thinking, this could be as difficult to implement as blowing up Glen Canyon Dam. Wilkinson (1992:305) favors this solution. To cross the next meridian, he has argued, we will have to do more than revamp the policies and laws he calls the "lords of yesterday." "It will require abolishing the philosophical ideas that fueled them and replacing those ideas with new ones." Some of the outmoded ideologies that may require rethinking include the humanist perspective that sees all human endeavor as the central purpose of life (Wakoski 1996), the West and wilderness as salvation, and notions of unlimited natural resources. We will need to shift our thinking to a more balanced approach that places humans in comparative scale against the rest of creation (Wakoski 1996)—to shed the antiquated dichotomous thinking that puts humans outside of the natural environment. We should abandon the nineteenth-century (and older) notion that the destiny of humanity is to possess the whole earth and the destiny of the earth is to be subject to humanity (Hepworth 1996:131–132).

Many of the antidam revolutionaries hold dear the outmoded notion of wilderness as spiritual salvation. For example, Farmer (1999:187) cites a letter to a newspaper editor stating that the core reason to drain Lake Powell was spiritual. Glen Canyon is the spiritual heart of the Colorado River, according to the writer, and recreational opportunities were a pitiful rationale to keep the lake when there is "a powerful spirit of peace and wisdom from our Mother Earth to be gained." The idea pervades the writings of preservationist icons such as Aldo Leopold, Wallace Stegner, and Edward Abbey. To confront the future of water in the West successfully, we need to shed the old, naive geography of hope. Freeing ourselves of the notion of the West as divine wilderness will help us go a long way toward developing practical policies to preserve, conserve, and use the land and its water wisely.

The nature and philosophy of water management in Arizona and the West have already begun to shift, and the change will be completed in the twenty-first century. The great dam-building, aqueduct-constructing, water-control era has ended. The Bureau of Reclamation has completed the job begun by the Reclamation Act of 1902, making Arthur Powell Davis's vision a reality. Few of the West's rivers are undammed and untamed, and the reservoirs behind Floyd Dominy's mighty dams could scarcely hold more water. According to Wilkinson (1992:259), the West's reservoirs hold more than 290 million acre-feet of water—the equivalent of 22 Colorado Rivers, enough to put Montana, Wyoming, Colorado, and New Mexico under a foot of water. According to *National Geographic* (National Geographic Society 2002), Colorado River water supports 25 million people. Instead of building new water-control projects, the Bureau of Reclamation and other agencies have turned to effective management and conservation of water resources. It is unlikely that, if the Central Arizona Project has outlived its usefulness by 2085, the Bureau of Reclamation will build a new system to replace it. In 2001, the agency listed its contemporary mission: "To manage, develop, and protect water and related resources in an

On Time and Gravity

Writer Jared Farmer (1999:200) on Glen Canyon Dam and Lake Powell:

> [T]he canyon can only get better. According to precedent, it will resurrect. In the recent geologic past (the last ten million years or so), a series of stupendous lava dams have plugged the Colorado River in Grand Canyon; each time, the river worked through and resumed its business of carrying silt to the sea. Glen Canyon Dam, too, is an aberrance. Time and gravity conspire against it. Someday, when the world is not much older, the song of the river will again echo between walls of sandstone. Wind and rain will uncover the classic desert varnish beneath the cheap white stain left by the reservoir. Flash floods, one at a time, will clear the glens of muck and debris. Cottonwoods will take root. Beavers will recolonize.

environmentally and economically sound manner in the interest of the American public." It is seeking a balanced program that will support water and economic development in the arid West while preserving biodiversity, conserving water, and protecting water quality and human health. By any measure, that's a tall order.

Will we seek to create another spectacular water-delivery system? One of the biggest plans ever to come out of politicians' and engineers' offices was an interbasin transfer of water from the water-rich Columbia River basin in the Pacific Northwest. A moratorium on even *discussing* diversion of this water to the Colorado was implemented after northwestern congressional members demanded it as their price for supporting the Central Arizona Project (Martin 1981:12). This moratorium has expired; politicians and engineers may even now be gearing up for a reintroduction of such a massive project, but this seems unlikely in today's political and social climate. Martin (1981:13) has written that an endless abundance of water—"the dream of a carefully managed relationship to land and resources that will sustain us forever—may light the way into a rich and fertile future."

Without a doubt, conservation will be necessary in the Arizona of 2085, regardless of what other strategies we might use. According to a Bureau of Reclamation booklet (U.S. Department of the Interior, Bureau of Reclamation 1998), the "fundamental equation of Western water today" is simple: "Supply is finite. Demand is growing. So conservation becomes essential." Water conservation is one of the Bureau of Reclamation's top priorities toward meeting the increasing demand for water, and the agency works with water users to develop management plans for efficient water use. Western states have attempted to deal with extended drought in a variety of ways. In many western cities, water restrictions have been implemented that prohibit car washing and refilling swimming pools and restrict outdoor watering to certain days and hours. Such restrictions are likely to be permanent in some areas.

It is clear that the dialogue between humans and nature is ongoing, constantly negotiated and consistently changing. We will never be able to achieve our goal of absolute sovereignty over nature, for "both continue to make and remake each other" (Worster 1985:22). As societies seek to remake nature, they remake themselves. We have seen this illustrated so well in the stories told in these pages. The rhetorical struggle over water control will continue in the Arizona of 2085, long after Glen Canyon was drowned, after the concrete in the dams and canals and bridges has begun to crumble, when the Central Arizona Project canals no longer carry water. There are fundamental questions to which we have no answers. "Should we let our technologies drive us, should we do whatever we're capable of doing in the certainty that science and engineering will enrich us? Or are we often wisest and most foresightful when we restrain ourselves, when we recognize natural limits, when we dare to leave the earth alone?" (Martin 1999:322).

Perhaps our paramount goal for the future should be to reconceptualize our environment, consider new ways of viewing land, water, and our relationship to these precious resources. We have to be clear about the West we are trying to restore and the values we employ in reconceptualizing our environment, however. Do we want the romantic, nineteenth-century West of our imagination? The West as it existed before Europeans arrived? The West before people arrived on the continent? (Flores 1998b:64). Or do we want the West that we would like to see, a land that is balanced with its population, whose resources are used respectfully, and whose management is considered with an eye to the future? We need to develop a sense of place, but it needs to be, as White (1991:633) reminds us, a sense about a real place. It cannot be the imaginary West of fiction, film, and story—the West as we would like it to be—but the real West, the West of scarcity and finite resources, of hunger and hardship.

Emergence

Robert Boissiere tells this story of the Hopi emergence into the Fourth World:

> So one by one, they climbed through the hollow reed,
> and went to ask permission to stay with Massoua.
> "This Earth has been created for all living things,"
> he said to them. "The animals, the plants, the birds,
> and humankind.
> Also the clouds in the sky, the water, and the fishes. . . .
> I am going to leave the Earth and all living things on it
> In your care. I appoint you guardians of this new world.
> Take care of it, protect it from pollution. It is your home.
> If you watch over it, it will feed you, clothe you,
> and keep your children and grandchildren healthy and happy.
> There will be hard times, when you will doubt.
> But never lose faith that what I told you today
> is the truth."

(Robert Boissiere, "The Emergence")

These goals are shared by many within the modern preservationist movement, the "deep ecology" that calls for a basic reevaluation of our attitudes toward nature and our place in the global ecosystem. Preservationism "calls for humans to recognize themselves not as masters but as wards and caretakers of the planet" (McNamee 1996:25). Williamson (1996:95) has pointed out that preservation of land, water, plants, and animal inhabitants can lead to preservation of the human species as well. In degrading nature, we are degrading ourselves, a connection that has been noted in philosophical movements of the twentieth century.

Holthaus (1997:29) has expressed this attitude well, writing:

> If the river stirs our fantasies, it is neither memory nor fancy but reality that tells us that the river is our parent. . . . Now. . . the life of the river is in our hands. We must care for it as once it cared for us.
>
> Though water has been one of the most complex and divisive issues in the West, it is also what draws us together in this place and allows us to stay. Water is the common bond that we share with one another and with all other creatures. It is one of the gifts that we have to have in order to live and that we therefore must share. Historically, if there has been any healing in the world, it has come from the rivers. . . . Water is not only a difficult, complex, and divisive issue; it is a source of our unity, a symbol of rest and health for mind and body, and our great hope.

In reconceptualizing and restoring the West and its water for the future, a new, redefined geography of hope may guide the way. In these pages, we have told stories of a stone-dry land that demonstrate a surpassing feat. Humans have made remarkable technological progress in the millennia since Late Archaic farmers first dropped kernels of seed corn into fields they cleared laboriously by hand. We have made prodigious strides in medicine and nutrition with concomitant extensions of life expectancy, improvements in quality of life, and overall well-being. Our major health problems stem from abundance, not privation. Technology brings fresh, clean water to most

Thoughts in A Desert Canyon

Barry Lopez (1981:31) shares some thoughts while experiencing a desert canyon on the Colorado Plateau:

> A thought that stayed with me was that I had entered a private place in the earth. I had seen exposed nearly its oldest part. I had lost my sense of urgency, rekindled a sense of what people were, clambering to gain access to high waterfalls where we washed our hair together; and a sense of our endless struggle as a species to understand time and to estimate the consequences of our acts.

Fannin-McFarland Aqueduct running through greater Phoenix metropolitan area. Photograph courtesy U.S. Bureau of Reclamation. Joe Madrigal, Jr., photographer.

homes and good water to farmlands. We have halted much of the wholesale degradation of land and water and have moved toward an effective compromise between resource utilization and conservation. We have the tools for reshaping our water-use policies; we need to implement new goals within an altered perspective.

Our hope for the future is to use technology wisely to preserve the only earth we have for generations to come. It won't be easy, of course; no great changes are ever easy. We need to improve economic opportunities for Arizona's residents to shed our dependence on extractive industries and profitless ranching and farming efforts. It is the poorest among us who must use their natural resources to death simply to stay alive. We must come to grips with the fact that nature cannot not be dominated or conquered without consequences to the larger web of life. We need to realistically assess our balance between population and water and ruthlessly promote conservation measures. We can hope that the dams will still stand and that water in the canals will still flow in the Arizona of 2085, but also that these technological marvels will bring water to enlightened residents who recognize the value of preserving the Copper State's natural wonders and available resources. We can promote Arizona not only as a place where climate, wilderness areas, and gorgeous scenery combine to offer a year-round recreational paradise, but also a place where these advantages are used wisely and for the benefit of future generations. We can create a new place, a best and perfect place, for today and tomorrow. This, then, can become our new geography of hope.

Appendix

Archaeology, Cultural Resource Management, and Legislative Overview

Central Arizona Project Archaeology illustrates the development of our nation's philosophy to preserve and protect its environmental, cultural, and historical resources. The project is a testament to changing American values, and we can read in its history the greater story of developing federal policy toward national resources. In this appendix, we discuss some of the important federal laws protecting cultural resources and look at how the **historic-preservation** process works in the context of cultural resource management.

We begin by looking at archaeology and how cultural resource management fits within this larger discipline. Archaeology in the United States is considered one of the four subfields of anthropology. Although most people think that archaeology deals with the past and equate archaeology with excavation, it is much broader. Archaeology studies material culture to understand broad patterns in the way people behave, whether in the past or present (Reid 1995; Reid and others 1975). It is this emphasis on *behavior* that makes archaeology part of the discipline of anthropology. Broadening the definition of archaeology beyond the excavation of the ruins of ancient societies helps us to understand archaeology's importance and how material culture functions in our lives.

Archaeology can be divided into four broad strategies that correlate material culture and behavior of the past and present (Reid 1995; Reid and others 1975). In Strategy 2, we can use the material culture of the present to derive principles to describe and explain behavior of the past (and present). Archaeologists called ethnoarchaeologists, who study living societies to derive information about how material culture is made and used, seek to apply this information in understanding past societies. Experimental archaeology, which studies modern material culture toward understanding physical principles, function, and so on, is another facet of archaeology that uses Strategy 2. Archaeologists who replicate ancient technologies and scientists who study the properties of ceramics and other classes of material culture are experimental archaeologists.

We can also use material culture of the present to understand modern societies (Strategy 3). The most famous example of this strategy is William Rathje's Garbage Project developed at the University of Arizona. Rathje and his students literally study garbage taken from waste-management operations and landfills to understand behaviors such as waste and recycling. Or, we can use material culture of the past to study living societies (Strategy 4). This is the least well known of the four archaeological strategies. Anthropologists who record the oral histories of Native Americans toward understanding their contemporary societies use this strategy.

The most common strategy and the one with which most people are familiar is Strategy 1, which uses past material culture to answer questions about past societies. This strategy is the subject matter of prehistoric and historical archaeology in the United States. Although most people commonly equate this strategy with excavating ancient Native American sites, it includes the material remains and archaeological sites of all people. Strategy 1 was used during the Central Arizona Project to excavate and interpret archaeological sites, most of which were occupied by ancient Native Americans.

Cultural resources, such as archaeological sites, historic buildings, historic landscapes, and so on, are therefore an important source of information as well as the record of history. Many of these resources are nonrenewable. Although we continue to generate archaeological sites through our activities, we can never replace those occupied by Paleoindians some 12,000 years ago, for example. Our nation recognized the importance of protecting these precious cultural resources by enacting laws to protect and preserve them. Federal laws protecting cultural resources are nearly a century old, and they have changed quite remarkably over time. Federal laws date back to 1906, when the Antiquities Act (16 U.S.C. 431–433) was passed to prohibit excavation of antiquities on public lands without permission from the Secretary of the Interior or from the Departments of Agriculture and War.

This landmark act—the first piece of preservation legislation in U.S. history—was intended to stop the rampant looting and destruction of archaeological sites by collectors and poorly qualified excavators. This had been a particularly critical problem in the U.S. Southwest, where sites had been mined by collectors who sold the artifacts. The growth of philanthropic institutions, research universities, and museums around the turn of the twentieth century sent many expeditions to the U.S. Southwest to collect anthropological and archaeological specimens (Fowler 2002). Much later in the twentieth century, these objects and the contentious issue of who owns the past would spur the creation of the Native American Graves Protection and Repatriation Act of 1990. The Antiquities Act established fines and imprisonment for damage to or appropriations from archaeological sites on federal lands. It also established a permitting system for legitimate investigation and authorized the president to create national monuments for purposes of preservation.

Ten years after the Antiquities Act was passed, the National Park Service was created to give the nation an agency for conservation of natural and cultural resources. The management of historic battlefields was transferred from the War Department to the National Park Service at that time (King 1998).

The Great Depression greatly affected the growth of historic preservation, as out-of-work professionals in different disciplines were hired to document historic buildings, write histories, and carry out archaeology in federal "make-work" programs. Reservoir salvage archaeology to excavate archaeological sites before they were inundated began in the 1930s as part of the Works Progress Administration (WPA). In 1935, the Historic Sites Act (16 U.S.C. 461–467) greatly expanded the role of the federal government in the arena of cultural resources. A piece of New Deal legislation, the act is considered a precursor to the National Historic Preservation Act. The Historic Sites Act created the National Historic Landmarks program, later to become the National Register of Historic Places. It also established the Historic American Buildings Survey and the Historic American Engineering Record, two programs that were designed to record the nation's architectural and engineering achievements and which are still used today. Importantly, the act declared a national policy to "preserve for public use historic sites, buildings, and objects of national significance for the inspiration and benefit of the people of the United States."

Not unexpectedly, World War II slowed the growth of historic preservation in the United States as the nation turned to other issues. In 1949, the National Trust for Historic Preservation, a private-sector, nonprofit organization to promote historic preservation across the nation, was chartered. In the 1950s, historic-preservation activities began to flourish once more. The U.S. Army Corps of Engineers began to build dams and reservoirs, and President Eisenhower launched the interstate highway program. Both of these would do "alarming damage to historic neighborhoods, buildings, structures, and archaeological sites, and the government responded—albeit rather haltingly"

(King 1998:14). The National Park Service and the Smithsonian Institution organized the River Basin Surveys to salvage archaeological sites threatened by reservoirs built by federal agencies. The 1960 Reservoir Salvage Act (16 U.S.C. 469) authorized the National Park Service to conduct salvage excavations at sites that were threatened with inundation. The act recognized that the federal government had a responsibility to protect the nation's cultural resources from destruction by government action; it was the first formal recognition of this responsibility. Some early Central Arizona Project investigations were conducted under the authority of this act.

The Kennedy and Johnson administrations were influential in producing legislation that would have tremendous impact on historic preservation and archaeology. In Chapter 3, we discussed the two most important pieces of legislation to come out of this era, which are the National Historic Preservation Act (16 U.S.C. 470) of 1966 and the National Environmental Policy Act of 1969. As enacted, Section 106 of the National Historic Preservation Act required agencies to consider impacts on places already included in the National Register of Historic Places. To avoid dealing with impacts, agencies could keep archaeological sites and properties from being nominated to the National Register. This problem was alleviated in 1972, when President Nixon issued Executive Order 11593. It directed federal agencies to treat eligible properties as though they were listed in the National Register and ordered the National Park Service to establish procedures for determining eligibility. After some early battles, agencies began to routinely incorporate preservation expertise and procedures into their environmental programs (King 1998:17).

Cultural resource management blossomed after Executive Order 11593 was issued. The term "cultural resource management" was coined in the 1970s by archaeologists working in the U.S. Southwest (Lipe and Lindsay 1974) and had the effect of generally equating historic preservation with archaeology, when it is actually much broader (King 1998:18). Although much of the information presented in this book was derived from archaeology, cultural resource management also includes the management of historical buildings and structures, rural historical landscapes, traditional cultural places, and more. And although we tend to focus on Native American archaeological sites, cultural resource management includes cultural and historical resources related to nonnative peoples of the historical period and all ethnic and cultural groups.

Intriguingly, cultural resource management began to flourish at a time when radical developments were taking place in academic archaeology. At that time, a new, explicitly scientific way of conducting archaeology emerged that has been variously labeled "the New Archaeology" and "processual archaeology." Processual archaeology was concerned with various processes shaping human behavior, hence the label. This revolution sought to go beyond the simple description of material remains to reconstruct and explain nonmaterial behavior, emphasizing how ancient people related to their environment and to other people (Reid and Whittlesey 1997:19). Researchers subscribing to this view saw archaeology as anthropology, the broader study of people and their culture. They emphasized the deductive nature of archaeology and were concerned with testing hypotheses about the past. The dual developments of the 1970s had the unfortunate effect of separating academic archaeologists, who practice and teach in university settings, from cultural resource management archaeologists, who are typically employed in the private sector or by various state and federal agencies. A less divisive way of viewing the differences between the two groups is to see academic archaeology as "pure" science and cultural resource management as "applied" science. Having said that, some academic institutions carry out cultural resource management programs, and some nonacademic organizations have applied for and received federal funds to sponsor research not related to cultural resource management. In short, the lines are becoming blurred, which is a good thing.

In 1974, the Archaeological and Historic Sites Preservation Act was passed to augment the Reservoir Salvage Act of 1960. The law required that the level of funding for preservation must be commensurate with the damage to cultural resources caused by governmental action. This would prevent low-budget "preservation" activities. Also in 1974, a federal case sparked a new act. The Antiquities Act of 1906 was found to be unconstitutionally vague in the Ninth Circuit Court of Appeals because it failed to indicate the age required for an object to be considered an antiquity. Elsewhere, the law was considered to be constitutional along with other parts of the law not related to antiquities (such as the power of a president to proclaim national monuments). Because new legislation was necessary to ensure uniformity, the case resulted in the Archaeological Resources Protection Act (16 U.S.C. 470aa–mm) of 1979.

This act clarified and greatly expanded the earlier law to include Indian rights and lands, artifact trafficking, the permitting process, and civil penalties. A felony conviction can bring two years in jail, a fine of as much as $250,000, and forfeiture of all equipment used in committing the crime. Sec. 2 of the act recognizes the importance of the nation's cultural heritage and the role of the federal government in protecting it, as follows:

(a) The Congress finds that—
   (1) archaeological resources on public lands and Indian lands are an accessible and irreplaceable part of the Nation's heritage;
   (2) these resources are increasingly endangered because of their commercial attractiveness;
   (3) existing Federal laws do not provide adequate protection to prevent the loss and destruction of these archaeological resources and sites resulting from uncontrolled excavations and pillage; and
   (4) there is a wealth of archaeological information which has been legally obtained by private individuals for noncommercial purposes and which could voluntarily be made available to professional archaeologists and institutions.
(b) The purpose of this Act is to secure, for the present and future benefit of the American people, the protection of archaeological resources and sites which are on public lands and Indian lands, and to foster increased cooperation and exchange of information between governmental authorities, the professional archaeological community, and private individuals having collections of archaeological resources and data which were obtained before the date of the enactment of this Act.

In 1978, the American Indian Religious Freedom Act (42 U.S.C. 1996) was passed. This increased protection of ancestral sites, spiritual places that were not archaeological sites, ceremonial uses of natural resources, and ancestral remains and artifacts.

The National Historic Preservation Act was amended several times throughout the 1970s and 1980s. The 1980 amendments identified the responsibilities of State Historic Preservation Officers and recognized the role of local governments (King 1998:21). The act was amended most recently in 1992. These amendments included a number of provisions designed to increase participation by Indian tribes, Alaska natives, and Native Hawaiians in historic preservation. One provision was to substitute tribal preservation programs and the Tribal Historic Preservation Officer for the State Historic Preservation Officer.

The 1980s witnessed a great increase in tribal participation in historic preservation and cultural resource management. It resulted in one of the most influential pieces of legislation relating to Native American remains and artifacts—the Native American Graves Protection and Repatriation Act of 1990. This act sparked return and reburial of skeletal remains, associated artifacts, and items of cultural patrimony from museums across the nation. It requires that federal agencies consult with tribes about the disposition of human remains and associated grave goods whenever such remains are discovered through federal actions on federal or Indian lands.

Since the 1980s, there has been a surge in preservation legislation on the state and local levels. In 1982, Arizona passed the State Historic Preservation Act that emulates the National Historic Preservation Act on the state level. Arizona has also enacted state laws designed to stop looting of human graves. The 1990 Arizona Burial Protection Laws apply to state and private land. It is unlawful to disturb an unmarked human grave, even on private land. Pima County has passed new requirements that require cultural resources studies to be carried out before construction can begin on projects necessitating county approval. Municipal governments have enacted similar regulations. Throughout the nation, similar requirements and legislation have been passed at local and state levels.

As a consequence of this long and complicated history, the legal structure for historic preservation is a patchwork of laws at municipal, county, state, and federal levels. Each set of regulations has its own requirements and involves different parties. Projects must comply with all applicable laws, however. This is one reason why cultural resource management is complicated, and highly specialized practitioners have arisen to negotiate through the complex web of legal, professional, and ethical requirements. Although there are literally hundreds of historic-preservation laws on the books, many cultural resource management activities are driven by the need for compliance with Section 106 of the National Historic Preservation Act. We look more closely at these requirements and how the process works in the following section.

Section 106 and Cultural Resource Management

Let's take a peek behind the scenes to see how all of this works on a practical level. First, let's look more closely at cultural resource management. Which organizations and agencies are required to undertake cultural resources studies? How does a sponsor planning a project, such as the Bureau of Reclamation, know how to proceed? How does it find qualified professionals to carry out the work? And who pays for the work? Many different agencies conduct cultural resource management activities because of Section 106 requirements, including those that administer public lands, such as the Bureau of Land Management and the U.S.D.A. Forest Service; carry out construction projects, such as the Federal Highways Administration and the U.S. Army Corps of Engineers; and serve as federal licensing agencies, such as the Federal Energy Regulatory Commission. Construction projects carried out by nonfederal organizations that employ federal funding in their activities (such as the Arizona Department of Transportation) and those that require a federal permit in their activities (such as a company building a pipeline across the state of Arizona that will require a permit from the Federal Energy Regulatory Commission), are also considered federal undertakings. Because of these requirements, federal archaeological projects may be carried out on private or state lands.

Many federal and state organizations as well as land-managing agencies, such as the Bureau of Land Management and the U.S.D.A. Forest Service, typically employ their own archaeologists, who understand the laws and the cultural resource management process. Although they may conduct the work themselves, more commonly such archaeologists prepare requests for proposals to select outside consultants to do the work, help to select consultants, oversee project costs and schedules, and serve as a liaison among the sponsor's contracting office, the consultant, and other players. Agency archaeologists review the studies of historic properties, weigh the project alternatives, and help the agency's managers to make decisions. For the most part, laws protecting cultural resources do not force a project sponsor to choose between building their project and protecting archaeological sites, historic buildings, and sacred places. Instead, the laws set up a process for making decisions that balance the importance of preserving our past with new development and infrastructure. Agency archaeologists and cultural resource management specialists help the agency negotiate this sometimes rocky road.

Federal organizations must advertise for qualified consultants to undertake the work by issuing a request for proposals. The request for proposals is usually prepared by the sponsor in collaboration with the land-managing agency and the historic preservation officer. It indicates the project's location, any previous archaeological work, and the scope of the proposed study. Potential projects are usually advertised in several formats; today, requests for proposals are often available on-line.

Consultants bid competitively on potential projects. Consultants who perform the archaeological work may be private consulting firms, museums, and university anthropology departments. There are no specifications other than that the organization and its personnel must be qualified, experienced, and have adequate facilities and equipment to conduct the work. Over the years, there has been a shift to securing private firms as archaeological consultants.

Typically, potential consultants prepare a technical proposal that indicates how the consultant will carry out the work. The proposal must demonstrate an understanding of the project's scope of work, and research designs are often submitted as part of the technical proposal. A cost proposal that specifies how much the proposed work will cost may or may not be part of the consultant's bid, depending on the organization who issues the request for proposals and the type of contract. The consultant is usually chosen by a committee selected from the various groups involved, who rate the proposals according to a preestablished set of criteria. These require that the work is done adequately to national standards by qualified organizations and in a culturally sensitive manner. Usually a consultant's track record, personnel, and facilities are considered to be most important. The proposed work is evaluated according to scientific research canons in addition to the other criteria. If cost of the archaeological work is part of the potential consultants' proposals, the evaluation process will include this factor, too, judging which firm offers the best value to the sponsor. Points are awarded according to a predetermined scale, and the highest-ranked bidder is selected. After selection, if cost has not already been part of the proposal, the project costs are negotiated with the sponsor. The entire process is typically overseen by and conducted through the sponsor's contracting office. Strict procedures are maintained to avoid accusations of favoritism and to maintain confidentiality.

A contract is issued to the winning consultant who performs the work under contractual specifications, which is why cultural resource management archaeology is often called "contract archaeology." When the contract is awarded, the consultant may begin the work.

Funding for cultural resource management studies comes directly from the federal agency that is conducting the project or approving it, such as the Bureau of Reclamation, or from the private party that needs agency approval for a project, such as a pipeline company requiring a federal permit. The Central Arizona Project archaeological studies were funded by the Bureau of Reclamation.

Now, let's turn to the details of Section 106. To recap, we have seen that Section 106 of the National Historic Preservation Act requires that a federal agency intending to undertake a project—such as the Bureau of Reclamation planning to build a dam—must deal with the listed or eligible cultural resources that will be impacted directly or indirectly by activities associated with the undertaking. (Note that many other federal and local laws and regulations may also require a concern with cultural resources, as discussed above. All of these laws must be complied with. For simplicity's sake, we'll ignore this complication.) Section 106 of the National Historic Preservation Act drives archaeology by requiring that federal agencies must: (1) take into account the effects of their actions on historic properties that are listed in or eligible for listing in the National Register of Historic Places, and (2) offer the Advisory Council on Historic Preservation an opportunity to comment on their actions.

The first step in this process is that the agency building the project (the sponsor) must identify the historic properties within the area that will be affected by the undertaking, called the area of potential effect. In other words, the sites must be found. The sponsor begins by plotting the area affected by the undertaking, such as the amount of acreage that will be inundated by the reservoir when a new dam is built, the land disturbed by construction staging sites, and the right-of-way for roads that will be built in the project area. This will determine the area that will be examined for the presence of cultural resources.

During the Central Arizona Project, the proposed project areas (for example, the route of Tucson Aqueduct Phase A) were often surveyed in the planning stages to determine if archaeological sites were present. Consultants usually carried out this task. There are several different levels of survey, ranging from a general overview and literature search to intensive, on-the-ground survey that covers the complete project area. These kinds of surveys are used as planning and management tools in different stages of project completion and were employed in this way during the Central Arizona Project.

Archaeologists usually begin a survey with site-file checks and records searches to determine if any surveys have already been made in the project area and if sites have already been recorded, listed in the National Register, or assessed as potentially eligible during a previous study. Such records are maintained at the Arizona State Museum, National Forest offices, offices of other land-managing agencies such as the U.S. Bureau of Land Management, and the State Historic Preservation Office. Other archival research is conducted, and the literature is searched for information relevant to the project area.

Next, archaeologists typically conduct an on-the-ground survey to look for artifacts and human-made features. Survey involves systematically walking over the construction right-of-way or area of potential effect. Surveys may be linear, as for a long, narrow aqueduct or highway right-of-way, or block, as for a proposed reservoir area. Several crew members walk parallel and spaced equally apart, the number depending on the width of the right-of-way. They make a sweep up one side of the right-of-way or block transect, then pivot and walk down the other side. This is repeated until the area has been covered. Compasses, Geographic Positioning Systems units, and different kinds of maps (engineering, topographic, and aerial photographs if available) are used to keep the line straight. During survey, newly discovered sites and isolated artifacts are mapped and recorded, and limited artifact collections may be made in some cases. Today the trend is toward what are called noncollection surveys, meaning no artifacts are collected. Maps are made, photographs are taken, and forms are filled out.

The first step in the cultural resource management process often involves other kinds of cultural resources as well as prehistoric archaeological sites. Anthropologists may conduct an ethnographic survey, interviewing elders of Native American tribes and other traditional communities to determine if places important to the history and traditions of these communities are located in the project area. Historians and historical archaeologists may conduct archival research, using historical records, maps, photographs, and interviews to determine the age and characteristics of historical buildings, townsites, roads, mines, and other historical resources. In short, all kinds of cultural resources must be considered, not just prehistoric archaeological sites.

When the survey is finished, the consultant prepares a report describing the sites in detail, recommending eligibility to the National Register if this was the survey goal, making management recommendations, and suggesting further action. If no cultural resources were found during the survey, this completes the sponsor's responsibilities under Section 106. In other words, having made a good-faith effort to locate archaeological sites and other historic places and finding none, the sponsor is off the hook.

Let's assume, however, that the survey located many prehistoric and historical sites. Using the information in the survey report, the sponsor must then determine if the properties are already listed in the National Register of Historic Places, and if they are not, determine if they are eligible for listing. This is the second step in the cultural resource management process. The sponsor consults with the State Historic Preservation Office, and in some cases, also with the Advisory Council on Historic Preservation. They apply the criteria established in Title 36 of the Code of Federal Regulations to determine if the sites are eligible for listing in the National Register of Historic Places.

During Section 106 review, the agency carrying out the project must collaborate with a variety of other players. These include the land-managing agency (the group that manages the public land, such as the U.S.D.A. Forest Service), the historic-preservation officer (state or tribal), Indian tribes whose lands or traditional religious and cultural values will be affected by the undertaking, local governments with jurisdiction over the areas affected, and any applicants for federal assistance or permits. Much of Central Arizona Project archaeology was conducted in consultation with Tonto National Forest, for example, because many individual projects were located on Tonto National Forest lands. A variety of other organizations and groups may be involved in the process, depending on its scope and level of interest to local communities.

The process of determining National Register eligibility appears deceptively simple, when it is actually rather complicated. National Register eligibility hinges on an elusive quality labeled "significance" and on the integrity of the property. Significance is assessed by applying a series of criteria found in the National Park Service regulations 36 CFR 60.4, labeled (a) through (d). The criteria read as follows.

> The quality of significance in American history, architecture, archeology, engineering, and culture is present in districts, sites, buildings, structures and objects that possess integrity of location, design, setting, materials, workmanship, feeling and association.
>
> (a) That are associated with events that have made a significant contribution to the broad patterns of our history; or
>
> (b) That are associated with the lives of persons significant in our past; or
>
> (c) That embody the distinctive characteristics of a type, period, or method of construction, or that represent the work of a master, or that possess high artistic values, or that represent a significant and distinguishable entity whose components may lack individual distinction; or
>
> (d) That have yielded, or may be likely to yield, information important to prehistory or history.

Criteria (a) through (c) are usually applied in properties with historical, architectural, artistic, and cultural importance. A property can be eligible under Criterion (a) if it is associated with a battle or an invention (an event) or a pattern of events, such as the westward movement or the developing of mining in frontier California. A Civil War battlefield might be eligible under Criterion (a). Events may also be traditional episodes in the oral history of native peoples. An example of a historical property considered eligible under Criterion (a) is Faraway Ranch in the Chiricahua Mountains of southeastern Arizona. First established in the 1880s as a pioneer homestead, the ranch exemplifies the changing history of rural life in the West. It includes the remains of a military camp established in 1885 by the "Buffalo Soldiers" of the 10th Cavalry during the Geronimo campaign. It has significance in the arenas of pioneer homesteading, cattle ranching and guest ranching industries, military history, and African-American history in Arizona (Baumler 1984).

Criterion (b) is straightforward, although important persons do not have to be people as famous as George Washington or Abraham Lincoln. They can also be people of lesser renown or even nonhuman entities, such as spirits. An archaeological site associated with a traditional culture hero might be eligible under this criterion, for example.

Under Criterion (c), important associations could be an architectural or building style, the best or only example of such a style, or an important piece of art such as a mural or a rock-art site. Districts can also be included, based on the idea that the whole is greater than the sum of its parts. Many rock-art sites in Arizona have been nominated to the National Register of Historic Places because they represent important examples of prehistoric rock-art styles, including the Ripley Intaglios along the lower Colorado River and the Hedgpeth Hills Petroglyphs site near Phoenix (Thiel 1995).

Criterion (d), by contrast, is usually used to assess the eligibility of prehistoric archaeological sites and often historical-period sites as well. It specifies that a property is eligible if it contains or may contain information important in history or prehistory. Criterion (d) can also apply to other types of properties. The information that a property yields or is likely to yield must be evaluated within the context of time, place, and research themes, which is called a historic context. Archaeologists typically prepare research designs that present the background information about a property's cultural setting, time of occupation, and environmental context when they prepare an overview or a plan of work for a survey. This information is used to create a set of research questions that information collected from the archaeological site might be used to answer.

Let's take as an example a hypothetical site discovered during survey of a Central Arizona Project aqueduct route. Say that the site was large with a dense scatter of artifacts on the surface. Ceramics were found that dated to the Pioneer period of the Hohokam culture. The extent of the site and associated artifacts suggested that it was used for habitation. Because relatively little is known about the Pioneer period compared to later times, archaeologists might craft a series of research questions to investigate subsistence, ceramic production and distribution, and household organization during the Pioneer period in the area of the site's location. Because a habitation site would be likely to yield architectural remains, household refuse deposits with many artifacts, and hearths for dating, thus providing considerable information about these topics, the site would probably be deemed eligible under Criterion (d). Research designs prepared for evaluating eligibility thus narrow the scope of investigation and ensure that important properties are investigated and time will not be wasted on poorly preserved or uninformative properties.

To be eligible under any criterion, a property must also display integrity, which is the ability of a property to convey its significance. That is, if a property has been so severely impacted by development, disturbance, or other processes as to destroy the qualities that made it significant, then it is usually not considered eligible. There are seven aspects of integrity—location, design, setting, materials, workmanship, feeling, and association. These are readily appreciated with properties eligible under Criteria (a) through (c). For example, a recent building fabricated to look like a historical building or a historical building restored with incompatible materials would not be eligible to the National Register because the integrity aspect of materials (and probably workmanship as well) has been compromised. The integrity of archaeological sites is usually evaluated in terms of preservation and disturbance. Returning to our hypothetical site discovered on survey, let's pretend that a dairy had been built on top of it. If construction of waterlines and continuous earthmoving activities had severely affected the subsurface deposits, the site might not have sufficient integrity to be considered eligible (the association of cultural remains would be ambiguous). If, however, earthmoving activities only affected the surface of the site, it might still be sufficiently intact to be considered eligible. In that case, testing might be warranted to determine the degree and extent of subsurface impacts.

Traditional cultural properties—properties of traditional religious and cultural importance to an ethnic group, segment of society, Indian tribe, Alaska native, or Native Hawaiian group—may also be determined to be eligible as amended by Congress in 1992. Such properties have traditional cultural significance derived from the role the property plays in a community's historically rooted beliefs, customs, and practices. Such properties might include a location associated with the traditional beliefs of a Native American group concerning its origins or places where Native American religious practitioners have gone to perform ceremonies. Otherwise, properties with religious importance, including cemeteries, churches, and commemorative shrines, are usually not eligible unless their historical significance can be established. Any cultural group can identify traditional cultural properties, not only indigenous peoples. Neighborhoods or districts associated with any ethnic group may be considered traditional cultural places based on cultural values reflected in architecture, organization of space, and activities.

Sometimes further information about a site is needed before recommendations for National Register eligibility can be made. This most often takes place when the extent, condition, or other information about a site is not known from surface indications, such that its integrity cannot be assessed (recall that sites must have integrity in order to be eligible). State Historic Preservation Offices are usually not inclined to approve extensive testing for eligibility purposes. More intensive testing may take place at a later time on an eligible site when data recovery is anticipated.

Test excavations, surface collections, and other limited work may be undertaken to determine the nature of deposits below the surface and their condition. Mechanical excavation (backhoe trenching or surface stripping of overburden deposits) is usually used on Hohokam sites where architectural features are not visible on the surface. This is accomplished by digging parallel trenches at systematic intervals over the surface of the site to locate pit houses and other subsurface features. At other kinds of sites, test pits may be hand excavated inside rooms, plazas, and other architectural features. When testing for National Register eligibility, archaeologists will usually try to place their test units in portions of the site that are already disturbed by erosion or other processes. Artifacts are collected from backhoe trenches and features; a limited number of samples for dating techniques and botanical analysis may be collected.

If no sites in the project area are determined to be eligible for listing in the National Register of Historic Places, the sponsoring agency's responsibilities under Section 106 are complete. If one or more sites are determined to be eligible to the National Register, however, the sponsoring agency, the historic preservation office, the Advisory Council, tribes, and other interested parties must then move on to the third step in cultural resource management, which is to evaluate the impacts of the proposed project on the site or sites. To do this, they must consider the kinds of effects on the eligible properties and the qualities that make those properties eligible to the

National Register. Impacts may be direct, in which construction affects the property directly, or indirect, resulting from activities made possible by the project or affecting a property from a distance, such as noise or air pollution. The kind of property must be considered, as well. Noise would not necessarily affect the integrity of an archaeological site and adversely impact it, but would have a significant adverse effect on a Native American religious site where solitude and quietude are considered to be important aspects of the religious experience.

The most common and most destructive impacts are those that result from ground disturbance, although the National Historic Preservation Act protects historic properties from a wide range of adverse effects, particularly for traditional cultural properties and historic buildings. Ground-disturbing activities are typically construction projects, such as building bridges, roads, dams, housing developments, and so on. For the Central Arizona Project, construction activities included building the aqueducts and siphons; blading roads to provide access to construction sites and making staging areas for equipment and materials; and building associated recreational facilities, such as campgrounds, boat ramps, and parking lots. Newly built dams created new reservoirs, and existing dams were modified to raise levels of their reservoirs. These processes would inundate many archaeological sites. Although not a ground-disturbing activity, inundation would obviously impact archaeological sites adversely. Other impacts that were considered include increased access to archaeological sites that might result in vandalism or destruction of sites. It short, all impacts of a project must be considered.

The sponsor, land-managing agency, State Historic Preservation Office, and other interested parties examine the effects that the project would have on each of the eligible historic properties within the project area and decide whether the properties will be adversely impacted. If none of them will be adversely impacted, the sponsor is off the hook again. If, however, the project will have an adverse impact on historic properties, the agency must decide what should be done to "take into account" those effects (recall that the agency must identify historic properties affected by the undertaking and take into account the affects of any projects it carries out, authorizes, or funds on historic properties). The agency must decide how to proceed, weighing the costs of the cultural resources studies against the construction costs. It is often possible to avoid sites by rerouting the project. Preservation is always the preferable alternative unless sites will be indirectly impacted. If the site cannot be avoided by moving the project, the parties will move on to the fourth step—they will try to reach an agreement about what to do, termed a Memorandum of Agreement. For prehistoric sites that will be physically destroyed by construction, usually such a memorandum requires that the cultural and historical values of the site be preserved through the excavation, analysis, and curation of the artifacts and other materials. This latter step, termed data recovery, is the fifth step in the cultural resource management process. The sponsor must pay for archaeological work spelled out in the Memorandum of Agreement before construction begins.

Data recovery is the most intensive type of archaeological project. It is designed to retrieve information from impacted sites and preserve it for the future, thereby mitigating the adverse effects of construction. Data recovery most often means excavation, particularly for prehistoric archaeological sites. During the Central Arizona Project, data recovery took place at archaeological sites where impacts could not be avoided by rerouting the project or other means. Many intensive data-recovery projects were carried out, particularly for the Tucson and Fannin-McFarland Aqueducts, modifications to Theodore Roosevelt Dam, and construction of New Waddell Dam.

Sometimes a site must be tested further before data recovery begins. This most often happens when the number and extent of subsurface features are unknown, so that it is impossible to decide where to excavate or how much excavation will cost. Archaeological testing usually involves a combination of mechanical trenching or scraping, hand excavation, and surface collection, as described above. If this step is undertaken, the consultant prepares a testing report for the sponsor. Testing reports are usually brief compared to those prepared for archaeological survey and data recovery. The report presents summary information about the extent of the site, the number of features and their condition, the kinds of subsurface deposits, the age of the site, and other information. A data-recovery plan may be presented that spells out proposed methods in detail. The plan may include a research design listing research themes and specific questions along with estimates of the effort and cost and the methods to be used if data recovery is deemed necessary.

If testing is not deemed necessary, the project moves into data recovery. The consultant usually prepares a plan of work and research design that will direct all aspects of excavation, analysis, and reporting. When data recovery is undertaken without a prior testing stage, excavation is usually phased. Phase 1 takes the place of testing, and consists of locating buried features, determining their condition, and estimating the quantity of artifacts. This information enables archaeologists to decide how many features to excavate and thereby estimate excavation costs. Usually the entire site is not excavated but only the portion that is directly affected. When construction plans are finalized, the area of potential effect is known and excavation concentrates on this area. The site is "sampled"—only a certain percentage of the site area or a particular number of features will be excavated. The rationale for this is that where many features are similar, a sample will be representative of the whole. This strategy not only reduces costs but also typically leaves a portion of the site intact for the future.

Excavation is usually carried out by hand regardless of the type of site, unless the locations of features are not known. If that is the case, backhoe trenches may be excavated to locate subsurface features that are then excavated by hand. Features may be completely or partially excavated. Excavation proceeds systematically in natural or cultural levels (roof fall, fill, floor) or arbitrary levels of equal depth. The feature may be divided into smaller horizontal units. At least a portion of the fill is screened to recover small artifacts. Artifacts and samples are bagged according to provenience and type (flaked stone, sherds, faunal bone, and so on). Photographs and notes are taken, forms are filled out, and other information is recorded during excavation. The excavation unit and any features it contains are mapped and profiled. Nonarchitectural features are excavated systematically; larger features may be sampled. Recording and mapping of prehistoric sites is accomplished with the metric system.

A plan of work for excavation always includes a data-recovery plan for treatment of human remains, should they be found. This specifies how burials will be excavated and recorded, what types of analyses, if any, can be carried out, and whether they will be conducted in the laboratory or in the field. The treatment plan is designed to comply with all applicable statutes and regulations and with Native American concerns and sensitivities.

All excavated units and features are recorded in similar systematic fashion. Last, the entire site is mapped with surveying instruments (optical or digital). If the site will not be destroyed by construction activities, the final step is usually backfilling (filling in the excavated portions of the site with dirt and rocks removed during excavation).

Historical-period sites are treated somewhat differently, particularly those with standing buildings. The English rather than metric system is used for recording measurements, for example, and mechanical trenching is seldom used. Buildings are recorded in detail and are mapped and photographed. Often special forms must be filled out for buildings. Imagine how difficult it would have been to record Theodore Roosevelt Dam before it was modified during the Central Arizona Project! "Data recovery" for such sites usually consisted of preparing a Historic American Buildings Survey form (for buildings) or a Historic American Engineering Record (for structures, such as dams and bridges), or both, which requires photodocumentation, among other requirements.

When the fieldwork has been completed, a brief report is usually submitted to the sponsor, the land-managing agency, the State Historic Preservation Office, and other reviewers. If the work is deemed satisfactory, the sponsor usually may proceed with the undertaking. Construction may be monitored by an archaeologist who watches carefully for important artifacts and features that might have been missed during excavation. This is particularly important if human burials are suspected to be present. Construction may be temporarily halted in the event that archaeological remains are discovered to permit their removal and recording, and then the work continues.

The research then proceeds into an analysis and reporting phase. Procedures for this phase of work are also spelled out in the data-recovery plan and describe how artifacts and other materials will be studied. Artifacts and samples (soil, ancient plant remains, samples for dating techniques) are processed in the laboratory with techniques suitable for the materials. They are then classified and recorded, and the resulting data are analyzed. Human remains may be studied by a physical anthropologist if this was approved and was not already carried out in the field. The features (or sites, if more than one site has been studied) are described and illustrated. Individual reports are written on classes of artifacts and other material remains. Specialists, such as palynologists, usually are subcontractors hired by the consultant, and they prepare their own reports, as do dating laboratories and other specialists.

All of this material is put together into the site report(s), which describe the data-recovery plan, how the plan was executed, and its results. Synthetic treatments may cover architecture, dating, how the site was organized in space, subsistence practices, burial patterns, and other higher-level questions of prehistory or history. The sponsor, land-managing agencies, and other reviewers read the draft report and provide comments. The consultant revises the report to take these comments into consideration. The revised final report is distributed to libraries, professional archaeologists, and the public.

When the final report is accepted, the artifacts, samples, data, photographs, field records, maps, and other information are curated at an approved facility (such as the Arizona State Museum or Museum of Northern Arizona), which protects the materials for perpetuity. A set curation fee is paid out of project monies to the repository for this service. Central Arizona Project materials are curated at a specific Bureau of Reclamation repository designated for this purpose. None of the artifacts collected from public lands may be discarded, and none may be kept by the archaeologists. All of the information is for the public trust, and qualified researchers and students may be given access to the collections for research purposes.

Often the consultant is asked to perform public-outreach tasks, which may include preparing a publication, booklet, or videotape for a general audience. Central Arizona Project contractors participated in a number of events for Arizona Archaeology Month during the Roosevelt Archaeology Project, for example, including site tours and exhibits. The sponsoring agency may elect to hold scientific symposia at national meetings or other venues. The Bureau of Reclamation sponsored two research seminars concerning Central Arizona Project archaeology at the Amerind Foundation in Dragoon, Arizona, which resulted in important publications. The book you are reading is another example of a public-outreach project sponsored by the Bureau of Reclamation. In this way, everyone participates in the historic-preservation process, including the interested public as well as professional archaeologists and historians.

When all the work has been performed satisfactorily and accepted, the federal agency notifies the historic preservation office and the Advisory Council on Historic Preservation that the Memorandum of Agreement has been successfully fulfilled. This represents the sixth and final stage in the cultural resource management process.

During the Central Arizona Project, all of the steps in the Section 106 cultural resource management process were carried out. The three kinds of archaeological studies that are commonly performed during cultural resource management—survey, testing, and data recovery—were completed. Often these phases of archaeological study were conducted by different organizations. A consultant who conducted data recovery may have employed a research design prepared by someone else, for example, and often the organization conducting data recovery was not the one who carried out the survey. Although cumbersome, this method helps to spread the work among different institutions, reduces overall costs and possible favoritism, and ensures that research is comparable across a large project area.

For further information, see: Thomas R. Hester, Harry J. Shafer, and Kenneth L. Feder, Field Methods in Archaeology *(7th ed., Mayfield, Mountain View, California, 1997); Thomas F. King,* Cultural Resource Laws and Practice: An Introductory Guide *(Altamira Press, Walnut Creek, California, 1998);* How to Apply the National Register Criteria for Evaluation *(National Register Bulletin 15, U.S.D.I. National Park Service, Washington, D.C., 1991); Patricia L. Parker and Thomas F. King,* Guidelines for Evaluating and Documenting Traditional Cultural Properties *(National Register Bulletin 38, U.S.D.I. National Park Service, Washington, D.C., 1994). A good introductory text in archaeology is by Brian M. Fagan,* Archaeology: A Brief Introduction *(8th ed., Prentice Hall, Upper Saddle River, New Jersey, 2003).*

Appendix References

Baumler, Mark F.

1984 *The Archeology of Faraway Ranch, Arizona: Prehistoric, Historic, and 20th Century.* Publications in Anthropology No. 24. Western Archeological and Conservation Center, Tucson.

Fowler, Don D.

2000 *A Laboratory for Anthropology: Science and Romanticism in the American Southwest, 1846–1930.* University of New Mexico Press, Albuquerque.

King, Thomas F.

1998 *Cultural Resource Laws and Practice: An Introductory Guide.* Altamira Press, Walnut Creek, California.

Lipe, William D., and Alexander J. Lindsay, Jr.

1974 Technical Series No. 14. Museum of Northern Arizona, Flagstaff.

Reid, J. Jefferson

1995 Four Strategies after Twenty Years: A Return to Basics. In *Expanding Archaeology,* edited by J. M. Skibo, W. H. Walker, and A. E. Nielsen, pp. 15–21. University of Utah Press, Salt Lake City.

Reid, J. Jefferson, Michael B. Schiffer, and William L. Rathje

1975 Behavioral Archaeology: Four Strategies. *American Anthropologist* 77:864–869.

Reid, Jefferson, and Stephanie Whittlesey

1997 *The Archaeology of Ancient Arizona.* University of Arizona Press, Tucson.

Thiel, J. Homer

1995 *Rock Art in Arizona: A Component of the Arizona Historic Preservation Plan.* Center for Desert Archaeology, Tucson. Submitted to the Arizona State Historic Preservation Office, Arizona State Parks Board, Phoenix.

Glossary

acequia: (Spanish) An irrigation ditch.

adobe: (Spanish) Clay-rich mud used as a wall plaster or construction material (Reid and Whittlesey 1997:277).

anthropology: The study of people and their cultures. Includes **archaeology;** physical anthropology, the study of the biological aspect of human beings; linguistics, the study of human languages; and cultural anthropology, the study of living societies and lifeways.

Antiquities Act of 1906: The first federal legislation enacted to protect cultural resources on federal lands. The Antiquities Act established fines and imprisonment for damage to or appropriations from archaeological sites, established a permitting system for legitimate investigation, and authorized the president to create national monuments for purposes of preservation.

archaeological feature: Concentrations of artifacts or organic residues (**ecofacts**), or both, and structural remains. A feature is considered to be the reflection in the archaeological record of some activity or set of activities (Hester and others 1997:44). An example would be a hearth or rock-filled roasting pit (cooking activities), a pit house (habitation activities), or a stone check dam (farming activities).

archaeological site: A discrete, bounded location where people lived, worked, or carried out a task and where physical evidence of their behavior can be recovered by the archaeologist (Hester and others 1997:42).

archaeological survey: Systematic method of locating and recording **archaeological sites,** usually pedestrian. May be linear (along a line, such as an aqueduct corridor) or block (a contiguous piece of land, such as the area to be inundated by a reservoir).

archaeology: One of the four subfields of **anthropology.** Most broadly defined as "the study of material objects regardless of time or space in order to describe and explain human behavior" (Reid 1995:16).

artifact: Any object modified by humans (tools, debris from making tools, objects that have use wear from activities, floral and faunal remains, and so on) (Hester and others 1997:44).

***bajada*:** (Spanish) A desert foothills slope.

ball court: An elliptical field defined by earthen or stone embankments. Used by the Hohokam for a version of the **Mesoamerican** ball game and for other public ceremonies and activities (Reid and Whittlesey 1997:277).

bichrome: Pottery of two colors (for example, black-on-red or red-on-buff).

***bosque*:** (Spanish) A thick growth of mesquite trees, usually found in the floodplain of a stream.

censer: A small, thick-walled, cup-shaped or cylindrical vessel of ceramic or stone, used by the Hohokam to burn incense or other substances.

ceramics: Artifacts, usually containers, made from clay and **temper** and produced by **firing**; used interchangeably with "pottery" in the Southwest (Reid and Whittlesey 1997:277).

check structure: Central Arizona Project canal structure that controls water flow.

chronometric date: Absolute date (date in calendar years) derived through mathematical or statistical methods, such as tree-ring or radiocarbon dating.

***cienega*:** (Spanish) A marshy area permanently saturated by water and characterized by sedges and other water-loving plants (Hendrickson and Minckley 1984:131).

cliff dwelling: A pueblo built into a rockshelter or against a cliff face (Reid and Whittlesey 1997:277).

Cochise culture: The Archaic (preceramic) hunting-gathering culture of the southern U.S. Southwest from the early Holocene until the appearance of pottery. First defined in 1941 by E. B. Sayles and geologist Ernst Antevs on the basis of buried sites in the Whitewater Draw region of southeastern Arizona. Some archaeologists restrict the label to southeastern Arizona. The Cochise developmental sequence is divided into three stratigraphically distinct stages: Sulphur Spring (10,000–8,000 radiocarbon years B.P.), Chiricahua (?–3,500 B.P.), and San Pedro (3,500–2,000 B.P.). Cochise has long been thought to be ancestral to the Mogollon culture.

coil-and-scrape technique: In pottery, a method of bonding coils and thinning vessel walls used throughout most of the central and northern Southwest. Clay coils are bonded together by pinching, then a scraper made from a gourd or piece of pottery is used to smooth the surface and thin the vessel walls (Reid and Whittlesey 1997:277–278).

compound: A walled enclosure defining domestic or ceremonial space, sometimes both (Reid and Whittlesey 1997:278).

coprolite: Preserved human feces.

corrugation: A method of finishing pottery that leaves the coils partially smoothed to give a textured exterior surface (Reid and Whittlesey 1997:278).

cultural resource management: A subfield in archaeology (more rarely, in environmental planning) that manages historic places of archaeological, architectural, and historical interest and considers such places with reference to environmental and historic-preservation laws (King 1998:6). It can be considered more broadly as a practical means of accommodating development with the preservation of important historical and cultural values.

cultural resources: Used in cultural resource management to mean an established or potential "**historic property**" as defined in the **National Historic Preservation Act,** Native American graves and cultural objects, shipwrecks, museum collections, historical documents, religious sites and practices, cultural uses of natural resources, folklife, tradition, social institutions, theater groups, orchestras, and other cultural resources and natural resources of cultural importance (King 1998:6).

culture: The collective knowledge of a people and the rules and regulations for transforming knowledge into appropriate social action. As used by archaeologists, a culture is a distinct collection of material traits, behavior, and organization in prehistory, such as the Hohokam culture (Reid and Whittlesey 1997:278).

ecofacts: Organic residues found in **archaeological sites** that are the result of human activities, although they may bear no evidence of modification (for example, plant remains, animal bone, charcoal) (Binford 1964).

environmental impact statement: The most detailed kind of environmental analysis carried out under the **National Environmental Policy Act.**

ethnography: An anthropological description of a cultural group focusing on lifeways.

fault: A fracture in the earth's crust along which movement has taken place (Baars 1995:1). Movement may be vertical or horizontal.

firing: Heating ceramic objects in an open fire or kiln to a sufficient temperature to fuse the clay particles into a hard, durable material.

flaked stone tools: Tools manufactured by removing flakes or chips of stone by percussion or pressure (Reid and Whittlesey1997:278).

flotation analysis: A technique used to recover charred plant parts and seeds (macrobotanical remains) from soil samples collected at **archaeological sites.** Water is used to "float" or separate the dirt and pebbles in the sample from the plant remains, which float to the surface and can be screened or scooped up. This can be done manually with tubs and screens or in more sophisticated mechanical flotation devices.

fugitive pigment: In pottery, pigment that is applied after **firing,** so that it is impermanent and tends to fade and rub off.

geoglyph (intaglio): Geometric, anthropomorphic, or zoomorphic figures made by scraping away the dark-colored stones of desert pavement to reveal the lighter color beneath.

great kiva: A large structure used for communal ceremonial and social activities (Reid and Whittlesey 1997:298). As with **kivas,** may be rectangular or circular; less frequently D-shaped.

ground stone tools: Tools shaped by grinding and polishing rather than flaking. Includes **manos, metates,** axes, palettes, and so on (Reid and Whittlesey 1997:278).

historic preservation: Loosely defined as the process by which places and things that are associated with history and culture are saved for the future. In Section 301[8] of the **National Historic Preservation Act,** more specifically defined as: "identification, evaluation, recordation, documentation, curation, acquisition, protection, management, rehabilitation, restoration, stabilization, maintenance, research, interpretation, (and) conservation [of **historic properties**] and education and training regarding the foregoing activities or any combination of the foregoing activities."

historic property: In the National Historic Preservation Act, "any prehistoric or historic district, site, building, structure or object included in, or eligible for inclusion on the National Register [of Historic Places], including artifacts, records, and material remains related to such a property" (National Historic Preservation Act, Sec. 301[5]).

jacal, pl. jacales: (Spanish) Wall construction of upright poles interlaced with twigs and plastered with adobe (Reid and Whittlesey 1997:278).

kachina, kachina dolls: Derived from the Hopi word *katsina.* Carved, wooden representations of *katsina* spirits traditionally made from cottonwood root. Among the Hopi, these small figures are a means of instructing children and are given respect. Kachina carving has become an art form among contemporary Hopi.

***katsina* (sing.; pl. *katsinam*):** (Hopi) A word with several meanings. It refers to both the incorporeal *katsina* spirits and the dancer that brings this spirit to life. The *katsina* spirits embody the spirits of nature in tangible form, act as intermediaries between the Creator and humans, and bring rain, goodness, and blessings to the Hopi. They also admonish and instruct children (Griffin-Pierce 2000:97). **Kachina** dolls, called *tihu* in Hopi, are small, carved wooden representations of *katsina* spirits.

kiva: Pueblo ceremonial room often built below ground and frequently detached from habitation areas (Reid and Whittlesey 1997:278). May be rectangular or circular, less frequently D-shaped.

laccolith: In geology, a dome formed by forceful injection of **magma** between sedimentary layers, pushing upper layers upward and outward (Chronic 1988:150).

magma: Molten rock.

mano: (Spanish for "hand") A hand-held stone used for grinding seeds and grains on a **metate** (Reid and Whittlesey 1997:278).

material culture or material remains: Any tool, construction, or alteration of the environment by human beings (Reid and Whittlesey 1997:279).

Mesoamerica: "Middle America," the land between North and South America. As used by archaeologists, it commonly refers to the complex societies of ancient Mexico and Guatemala. The northern border is difficult to define, but it is typically placed several hundred miles south of the international border.

metate: (Spanish) A flat, basin-shaped, or trough-shaped stone on which seeds and corn are ground with a **mano** (Reid and Whittlesey 1997:279).

midden: A deposit of household refuse.

Mogollon culture: The prehistoric archaeological culture of the mountain Transition Zone in Arizona, New Mexico, and to a lesser extent, in Chihuahua and Sonora. Characterized by mixed hunting-gathering-farming lifeways, brown and red-**slipped** smoothed and textured pottery, red-on-brown painted pottery, pit-house and later masonry **pueblo** architecture, and inhumation burial of the deceased.

monocline: The simplest of geologic folds, with one side raised higher than the other (Chronic 1988:6).

National Environmental Policy Act of 1969: Federal legislation requiring federal agencies to consider the effects of their actions upon natural and cultural resources.

National Historic Preservation Act of 1966: Federal legislation requiring federal agencies to consider the effects of their actions on historic properties listed in or eligible for listing in the **National Register of Historic Places.**

National Register of Historic Places: The nation's inventory of historic places and the national repository of documentation on the variety of historic property types, their significance and abundance, and other information.

obliterated corrugated: A kind of pottery with smoothed **corrugations.**

olla: (Spanish) A pottery jar with a narrow opening, commonly used for water and food storage (Reid and Whittlesey 1997:279).

orogeny: A mountain-building episode in geologic history (Baars 1995:2).

paleobotanical remains: Ancient plant remains (seeds, plant parts, or pollen) found in **archaeological sites.**

paleofaunal remains: Ancient animal (faunal) bones found in **archaeological sites.**

Paleoindians: Archaeological name for the big-game hunters of North and South America during the Pleistocene, such as the Clovis culture.

palynologist: A scientist who studies plant pollen. The science is called palynology.

Patayan culture: Archaeological name for the prehistoric people who lived along the Colorado River and in the surrounding desert between about A.D. 700 and 1400.

period: The largest time unit of cultural classification, usually further subdivided into phases (Reid and Whittlesey 1997:279).

petroglyph: An image scratched, hammered, or pecked onto rock (Reid and Whittlesey 1997:279).

phase: The smallest unit of culture history, representing a prehistoric culture at a specific point in time and identified by pottery types, house construction, mortuary practices, and other traits (Reid and Whittlesey 1997:279).

phyllite: A foliated (layered), tabular metamorphic rock with a dull gray or purplish, opaque color. Used by the Hohokam to make palettes and crushed as pottery **temper.**

physical anthropology: Branch of anthropology that studies past and present human bodies, human evolution, and adaptation.

plain ware pottery: Pottery that has not been **slipped,** painted, or textured (Reid and Whittlesey 1997:279).

platform mound: An earthen tumulus associated with Hohokam and Salado ceremonialism, ultimately derived from Mesoamerica (Reid and Whittlesey 1997:279).

polychrome: Pottery decorated with three or more colors (Reid and Whittlesey 1997:279).

prehistory: The time before written records.

projectile point: A spear point, dart point, or arrowhead (Reid and Whittlesey 1997:279).

pueblo: In archaeology, a single-story or multistory dwelling built of stone blocks or adobe, usually composed of rectangular rooms.

Pueblo: One of the living Native American groups of the American Southwest who occupied pueblos. Eastern Pueblos include those along the Río Grande in New Mexico and Western Pueblos include Hopi, Zuni, and Acoma.

puebloan: In archaeology, ancient peoples who lived in pueblos and had a lifestyle much like that of living Pueblo peoples (settled village farmers who depended heavily on corn).

radiocarbon dating: A method of chronometric dating using carbon isotopes.

schist: A kind of metamorphic rock containing mica and other minerals. Composed of layers (a "foliated" stone). When crushed, used by the Hohokam to **temper** pottery vessels.

sherd: A piece of a broken ceramic pot, also called a potsherd or shard (Reid and Whittlesey 1997:279).

Sinagua culture: Name archaeologists use for the prehistoric inhabitants of the Flagstaff area and the Verde Valley. First living in pit houses and then in masonry pueblos, the Sinagua made brown and red pottery using the paddle-and-anvil technique—much of it tempered with volcanic materials after the eruption of Sunset Crater Volcano. Walnut Canyon National Monument and Tuzigoot National Monument are Sinagua ruins that can be visited today.

siphon: In the Central Arizona Project, covered tunnels that funnel water under obstacles such as rivers and major washes to prevent erosion during storms and flood events.

slip: A thin mixture of clay and water applied to the surface of a pottery vessel to form an overall color treatment.

stratigraphy: The archaeological study of stratification, which is the deposition or accumulation of sediments and cultural material. In an orderly, undisturbed sequence, the oldest deposits are the lowest (Reid and Whittlesey 1997:280). Stratigraphic deposits are laid down according to the principles of stratification.

temper: In pottery, any nonclay material added to clay when making ceramic vessels to provide strength and prevent cracking. May be sand, crushed rock, horse manure, or other materials (Reid and Whittlesey 1997:280).

Trincheras culture: Prehistoric culture centered in the Altar and Magdalena River valleys of Sonora, Mexico, and dating from about A.D. 700 to 1100. Characterized by purple-on-red **bichrome** and **polychrome** pottery, pit-house architecture, and mixed subsistence.

turnout: Central Arizona Project canal structure that delivers water to user-distribution systems.

U.S. Southwest: As used in this book, the American Southwest includes the Four Corners states of Arizona, Colorado, New Mexico, and Utah. "Southwest" is more broadly defined on the basis of environmental and cultural similarities to include the Mexican states of Chihuahua and Sonora.

References Cited

Abbey, Edward
1968 *Desert Solitaire: A Season in the Wilderness.* Simon and Schuster, New York.

Abruzzi, William S.
1989 Ecology, Resource Distribution, and Mormon Settlement in Northeastern Arizona. *American Anthropologist* 91:642–655.

Adams, E. Charles
1991 *The Origin and Development of the Pueblo Katsina Cult.* University of Arizona Press, Tucson.

2000 Salado: The View from the Colorado Plateau. In *Salado,* edited by Jeffrey S. Dean, pp. 263–274. Amerind Foundation New World Studies Series 4. Amerind Foundation, Dragoon, Arizona, and University of New Mexico Press, Albuquerque.

Ambrose, Stephen E.
1996 *Crazy Horse and Custer.* Anchor Books, Doubleday, New York.

Austin, Mary
1985 *The Land of Journey's Ending.* Reprinted, with an introductory essay by Larry Evers. University of Arizona Press, Tucson. Originally published 1924, George Allen & Unwin, London.

Baars, Donald L.
1995 *Navajo Country: A Geology and Natural History of the Four Corners Region.* University of New Mexico Press, Albuquerque.

Bahr, Donald, Juan Smith, William S. Allison, and Julian Hayden
1994 *The Short Swift Time of Gods on Earth: The Hohokam Chronicles.* University of California Press, Berkeley.

Bahre, Conrad Joseph
1991 *A Legacy of Change: Historic Human Impact on Vegetation in the Arizona Borderlands.* University of Arizona Press, Tucson.

Barnes, Will C.
1988 *Arizona Place Names.* Reprinted. University of Arizona Press, Tucson. Originally published 1935.

Basso, Keith H.
1971 *The Cibecue Apache.* Holt, Rinehart and Winston, New York.

1983 Western Apache. In *Southwest*, edited by Alfonso Ortiz, pp. 462–488. Handbook of North American Indians, vol. 10, William C. Sturtevant, general editor. Smithsonian Institution, Washington, D.C.

1996 *Wisdom Sits in Places: Landscape and Language among the Western Apache.* University of New Mexico Press, Albuquerque.

Batman, Richard
1984 *James Pattie's West: The Dream and the Reality.* University of Oklahoma Press, Norman.

Bayham, Frank E., and Donald H. Morris
1986 Episodic Use of a Marginal Environment: A Synthesis. In *Prehistoric Hunter-Gatherers of South Central Arizona: The Picacho Reservoir Archaic Project,* edited by Frank E. Bayham, Donald H. Morris, and M. Steven Shackley, pp. 359–381. Anthropological Field Studies 13. Office of Cultural Resource Management, Department of Anthropology, Arizona State University, Tempe.

Bayham, Frank E., Donald H. Morris, and M. Steven Shackley
1986 *Prehistoric Hunter-Gatherers of South Central Arizona: The Picacho Reservoir Archaic Project.* Anthropological Field Studies 13. Office of Cultural Resource Management, Department of Anthropology, Arizona State University, Tempe.

Bierhorst, John (editor and translator)
1974 *Four Masterworks of American Indian Literature: Quetzalcoatl/The Ritual of Condolence/Cuceb/The Night Chant.* Farrar, Straus and Giroux, New York.

Binford, Lewis R.
1964 A Consideration of Archaeological Research Design. *American Antiquity* 29:425–444.

Bischoff, Matt C., Joseph A. Ezzo, Teresita Majewski, Robert M. Wegener, and Stephanie M. Whittlesey
2000 *Archaeological Research Design for the Northeastern Great Basin.* Technical Report 99-29. Statistical Research, Tucson.

Black, Robert C.
1969 *Island in the Rockies.* Pruett, Boulder, Colorado.

Bohrer, Vorsila L.
1971 Paleoecology of Snaketown. *The Kiva* 36:11–19.

Boissiere, Robert
1986 *Meditations with the Hopi.* Bear and Co., Santa Fe.

Bourke, John G.
1971 *On the Border with Crook.* University of Nebraska Press, Lincoln.

Bowden, Charles
1977 *Killing the Hidden Waters: The Slow Destruction of Water Resources in the American Southwest.* University of Texas Press, Austin.

1986 *Blue Desert.* University of Arizona Press, Tucson.

Bowden, Martyn
1992 The Invention of the American Tradition. *Journal of Historical Geography* 18:3–26.

Brooks, Juanita
1985 *John Doyle Lee: Zealot, Pioneer Builder, Scapegoat.* Utah University Press, Logan.

Brown, Patricia Eyring, and Connie Lynn Stone (editors)
1982 *Granite Reef: A Study in Desert Archaeology.* Anthropological Research Papers No. 28, Anthropological Field Studies 3. Office of Cultural Resource Management, Department of Anthropology, Arizona State University, Tempe.

Browning, Sinclair
1982 *Enju: The Life and Struggle of an Apache Chief from the Little Running Water.* Northland Press, Flagstaff, Arizona.

Buskirk, Winfred
1986 *The Western Apache: Living with the Land Before 1950.* University of Oklahoma Press, Norman.

Byrkit, James W.
1992 Land, Sky, and People: The Southwest Defined. *Journal of the Southwest* 34:257–387.

Cahalan, James
2001 *Edward Abbey: A Life.* University of Arizona, Tucson.

Cañizo, Susanna
2002 County's Population at 900,000. *Arizona Daily Star* 10 November:A1.

Carothers, S. W., R. R. Johnson, and S. W. Atchison
1974 Population Structure and Social Organization in Southwestern Riparian Birds. *American Zoologist* 14:97–108.

Castetter, Edward F., and Willis H. Bell
1942 *Pima and Papago Indian Agriculture.* University of New Mexico Press, Albuquerque.

Cather, Willa
1915 *The Song of the Lark.* Houghton Mifflin, Boston.

Central Arizona Project (CAP)
2003 Central Arizona Project, CAP Web home page [Online]. Available at http://www.cap-az.com (modified: frequently; accessed 20 July 2002; verified 22 January 2003). Central Arizona Project, Phoenix, Arizona.

Childs, Craig
2000 *The Secret Knowledge of Water: Discovering the Essence of the American Desert.* Little, Brown and Company, New York. Originally published by Sasquatch Books, Seattle.

Chronic, Halka
1988 *Pages of Stone: Grand Canyon and the Plateau Country: Geology of Western National Parks & Monuments.* 5th printing, 2000. The Mountaineers, Seattle.

Cohodas, Marvin
1991 Ballgame Imagery of the Maya Lowlands: History and Iconography. In *The Mesoamerican Ballgame,* edited by Vernon L. Scarborough and David R. Wilcox, pp. 251–288. University of Arizona Press, Tucson.

Comer, Krista
1999 *Landscapes of the New West: Gender and Geography in Contemporary Women's Writing.* University of North Carolina Press, Chapel Hill.

Connelly, John C.
1979 Hopi Social Organization. In *Southwest,* edited by Alfonso Ortiz, pp. 539–553. Handbook of North American Indians, vol. 19, William C. Sturtevant, general editor. Smithsonian Institution, Washington, D.C.

Cooke, Ronald U., and Richard W. Reeves
1976 *Arroyos and Environmental Change in the American South-West.* Clarendon Press, Oxford.

Corle, Edwin
1951 *The Gila: River of the Southwest.* University of Nebraska Press, Lincoln.

Craig, Douglas B.
1995 The Social Consequences of Irrigation Agriculture: A Perspective from Meddler Point. In *The Roosevelt Community Development Study: New Perspectives on Tonto Basin Prehistory,* edited by Mark D. Elson, Miriam T. Stark, and David A. Gregory, pp. 227–249. Anthropological Papers No. 15. Center for Desert Archaeology, Tucson.

Crampton, C. Gregory
1972 *Land of Living Rock: The Grand Canyon and the High Plateaus: Arizona, Utah, Nevada.* Gibbs Smith and Peregrine Smith Books, Layton, Utah.

Crown, Patricia L.
1984a Hohokam Subsistence and Settlement in the Salt-Gila Basin. In *Synthesis and Conclusions,* edited by Lynn S. Teague and Patricia L. Crown, pp. 87–113. Hohokam Archaeology along the Salt-Gila Aqueduct, Central Arizona Project, vol. 9. Archaeological Series 150, vol. 9. Cultural Resource Management Division, Arizona State Museum, University of Arizona, Tucson.

1984b Identification and Documentation of Agricultural Features on the Salt-Gila Aqueduct Project. In *Environment and Subsistence,* edited by Lynn S. Teague and Patricia L. Crown, pp. 33–36. Hohokam Archaeology along the Salt-Gila Aqueduct: Central Arizona Project, vol. 7. Archaeological Series 150, vol. 7. Cultural Resource Management Division, Arizona State Museum, University of Arizona, Tucson.

1984c Prehistoric Agricultural Technology in the Salt-Gila Basin. In *Environment and Subsistence,* edited by Lynn S. Teague and Patricia L. Crown, pp. 207–260. Hohokam Archaeology along the Salt-Gila Aqueduct: Central Arizona Project, vol. 7. Archaeological Series 150, vol. 7. Cultural Resource Management Division, Arizona State Museum, University of Arizona, Tucson.

Crumley, Carole L., and William H. Marquardt
1990 Landscapes: A Unifying Concept in Regional Analysis. In *Interpreting Space: GIS and Archaeology,* edited by Kathleen M. S. Allen, Stanton W. Green, and Ezra B. W. Zubrow, pp. 73–79. Taylor & Francis, London.

Czaplicki, Jon S.
1989 The Tucson Aqueduct Phase B Project: Review and Summary. In *Syntheses and Interpretations,* edited by Jon S. Czaplicki and John C. Ravesloot, pp. 1–25. Hohokam Archaeology along Phase B of the Tucson Aqueduct, Central Arizona Project, vol. 1. Archaeological Series 178, vol. 1. Cultural Resource Management Division, Arizona State Museum, University of Arizona, Tucson.

Czaplicki, Jon S., and John C. Ravesloot
1989 *Excavations at Water World (AZ AA:16:94): A Rillito Phase Ballcourt Village in the Avra Valley.* Hohokam Archaeology along Phase B of the Tucson Aqueduct, Central Arizona Project, vol. 3. Archaeological Series 178, vol. 3. Cultural Resource Management Division, Arizona State Museum, University of Arizona, Tucson.

Davis, G. H., S. R. Showalter, G. S. Benson, L. S. McCalmont, and F. W. Cropp III
1981 Guide to the Geology of the Salt River Canyon Region, Arizona. *Arizona Geological Digest* 24:48–97.

Dean, Jeffrey S.
2000 Preface. In *Salado,* edited by Jeffrey S. Dean, pp. xv–xix. Amerind Foundation New World Studies Series 4. Amerind Foundation, Dragoon, Arizona, and University of New Mexico Press, Albuquerque.

DeJong, David H.
1992 "See the New Country": The Removal Controversy and Pima-Maricopa Water Rights, 1869–1879. *The Journal of Arizona History* 33:367–396.

Dering, J. Phil
1996 Plant Remains from the Schoolhouse Point Mound, U:8:24/13a. In *The Place of the Storehouses: Roosevelt Platform Mound Study: Report on the Schoolhouse Point Mound, Pinto Creek Complex*, by Owen Lindauer, pp. 623–639. Roosevelt Monograph Series 6, Anthropological Field Studies 35, Pt. 1. Office of Cultural Resource Management, Department of Anthropology, Arizona State University, Tempe.

1997 Plant Remains from U:4:33/132, the Cline Terrace Mound. In *A Salado Platform Mound on Tonto Creek: Roosevelt Platform Mound Study: Report on the Cline Terrace Mound, Cline Terrace Complex*, by David Jacobs, pp. 529–544. Roosevelt Monograph Series 7, Anthropological Field Studies 36. Office of Cultural Resource Management, Department of Anthropology, Arizona State University, Tempe.

1998 Macrobotanical Remains from Classic Period Farming Villages in Tonto Basin. In *Environment and Subsistence in the Classic Period Tonto Basin: The Roosevelt Archaeology Studies, 1989 to 1998*, edited by Katherine A. Spielmann, pp. 87–132. Roosevelt Monograph Series 9, Anthropological Field Studies 39. Office of Cultural Resource Management, Department of Anthropology, Arizona State University, Tempe.

Dimmitt, Mark A.
2000a Biomes & Communities of the Sonoran Desert Region. In *A Natural History of the Sonoran Desert*, pp. 3–18. Arizona-Sonora Desert Museum, Tucson.

2000b Flowering Plants of the Sonoran Desert. In *A Natural History of the Sonoran Desert*, pp. 153–264. Arizona-Sonora Desert Museum, Tucson.

Di Peso, Charles C.
1958 *The Reeve Ruin of Southeastern Arizona: A Study of Prehistoric Western Pueblo Migration in the Middle San Pedro Valley*. Publication No. 8. Amerind Foundation, Dragoon, Arizona.

Dobyns, Henry F.
1981 *From Fire to Flood: Human Destruction of Sonoran Desert Riverine Oases*. Ballena Press, Socorro, New Mexico.

Dobyns, Henry F., and Robert C. Euler
1972 *The Navajo Indians*. Indian Tribal Series, Phoenix.

Doelle, William H., David A. Gregory, and Henry D. Wallace
1995 Classic Period Platform Mound Systems in Southern Arizona. In *The Roosevelt Community Development Study: New Perspectives on Tonto Basin Prehistory*, edited by Mark D. Elson, Miriam T. Stark, and David A. Gregory, pp. 385–440. Anthropological Papers No. 15. Center for Desert Archaeology, Tucson.

Doolittle, William E.
1990 *Canal Irrigation in Prehistoric Mexico: The Sequence of Technological Change*. University of Texas Press, Austin.

Doyel, David E.
1984 From Foraging to Farming: An Overview of the Preclassic in the Tucson Basin. *The Kiva* 49:147–165.

1991 Hohokam Cultural Evolution in the Phoenix Basin. In *Exploring the Hohokam: Prehistoric Desert Peoples of the American Southwest*, edited by George J. Gumerman, pp. 231–278. Amerind Foundation New World Studies Series 1. University of New Mexico Press, Albuquerque.

1992 On Models and Methods: Comments on the History of Archaeological Research in the Southern Southwest. In *Proceedings of the Second Salado Conference Globe, AZ*, edited by Richard C. Lange and Stephen Germick, pp. 345–351. Occasional Paper 1992. Arizona Archaeological Society, Phoenix.

Drucker, Philip
1941 Yuman-Piman. *Anthropological Records* 6(3):19–230. Culture Element Distributions 17. University of California Press, Berkeley.

Dunbier, Roger
1968 *The Sonoran Desert: Its Geography, Economy, and People*. University of Arizona Press, Tucson.

Dutton, Clarence E.
1882 *The Tertiary History of the Grand Cañon District, with Atlas*. Government Printing Office, Washington, D.C.

Ekholm, Susanna M.
1991 Ceramic Figurines and the Mesoamerican Ballgame. In *The Mesoamerican Ballgame*, edited by Vernon L. Scarborough and David R. Wilcox, pp. 241–249. University of Arizona Press, Tucson.

Ellis, Reuben (editor)
1997 *Stories and Stone: Writing the Anasazi Homeland*. Pruett, Boulder, Colorado.

Ellison, "Slim"
1968 *Cowboys Under the Mogollon Rim*. University of Arizona Press, Tucson.

Elson, Mark D., Miriam T. Stark, and David A. Gregory
2000 Tonto Basin Local Systems: Implications for Cultural Affiliation and Migration. In *Salado*, edited by Jeffrey S. Dean, pp. 167–191. Amerind Foundation New World Studies Series 4. Amerind Foundation, Dragoon, Arizona, and University of New Mexico Press, Albuquerque.

Elson, Mark D., Miriam T. Stark, and James M. Heidke
1992 Prelude to Salado: Preclassic Period Settlement in the Upper Tonto Basin. In *Proceedings of the Second Salado Conference, Globe, AZ*, edited by Richard C. Lange and Stephen Germick, pp. 274–285. Occasional Paper 1992. Arizona Archaeological Society, Phoenix.

Farmer, Jared
1999 *Glen Canyon Dammed: Inventing Lake Powell and the Canyon Country.* University of Arizona Press, Tucson.

Felger, Richard S., Bill Broyles, Michael Wilson, and Gary Paul Nabhan
1997 The Binational Sonoran Desert Biosphere Network and Its Plant Life. *Journal of the Southwest* 39:411–560.

Ferg, Alan, William H. Leisenbein, Peter J. Pilles, Jr., and Pamela Haas
1988 *Historical Archaeology at Joseph City, Arizona.* Arizona Archaeologist 22. Arizona Archaeological Society, Phoenix.

Ferg, Alan, and Jim I. Mead
1993 *Red Cave: A Prehistoric Cave Shrine in Southeastern Arizona.* Arizona Archaeologist 26. Arizona Archaeological Society, Phoenix.

Fish, Paul R., and Suzanne K. Fish
1991 Hohokam Political and Social Organization. In *Exploring the Hohokam: Prehistoric Desert Peoples of the American Southwest,* edited by George J. Gumerman, pp. 151–175. Amerind Foundation New World Studies Series 1. Amerind Foundation, Dragoon, Arizona, and University of New Mexico Press, Albuquerque.

Fish, Paul R., Suzanne K. Fish, Stephanie M. Whittlesey, Hector Neff, Michael D. Glascock, and J. M. Elam
1992 An Evaluation of the Production and Exchange of Tanque Verde Red-on-Brown Ceramics in Southern Arizona. In *Chemical Characterization of Ceramic Pastes in Archaeology,* edited by Hector Neff, pp. 233–254. Monographs in World Archaeology No. 7. Prehistory Press, Madison, Wisconsin.

Fish, Suzanne K.
1984 Agriculture and Subsistence Implications of the Salt-Gila Aqueduct Project Pollen Analysis. In *Environment and Subsistence*, edited by Lynn S. Teague and Patricia L. Crown, pp. 111–138. Hohokam Archaeology along the Salt-Gila Aqueduct, Central Arizona Project, vol. 7. Archaeological Series 150, vol. 7. Cultural Resource Management Division, Arizona State Museum, University of Arizona, Tucson.

1989 From the Avra Valley to the Picacho Mountains: A Comparative Assessment of Hohokam Subsistence Based on the Pollen Record. In *Syntheses and Interpretations,* edited by Jon S. Czaplicki and John C. Ravesloot, pp. 239–252. Hohokam Archaeology along Phase B of the Tucson Aqueduct, Central Arizona Project, vol. 1. Archaeological Series 178, vol. 1. Cultural Resource Management Division, Arizona State Museum, University of Arizona, Tucson.

1997 Pollen Results from U:4:33/132, the Cline Terrace Mound. In *A Salado Platform Mound on Tonto Creek: Roosevelt Platform Mound Study: Report on the Cline Terrace Mound, Cline Terrace Complex*, by David Jacobs, pp. 545–552. Roosevelt Monograph Series 7, Anthropological Field Studies 36. Office of Cultural Resource Management, Department of Anthropology, Arizona State University, Tempe.

1998 A Pollen Perspective on Variability and Stability in Tonto Basin Subsistence. In *Environment and Subsistence in the Classic Period Tonto Basin: The Roosevelt Archaeology Studies, 1989 to 1998,* edited by Katherine A. Spielmann, pp. 49–86. Roosevelt Monograph Series 9, Anthropological Field Studies 39. Office of Cultural Resource Management, Department of Anthropology, Arizona State University, Tempe.

Fish, Suzanne K., Paul R. Fish, and John H. Madsen
1992 Evolution and Structure of the Classic Period Marana Community. In *The Marana Community in the Hohokam World,* edited by Suzanne K. Fish, Paul R. Fish, and John H. Madsen, pp. 20–40. Anthropological Papers No. 56. University of Arizona Press, Tucson.

Fish, Suzanne K., Paul R. Fish, Charles Miksicek, and John H. Madsen
1985 Prehistoric Agave Cultivation in Southern Arizona. *Desert Plants* 7(2):102–112.

Fish, Suzanne K., and Gary P. Nabhan
1991 Desert as Context: The Hohokam Environment. In *Exploring the Hohokam: Prehistoric Desert Peoples of the American Southwest,* edited by George J. Gumerman, pp. 29–60. Amerind Foundation New World Studies Series 1. Amerind Foundation, Dragoon, Arizona, and University of New Mexico Press, Albuquerque.

Flores, Dan L.
1998a Environmentalism and Multiculturalism. In *Reopening the American West,* edited by Hal K. Rothman, pp. 24–37. University of Arizona Press, Tucson.

1998b Making the West Whole Again. In *Reclaiming the Native Home of Hope: Community, Ecology and the American West,* edited by Robert B. Keiter, pp. 58–68. University of Utah Press, Salt Lake City.

Fontana, Bernard L.
1983 Pima and Papago: An Introduction. In *Southwest,* edited by Alfonso Ortiz, pp. 125–136. Handbook of North American Indians, vol. 10, William C. Sturtevant, general editor. Smithsonian Institution, Washington, D.C.

1989 *Of Earth and Little Rain.* University of Arizona Press, Tucson.

Forbes, R. D.
1916 Extensive Land Classification, Tonto National Forest, Arizona, District 3. Manuscript on file, Tonto National Forest, Phoenix.

Ford, Richard I.
1999 Ethnoecology Serving the Community: A Case Study from Zuni Pueblo, New Mexico. In *Ethnoecology: Situated Knowledge/Located Lives,* edited by Virginia D. Nazarea, pp. 71–87. University of Arizona Press, Tucson.

Fowler, Don D.
1998 Foreward to *Glen Canyon: An Archaeological Summary,* by Jesse D. Jennings. University of Utah Press, Salt Lake City.

2000 *A Laboratory for Anthropology: Science and Romanticism in the American Southwest, 1846–1930.* University of New Mexico Press, Albuquerque.

Fradkin, Philip L.
1968 *A River No More: The Colorado River and the West.* University of Arizona Press, Tucson.

Geary, Michael M.
1999 *A Quick History of Grand Lake: Including Rocky Mountain National Park and the Grand Lake Lodge.* Western Reflections, Ouray, Colorado.

Geib, Phil R.
1996a Competing Models of Pueblo II Anasazi Settlement-Subsistence Strategies in Glen Canyon. In *Glen Canyon Revisited,* by Phil R. Geib, pp. 180–184. Anthropological Papers No. 119. University of Utah Press, Salt Lake City.

1996b *Glen Canyon Revisited.* Anthropological Papers No. 119. University of Utah Press, Salt Lake City.

Ghiglieri, Michael P., and Thomas M. Myers
2001 *Over the Edge: Death in Grand Canyon: Gripping Accounts of All Known Fatal Mishaps in the Most Famous of the World's Seven Natural Wonders.* Puma Press, Flagstaff, Arizona.

Gladwin, Harold S., Emil W. Haury, E. B. Sayles, and Nora Gladwin
1937 *Excavations at Snaketown: Material Culture.* Medallion Papers No. 25. Gila Pueblo, Globe, Arizona.

Goff, John F.
1983 *Arizona Biographical Dictionary.* Black Mountain Press, Cave Creek, Arizona.

Goodwin, Grenville
1969 *The Social Organization of the Western Apache.* University of Arizona Press, Tucson.

1994 *Myths and Tales of the White Mountain Apache.* University of Arizona Press, Tucson.

Graves, Michael W.
1982 Apache Adaptation to the Mountains. In *The Q Ranch Region,* edited by J. Jefferson Reid, pp. 193–215. Cholla Project Archaeology, vol. 3. Archaeological Series 161, vol. 3. Cultural Resource Management Division, Arizona State Museum, University of Arizona, Tucson.

Green, Margerie (editor)
1989 *Settlement, Subsistence, and Specialization in the Northern Periphery: The New Waddell Project.* 2 vols. Cultural Resources Report No. 65. Archaeological Consulting Services, Tempe.

Greenwald, David H., and Pat H. Stein
1993 Prehistoric Phoenix: Examination and Comparison of Prehistoric and Historic Settlement in the Phoenix Basin. In *Special Studies, Synthesis, and Conclusions,* edited by David H. Greenwald and Jean H. Ballagh, pp. 1–15. Early Desert Farming and Irrigation Settlements: Archaeological Investigations in the Phoenix Sky Harbor Center, vol. 4. Archaeological Report No. 93-17. SWCA Environmental Consultants, Flagstaff.

Gregory, David A.
1991 Form and Variation in Hohokam Settlement Patterns. In *Chaco & Hohokam: Prehistoric Regional Systems in the American Southwest,* edited by Patricia L. Crown and W. James Judge, pp. 159–193. School of American Research Press, Santa Fe.

Greider, Thomas, and Lorraine Garkovich
1994 Landscapes: The Social Construction of Nature and the Environment. *Rural Sociology* 59:1–24.

Griffin-Pierce, Trudy
2000 *Native Peoples of the Southwest.* University of New Mexico Press, Albuquerque.

Griffith, James S.
1992 *Beliefs and Holy Places: A Spiritual Geography of the Pimería Alta.* University of Arizona Press, Tucson.

Gussow, Alan
1995 Beauty in the Landscape: An Ecological Viewpoint. In *Landscape in America,* edited by George F. Thompson, pp. 223–231. University of Texas Press, Austin.

Hackbarth, Mark R., and Nick Lancaster
1992 Irrigation along the Lower Verde River: Investigations of the Velasco Ditch. In *Prehistoric and Historic Occupation of the Lower Verde River Valley: The State Route 87 Verde Bridge Project,* by Mark R. Hackbarth, pp. 423–449. Northland Research, Flagstaff, Arizona.

Halbirt, Carl D., Kurt E. Dongoske, and T. Kathleen Henderson
1993 Coffee Camp: A Late Archaic Site on the Santa Cruz Flats. In *Archaic Occupation on the Santa Cruz Flats: The Tator Hills Archaeological Project,* edited by Carl D. Halbirt and T. Kathleen Henderson, pp. 55–114. Northland Research, Flagstaff, Arizona.

Halbirt, Carl D., and T. Kathleen Henderson (editors)
1993 *Archaic Occupation on the Santa Cruz Flats: The Tator Hills Archaeological Project.* Northland Research, Flagstaff.

Hamilton, Patrick
1884 *Resources of Arizona.* A. L. Bancroft & Company, printers, San Francisco.

Hardesty, Donald L.
1999 Archaeological Models of the Modern World in the Great Basin: World Systems and Beyond. In *Models for the Millennium: Great Basin Anthropology Today,* edited by Charlotte Beck, pp. 213–219. University of Utah Press, Salt Lake City.

Hartmann, William K.
1989 *Desert Heart: Chronicles of the Sonoran Desert.* Fisher Books, Tucson, Arizona.

Harvey, Mark William Thornton
1994 *A Symbol of Wilderness: Echo Park and the American Conservation Movement.* University of New Mexico Press, Albuquerque.

Haury, Emil W.
1936 *The Mogollon Culture of Southwestern New Mexico.* Medallion Papers No. 20. Gila Pueblo, Globe, Arizona.

1937 Pottery Types at Snaketown. In *Excavations at Snaketown: Material Culture,* by Harold S. Gladwin, Emil W. Haury, E. B. Sayles, and Nora Gladwin, pp. 169–229. Medallion Papers No. 25. Gila Pueblo, Globe, Arizona.

1945 *The Excavations of Los Muertos and Neighboring Ruins in the Salt River Valley, Southern Arizona.* Papers No. 24(1). Peabody Museum of American Archaeology and Ethnology, Harvard University, Cambridge, Massachusetts.

1950 *The Stratigraphy and Archaeology of Ventana Cave, Arizona.* University of Arizona Press, Tucson, and University of New Mexico Press, Albuquerque.

1958 Evidence at Point of Pines for a Prehistoric Migration from Northern Arizona. In *Migrations in New World Culture History,* edited by Raymond H. Thompson, pp. 1–6. Social Science Bulletin No. 27. University of Arizona, Tucson.

1976 *The Hohokam: Desert Farmers and Craftsmen: Excavations at Snaketown, 1964–1965.* University of Arizona Press, Tucson.

Hawley, Florence G.
1965 Chemical Investigation of the Incrustation on Pottery Vessels from Snaketown. In *Excavations at Snaketown,* by Harold S. Gladwin, Emil W. Haury, E. B. Sayles, and Nora Gladwin, Appendix 4, pp. 282–289. Reprinted. University of Arizona Press, Tucson. Originally published 1937, Medallion Papers No. 25, Gila Pueblo, Globe, Arizona.

Henderson, T. Kathleen
1993 The Archaic Occupation of the Santa Cruz Flats. In *Archaic Occupation on the Santa Cruz Flats: The Tator Hills Archaeological Project,* edited by Carl D. Halbirt and T. Kathleen Henderson, pp. 373–392. Northland Research, Flagstaff.

Hendrickson, Dean A., and W. L. Minckley
1984 Cienegas—Vanishing Climax Communities of the American Southwest. *Desert Plants* 6(3):131–175.

Hepworth, James R.
1996 *Canis Lupus Amorus Lunaticum.* In *Resist Much, Obey Little: Remembering Ed Abbey,* edited by James R. Hepworth and Gregory McNamee, pp. 117–137. Sierra Club Books, San Francisco.

Hester, Thomas R., Harry J. Shafer, and Kenneth L. Feder
1997 *Field Methods in Archaeology.* 7th ed. Mayfield, Mountain View, California.

Holthaus, Gary
1997 *Wide Skies: Finding a Home in the West.* University of Arizona Press, Tucson.

House, Dorothy A.
1994 *Landscapes of the Colorado Plateau.* Plateau 65(3).

Howard, Ann Valdo
1993 Marine Shell Artifacts and Production Processes at Shelltown and the Hind Site. In *Shelltown and the Hind Site: A Study of Two Hohokam Craftsman Communities in Southwestern Arizona,* vol. 1, edited by William S. Marmaduke and Richard J. Martynec, pp. 321–423. Northland Research, Flagstaff., Arizona.

Huntington, Frederick W.
1986 Mortuary Practices. In *Archaeological Investigations at the West Branch Site: Early and Middle Rincon Occupation in the Southern Tucson Basin,* by Frederick W. Huntington, pp. 333–348. Anthropological Papers No. 5. Institute for American Research, Tucson.

Ingram, Mrill
2000 Desert Storms. In *A Natural History of the Sonoran Desert*, pp. 41–50. Arizona-Sonora Desert Museum, Tucson.

Jackson, John B.
1995 In Search of the Proto-Landscape. In *Landscape in America*, edited by George F. Thompson, pp. 43–50. University of Texas Press, Austin.

Jackson, Richard H.
1994 People and Place in a Harsh Land: The Cultural Geography of the Great Basin. In *Natural History of the Colorado Plateau and Great Basin*, edited by Kimball T. Harper, Larry L. St. Clair, Kaye H. Thorne, and Wilford M. Hess, pp. 125–145. University Press of Colorado, Niwot.

Jacobs, David
1997 *A Salado Platform Mound on Tonto Creek: Roosevelt Platform Mound Study: Report on the Cline Terrace Mound, Cline Terrace Complex.* Roosevelt Monograph Series 7, Anthropological Field Studies 36. Office of Cultural Resource Management, Department of Anthropology, Arizona State University, Tempe.

Jehl, Douglas
2002 Santa Fe's Water Plan: More Low-Flow Toilets. *Arizona Daily Star* 3 November:A6.

Jennings, Jesse D.
1998 *Glen Canyon: An Archaeological Summary.* University of Utah Press, Salt Lake City.

Johnson, Rich
1977 *The Central Arizona Project 1918–1968.* University of Arizona Press, Tucson.

Joseph, Alice, Rosamond B. Spicer, and Jane Cheskey
1949 *The Desert People: A Study of the Papago Indians.* University of Chicago Press, Chicago. Midway reprint 1974.

Kamp, Kathryn
1998 *Life in the Pueblo: Understanding the Past through Archaeology.* Waveland Press, Prospect Heights, Illinois.

Keiter, Robert B.
1998 In Search of a Western Ethic: Lessons from Public Land and Natural Resource Policy. In *Reclaiming the Native Home of Hope: Community, Ecology and the American West*, edited by Robert B. Keiter, pp. 23–32. University of Utah Press, Salt Lake City.

Kelley, J. Charles
1966 Mesoamerica and the Southwestern United States. In *Archaeological Frontiers and External Connections,* edited by G. F. Ekholm and Gordon R. Willey, pp. 95–111. Handbook of North American Indians, vol. 4. University of Texas Press, Austin.

1993 Zenith Passage: The View from Chalchihuites. In *Culture and Contact: Charles C. Di Peso's Gran Chichimeca*, edited by Anne I. Woosley and John C. Ravesloot, pp. 227–250. Amerind Foundation New World Studies Series 2. Amerind Foundation, Dragoon, Arizona, and University of New Mexico Press, Albuquerque.

Kelley, Klara Bonsack, and Harris Francis
1994 *Navajo Sacred Places.* Indiana University Press, Bloomington and Indianapolis.

Kelly, William H.
1953 *Indians of the Southwest: A Survey of Indian Tribes and Indian Administration in Arizona.* First Annual Report of the Bureau of Ethnic Research, University of Arizona, Tucson.

Khera, Sigrid, and Patricia S. Mariella
1983 Yavapai. In *Southwest*, edited by Alfonso Ortiz, pp. 38–54. Handbook of North American Indians, vol. 10, William C. Sturtevant, general editor. Smithsonian Institution, Washington, D.C.

King, Thomas F.
1998 *Cultural Resource Laws and Practice: An Introductory Guide.* Altamira Press, Walnut Creek, California.

Kohler, Timothy A.
2000 The Final 400 Years of Prehispanic Agricultural Society in the Mesa Verde Region. *Kiva* 66:191–204.

Kresan, Peter L.
1997 A Geologic Tour of the Lower Colorado River Region of Arizona and Sonora. In "Dry Borders," a special issue. *Journal of the Southwest* 39:567–612.

Krech, Shepard III
1999 *The Ecological Indian: Myth and History.* W. W. Norton and Company, New York.

Krutch, Joseph Wood
1951 *The Desert Year.* University of Arizona Press, Tucson.

1989 *Grand Canyon: Today and All Its Yesterdays.* University of Arizona Press, Tucson.

Lansing, J. Stephen
1991 *Priests and Programmers: Technologies of Power in the Engineered Landscape of Bali.* Princeton University Press, Princeton.

La Rue, Eugene C.
1916 *Colorado River and Its Utilization.* Water-Supply Paper No. 395. U.S. Geological Survey, Washington, D.C.

Lavender, David
1984 *The History of Arizona's Pipe Spring National Monument.* Zion Natural History Association. Paragon Press, Salt Lake City.

Lawrence, D. H.
1982 *Mornings in Mexico.* Reprinted. G. M. Smith, Salt Lake City. Originally published 1927, Alfred A. Knopf, New York.

Lekson, Stephen H.
1992 Para-Salado, Perro Salado, or Salado Peril? In *Proceedings of the Second Salado Conference, Globe, AZ,* edited by Richard C. Lange and Stephen Germick, pp. 334–336. Occasional Paper 1992. Arizona Archaeological Society, Phoenix.

Leone, Mark P.
1979 *Roots of Modern Mormonism.* Harvard University Press, Cambridge.

Leopold, Aldo
1949 *A Sand Country Almanac and Sketches Here and There.* Oxford University Press, New York.

Levy, Jerrold E.
1992 *Orayvi Revisited: Social Stratification in an "Egalitarian" Society.* School of American Research Press, Santa Fe, New Mexico.

Limerick, Patricia Nelson
1987 *The Legacy of Conquest: The Unbroken Past of the American West.* W. W. Norton and Company, New York.

Limerick, Patricia Nelson, and William Travis
2002 Will the West See Message in the Flames? *Arizona Republic* 11 July:B11.

Lincoln, Charles E.
1990 Ethnicity and Social Organization at Chichen Itza, Yucatan, Mexico. Unpublished Ph.D. dissertation, Department of Anthropology, Harvard University, Cambridge, Massachussetts.

Lincoln, Thomas R.
2000 A Brief History of Salado Archaeology. In *Salado,* edited by Jeffrey S. Dean, pp. 17–25. Amerind Foundation New World Studies Series 4. Amerind Foundation, Dragoon, Arizona, and University of New Mexico Press, Albuquerque.

Lindauer, Owen
1995 Understanding the Salado through Work at Bass Point Mound, U:8:23/177. In *Where the Rivers Converge: Roosevelt Platform Mound Study, Report on the Rock Island Complex,* by Owen Lindauer, pp. 425–443. Roosevelt Monograph Series 4, Anthropological Field Studies 33. Office of Cultural Resource Management, Department of Anthropology, Arizona State University, Tempe.

1996 *The Place of the Storehouses: Roosevelt Platform Mound Study: Report on the Schoolhouse Point Mound, Pinto Creek Complex.* Roosevelt Monograph Series 6, Anthropological Field Studies 35, Pt. 1. Office of Cultural Resource Management, Department of Anthropology, Arizona State University, Tempe.

2000 A Schoolhouse Point Mesa Perspective on Salado Community Development. In *Salado,* edited by Jeffrey S. Dean, pp. 219–240. Amerind Foundation New World Studies Series 4. Amerind Foundation, Dragoon, Arizona, and University of New Mexico Press, Albuquerque.

Lingenfelter, Richard E.
1978 *Steamboats on the Colorado River 1852–1916.* University of Arizona Press, Tucson.

Loeffler, Jack
1996 Edward Abbey, Anarchism, and the Environment. In *Resist Much, Obey Little: Remembering Ed Abbey,* edited by James R. Hepworth and Gregory McNamee, pp. 31–39. Sierra Club Books, San Francisco.

Lopez, Barry
1981 Into the Earth: A Journey for the Soul. *Notre Dame Magazine* May 1981:30–34.

1998 *About this Life: Journeys on the Threshold of Memory.* Alfred A. Knopf, New York.

Lowenthal, David
1985 *The Past is a Foreign Country.* Cambridge University Press, New York.

Luckert, Karl W.
1979 *Coyoteway: A Navajo Holyway Healing Ceremonial.* University of Arizona Press, Tucson, and Museum of Northern Arizona Press, Flagstaff.

Mabry, Jonathan B., Deborah L. Swartz, Helga Wöcherl, Jeffery J. Clark, Gavin H. Archer, and Michael W. Lindeman
1997 *Archaeological Investigations of Early Village Sites in the Middle Santa Cruz Valley: Descriptions of the Santa Cruz Bend, Square Hearth, Stone Pipe, and Canal Sites.* Anthropological Papers No. 18. Center for Desert Archaeology, Tucson.

MacDougal, Daniel Trembly
1937 Foreward to *The Colorado Delta,* by Godfrey Sykes. American Geographical Society Special Publication No. 19. Carnegie Institution, Washington, D.C., and American Geographical Society, New York.

Mangum, Richard K., and Sherry G. Mangum
1997 *One Woman's West: The Life of Mary-Russell Ferrell Colton.* Northland Publishing, Flagstaff, Arizona.

1999 *Grand Canyon–Flagstaff Stage Coach Line: A History and Exploration Guide.* Hexagon Press, Flagstaff, Arizona.

Markman, Roberta H., and Peter T. Markman
1992 *The Flayed God: The Mythology of Mesoamerica: Sacred Texts and Images from Pre-Columbian Mexico and Central America.* HarperSan Francisco, New York.

Marquardt, William H., and Carole L. Crumley
1987 Theoretical Issues in the Analysis of Spatial Patterning. In *Regional Dynamics: Burgundian Landscapes in Historical Perspective,* edited by Carole L. Crumley and William H. Marquardt, pp. 1–18. Academic Press, San Diego.

Martin, Patricia Preciado
1992 *Songs My Mother Sang to Me.* University of Arizona Press, Tucson.

Martin, Russell
1981 Bargaining for Time: Water on the Plateau. *Plateau* 53:4–13.

1999 *A Story that Stands Like a Dam: Glen Canyon and the Struggle for the Soul of the West.* University of Utah Press, Salt Lake City.

Masse, W. Bruce
1991 The Quest for Subsistence Sufficiency and Civilization in the Sonoran Desert. In *Chaco & Hohokam: Prehistoric Regional Systems in the American Southwest,* edited by Patricia L. Crown and W. James Judge, pp. 195–223. School of American Research Press, Santa Fe.

Matson, R. G.
The Origins of Southwestern Agriculture. University of Arizona Press, Tucson.

McAuliffe, Joseph R.
2000 Desert Soils. In *A Natural History of the Sonoran Desert,* pp. 87–104. Arizona-Sonora Desert Museum, Tucson.

McClintock, James H.
1985 *Mormon Settlement in Arizona.* University of Arizona Press, Tucson.

McGuire, Thomas R.
1980 *Mixed-Bloods, Apaches, and Cattle Barons: Documents for a History of the Livestock Economy on the White Mountain Apache Reservation, Arizona.* Archaeological Series 142. Cultural Resource Management Division, Arizona State Museum, University of Arizona, Tucson.

McNamee, Gregory
1994 *Gila: The Life and Death of an American River.* University of New Mexico Press, Albuquerque.

1996 Scarlet "A" on a Field of Black. In *Resist Much, Obey Little: Remembering Ed Abbey,* edited by James R. Hepworth and Gregory McNamee, pp. 18–30. Sierra Club Books, San Francisco.

McNamee, Gregory (editor)
1993 *Named in Stone and Sky: An Anthology.* University of Arizona Press, Tucson.

McPherson, Robert S.
1992 *Sacred Land Sacred View: Navajo Perceptions of the Four Corners Region.* Brigham Young University, Salt Lake City, Utah.

Meeker, Joseph W.
1997 *The Comedy of Survival: Literary Ecology and a Play Ethic.* University of Arizona Press, Tucson.

Merrill, W. Earl
1975 Rio Verde Project Fell Through. *Mesa Tribune* 17 January.

Meyer, Michael C.
1984 *Water in the Hispanic Southwest: A Social and Legal History,* 1550–1850. University of Arizona Press, Tucson.

Miksicek, Charles H.
1984 Historic Desertification, Prehistoric Vegetation Change, and Hohokam Subsistence in the Salt-Gila Basin. In *Environment and Subsistence,* edited by Lynn S. Teague and Patricia L. Crown, pp. 53–80. Hohokam Archaeology along the Salt-Gila Aqueduct, Central Arizona Project, vol. 7. Archaeological Series 150, vol. 7. Cultural Resource Management Division, Arizona State Museum, University of Arizona, Tucson.

1995 Temporal Trends in the Eastern Tonto Basin: An Archaeobotanical Perspective. In *Paleobotanical and Osteological Analyses,* edited by Mark D. Elson and Jeffery J. Clark, pp. 43–83. The Roosevelt Community Development Study, vol. 3. Anthropological Papers No. 14. Center for Desert Archaeology, Tucson.

Miller, Mary, and Karl Taube
1993 *An Illustrated Dictionary of the Gods and Symbols of Ancient Mexico and the Maya.* Thames and Hudson, New York.

Morton, Larry D.
1996 *Oral History Interviews: Larry D. Morton.* Bureau of Reclamation Oral History Program. 2 vols. U.S. Department of the Interior, Bureau of Reclamation, Phoenix Area Office, Phoenix.

Mrozowski, Stephen A., and Mary C. Beaudry
1990 Archaeology and the Landscape of Corporate Ideology. In *Earth Patterns: Essays in Landscape Archaeology,* edited by William M. Kelso and Rachel Most, pp. 189–208. University Press of Virginia, Charlottesville.

Nabhan, Gary Paul
1982 *The Desert Smells Like Rain: A Naturalist in O'odham County.* University of Arizona Press, Tucson.

1985 *Gathering the Desert.* University of Arizona Press, Tucson.

Nabhan, Gary, James Berry, Cynthia Anson, and Charles Weber
1980 Papago Indian Floodwater Fields and Tepary Bean Protein Yields. *Ecology of Food and Nutrition* 10:71–78.

Nasdijj
2000 *The Blood Runs Like a River through My Dreams: A Memoir.* Houghton Mifflin, Boston.

National Geographic Society
2002 *A Thirsty Planet.* A National Geographic Magazine Map. National Geographic Society, Washington, D.C.

National Park Service
2003 The National Historic Preservation Act of 1966, As Amended [Online]. Available at http://www2.cr.nps.gov/laws/NHPA1966.htm (accessed 20 July 2002; verified 18 February 2003). ACHP, Washington, DC.

Neitzel, Jill E.
1991 Hohokam Material Culture and Behavior: The Dimensions of Organizational Change. In *Exploring the Hohokam: Prehistoric Desert Peoples of the American Southwest,* edited by George J. Gumerman, pp. 177–230. Amerind Foundation New World Studies Series 1. University of New Mexico Press, Albuquerque.

Neumann, Mark
1999 *On the Rim: Looking at the Grand Canyon.* University of Minnesota Press, Minneapolis.

Nials, Fred L., David A. Gregory, and Donald A. Graybill
1989 Salt River Stream Flow and Hohokam Irrigation Systems. In *Environment and Subsistence,* by David A. Gregory, William L. Deaver, Suzanne K. Fish, Ronald Gardiner, Robert W. Layhe, Fred L. Nials, and Lynn S. Teague, pp. 59–76. The 1982–1984 Excavations at Las Colinas, vol. 5. Archaeological Series 162, vol. 5. Cultural Resource Management Division, Arizona State Museum, University of Arizona, Tucson.

Nicolson, John (editor)
1974 *The Arizona of Joseph Pratt Allyn, Letters from a Pioneer Judge: Observations and Travels, 1863–1866.* University of Arizona Press, Tucson.

Noble, Marguerite
1979 *Filaree: A Novel of American Life.* University of New Mexico Press, Albuquerque.

Olmstead, Frank H.
1919 *Gila River Flood Control—A Report on Flood Control of the Gila River in Graham County, Arizona.* S. Doc. 436, 65th Congress, 3rd Session. U.S. Government Printing Office, Washington, D.C.

Parsons, Elsie Clews
1939 *Pueblo Indian Religion.* University of Chicago Press, Chicago.

Patten, Duncan T.
1998 Restoration as the Order of the 21st Century: An Ecologist's Perspective. In *Reclaiming the Native Home of Hope: Community, Ecology and the American West,* edited by Robert B. Keiter, pp. 69–77. University of Utah Press, Salt Lake City.

Pattie, James O.
1984 *The Personal Narrative of James O. Pattie.* University of Nebraska Press, Lincoln.

Pedrick, Kathryn E.
1992 Introduction to *Developing Perspectives on Tonto Prehistory,* edited by Charles L. Redman, Glen E. Rice, and Kathryn E. Pedrick, pp. 1–4. Roosevelt Monograph Series 2, Anthropological Field Studies 26. Office of Cultural Resource Management, Department of Anthropology, Arizona State University, Tempe.

Peirce, H. Wesley
1985 Arizona's Backbone: The Transition Zone. *Fieldnotes* 15(3):1–6. Arizona Bureau of Geology and Mineral Technology, Tucson.

Perry, Richard J.
1991 *Western Apache Heritage: People of the Mountain Corridor.* University of Texas Press, Austin.

1993 *Apache Reservation: Indigenous Peoples and the American State.* University of Texas Press, Austin.

Peterson, Charles S.
1973 *Take Up Your Mission: Mormon Colonizing along the Little Colorado River, 1870–1900.* University of Arizona Press, Tucson.

Peterson, Frederick A.
1959 *Ancient Mexico: An Introduction to the Pre-Hispanic Cultures.* George Allen and Unwin, London.

Pimental, O. Ricardo
2002 Stupidity and Greed Lit Fires, Not Racial Issues. *The Arizona Republic* 11 July:B11.

Polzer, Charles W.
1982 *Kino Guide II: His Missions and Monuments.* Southwestern Mission Research Center, Tucson, Arizona.

Porter, Joseph C.
1986 *Paper Medicine Man.* University of Oklahoma Press, Norman.

Powell, John Wesley
1895 *Canyons of Colorado.* Flood & Vincent, Meadville, Pennsylvania.

1983 *Report on the Lands of the Arid Regions of the United States, with a More Detailed Account of the Lands of Utah.* Reprinted. Harvard Common Press, Harvard, Massachussets. Originally published 1879, Government Printing Office, Washington, D.C.

Preucel, Robert W.
1996 Cooking Status: Hohokam Ideology, Power, and Social Reproduction. In *Interpreting Southwestern Diversity: Underlying Principles and Overarching Patterns,* edited by Paul R. Fish and J. Jefferson Reid, pp. 125–131. Anthropological Research Papers No. 48. Office of Cultural Resource Management, Arizona State University, Tempe.

Pyne, Stephen J.
1998 *How the Canyon Became Grand: A Short History.* Viking Press, New York.

Qoyawayma, Polingaysi
1964 *No Turning Back: A Hopi Indian Woman's Struggle to Live in Two Worlds.* University of New Mexico Press, Albuquerque.

Rabbit, Thomas
1995 A Flat Rock, Poetry, Perception, and Landscape. In *Landscape in America,* edited by George F. Thompson, pp. 171–182. University of Texas Press, Austin.

Ravesloot, John C., and Jon S. Czaplicki
1989 Concluding Thoughts. In *Excavations at Water World (AZ AA:16:94), A Rillito Phase Ballcourt Village in the Avra Valley,* edited by Jon S. Czaplicki and John C. Ravesloot, pp. 305–314. Hohokam Archaeology along Phase B of the Tucson Aqueduct, Central Arizona Project, vol. 3. Archaeological Series 178, vol. 3. Cultural Resource Management Division, Arizona State Museum, University of Arizona, Tucson.

Ravesloot, John C., and Marcia H. Regan
2000 Demographic, Health, Genetic, and Mortuary Characteristics of Late Prehistoric Central Arizona Populations. In *Salado,* edited by Jeffrey S. Dean, pp. 57–79. Amerind Foundation New World Studies Series 4. Amerind Foundation, Dragoon, Arizona, and University of New Mexico Press, Albuquerque.

Rea, Amadeo M.
1983 *Once A River: Bird Life and Habitat Changes on the Middle Gila.* University of Arizona Press, Tucson.

1997 *At the Desert's Green Edge: An Ethnobotany of the Gila River Pima.* University of Arizona Press, Tucson.

Redman, Charles L.
1999 *Human Impact on Ancient Environments.* University of Arizona Press, Tucson.

Reid, J. Jefferson
1989 A Grasshopper Perspective on the Mogollon of the Arizona Mountains. In *Dynamics of Southwest Prehistory,* edited by Linda S. Cordell and George J. Gumerman, pp. 65–97. Smithsonian Institution Press, Washington, D.C.

Reid, J. Jefferson (editor)
1982 *Cholla Project Archaeology.* 5 vols. Archaeological Series 161. Cultural Resource Management Division, Arizona State Museum, University of Arizona, Tucson.

Reid, J. Jefferson, and Stephanie M. Whittlesey
1997 *The Archaeology of Ancient Arizona.* University of Arizona Press, Tucson.

1999 *Grasshopper Pueblo: A Story of Archaeology and Ancient Life.* University of Arizona Press, Tucson.

Reisner, Marc
1986 *Cadillac Desert: The American West and Its Disappearing Water.* Penguin Books, New York.

Rice, Glen E., and Thomas R. Lincoln
1998 The Bureau of Reclamation Archaeology Projects in Tonto Basin. In *A Synthesis of Tonto Basin Prehistory: The Roosevelt Archaeology Studies, 1989 to 1998,* edited by Glen E. Rice, pp. 1–9. Roosevelt Monograph Series 12, Anthropological Field Studies 41. Office of Cultural Resource Management, Department of Anthropology, Arizona State University, Tempe.

Rice, Glen E., Charles L. Redman, David Jacobs, and Owen Lindauer
1998 Architecture, Settlement Types, and Settlement Complexes. In *A Synthesis of Tonto Basin Prehistory: The Roosevelt Archaeology Studies, 1989 to 1998,* edited by Glen E. Rice, pp. 55–83. Roosevelt Monograph Series 12, Anthropological Field Studies 41. Office of Cultural Resource Management, Department of Anthropology, Arizona State University, Tempe.

Roberts, Brian K.
1993 *Landscapes of Settlement: Prehistory to the Present.* Routledge, London.

Robinson, Michael C.
1979 *Water for the West: The Bureau of Reclamation 1902–1977.* Public Works Historical Society, Chicago.

Rogge, A. E.
1983 Little Archaeology, Big Archaeology: The Changing Context of Archaeological Research. Unpublished Ph.D. dissertation, Department of Anthropology, University of Arizona, Tucson.

Rogge, A. E., D. Lorne McWatters, Melissa Keane, and Richard P. Emanuel
1995 *Raising Arizona's Dams: Daily Life, Danger, and Discrimination in the Dam Construction Camps of Central Arizona, 1890s–1940s.* University of Arizona Press, Tucson.

Rogge, A. E., and Cindy L. Meyers (editors)
1987 *A Plan for Archaeological Investigations of Historic Dam Construction Camps of Central Arizona.* Dames and Moore Intermountain Cultural Services, Phoenix.

Sahagún, Fray Bernardino de
1946 *Historia General de las Cosas de Nueva España,* vol. 3. Editorial Nueva España, Mexico.

1953 *Florentine Codex: General History of the Things of New Spain.* Translated from the Aztec into English by Arthur J. O. Anderson and Charles E. Dibble. Book 7, The Sun, Moon, and Stars, and the Binding of the Years. University of Utah, Salt Lake City, and School of American Research, Santa Fe, New Mexico.

Salt River Project (SRP)
2003 Roosevelt Dam [Online]. Available at http://www.srpnet.com/water/lakes/rooseveltdam.asp (accessed 20 July 2002; verified 22 January 2003). SRP, Tempe, Arizona.

Saxton, Dean, and Lucille Saxton
1973 *O'othham Hoho'ok A'agitha: Legends and Lore of the Papago and Pima Indians.* University of Arizona Press, Tucson.

Scarborough, Robert
2000 The Geologic Origin of the Sonoran Desert. In *A Natural History of the Sonoran Desert,* pp. 71–85. Arizona-Sonora Desert Museum, Tucson.

Schaafsma, Polly
1999 Tlalocs, Kachinas, Sacred Bundles, and Related Symbolism in the Southwest and Mesoamerica. In *The Casas Grandes World,* edited by Curtis F. Schaafsma and Carroll L. Riley, pp. 164–192. University of Utah Press, Salt Lake City.

Schroeder, Albert H.
1979 Prehistory: Hakataya. In *Southwest,* edited by Alfonso Ortiz, pp. 100–107. Handbook of North American Indians, vol. 9, William C. Sturtevant, general editor. Smithsonian Institution, Washington, D.C.

Schuck, Leora
1978 The Homesteaders: Neils Hansen Believed in Future, Worked for Progress. *Pinetop-Lakeside News* 28 September:4.

Schwalen, H. C., and R. J. Shaw
1957 *Water in the Santa Cruz Valley.* Bulletin No. 288. Agricultural Experiment Station, University of Arizona, Tucson.

Séjourné, Laurette
1976 *Burning Water: Thought and Religion in Ancient Mexico.* Shambhala, Berkeley.

Sekaquaptewa, Helen
1969 *Me and Mine: The Life Story of Helen Sekaquaptewa.* As Told to Louise Udall. 11th printing. University of Arizona Press, Tucson.

Shaul, David Leedom, and Jane H. Hill
1998 Tepimans, Yumans, and other Hohokam. *American Antiquity* 63:375–396.

Sheridan, Thomas E.
1995 *Arizona: A History.* University of Arizona Press, Tucson.

Shreve, Forrest
1951 *Vegetation of the Sonoran Desert.* Carnegie Institution of Washington, Washington, D.C.

Siminski, Peter
2000 The Desert Adaptations of Birds and Mammals. In *A Natural History of the Sonoran Desert,* pp. 367–372. Arizona-Sonora Desert Museum, Tucson.

Simon, Arleyn W.
1997 Plain, Red, and Other Ceramic Wares from U:4:33/132, the Cline Terrace Mound. In *A Salado Platform Mound on Tonto Creek, Roosevelt Platform Mound Study: Report on the Cline Terrace Mound, Cline Terrace Complex,* by David Jacobs, pp. 291–362. Roosevelt Monograph Series 7, Anthropological Field Studies 36. Office of Cultural Resource Management, Department of Anthropology, Arizona State University, Tempe.

Smith, Henry Nash
1971 *Virgin Land: The American West as Symbol and Myth.* Harvard University Press, Cambridge.

Snow, David H.
1990 Tener Comal y Metate: Protohistoric Rio Grande Maize Use and Diet. In *Perspectives on Southwestern Prehistory,* edited by Paul E. Minnis and Charles L. Redman, pp. 289–300. Westview Press, Boulder, Colorado.

Solheim, Dave, and Rob Levin
1996 The *Bloomsbury Review* Interview. In *Resist Much, Obey Little: Remembering Ed Abbey*, edited by James R. Hepworth and Gregory McNamee, pp. 138–155. Sierra Club Books, San Francisco.

Spicer, Edward H.
1962 *Cycles of Conquest: The Impact of Spain, Mexico, and the United States on the Indians of the Southwest, 1540–1960.* University of Arizona Press, Tucson.

Stegner, Wallace
1953 *Beyond the Hundredth Meridian: John Wesley Powell and the Second Opening of the West.* Penguin Books, New York.

1981 Introduction: Water Warnings, Water Futures. Water on the Plateau. *Plateau* 53:2–3.

Stevens, Joseph E.
1988 *Hoover Dam: An American Adventure.* University of Oklahoma Press, Norman.

Stewart, Kenneth
1983 Mojave. In *Southwest*, edited by Alfonso Ortiz, pp. 55–70. Handbook of North American Indians, vol. 10, William C. Sturtevant, general editor. Smithsonian Institution, Washington, D.C.

Sullivan, T. D.
1974 *Tlaloc: A New Etymological Interpretation of the God's Name and What it Reveals of His Essence and Nature.* Proceedings of the 40th International Congress of Americanists 2:213–219. Rome.

Summerhayes, Martha
1979 *Vanished Arizona: Recollections of the Army Life of a New England Woman.* Reprinted. University of Nebraska Press, Lincoln. Originally Published Salem Press, Salem, 1911 (2nd ed.).

Swanton, John R.
1952 *Indian Tribes of North America.* Smithsonian Institution, Bureau of American Ethnology, Bulletin No. 145. Government Printing Office, Washington, D.C.

Sykes, Godfrey
1937 *The Colorado Delta.* American Geographical Society Special Publication No. 19. Carnegie Institution, Washington, D.C., and American Geographical Society, New York.

Szuter, Christine R.
1984 Paleoenvironment and Species Richness along the Salt-Gila Aqueduct. In *Environment and Subsistence*, edited by Lynn S. Teague and Patricia L. Crown, pp. 81–93. Hohokam Archaeology along the Salt-Gila Aqueduct, Central Arizona Project, vol. 7. Archaeological Series 150, vol. 7. Cultural Resource Management Division, Arizona State Museum, University of Arizona, Tucson.

1988 Environment and Subsistence in the Tucson Basin: The Faunal Data from Hohokam Sites. In *Recent Research on Tucson Basin Prehistory: Proceedings of the Second Tucson Basin Conference*, edited by William H. Doelle and Paul R. Fish, pp. 39–45. Anthropological Papers No. 10. Institute for American Research, Tucson.

1991 *Hunting by Prehistoric Horticulturalists in the American Southwest.* Garland, New York.

Teague, Lynn S.
1992 Textiles in Late Prehistory. In *Proceedings of the Second Salado Conference, Globe, AZ*, edited by Richard C. Lange and Stephen Germick, pp. 304–311. Occasional Paper 1992. Arizona Archaeological Society, Phoenix.

1998 *Textiles in Southwestern Prehistory.* University of New Mexico Press, Albuquerque.

Teague, Lynn S., and Patricia L. Crown (editors)
1984 *Hohokam Archaeology along the Salt-Gila Aqueduct, Central Arizona Project.* 9 vols. Archaeological Series 150. Cultural Resource Management Division, Arizona State Museum, University of Arizona, Tucson.

Tellman, Barbara, Richard Yarde, and Mary G. Wallace
1997 *Arizona's Changing Rivers: How People Have Affected the Rivers.* Issue Paper No. 19. Water Resources Research Center, College of Agriculture, University of Arizona, Tucson.

Thomas, Charles Matthew, and Jeffrey Howard King
1985 Hohokam Figurine Assemblages: A Suggested Ritual Context. *Proceedings of the 1983 Hohokam Symposium*, edited by Alfred E. Dittert, Jr., and Donald E. Dove, pp. 687–732. Occasional Paper No. 2, Pt. II. Arizona Archaeological Society, Phoenix.

Thompson, George F.
1995 A Message to the Reader. In *Landscape in America*, edited by George F. Thompson, pp. xi–xiv. University of Texas Press, Austin.

Thompson, John Eric Sidney
1970 *Maya History and Religion.* University of Oklahoma Press, Norman.

Tilley, Christopher
1994 *A Phenomenology of Landscape: Places, Paths and Monuments.* Berg, Oxford.

Time Traveler Maps
1999 *The Colorado Plateau: Map & Guide to Public Lands on the Colorado Plateau and its Borderlands.* The Peaks, Plateaus & Canyons Association, Mancos, Colorado.

Titiev, Mischa
1992 *Old Oraibi: A Study of the Hopi Indians of Third Mesa.* University of New Mexico Press, Albuquerque.

Tobin, Mitch
2001 Unending Water Fight. *Arizona Daily Star* 30 April:A1.

Townsend, Richard F.
1992 The Renewal of Nature at the Temple of Tlaloc. In *The Ancient Americas: Art from Sacred Landscapes,* edited by Richard F. Townsend, pp. 171–186. Art Institute of Chicago, Chicago.

Trimble, Stephen
1993 *The People.* School of American Research Press, Santa Fe.

1998 Letting Go of the Rim. In *Reclaiming the Native Home of Hope: Community, Ecology and the American West,* edited by Robert B. Keiter, pp. 136–143. University of Utah Press, Salt Lake City.

Turner, Christy G. II
1993 Southwest Indian Teeth. *National Geographic Research & Exploration* 9:32–53.

Turner, Christy G., Marcia H. Regan, and Joel D. Irish
1994 Physical Anthropology and Human Taphonomy. In *Prehistoric Rural Settlements in the Tonto Basin,* edited by Richard Ciolek-Torrello, Steven D. Shelley, and Su Benaron, pp. 559–583. The Roosevelt Rural Sites Study, vol. 2. Technical Series 28. Statistical Research, Tucson.

Underhill, Ruth Murray
1965 *Red Man's Religion: Beliefs and Practices of the Indians North of Mexico.* University of Chicago Press, Chicago.

1979 *Papago Woman.* Holt, Rinehart and Winston, New York.

1993 *Singing for Power: The Song Magic of the Papago Indians of Southern Arizona.* University of Arizona Press, Tucson.

Urrea, Luis Alberto
1996 Down the Highway with Edward Abbey. In *Resist Much, Obey Little: Remembering Ed Abbey,* edited by James R. Hepworth and Gregory McNamee, pp. 40–47. Sierra Club Books, San Francisco.

U.S. Department of Energy
2003 U.S. Department of Energy's NEPA Web site [Online]. Available at http://ceq.eh.doe.gov/nepa/regs/nepa/nepaeqia.htm (accessed 20 July 2002; verified 18 February 2003). U.S. Department of Energy.

U.S. Department of the Interior, Bureau of Reclamation
2003a A Brief History of Roosevelt Dam [Online]. Available at http://www.apo.lc/usbr/gov/ (modified 9 January 2003; accessed 20 July 2002; verified 18 February 2003). U.S. Department of the Interior, Bureau of Reclamation Phoenix Area Office, Phoenix, Arizona.

2003b Hoover Dam [Online]. Available at http://www.usbr/gov.lc/hooverdam/History/fatalities/fatal.html (modified November 2000; accessed 20 July 2002; verified 18 February 2003). U.S. Department of the Interior, Bureau of Reclamation Phoenix Area Office, Phoenix, Arizona.

2003c Theodore Roosevelt Dam Fact Sheet [Online]. Available at http://www.apo.lc/usbr/gov/ (modified 9 January 2003; accessed 20 July 2002; verified 18 February 2003). U.S. Department of the Interior, Bureau of Reclamation Phoenix Area Office, Phoenix, Arizona.

Van West, Carla R., and Jeffrey H. Altschul
1994 Agricultural Productivity and Carrying Capacity in the Tonto Basin. In *Changing Land Use in the Tonto Basin,* edited by Richard Ciolek-Torrello and John R. Welch, pp. 361–435. The Roosevelt Rural Sites Study, vol. 3. Technical Series 28. Statistical Research, Tucson.

Van West, Carla R., Richard S. Ciolek-Torrello, John R. Welch, Jeffrey H. Altschul, Karen R. Adams, Steven D. Shelley, and Jeffrey A. Homburg
2000 Subsistence and Environmental Interactions. In *Salado,* edited by Jeffrey S. Dean, pp. 27–56. Amerind Foundation New World Studies Series 4. Amerind Foundation, Dragoon, Arizona, and University of New Mexico Press, Albuquerque.

Wakoski, Diane
1996 Joining the Visionary "Inhumanists." In *Resist Much, Obey Little: Remembering Ed Abbey,* edited by James R. Hepworth and Gregory McNamee, pp. 168–174. Sierra Club Books, San Francisco.

Walka, Ann Weiler
1993 *Waterlines: Journeys on a Desert River.* Red Lake Books, Flagstaff, Arizona.

2002 *Walking the Unknown River and other Travels in Escalante Country.* Bluff City Books, Flagstaff, Arizona, and Bluff, Utah.

Wallace, Henry D., and James P. Holmlund
1986 *The Petroglyphs of the Picacho Mountains, South-Central Arizona.* Anthropological Papers No. 6. Institute for American Research, Tucson.

Walters, Harry, and Hugh C. Rogers
2001 Anasazi and Anaasázi: Two Words, Two Cultures. *Kiva* 66:317–326.

Wasley, William W., and David E. Doyel
1980 Classic Period Hohokam. *The Kiva* 45:337–352.

Waters, Frank
1984 *The Colorado.* Reprinted. Ohio University Press/Swallow Press, Athens, Ohio. Originally published 1946, Holt, Rinehart, and Winston, New York.

Waters, Michael R.
1989 The Influence of Late Quaternary Landscape Processes on Hohokam Settlement Patterning in Southern Arizona. In *Syntheses and Interpretations,* edited by Jon S. Czaplicki and John C. Ravesloot, pp. 79–130. Hohokam Archaeology along Phase B of the Tucson Aqueduct, Central Arizona Project, vol. 1. Archaeological Series 178, vol. 1. Cultural Resource Management Division, Arizona State Museum, University of Arizona, Tucson.

1998 Geoarchaeological Investigations in the Tonto Basin. In *Environment and Subsistence in the Classic Period Tonto Basin: The Roosevelt Archaeology Studies, 1989 to 1998,* edited by Katherine A. Spielmann, pp. 7–47. Roosevelt Monograph Series 9, Anthropological Field Studies 39. Office of Cultural Resource Management, Department of Anthropology, Arizona State University, Tempe.

Watkins, T. H.
1983 Introduction to *Report on the Lands of the Arid Regions of the United States, with a More Detailed Account of the Lands of Utah,* by John Wesley Powell. Reprinted. Harvard Common Press, Harvard, Massachussets. Originally published 1879, Government Printing Office, Washington, D.C.

Weaver, M. P.
1981 *The Aztecs, Maya, and Their Predecessors: Archaeology of Mesoamerica.* 2nd ed. Studies in Archaeology, Academic Press, New York.

Webb, George
1959 *A Pima Remembers.* University of Arizona Press, Tucson. 7th printing, 1992.

Welch, John R.
1992 Irrigation Agriculture in the Tonto Basin. In *Proceedings of the Second Salado Conference, Globe, AZ,* edited by Richard C. Lange and Stephen Germick, pp. 161–171. Occasional Paper 1992. Arizona Archaeological Society, Phoenix.

1994a Archaeological Studies of Agricultural Contexts. In *Changing Land Use in the Tonto Basin,* edited by Richard Ciolek-Torrello and John R. Welch, pp. 223–251. The Roosevelt Rural Sites Study, vol. 3. Technical Series 28. Statistical Research, Tucson.

1994b Environmental Influences on Tonto Basin Agricultural Productivity and Sustainability. In *Changing Land Use in the Tonto Basin,* edited by Richard Ciolek-Torrello and John R. Welch, pp. 19–39. The Roosevelt Rural Sites Study, vol. 3. Technical Series 28. Statistical Research, Tucson.

1994c Ethnographic Models for Tonto Basin Land Use. In *Changing Land Use in the Tonto Basin,* edited by Richard Ciolek-Torrello and John R. Welch, pp. 79–120. The Roosevelt Rural Sites Study, vol. 3. Technical Series 28. Statistical Research, Tucson.

Welch, John R., and Richard Ciolek-Torrello
1994 Nineteenth- and Twentieth-Century Land Use in the Tonto Basin. In *Changing Land Use in the Tonto Basin,* edited by Richard Ciolek-Torrello and John R. Welch, pp. 57–78. The Roosevelt Rural Sites Study, vol. 3. Technical Series 28. Statistical Research, Tucson.

White, Richard
1991 *"It's Your Misfortune and None of My Own": A New History of the American West.* University of Oklahoma Press, Norman.

Whiteley, Peter M.
1998 *Rethinking Hopi Ethnography.* Smithsonian Institution Press, Washington, D.C.

Whiting, Alfred F.
1939 *Ethnobotany of the Hopi.* Bulletin No. 15. Museum of Northern Arizona, Flagstaff.

Whittlesey, Stephanie M.
1998a Archaeological Landscapes: A Methodological and Theoretical Discussion. In *Overview, Synthesis, and Conclusions,* edited by Stephanie M. Whittlesey, Richard Ciolek-Torrello, and Jeffrey H. Altschul, pp. 17–28. Vanishing River: Landscapes and Lives of the Lower Verde Valley: The Lower Verde Archaeological Project. SRI Press, Tucson.

1998b Landscapes and Lives along the Lower Verde River. In *Vanishing River: Landscapes and Lives of the Lower Verde Valley: The Lower Verde Archaeological Project,* edited by Stephanie M. Whittlesey, Richard Ciolek-Torrello, and Jeffrey H. Altschul, pp. 703–721. SRI Press, Tucson.

1998c Rethinking the Core-Periphery Model of the Pre-Classic Period Hohokam. In *Overview, Synthesis, and Conclusions,* edited by Stephanie M. Whittlesey, Richard Ciolek-Torrello, and Jeffrey H. Altschul, pp. 597–628. Vanishing River: Landscapes and Lives of the Lower Verde Valley: The Lower Verde Archaeological Project. SRI Press, Tucson.

1998d Toward a Unified Theory of Ceramic Production and Distribution: Examples from the Central Arizona Deserts. In *Overview, Synthesis, and Conclusions*, edited by Stephanie M. Whittlesey, Richard Ciolek-Torrello, and Jeffrey H. Altschul, pp. 417–446. Vanishing River: Landscapes and Lives of the Lower Verde Valley: The Lower Verde Archaeological Project. SRI Press, Tucson.

1998e The Vanished River: Historical-Period Impacts to Desert Landscapes and Archaeological Implications. In *Overview, Synthesis, and Conclusions*, edited by Stephanie M. Whittlesey, Richard Ciolek-Torrello, and Jeffrey H. Altschul, pp. 29–57. Vanishing River: Landscapes and Lives of the Lower Verde Valley: The Lower Verde Archaeological Project. SRI Press, Tucson.

Whittlesey, Stephanie M., and Su Benaron
1998 Yavapai and Western Apache Ethnohistory and Material Culture. In *Overview, Synthesis, and Conclusions*, edited by Stephanie M. Whittlesey, Richard Ciolek-Torrello, and Jeffrey H. Altschul, pp. 143–183. Vanishing River: Landscapes and Lives of the Lower Verde Valley: The Lower Verde Archaeological Project. SRI Press, Tucson. SRI Press, Tucson.

Whittlesey, Stephanie M., Richard Ciolek-Torrello, and J. Jefferson Reid
2000 Salado: The View from the Arizona Mountains. In *Salado*, edited by Jeffrey S. Dean, pp. 241–261. Amerind Foundation New World Studies Series 4. Amerind Foundation, Dragoon, Arizona, and University of New Mexico Press, Albuquerque.

Whittlesey, Stephanie M., Richard S. Ciolek-Torrello, and Matthew A. Sterner
1994 *Southern Arizona: The Last 12,000 years: A Cultural-Historic Overview for the Western Army National Guard Aviation Training Site.* Technical Series 48. Statistical Research, Tucson.

Whittlesey, Stephanie M., Teresita Majewski, John R. Welch, Matthew C. Bischoff, and Richard Ciolek-Torrello
1998 Euroamerican History, 1540 to the Present. In *Overview, Synthesis, and Conclusions*, edited by Stephanie M. Whittlesey, Richard Ciolek-Torrello, and Jeffrey H. Altschul, pp. 281–336. Vanishing River: Landscapes and Lives of the Lower Verde Valley: The Lower Verde Archaeological Project. SRI Press, Tucson.

Whittlesey, Stephanie M, and J. Jefferson Reid
1982 Cholla Perspectives on Salado. In *Introduction and Special Studies,* edited by J. Jefferson Reid, pp. 63–80. Cholla Project Archaeology, vol. 1. Archaeological Series 170, vol. 1. Cultural Resource Management Division, Arizona State Museum, University of Arizona, Tucson.

Wilcox, David R.
1991 The Mesoamerican Ballgame in the Southwest. In *The Mesoamerican Ballgame*, edited by Vernon L. Scarborough and David R. Wilcox, pp. 101–125. University of Arizona Press, Tucson.

Wilcox, David R., Thomas R. McGuire, and Charles Sternberg
1981 *Snaketown Revisited.* Archaeological Series 155. Cultural Resource Management Division, Arizona State Museum, University of Arizona, Tucson.

Wilcox, David R., and Charles Sternberg
1983 *Hohokam Ballcourts and Their Interpretation.* Archaeological Series 160. Cultural Resource Management Division, Arizona State Museum, University of Arizona, Tucson.

Wilkinson, Charles F.
1992 *Crossing the Next Meridian: Land, Water, and the Future of the West.* Island Press, Washington, D.C.

Williamson, Chilton, Jr.
1996 Abbey Lives! In *Resist Much, Obey Little: Remembering Ed Abbey*, edited by John R. Hepworth and Gregory McNamee, pp. 89–95. Sierra Club Books, San Francisco.

Wittfogel, Karl A.
1957 *Oriental Despotism: A Comparative Study of Total Power.* Yale University Press, New Haven.

Wood, J. Scott
2000 Vale of Tiers Palimpsest: Salado Settlement and Internal Relationships in the Tonto Basin Area. In *Salado*, edited by Jeffrey S. Dean, pp. 107–141. Amerind Foundation New World Studies Series 4. Amerind Foundation, Dragoon, Arizona, and University of New Mexico Press, Albuquerque.

Wood, J. Scott, and Martin E. McAllister
1980 Foundation and Empire: The Colonization of the Northeastern Hohokam Periphery. In *Current Issues in Hohokam Prehistory: Proceedings of a Symposium*, edited by David E. Doyel and Fred Plog, pp. 180–204. Anthropological Research Papers No. 23. Arizona State Museum, University of Arizona, Tucson.

Wood, J. Scott, Glen E. Rice, and David Jacobs
1992 Factors Affecting Prehistoric Salado Irrigation in the Tonto Basin. In *Developing Perspectives on Tonto Basin Prehistory*, edited by Charles L. Redman, Glen E. Rice, and Kathryn E. Pedrick, pp. 27–32. Roosevelt Monograph Series 2, Anthropological Field Studies 26. Office of Cultural Resource Management, Department of Anthropology, Arizona State University, Tempe.

Woodin, Ann
1994 *Home is the Desert.* Reprinted. Oracle Press, Oracle, Arizona. Originally published 1964, University of Arizona Press, Tucson.

Woodson, Michael Kyle
1995 The Goat Hill Site: A Western Anasazi Pueblo in the Safford Valley of Southeastern Arizona. Unpublished Master's thesis, Department of Anthropology, University of Texas, Austin.

Worster, Donald
1985 *Rivers of Empire: Water, Aridity, and the Growth of the American West.* Oxford University Press, New York.

2001 *A River Running West: The Life of John Wesley Powell.* Oxford University Press, New York.

Young, Herbert V.
1983 *Water by the Inch: Adventures of a Pioneer Family on an Arizona Desert Homestead.* Northland Press, Flagstaff, Arizona.

Zarbin, Earl
1984 *Roosevelt Dam: A History to 1911.* Salt River Project, Phoenix.

Zepeda, Ofelia
1995 *Ocean Power: Poems from the Desert.* University of Arizona Press, Tucson.

Zwinger, Ann
1996 *The Mysterious Lands.* Reprinted. University of Arizona Press, Tucson. Originally published 1989, Dutton, New York

Text Acknowledgments

From DESERT SOLITAIRE by Edward Abbey. Reprinted by permission of Don Congdon Associates, Inc. © 1968 by Edward Abbey, renewed 1996 by Clarke Abbey.

"An American Symbol" excerpt used by permission of the Buffalo Bill Historical Center, Cody Wyoming.

Excerpt from THE SHORT SWIFT TIME OF GODS ON EARTH: THE HOHOKAM CHRONICLES by Donald Bahr, Juan Smith, William A. Allison, and Julian Hayden. Copyright © 1994 The Regents of the University of California. Used by permission of the University of California Press.

Excerpts from MEDITATIONS WITH THE HOPI: A CENTERING BOOK by Robert Boissiere, Bear & Co., a division of Inner Traditions, Bear & Co., Rochester, VT 05767. Copyright © 1986 by Robert Bossiere.

Excerpts from BLUE DESERT, by Charles Bowden. © 1986 The Arizona Board of Regents. Reprinted by permission of the University of Arizona Press.

From KILLING THE HIDDEN WATERS by Charles Bowden, Copyright © 1977. By permission of the University of Texas Press.

Excerpt from ENJU: THE LIFE AND STRUGGLE OF AN APACHE CHIEF FROM THE LITTLE RUNNING WATER by Sinclair Browning, published by Northland Press. Copyright © 1982 by Sinclair Browning. Reprinted with the permission of Sinclair Browning.

Excerpt from "Three Poems for the Indian Steelworkers in a Bar Where I Used to Drink," in INDIAN MOUNTAIN AND OTHER POEMS, by Joseph Bruchac. Copyright © 1971 by Joseph Bruchac. Reprinted by permission of Barbara S. Kouts.

© 2002 by Craig Childs. All rights reserved. Excerpted from THE SECRET KNOWLEDGE OF WATER by permission of Sasquatch Books.

Excerpt from THE SONORAN DESERT: ITS GEOGRAPHY, ECONOMY, AND PEOPLE, by Roger Dunbier. Copyright © 1968 The Arizona Board of Regents. Reprinted by permission of the University of Arizona Press.

Excerpt from GLENN CANYON DAMMED: INVENTING LAKE POWELL AND THE CANYON COUNTRY, by Jared Farmer. Copyright © 1999 The Arizona Board of Regents. Reprinted by permission of the University of Arizona Press.

Excerpt from MYTHS AND TALES OF THE WHITE MOUNTAIN APACHE by Grenville Goodwin, copyright © Grenville Goodwin. Used courtesy of the American Folklore Society.

Excerpt from the exhibit *Mountain Family Spirit: Art and Culture of the Ute Indians*, organized by the Taylor Museum of the Colorado Springs Fine Arts Center. Used by permission of Dr. James A. Goss.

Excerpt from the poem "Dry Bones" from POEMS OF A RANCH WOMAN, by Sharlot Hall. Copyright © 1953 The Prescott Historical Society/Sharlot Hall Museum. Reprinted by permission of the Sharlot Hall Museum Archives and Library.

Excerpt from the poem "Water Rising," by Linda Hogan, in HOME PLACES: CONTEMPORARY NATIVE AMERICAN WRITING FROM SUN TRACKS, published in 1995 by the University of Arizona Press. Copyright © Linda Hogan. Reprinted by permission of Linda Hogan.

Excerpts from WIDE SKIES: FINDING A HOME IN THE WEST, by Gary Holthaus. Copyright © 1997 The Arizona Board of Regents. Reprinted by permission of the University of Arizona Press.

From THE COLLECTED POEMS OF LANGSTON HUGHES by Langston Hughes, copyright ©1994 by The Estate of Langston Hughes. Used by permission of Alfred A. Knopf, a division of Random House, Inc.

Excerpt from page 25 of GLEN CANYON: AN ARCHAEOLOGICAL SUMMARY by Jesse Jennings, copyright © 1998. Reprinted with the permission of University of Utah Press.

Excerpt from NAVAJO SACRED PLACES by Klara Kelley and David Francis. Copyright ©1994 by Indiana University Press. Reprinted with the permission of Indiana University Press.

Excerpt by Richard Lange from "Pots, People, Politics, and Precipitation: Just Who or What Are the Salado Anyway?" on page 333 of THE PROCEEDINGS OF THE SECOND SALADO CONFERENCE, GLOBE, AZ. Copyright © 1992 by The Arizona Archaeological Society. Reprinted by permission of The Arizona Archaeological Society.

Excerpt by Barry Lopez reprinted from "Gone Back into the Earth" from CROSSING OPEN GROUND by Barry Lopez. Copyright © 1981 by Barry Holstun Lopez. Reprinted by permission.

Excerpt from THE PAST IS A FOREIGN COUNTRY, by David Lowenthal, Copyright © 1985 Cambridge University Press. Reprinted with the permission of Cambridge University Press.

Excerpt from COYOTEWAY: A NAVAJO HOLYWAY HEALING CEREMONIAL by Karl W. Luckert and Johnny C. Cooke, published in 1979 by the University of Arizona Press. Copyright ©1979 Karl W. Luckert. Reprinted with the permission of Karl W. Luckert.

Excerpts from SONGS MY MOTHER SANG TO ME, by Patricia Preciado Martin. Copyright © 1992 The Arizona Board of Regents. Reprinted by permission of the University of Arizona Press.

Excerpts from FILAREE by Marguerite Noble, published in 1979 by the University of New Mexico Press. Copyright ©1979 Marguerite Noble. Reprinted with the permission of Marguerite Noble.

Excerpt from GRASSHOPPER PUEBLO: A STORY OF ARCHAEOLOGY AND ANCIENT LIFE, by J. Jefferson Reid and Stephanie Whittlesey. Copyright © 1999 The Arizona Board of Regents. Reprinted by permission of the University of Arizona Press.

Excerpt from ME AND MINE: THE LIFE STORY OF HELEN SEKAQUAPTEWA, AS TOLD TO LOUISE UDALL. Copyright © 1969 The Arizona Board of Regents. Reprinted by permission of the University of Arizona Press.

Excerpts from O'OTHHAM HOHO'OK A'AGITHA: LEGENDS AND LORE OF THE PAPAGO AND PIMA INDIANS, by Dean and Lucille Saxton, published by the University of Arizona Press. Copyright © 1973 Dean and Lucille Saxton. Reprinted by permission of Dean and Lucille Saxton.

Excerpt by William Stegner from *Plateau Magazine* used by permission of the Museum of Northern Arizona.

Excerpt from "Dust Precedes the Rain," in BLUE HORSES RUSH IN: POEMS AND STORIES, by Luci Tapahonso. Copyright © 1997 Luci Tapahonso. Reprinted by permission of the University of Arizona Press.

Excerpt from SINGING FOR POWER by Ruth Murray Underhill. Copyright © 1993 The Regents of the University of California. Used by permission of the University of California Press.

Excerpts from WALKING THE UNKNOWN RIVER AND OTHER TRAVELS IN ESCALANTE COUNTRY, published in 2002 by Bluff City Books. Copyright © 2002 by Ann Weiler Walka. Reprinted with the permission of Ann Weiler Walka.

"Havasupai Medicine Song," from SPIRIT MOUNTAIN: AN ANTHOLOGY OF YUMAN STORY AND SONG, edited by Lucille Watahomogie and Leanne Hinton. © 1984 Arizona Board of Regents. Reprinted by permission of the University of Arizona Press.

From RED: PASSION AND PATIENCE IN THE DESERT by Terry Tempest Williams, copyright © 2001 by Terry Tempest Williams. Used by permission of Pantheon Books, a division of Random House, Inc.

Excerpts from HOME IS THE DESERT by Ann Woodin, published in 1994 by Oracle Press. Copyright © 1994 by Ann Woodin. Reprinted by permission of Ann Woodin.

Excerpts from A RIVER RUNNING WEST by Donald Worster, copyright © 2000 by Donald Worster. Used by permission of Oxford University Press, Inc.

Excerpts from OCEAN POWER: POEMS FROM THE DESERT, by Ofelia Zepeda. Copyright © 1995 Ofelia Zepeda. Reprinted by permission of the University of Arizona Press.

Excerpts from THE MYSTERIOUS LANDS by Ann Zwinger, published in 1996 by the University of Arizona Press. Copyright © 1996 by Ann H. Zwinger. Reprinted by permission of Ann H. Zwinger.

INDEX

Italicized page numbers refer to photographic images, drawings, or maps. They appear after the text reference page numbers. For aqueducts, archaeological consultants, archaeological sites, archaeological projects, creeks, dams, *and* washes, *please look for the specific names under those headings. For definitions see* Glossary.

A

B

C

D

E

F

G

H

I

J

M

n

Q

R

S

T

U

V

W

Y

Z

About the Author

Stephanie Whittlesey is a senior principal investigator with Statistical Research, Inc. She holds a Ph.D. in anthropology from the University of Arizona and has devoted her professional career to southwestern archaeology. She believes strongly that writing about archaeology for the public is the best way to ensure that the discipline continues to enjoy public support. She divides her time between Flagstaff and Tucson, Arizona, traveling with an entourage of four cats. Her previous books about Arizona archaeology for the nonarchaeologist include *The Archaeology of Ancient Arizona* and *Grasshopper Pueblo: A Story of Archaeology and Ancient Life* (coauthored with Jefferson Reid and published by the University of Arizona Press).

Statistical Research, Inc., is committed to distributing the results of cultural resource management studies to a wide audience. Toward this goal, we maintain three publication series, designed to achieve different objectives and reach different readers.

SRI Press produces broad-interest volumes in archaeology, anthropology, history, and ethnography. These studies will appeal to professional archaeologists, avocational archaeologists, and general readers. Titles include:

- Vanishing River: Landscapes and Lives of the Lower Verde Valley. CD (3 volumes) and book. 1998.
- Sixty Years of Mogollon Archaeology: Papers from the Ninth Mogollon Conference, Silver City, New Mexico, 1996 edited by Stephanie M. Whittlesey. 1999.
- Islanders and Mainlanders: Prehistoric Context for the Southern California Bight, edited by Jeffrey H. Altschul and Donn R. Grenda. 2002.

The SRI Technical Series presents the results of our most significant cultural resource management projects and is aimed toward a professional audience. A limited number of these reports are offset printed and perfect bound. Out-of-print volumes can be photocopied as requested. Readers of this volume will find the following studies of special interest:

- From the Desert to the Mountains: Archaeology of the Transition Zone: The State Route 87–Sycamore Creek Project. Vol. 1: Prehistoric Sites, edited by Rein Vanderpot, Eric Eugene Klucas, and Richard Ciolek-Torrello (Technical Series 73, 1999). The results of archaeological investigations at 29 prehistoric sites in the Sycamore Creek valley and Mazatzal Mountains of central Arizona.
- Early Farmers of the Sonoran Desert: Archaeological Investigations at the Houghton Road Site, Tucson, Arizona, edited by Richard Ciolek-Torrello (Technical Series 72, 1998). An investigation of early farmers of the Sonoran Desert through archaeological evidence recovered from the eastern Tucson Basin of southern Arizona.
- Prehistoric Painted Pottery of Southeastern Arizona, by Robert A. Heckman, Barbara K. Montgomery, and Stephanie M. Whittlesey (Technical Series 77, 2000). A guide to southeastern Arizona painted pottery of the period between A.D. 650 and 1450 with special focus on the Garden Canyon site.
- Watering the Desert: Late Archaic Farming at the Costello-King Site, by Joseph A. Ezzo and William L. Deaver (Technical Series 68, 1998). Archaeological investigations of a 2,500–3,000-year-old farming camp, with evidence of ditch irrigation, on the Santa Cruz River near Tucson, Arizona.

SRI's Technical Report series provides an outlet for all cultural resource management reports conducted under contract. These compliance reports can be photocopied as needed. The titles listed above, along with selected others, can be obtained from the University of Arizona Press at 1230 North Park Avenue, Suite 102, Tucson, AZ 85719, or (800) 426-3797 (outside Arizona) or (520) 626-4218. For a complete list of the three series, write to SRI at P.O. Box 31865, Tucson, AZ 85751-1865.